REWRITING HISTORIES OF THE USE OF FORCE

It is commonly taught that the prohibition of the use of force is an achievement of the twentieth century and that beforehand States were free to resort to the arms as they pleased. International law, the story goes, was 'indifferent' to using force. 'Reality' as it stems from historical sources, however, appears much more complex. Using tools of history, sociology, anthropology and social psychology, this monograph offers new insights into the history of the prohibition of the use of force in international law. Conducting in-depth analysis of nineteenth-century doctrine and State practices, it paves the way for an alternative narrative on the prohibition of force and seeks to understand the origins of international law's traditional account. In so doing, it also provides a more general reflection on how the discipline writes, rewrites and chooses to remember its own history.

AGATHA VERDEBOUT holds a PhD in Public International Law from the Université Libre de Bruxelles (ULB). Her main research interests lie in critical histories of international law and the use of force. She is the recipient of several prizes, awards and research grants, notably the 2017 Henri Rolin Prize.

Cambridge Studies in International and Comparative Law: 160

Established in 1946, this series produces high quality, reflective and innovative scholarship in the field of public international law. It publishes works on international law that are of a theoretical, historical, cross-disciplinary or doctrinal nature. The series also welcomes books providing insights from private international law, comparative law and transnational studies which inform international legal thought and practice more generally.

The series seeks to publish views from diverse legal traditions and perspectives, and of any geographical origin. In this respect it invites studies offering regional perspectives on core *problématiques* of international law, and in the same vein, it appreciates contrasts and debates between diverging approaches. Accordingly, books offering new or less orthodox perspectives are very much welcome. Works of a generalist character are greatly valued and the series is also open to studies on specific areas, institutions or problems. Translations of the most outstanding works published in other languages are also considered.

After seventy years, Cambridge Studies in International and Comparative Law sets the standard for international legal scholarship and will continue to define the discipline as it evolves in the years to come.

A list of books in the series can be found at the end of this volume.

REWRITING HISTORIES OF THE USE OF FORCE

The Narrative of 'Indifference'

AGATHA VERDEBOUT
Lille Catholic University

CAMBRIDGE
UNIVERSITY PRESS

CAMBRIDGE
UNIVERSITY PRESS

University Printing House, Cambridge CB2 8BS, United Kingdom

One Liberty Plaza, 20th Floor, New York, NY 10006, USA

477 Williamstown Road, Port Melbourne, VIC 3207, Australia

314–321, 3rd Floor, Plot 3, Splendor Forum, Jasola District Centre, New Delhi – 110025, India

103 Penang Road, #05–06/07, Visioncrest Commercial, Singapore 238467

Cambridge University Press is part of the University of Cambridge.

It furthers the University's mission by disseminating knowledge in the pursuit of education, learning, and research at the highest international levels of excellence.

www.cambridge.org
Information on this title: www.cambridge.org/9781108838184
DOI: 10.1017/9781108937375

First published 2021

A catalogue record for this publication is available from the British Library.

Library of Congress Cataloging-in-Publication Data
Names: Verdebout, Agatha, 1987– author.
Title: Rewriting histories of the use of force : the narrative of 'indifference' / Agatha Verdebout, Université Catholique de Lille.
Description: Cambridge, United Kingdom ; New York, NY : Cambridge University Press, 2021. | Series: Cambridge studies in international and comparative law ; 160 | Based on author's thesis (doctoral–Université libre de Bruxelles, 2017) issued under title: Deconstructing 'indifference' : a critical analysis of the traditional historical narrative on the use of force. | Includes bibliographical references and index.
Identifiers: LCCN 2021026838 (print) | LCCN 2021026839 (ebook) | ISBN 9781108838184 (hardback) | ISBN 9781108947770 (paperback) | ISBN 9781108937375 (epub)
Subjects: LCSH: Intervention (International law)–History.
Classification: LCC KZ6368 . V463 2021 (print) | LCC KZ6368 (ebook) | DDC 341.5/84–dc23
LC record available at https://lccn.loc.gov/2021026838
LC ebook record available at https://lccn.loc.gov/2021026839

ISBN 978-1-108-83818-4 Hardback

CONTENTS

FOREWORD

'The prohibition of the use of force is a peremptory norm of law that was enshrined in the Charter of the United Nations, after having been incompletely enunciated in the Covenant of the League of Nations and then in the Briand Kellogg Pact'. Declined in various forms, this is the account found in the vast majority of contemporary doctrine. In her book, Agatha Verdebout not only questions the relevance of this narrative of 'indifference' (i.e., the use of force would have been neither prohibited nor authorized by international law) but also explains its emergence and success.

The narrative of indifference is essentially based on two arguments: one empirical, and the other more theoretical.

According to the first, throughout the nineteenth and early twentieth centuries, States would have never admitted a legal limitation of their ultimate sovereign prerogative to wage war. *Jus ad bellum* was therefore a matter of fact and of power, but not of law. No text, conventional or otherwise, contained such a limitation, nor could anything of the kind be inferred from custom. Based on an in-depth study of practice, Agatha Verdebout firmly rejects this argument. She shows how intervening powers did put justifications based on international law forward; sometimes invoking consideration of collective security resulting from applicable treaties, sometimes more humanitarian considerations but always linked to rules of law. By carefully dissecting archival documents, Agatha Verdebout demonstrates that, alongside politics and morals, law was equally used as a specific resource and register of legitimization. Upon reading these documents, one cannot but realize that this image of a deformalized international law (in the sense that it could not be distinguished from ethics) was created a posteriori and does not correspond to the relevant empirical material at all. In the same spirit, Agatha Verdebout also analyses nineteenth-century doctrine with great finesse. She shows that the prohibition of the use of force was accepted by the majority of authors, not only among *jusnaturalists* but also, with a few exceptions, within the positivist doctrine. In short, if we confine ourselves to a technical analysis of existing law, we must make a nuanced observation. On the one hand, State practice and doctrine did not conceive of the use of force as an unlimited right; on the other hand, it is true that the latter only set very loose limits, admitting a whole series of justifications for the use of force, which left a wide margin of appreciation to States, especially since the control exercised by international institutions, particularly judicial, was weak, if not nonexistent.

But a second, more theoretical argument, has been put forward to support the historical narrative according to which the prohibition of the use of force was inexistent before the interwar period. In the nineteenth century, it has been argued, there was no international legal order in the proper sense of the term. In the absence of international institutions and even genuine secondary rules governing the creation, interpretation and application of primary rules of conduct, law had barely, if at all, invested the international arena. It is therefore in this context that we should understand the States' justifying discourses when they resorted to force: as discourses, which when they referred to law, truly referred to a form of natural, rather than positive, law. In addition to the fact that it has just been shown that this claim cannot resist an empirical analysis that takes archive documents seriously, it also immediately stands out as tautological: there was no positive international law at the time, so States did not justify the use of force based on positive law; and since States did not justify their behaviour in light of positive law, positive law did not exist at the time. The proponents of this argument are also faced with a problem of coherence. By following it to the end, they would have to conclude that international law itself only came into being after the First, or even the Second, World War. And yet, all the while enshrining the narrative of indifference, historical introductions to most textbooks illustrate that this idea is far from widespread.

But, if the thesis of indifference is so difficult to defend, both empirically and theoretically, how can its success be explained? It is at this stage that Agatha Verdebout's contribution is the most original. In the last part of her book, she traces the genealogy of the narrative of indifference, which emerged with the end of the World War I. At that precise moment, the profession of international law was confronted with a kind of cognitive dissonance: on the one hand, the progress of law as a peaceful means of settling disputes had been praised (with the Hague conferences of 1899 and 1907 in particular); but, on the other hand, it had in no way prevented the outburst and terrible ravages caused by the Great War. One way of overcoming this dissonance was to rewrite history, to construct a narrative according to which the problem lay in the inadequacies of the law of the time – inadequacies that it was therefore sufficient to remedy in order to avoid the outbreak of new wars. It was at this point, therefore, that it began to be asserted that the prohibition of the use of force had previously been nonexistent, and that its formalization into conventional texts should make it possible to guarantee peace through law. It was also at this point that internationalists once again presented themselves as the vanguard of the pacification of international relations. Of course, history has shown all the vanity of this prophecy and corporatist representation. In any case, the episode confirms that this idealistic vision of peace through law is deeply rooted in the 'subconscious' of internationalists. Agatha Verdebout explains how this vision has been very precisely applied in the central domain of the framing of force by law. She also warns us about a defect that is too widespread among internationalists. It is not enough to accept, in principle, that this idealistic vision has limits; one must also draw all the consequences when one considers the historical evolution of a particular legal rule, avoiding relaying anachronisms and making the effort to deconstruct them, even if they have been firmly anchored in the doctrine for decades.

It is clear that this is a landmark work, both in the field of the use of force and, more broadly, in that of the history of international law. Particularly appreciated by her thesis jury and already abundantly commented on in the literature through an article outlining its main lines, it has already been awarded the Henri Rolin Prize (2017) and the Alice Seghers Prize (2018). Let us bet that this book will seduce many more readers in the short, medium and long terms. With this book, we are decidedly talking about history.

Olivier Corten

ACKNOWLEDGEMENTS

I observe a lot and hesitate for a long time. Perhaps this is a quality for a researcher, but it is a condition that requires being well guided and surrounded to carry out the intense and grueling project that is a doctoral thesis and its transformation into a monograph. I was lucky, I lacked neither one nor the other.

My gratitude, first of all, goes to Olivier Corten, who supervised the thesis from which this book is issued. I am thankful for his availability and his trust; his confidence and his encouragements made me audacious. Throughout my doctoral research, I was also privileged to benefit from the advice and feedback of an interdisciplinary PhD supervision committee. I am especially in debt to Anne Lagerwall for her continuous investment and her (always well-informed) advice; to Pieter Lagrou for his instructive and wise remarks, which helped me get a better grasp of the methods of history; and to Emmanuelle Tourme-Jouannet for those two weekends at Gometz-le-Châtel, which had a decisive impact on the theoretical turn the research eventually took. My thanks also go to Randall Lesaffer and Martti Koskenniemi for accepting to be part of the PhD examination committee and for their support in the publication of this monograph. Jean Salmon has also been a guiding force throughout this research; I feel extremely privileged for his support and guidance.

This book would not be what it is if it was not for the research stays I was able to carry out at the Lauterpacht Centre for International Law of the University of Cambridge in 2015 and the Law Faculty of McGill in 2016–2017. In Cambridge, my thanks go to the Lauterpachyosaurus Lex for making it such an enjoyable and fruitful experience; in Montréal, to Frédéric Mégret, as well as to Olivier Barsalou, Michael Hennecy-Picard and Bérénice Schramm for their warm welcome and our (late-night) discussions on the theories of international law. These trips would not have been possible without the financial help of the Belgian Fonds national de la recherche scientifique (FNRS), of the Fondation Roi Baudoin and of the Sofina–Boël Fellowship.

The Centre of International Law of the Université Libre de Bruxelles (ULB) provided me with an ideal working environment. Many colleagues have become friends. I am very grateful for Martyna Fałkowska-Clarys's, Arnaud Louwette's, Marie-Laurence Hébert-Dolbec's, Vaios Koutroulis's, François Dubuisson's, Pierre Klein's, Vincent Chapaux's, Nicolas Angelet's and Eric David's friendship and kindness. You have all contributed to make the seven years I have spent at the Centre a wonderful experience. My thanks also go to my new colleagues at the European School of Political and Social Sciences (ESPOL) in Lille for their incredible team spirit and combativity. As a the only international lawyer of the department, I look forward to continuing to learn from you and enriching my knowledge of social sciences for the study of international law.

ABBREVIATIONS

AFSdN	Association française pour la Société des Nations
APD	Association pour la paix et le droit
ASIL	American Society for International Law
BFSP	British and Foreign State Papers
FO	Foreign Office
GUSdN	Groupe universitaire pour la Société des Nations
ICJ	International Court of Justice
IDI	Institut de droit international
IIFFMCG	Independent International Fact-Finding Mission on the Conflict in Georgia
ILC	International Law Commission
IPB	International Peace Bureau
IULNA	International Union of League of Nations Associations
LEP	League to enforce peace
LN	League of Nations
LNU	League of Nations Union
MAE	Ministère des affaires étrangères (France)
PCIJ	Permanent Court of International Justice
UN	United Nations
USSD	United States State Department
WWI	World War I
WWII	World War II

Introduction

I

There is a strange paradox in the contemporary literature on the use of force. While authors continue to relentlessly debate the scope and meaning of the current prohibition resort to armed force as embedded in Article 2(4) of the United Nations (UN) Charter, an element appears to enjoy relative consensus. This element is the history of the rule.

Most international law manuals indeed teach that the prohibition of the use of force is an achievement of the twentieth century and that, beforehand, States were free to resort to armed force as they pleased. Following this general narrative weave, the nineteenth century is, in particular, presented as the 'golden age of positivism'; as a time when any attempt to restrict the use of force would have been doomed to fail in face of the States' unwillingness to restrain their own sovereign prerogatives.[1] It is thus far from uncommon to read that 'in the Westphalian legal order it was admitted that the States could resort to force';[2] that 'the *ius publicum europaeum* admitted war regardless of any *justa causa*';[3] that 'the right to use force was recognised as an inherent right of every independent sovereign State';[4] or yet that 'never until the twentieth century has the use of force been banned by positive international law, nor would it even have been possible to ban it in a society without any

[1] For a critical analysis of international law's general representation of the nineteenth century in traditional historiography, see David Kennedy, 'International Law in the Nineteenth Century: History of an Illusion' (1996) 65 *Nordic Journal of International Law* 385–420.

[2] Nico Schrijver, 'Article 2, paragraphe 4', in Jean-Pierre Cot et Alain Pellet (eds.), *La Charte des Nations Unies. Commentaire articles par articles* (3rd éd., Economica, 2005) p. 440. Translation by the author.

[3] Hans Wehberg, 'L'interdiction du recours à la force. Le principe et les problèmes qui se posent' (1951) 78 *Recueil des cours de l'académie de droit internationa* 25–26 Emphasis in the original. Translation by the author.

[4] Rebecca M. Wallace, *International Law* (4th ed., Sweet & Maxwell, 2002) p. 253.

central authority to enforce the ban'.[5] In the nineteenth century, the story goes, international law was 'indifferent' to the use of armed force: it did not prohibit it but did not explicitly authorize it either. Today, this historical account – which has come to be known as the 'narrative of indifference'[6] – has become so widely and deeply accepted that some

[5] Jan Verzijl, *International Law in Historical Perspective*, 5 vols. (A. W. Stijhoff, 1968), vol. 1, p. 215. See also *inter alia* Philip C. Jessup, *A Modern Law of Nations. An Introduction* (MacMillan, 1950), p. 157; Marcel Sibert, *Traité de droit international public* (Dalloz, 1951) vol. 2, 625; Paul Reuter, *Droit international public* (Presses Universitaire de France, 1963), p. 285; Louis Delbez, *Les principes généraux du droit international public* (3rd éd., LGDJ, 1963), p. 395; Krzysztof Skubiszewski, 'Use of Force by States and Collective Security. Law of War and Neutrality', in Max Sørensen (ed.), *Manual of Public International Law* (MacMillan, 1968), pp. 741–742; Georg Schwarzenberger, *International Law as Applied by International Courts and Tribunals*, 2 vols. (Stevens and Sons, 1968), vol. 2, pp. 38–39; Ian Brownlie, *International Law and the Use of Force by States* (Clarendon Press, 1968), pp. 19–50; Antoine Favre, *Principes du droit des gens* (LGDJ, 1974), pp. 711–713; Hersch Lauterpacht (edited by Elihu Lauterpacht), *International Law. Collected Papers* (Cambridge University Press, 1975), vol. 2, p. 96; Philippe Manin, *Droit International Public* (Masson, 1979), pp. 333–334; J. G. Starke, *Introduction to International Law* (9th ed., Butterworths, 1984), p. 508; Anthony Clark Arend and Robert J. Beck, *International Law and the Use of Force: Beyond the UN Charter* (Routledge, 1993), pp. 16–17; Peter Malanczuk, *Akehurst's Modern Introduction to International Law* (7th ed., Routledge, 1997), p. 10; Antonio Cassese, *International Law* (Oxford University Press, 2001) pp. 27 and 33; John O'Brien, *International Law* (Cavendish Publishing Limited, 2001), pp. 676–677; Ahmed Abou-Al-Wafa, *Public International Law* (Dar-Al-Nahda Al Arabia, 2002), p. 609; Slim Laghmani, *Histoire du droit des gens du jus gentium impérial au jus publicum europaeum* (Pedone, 2003), pp. 180–182; Modesto Seara Vásquez, *Derecho internacional público* (Editorial Porrúa, 2004), pp. 361-362; Martin Dixon, *International Law* (6th ed., Oxford University Press, 2007), p. 310; Robert Kolb and Richard Hyde, *An Introduction to the International Law of Armed Conflicts* (Hart Publishing, 2008), pp. 9–10; John H. Currie, *Public International Law* (2nd ed., Irwin Law, 2008), pp. 452–453; Jean Combacau et Serge Sur, *Droit international public* (8th ed., Montchrestien, 2008), p. 619; (Nguyên Quôc Dinh), Patrick Daillier, Mathias Forteau et Alain Pellet, *Droit international public* (8e éd., LGDJ, 2009), p. 1032; Alina Kaczorowska, *Public International Law* (4th ed., Routledge, 2010), p. 689; John Duggard, *International Law. A South African Perspective* (4th ed., Juta, 2011), p. 465; Enzo Cannizzaro, *Corso di diritto internazionale* (Giuffrè Editore, 2011), p. 6; Gideon Boas, *Public International Law. Contemporary Principles and Perspectives* (Edward Elgar, 2012), pp. 310–311; Pierre-Marie Dupuy et Yann Kerbat, *Droit international public* (Dalloz, 2012), p. 615; Rebecca M. Wallace and Olga Martin-Ortega, *International Law* (7th ed., Sweet & Maxwell, 2013), p. 294; Oliver Dörr, 'Prohibition of the Use of Force' *Max Planck Encyclopedia of Public International Law Online* (last update: September 2015) par. 4; Lung-chu Chen, *An Introduction to Contemporary International Law. A Policy-Oriented Perspective* (3rd ed., Oxford University Press, 2015), p. 378.

[6] Some may dislike the word 'indifference' because of the pejorative connotation it holds and prefer terms such as 'neutrality', 'tolerance' or 'acceptance' to describe classical

authors have not hesitated to qualify any attempt to question it as 'absurd'.[7]

Yet, upon closer inspection, the narrative of indifference appears riddled with ambiguities. It more particularly seems to be at odds with 'reality' as it stems from nineteenth century sources. Most nineteenth century international lawyers, in fact, appeared to consider that the use of force was far from an unrestricted prerogative of States. In 1900, for instance, Théophile Funck-Brentano and Albert Sorel asserted that war was not a right for States because saying so would be 'tantamount to saying that there is no law but force'.[8] Johann-Caspar Bluntschli (1808–1881) likewise insisted that 'war is just when authorized by the law of nations',[9] thus inverting the idea that war is legal when it is just. In practice as well, it seems that heads of States usually felt the urge to justify their actions when they had resort to measures of a military nature. The *Caroline* incident (1837), in the course of which Great Britain claimed the destruction of the eponym American steamboat was justified as a matter of self-defence, immediately comes to mind.[10] This incident, in fact, resulted in lengthy diplomatic exchanges between London and Washington, in which the two nations came to the conclusion that, although they agreed on 'the great principles of public international law',[11] they disagreed on whether the conditions for self-defence were *in casu* fulfilled.

Faced with these conflicting elements, modern-day scholarship has brought several explanations forward in defence of the traditional narrative of indifference. As regards doctrine, it generally argues that nineteenth-century authors who claimed the use of force to be ring-fenced by

international law's attitude towards the use of force. However, for the sake clarity, to avoid a multiplication of terms and because this is how the traditional historical account has generally come to be known in the literature, the following pages will continue using the terms 'narrative of indifference'. See Paul Guggenheim, *Traité de droit international public*, 2 vols. (Librairie de l'Université de Genève, 1954), vol. 2, p. 94; Robert Kolb, *Ius contra bellum. Le droit international relatif au maintien de la paix* (Bruylant, 2009), p. 28.

7 Albane Geslin, 'Du *bellum justum* au *jus ad bellum*: glissements conceptuels ou simples variations sémantiques?' (2009) 64 *Revue de métaphysique et de morale* 463.

8 Théodore Funck-Brentano et Albert Sorel, *Précis de droit gens* (Plon 1900) 232. Translation by the author.

9 Johan-Caspar Bluntschli, *Le droit international codifié* (Guillaume et Cie. 1870) 273. Translation by the author.

10 On the *Caroline* incident see John Bassett Moore, *A Digest of International Law*, 8 vols. (Government Printing Office, 1906), vol. 2, pp. 404–414.

11 Mr. Weber, Sec. of State, to Lord Ashburton, quoted in ibid. 412.

international law were more concerned with the law as they thought it ought to be rather than as it truly was. Said differently, these authors were naturalists, or at least still too much imbued in old natural law theories of just war for any positive law credit to be given to their writings. As Hans Wehberg put it: 'the moral influence of the theories of *bellum justum* at the beginning of the *ius publicum europaeum* era was so great that we did not dare purely and simply reject it'.[12] In what concerns practice, modern writers usually contend that, albeit States justified their actions, legal considerations were either non-existent or lost in the bulk of political and ethical arguments. The practice of justifying the use of force in the nineteenth century, in other words, was the mere reflection of a sense of moral and diplomatic propriety rather than legal duty. Justification discourses did not produce any effect in positive international law. Wilhelm Grewe, for example, was adamant that while 'it is true that States in general did not stop making solemn assurances of the justice of their cause when declaring and proclaiming war, they themselves did not normally attribute such assurances with anything more than propaganda value'.[13]

Lately, a few authors have started to express doubts regarding the overall narrative of indifference. They feel that contemporary scholarship might have been a little 'too prompt to disqualify classical international law'.[14] So far, however, these doubts have not gone beyond the stage of intuition. An in-depth analysis of the indifference narrative is, in sum, still missing. This is the gap the present book intends to fill. It will challenge international law's dominant historical account on the use of force in two ways. First, by investigating the discrepancy between the present-day narrative and historical sources further: Was international law really indifferent to the use of force before 1919, or has contemporary scholarship indeed been too quick to discard classical international law? Second, by seeking to trace the origins and understand the roots of the narrative of indifference: where

[12] Wehberg, 'L'interdiction du recours à la force', 21. Translation by the author.

[13] Wilhelm Grewe, *The Epochs of International Law* (Walter de Gruyter, 2000), p. 531.

[14] Emmanuelle Jouannet, *The Liberal Welfarist Law of Nations. A History of International Law* (Cambridge University Press, 2012), p. 130. See also Olivier Corten, 'Droit, force et légitimité dans une société internationale en mutation' (1996) 37 *Revue interdisciplinaire d'études juridiques* 89–94; Randall Lesaffer, 'Too Much History: From War as Sanction to the Sanctioning of War', in Marc Weller (ed.), *The Oxford Handbook on the Use of Force in International Law* (Oxford University Press, 2015), p. 46; Mary O'Connell, 'The Prohibition of the Use of Force', in Nigel D. White and Christian Henderson (eds.), *Research Handbook on International Conflict and Security Law* (Edward Elgar, 2013), p. 95. For a more thorough review of these authors' works, see below (8.2.3.).

does this narrative come from? Why and how did it become the discipline's standard account of the history of the use of force? Through these questions, this book not only wishes to interrogate how the discipline of international law 'remembers' its past and writes its history, but also the nature and the purpose(s) of that (hi)story. From this point of view, one could say that is not so much a study about the 'past history' of international law as it is about the 'present memory' of international law's past. Thus, defined and circumvented, the research object and problem(s) of this book suggest a critical outlook on international law and its history, the details of which shall now be presented.

II

For the past two decades or so, history of international law has boomed. Many have traced this renewed interest for history to the end of the Cold War and the need to find a new direction and guidance for the discipline.[15] International law, it in fact seems, has made a habit of revolving to the past in times of crisis and uncertainty. Unlike previous 'turns to history' however, the last one has taken distinctly critical twist. It would be beside the point here to try to anthologise critical legal histories of international law. From Martti Koskenniemi, David Kennedy and Emmanuelle Tourme-Jouannet to Anne Orford, Anthony Anghie and Samuel Moyne, these are indeed by now relatively well known by most of international legal scholarship.[16]

It is nevertheless interesting to highlight some of the main common features that these 'critical histories' assume. Thomas Skouteris identifies

15 See, e.g., Martti Koskenniemi, 'Why History of International Law Today?' (2004) 4 *Rechtsgeschichte* 61–66; George Rodrigo Bandeira Galindo, 'Martti Koskenniemi and the Historiographical Turn in International Law' (2005) 16 *European Journal of International Law* 539–559; Randall Lesaffer, 'International Law and Its History: The Story of an Unrequited Love', in Matthew Craven, Malgosia Fitzmaurice and Maria Vogiatzi (eds.), *Time, History and International Law* (Martinus Nijhoff, 2007), pp. 27–41; Emmanuelle Tourme-Jouannet and Anne Peters, 'The *Journal of the History of International Law*: A Forum for New Research' (2014) 16 *Journal of the History of International Law* 1–8; Matthew Craven, 'Theorizing the Turn to History in International Law', in Anne Orford and Florian Hoffman (eds.), *The Oxford Handbook of the Theory of International Law* (Oxford University Press, 2016), pp. 21–37.

16 Martti Koskenniemi, *The Gentle Civiliser of Nations. The Rise and Fall of International Law 1870–1960* (Cambridge University Press, 2001); Antony Anghie, *Imperialism, Sovereignty and the Making of International Law* (Cambridge Univerity Press, 2007); Samuel Moyne, *The Last Utopia. Human Rights in History* (Harvard University Press, 2010); Jouannet, The Liberal Welfarist Law of Nations.

three.[17] The first consists in approaching legal history as a discursive construction. Critical histories, in other words, rely on the idea that the past can never be fully accounted for and that 'historical truth' is unattainable. (Hi)stories are products of certain conscious or unconscious premises and biases and pursue some conscious or unconscious political or ideological purposes. The work of critical legal historians has thus generally been aimed at unveiling these biases and purposes. The second common feature, according to Skouteris, is a rejection of 'cause-and-effect' relationship between law and social context. This is to say that law is not an objective and quasi-automatic reaction to a determinate historical and socio-political context. Instead, law is viewed as contingent and the result of a complex nexus of factors, whether power relationships or personal games of influence. Third and last, is the proposition that humanity does not follow an evolutionary path. As we shall see, mainstream histories are in fact often built on narrative structures that highlight continuity and progress.[18] By contrast, critical legal historians have sought to emphasise contingency and discontinuity in the creation and evolution of rules of international law.

All the above is why it has become quite common to speak of critical histories as 'deconstructions' of mainstream histories. The term 'deconstruction' is then used in a generic sense rather than in a strictly 'derridean' understanding (even though Jacques Derrida's philosophy certainly had an influence on critical legal scholars). In social sciences, in fact, deconstruction has been associated with the notion of discourse. In this context, a 'discourse' is much more than a text consisting of words and sentences. It can be an attitude, an act or a speech that is the expression of a particular system of beliefs, of ideas and of values.[19] Deconstruction consists in a technique for discourse analysis that aims to show that discourse actually say more than what they enunciate. It seeks to understand the underlying meaning of a discourse, as well as process through which this meaning is created. The method advocated by Derrida supposes to identify the structures and units of a given discourse,

[17] Thomas Skouteris, 'Engaging History in International Law', Randall Lesaffer, 'International Law and Its History: The Story of an Unrequited Love', in Matthew Craven, Malgosia Fitzmaurice and Maria Vogiatzi (eds.), *Time, History and International Law* (Martinus Nijhoff, 2007), pp. 27–41, 112–116.

[18] See below (8.1.3).

[19] See Michel Foucault, 'The Order of Discourse', in Robert Young (ed.), *Untying the Text: A Post-Structuralist Reader* (Routledge, 1981), pp. 51–78.

and attempt to elucidate the relations between these different units.[20] This approach suggests that meaning is not created by reference to any elements outside of the discourse itself, but in a strictly internal and self-contained manner. A discourse, in sum, constructs its own coherence and validity. Derrida's process breaks the impression that knowledge, social practices and norms are self-evident and objective facts by highlighting the circular pattern of how they are produced.[21]

In light of this, and inasmuch as it shares the three common features evidenced above and seeks to interrogate the narrative of indifference by reference to international law's broader discourse about itself and its history, the present book also qualifies as a 'deconstruction'; a deconstruction of indifference. That said, although it follows the tide of critical histories of international law, the inspiration for the overall theoretical approach does not come from the existing legal history literature. It finds a more direct source in a body of work on the theory of history that has not really been exploited by international legal historians yet: mnemohistory.

III

Mnemohistory literally translates as the 'history of memory'. The notion was first introduced by Egyptologist Jan Assmann in his book *Moses and the Egyptian* (1997). Assmann defined mnemohistory by reference and by contrast to the concept of 'history'. He explains that 'unlike history, mnemohistory is concerned not with the past as such, but only with the past as it is remembered'.[22] Mnemohistorians are interested with the representations of the past that prevail in a given group or society: with 'collective memory' in sum.[23] They contend that the manner in which the

20 Jacques Derrida, *Positions* (The University of Chicago Press, 1981), p. 41; and by the same author, *Margins of Philosophy* (The University of Chicago Press, 1982), p. 329.

21 See Martti Koskenniemi, *From Apology to Utopia. The Structure of International Legal Argument* (re-issue with new epilogue) (Cambridge University Press, 2005), p. 12.

22 Jan Assmann, *Moses and the Egyptian. The Memory of Egypt in Western Monotheism* (Harvard University Press, 1997), pp. 8–9.

23 The paternity of the concept of 'collective memory' is usually attributed to French sociologist Maurice Halbwachs, see *Les actes sociaux de la mémoire* (Librairie Félix Alcan, 1925); and *La mémoire collective* (édition critique établie par Gérard Namer, first edition: 1950) (Albin Michel, 1997). Since its apparition in 1925, the notion of 'collective memory' has, however, spurred numerous debates, in particular, regarding a group's capacity to 'remember' and have a 'memory'. See, in particular, Reinhart Koselleck, 'Gibt es ein kollektives Gedächtnis?' (2004) 19 *Divanatio* 1–6; and Susan Sontag,

past is remembered and events are believed to have taken place is more important, and therefore more interesting, than the way things truly happened.[24] Mnemohistory thus does not seek to elucidate the past, or even assess the veracity of historical narratives against historical evidence. What matters is the discourse on the past and to understand why a particular event is represented and remembered the way it is represented and remembered. The past, Assmann writes, is 'not a natural growth but a cultural creation' and 'the task of mnemohistory consists in analysing the mythical elements in tradition and discovering their hidden agenda'.[25]

As such, mnemohistory is not a fundamentally new type of endeavour. In fact, the interest of historiography for memory and the construction of historical narratives dates back at least to the mid-nineteenth century.[26] Assmann himself acknowledges that 'only the difference between history and mnemohistory is new'. This difference, he however insists, is important: 'without awareness of the difference, the history of memory, [. . .], turns too easily into a historical critique of memory'.[27] This is, in fact, where the term 'mnemohistory' has added value. It highlights the meta-historical dimension of the inquiry and, in so doing, anticipates the criticism that has regularly been addressed to memory studies. Best synthetized by Alon Confino and Wulf Kansteiner, this criticism revolves around two axes. First, is the fact that memory studies have too often consisted in describing the representations of the past that prevail in a given society without interrogating their origins and raison d'être.[28] Second, is the observation that literature has had a tendency to view the creation of collective memory solely as deliberate ideological constructions aimed at promoting a specific political agenda, while leaving

Regarding the Pains of Others (Picador 2003). In defence of the notion of 'collective memory', see Aleida Assmann, 'Transformations between History and Memory' (2008) 75 *Social Research* 49–72. Along the same lines, Philip Allott claims that 'History is public memory', in 'International Law and the Idea of History' (1999) 1 *Journal of the History of International Law* 3.

[24] Marek Tamm, 'Introduction: Afterlife of Events: Perspective on Mnemohistory', in Marek Tamm (ed.), *Afterlife of Events: Perspective on Mnemohistory* (Palgrave MacMillan, 2015), p. 3.

[25] Assmann, *Moses and the Egyptian*, p. 10.

[26] See Marek Tamm, 'Beyond History and Memory: New Perspectives in Memory Studies' (2013) 11 *History Compass* 458–473.

[27] Assmann, *Moses and the Egyptian*, pp. 12–13.

[28] Alon Confino, 'Collective Memory and Cultural History: Problems and Method' (1997) 102 *American Historical Review* 1388.

other unconscious grassroots factors (such as values and beliefs) to the side.[29] As it is, mnemohistory – and for that matter most of recent meta-historical works of deconstructionist inspiration – emphasise the dynamic process behind the construction of historical narratives. Assmann particularly stresses the role of identity in that process. Not only is the development of historical narratives influenced by pre-existing 'intellectual and cultural traditions' that frame the identity of the group, but the narratives thus created reinforce these traditions and therefore this identity.[30] As Hans Mol then argues, it is a circular 'need for identity' instead of 'theoretical curiosity' that prompts demand for history.[31] The (hi)stories told are both the reflection of how a group imagines and projects itself in the world, and a mechanism for the preservation of these collective beliefs and representations of self and others. History and identity, in fewer words, are the two sides of the same coin.

The present research draws from this idea and will emphasise the role of disciplinary identity in the creation of the narrative on the indifference. As already mentioned, it will analyse this narrative considering international law's more general discourse about itself and its history. For all that, it will not necessarily abide by all the theoretical and methodological cannons of mnemohistory as set by Assmann. The Egyptologist relinquishes any sort of positive inquiry into history and, as we saw, indeed defines his approach by opposition to it. 'Historical positivism', he writes, 'consists in separating the historical from the mythical elements in memory' but the issue is that 'history turns into myth as soon as it is remembered, narrated and used'.[32] History cannot objectively be accounted for because the raw data is necessarily selected, mediated, narrated and, as a result, deformed. As soon as historical events are told (instead of simply chronicled), the line between 'scientific history' and 'historical fiction' is blurred.[33] As Hayden White, Assmann thus appears to believe that factuality is uninteresting and that classical historical

[29] Ibid. 1393–1394; Wulf Kansteiner, 'Finding Meaning in Memory: A Methodological Critique of Collective Memory Studies'(2002) 41 *History and Theory* 180.

[30] Jan Assmann, 'Collective Memory and Cultural Identity' (1995) 65 *New German Critique* 130. See also Kansteiner, 'Finding Meaning in Memory' 180.

[31] Assmann, 'Collective Memory and Cultural Identity', 130; Kansteiner, 'Finding Meaning in Memory', 180.

[32] Assmann, *Moses and the Egyptian*, pp. 10 and 14.

[33] Hayden White, 'The Question of Narrative in Contemporary Historical Theory' (1984) 23 *History and Theory* 1–33.

methodology based on primary sources is somewhat irrelevant.[34] While agreeing that history is just a story amongst other stories (i.e., a social and literary construct), many historians have criticised this attitude as too relativistic. Roger Chartier, for instance, argues that history, unlike fiction, is guided by an intention of truth; a truth is external to the historical narrative. Although that 'reality' can never be fully grasped and accounted for, it remains that elements of 'reality' can be captured provided the tenets of historical methodology are respected.[35] Each account of history, in spite but also thanks to its own biases and preoccupations, offers a certain glimpse into the past. What is important it so be aware of the limits, caveats, and tropisms of one's own research and of the way in which these orient the story being told.

This book subscribes to this latter view. This is not only for epistemological reasons, but also because positivistic inquiry is sometimes a prerequisite of meta-historical analysis. At least, such is the case here and such is equally the case, to a certain extent, in Assmann's own work. As a matter of fact, when he examines the uses of the figure of Moses by western monotheist religions in *Moses and the Egyptian* (1997), Assmann's project hinges on the idea that these images are mythologized: that is, that they do not correspond to reality, whatever that reality might have been. Likewise, this research starts from the observation that there seems to be a discrepancy between the current narrative of indifference and 'reality' as it stems from historical sources. Unlike Assmann, however, before any meta-historical argument can be compellingly presented to explain the 'hidden agenda' of the narrative of indifference, the discrepancy needs to be demonstrated. When some authors qualify attempts to discuss 'indifference' as *ab initio* 'absurd', the presence of mythologized elements in the discourse cannot simply be stated, it needs

[34] See also Hayden White, *Metahistory: The Historical Imagination in Nineteenth Century Europe* (The Johns Hopkins University Press, 1973), pp. 1–42.

[35] Roger Chartier, *Au bord de la falaise. L'histoire entre inquiétude et certitude* (Albin Michel, 1998), pp. 16 and 18. See also by the same author, 'Le monde comme représentation' (1989) 44 *Annales. Economies, Sociétés, Civilisations* 1505–1520. See also Henri-Irénée Marrou, *De la connaissance historique* (Editions du Seuil, 1954), pp. 26–46; John H. Zammito, 'Are We Being Historical Yet? The New Historicism, the New Philosophy of History, and 'Practising Historians'' (1993) 65 *Journal of modern History* 783–814; William W. Fisher III, ''Texts and Context'. The Application to American Legal History of the Methodologies of Intellectual Histories' (1997) 49 *Stanford Law Review* 1065–1110.

to be established. This not only impacts the methodology, but the general structure of the book as well.

IV

As is probably clear by now, the scope of this research is broader than the mere history of the prohibition of the use of force in international law. The ultimate purpose is not so much to offer an alternative, supposedly more accurate, version of that history, but rather to examine the preconceptions (and misconceptions) upon which our present-day narrative relies. It follows that, maybe to the surprise of some, this book does not dwell on the theories of 'just war' and on the work of authors such as Vitoria, Grotius, Vattel, Bynkershoek or yet Gentili. Although they probably had an impact, their work falls outside the scope of this research. Likewise, little attention is given to the technical analysis of 'land-mark' conventions, doctrines or case law, such as the *Alabama Claims* arbitration, the Hague Conventions, the Bryan Treaties, the Locarno Treaties or yet the Briand-Kellogg Pact.

Still, as mentioned, a certain degree of 'positivistic' inquiry cannot be avoided. More particularly, before any convincing argument can be made about the meaning and origins of the narrative of indifference, the two backbones upon which this narrative rests have to be addressed. Failing this, the meta-historical argument might not be heard, and some may be tempted to simply discard it by repeating the scholarship's traditional '*ritornello*' about nineteenth-century doctrine and State practice. As a result, this analysis of the narrative of indifference is divided into three main parts. Each of these three parts examines a different aspect of the narrative of indifference, based on a different set of materials and using a different (adapted) methodology.

Part 1 starts by examining nineteenth- and early twentieth-century scholarship to test the assumption according to which the authors who considered the use of force to be ring-fenced by international law were, generally speaking, 'naturalists'. Analysing textbooks dating from 1815 to 1914, it attempts to resituate the conclusions that the lawyers of the time reached regarding the legality of resort to armed force in their theoretical and methodological contexts. It seeks to understand how these writers thought about international law and how this affected the manner in which they thought about the use of force. More than a mere description of what the literature said about the rules of *ius ad bellum*, it hence truly aims to evidence the mechanics and logics behind classical international legal doctrine. It highlights the tensions, the ambivalences, and the ambiguities that characterised nineteenth-century lawyers' discourse about international law and the use of force. This first part of the book comes to the conclusion that, albeit pre-1914 scholarship often mixed elements of naturalism and positivism in their theories, and elements of deduction and induction in their methodologies, claiming that those who asserted that the right to use force was limited by international law were 'naturalists' is a clear simplification. Far from being the prerogative of a few 'naturalist' lawyers, this conviction was shared by an overwhelming majority of authors, from all theoretical backgrounds.

Part 2 then turns to nineteenth- and early twentieth-century State practice. Its purpose is to question the second backbone of the narrative of indifference, i.e., the affirmation that the justification discourses brought forward by States were the reflections of political and moral considerations that had no repercussions on the positive law of nations. It conducts an analysis of the argument deployed by States to justify the use of armed force in 13 different precedents.[36] The aim of this analysis, it should be stressed, is neither to determine the precise content of the rules nor to judge the legality or illegality of this or that intervention. The purpose is simply to examine the nature of the arguments put forth by States to justify the use of force and to verify whether law was, or not, a consideration. Without being oblivious of the sociopolitical context in which these interventions took place, this second part of the book shows that States not only quasi-systematically referred to law to justify their actions, but also that the arguments they brought forth appeared to have decisive importance. The care with which governments developed articulated legal reasoning to explain their behaviour, indeed, suggests that their practice of justifying the use of force was derived from more than diplomatic propriety.

The discrepancy between the modern-day account and historical sources having thus been evidenced and the rationalisations offered by doctrine set aside, Part 3 finally investigates the reasons for the emergence of the narrative of indifference. This is where the mnemohistory framework previously presented unfolds to its fullest. It seeks to understand the meaning and function of the narrative of indifference by analysing its rhetorical structures and their relations with international law's broader discourse about itself and its history. It argues that our

[36] For details about how the selection of these 13 case studies was operated, see the introduction of the second part of the book.

present-day bleak representation of classical *ius ad bellum* finds its roots in the confrontation between international law's deep-founded disciplinary beliefs and the events of the World War I. The outburst of violence shook the discipline to its very core and, in particular, challenged the idea that law can ensure the pacific co-existence of States. For, in fact, if international law restricted the use of force before 1914, how could the Great War have taken place? The narrative of indifference reconciled the discipline with the benevolent image it had of itself. It enabled the field to move past the failure of 1914, preserve its identity and restore its credibility by blaming the war on the lack of pre-existing rules.

PART I

The Use of Force in Nineteenth-Century Doctrine

More than a Naturalist Fantasy

Introduction: Aim, Methodology and Outline

Nineteenth-century international legal scholarship suffers from bad press in traditional histories of international law. The portrait they paint is negative and paradoxical at the same time. On the one hand, the nineteenth century is generally presented as the 'golden age of positivism'; a neo-Hegelian and 'apologetic' positivism in which law was deprived of any autonomy *vis-à-vis* the political will of States.[1] The rise of this positivism, it is said, went hand in hand with the dismissal of the theories of just war and the consecration of an absolute war prerogative for sovereign States.[2] On the other hand, however, the writings of the authors who asserted the use of force to be ring-fenced by law are promptly deprecated as 'utopian' and disconnected from the realities of their time. As Randall Lesaffer notes, we are in a configuration in which everything that corroborates our

[1] On the emergence of this 'apologetic' representation of nineteenth-century international legal positivism, see Richard Collins, 'Classical Legal Positivism in International Law Revisited', in Jörg Kammerhofer and Jean d'Aspremont (eds.), *International Legal Positivism in a Post-Modern World* (Cambridge University Press, 2014), pp. 23–49.

[2] See Hans Wehberg, 'L'interdiction du recours à la force. Le principe et les problèmes qui se posent' (1951) 78 *Recueil des cours de l'académie de droit international* 21; Charles de Visscher, *Théories et réalités en droit international public* (2e éd., Pedone, 1955), p. 362; Ian Brownlie, *International Law and the Use of Force by States* (Clarendon Press, 1968), p. 41; Anthony Clark Arend and Robert J. Beck, *International Law and the Use of Force* (Routledge, 1993), p. 15; Sean D. Murphy, *Humanitarian Intervention. The United Nations in an Evolving World* (University of Pennsylvania Press, 1996), p. 47; (Nguyên Quôc Dinh), Patrick Daillier, Mathias Forteau et Alain Pellet, *Droit international public* (LGDJ, 2009), p. 1032; Robert Kolb, *Ius contra bellum. Le droit international relatif au maintien de la paix* (Bruylant, 2009), p. 32; Albane Geslin, 'Du justum bellum au jus ad bellum: glissements conceptuels ou simples variations sémantiques?', (2009) 64 *Revue de métaphysique et de morale* 463; Yoram Dinstein, *War, Aggression and Self-Defence* (Cambridge University Press, 2011), p. 69; Mary Ellen O'Connell, 'War and Peace', in Bardo Fassbender & Anne Peters (eds.), *The Oxford Handbook on the History of International Law* (Oxford University Press, 2012), p. 277; Eliav Lieblich, *International Law and Civil Wars - Intervention and consent* (Routledge, 2013), p. 74.

over-realistic understanding of classical international law is put 'in the spotlight and called fundamental to the system' while the elements 'that detract from it [are] pushed into the shadows and rejected as exceptional'.[3] Drawing a synoptic and yet critical picture of the way the use of force was addressed by nineteenth century scholars, the pages that follow nuance this 'apologetic positivism vs. utopian naturalism' caricature. They show that not only did a substantial part of the literature assert that the right to use force was limited by international law, but also that this assertion was far from being a prerogative of a few 'naturalist' authors.

With this objective in mind, the material for analysis essentially consists of nineteenth and early twentieth-century manuals of international law. Manuals, in fact, have specific historical value. They are often considered to be the best reflection of the spirit and ideas that prevailed in a given society at a given time.[4] But the decision to study textbooks also has another advantage. Since the aim, is not solely to give an overview of what nineteenth century authors believed the rules on the use of force to be but also to understand the theoretical and methodological underpinnings of how they approached these rules, textbooks are extremely valuable. Before presenting the content of the rules, authors often laid out their general vision of international law, of its nature and of how it should be addressed. Seldom made in articles and monographs, these precisions give important indications concerning the theoretical and methodological preferences of a given author. Placing the focus on manuals, in other words, allows to make direct links between a specific discourse on law and method on the one hand, and the conclusions reached regarding the use of armed force on the other.

Around eighty manuals of international law dating from 1815 to 1914 are scrutinized. The selection was operated based on three criteria: impact, chronology and geography. Care was taken to include the most influential textbooks. The study would have, been incomplete had it not examined the writings of authors such as Henry Wheaton, Johann-Caspar Bluntschli, Carlos Calvo, Friedrich Martens or yet Lassa Oppenheim, to name a few. To have a representative view of classical international law, it was moreover important to have textbooks covering

[3] Randall Lesaffer, 'International Law and Its History: The Story of an Unrequited Love', in Matthew Craven, Malgosia Fitzmaurice and Maria Vogiatzi (eds.), *Time, History and International Law* (Martinus Nijhoff, 2007), p. 36.

[4] See, e.g., Alain Chopin, 'L'histoire des manuels scolaire: une approche globale' (1980) 9 *Histoire de l'éducation* 1–25; John Issitt, 'Relfections on the Study of Textbooks' (2004) 33 *History of education* 683–696; Michèle Verdelhan-Bourgade, Béatrice Bakhouche, Pierre Boutan et Richard Etienne (dirs.), *Les manuels scolaires, miroir de la nation?* (L'Harmattan, 2007).

the beginning, the middle, as well as the end of our period of interest. Finally, the idea was also to try to have as broad a geographical spectrum as possible by including the work of writers of different nationalities as well as different cultural and legal backgrounds. But there are practical limitations, language barrier and availability being the main ones. Despite this, amongst the studied manuals, books from England, France, Germany, Italy, Spain, Russia, the United States, as well as Argentina, Peru and Bolivia, can be found. Still, one must admit that this material remains, all in all, rather 'western'. This 'eurocentrism', however, is not really problematic in the context of this research, as the aim is to examine a narrative that has itself been built on 'eurocentric' premises.

There are several ways in which this material can be approached. The traditional taxonomy applied to nineteenth-century scholarship consists in distinguishing between 'naturalists', 'eclectics' (also called 'grotians') and 'positivists'.[5] Naturalists are generally considered to be those writers who acknowledged no law besides the law of nature; eclectics as those who recognised both natural and positive law; and positivists as those who only admitted 'man-made' rules.[6] This taxonomy has been criticised as reductive as it seems to offer a rather simplified picture of pre-1914 scholarship.[7] This representation, in fact, does not do justice to the far more complex and subtle theories of and approaches to international law developed by nineteenth century scholars. Tourme-Jouannet, for instance, underlines that most authors found themselves in what she calls a 'vattelian dualism', that is to say, a vision of law, which torn between tradition and modernity, constantly oscillated between naturalism and positivism.[8] Koskenniemi, likewise, notes that the international

[5] Using this classic taxonomy, see, e.g., Lassa Oppenheim, *International Law - A Treatise*, 2 vols. (Longmans, Green & Co. 1905), vol. 1, pp. 82–87; Stephen C. Neff, *Justice among Nations. A History of International Law* (Harvard University Press, 2014), pp. 222–269; Dominique Gaurier, *Histoire du droit international. Auteurs, doctrines et développement de l'Antiquité à l'aube de la période contemporaine* (Presses Universitaires de Rennes, 2005), pp. 229–239.

[6] See, e.g., Oppenheim, International Law, pp. 82–87.

[7] Martti Koskenniemi, *The Gentle Civilizer of Nations. The Rise and Fall of International Law, 1870–1960* (Cambridge University Press, 2001), p. 92.

[8] Emmanuelle Jouannet, *The Liberal Welfarist Law of Nations. A History of International Law* (Cambridge University Press, 2012), p. 115. See also Martti Koskenniemi, *From Apology to Utopia. The Structure of International Legal Argument* (re-issue with new epilogue) (Cambridge University Press, 2005), p. 131. Other authors sometimes speak of 'consensual positivism', see Alexander Orakhelashvili, 'The Origins of Consensual Positivism - Pufendorf, Wolff and Vattel', in Alexander Orakhelashvili (ed.), *Research Handbook on the Theory and History of International Law* (Edward Elgar, 2011), pp. 93–110.

lawyers of the time were 'reluctan[t] to occupy confidently any one of the three major positions of the period's legal theory (rationalism, naturalism and positivism)' and 'cons[antly] borrow[ed] aspects of each'.[9] Against this background, natural law principles, he argues, generally served as a structure that determined the contours of the law, whereas positivism provided a method to unveil the detailed content of the rules.[10]

Nevertheless, as we shall see in further details, variations existed in the manner in which the interaction between these two 'bodies' of law was construed. As H. B. Jacobini indeed underlines, shades of 'eclecticism' with a more or less unified set of common features leaning more towards naturalism or positivism can be identified.[11] It follows that, provided it be slightly redefined and refined, the traditional taxonomy might still offer a relevant tool for analysis. It allows to highlight broad theoretical inclinations and, most importantly, to challenge 'mainstream' literature on its own grounds (i.e. using its own methodological tools and its own epistemological system of reference). In this respect, it is also worth noting that this taxonomy was the one used by nineteenth century scholars themselves. Drawing on this taxonomy then, the pages that follow distinguish between three models of interaction between natural law and positive law. For each of these models, the idea is to: evidence the main features of how the interplay between natural law and positive law was conceptualised; examine how this affected the methodology for the determination of customary rules; and finally, how it influenced the way in which the rules on the use of force were addressed. Successively analysing the works of 'naturalist' inclination (Chapter 2), of 'eclectic' inclination (Chapter 3) and of 'positivist' inclination (Chapter 4), we will see, as announced, that the vast majority of nineteenth century authors asserted that the right to use armed force was not an absolute prerogative of States, and that this assertion was not the prerogative of a few 'naturalists'. Before diving into the matter at heart, however, some brief conceptual clarifications on the notion of 'use of force' and its use in the context of nineteenth century international law are in order (Chapter 1).

[9] Koskenniemi, *The Gentle Civilizer of Nations*, p. 92.

[10] Martti Koskenniemi, 'Into Positivism: Georg Friedrich von Martens (1756–1821) and the Modern International Law' (2008) 15 *Constellations* 190; and by the same author, 'The Legacy of the Nineteenth Century', in David Armstrong (ed.), *Routledge Handbook of International Law* (Routledge, 2009), p. 147. On the relations between natural and positive law in general, see Simone Goyard-Fabre, *Les embarras philosophiques du droit naturel* (J. Vrin, 2002), pp. 127–230.

[11] H. B. Jacobini, *A Study of the Philosophy of International Law as Seen in Works of Latin American Writers* (Martinus Nijhoff, 1954), p. 38.

1

The 'Use of Force' in the Nineteenth Century

Some Conceptual Clarifications

Can it be truly spoken of 'use of force' when studying nineteenth- and early twentieth-century international law? As a legal concept, the 'use of force' was only consecrated by Article 2(4) of the UN Charter, which, as we know, provides that 'all members shall refrain in their international relations from the threat or use of force'.[1] Even though nineteenth-century literature sometimes used this expression, it is hard to say whether it had its own legal meaning.[2] Instead, scholarship spoke of 'coercive measures short of war' and of 'war' to describe the different forms that the use of military force could take. But what was the meaning of these different notions? What did they encompass, and how did they differ, relate and connect to one another?

According to present-day literature, classical international law operated a strict distinction between the uses of armed force that did not amount to war and those that amounted to war.[3] It is usually said that these two types of armed actions depended on distinct legal regimes: the laws of peace on the one hand and the laws of war on the other. It is, indeed, not rare to read that there was no 'twilight zone' between peace and war in classic international law.[4] Either a State declared war, in

[1] Art. 2(4), United Nations Charter, San Francisco, 26 June 1945, in force 24 October 1945.

[2] See, e.g., John T. Abdy, *Kent's Commentaries on International Law* (2nd ed., Deighton and Sons, 1878), p. 54; Thomas Lawrence, *The Principles of International Law* (D. C. Heath & Co., 1900), p. 293.

[3] See Philip C. Jessup, *A Modern Law of Nations* (Macmillan, 1950), p. 157; Ian Brownlie, *International Law and the Use of Force by States* (Clarendon Press, 1968), pp. 26–28; Christopher Greenwood, 'The Concept of War in Modern International Law' (1987) 36 *The International and Comparative Law Quarterly* 284–285; Anthony Clark Arend & Robert J. Beck, *International Law and the Use of Force: Beyond the UN Charter Paradigm* (Routledge, 1993), p. 17; Malcolm Shaw, *International Law* (6th ed., Cambridge University Press, 2008), p. 1121; Robert Kolb, *Ius contra bellum: Le droit international relatif au maintien de la paix* (Bruylant, 2009), p. 32; (Nguyên Quôc Dinh), Patrick Daillier, Mathias Forteau et Alain Pellet, *Droit international public* (LGDJ, 2009), p. 1032.

[4] See, e.g., David Kennedy, *Of Law and War* (Princeton University Press, 2006).

which case the use of force was an act of war that triggered the application of the laws of war (*ius in bello*, suspension of treaty relations and neutrality), or a State did not, in which case the use of force had to be considered as a coercive measure compatible with the maintenance of pacific relations and with the laws of peace. Another common assumption is that 'measures short of war' consisted in smaller-scale uses of armed force, while war suggested a larger outburst of violence. The criteria for distinction are thus believed to have been based on the intention of the parties involved and/or on the material scope of hostilities.

Even so, the distinction between measures short of war and war was not an easy task and was not as straightforward as one might think. The ambiguity was reinforced by the fact that coercive measures and war generally entailed similar acts of force, as well as by the fact that they were believed to be permissible on the same grounds. Armed operations thus often left international lawyers, as well as States, confused as to whether a state of war existed or not. It follows that it is unclear whether the right to resort to measures short of war or to war truly depended on separate sets of rules. In trying to highlight the ambiguities surrounding the notion of 'coercive measures short of war' (Section 1.2) and 'war' (Section 1.3), this chapter argues that, in order to have a clear view of nineteenth-century *ius ad bellum*, they both have to be resituated within the broader concept of intervention (Section 1.1), of which they were but particular forms of expression.

1.1 'Intervention': Unarmed and Armed Measures of Coercion

Back in the nineteenth century, intervention was already considered a particularly ambiguous and multifaceted notion, the definition of which was an arduous task.[5] The authors of the time underlined the difficulties surrounding the concept of 'intervention' and noted that many international lawyers, as a result, avoided defining it altogether. In *De l'intervention au point de vue du droit international* (1884), Jean Tanoviceano observed that

> '[t]he definition of *intervention*, from an international law perspective, is not easy: some authors give none, others provide a clearly inexact definition; [. . .]. Fuzziness reigns over the very notion of intervention and this has greatly contributed to the confusion and to the dissent that exists amongst the authors that have dealt with this topic'.[6]

[5] On the ambiguities of the notion of intervention in contemporary international law, see, e.g., James N. Rosenau, 'The Concept of Intervention' (1968) 22 *Journal of International Affairs* 165–176.

[6] Jean Tanoviceano, *De l'intervention au point de vue du droit international* (L. Larose et Forcel, 1884), p. 2. Also underlining the difficulties that surround the concept of

Instead of giving a general definition, many authors preferred to directly expound the circumstances in which they deemed intervention to be justified,[7] or to categorise, classify and describe the different types of interventions that had taken place in history at that time. These classifications were generally based on the object, the motivations, the means employed or even the circumstances in which interventions had taken place. Carlos Calvo, for instance, spoke of unofficial (diplomatic but not public) or official (public) interventions and of pacific or armed interventions.[8] Henry Bonfils added a distinction between interventions in a State's internal affairs – to impose a form of government or political organisation – and external affairs – to dictate foreign policy.[9] Theodore D. Woolsey noted that interventions had taken place to maintain the balance of power, to prevent revolutions in favour or against established governments, or yet on the basis of religious and humanitarian considerations.[10] Paul Pradier-Fodéré identified up to ten different types of intervention: intervention to prevent a revolution from spreading to a neighbouring country; intervention to maintain the balance of power; intervention in civil war at the request of the government or of the opposition; intervention following a diplomatic protest resulting from the actions of a State or of its citizens; intervention in favour of a State's own citizens to obtain the execution of contract obligations; intervention in a religious war; intervention of humanity; intervention to bring civilisation and ameliorate the institutions of another State; and so on.[11] Most of these categories overlapped, and their profusion contributed to the overall confusion deplored by Tanoviceano and others.

That said, some writers did seek to provide a general definition of 'intervention'. These definitions were often very broad: intervention was

intervention, see Gustave Rolin-Jaequemyns, 'Note sur la théorie du droit d'intervention: A propos d'une lettre de M. le Professeur Arntz' (1876) 8 *Revue de droit international et de législation comparée* 676–677; Giuseppe Carnazza-Amari, 'Nouvel exposé du principe de non-intervention' (1873) 5 *Revue de droit international et de législation comparée* 352.

[7] See, e.g., Alphonse Rivier, *Principes du droit des gens*, 2 vols. (A. Rousseau, 1896), vol. 1, p. 389 ff; Alexandre Mérignhac, *Traité de droit international public*, 3 vols. (LGDJ, 1908–1912), vol. 1, p. 284 ff.

[8] Charles Calvo, *Dictionnaire de droit international public et privé*, 2 vols. (Puttkamer & Mühlbrecht, 1885), vol. 1, p. 402. See also Charles Calvo, *Manuel de droit international public et privé*, 2 vols. (Arthur Rousseau, 1892), vol. 2, p. 101.

[9] Henry Bonfils, *Manuel de droit international public* (Arthur Rousseau, 1894), pp. 153–154.

[10] Theodore D. Woolsey, *Introduction to the Study of International Law* (3rd ed., Charles Scribner & Co., 1872), pp. 58–74.

[11] Paul Pradier-Fodéré, *Traité de droit international public européen et américain suivant les progrès de la science et de la pratique contemporaine*, 9 vols. (Pedone-Lauriel, 1883–1894), vol. 1, p. 559 ff.

described as 'a dictatorial interference by a state in the affairs of another state for the purpose of maintaining or altering the actual condition of things';[12] as 'the use of moral or material force, or of both, to compel a people or a government to change conduct';[13] or yet as an 'interfere[nce] in the domestic affairs of another state irrespectively of the will of the latter for the purpose of either maintaining or altering the actual conditions of things within it'.[14] Two main elements emerge from these definitions: (i) the question of the purpose of the intervention and (ii) the issue of means used to attain this purpose.

An intervention's purpose, as the definitions quoted above state, was to 'maintain or alter the state of things'[15] and to 'compel [a State] to do something which if left to itself, it would not do, or refrain from doing something, which if left to itself, it would do'.[16] This was rather vague and susceptible of including a wide variety of situations. Actions carried out to recover debts that would have otherwise not been paid, to repel an attack that would have otherwise taken place, to prevent a violation of a treaty that would have otherwise been violated, or yet to help a rebel movement overthrow a government, were all susceptible of falling within this definition.[17] An intervention, in sum, was aimed at bending the will of another State and forcing it to act against its original intentions.

It follows that the purpose of the intervention was construed as intrinsically and inextricably linked to the issue of the means employed to attain it. If the objective was coericing a State to do or not to do something, the method unavoidably necessitated the presence of an element of 'force'. In the absence of that element – that is to say, if the State willingly abided by the requests of another nation – the aforementioned State was merely freely exercising its sovereign prerogatives.

[12] Lassa Oppenheim, *International Law: A Treaties*, 2 vols. (Longmans, Green & Co., 1905), vol. 1, p. 181.

[13] Calvo, *Dictionnaire*, vol. 1, p. 402. Translation by the author.

[14] William E. Hall, *Treatise on International Law* (3rd ed., Clarendon Press, 1890), p. 281. See also Giuseppe Carnazza-Amari, *Tratatto sul diritto internazionale pubblico di pace* (2nd ed., V. Maisner e compagnia, 1875), p. 361; and by the same author, 'Nouvel exposé', 353; Tanoviceano, *De l'intervention*, p. 2; Henry Bonfils et Paul Fauchille, *Manuel de droit international public* (7th ed., Arthur Rousseau, 1914), p. 185.

[15] Oppenheim, *International Law*, vol. 1, p. 181.

[16] Lawrence, *The Principles of International Law*, p. 115.

[17] On the changing purposes of intervention through history, see Martha Finnemore, *The Purpose of Intervention: Changing Beliefs about the Use of Force* (Cornell University Press, 2003).

As a result, many authors considered that the means (i.e., the use of coercion) was the determinant element of intervention.[18] Thomas Lawrence, for example, insisted that

> [the] essence of intervention is force, or threat of force, in case the dictates of the intervening power are disregarded. It is, therefore, clearly differentiated from mere *advice* tendered by a friendly state without any idea of compulsion, from *mediation* entered upon a third power at the request of the parties [...], and from *arbitration*, which takes place when the contestants agree to refer the dispute to an independent tribunal [...] There can be no intervention without, on the one hand the presence of force, naked or veiled, and, on the other hand, the absence of consent.[19]

But what form did this force, or coercion, need to take? Again definitions were broad and the nature of the coercion did not really matter: it could be both armed or unarmed – 'material' or 'moral' in Calvo's terms and 'naked' or 'veiled' in Lawrence's – as long as the intention was for it to have a compelling effect.[20] Armed intervention entailed the threat or the effective use of military power, while diplomatic (or unarmed) intervention could take place through simple diplomatic notes and correspondence.[21] Concrete examples of intervention will be given and analysed later on and we shall also see how intervention was deemed permissible in a circumscribed number of circumstances – when it was aimed at redressing a preventing a wrong.[22] But already at this stage, we can sense how the notion of intervention included those of coercive measures short of war and, eventually, war.

[18] In an article examining the notion of intervention in contemporary international law, Eric David defends the opposite view – that is to say, the objective and not the means is the determinative element of intervention. See Eric David, 'Portée et limite du principe de non-intervention' (1990) 23 *Revue belge de droit international* 352.

[19] Lawrence, *The Principles of International Law*, p. 116. Emphasis in the original. In this sense, see also Montague Bernard, *On the Principle of Non-intervention: A Lecture* (J. H. and Jas. Parker, 1860), p. 1; Carnazza-Amari, 'Nouvel exposé', 353; and Trattato, p. 363; Tanoviceano, *De l'intervention*, p. 5; Rivier, *Principes du droit des gens*, vol. 1, p. 390; W. E. Lingelbach, 'The Doctrine and Practice of Intervention in Europe' (1900) 16 *The Annals of the American Academy of Political and Social Science* 1; Oppenheim, *International Law*, vol. 1, p. 181.

[20] Calvo, *Dictionnaire*, vol. 1, p. 402.

[21] See, e.g., Henry Halleck, *International Law: or Rules Regulating the Intercourse of States in Peace and War* (D. Van Nostrand, 1861), p. 335; Carnazza-Amari, Trattato, p. 363; Tanoviceano, *De l'intervention*, pp. 3–4; Rivier, *Principes du droit des gens*, vol. 1, p. 390.

[22] See Sections (2.4), (3.4) and (4.4).

1.2 'Coercive Measures Short of War': Small-Scale Armed Interventions for the Purpose of Self-Help?

Coercive measures short of war were part of the broader category of coercive measures. Coercive measures were understood as unamicable but pacific means of settling an international dispute and were defined as measures 'containing a certain amount of compulsion taken by a State for the purpose of making another State consent to such settlement of difference as is required by the former'.[23] The purpose of coercive measures, as can be seen, was similar to that of intervention: compel a State to do or agree to something that it would have otherwise not done or agreed to. They were deemed permissible once amicable means – such as negotiation, mediation and arbitration – had been exhausted[24] and included retorsions, reprisals, and embargoes and pacific blockades as popular forms of reprisals.[25] Their existence was justified by the absence of any central authority capable of enforcing the law. Oppenheim indeed emphasised how, if a permanent and efficient mechanism for the settlement of international disputes was not put in place, States would have to rely on such means of self-help.[26]

The difference between retorsions and reprisals was the same as nowadays: retorsions were unamicable but intrinsically legal actions; reprisals consisted in the adoption of unamicable and, a priori, illegal measures. Because the latter were more 'aggressive', they were also deemed to be permissible on different grounds as retorsions. Retorsions, Calvo explained, 'consisted in responding to an act contrary to equity'.[27] Travers Twiss and Theodor Woolsey spoke of acts 'contrary

[23] Oppenheim, *International Law*, vol. 2, p. 29. See also Leopold von Neumann, *Elements de droit des gens moderne européen* (Arthur Rousseau, 1886), p. 136; Carlos Calvo, *Le droit international théorique et pratique*, 6 vols. (4th ed., Guillaumin & Cie., 1887), vol. 4, p. 516; Hall, *Treatise on International Law*, p. 366; Rivier, *Principes du droit des gens*, vol. 2, p. 194.

[24] See, e.g., von Neumann, *Eléments*, p. 136; Calvo, *Le droit international théorique et pratique*, vol. 4, p. 516; *Rivier, Principes du droit des gens*, vol. 2, p. 194; Oppenheim, *International Law*, vol. 2, p. 29; Bonfils et Fauchille, *Manuel*, p. 543

[25] See, e.g., von Neumann, *Eléments*, pp. 141 and 142; Hall, *Treatise on International Law*, p. 366; Rivier, *Principes du droit des gens*, vol. 2, pp. 195–196; Oppenheim, *International Law*, vol. 2, pp. 40, 43; Bonfils et Fauchille, *Manuel*, p. 549.

[26] Oppenheim, *International Law*, vol. 2, p. 42.

[27] Calvo, *Dictionnaire*, vol. 2, p. 174. See also von Neumann, *Eléments*, p. 136.

to comity';[28] Oppenheim spoke of 'discourteous or unkind and unequitable acts'.[29] Reprisals, on the other hand, could be exercised when 'simple measure of retorsions' would not be sufficient to obtain satisfaction[30] and were 'admissible for international delinquencies only and exclusively'.[31] In other words, they responded to a previous violation of international law, rather than 'equity' of 'comity'. The use of both types of coercive measures needed to remain proportionate, meaning that retorsions could not involve the use of armed force. Calvo even specified that the very purpose of the institution of retorsions was to give States the necessary tools to empty a dispute without having recourse to the arms.[32] The main examples of measures of retorsions given by nineteenth-century scholars included raising tariffs on the import and transit of goods, modifying the tax regime for the citizen of the target State or yet adopting discriminating legislation against the citizens of that same State.[33] Reprisals, for their part, could include not just the suspension or denunciation of a treaty, seizing goods or properties belonging to the target State or its citizens and androlepsy but also measures of force short of war such as embargoes, pacific blockades or yet bombardments and military occupations.[34] In these last cases, the line between peace and war became particularly thin. The use of such measures, often led to situations in which it was unclear whether the relations between the protagonists could still truly qualify as 'peaceful'.

Embargoes consisted in sequestering the ships of a delinquent State in ports or seizing them on the high seas for the purpose of compelling said State to give reparations.[35] An illustration sometimes given by scholarship was the British embargo on Sicilian ships carried out in 1840 in the

[28] Travers Twiss, *The Law of Nations Considered as Independent Political Communities* (Clarendon Press, 1884), p. 18; Woolsey, *Introduction to the Study of International Law*, p. 181.

[29] Oppenheim, *International Law*, vol. 2, p. 31.

[30] Calvo, *Dictionnaire*, vol. 1, p. 161.

[31] Oppenheim, *International Law*, vol. 2, p. 35.

[32] Calvo, *Dictionnaire*, vol. 2, p. 174.

[33] See, e.g., ibid., p. 174; Hall, *Treatise on International Law*, p. 364; Johann-Caspar Bluntschli, *Le droit international codifié* (Guillemin & Cie., 1870), p. 285.

[34] Rivier, *Principes du droit des gens*, vol. 2, p. 195.

[35] Ibid., p. 194; Oppenheim, *International Law*, vol. 2, p. 40; von Neumann, *Eléments*, p. 141; Mérighnac, *Traité de droit international public*, vol. 2, p. 57; Lawrence, *The Principles of International Law*, p. 295.

context of the Sulphur Crisis.[36] This crisis resulted from the decision of the King of the Two-Sicilies to grant a monopoly on the extraction of sulphur to a French company despite a treaty securing commercial privileges to Great Britain. In reprisal of this decision, London decided to immobilize the Sicilian merchant ships present in Malta's harbours and seize others sailing in the Mediterranean. The purpose of the measure was to force Ferdinand II to abide by his treaty obligations and rescind his contract with the French. It is also interesting to note how, despite Great Britain's clear military superiority and in the absence of any direct military confrontation, European courts feared the situation would degenerate into war. The dispute was eventually peacefully resolved thanks to the mediation of France, leading to the release of the Two-Sicilies' ships.[37] Other examples of embargoes were the Christie Question and the Batsch Affair. The Christie Question originated in two separate incidents: first, the plunder of a wrecked British merchant vessel and the suspected murder of crew members on the southern coast of Brazil; and, second, the arrest of two British sailors suspected of encouraging mutinies in Rio de Janeiro. Great Britain's ambassador, William Douglas Christie, believed that Brazilian authorities had not investigated these two events as they should have and demanded compensation for the offences suffered by its nationals.[38] Brazil, however, refused and Christie ordered the capture of Brazilian ships in the Atlantic as reprisal. The former Portuguese colony eventually agreed to pay indemnities and to submit the matter of the sailors' arrest to arbitration. The arbitrators ruled in favour of Brazil and considered that it had meant no offense or insult to Great Britain. It was the latter's refusal to comply with this decision and give the captured ships back that precipitated the 1863 Anglo-Brazilian War. The Batsch Affair, for its part, was connected to the destruction of German citizens' business as the result of the bombardment of Cap-Haitien by British ships in 1865. Berlin asked the island's authorities to compensate these losses and, following several years of negotiations, resolved to sail to Port-au-Prince and capture

[36] Oppenheim, *International Law*, vol. 2, p. 40 and 35. See also Calvo, *Le droit international*, vol. 3, p. 530.

[37] About the Sulphur Crisis of 1840, see Miroslav Šedivý, 'Metternich and the Anglo-Neapolitan Sulphur Crisis of 1840' (2011) 16 *Journal of Modern Italian Studies* 1–18; and by the same author, *The Decline of the Congress System: Metternich Italy and European Diplomacy* (I. B. Tauris, 2018), pp. 107–123.

[38] William Douglas Christie, *Notes on the Brazilian Question* (Macmillan, 1865), pp. 177–178.

two Haitian corvettes. Haiti promptly paid the debt, and the vessels were restituted.

Embargoes were sometimes completed by the establishment of the pacific blockade, which consisted in blocking the coasts of the target State to prevent supplies from entering or leaving its ports. Such measures were originally used during wartime to hinder the enemy's war effort. Their use as pacific reprisals was fairly new at the time.[39] They were usually traced back to the 1827 intervention of Great Britain, France and Russia in the Greek War of Independence. Claiming that the ongoing war was causing damage to their commerce in the Mediterranean, the three powers had indeed convened to establish a blockade around the coast of Morea (modern-day Peloponnese).[40] The purpose, as stated in the powers' agreement, was to force the Ottoman Empire to accept mediation and put an end to the conflict.[41] Interestingly, the instructions received by the commanders of the allied fleet insisted that 'great care should be taken so as to avoid the measures adopted against the Ottoman navy from degenerating into hostilities'.[42] London, Paris and Saint-Petersburg were thus well aware of the 'borderline' character of their actions. The Battle of Navarino, during which most of the Turkish fleet was destroyed and which left European capitals and Constantinople puzzled as to whether a state of war now existed, came as a further illustration of the ambiguous nature of 'pacific' blockades.[43] In his book *Le blocus pacifique* (1919), Horst Falcke listed around twenty-seven other instances of pacific blockades throughout the nineteenth and early twentieth centuries, the majority of which however had taken place in times of war.[44] This probably explains why many

[39] See, e.g., Rivier, *Principes du droit des gens*, vol. 2, p. 198; Mérignhac, *Traité de droit international public*, vol. 3, p. 60.

[40] This agreement was enacted in the Treaty for the Pacification of Greece signed in London on 6 July 1827. The preamble of the treaty stated that the Powers were acting 'penetrated by the necessity of putting an end to the sanguinary struggle [. . .] which daily causes fresh impediments to the commerce of the States of Europe, and gives opportunity for acts of piracy which not only expose the subjects of the high contracting parties to grievous losses, but also renders necessary measures which are burthensome for their observation and suppression'.

[41] Article 1, Treaty for the Pacification of Greece, London, 6 July 1827.

[42] 'Secondes instructions communes aux Officiers commandants dans les mers du Levant, Londres 12 juillet 1827', in Foreign Office, *Papers Relative to the Affairs of Greece, 1826–1832* (J. Harrison and Son, 1835), p. 10.

[43] See Will Smiley, 'War without War: The Battle of Navarino, the Ottoman Empire, and the Pacific Blockade' (2016) 18 *Journal of the History of International Law* 42–69.

[44] Horst P. Falcke, *Le blocus pacifique* (Rossberg, 1919), pp. 13–222.

nineteenth-century authors had an ambivalent attitude towards pacific blockades. Alphonse Rivier, for instance, stated that he had 'serious objections against this practice, which surreptitiously introduces war in peace'.[45] The debates that took place during the 1887 session of the *Institut de droit international* in Heidelberg also reflected the division among doctrine well. On the one hand, those in favour of pacific blockades – among which was Rapporteur Ferdinand Prenels – insisted that they were useful means of avoiding full-blown war.[46] On the other hand, those against – at the forefront of which was Heinrich Geffcken, who presented a counter-report – felt not only that blockades were intrinsically hostile but also that their inclusion in the category of pacific reprisals was a plain consecration of the right of the powerful over the weak.[47] The synthesis of this opposition was the adoption of a declaration, in which the IDI stated that pacific blockades could only be considered as permissible under three conditions: (i) that it did not affect third States, (ii) that it be declared and officially notified, and (iii) that the seized ships be restituted as soon as the blockade ended.[48]

Arguably, however, pacific blockades were not the most aggressive form that reprisals could take. Bombardments and military occupations, in fact, were also sometimes used for the purpose of obtaining redress for an offence. Examples were, amongst others, the occupation of the Nicaraguan port of Corinto by Great Britain in 1896, the occupation of the city of Oujda in Morocco by France in 1897 and the occupation of the port of Veracruz by the United States in 1914.[49] The latter precedent offers a particularly good illustration of the tenuous nature of the distinction between peace and war. The dispute found its roots in the Tampico Affair in the context of the Mexican faction wars. Hostilities were intensifying in the region of the port of Tampico, which concentrated many US interests. The United States already had several ships mooring off the coast. On 9 April 1914, nine unarmed sailors were sent ashore on a whaling boat flying the American flag in order to get gasoline supplies. They were arrested by governmental forces, but promptly

[45] Rivier, *Principes du droit des gens*, vol. 2, p. 198.

[46] 'Report of M. Perels, 'Rapporteur de la sixième commission détude – Droit de blocus en temps de paix' (1887) 9 *Annuaire de l'Institut de droit international* 282–283.

[47] 'Counter-Report of M. Geffecken', ibid., pp. 286–295.

[48] IDI, *Declaration concernant le blocus en dehors de l'état de guerre* (Heidelberg Session, 1887).

[49] Paul Fauchille, *Traité de droit international public*, 2 vols. (Rousseau et cie. 1926), vol. 1, Partie 3, pp. 693–694.

released with an apology. The commander of the US force, Henry T. Mayo, however, felt that this offence required full reparations. He demanded a formal disavowal, the punishment of those responsible and for the American flag to be hoisted in a prominent position on the shore and saluted by twenty-one gunshots. The Mexican government refused this last request, which was perceived as particularly humiliating and as tantamount to recognising the sovereignty of a foreign State on its own territory. In response, President Woodrow Wilson ordered the capture of the port of Veracruz. Interestingly, although he underlined that it was within his constitutional powers to act without the consent of Congress 'to enforce respect for [the United States']',[50] Wilson sought congressional approval. He thus seemed to be well aware of the equivocal nature of such a measure of reprisal. The disembarkment of US troops in Veracruz was met with resistance; it is estimated that 174 soldiers and 150 civilians lost their lives.[51] The Mexican government explained that, 'according to international law, those acts of the armed forces of the United States [...] must be understood as an initiation of war',[52] and severed diplomatic relations with Washington.[53] The dispute was eventually resolved following the mediation of Argentina, Brazil and Chile. An agreement was made at Niagara Falls in May 1914: Mexico established a new provisional government, and the United States relinquished its requests for financial reparations.[54] The occupation of Veracruz was lifted on 23 November 1914. Maybe because they took place around the same time as the outbreak of World War I, the events of Veracruz were not widely commented by doctrine. Paul Fauchille nonetheless underlined that such actions could hardly be seen as compatible with a state of peace.[55] As we know, this issue would resurface in 1923 when Italy

[50] 'Address of the President delivered at a joint session of the two Houses of Congress, April 20 1914, on "The Situation in our dealings with General Victoriano Huerta and Mexico City"', in US Department of State, *Papers Relating to Foreign Affairs 1914* (Government Printing Office, 1922), p. 476.

[51] Niheer Dasandi, 'United States Occupation of Vera Cruz' in *Encyclopaedia Britannica* (published on 14 April 2019).

[52] 'The Minister for Foreign Affairs to Chargé O'Shaughnessy, Foreign Office, Mexico, April 22 1914' enclosed to 'Chargé O'Shaughnessy to Secretary of State, Vera Cruz, April 25 1914' in US Department of State, Papers 1914, p. 490.

[53] 'Chargé O'Shaughnessy to Secretary of State, American Embassy, Mexico, April 22 1914' in ibid., pp. 484–485.

[54] See Michael Small, *The Forgotten Peace. Mediation at Niagara Falls, 1914* (University of Ottawa Press, 2009).

[55] Fauchille, *Traité de droit international public*, vol. 1, p. 695.

bombarded and occupied the Island of Corfu as reprisal for the assassination of three of its officers along the Greco-Albanian border, once more highlighting the porosity between peace and war.

1.3 'War': Large Scale Armed Intervention as the Last Resort Mean of Self-Help?

In 1870, Johann-Caspar Bluntschli defined war as 'all acts by which a State or people ensures respect for its rights by fighting arms in hand against another State or another people'.[56] A few years later, Travers Twiss, gave a similar definition: '[W]ar may be regarded as an alternative state of international relations, which supersedes the relation of Peace, whenever Nations prosecute their right by force'.[57] Like them, most late nineteenth-century authors insisted that war was a mean to settle a dispute between two or more States.[58] War hence simply appeared to be another, specific, armed coercive measure: the 'extreme means of coercion' to use Rivier's words.[59] And, in fact, it was not uncommon for nineteenth-century textbooks to examine resort to war in the same chapter or section as armed reprisals,[60] once more evidencing that war could be seen as a special, particularly grave, form of armed reprisal and, therefore, of armed intervention. Authors nevertheless insisted that war was a measure of absolute last resort, to be used only if all the amicable and unamicable (but still 'pacific') dispute settlement mechanisms had failed. Leopold von Neumann wrote that a war would have to be considered unjust 'if it were to be started before all pacific means have been exhausted to obtain satisfaction'.[61] While he did not disagree with his colleagues, Oppenheim nevertheless insisted that war differed from armed reprisals in at least one fundamental way: it gave rise to a state

[56] Bluntschli, *Le droit international codifié*, p. 270.

[57] Twiss, *The Law of Nations*, p. 49.

[58] For an index of definitions, see Calvo, *Le droit international*, vol. 4, pp. 15–16.

[59] Rivier, *Principes de droit des gens*, vol. 2, p. 200.

[60] See, e.g., August Wilhelm Heffter, *Le droit international de l'Europe* (E.-H. Schroeder, 1873), pp. 220 ff.; Lawrence, *The Principles of International Law*, p. 290 ff.; Mérighnac, *Traité de droit international public*, vol. 3, p. 60 ff.; Twiss, *The Law of Nations*, p. 49 ff.; von Neumann, *Eléments*, p. 129 ff.; John Westlake, *International Law*, 2 vols. (Cambridge University Press, 1913), vol. 2, p. 1 ff.

[61] von Neumann, Elements, p. 145; Heffter, Le droit international de l'Europe, p. 221; Antoine Pillet, *Les lois actuelles de la guerre* (Arthur Rousseau, 1898), p. 65; Bonfils and Fauchille, Manuel, p. 711.

of war.[62] The state of war was characterised by the suspension of the belligerents' trade and treaty relations, as well as by the application of the laws of armed conflict and neutrality. In other words, their *effects* were completely different. For States, belligerents and bystanders, to understand their obligations it was therefore crucial to understand how an act of war could be distinguished from a coercive measure short of actual war.

As previously stated, it is commonly assumed that this distinction was fairly easy to operate and rested on the existence of the parties 'intent of war' (*animus belligerandi*). It is moreover not rare to read that in the nineteenth century wars were usually preceded by declarations or ultimatums, which some assume were even a legal prerequisite of war. But, the issue of a formal war declaration or ultimatum only became mandatory with the adoption of the Hague Convention (III) on the Opening of Hostilities in 1907.[63] Many nineteenth-century scholars asserted war declaration to be an obsolete institution and that States scarcely employed them.[64] In 1900, Lawrence thus observed that 'the nearer we approach to modern times the rarer do formal declarations become'.[65] Conducting an historical survey on the use of war declarations, Brevet Lieutenant Colonel J. F. Maurice concluded that between 1700 and 1870 only 10 out of the 117 wars that took place had been formally declared.[66] Yet, nineteenth century authors generally agreed that the main criteria for distinction was, indeed, the presence of an *animus belligerendi*. But, if war declarations were not mandatory and it was not within the mores of States to use them, how could a belligerent intention be enacted?

62 Oppenheim, International Law, vol. 2, pp. 29–30.

63 Article 1, Convention (III) on the Opening of Hostilities, The Hague, 18 October 1907, in force 26 January 1910.

64 Affirming the obsolete character of war declarations, see, e.g., Henry Wheaton, *Elements of International Law*, 2 vols. (Carey, Lea & Blanchard, 1836), vol. 2, p. 11; Halleck, The Law of Nations, p. 352; von Neumann, Eléments, p. 57; Lawrence, The Principles of Internatinal Law, p. 301. Note that a minority of authors nevertheless considered them to be mandatory, see, e.g., Bluntschli, Le droit international codifié, p. 275; Calvo, Manuel, vol. 2, p. 317; Pillet, Les lois actuelles, pp. 64–65. See also the debates during the IDI session of 1906 in (1906) 21 *Annuaire de l'Institut de droit international* 29–33.

65 Lawrence, *The Principles of International Law*, p. 300. See also Westlake, *International Law*, vol. 2, pp. 23–25; Twiss, The Law of Nations, p. 65; von Neumann, Elements, p. 157; Rivier, Principes de droit des gens, vol. 2, p. 21.

66 Brevet Lieutenant Colonel J. F. Maurice, *Hostilities without Declaration of War* (H.M. Stationary Office, 1883), p. 4. See also Brien Hallett, *The Lost Art of Declaring War* (University of Illinois Press, 1998).

Stephen Neff identifies two main approaches for establishing the existence of an *animus belligerendi* in nineteenth-century scholarship: a *subjective* approach, which focused on the explicit expression of an intent of war; and an *objective* approach, which put the emphasis on the presence and nature of material hostilities.[67] With the exception of John Bassett Moore few writers followed a strictly subjective or objective method. For Moore, the expression of a belligerent intention by itself sufficed to create a state of war even in the absence of actual armed clashes: 'if two nations declare war', he wrote, 'war exists, though no force whatsoever may as yet have been employed'.[68] This position could lead to somewhat bizarre and paradoxical situations in which war existed despite the absence of hostilities or, on the contrary, in which war did not exist despite ferocious and widespread combat. The advocates of a purely objective approach were just as scarce and, in fact, authors usually preferred to adopt a mix of both approaches.[69] A state of war could then result from an explicit expression of a belligerent intention through a declaration or an ultimatum, or from facts, interpreted as an implicit expression of that same intention. William E. Hall, for instance, underlined that 'an act of hostility, [. . .] is in itself a full declaration of intention'.[70] But this view was not without problems either since, as previously highlighted, measures short of war were *prima facie* hostile

[67] Stephen C. Neff, *War and the Law of Nations. A General History* (Cambridge University Press, 2005), pp. 172–175. See also Greenwood, 'The Concept of War', 286; Ingrid Detter, *The Law of War* (2nd ed., Cambridge University Press, 2000), p. 10.

[68] John Bassett Moore, *A Digest of International Law*, 8 vols. (Government Printing Office, 1906), vol. 7, p. 153.

[69] See, for example, Georg-Friedrich Von Martens, *A compendium of the Law of Nations* (2nd ed., Corbett and Morgan, 1802), pp. 281–282; Wheaton, Elements of International Law, vol. 2, p. 10; Halleck, *International Law*, pp. 354–355; Theophile Funck-Brentano et Albert Sorel, *Précis de droit des gens* (E. Plon et Cie., 1877), p. 247; Bonfils, *Manuel*, p. 579; Rivier, Principes de droit des gens, vol. 2, p. 228; Louis-J.-D. Féraud-Giraud, 'Des hostilités sans déclaration de guerre' (1885) 18 *Revue de droit international et de législation comparée* 19–49.

[70] The position of William E. Hall might in this respect appear somewhat ambiguous. He was of the opinion that '[a]n act of hostility, [. . .] is in itself a full declaration of intention; any sort of previous declaration therefore is an empty formality' and that as a consequence '[t]he date of the commencement of a war can be perfectly defined by the first act of hostility'. It thus appears that the most important element for him was the presence of material hostilities. At the same time, however, he insisted that this was because they were tantamount to a declaration of war thus emphasising the criteria of the existence of an intention. See Hall, *Treatise*, pp. 374–375.

acts that could hardly be materially differentiated from acts of war, especially in the first stages of the operation.

It has nevertheless been argued, that measures short of war and war could be distinguished based on the gravity and widespread nature of the acts of force involved.[71] Armed reprisals are then represented as more limited temporally, geographically and materially. War, on the other hand, is seen as a more generalised outburst of violence. This is to some extent exact because war suggested *reciprocal* hostilities (action-reaction), while reprisals usually were unilateral acts of force (action without reaction). When an act of force is reciprocated, there is a good chance that the conflict will spread and last longer. Still, reciprocity, rather than the scope of the conflict, appeared to be the determinant element.[72] And yet, we just saw that the reaction of the Mexican authorities to US soldiers disembarking to Veracruz was not considered as having given rise to a proper state of war between these two nations. It follows that, for better or for worst, acts of armed reprisals could not be distinguished from acts of war at the moment in which they were being resorted to. Ultimately, whether a use of force created a state of war depended on the capacity of the target State to retaliate as well as on the willingness of the States involved to consider that they were at war with each other, with all the detrimental consequences this could have on their commerce, treaties and relations with neutral powers.

* * *

The purpose of this brief chapter was to provide some conceptual clarification around the notion of 'use of force' in the context of nineteenth-century international law. In fact, although the authors of the time sometimes used this expression, it was not consecrated as a self-standing legal concept before the adoption of the UN Charter in 1945. Present day doctrine generally assumes that the use of force at the time was divided into two broad categories: measures short of war, on the one hand, and war, on the other. It is claimed that resort to these two different 'types' force depended in two distinct legal regimes and were, moreover, relatively easy to distinguish. Measures short of war, it is said,

[71] See Brownlie, *International Law and the Use of Force by States*, p. 28.

[72] The criteria of the geographical and temporal scope of the conflict was used by nineteenth century scholarship to distinguish between 'perfect' wars – which implicated the nations as a whole – and 'imperfect' wars – which only involved a part of the nation. See, for example Calvo, *Le droit international*, vol. 4, p. 20.

fell within the purview of the laws of peace and consisted in more limited uses of military force, while resort to war was (un)regulated by the laws of war and implied a generalised state of violence between at least two States.

The above examination of doctrine, complemented by some elements of State practice, shows that the distinction was not as clear-cut. A 'twilight zone' between peace and war did exist. Commentators as well as States were often confused as to whether a particular act of force should be interpreted a measure of armed reprisal or of war. Both, in fact, involved actions of a priori hostile nature and, unless it was preceded by a formal war declaration, there was no clear criteria to distinguish one from the other at the moment in which they were being used. Several authors furthermore underlined that measures short of war often served as premises for, or resulted in, war. The Christie Question discussed above, which led to the Anglo-Brazilian War of 1863 offers an illustration. Another example was the Russo-Turkish War of 1828 and the Spanish-American War of 1898 which were respectively the direct consequence of the pacific blockade established by the British, French and Russian in Morea, on the one hand, and of the United States' intervention in the Cuban War of Independence on the other.

To add to the ambiguity, resort to measures short of war and war were justified on same grounds. Both were presented as means of self-help permissible to redress an offence, understood as a previous violation of international law. Measures short of war were indeed defined as actions undertaken 'for the purpose of compelling [a State] to consent to a satisfactory settlement of a dispute created by its own delinquency',[73] while war was claimed to be the 'extreme mean of coercion'[74] used by nations 'to prosecute their Right by force'[75] when all other mechanisms had failed. Armed reprisals and war thus essentially seemed to be placed on a continuum: a same incident could warrant resort to measure short of war and, if these had failed, to war. It follows that these two categories of uses of armed force did not depend on separate legal regimes but a single, identical set of rules. And, in fact, as previously stated, they were often analysed in the same section or chapter immediately before expounding the rules of *ius in bello* and neutrality. This chapter argues that measures short of war and war belonged to the broader category of

[73] Oppenheim, *International Law*, vol. 2, p. 34.
[74] Rivier, *Principes du droit des gens*, vol. 2, p. 200.
[75] Twiss, *The Law of Nations*, p. 49.

intervention and, more specifically, of armed intervention. As a result, to understand if and how classic international law ring-fenced the use of force we need to further investigate the legal regime applicable to intervention. This is the task carried out in the next three chapters, which aim to resituate the conclusions nineteenth century scholars reached on this subject within the broader context of how they thought about international law as a normative system.

2

The Use of Force in Writings of 'Naturalist' Inclination

The claim of the narrative of indifference vis-à-vis the use of force in nineteenth-century doctrine is a claim about theory and method. States' war prerogatives are, in fact, said to have been the consequence of the rise of positivism and concomitant dismissal of the theories of just war. Following this line of thought, the work of the authors who still asserted that rules regulating the right for States to use force existed are immediately pushed to the side as 'naturalist' and their writings discarded as not representative of law as it applied. But what did it mean to be a 'naturalist' in the nineteenth century? How did they think about the international legal system? Was their method top-down and disconnected from any 'practical' considerations? How did this affect the conclusions they reached regarding the use of force?

In this chapter, we shall see that positive law and State practice were not absent from the writings of nineteenth century authors leaning more towards 'naturalism'. The manner in which they conceived the international legal system originated in the 'rationalist' conceptions that took root in the literature from the sixteenth century onwards, out of the necessity to find a new, non-strictly theological, basis for the law of nations following the religious schism and the secularisation of State power.[1] By placing human nature and men's inherent rationality instead of God at the centre of law, thinkers such as Grotius and Hobbes opened the way for an increased role of positive ('man-made') law into legal philosophy and theory. Nineteenth-century writings of 'naturalist' inclination thus often acknowledged the existence of both natural and positive law, even though they considered the former to be normatively superior to the latter (Section 2.1). All the rules of international law were considered to ultimately derive from nature and reason. This translated into

[1] See Simone Goyard-Fabre, *Les embarras philosophiques du droit naturel* (J. Vrin, 2002), pp. 27–126; Randall Lesaffer, 'The Grotian Tradition Revisited: Change and Continuity in International Law' (2002) 73 *British Yearbook of International Law* 103–139.

a method for custom determination that was predominantly deductive, although it took State practice into consideration (Section 2.2). When it came to the use of force, however, it must be admitted that 'naturalist' authors left little space for the analysis of actual practice. The general rule of non-intervention was foremost deduced from the principles of independence and of equality of States (Section 2.3). State practice, on the other hand, was much more thoroughly examined to establish the exceptions to the rule, even though, as we shall see, their truly legal character was still considered to rest on their concordance with the principles derived from nature and reason, in particular the principle of self-preservation (Section 2.4).

2.1 The 'Naturalist' Legal Order: Positive Law as an Emanation of Natural Law

In 1905, Oppenheim explained that naturalists were 'those writers who den[ied] that there is any positive Law of Nations whatever as the outcome of custom or treaties, and who maintain[ed] that all Law of Nations is only part of the Law of Nature'.[2] If such a narrow definition was to be kept, few nineteenth century authors would qualify as 'naturalists'. From the sixteenth century onwards, in fact, authors such Gentili and Grotius already recognised the existence of positive 'man-made' rules alongside natural law dictated by necessity and reason. In *De Jure Belli Ac Pacis* (1625), for instance, Grotius explained that the law of nations was 'that law which is common to many Nations or Rulers of Nations, whether derived from nature, or instituted by Divine Comments, *or introduced by Custom and tacit consent*'.[3] A few years earlier, in 1612, Gentili had made a similar contention.[4] The two

[2] Lassa Oppenheim, *International Law. A Treatise*, 2 vols. (Longmans Greens, 1905), vol. 1, p. 82.

[3] Hugo Grotius, *The Rights of War and Peace* (translated from Latin by Jean de Barbeyrac, original ed.: 1625) (W. Innys & al., 1738), Book I, Preliminary discourse, par. I, p. xiii. Emphasis added. According to Stephen C. Neff the first author to make the difference between the 'law of nature' and the 'law of nations' was Isidore of Seville in *Hugo Grotius. On the Law of War and Peace* (edited and annotated by Stephen C. Neff) (Cambridge University Press, 2012), p. xxxiv. See also H. B. Jacobini, *A Study of the Philosophy of International Law as Seen in Works of Latin American Writers* (Martinus Nijhoff, 1954), p. 14.

[4] Alberico Gentili, *De Iure Belli Libri Tres* (translated from Latin by John C. Rolphe, original ed.: 1612), 2 vols. (Clarendon Press, 1933), vol. 2, p. 8. On the relation between Gentili's and Grotius's works, see Peter Haggenmacher, 'Grotius and Gentili: a Reassessment of

scholars, however, also agreed that although 'man-made' rules were part of the law of nations they were normatively inferior to the laws of nature.[5] For Grotius, the binding nature of positive law rules was simply the result of human beings' inherent rationality and sociability, which, he argued, led them to naturally abide by their engagements and promises. Gentili's theory was slightly different. He considered that 'man-made' rules were part of the law of nations only inasmuch as they were compatible with the principles of natural law. In this perspective, natural law served as a benchmark to assess the binding and normative value of customs and treaties: if they were compatible, they were binding, but if they were not compatible, they could not be considered as rules of law. During the Enlightenment era, this idea of a 'legality-test' was notably taken over by Emer de Vattel. In *Le droit des gens ou principes de la loi naturelle* (1758), he distinguished between 'necessary' (natural) and 'voluntary' (positive) law, insisting that:

> … as this law [natural law] is immutable, and the obligations that arise from it necessary and indispensable, nations can neither make any changes to it by the conventions, dispense with it in their own conduct, nor reciprocally release each other from the observance of it.
>
> This is the principle by which we distinguish *lawful* conventions or treaties from those that are not lawful, and innocent and rational customs from those that are unjust or censurable.[6]

Vattel thus viewed the principles of natural law as eternal and immutable, which meant that the legally constraining character of positive rules depended on their conformity with these principles. Customs and treaties that went against 'necessary' law had to be considered as 'not lawful'. It follows that, the content of positive law could not fundamentally or substantially differ from that of natural law. In some ways, positive law was a mere emanation, or expression under a different form, of natural law.

Thomas E. Holland Inaugural Lecture 1', in Hedley Bull, Benedict Kingsbury and Adam Roberts (eds.), *Hugo Grotius and International Relations* (Clarendon Press, 1992), pp. 133–176.

[5] Gentili, *De Iure Belli*, vol. 2, p. 8. On this topic see also Gezina van der Molen, *Alberico Gentili and the Development of International Law. His life, Work and Times* (H. J., 1937).

[6] Emmer de Vattel, *The Law of Nations; or, Principles of Natural Law Applied to the Conduct and Affaires of Nations and Sovereigns* (original ed.: 1758) (T. & J. W. Johnson, 1853), Book 1, par. 9, p. viii. Emphasis in the original.

The influence of these authors on nineteenth century literature has often been highlighted.[7] And, in fact, the premises of sociability, rationality and immutability of natural law as well as the belief in the necessity to distinguished 'good' from 'bad' customs were amongst the most salient features of nineteenth century writings inclined towards naturalism. Amanda Perreau-Saussine thus explained that the naturalistic inclinations of Sir Robert J. Phillimore, for instance, were evident from the fact that he tempered his analysis of State practice by referring to morals and discriminated between 'good' and 'bad' positive rules.[8] Phillimore was born in a family of ecclesiastical lawyers and was himself foremost trained in canon law.[9] This might explain why he leaned more towards 'naturalist' approaches to international law, but also why he preferred the expression 'divine law' to that of 'natural law'. As a barrister and later as a judge, Phillimore essentially practiced civil law and most of his publications dealt with British private law. From 1854 to 1861, however, while a member of the House of Commons, he published a four-volume textbook on international law entitled *Commentaries upon International Law*. The book was re-edited several times throughout the nineteenth century (in 1854, 1871 and 1879) and was even translated into Chinese in the late 1870s.[10] In it, Phillimore explained that 'states are governed, in their mutual relations, partly by divine, and partly by positive law',[11] but that 'the primary source of International jurisprudence is Divine law'[12] and that, as a consequence, 'positive law, [. . .] may add to, but cannot

[7] See Emmanuelle Jouannet, *The Liberal-Welfarist Law of Nations. A History of International Law* (Cambridge University Press, 2012), p. 111; Martti Koskenniemi, *From Apology to Utopia. The Structure of International Legal Argument* (re-issue with new epilogue) (Cambridge University Press, 2005), p. 124.

[8] Amanda Perreau-Saussine, 'Three ways of writing a treatise on public international law: textbooks and the nature of customary international law' in Amanda Perreau-Saussine and James B. Murphy (eds.), *The Nature of Customary Law. Legal, Historical and Philosophical Perspectives* (Cambridge University Press, 2007), pp. 239–240.

[9] His father was renowned ecclesiastical and civil law professor at Oxford, Joseph Phillimore. About Robert Phillimore see for e.g. John H. Baker, 'Famous English Canon Lawyers: X Sir Robert Phillimore, QC, DCL († 1885) and the Last Practising Doctors of Law' (1994) 21 *Ecclesiastical Law Journal* 709–719.

[10] Rune Svarverud, *International Law as a World Order in Late Imperial China. Translation, Reception and Discourses* (Brill, 2007), p. 115.

[11] Robert Phillimore, *Commentaries upon International Law*, 3 vols. (T. & J. W. Johnson, 1854), vol. 1, p. 56.

[12] Ibid.

take from prohibition of Divine law'.[13] Another distinguished Anglo-Saxon scholar, Henry Halleck, shared this view.[14] He believe that:

> 'The rules which ought to regulate the conduct of nations in their mutual intercourse are undoubtedly deduced, in part, from reason and justice, and from the nature of society existing between independent states or bodies politic; and, in part, from usage, and the agreements or compacts entered into between different nation'.[15]

He added, furthermore, that: 'it is to these principles, or rules of right reason, or natural law, that all other laws, whether founded on custom or treaty, must be referred, and their binding force determined'.[16] This conception of the international legal order was also quite popular in the Latin American literature, in particular in the writings of Gregorio Perez Gomar, José Silva Santisteban, Agustin Aspiazu or yet of José Maria Pando. Aspiazu, for example, was of the opinion that 'the discipline that we are going to study does not deserve the name of law, if it is not in conformity with the prescriptions of reason'.[17] As a result, if treaties or customs 'are contrary to good sense, then we should not take as rules of our conduct that which is unfair or arbitrary'.[18]

Alongside this 'weak naturalism', as it has sometimes been called, doctrine claims that a stronger iteration of naturalism (more in keeping with Oppenheim's definition) could also be observed in nineteenth-century scholarship.[19] This other strand of naturalism is sometimes described as being of 'pufendorfian' legacy. Although he recognised the existence of positive law at the domestic level, Samuel von Pufendorf (1632–1694) was indeed of the opinion that, in the absence of a supranational authority, such law could not exist at the international level.[20]

[13] Ibid., p. 63.

[14] In addition to being an academic, Henry Halleck was also a General in the Union Army during the American Secession War.

[15] Henry Halleck, *International Law: Or Rules Regulating the Intercourse of States in Peace and War* (D. Van Nostand, 1861), p. 43. See also Sir Sherston Baker, *Halleck's International Law* (2nd ed., C. Kegan Paul & Co., 1878), pp. 42 ff.

[16] Halleck, *International Law*, p. 51.

[17] Agustin Aspiazu, *Dogmas del derecho internacional* (Hallet & Breen, 1872), p. 3. Translation by the author.

[18] Ibid., p. 4. Translation by the author.

[19] See Casper Sylvest, *British Liberal Internationalism, 1880–1930. Making Progress?* (Manchester University Press, 2009), p. 78.

[20] Samuel Von Pufendorf, *Of the Law of Nature and Nations* (translated from Latin by Mr Carew, original ed.: 1672) (J. Walthoe, R. Wilkin, J. and J. Bonwicke, S. Birt, T. Ward, and T. Osborne 1729), Book II, Chapter 3, par. 23, p. 150.

Sovereigns, he felt, evolved in a state of nature and only the principles of nature deduced by reason could regulate their relations. James Lorimer and Antonio Saénz have sometimes been considered as representatives of this 'stronger' naturalism. Oppenheim, in fact, described Lorimer as a 'naturalist pure and simple',[21] and H. B. Jacobini deemed Saénz a 'complete naturalist'.[22] Yet, despite insisting that the international law was 'the law of nature realised in the relations of separate entities',[23] Lorimer dedicated approximately twenty pages to the discussion of custom and treaties and of their relations with natural law principles in his well-known book *The Institutes of the Law of Nations* (1883).[24] This suggests that he did not only acknowledge the existence of 'man-made' rules but also that he considered them as relevant from a legal point of view. The fact that Lorimer entitled his chapter on custom 'Of international customs as unconscious interpreters of the law of nature in international relations'[25] only seems to confirm that intuition, as do many other passages of his work.[26] Moreover, just as the writings of 'weak' naturalist inclination, Lorimer was an advocate of the 'legality-test'. He considered that 'good' and 'bad' customs needed to be distinguished using natural law as the benchmark:

> 'There is no direction in which it is more necessary that we should keep the subjective channel to natural law distinctly before us than when we are called upon to distinguish between good and bad customs, because customs themselves claim to be the objective witnesses to the very law by which their qualities must be tested'.[27]

As can then be seen, writings of 'naturalist' inclination generally integrated elements of positivism in their theory of international law. Positive law, although legally relevant, was nonetheless deemed to have a lesser normative value than natural law. As may already be assumed, this hierarchy between these two components of the law of nations, translated

[21] Oppenheim, *International Law*, vol. 1, p. 93, footnote no 1.

[22] Jacobini, *Study of the Philosophy of International Law*, p. 67. See Antonio Saénz, Instituciones elementales sobre el derecho natural y de gentes: *curso dictado en la Universidad de Buenos Aires en los años 1822 23* (A Boiça y cia. 1939) 56–57.

[23] James Lorimer, *The Institutes of the Law of Nations. A Treatise of the Jural Relations of Separate Political Communities*, 2 vols. (W. Blackwood and sons, 1883), vol. 1, p. 1.

[24] Ibid., pp. 27–50.

[25] Ibid., p. 27. See also pp. 2 and 19 where he speaks of custom as a 'secondary source' of the law of nations.

[26] See in particular James Lorimer, *The Institutes of Law. A Treatise of the Principles of Jurisprudence, as Determined by Nature* (T. & T. Clark Publishers, 1872), p. 9.

[27] Lorimer, The Institutes of the Law of Nations, vol. 1, pp. 34–35.

into a methodology for custom determination that, while trying to take practice into consideration, was still in essence predominantly deductive.

2.2 The 'Naturalist' Approach to Custom: Practice under the 'Marginal' Control of Natural Law Principles

The decisive impact of theoretical inclinations on methods for the determination of customary international law is evident and has long been emphasized and discussed by scholarship. Traditionally, naturalism is associated with deductive (or 'descending') reasoning,[28] that is to say, a method that relies on broad principles rather than facts and goes from the general to the specific proceeding in an a priori fashion.[29] Although nineteenth century scholarship rarely frontally addressed issues of method, the analysis of the works of naturalist inclination roughly seems to confirm this assumption. The overall approach to custom was indeed, and despite hints of induction, essentially deductive. The method for the identification and determination of custom in this strand of the literature can be described as a two-step process: first, identification of a potential customary rule through the analysis of State practice (inductive phase), and second, confirmation or invalidation of the rule through the 'legality-test' (deductive phase). Two issues then surface: how was State practice analysed to identify potential customary rules? And against which natural law principles was their validity assessed?

In respect to the first question, it should probably first be noted that nineteenth century scholarship, including that of naturalist inclination, adopted the classical two-element definition of customary international law.[30] Halleck and Pando, for instance, defined custom as the law that 'is founded on the tacit or implied consent of nations as deduced from their

[28] See, e.g., Koskenniemi, *From Apology to Utopia*, p. 410; Olivier Corten, 'Controversies Over the Customary Prohibition on the Use of Force: A Methodological Debate' (2005) 16 *European Journal of International Law*, pp. 803–822; and by the same author, *Méthodologie du droit international* (Editions de l'Université de Bruxelles, 2009), pp. 51–57.

[29] See William Thomas Worster, 'The Inductive and Deductive Methods in Customary International Law Analysis: Traditional and Modern Approaches' (2014), 45 *Georgetown Journal of International Law* 455–456.

[30] Halleck, *International Law*, p. 48; José María Pando, *Elementos de derecho internacional* (Imprenta de Alegría y Charlain, 1843), p. 10. See also Phillimore, *Commentaries*, vol. 1, p. 70; Pasquale Fiore, *Il diritto internazionale codificato e la sua sanzione giuridica* (Unione Tipografico-Editrice, 1890), p. 40.

intercourse which each other',[31] and as the rules born out of tacit agreement, as by voluntarily adopting a certain practice, we bound ourselves to be ruled by them'.[32] The material and psychological element of custom are both present in these definitions, but it also seems that the second is considered to follow from the first – or, said clearly, practice is considered to be proof of *opinio juris*. Theoretically, this would tend to suggest a method for custom determination relying foremost on the analysis of State practice to identify a potential rule. Lorimer, for instance, distinctly advocated for an empirical and historical method, as he stated that:

> 'custom, or usage, is the earliest form in which positive law declares itself; and it is in *observing and recording* this spontaneous manifestation of it that *historical method* of its discovery consists. He who would make a better road to kirk or market must first observe the road that has been beaten by the feet of the previous travellers'.[33]

In the same manner, Phillimore's approach to custom has sometimes been described as consisting in a 'detailed discussion of practice'.[34] The British lawyer insisted that custom had to be evidenced through

> 'precedents recorded in History, by being embodied and recorded in Treaties; in public documents of states; in the Marine Ordinances of States; in the decisions of International Tribunals; in the works of eminent writers upon International Jurisprudence'.[35]

Still in the same vein, Halleck explained that:

> 'What is called the voluntary, or positive law of nations, is mainly derived from usage and custom, and to determine these we must have recourse to the history of what has passed from time to time among the several nations of the world'.[36]

Leaving aside the complex controversies that today surround the status of treaties, State papers and so forth as proof of either practice or *opinio juris*, what must be remembered is that the first step of the process for custom

[31] Halleck, *International Law*, p. 48.
[32] Pando, *Elementos*, p. 10. Translation by the author.
[33] Lorimer, *The Institutes of the Law of Nations*, vol. 1, p. 27. Emphasis added.
[34] Perreau-Saussine, 'Three Ways of Writing', p. 239. See also Michael Lobban, 'English Approaches to International Law in the Nineteenth Century' in Matthew Craven, Malgosia Fitzmaurice & Maria Vogiatzi (eds.), *Time, History and International Law* (Martinus Nijhoff, 2007), p. 68.
[35] Phillimore, *Commentaries*, vol. 1, p. 86.
[36] Halleck, *International Law*, p. 55.

determination was empirical, inductive and historical. Customary rules were thus not directly deduced from higher moral or divine principles of law. These principles only intervened in the second phase of the process.

The second step consisted in applying the 'legality-test' to determine the legal value and binding character of the potential customary rule. But against which natural principles did these potential customary rules have to be tested? From where did these principles come from and what purpose did they serve in the 'naturalist' international legal order?

To fully grasp the logics behind the 'naturalist' framework, it is important to underline that, inspired by seventeenth-century political philosophy, the 'contractualist' theories of the State were often used as a starting point to think about the international legal order. It was considered that, while at the national level men had agreed to abandon a part of their liberty to a higher authority in exchange for security, such higher authority did not exist at the international level. States evolved with each other in a state of nature. Following the 'rationalist' train of thought, they however felt that this state of nature was not tantamount to international anarchy. Because men are by nature reasonable creatures, rules of cooperation, conduct and coexistence necessarily and naturally emerge and impose themselves.[37] These necessary principles were generally deemed to be in the number of three: independence (or sovereignty), equality and self-preservation (sometimes considered be a corollary of independence).[38] Using Phillimore's words, it was believed that 'together [they] constitute[d] the basis of International Law'[39] – a naturally imposed social contract of some sort, from which all the international rules derived and could be deduced. It thus seems that it is against these three fundamental principles that potential customary rules had be tested and their value assessed, for if they contradicted them, the whole international social order would have been jeopardised. The 'legality-test' thus gave a final and decisive deductive inflexion to the process of custom determination as presented in 'naturalist' literature.

Although considerations of nature and reason formally only intervened a posteriori to confirm or invalidate customary rules, in truth, it

[37] Phillimore, *Commentaries*, vol. 1, p. 49; Halleck, *International Law*, p. 55; Lorimer, The Institutes of the Law of Nations, vol. 1, p. 3; Cushman K. Davis, *A Treatise on International Law Including American Diplomacy* (Keefe Davidson Law Book Co., 1901), p. 22.

[38] Phillimore, *Commentaries*, vol. 1, p. 149.

[39] Ibidem. See also Davis, *A Treatise*, p. 27.

seems that they also played an incepting role on the actual formation of customs. Many authors indeed believed that the actions of States were, upstream, guided by reason. Lorimer, as a matter of illustration, insisted that:

> '[t]hough customs appear to arise spontaneously, and are rarely traceable to premeditation, *they must always have rested on a previous conception* of an object to be attained, and of means of attaining it'.[40]

In sum, the rules discovered through the inductive phase were considered to already partly be the result of a descending phenomenon. Conceptually then, although procedurally and formally custom determination was presented as a two-step process, the content of the rules seemed to depend on the laws of nature both upstream and downstream. How did this method apply to the issue of the use of force? We will see in the following two sections, that although it was not thoroughly respected for the establishment of the general rule of non-intervention, it was more faithfully applied for the establishment of the exceptions to this rule.

2.3 Non-Intervention as a Consequence of the Principles of Independence and Equality

The general rule of non-intervention was essentially deemed to be a consequence of the principles of independence and equality. Since the principle of independence was defined as the fact of not being submitted to any foreign rule or influence,[41] and that States had to respect their mutual independence as a result of the principle of equality,[42] a general principle of non-intervention quite logically followed. As Halleck explained:

> 'The right of every sovereign state to establish, alter, or abolish, its own municipal constitution and form of government, would seem to follow, as a necessary conclusion from these premises. And from the same course of reasoning, it will be inferred, that no foreign state can interfere with the exercise of this right'.[43]

[40] Lorimer, *The Institutes of the Law of Nations*, vol. 1, p. 28. Emphasis added.
[41] Phillimore, *Commentaries*, vol. 1, p. 149; Halleck, International Law, p. 81.
[42] Phillimore, *Commentaries*, vol. 1 149; Robert Phillimore, *Commentaries upon International Law* (3rd ed., Butterworths, 1879), vol. 1, p. 216; Halleck, *International Law*, p. 97; Pando, *Elementos*, p. 60.
[43] Halleck, *International Law*, p. 82. See also Henry Halleck, *Elements of International Law and the Laws of War* (J. B. Lippincott, 1866), p. 52.

Pando and Lorimer likewise respectively considered that: 'it is not lawful for any of them [States] to wish to dictate to another the form of government, the religion, or the administration which it should adopt; nor to call it to account for what happens between its own citizens, or between the government and its subjects';[44] and that: 'the capacity for self-support and self-government being, as we have seen conditions of recognition, non-interference may be enunciated as the primary duty which separate communities, simply as such, owe to each other'.[45] Phillimore and Aspiazu were arguably even more explicit. Phillimore – who, as a reminder, mainly practiced civil law – drew an analogy between individuals and State and between sovereignty and the right of ownership in order to explain that States have a right to 'territorial inviolability'.[46] The corollary to this right was a duty of others to abstain from penetrating or violating the territory of a fellow nation:

> A State, like an individual, is capable of possessing property. The property of a State is marked by the same characteristics relatively to other States, as the property of individuals; that is to say, it is exclusive of all foreign interference, and susceptible of free disposition.
>
> [...]
>
> A State in the lawful possession of a territory has an exclusive right of property therein, and no stranger can be entitled, without her permission, to enter within her boundaries, much less to interfere with her full exercise of all the rights incident to that supreme dominion, [...].[47]

Aspiazu, for his part, wrote that: 'the territory of a state is inviolable. [...] Penetrating with armed force on the territory of a foreign state is an act of violation'.[48] It is therefore not surprising that when examining coercive measures of dispute settlement (including war) these authors usually immediately exposed the circumstances in which they could be resorted to, without restating the fact that they were, in principle, not part of the normal relations of States, not to say 'forbidden'.

More intriguing when analysing the statement of the prohibition of intervention in the writings of naturalist inclination is the absence of any reference to State practice. The establishment of the rule was the result of a top-down and deductive process from the principles of independence

[44] Pando, *Elementos*, p. 74. Translation by the author.
[45] Lorimer, *The Institutes of the Law of Nations*, vol. 1, p. 231.
[46] Phillimore, *Commentaries*, vol. 1, p. 150.
[47] Ibid., pp. 150–151 and 554.
[48] Aspiazu, Dogmas, pp. 64 and 27. Translation by the author.

and equality. It seems that the authors of naturalist sensibility did not feel it was necessary to refer to any other type of element or argument. Phillimore, for example, considered that: '[t]his elementary proposition of International Law is so unquestionable that it would be superfluous to cite authorities in support of it'.[49] In the same vein, Halleck was of the opinion that examining State practice would, in any case, be trivial because:

> 'If foreign interference in internal affairs of a sovereign state, [...], is contrary to natural law, as the fundamental principle of international jurisprudence, usage, and custom, cannot make it justifiable or lawful, for no length of usage can justify a wrong'.[50]

Interestingly, he further added a criticism of how practice was analysed in the rest of the doctrine, insisting that: 'Unfortunately historians and jurisconsults are too apt to draw their argument from the *fact* to the *right*, and to infer the right of interference from the numerous examples of its actual exercise without testing the legality of the usage by reference to fundamental principles'.[51]

In other words, the fact that States resorted to armed force and intervened in each other's affairs, could not question the rule of non-intervention. But, while practice was not enough to bend the overarching principle of non-intervention, it was relevant to determine the exceptions to that principle.

2.4 The Exceptions Resulting from State Practice and Confirmed by the Principle of Self-Preservation

According to the third fundamental principle of the law of nations (self-preservation), States had a right, sometimes even the duty, to ensure their security as well as the protection of their interests and those of their nationals.[52] Among the measures that could be taken in pursuance of this right were the establishment of treaties of alliance and commerce, maintaining an army, building fortifications but also of seeking redress for an

[49] Phillimore, *Commentaries*, vol. 1, p. 150.

[50] Halleck, *International Law*, p. 84.

[51] Ibidem. Emphasis in the original. See also Aspiazu, Dogmas, p. 28: 'Verdad es que frecuentemente los estados poderosos se han arrogado el derecho de intervenir en los asuntos domésticos de otro; pero también lo es que la opinión general se ha sublevado contra semejantes atentados'.

[52] Pando, *Elementos*, p. 77; Phillimore, *Commentaries*, vol. 1, p. 187; Halleck, *International Law*, p. 91; Davis, *A Treatise*, p. 93.

endured wrong. 'Under certain circumstances, and to a certain extent', Phillimore explained, self-preservation could also 'modify the Right of Territorial Inviolability'.[53] For all that, self-preservation did not amount to a right for States to do whatever they claimed necessary to guarantee their security and interest; the equal rights (of self-preservation, of independence and of equality) of the other nations limited their liberty in this respect.

To establish under what circumstances States could resort to coercion, the 'naturalists' seemed to proceed in a manner more consistent with the method previously described. As Halleck explained:

> 'That the general rule of natural law is opposed to all interference in the internal affairs of another State, cannot be doubted. [...] It must nevertheless be admitted that there are exceptions to this rule. *The principal difficulty is in confining the exceptions so as not to infringe upon the principle of the rule*'.[54]

The way this strand of the doctrine apprehended the determination of the exceptions to non-intervention, nonetheless, greatly varied depending on the author.

Aspiazu and Pando, for instance, were quite succinct in their presentation and appreciation of the circumstances in which intervention could be legal and mostly focused their attention on the issue of self-defence. The existence of the exception of self-defence was uncontroversial; it was the most direct and logical consequence and application of the principle of self-preservation. Its scope, and in particular the definition of what constituted a sufficient and proper threat to justify the use of arms as a matter of self-defence was, however, more problematic. Could internal revolts in a foreign State be a sufficient threat to the neighbouring countries to justify interference? Were the expansionist policies of another nation necessarily disruptive of the balance of power and menacing of the other nations' security?

These issues, specifically intervention to repress internal revolts had generated a controversial practice and extensive debates amongst the European Powers at the beginning of the nineteenth century. Aspiazu, Pando and the others directly referred to this practice and often expressly quoted extracts of the exchange of views that had opposed Russia and Austria to Great Britain during the different congresses that took place

[53] Phillimore, *Commentaries*, vol. 1, p. 187.

[54] Halleck, *International Law*, p. 84. Emphasis added.

between 1818 and 1822.[55] At the Congress of Aix-la-Chapelle (1818), in particular, boasting on the successes of the Quadruple Alliance during the French campaign and wishing to integrate the Holy Alliance within the framework of the European Concert, Tsar Alexander I had issued a '*Mémoire confidentiel*' in which he pleaded in favour of systematic intervention to repress liberal revolts.[56] The Tsar had a very extensive interpretation of what constituted a sufficient threat to justify intervention. He believed that internal and external politics were intimately linked and that the rise to power of liberal governments *ipso facto* represented a threat to the general peace and security of Europe.[57] A general and abstract menace was, in others words, enough to trigger a preventive right of intervention as a matter of self-defence. The British Foreign Affairs Secretary, Lord Castlereagh, strongly disagreed. In a memorandum on the interpretation of the 1814–1815 Peace Treaties, he was adamant that: 'The Allies could only justify an Interference in the affairs of a Foreign State, upon the ground of considering *their own safety* compromised and that, independently of such a Consideration, they c[ould] not claim any right of interference'.[58] Although it could still be preventive, the threat had to be personal and certain to justify intervention. The British view did not, however, prevent the Austrian intervention to quell the Carbonari insurrection in Naples in 1821, nor the

[55] Pando, *Elementos*, pp. 77–78; Aspiazu, Dogmas, p. 29; Halleck, *International Law*, pp. 342–343. Phillimore also refers to the eighteenth-century practice, in particular to the precedent of the French Revolution, see Commentaries, pp. 315–316.

[56] 'Mémoire confidentiel du Cabinet Russe, Aix-la-Chapelle, le 26 septembre (8 oct.) 1818', available in Arthur R. Wellesley (2nd Duke of Wellington) (ed.), *Supplementary Despatches, Correspondence and Memoranda of Field Marshal Arthur Duke of Wellington, K.G.*, 15 vols. (John Murray, 1865), vol. 12, pp. 743–749.

[57] Ibid., p. 746.

[58] 'Memorandum on the Treaties of 1814–1815', Aix-la-Chapelle, October 1818, available in C. K. Webster (ed.), *The Congress of Vienna 1814–1815* (Oxford University Press, 1918), p. 169. Emphasis added. The Foreign Secretary also took this occasion to specify that, unlike the Tsar, Great Britain had to take the opinion of its population into consideration and that the latter was more concerned with economic growth than with the political intrigues of the Continent, see Adolphus W. Ward and George P. Gooch, *The Cambridge History of British Foreign Policy (1783–1919)*, 3 vols. (Cambridge University Press, 1923), vol. 2, pp. 26–27; R. J. Vincent, *Nonintervention and International Order* (Princeton University Press, 1974), pp. 73–90. This position will later be reiterated in the State Paper of 5 May 1820, which is generally considered to have laid down the basis of the British foreign policy, full text available in Harold Temperley and Lilian Penson, *Foundations of British Foreign Policy from Pitt (1792) to Salisbury (1902)* (Cambridge University Press, 1923), p. 52.

French from restoring Ferdinand II on the throne of Spain in 1822.[59] The Foreign Office itself recognised that it might have been isolated on this matter.[60] In spite of this, and of State practice that seemed to establish otherwise, the literature of naturalist inclination generally supported and adopted the restrictive interpretation of what constituted a proper threat.[61] This choice, it seems, was conditioned by the understanding that 'naturalist' authors had of the principle of self-preservation to begin with. After examining State practice and the debates that had taken place between the European Powers, Aspiazu, for instance, insisted that 'self-preservation authorizes us, it is true, to defend ourselves against the attacks that might compromise our security; but it can never justify an aggression against someone who has not offended us'.[62] In sum, in accordance to the principle of self-preservation the intervening State needed to be actually and personally offended in order for the intervention to be justified.

Phillimore and Halleck were more exhaustive in their analysis of the exceptions to the rule of non-intervention. In addition to self-defence, they identified and analysed at least three other frequently alleged grounds for intervention: treaty stipulations, solicited intervention in a civil war and humanitarian (or religious) considerations.[63] They applied the same methodology as Aspiazu with respect to self-defence: they referred to practice but the legally binding character of the alleged exceptions ultimately depended on their compatibility with principles of natural law, and especially the principle of self-preservation that, they

[59] On the intervention of certain European Powers in Spain and Naples, see among others Cynthia Weber, *Simulating Sovereignty. Intervention, the State and the Symbolic Exchange* (Cambridge University Press, 1995), pp. 40–60; Mark Jarrett, *The Congress of Vienna and Its Legacy. War and Power Diplomacy after Napoleon* (Oxford University Press, 2014), pp. 223–247.

[60] In the context of the early stages of the crisis in Greece in 1821, Lord Castlereagh sent a letter to the Tsar in which, referring to the Aix-la-Chapelle debates, he wrote: 'whatever degree of divergence of opinion may have occurred in late discussions on abstract theories of international law, and however the position of the British Government may have been rendered distinct from that of the three Allied Courts…', in 'Letter of the Marquess of Londonberry (Lord Castlereagh) to his Imperial Majesty the Emperor of all Russias, Foreign Office, London, July 16 1821', available in Charles W. V. Marquess of Londonberry (ed.), *Correspondence, Despatches and other papers of the Viscount Castlereagh* (John Murray, 1853), p. 407.

[61] Pando, Elementos, p. 329; Phillimore, *Commentaries*, vol. 1, pp. 315–316; Halleck, *International Law*, p. 83; Aspiazu, *Dogmas*, p. 29.

[62] Aspiazu, *Dogmas*, p. 29. Translation by the author.

[63] Halleck, *International Law*, p. 83 ff; Phillimore, *Commentaries*, vol. 1, p. 315 ff and 559 ff.

too, interpreted restrictively. Both felt that self-defence was very likely to be abused as an excuse to use force and, consequently, as their Latin American colleagues, believed a threat should be actual (or at least immediate) and personal to warrant intervention.[64] Pointing to the difference between causes and motives for war – the former relating to the *'right'* to use force and the latter to the *'expediency'* of doing so[65] – Halleck insisted that 'the justifiable causes of war are injuries received or threatened' and that 'there must be strong probability that the threat may be attempted to be carried into execution, as mere empty words will seldom justify us in declaring war'.[66]

But to what results did this restrictive understanding of the right to self-preservation lead with respect to the other alleged grounds for intervention?

Intervention based on treaty stipulations mainly referred to the hypothesis of treaties of guarantee – that is, treaties whereby a State vouched to protect another State or a specific population from attacks or violations of their rights. Classic illustrations of such treaties were the 1839 Treaty of London, through which the newly independent State of Belgium agreed to perpetual neutrality in exchange for the Great Powers' protection should it be attacked, and the 1774 Treaty of Kütchük Kaynarca between Russia and the Ottoman Empire – through which the Russians were granted a right of inspection and protection over the Orthodox populations of Wallachia and Moldavia.[67] Halleck did not elaborate much on this alleged ground for intervention. He simply noted that a treaty could not give a general right of interference on the territory of another State without seriously impinging on the principle of independence.[68] Treaties, he explained, could not make a use of armed force that could not otherwise be justified as a matter of self-defence/self-preservation, legal.[69] Although treaties of guarantee were not

64 Halleck, *International Law*, p. 83; Phillimore, *Commentaries*, vol. 1, pp. 315 ff and 562 ff.

65 Halleck, *International Law*, p. 312. Emphasis in the original.

66 Ibid., p. 313.

67 Art. 7, Treaty of Kütchük Kaynarca, 10/21 of July 1774, Kütchük Kaynarca, available in Gabriel Noradounghian (ed.), *Recueil des actes internationaux de l'Empire ottoman*, 3 vols. (Librarie Cotillon et F. Pichon, 1897), vol. 1, p. 323.

68 Halleck, *International Law*, p. 86: 'will the stipulation of mediation or guarantee justify generally the interference of one State in the affaires of another, contrary to the wishes of the latter? If the interference is in itself unlawful, can any previously existing stipulation make it lawful? We think not; for the reason that a contract against public morals has no binding force'.

69 Ibid., p. 338.

uncommon, Phillimore was of a similar opinion. His concern was more particularly directed towards treaties whose object was to guarantee the rights of a particular population within a State, or yet a particular constitution or form of political organisation. Because these related to the internal affairs of the State, he felt that such treaties were 'in theory not consistent with the perfect uncontrolled freedom which is of the essence of [the] State'.[70] Ad hoc agreements, on the other hand, could be admissible under certain circumstances.

The issue of intervention based on treaty stipulations was, in fact, partly linked to the question of the admissibility of solicited intervention in a civil conflict. Such interventions were also deemed potentially very problematic considering the principle of self-preservation and independence. They had, moreover, given rise to highly ambiguous State practice. Even amongst them, 'naturalist' lawyers could not agree on the legality of such operations. While he felt that a State could not give a general surrender of part of its sovereignty to another nation, Phillimore was not opposed to solicited intervention on an ad hoc basis. He indeed considered that solicited intervention in case of civil strife, whether in favour of the governmental authorities or of the rebels, 'must be admitted to have continual sanction from the practice of nations'.[71] He gave the aid provided by Queen Elizabeth I to the Dutch against their Spanish rulers in 1585, the help given by Tsar Nicholas I to Austria to quell the Hungarian revolt of 1848, as well as the joint intervention carried out by Great-Britain, France and Russia during the Greek War of Independence in 1827 as illustrations of this practice. In order for such actions to be justified, however, Phillimore believed that power needed to be vacant because then the intervention was not actually taking place against the independence of the State or of its people. Halleck, who was to become a Union Army General during the American Secession War and whose manual was published in 1861, was more cautious and restrictive. While he shared Phillimore's idea that there should be a vacancy of power to warrant the intervention of a third party, he felt that this could only take place if the intervention was solicited by both of the contending parties.[72] This was the hypothesis of a mediation. On the other hand, he was categorical that intervention on the invitation of one of the belligerents only could not be accepted:

[70] Phillimore, *Commentaries*, vol. 2, p. 85.
[71] Ibid., p. 320.
[72] Halleck, *International Law*, p. 339.

'the invitation of one party to a civil war can afford no right of foreign interference, as against the other party. The same reasoning holds good with respect to armed intervention, whether belligerent states, or between belligerent parties in the same state'.[73]

To the argument based on practice, Halleck retorted that albeit the invitation of a party was indeed often put forth, it was seldom put forth alone, but rather 'in connection to other reasons'.[74] In 1585, Queen Elizabeth I, he underlined, also invoked the protection she owed to her protestant subjects in the Low Countries, while Great Britain, France and Russia had put three justifications forth to intervene in the Greek war of independence: the invitation of the Greeks, the need to stay the effusion of blood, and protecting the European trade in the Mediterranean. State practice, in sum, was in his opinion inconclusive.

Halleck adopted a similar train of thought to reject considerations of humanity (and/or religion) as a legal ground for intervention. While believing that mediation could – and in fact should – be proposed to stay the 'effusion of blood', Halleck doubted that 'the general interest of humanity justif[ied] interference to the extent of war of intervention'.[75] Phillimore shared this view. Their rejection of considerations of humanity as a sufficient ground for armed intervention was based on two complementary arguments: first, was the absence of conclusive State practice; and second, was the fact that such an exception would be too vulnerable to political manipulation and, consequently, be disruptive of the international social order. They explained:

> Intervention urged on behalf of the general interests of humanity, has been frequently put forward, and especially in our own times, *but rarely, if ever, without others of greater and more legitimate weight to support it*; [...] As an accessory to others, this ground may be defensible; but as a substantive and solitary justification of Intervention in the affairs of another country, it can scarcely be admitted into the code of International Law, since it is manifestly open to abuses, tending to the violation and destruction of the vital principles of that system of Jurisprudence.[76]

[73] Ibidem.

[74] Ibidem. Emphasis added.

[75] Ibid., p. 340.

[76] Phillimore, *Commentaries*, vol. 1, p. 320. Emphasis added. Henry Halleck expressly quotes Phillimore, see Halleck, *International Law*, p. 340.

Halleck once more referred to the justifications brought forward by the Powers to intervene in Greece in 1827, underlining that in addition to considerations of humanity the right to preserve their commercial interests and protect their citizens in the Mediterranean was also invoked.[77] Phillimore likewise considered that considerations of humanity were 'by no means the only justification advanced for that intervention'.[78] In spite of the many 'humanitarian interventions' that took place in the 1860s and 1870s, Phillimore stood firm on his ground in the 2nd and 3rd editions of his *Commentaries upon International Law* respectively published in 1871 and 1879.[79]

Practice, as we can see, played an important role in the determination of the exceptions to the rule of non-intervention. Albeit interpretations varied, historical precedents were engaged with to see in what circumstances a right to intervention had been claimed, but also appeared to have a real weight in the authors' conclusions. The validity of the alleged exceptions, however, still ultimately rested on their compatibility with the necessary law of nations and, more particularly, with self-preservation as the only principle capable of tempering the right to independence of other nations. As Halleck insisted in his 1861 manual after having examined the different pretexts under which a right of intervention had been claimed:

> These various grounds, upon which wars of intervention in the international affairs of states were formerly attempted to be justified, are now abandoned by the best modern writers on international law, and the present rule is, that stated in another chapter: 'No government has a right to interfere in the affairs of another government, *except in the case where the security and immediate interests of the first government are compromised*'.[80]

* * *

This chapter examined how the authors of naturalist inclination tackled the issue of the use of force. It sought to resituate their conclusions in the general framework of how they thought about the international law and the international legal system more generally. We saw that, following the

[77] Halleck, *International Law*, p. 340.
[78] Phillimore, *Commentaries*, vol. 1, p. 321.
[79] Robert Phillimore, *Commentaries upon International Law* (2nd ed., Butterworths, 1871), vol. 1, p. 476; and (3rd ed., Butterworths, 1879), vol. 1, p. 571.
[80] Halleck, *International Law*, p. 340.

rationalist premises of their sixteenth century predecessors, nineteenth century 'naturalist' authors usually recognised the existence of both natural and positive law, but considered the former to be normatively superior to the latter. The legal superiority of natural law manifested itself in the fact that it was deemed immutable, and that, consequently, 'man-made' rules were considered as binding only insofar as they were compatible with the principles of natural law. When it came to custom determination, this meant that all the rules that seemingly emerged from practice had to be tested against the backdrop of the principles of independence, equality and self-preservation in order for their legal value to be confirmed or, on the contrary, rejected. This method, however, was not always thoroughly followed to establish the rule of non-intervention. In fact, the rule was such a direct and logical consequence of the principles of independence and equality that no one denied its existence and that reference to State practice was deemed superfluous. In a way, non-intervention was itself part of the naturally imposed social contract amongst the nations. On the other hand, 'naturalist' writings profusely used State practice to attempt to determine the circumstances in which States could interfere in the affairs of another State including, if need be, by using force. Authors did not always interpret State practice the same way. Still, they agreed that, in order to have legal value, the exceptions that emerged from practice had to fall within the scope of the principle of self-preservation which was the only one capable of tempering the two other necessary principles of the law of nations – that is, independence and equality. Concretely, this meant that force could be used only to prevent or repel an attack against the actual security or the interest of the State – as a sanction, in sum.

This proposition, of course, is not without recalling the theories of 'just war' modern-day doctrine precisely argues nineteenth century lawyers were still too much imbued with for genuine credit to be given to their writings. As we in fact know, the theories of 'just war', in particular Grotius's, equally rested on the idea that war could not be waged without a 'just' cause, i.e. to redress a wrong.[81] That said, although the works of Thomas of Aquinas, of the Salamanca School or yet of Grotius or Vattel, certainly had an impact on nineteenth century 'naturalist' authors, it must be emphasised that they seldom mentioned their illustrious predecessors when discussing intervention, armed coercive measures or war.

[81] About Grotius's theory of just war see Peter Haggenmacher, *Grotius et la doctrine de la guerre juste* (Graduate Institute Publications, 1983).

Their reasoning with respect to the 'causes of war' was, as we saw, anchored in the discussion of State practice rather than on exegesis from ancient doctrinal texts. Instead, the hypothesis that the theories of 'just war' have slowly worked their way from ethics, theology and philosophy into diplomacy, practice and, therefore, positive international law might have to be embraced. This hypothesis finds a certain confirmation in the analysis of the rest of the nineteenth-century scholarship. Moving on to the analysis of the writings of eclectic inclination, we will see that, although the three necessary principles of international law retained a central role, their descending influence was less overpowering. The increased space and role that this left to positive law and inductive methodologies did not, for all that, change the conclusions authors reached regarding *ius ad bellum*: far from indifference, international law was still asserted to regulate the use of force by States.

3

The Use of Force in Writings of 'Eclectic' Inclination

Midway through the evolution of 'rational naturalism' towards positivism, writings of eclectic inclination probably formed the bulk of nineteenth century international legal scholarship. Yet, the 'eclectics' (also sometimes referred to as 'Grotians') may seem somewhat absent from the naturalist vs. positivist diptych that underlies the narrative of indifference. The argument of modern-day doctrine, however and as previously stated, is about method. The advocates of 'indifference' might contend that because 'eclectics' still took natural law into consideration we can assume that those who asserted the use of force was ring-fenced reached this conclusion based on naturalist premises. The previous chapter already demonstrated that even the authors who leaned more towards 'naturalism' did not rely on purely deductive methodologies. Albeit some may argue only incompletely or marginally, nineteenth century 'naturalists' took State practice into consideration when they discussed *ius ad bellum*.

The same holds true for the 'eclectics', who actually gave more space to positive 'man-made' rules and inductive methodologies. The 'eclectic' system of international law was built on the same theories of sociability and reason that characterised the work of 'naturalists'. Authors believed in the inherently sociable and rational nature of men and adopted a dualist vision of international law that recognised the existence of both positive and natural law. However, they established no formal normative hierarchy between the two. The interaction between positive and natural law was more complex: 'man-made' rules were considered as autonomous from natural principles, but these retained a strong structuring, influential and supplementary value (Section 3.1). There was a tension between 'ideal' and 'real' law (as they were also called). This tension translated into a method for custom determination that clearly gave preference to induction and to the analysis of State practice (Section 3.2). This is not to say that the 'eclectics' method was devoid of ambiguity, especially since many writers felt that law could not be fully detached from the ideals of justice and welfare. As a result, they often strove to make the 'practical' rule coincide with the 'theoretical' principle. This urge was unproblematic and easy to fulfil regarding the establishment of the rule of non-intervention. State practice and the principles of independence and equality all pointed to the same direction: (Section 3.3). On the other hand, when it came to the exceptions to the rule, the concordance of practice with the principle of self-preservation was less evident. Even though their assessment of practice differed, 'eclectic' authors all seemed to seek to legitimize their interpretation by linking the exceptions they believed existed back to the general principle of self-preservation (Section 3.4).

3.1 The 'Eclectic' Legal Order: Autonomy of Positive Law, Structuring and Suppletive Value of Natural Law

The term 'eclectic' originates from the history of philosophy where it is used to refer to those thinkers from the antiquity who did not belong to any particular school of thought but, instead, borrowed elements from different theories without any apparent coherence.[1] In international legal theory, this term has been used since the nineteenth century to describe the work of those writers who, in Oppenheim's terms, 'st[ood] midway between Naturalists and Positivists'.[2] Unlike the philosophers of the antiquity, in their complex combination of naturalism and positivism, the writings of eclectic inclination attained a certain degree of syncretism, in which, despite the absence of formal normative hierarchy, natural and positive law each assumed a precise and delimited function.The first main feature of the writings of eclectic inclination was that they considered natural and positive law as the two, normatively equal, components of the law of nations. This view was widespread in the nineteenth and early twentieth century literature. Yet it was rarely expressed in such explicit, straightforward, terms. Like Georg-Friedrich von Martens, and Paul Fauchille almost a century

[1] The editors of Encyclopaedia Britannica, 'Eclecticism – Philosophy and Theology', *Encyclopaedia Britannica Online* (available at: www.britannica.com/topic/eclecticism, last update: 25 July 2015).

[2] Lassa Oppenheim, *International Law. A Treatise*, 2 vols. (Longman Greens, 1905), vol. 1, p. 85. See also Edwin De Witt Dickinson, *The Equality of States in International Law* (Harvard University Press, 1920), p. 95; H. B. Jacobini, *A Study of the Philosophy of International Law as Seen in Works of Latin American Writers* (Martinus Nijhoff, 1954), p. 20; Christopher Joyner, *International Law in the 21st Century. Rules for Global Governance* (Rowman & Littlefield Publishers, 2005), p. 17.

later, most authors simply stated that: 'international law is divided into two branches: *theoretical* or *rational* law, *positive* or *voluntary* law'.[3] Still, the fact that they considered natural and positive law to have the same normative value was clear from various elements.The first and most important of these elements was the fact that natural law was not believed to be immutable. Although 'eclectics' used the contracturalist theories of the State and Grotius's theory of sociability as a starting point of their reflexion about the international legal system, they did not sacralise 'necessary' principles. Some fundamental rules of coexistence were thought to necessarily emerge from the primary interaction of States, but this naturally imposed international social contract was not viewed as set in stone. Henry Wheaton's definition of international law illustrates this:

> 'The law of nations, or international law, [...] may be defined as consisting of those rules of conduct which reason deduces, as consonant to justice, from the nature of society existing among independent nations; with such definitions and modifications as may be established by general consent'.[4]

Along the same lines, James Reddie equally insisted that 'even the imperative, or prohibitory rules of natural law, may in certain instances, be departed from, with the consent of the parties interested'.[5] Necessary

[3] Henry Bonfils et Paul Fauchille, *Manuel de droit international public* (7e ed., Arthur Rousseau, 1914), p. 14. Emphasis in the original. Translation by the author. See also Georg Friedrich von Martens, *Précis de droit des gens moderne de l'Europe fondé sur les traités et l'usage* (3e éd., Librairie de Dieterich, 1821), p. 7; Johann-Ludwig Klüber, *Droit des gens moderne de l'Europe*, 2 vols. (Librairie J. G. Cotta, 1819), vol. 1, p. 12; James Kent, *Commentaries on American Law*, 4 vols. (9th ed., Little, Brown and Company, 1858), vol. 1, pp. 2–3; James Reddie, *Inquiries into International Law, Public and Private* (2nd ed., William Blackwood and Sons, 1851), p. 130; Henry Wheaton, *Elements of International Law*, 2 vols. (Carey, Lea & Blanchard, 1836) vol. 1, p. 54; August-Wilhelm Heffter, *Le droit international de l'Europe* (E. H. Schroerder, 1873), pp. 4–5; Johann-Caspar Bluntschli, *Le droit international codifié* (Guillaumin et Cie., 1870), p. 53; Travers Twiss, *The Law of Nations Considered as Separate Political Communities*, 2 vols. (2nd ed., Clarendon Press, 1884), vol. 1, pp. 145–146; Leopold von Neumann, *Eléments de droit des gens moderne européen* (Athur Rousseau, 1886), p. 2; Paul Pradier-Fodéré, *Traité de droit international public européen et américain suivant les progrès de la science et de la pratique contemporaine*, 6 vols. (Pedone-Lauriel, 1885), vol. 1, p. 19. See also Theodor D. Woolsey, *Introduction to the Study of International Law* (3rd ed., Charles Scribner & Co., 1872), p. 14; Louis Renault, *Introduction à l'étude du droit international* (L. Larose, 1879), p. 33; Leone Levi, *International Law: With Materials for a Code of International Law* (D. Appleton and Company, 1888), p. 1.

[4] Wheaton, *Elements of International Law*, vol. 1, p. 54.

[5] Reddie, *Inquiries*, p. 129. See also Renault, Introduction, p. 13; Henry Bonfils, *Manuel de droit international public* (Arthur Rousseau, 1894), p. 17.

principles could, in sum, be amended, modified and sometimes even overturned by voluntary law. This meant that positive law was, at least in part, autonomous from natural law. The interaction between these two components of the law of nations was not one of dependence, but rather of interdependence. Leopold von Neumann spoke of 'two primitive forces that mutually influence and penetrate each other',[6] while Pradier-Fodéré explained that: 'the *droit-type* [and] the *droit-réel* enlighten each other: the *droit-type* is tested by the *droit-réel*, the *droit-réel* is purified by the *droit-type*'.[7] The question remains of how was this relation of interdependence was more precisely articulated. In particular, if positive rules and natural principles mutually influenced each other and none superseded the other, how was the conflict between them to be resolved?

Overall, it appears that natural law principles were considered to form the basis of international law; the structural foundations from which States could elaborate (i.e., deduce) further rules, but also upon which the rules established by States could graft (i.e., add) themselves. Von Martens thus explained that even though natural principles were sufficient to apprehend and order the elementary interaction of States, they became too vague and general if two nations wished to develop closer ties. The States that wanted to enhance their cooperation and establish stronger political and commercial agreements needed to elaborate new rules. He wrote:

> As soon as two nations interact and want to establish a steady trade, natural law will no longer suffice. Different motives must lead them to sometimes mitigate the rigor of natural law, sometimes to determine the doubtful points, or to settle those which it ignores, sometimes even to depart from this reciprocity of rights which universal law establishes for all nations.[8]

[6] von Neumann, Eléments, p. 31. Translation by the author.

[7] Pradier-Fodéré, Traité de droit international public, vol. 1, p. 66. Translation by the author.

[8] von Martens, *Précis de droit des gens*, p. 7. Translation by the author. See also, Klüber, Droit des gens moderne, vol. 1, 1819, pp. 70–71; Théodore Ortolan, *Règles de droit international et de diplomatie de la mer*, 2 vols. (J. Dumaine, Cosse et N. Delamotte, 1845), vol. 1, p. 5; Bluntschli, *Le droit international codifié*, p. 53; Heffter, Le droit international de l'Europe, p. 3; Pradier-Fodéré, Traité de droit international public, vol. 1, pp. 16–19; Twiss, *The Law of Nations*, p. 7; Amancio Alcorta, *Cours de droit international public*, 2 vols. (L. Larose et Forcel, 1887), vol. 1, p. 24; Franz von Holtzendorff, *Introduction au droit des gens* (Verlagsanstalt und Druckerei A.-G., 1889), p. 6.

Henry Bonfils shared his German colleague and predecessor's view:

> In the absence of customs, reason alone provides and formualtes orver-riding principles. [...]. This branch of law [natural law] is limited: its precepts are mainly of a *negative* nature. They more often command abstention than action. They all relate to the essential principle of not harming, of not impeding freedom, of respecting the independence and honour of others.
>
> The development of relations between States [...] continuously facilitated and deepened by the progress of science and industry, has given rise to *contingent*, *variable*, *secondary* rights and duties, established by international custom or regulated by conventions and treaties.[9]

Temporally natural law and necessary principles were pre-existent to positive law. 'Man-made' rules could be elaborated based on these principles to give them a more detailed and practical content, but could also, as mentioned above, put them aside if necessary. If, however, the natural principles formed the backbone of international law, and that positive rules could overturn these principles, one may wonder how the 'eclectic' legal system did not collapse. The key seemed to be that positive law was considered to pursue the same aim as natural law, that is the peaceful co-existence and prosperity of States. As Neumann put it:

> From the moment a State has entered the society of peoples governed by the law of nations, it must be imbued, in all matters relating to its legislation and government, with the idea that it does not exist solely for itself, but that since it cannot satisfy its material and moral needs without recourse to the assistance of other States, it is obliged to co-operate for its part in the achievement of a common goal. This common purpose is the higher interests of mankind.[10]

The idea was that when they established rules of conduct to strengthen their ties, States would rarely go against the principles that regulated their primary intercourse. Moreover, considering that the conventions and obligations thus set only bound the States that had agreed to them, positive rules rarely had universal value.[11] Even if 'man-made' rules contradicted the principles of necessary law, their impact on the overall system was, in any case, limited. It also follows that in case of conflict priority would be given to the particular rules that the States had

[9] Bonfils, *Manuel*, pp. 16–17. Emphasis in the original. Translation by the author.

[10] von Neumann, *Eléments*, p. 43. Translation by the author.

[11] On the inexistence of universal positive international law, see von Martens, *Précis de droit des gens*, p. 9; Wheaton, *Elements of International Law*, vol. 1, p. 50.

established for their mutual relations rather than to the general principles. This was not because positive law was in anyway viewed as having a superior normative value, but just a sort of application of the *lex specialis* and *lex posterior* maxims.

That being said, natural law did not lose all relevance as soon as treaties or customs came into play. Natural law kept a crucial role. Aside from the structuring function just described, it acted in essentially two other ways: as a driving force that influenced the content of voluntary law, and as a supplementary regime to fill the lacunae left by 'man-made' rules. Natural law was indeed considered to embody the law of nations as it should be – 'le *droit idéal*' in the words of Pradier-Fodéré. It represented the ideal towards which the positive law of nations should develop, as well as a measuring rod to assess the moral progress of the international community. Pradier-Fodéré was very emphatic in stressing that most of the progress in which civilization took pride resulted from natural law and that, without it, States 'would soon go back to their vulgar impulsions of egoistic nationalism'.[12] 'Ideal, theoretical international law', he further insisted, 'offers itself to reason as the model to be followed'.[13] In the same vein, Franz von Holtzendorff spoke of the 'fertile action'[14] of ideal law on real law, and Bonfils considered that:

> 'The principles of rational or theorerical law provide the necessary criteria for assessing the real value of rules of positive law. They provide the means to sustain the progress achieved, to fill in the gaps, to prepare improvement and justify modifications'.[15]

Necessary law, in sum, maintained an inspirational function: it could act as a driving force to foster the evolution of the positive law of nations. In this quote, Bonfils also alluded to the supplementary character of natural law. Like him, many authors felt that reason and common sense could usefully fill the gaps left by customs and treaties.

[12] Pradier-Fodéré, *Traité de droit international public*, vol. 1, p. 25. Translation by the author. See also Théodore Ortolan, *Règles de droit international*, vol. 1, p. 67; Franz von Holtzendorff, *Introduction au droit des gens*, p. 44; Woolsey, *Introduction*, p. 21; Alcorta, Cours de droit international public, vol. 1, p. 107.

[13] Pradier-Fodéré, *Traité de droit international public*, vol. 1, p. 67. Translation by the author.

[14] von Holtzendorff, *Introduction au droit des gens*, p. 27.

[15] Bonfils, *Manuel*, p. 17. Translation by the author.

In the 1858 *Commentaries on American Law*, James Kent (1763–1847) was remarkably clear:

> 'in the absence of these latter regulations, the intercourse and conduct of nations are to be governed by principles fairly to be deduced from the right and duties of nations, and nature of moral obligations'.[16]

Because it did not require the consent of nations and derived directly from reason, natural law had a universal value and could thus act as a default legal regime.

To summarize, in the international order as it was conceptualized in the writings of eclectic inclination, natural law and positive law entertained a relation of autonomy and interdependence. They were 'intermixed or separate',[17] to quote Leone Levi. Positive rules enjoyed a certain degree of independence with respect to natural principles, although these retained a strong structural, influential and supplementary role. The ambivalence of the interplay between necessary and voluntary law in the 'eclectic' framework of international law was, as we will now see, heavily reflected in a method for custom determination that was marked by a wish to make the real rule match the ideal principle as much as possible.

3.2 The 'Eclectic' Approach to Custom: Making the 'Real' Rule Match the 'Ideal' Principle

The 'eclectic' system of international law, as we just saw, provided a certain autonomy to positive law. Custom was part of the voluntary or 'real' law of nations.[18] Its binding force therefore rested 'upon the will or consent of nations, express or implied'[19], not on its conformity with abstract principles of theoretical law. It should then follow that the 'eclectic' approach to custom determination was mainly inductive and based on the analysis of State practice. This intuition is reinforced by the definition of custom this strand of the literature adopted. Paul Pradier-Fodéré spoke of 'an unequivocal usage of nations and of their governments [that] proves a tacit agreement that has the same value as an

16 Kent, *Commentaries on American Law*, vol. 1, p. 3. See also Twiss, *The Law of Nations*, p. 176.

17 Levi, *International Law*, p. 2.

18 See Wheaton, *Elements of International Law*, vol. 1, p. 56; Reddie, *Inquiries*, p. 124; Twiss, *The Law of Nations*, p. 150.

19 See Reddie, Inquiries, p. 124. See also Wheaton, Elements of International Law, vol. 1, p. 56; Ortolan, *Règles de droit international*, vol. 1, pp. 66–67; Woolsey, Introduction, p. 26; Pradier-Fodéré, *Traité de droit international public*, vol. 1, p. 87.

express agreement'.[20] In other words, once again, clear and continuous practice was *a priori* seen as a proof of *opinio juris*.

But what did these writers mean by 'usage' and 'practice'? Through what type of documents did they believe these could be established and proven? In *The Law of Nations Considered as Independent Political Communities* (1884), Twiss explained that '[t]he *Jus Consuetudinarium* of Nations [could] be gathered from a variety of sources,'[21] and discussed the value of collection of usages, treaties and ordinances of princes as useful material for analysis.[22] Other authors also mentioned records of treaty negotiations, State papers or yet diplomatic correspondence as elements that should be taken into consideration.[23] Most did not address the issue frontally, but in practice also examined such documents to determine the content of international customary rules.[24] In sum, the 'eclectic' writings generally seemed to advocate a methodology based on historical inquiry consisting in the collection and analysis of State practice through time.[25]

Yet, their historical method was far from being a purely factual one. Their understanding of 'practice' was broader than the mere 'material' action of States; it also seemed to include the 'rhetorical' practice of States (i.e., how they rationalised or justified their behaviour). Wheaton, for example, insisted that historical research was necessary

> 'not because any constant and uninterrupted practice in matters which are indifferent by the law of nature can be collected from thence; but because *we shall there find what has been generally approved, and what has been generally condemned* in the variable and contradictory practice of nations'.[26]

Similarly, Franz von Holtzendorff stressed that one had to 'look for the facts, which dominate in an incontestable manner the relations and the state of society, and then, *examine what the legal conscience of nations thinks*

[20] Pradier-Fodéré, *Traité de droit international public*, vol. 1, p. 86. Translation by the author. See also

von Martens, *Précis de droit des gens*, p. 123; Wheaton, *Elements of International Law*, vol. 1, p. 48; Reddie, Inquiries, p. 125; Woolsey, Introduction, p. 42; Renault, Introduction à l'étude du droit international, p. 41; Twiss, *The Law of Nations*, vol. 1, pp. 150–151; Alcorta, Cours de droit international public, vol. 1, p. 120.

[21] Twiss, *The Law of Nations*, vol. 1, p. 159.

[22] Ibid., pp. 159–161.

[23] Renault, *Introduction à l'étude du droit international*, p. 42.

[24] See below (Section 3.(Section 3.4) and (Section 3.(Section 3.5).

[25] See, e.g., Klüber, *Droit des gens moderne*, vol. 1, p. 23.

[26] Wheaton, *Elements of International Law*, vol. 1, p. 41. Emphasis added. See also Reddie, Inquiries, p. 126.

of that, whether it recognises it or contests it'.[27] Factual practice (or usage) was not enough to establish and define the contours of customary rules. It needed to be read considering the discursive practice and of the reactions it had provoked amongst the other members of the international society. *Opinio juris* was, hence, given the predominant role; *opinio juris* was the element that transformed a mere usage into international customary law.[28]

At first glance, the above appears to exclude considerations of natural law from the process of custom determination and to resolutely opt for a positivist and inductive methodology. In truth, however, reason and justice were not completely evacuated from the process. The tension between the will to describe the law as it was and to push it towards what it ought to be was strong. This tension was evident in Pradier-Fodéré's work for instance. He stressed that: '[w]hen, in one word, we look for the laws that must rule the nations, we have to keep an eye on the past, the present and the future: philosophy has to shed light on the facts without however leaving the realm of reality'.[29] It was equally so in Theodor Woolsey's *Introduction to the Study of International Law* (1871). Woolsey noted that one had to wonder:

> '[first] [w]hat is the actual understanding and practice of nations? [O]therwise we have a structure that floats in the air, subjective speculation without authority; and *the second*, [o]n what rational and moral

[27] von Holtzendorff, Introduction au droit des gens, p. 73. Emphasis added. Translation by the author.

[28] The approach advocated by the 'eclectics' is not without recalling the method used by the International Court of Justice in the *Continental Shelf* and *Nicaragua* cases, but also still advocated by a great part of the contemporary scholarship, including the International Law Commission. In the introduction of his second report on the identification of customary international law the Special Rapporteur, Michael Wood, indeed underlines that: 'There was general support amongst the members of the Commission for the "two-element" approach, that is to say, that the identification of a rule of customary international law requires an assessment of both general practice and acceptance of that practice as law. Virtually all those who spoke expressly endorsed this approach, which was also supported by the wide array of materials covered in the first report, and none questioned it', Michael Wood, Special Rapporteur, *Second Report on identification of customary international law* (International Law Commission, 66th session, Geneva 5 May–6 June and 7 July–8 August 2014), A/CN.4/672, 22 May 2014, par. 3 (a), p. 2. See also ICJ, *North Sea Continental Shelf* (Federal Republic of Germany vs. Denmark; Federal Republic of Germany vs. Netherlands), Judgment of 20 February 1969, *I.C.J. Reports 1969*, in particular par. 77, p. 44; ICJ, *Military and paramilitary activities in and against Nicaragua* (Nicaragua vs. United-States of America), Merits, Judgment of 27 June 1986, *I.C.J. Reports 1986*, in particular par. 186, p. 98.

[29] Pradier-Fodéré, *Traité de droit international public*, vol. 1, p. 26. Translation by the author. See also p. 66.

> ground can this practice be explained and defended? [O]therwise it is divorced from *truth* and *right*, [...]'.[30]

He also added that 'if international law were not made up of rules for which reasons could be given, satisfactory to man's intellectual and moral nature; if it were not built on principles of right; it would be even less of a science [...]'.[31] Repercussing this last preoccupation, Neumann, and Johann-Ludwig Klüber before him advocating of a 'dogmatico-historical' method,[32] argued for a method mixing historical, dogmatic and philosophical approaches to law. He was of the opinion that history and dogma without philosophy would amount to a simple enumeration of fact (a 'mechanical alignment of formulas')[33], and that philosophy, which in any case found in roots in history and reality, helped ordain the law of nations into a scientific ensemble.[34] The tension between the need to describe a body of rules in touch with reality but not fully disconnected from the ideal of justice is, in sum, palpable.

How did these preoccupations reconcile with a method for custom determination that was openly proclaimed to rest on induction and historical inquiry? As in the work of naturalist inclination, 'eclectic' writers often seemed to consider that the actions of States where guided by reason in the first place. It, in fact, has to be remembered that the 'eclectic' legal framework was built on the 'rationalist' premises of reason and sociability. As a result, as Théodore Ortolan probably best expressed: '[c]ustom is often in conformity with the Enlightenment of reason in regard to what is just or unjust, because they stem from societies, or collections of reasonable beings'.[35] In other words, customary rules could be presumed to be consistent with natural law and, even if they were not, it had to be assumed that States in acting the way they had acted thought their behaviour reasonable. As Bonfils explained: 'international usages were established because they appeared (sometimes wrongfully so) in line with the ideas of justice, equality and independence'.[36] Incidentally, this also meant that, in the 'eclectic' frame of mind, it was believed that when States would come to realise that their behaviour deviated from what was truly just and

30 Woolsey, Introduction, p. 14. See also Ortolan, *Règles de droit international*, vol. 1, p. 46.
31 Woolsey, *Introduction*, p. 13.
32 Klüber, *Droit des gens moderne*, vol. 1, p. 23.
33 von Neumann, *Eléments*, p. 12. Translation by the author.
34 Ibid.
35 Ortolan, *Règles de droit international*, vol. 1, p. 66. Translation by the author.
36 Bonfils, *Manuel*, p. 26. Translation by the author.

reasonable, they would rectify it. As a result, in due course of time, 'practical' law would eventually and increasingly overlap with 'ideal' law.[37]

Under proclaimed induction, the method for custom determination was thus marked by an underlying propensity for deduction. We will see in the following two sections, that this tension and ambiguity between the 'real' and the 'ideal', found a privileged ground of expression regarding intervention and the use of force.

3.3 The Concordance of the 'Real' Rule and of the 'Ideal' Principle of Non-Intervention

We have already mentioned how the 'eclectic' system of international law was built on the 'rationalist' premises of sociability and on the idea that some rules of conduct necessarily emerged from the interaction of States in the state of nature.[38] The principles of independence, equality and self-preservation were, again, viewed as forming an international social contract, and the *sine qua non* condition for the existence of an international society.[39] Again as well, instead of starting by analysing the practice of States, the writings of 'eclectic' tendency directly drew the rule of non-intervention from the principles independence and equality. Wheaton, for instance, insisted that:

> 'every state, as a distinct moral being independent of every other, may freely exercise all its sovereign rights in a manner not inconsistent with the equal rights of the other states. [...] *No foreign state can lawfully interfere with the exercise of this right,* [...]'[40]

[37] As Koskenniemi points out, one of the reasons this literature can understand itself as coherent is notably due to the assumption that '(descending) norms and (ascending) behaviour coalesced in the inevitable march of history towards progress and enlightenment', in *From Apology to Utopia*, p. 143.

[38] See above (Section 3.2).

[39] Klüber, *Droit des gens moderne,* vol. 1, p. 69; Wheaton, Elements of International Law, vol. 1, p. 107; Ortolan, *Règles de droit international,* vol. 1, pp. 46–50; Reddie, Inquiries, p. 183; Kent, *Commentaries on American Law,* vol. 1, p. 21,
Bluntschli, *Le droit international codifié,* pp. 81 and 88; Woolsey, Introduction, pp. 16 and 50; Heffter, *Le droit international de l'Europe,* pp. 56–57; Pradier-Fodéré, Traité de droit international public, vol. 1, p. 307; von Neumann, *Eléments,* p. 30; Levi, *International Law,* p. 103; Bonfils, *Manuel,* pp. 122–123; Bonfils et Fauchille, *Manuel,* p. 152. On the 'fundamental' rights of States in general see: Antoine Pillet, *Recherches sur les droits fondamentaux des Etats dans l'ordre des rapports internationaux et sur la solution des conflits qu'ils font naître* (A. Pedone, 1899).

[40] Wheaton, *Elements of International Law,* vol. 1, p. 95.

August-Wilhelm Heffter and Pradier-Fodéré were very clear as well. After having described the content and meaning of the 'fundamental rights' (as he called them), Heffter concluded that: 'it clearly results from all that we have established so far that in general no power has a right to interfere in the internal affairs of a foreign State'.[41] Pradier-Fodéré was even more categorical and decidedly asserted that: '[t]here is no right of intervention because there is no right against the law. The law is independence: intervention is a violation of independence'.[42]

At first glance, the writings of 'eclectic' inclination give the impression that the rule of non-intervention was just the product of a logico-deductive reasoning. Considering that in the 'eclectic' legal framework natural law and positive law were considered to have a similar normative value, the extent to which the prohibition of intervention was also thought to be part of the practical law may then be questioned. Opinions were contrasted. Travers Twiss held that:

> A scrupulous respect for the independence of Individual States, evidenced by a systematic abstinence from all encroachments upon that independence, is a necessary condition of Permanent Fellowship amongst Nations. *Non-interference* to such an extent would thus seem to be a *natural law* of international life, and it is superfluous to presume a *consent of Nations* as an authority for the rule of such non-interference.[43]

In other terms, the rule of non-intervention was foremost a principle of natural law, but a principle so necessary to the existence of an international society that it was irrelevant whether States had consented to it or not. Twiss added that treating the rule of non-intervention as voluntary law was not advisable as it would weaken the sanction and, hence, the strength of the rule. He believed that since natural principles were indispensable and necessary for the existence of an international society their violation would result in the dissolution of that society. The consequences of disobeying positive rules were less dramatic: it only resulted in the social isolation of the delinquent State.[44] What, however, remained

[41] Heffter, *Le droit international de l'Europe*, p. 94. Translation by the author.

[42] Pradier-Fodéré, Traité de droit international public, vol. 1, p. 547. Translation by the author. See also Klüber, Droit des gens moderne, vol. 1, p. 87; von Martens, Précis de droit des gens, p. 215; Reddie, *Inquiries*, p. 185; Kent, *Commentaries on American Law*, vol. 1, p. 21; Bluntschli, Le droit international codifié, p. 82; Woolsey, Introduction, pp. 56–57; Twiss, *The Law of Nations*, vol. 1, p. 149; von Neumann, Eléments, p. 48; Bonfils, *Manuel*, p. 153; Bonfils et Fauchille, *Manuel*, p. 186.

[43] Twiss, The Law of Nations, vol. 1, p. 149.

[44] Ibid., p. 146.

unclear in Twiss's work is why a rule could not be simultaneously part of natural and positive law. As a matter of fact, if most States abided by a principle of the 'theoretical' law of nations, there was no reason why this principle could not also become part of the 'practical' law of nations. This was the view held by von Holtzendorff. He wrote:

> 'For a principle to have a positive character, it is sufficient that it is the necessary consequence of the legal community that the existence of States supposes, that it results from the sequence of common principles recognised and transmitted by historical and legal tradition, or that it has been admitted from one country to another'.[45]

Said differently, to be part of the 'real' law of nations, a principle or a rule just had to either be: (i) a consequence of the existence of an international society, (ii) a consequence of other previously established principles of law or (iii) generally recognized by States. It followed from this that the rules deduced from the principles of independence, equality or self-preservation were automatically considered to be part of positive international law. In this regard, however, Holtzendorff's position may be viewed as paradoxical because it made the distinction between 'ideal' and 'real' law somewhat cosmetic and inoperative.

At any rate, even though the rule of non-intervention was initially deduced from the necessary principles of independence and equality, 'eclectic' writings generally looked for confirmation of the rule in State practice. This was particularly true from the second half of the nineteenth century onwards. In 1894, Bonfils thus explained that after having established the 'duty' of non-intervention and reviewed the opinions expressed in doctrine, State practice now needed to be examined.[46] When analysing practice, the authors of the time frequently highlighted its contrasted, contradictory, ambiguous and contingent nature. They observed that 'modern and recent history offers us many instances, maybe too many, of interventions of all sorts',[47] and that 'States have successively invoked and rejected the duty of non-intervention depending on their interests'.[48] At the same time, these same writers noted that during the Châtillon-sur-Seine Congress in 1814, after

45 von Holtzendorff, *Introduction au droit des gens*, p. 20. Translation by the author.

46 Bonfils, *Manuel*, p. 156.

47 von Neumann, *Eléments*, p. 51. Translation by the author.

48 Bonfils, *Manuel*, p. 156. Translation by the author. See also Kent, *Commentaries on American Law*, p. 22; Woolsey, Introduction, p. 66; Pradier-Fodéré, *Traité de droit international*, vol. 1, p. 546.

thirteen years of Napoleonic wars and twenty-six years of disorder on the European scale, the allied forces had solemnly announced that: '[i]t is time, at last, that princes may, without foreign interference, ensure the well-being of their people; *that nations respect their mutual independence*'.[49] They also frequently referred to the declarations made by the Great Powers at the Aix-la-Chapelle Congress (1818), in which it was stated that:

> 'In forming this august union, Sovereigns regarded the invariable resolve to never depart [...] from the strictest observance of the law of nations, principles which in their application to a state of permanent peace are the only ones capable of effectively guaranteeing the independence of each government and the stability of the general association, as a fundamental basis'.[50]

The Monroe Doctrine was equally mentioned as yet another element showing that States, in practice, recognised the rule of non-intervention.[51] The fact that history offered so many instances of intervention was therefore not believed to call the rule into question. As Bluntschli, among others, underlined: 'the very history of these numerous interventions and the fact that government have from time to time recognised and practiced the principle of non-intervention are sufficient to demonstrate the accuracy of this principle'.[52] In truth, many of these so-called interventions, they argued, were nothing more than the exercise of a legitimate right: a legal exception to the rule of non-intervention.[53]

[49] 'Déclaration des Puissances alliées sur la rupture du Congrès de Châtillon-sur-Seine, 16 mars 1814', available in Charles de Martens, *Guide diplomatique*, 2 vols. (P. Aillaud, 1837), vol. 2, p. 12. Emphasis added. Translation by the author. See also Ernest Nys, 'Le Concert européen et la notion de droit international' (1899) 31 *Revue de droit international et de législation comparée* 273–313.

[50] 'Déclaration de Metternich, Richelieu, Castlereagh, Wellington, Hardenberg, Bernstorff, Nesselrode et Capo d'Istria à Aix-La-Chapelle, 15 novembre 1818', available in de Martens, *Guide diplomatique*, vol. 2, p. 561. Translation by the author.

[51] Scholarship was divided cocnerning the real content and meaning of President James Monroe's 1823 annual message to the Congress. While the US President proclaimed a principle of absolute non-intervention for the European Powers in the affairs of the American continent, some authors considered that his declaration had, in parallel, consecrated a right of interference for the United States into the affairs of Latin America. See e.g., Bluntschli, Le droit international codifié, p. 254, footnote no 3; Woolsey, Introduction, p. 68; Pradier-Fodéré, *Traité de droit international public*, vol. 1, p. 557; Bonfils, *Manuel*, p. 157.

[52] Bluntschli, *Le droit international codifié*, p. 253, footnote no 2. Translation by the author.

[53] Pradier-Fodéré, Traité de droit international public, vol. 1, p. 559; Bonfils, *Manuel*, p. 158.

'Eclectic' literature was hence unanimous in considering that the 'ideal' rule and the 'practical' rule of non-interference coincided. Non-intervention was not only a rule directly issued from the necessary principles of independence and equality, but also a rule that States recognised and actively proclaimed to be a rule of international law. On the other hand, when it came to the exceptions to the rule of non-intervention, the assessment of State practice was not as unanimous, and the coincidence of the 'real' exceptions with the 'ideal' principle not as clear-cut.

3.4 Exceptions Resulting from State Practice and Legitimised by the Principle of Self-Preservation

Intervention, nineteenth-century scholarship often insisted, was probably the most contentious and complex issue of international law.[54] The dissensions did not concern the principle as such, but rather the number, scope and content of the exceptions. Woolsey noted:

> 'The rule of non-intervention in the affairs of other states is then an established principle. But the exceptions to it which are admitted, or which are claimed to exist, are of great importance and there is considerable difficulty in determining what is lawful interference and what is unlawful'.[55]

In this difficult process of determination, the method employed by 'eclectic' writers seemed more consistent with the approach to custom previously presented (i.e., a method that officially relied on induction and State practice analysis).[56] 'Eclectic' textbooks generally started out by relying on historical precedents, and analysing the arguments put forward by States to justify their actions. This did not, however, lead to a similar and uniform set of conclusions. On the contrary, the assessments of practice greatly differed and authors sometimes adopted self-contradictory positions depending on the examined ground for intervention. Whatever the conclusions, it is nevertheless interesting to note that these were almost systematically brought back to the principle of self-preservation, which was alternatively broadly or restrictively understood to either include or exclude a specific exception to non-intervention. The

[54] See e.g., Pradier-Fodéré, Traité de droit international public, vol. 1, p. 546.
[55] Woolsey, *Introduction*, p. 57.
[56] See above (Section 3.3).

establishment of this link between the rules emerging from practice and the 'ideal' principle appeared to legitimize the exceptions by giving them 'objective' authority.

Humanitarian intervention offers a particularly good illustration. The 'eclectic' writings were fairly divided regarding its admissibility as a legal ground for intervention, but both its opponents and its defenders ultimately referred to the principle of self-preservation, not to test the legitimacy of the rule, but to strengthen their position and argument. Pradier-Fodéré, Neumann, Bonfils and Fauchille were among the clearest adversaries to humanitarian intervention.[57] Bonfils and Fauchille considered that while such intervention could be an act of high and far-sighed politics, 'it is not the exercise of a right; it is the perpetration of an act of war against the State under the domination of which this people is placed.'[58] Pradier-Fodéré stressed the risk of abuses such a doctrine could give rise to and also noted that so-called humanitarian interventions had barely ever been justified on grounds of humanity alone. The interference of the Great Powers in the Ottoman Empire, he insisted, mostly found their justifications in the various treaties and special concessions made by the Sultan to the Europeans.[59] Likewise, Napoleon III's 1860 expedition to Lebanon in order to put an end to the massacres of the Maronites by the Druzes had been undertaken only once the consent of the Turkish authorities had been secured.[60] Practice, in other terms, did not support the hypothesis of humanitarian intervention as a legal exception to the rule of non-interference. As a closing argument, some writers moreover added that:

> 'This intervention is not legitimate because it constituted an infringement on the independence of States; powers are not directly and immediately injured by these inhuman acts, and are [consequently] in no way justified to intervene, . . .'.[61]

The principle of self-preservation was here restrictively interpreted: only a direct and imminent threat could justify intervention. Such was also the

[57] Heffter, *Le droit international de l'Europe*, p. 98; Pradier-Fodéré, *Traité de droit international public*, vol. 1, p. 663; von Neumann, *Eléments*, p. 49; Bonfils, *Manuel*, p. 162; Bonfils et Fauchille, *Manuel*, p. 201.

[58] Bonfils, *Manuel*, p. 162. Translation by the author.

[59] Pradier-Fodéré, *Traité de droit international*, vol. 1, p. 643.

[60] Ibid., p. 644; Bonfils, *Manuel*, p. 165.

[61] Pradier-Fodéré, *Traité de droit international public*, vol. 1, p. 663. Translation by the author. See also Bonfils, *Manuel*, p. 166.

opinion of Heffter, who insisted that: '[r]egardless of how blameworthy the conduct of a sovereign might be, it does not give a right of intervention to the other sovereigns as long as their rights are not affected or threatened'.[62]

The advocates of humanitarian intervention, on the other hand, argued that when a State disregarded the basic laws of humanity, the international community as a whole was affected and that each and every member of that community had a right to react to these violations. Such was the position of Wheaton, Woolsey, Bluntschli and Kent for instance. Ethical and moral considerations assuredly were part of the elements that encouraged these scholars to accept this type of intervention. When he spoke of the events of the Greek war of independence, Wheaton undeniably used a vernacular that appealed to human sensibilities rather than to the 'rational' legal mind. He wrote:

> Still more justifiable was the interference of the Christian powers of Europe to rescue a whole nation, not merely from religious persecution, but from the cruel alternative of being transported from their native land into Egyptian bondage, or exterminated by their merciless oppressors. The right of human nature, wantonly outraged by this cruel warfare, prosecuted for six years against a civilized and Christian people, to whose ancestors' mankind are so largely indebted [. . .].[63]

A few sentences later he furthermore added that, in any case, such intervention in 'its principle was fully justified by the great paramount law of self-preservation'.[64] Wheaton did not explain the reasoning behind this affirmation, and neither did Woolsey and Kent who expressly referred to their American colleague in their work.[65] Bluntschli was more explicit. He explained that '[w]e are authorised to intervene when the violation of international law constitutes a general danger',[66] and considered that amongst the violations that could represent a threat to the 'universal public order' was the brutal oppression by a State of its

[62] Heffter, *Le droit international de l'Europe*, p. 98. Translation by the author. Heffter's position about humanitarian intervention may be viewed as ambiguous: he believed that such intervention became permissible but only in a situation of civil war and if one of the parties to the conflict requested the intervention. In that case, however, the legal basis of the intervention was the consent given by either the government or the rebels and not considerations of humanity.

[63] Wheaton, *Elements of International Law*, vol. 1, p. 129.

[64] Ibid., pp. 129–130.

[65] Woolsey, Introduction, p. 73; Kent, *Commentaries on American Law*, vol. 1, p. 26.

[66] Bluntschli, *Le droit international codifié*, p. 255 (footnote no 1). Translation by the author.

population.[67] Although they were not directly affected, the other States had a collective interest in ensuring compliance with the law of nations. The logics seemed to be as follows: by sanctioning the violations of international law, States preserved the existence of the international community and, by the same token, their own survival. Considering, however, that the intervention was meant to sanction the violation of a right that was deemed due to the international community, such intervention could only be undertaken collectively. The principle of self-preservation was, in this case, broadly understood: beyond an 'individual' right to redress the wrongs directly endured, States had a collective right to redress the wrongs collectively endured.

Intriguingly, the writers that adopted a broad understanding of self-preservation in the case of humanitarian intervention sometimes defended a restrictive interpretation of that same principle in other, but related, issues. The contrast with the position most authors took regarding the question of intervention to repress revolutionary movements was especially striking. While he considered that foreign powers could interfere in the affairs of another State to put an end to the effusions of blood, James Kent insisted that they could not help a government crush a social or political uprising. In his 1858 manual, he quoted and adopted the British position as expressed during the Congress of Aix-la-Chapelle (1818), of Troppau (1821), of Laybach (1821) and of Verona (1822) on the occasions of which Lord Castlereagh had defended a restrictive interpretation of self-preservation, insisting that a threat needed to be imminent and personal to justify intervention.[68] Kent also argued that although the British position had not prevented the Austrians from interfering in Naples and the French from re-establishing Ferdinand II on the throne of Spain, the arguments put forward by both Austria and France had truly shown deference to Castlereagh's view. In his opinion in fact:

> 'The allied sovereigns who assembled at Laybach and Verona, do not appear to have differed essentially with Great Britain, as to the general principles which ought to regulate the interference of the other states in the internal affairs of Naples and Spain, but they differed in the application of those principles to the cases before them'.[69]

[67] Ibid., p. 251, footnote no 1, and p. 252.

[68] See 'Memorandum on the Treaties of 1814–1815, Aix-la-Chapelle, October 1818', available in C. K. Webster (ed.), *The Congress of Vienna 1814–1815* (Oxford University Press, 1918) p. 169.

[69] Kent, *Commentaries on American Law*, vol. 1, p. 26, footnote (a).

The other authors who opposed intervention to suppress internal revolts used the same elements of practice and restrictive understanding of the principle of self-preservation. Wheaton, Bluntschli and Woolsey – who like Kent had a broad understanding of concept in the case of humanitarian intervention – equally referred to and shared the British liberal and restrictive view on this other matter.[70]

Although 'eclectic' writings were quite unanimous in rejecting interventions to repress revolts, their positions once again became much more contrasted once the situation deteriorated from simple internal turmoil to actual civil war.[71] Von Martens, Kent and Heffter, despite denying any right of interference against or in favour of the government in case of internal disorders, adopted a diametrically opposed position regarding intervention in civil wars. They considered that foreign nations could assist whichever of the parties to the conflict whose claim they believed to be most founded in justice.[72] Usually, the party that would be considered to have 'justice' on its side was the one that could be considered as the rightful representative of the people. 'Moral', von Martens wrote, 'authorizes to rescue the oppressed and forbids to support the usurper'.[73] The writers who opposed intervention in a civil war usually underlined that, to the exception of counter-intervention, it was impossible to determine on whose side 'justice' laid and which party was the rightful representative of the nation.[74] They felt that by requesting the help of a foreign power, a government admitted to its own forfeiture and to the fact that it had lost the support of its population.[75] The rebels, on the other hand, had never been the legitimate representatives of the nation.[76] Foreign powers had no right to decide which constitution or political organisation was worth saving, promoting and imposing upon a population,

[70] Wheaton, *Elements of International Law*, vol. 1, pp. 115–116; Bluntschli, *Le droit international codifié*, p. 253 (footnote 3); Woolsey, *Introduction*, pp. 61–68. See also Heffter, Le droit international de l'Europe, p. 97; Pradier-Fodéré, Traité de droit international public, vol. 1, pp. 560–567; Bonfils, *Manuel*, pp. 160–161.

[71] On the principle of neutrality in civil wars, see Olivier Corten, 'La rébellion et le droit international: le principe de neutralité en tension' (2014) 374 *Recueil des cours de l'académie de droit international*, 88–100.

[72] von Martens, *Précis de droit des gens moderne*, p. 151; Kent, *Commentaries on American Law*, vol. 1, pp. 26–27; Heffter, Le droit international de l'Europe, p. 98.

[73] von Martens, Précis de droit des gens moderne, p. 151. Translation by the author.

[74] Bluntschli, Le droit international codifié, p. 255; Heffter, Le droit international de l'Europe, p. 59; von Neumann, *Eléments*, p. 49; Bonfils, *Manuel*, p. 167.

[75] Pradier-Fodéré, *Traité de droit international public*, vol. 1, p. 585; Bonfils, *Manuel*, p. 163.

[76] Pradier-Fodéré, *Traité de droit international public*, vol. 1, p. 587.

unless, once more, 'it is about preserving *oneself* from a certain danger, an immediate threat'.[77] To this argument, von Martens, Kent and Heffter opposed a broader understanding of self-preservation. In such circumstances, intervention was about ensuring the survival of the nation that found itself in a state of civil war and, in so doing, preserve the community from the disorders and inconveniences an on-going conflict could create for the neighbouring States. As Heffter explained: 'the Nations that acknowledge the existence of a common law between them [. . .] have an unquestionable right to put an end, by common consent, to an internal war which devours one or more countries'.[78] Formally speaking, the legal basis of the intervention was the consent given by one of the parties to the conflict, but such actions were, in addition, justified as a way to safeguard the general tranquillity of nations – the threat could be consequently be general and remote.

The above shows that, as in the 'naturalist' literature, the principle of self-preservation maintained a central role. It was not, however, the content of the principle that shaped the exceptions to the rule of non-intervention, but rather the exceptions that a given author believed to exist as legal grounds for intervention that shaped the principle.

* * *

After examining how the nineteenth-century authors whose work had a naturalist inclination approached *ius ad bellum* and showing that even they took State practice into consideration, this second chapter took a leap into the 'eclectic' literature. It aimed to further nuance the narrative of indifference's claim that the authors of the time were still too influenced by naturalism and the classical theories of just war for any genuine credit to be given to their assertion that the use of force was not an absolute prerogative of States. As in Chapter 2, it sought to understand how 'eclectic' authors thought about the international legal system more generally, in order to fully grasp how they proceeded to establish the principle of non-intervention and the exceptions to the said principle.

It has shown that the writings of 'eclectic' inclination, like those of 'naturalist' inclination, recognised the existence and normative character of both natural and positive law. Unlike them, however, they established no formal hierarchy between the two. The relation between natural and

77 Ibid., p. 576. Emphasis added. Translation by the author.

78 Heffter, *Le droit international de l'Europe*, p. 96. Translation by the author.

positive law was quite complex: 'man-made' rules were considered autonomous from 'necessary' principles, but the latter retained a strong power of influence. In several respects, the 'eclectic' legal order could be viewed as an attempt to synthetize and conciliate the scientific requirements for a positive methodology with international law's project of creating a peaceful international community. And, in fact, although the 'eclectics' clearly put the emphasis on positive rules and inductive methodologies, they always seemed to be guided by the wish to make the 'real' rule match, or at least appear to match, the 'ideal' principles. The concordance of positive rules with natural principles theoretically was not necessary, but it was desirable. It was not a proof of the legality of the rules but reinforced their legitimacy. This peculiar interaction of positive and natural law was particularly evident in the way in which 'eclectic' authors established the exceptions to the rules of non-intervention. Their method was primarily based on State practice, yet their assessment of practice regularly differed. In spite of this, they all attempted to reattach their views on which grounds could or could not justify the use of arms to the principle of self-preservation, as if to adorn them with the superior moral authority of natural law. In the end, content-wise, the right to resort to force all boiled down to the interpretation of what constituted a proper threat to the rights and interest of the intervening State.

Once again, this is not without recalling the theories of just war and one may be tempted to take this conclusion as proving the indifference-narrative right. This point was already addressed in the conclusion of Chapter 2, and what was said there holds true here as well. First, is the fact that the classical theories of just war were barely (if ever) mentioned by the 'eclectic' authors when they discussed *ius ad bellum*, or intervention more generally. Practice, on the contrary, and as we saw, was omnipresent. Second, the boundary between theory and practice is rarely hermetic, and theories have a tendency of working their way into the practice of States. And, in fact, the idea that force could only be used as a sanction was equally held by the more positivist strand of nineteenth-century scholarship even though they relied on inductive methodologies far more than their 'naturalist' and 'eclectic' colleagues.

4

The Use of Force in Writings of 'Positivistic' Inclination

According to the narrative of indifference, the dismissal of the theories of 'just war' and the recognition of an absolute war prerogative for States resulted from the rise of positivism in the nineteenth century. Nineteenth-century positivism is portrayed as 'neo-Hegelian' – i.e. solely based on the will of States and totally deferent to that will. Following this line of thought it is claimed that it was impossible for positivists to assert that international law ring-fenced the use of force. States, in fact, would have never agreed to such a limitation of their sovereignty. Positivist writers would have contradicted themselves, disavowed the premises of their work and fallen back into the old tropisms of naturalism and just war. For sure, there existed different iteration of positivism, some of which were fairly close to the above 'neo-Hegelian' description.[1] For the most part, however, 'mainstream' nineteenth-century positivism was not as extreme, and its stand on the right to use force was not one of indifference.

Legal positivism in international law truly gained momentum from the 1870s onwards. With the progressive consolidation of international law as a self-standing discipline, the desire for 'scientificity' took on a new form. In accordance with the methodological canons of the time, legal positivism pleaded for a science of law based on empirical observation alone. Under the guise of rejecting naturalism, however, writings of positivist inclination still found their roots in rationalist philosophy. This was not without creating some ambiguities.[2] 'Positivists', in fact, generally kept and 'positivized' naturalist premises, especially that of an

[1] See below (Section 4.2.).

[2] One may wonder to what extent these ambiguities are not still a trademark of modern-day international legal doctrine. See below Conclusion to Part 1. See also David Kennedy, *International Legal Strcutures* (Nomos Verslagsgesellschaft, 1987); Martti Koskkeniemi, *From Apology to Utopia, The Structure of International Legal Argument* (re-issue with new epilogue) (Cambridge University Press, 2005).

international community of States and legal order structured around three fundamental principles of law (Section 4.1). In the same vein, although highly critical of deductive thinking and advocating for a strictly inductive approach to custom, 'positivist' author often shared the idealist vision of, and project for, international law (Section 4.2). Strictly speaking, their method nevertheless remained inductive and based on the analysis of State practice. The ambivalent attitude of 'positivists' vis-à-vis their 'rationalist' heritage was well reflected in the way they approached *ius ad bellum*. Some authors separated war from the general regime of intervention and used methodologies that did not always give the same weight to fundamental principles of law when determining whether these measures were forbidden or not by international law (Section 4.3). Still, most believed war and intervention to be prohibited on the same grounds and permissible in the same circumstances. These circumstances were either induced from the analysis of practice or deduced from fundamental principles of law (Section 4.4).

4.1 The 'Positivist' Legal Order: The Rejection of Natural Law and the 'Positivation' of Naturalist Premises

Positivism has been understood as an approach that seeks to describe the law as it is and as it stems from the will of States, rather than, as it ought to be. These are the elements that usually surface in traditional definitions of positivism,[3] but also in the way part of nineteenth and early twentieth-century literature characterized its own approach to the law of nations. It insisted that international law 'consists in certain rules of conduct which modern civilized states regard as being binding on them in their relations with one another'[4] and that the task of the jurist was to 'an inquir[e] into what is, not into what ought to be'.[5] Alphonse Rivier, for instance, explained that 'the positivist tendency is a realist tendency, above all seeking to determine the law that is materially and effectively in

[3] See, e.g., Jean Salmon (dir.), *Dictionnaire de droit international public* (Bruylant, 2001), p. 852; Carlo Focarelli, *International Law as a Social Construct. The Struggle for Global Justice* (Oxford University Press, 2012), p. 103.

[4] William E. Hall, *A Treatise on International Law* (3rd ed., Clarendon Press, 1890), p. 1. See also John Westlake expressly quoting Hall in *International Law*, 2 vols. (Cambridge University Press, 1910), vol. 1, p. 8.

[5] Thomas Lawrence, *The Principles of International Law* (D.C. Heath & Co. Publishers, 1900) p. 20. See also Lassa Oppenheim, 'The Science of International Law: Its Tasks and Methods' (1908) 2 *American Journal of International Law* 314–315.

operation'.[6] By contrast, the naturalist perspective was perceived as 'idealist', 'abstract', 'speculative' and as 'confus[ing] facts and theory'.[7] Even the authors who, to some extent, acknowledged natural law stressed that it did not created any obligations and that its violation had no legal consequences. As Théophile Funck-Brentano and Albert Sorel wrote in their *Précis de droit des gens* (1900):

> This natural law, this moral, this philosophy is presented as the expression of absolute truth; and yet authors conceptualise them and expound them differently. [. . .] The theoretical law of nations does not create positive obligations nor practical rules, because it is interpreted in a diversity of ways and it is not respected nor recognised by all the peoples whose conduct and relations it is meant to guide.[8]

In fewer words, the content of natural law could not be defined with precision and it therefore could not be given any normative value. Other authors were more virulent in their criticism of natural law theories. John T. Abdy, an English barrister and professor at the University of Cambridge, for instance, qualified the naturalist point of view as 'absurd'. He insisted that:

> 'the sole source of this law, the fountain from which it flows, whether in its customary, conventional, or judicial-customary shape, is the consent of nations. [...] neither the law of God, nor positive rules of morality, or the law of nature (whatever that may be), can be considered as the source or foundation of International Law, [...]'.[9]

In the same vein, Lassa Oppenheim, would later explain that 'the place of the theory of the law of nature is no longer in our textbooks, law schools, and universities, but in the museums',[10] and 'that the mere term "science" implies knowledge, and that it is a demand of science to stick to the facts, and not to hunt phantasms. And the law of nature is nothing else

[6] Alphonse Rivier, *Principes du droit des gens*, 2 vols. (Arthur Rousseau, 1896), vol. 1, p. 19. Translation by the author. See also Frédéric de Martens, *Traité de droit international*, 3 vols. (Librairie Marescq Ainé, 1883), vol. 1, p. 233; Alexandre Mérignhac, *Traité de droit public international*, 3 vols. (LGDJ, 1905–1912), vol. 1, p. 14.

[7] See, e.g. Lawrence, *The Principles of International Law*, pp. 18–19.

[8] Théophile Funck-Brentano et Albert Sorel, *Précis de droit des gens* (E. Plon et Cie., 1900), p. 2. Translation by the author. See also Rivier, Principes du droit des gens, vol. 1, pp. 24 and 30.

[9] John T. Abdy, *Kent's Commentaries on International Law* (2nd ed., Deighton and sons, 1878), p. 4.

[10] Oppenheim, 'The Science of International Law', 329.

than a phantasm!'.[11] In an effort to prove that international law could be a science, and indeed law, 'positivists' advocated for an approach anchored in the observation of facts and reality, unballasted from any 'metaphysical' considerations.

This definition of positivism is still very broad and different subconceptions of the international legal order can be identified within it. Focusing on the nineteenth and early twentieth centuries, Stephen Neff distinguishes three types of positivist theories: 'empirical', 'common-will' and 'voluntarist'.[12] This taxonomy, however, mixes two types of issues: first, is the question of what was the 'force' that created rules of international law, and second, that of how these rules concretely manifested themselves. 'Empirical' positivism is described as placing the emphasis on the analysis of State practice, because the behaviour of States was the medium through which they expressed their will to be bound by a specific rule.[13] But this seemed to be equally true in the two other 'positivisms'. Presented as the leading figures of 'common-will' positivism,[14] Dionisio Anzilotti and Heinrich Triepel also believed that 'the will for something to become law is expressed through words and acts'.[15] It is true that, unlike the 'empiricists', the two other strands of positivism favoured treaties over custom as the main source of the law of nations, so that their outlook and method may be viewed as less 'historical'.[16] That being said, the adoption of a treaty is as much a 'behaviour' or 'action' of a State as the establishment of national legislation, the drafting of State papers, of diplomatic correspondence or other elements upon which

[11] Ibid., 330.

[12] Stephen C. Neff, 'Jurisprudential Polyphony: The Three Variations on the Positivist Theme in the 19th century', in Pierre-Marie Dupuy et Vincent Chetail (eds.), *The Roots of International Law/Les fondements du droit international – Liber Amicorum Peter Haggenmacher* (Martinus Nijhoff, 2013), pp. 301–334; and by the same author, *Justice among Nations. A History of International Law* (Harvard University Press, 2014), pp. 226–243.

[13] Neff, 'Jurisprudential Polyphony', 304; and *Justice among Nations*, p. 226.

[14] Neff, 'Jurisprudential Polyphony', 313; and *Justice among Nations*, p. 232.

[15] Heinrich Triepel, *Droit international et droit interne* (original edition: 1899) (Pedone, 1920), p. 90. Translation by the author. See also Dionisio Anzilotti, *Cours de droit international*, (translation of the Italian 3rd ed.: 1927) (LGDJ, 1999), p. 67.

[16] Anzilotti, for instance, insisted that: 'il n'est pas vrai de dire, bien que la phrase soit courante, que le droit international est un droit essentiellement coutumier; en réalité, la plus grande partie des rapports entre les Etats est d'ores et déjà réglée par des traités', in Cours de droit international, p. 74. See also Neff, 'Jurisprudential Polyphony', 314; Martti Koskenniemi, *The Gentle Civilizer of Nations. The Rise anf Fall of International Law, 1870–1960* (Cambridge University Press, 2001), p. 211.

custom could be established. Furthermore, the seemingly more 'empirical' approach of the 'empiricists' may also simply be due to the fact that their outlook on international law was, overall, more pragmatic and less theoretical. As Antony Carty underlined, they thought that their task was to uncover and describe the content of international rules, not to theorise about the legal phenomena.[17]

This does not, however, mean that the 'empiricists' did not occasionally touch upon more theoretical issues.[18] In this respect, the dissensions between the different iterations of positivism highlighted by Neff were most evident regarding what the 'will of States' was really understood to be. These differences, it seems, may be better understood if analysed along two axes: (i) common-will (will of State*s*) *vs.* individual-will (will of *a* State), and (ii) international society *vs.* international community. The first axis sees the opposition of 'empirical' and 'common-will' positivism to 'voluntarist' positivism. Even though Triepel and Anzilotti developed the notion of 'agreement' more thoroughly, the 'empiricists' shared their view. Thomas Lawrence and Fyodor Martens, for instance, insisted that a rule became part of international law 'if it wins *general* assent'[19] and that 'the laws that nowadays determine the relations between the different countries are the product of *agreements* between them'.[20] More explicitly still, Oppenheim affirmed that '*common consent* is the basis of all law'.[21] Of course Triepel's and Anzilotti's writings, notably in relation to the concept of *Vereinbarung* and the distinction between contract-treaties

[17] In relation to the work of Oppenheim, Antony Carty explains that he 'was not a theorician but merely the humblest scriber of student manuals', in 'Why Theory? The Implications for International Law Teaching', in Philip Allott, Antony Carty, Martti Koskenniemi and Colin Warbrick (eds.), *Theory and International Law: An Introduction* (British Institute of International and Comparative Law, 1991), p. 80.

[18] In reaction to Carty's assertion, Benedict Kingsbury explains that 'despite his elementary style and the sparcity of the explicit theorizing in his international law works, Oppenheim must be regarded as a more sophisticated theorist then Carty's appraisal suggests', in 'Legal Positivism as Normative Politics: International Society, Balance of Power and Lassa Oppenheim's Positive International Law' (2002) 13 *European Journal of International Law* 406.

[19] Lawrence, *The Principles of International Law*, p. 106. Emphasis added. See also Carlos Calvo, *Le droit international théorique et pratique*, 6 vols. (Guillaumin & Cie., 1887), vol. 1, p. 144; Rivier, Principes du droit des gens, vol. 1, pp. 7–8; Hall, *A Treatise*, p. 5; Funck-Brentano et Sorel, Précis de droit des gens, p. 3; Mérignhac, Traité de droit public international, vol. 1, p. 21; Westlake, *International Law*, vol. 1, p. 7.

[20] de Martens, Traité de droit international, vol. 1, p. 15. Emphasis added. Translation by the author.

[21] Oppenheim, International Law, vol. 1, pp. 15 and 17. Emphasis added.

and law-treaties, were much more elaborate.[22] The logics were nonetheless the same: international law required a plurality of States and its content was the product of the meeting of the concordant wills of these States. By contrast, for the 'voluntarists', international law rested on the individual will of the State, meaning that a State promulgated for itself and on its own the rules it intended to see regulate its relations with other nations. This perspective, characteristic of the 'German' literature, has often been described as viewing international law as a form of 'external public law': the legislator was the same as in national law, only the subject matter differed.[23] Notwithstanding the nuances and differences between their theories, Adolph Lasson, Carl Bergbohm, Philipp Zorn and Georg Jellinek are traditionally considered to be the main representatives of this school of thought.[24] In addition to being individual, the will of States was also believed to be free, which brings us to the second axis.

Linked to the question of the prevalence of a higher degree of normativity issuing from the existence of a 'community' between States, the second axis is closely connected to the first one: a 'voluntarist' was, in fact, unlikely to assert or recognize the existence of a community of values above the State. More interestingly, this axis sees a fracture between Triepel, whose thought was closer to that of his German-speaking fellowmen, and Anzilotti. Although with the concept of '*vereinbarung*' Triepel contended that the 'common-will' was superior to the

[22] In English the term *Vereinbarung* literally translates into 'agreement'. In international legal theory it refers to the process by which the concordant individual wills of States meet and create a common-will which bares general rules meant to permanently regulate the relations of the concerned States. The concept was developed by Triepel in *Landesrecht und Völkerrecht* (1899) and later taken up by Anzilotti. See Triepel, Droit international et droit interne, pp. 62–73; Dionisio Anzilotti, *Teoria generale della responsabilità dello Stato nel diritto internazionale*, 2 vols. (F. Lumachi, 1902) vol. 1, pp. 37 and 42. On these concepts, see Gérard Cahin, 'Traité-contrat et traité-loi à partir d'Heinrich Triepel', in *Grandes pages du droit international* (Editions A. Pedone, 2016), vol. 2, pp. 21–54.

[23] Neff, 'Jurisprudential Polyphony', 317–326.

[24] Ibid., 320–322. For detailed discussions of these authors' theories see Wihelm G. Grewe, *The Epochs of International Law* 'Walter De Gruyter, 2000), pp. 503–506; Martti Koskenniemi, *The Gentle Civilizer of Nations*, pp. 179–265; Amnon Lev, 'The transformation of international law in the 19th century', in Alexander Orakhelashvili (ed.), *Research Handbook on the Theory and History of International Law* (Edward Elgar, 2011), pp. 134–137; Jochen von Bernstorff, 'Georg Jellinek and the Origins of Liberal Constitutionalism' (2012) 4 *Goettingen Journal of International Law* 659–675; and by the same author, 'German intellectual historical origins of international legal positivism', in Jean d'Aspremont and Jörg Kammerhofer (eds.), *International Legal Positivism in the Post-Modern World* (Cambridge University Press, 2014), pp. 50–80.

individual-will of States, he stood firm on the fact that 'it is not necessary nor admissible to consider this legal rule as an expression of the will of an *international collectivity* or of an *interstate system* composed of States and superimposed on them as a sort of association or person'.[25] At the end of the day, most 'voluntarists' admitted that psycho-sociological factors had an influence on the determination and content of the will of States.[26] But this was only an influence and not an imposition issuing from the existence of an international community with common values baring some sort of a higher degree of normativity. This also meant that it was believed that many States could not dictate rules to those that were not willing to accept them, and that, unless a rule achieved unanimity, general international law could not exist.[27]

Anzilotti was more ambiguous. Despite stressing that the necessity of law did not determine its content and praising German literature,[28] he emphasized the role of the 'social conscience' and seemed to admit the existence of an overbearing impetus emanating from 'the requirements that spurt from reality'.[29] To a certain extent then, he fell within the criticism he himself addressed to mainstream 'empirical' positivism: the mixing of a positivist approach to law and of remnant traditional ideas.[30] The existence of a 'community' with common values and Grotius's theory of sociability were, in fact, still very influential in most of the nineteenth- and early twentieth-century writings of positivist inclination.[31] The rules of international law established by States were considered to be the expression of a 'common legal conscience',[32] of the 'essential facts of the existence of a society',[33] or yet of a 'family of nations'.[34] As Martens then affirmed: 'the bias of the scientific system

[25] Triepel, Droit international et droit interne, p. 75. Emphasis in the original. Translation by the author.
[26] Koskenniemi, *The Gentle Civilizer of Nations*, p. 206.
[27] Triepel, *Droit international et droit interne*, p. 82.
[28] Anzilotti, *Teoria generale*, pp. 38–39.
[29] Anzilotti, *Cours de droit international*, p. 67. Translation by the author. On this aspect of Anzilotti's work see Denis Alland, *Anzilotti et le droit international. Un essai* (Pedone, 2012), pp. 39–44; Carlo Santulli, 'Quels sont les pères volontaristes du droit international? Anzilotti et Triepel', in *Grandes pages du droit international* (Pedone, 2016), vol. 2, pp. 5–19.
[30] Giogio Gaja, 'Positivism and Dualism in Dionisio Anzilotti' (1992) 3 *European Journal of International Law* 125.
[31] See in particular Lawrence, *The Principles of International Law*, p. 3.
[32] Rivier, *Principes du droit des gens*, vol. 1, p. 27.
[33] Hall, *A Treatise*, p. 6.
[34] Oppenheim, International Law, vol. 1, p. 15, see also p. 10.

of contemporary international law is the *idea of an international community* according to which each State is bound to the others by interests and common laws, forming an organic whole in which they nevertheless maintain their independence'.[35] In this perspective, it was not necessary for all the members of the community to assent to a particular rule for it to become applicable and binding upon all States: general international law required majority and not unanimity.[36] Hence, as Antony Anghie emphasized, 'society, rather than sovereignty [was] the central concept used to construct the system of international law'.[37] The descending movement that had, at first glance, been evacuated from the process of creation of international rules with the rejection of natural law, was thus reintroduced by a byroad. The fact that 'empirical' positivists kept the idea of the existence of 'fundamental principles' of international law (independence, equality and self-preservation) is, in that respect, quite compelling.[38] William E. Hall, for instance, considered that: 'the ultimate foundation of international law is an assumption that states possess rights and are subject to duties corresponding to the facts of their postulated nature'.[39] Oppenheim similarly noted that, in spite of the disagreements regarding their number, 'these fundamental rights are a matter of course and self-evident, since the Family of Nations consists of sovereign States'.[40] This comes to show how mainstream 'empirical' positivism conserved the classical structure of the international legal order inherited from natural law theories. For all that, it cannot be fully affirmed, as Wilhelm Grewe does, that: 'even those of their protagonists who converted to positivism in respect of national law continued to think in traditional, natural law categories as far as the foundations of

[35] de Martens, Traité de droit international, vol. 1, p. 232. Emphasis in the original. Translation by the author.

[36] John Westlake was particularly clear in this respect: 'When one of those rules is invoked against a state it is not necessary to show that the state in question has assented to the rule either diplomatically or by having acted on it, though it is a strong argument if you can do so', in *International Law*, vol. 1, p. 16.

[37] Antony Anghie, *Imperialism, Sovereignty and the Making of International Law* (Cambridge University Press, 2007), p. 48. See also Collins, 'Classical Legal Positivism', 41; Kingsbury, 'Legal Positivism as Normative Politics', 409; Mathias Schmoeckel, 'The Internationalists as a Scientist and a Herald: Lassa Oppenheim' (2000) 11 *European Journal of International Law* 707.

[38] See, e.g., Abdy, *Kent's Commentaries*, p. 40; de Martens, Traité de droit international, vol. 1, p. 387; Rivier, Principes du droit des gens, vol. 1, p. 255; Mérignhac, Traité de droit public international, vol. 1, p. 89. Contra: Westlake, *International Law*, vol. 1, p. 307.

[39] Hall, *A Treatise*, p. 45.

[40] Oppenheim, *International Law*, vol. 1, p. 158.

international law were concerned'.[41] As a matter of fact, while the basic structure of international law was indeed borrowed from the naturalist tradition, 'positivist' writings did not think in 'natural law categories' per se. Fundamental principles were believed to be part of the positive law of nations. They were considered to be fundamental not only because they were inherent to States as the main entities and actors of the international scene, but also because States themselves recognised them as such. Lawrence, for instance, noted that: 'no one doubts the existence of the right of independence or of the duty of self-preservation'.[42] As a result, when they spoke of independence, equality and self-preservation, writings of positivist inclination did not think in natural law categories but in terms of positive law.

4.2 The 'Positivist' Approach to Custom: An Inductive Methodology for an Idealist Project

Since different shades of positivism could be observed in nineteenth and early twentieth century scholarship, it could be expected that each of these shades had its own conception of and approach to customary international law. However, since they considered treaties to be the most important source of the law of nations, 'voluntarist' and 'common-will' positivists barely examined how customary rules should be established. Because they considered custom to be the most important source of the law of nations, the 'empiricists', while less concerned with the theory, scrupulously discussed methodological questions.[43]

Unsurprisingly, 'empirical' positivism developed a discourse that advocated for the rejection of deduction and was in favour of a process based on induction and historical inquiry. Most writings, indeed, insisted that 'the science of the law of nations must be a science of application, not of speculation and pure reasoning',[44] and that, as a consequence, 'it is essentially in history that the science looks for and finds their [custom

[41] Grewe, *The Epochs of International Law*, p. 506.

[42] Lawrence, *The Principles of International Law*, p. 23, see also p. 117.

[43] Oppenheim and Rivier, for instance, respectively insisted that: 'Custom is the older and original source of international law'; and that: 'le droit des gens, [. . .] est par sa nature même un droit coutumier'. Oppenheim, *International Law*, vol. 1, p. 22; Rivier, Principes du droit des gens, vol. 1, p. 36.

[44] Rivier, *Principes du droit des gens*, vol. 1, p. 28. Translation by the author.

and treaties] manifestations'.[45] For the purpose of this historical inquiry, authors quite classically stressed the useful character of arbitrary and prize court awards, of national case law, treaties, state papers, diplomatic correspondence and so forth to determine the existence and content of customary law.[46] John Westlake wrote in 1910:

> 'The best evidence of the consent which makes international law is the practice of states appearing in their actions, in the treaties they conclude, and in the judgement of their prize and other courts, [. . .].
>
> The arguments adduced by statesmen in despatches and other public utterances are very important as showing what were the principles proceeded on, [. . .]'.[47]

As this extract also suggests, the 'positivist' method for custom determination, although rooted in the analysis of practice, was not purely 'materialistic'. The re-collection of these documents was not only a means to establish the 'factual' practice of State, but also to determine the attitudes and positions formulated in relation to that practice. Like the rest of nineteenth and early twentieth century scholarship, they urged the difference between mere usage and proper practice: 'Jurists', Oppenheim wrote, 'speak of custom when a clear and continuous habit of doing certain actions had grown up under the aegis of the conviction that these actions are legally necessary or legally right'.[48] In sum, they adopted the classical two-element definition of custom and considered *opinio juris* to be the determinative element. As Carlos Calvo underlined, 'to determine if a particular act is sanctioned or prohibited by law, it is necessary to search whether it has been approved or disapproved by civilised nations in general, or at least by the nations concerned by this act in some way or another'.[49] Beside 'factual'

[45] Ibid., p. 30. Translation by the author. See also Calvo, Le droit international vol. 1, p. 160; Hall, *A Treatise*, p. 5; Funck-Brentano et Sorel, Précis, pp. 2–3.

[46] Abdy, *Kent's Commentaries*, p. 7; de Martens, Traité de droit international, vol. 1, pp. 247–248; Calvo, Le droit international, vol. 1, pp. 160–164; by the same author, *Manuel de droit international public et privé*, 2 vols. (Arthur Rousseau, 1892), vol. 1, pp. 80–82; Rivier, Principes du droit des gens, vol. 1, p. 35, Lawrence, *The Principles of International Law*, pp. 100–106; Mérignhac, *Traité de droit public international*, vol. 1, p. 89; Oppenheim, International Law, vol. 1, p. 24; by the same author, 'The Science of International Law', 336 and 341; Westlake, *International Law*, vol. 1, p. 16.

[47] Westlake, *International Law*, vol. 1, p. 16.

[48] Oppenheim, *International Law*, vol. 1, p. 22. See also Westlake, *International Law*, vol. 1, p. 14.

[49] Calvo, *Le droit international*, vol. 1, p. 144.Translation by the author. See also Westlake, *International Law*, vol. 1, p. 16.

practice, particular attention thus needed to be paid to the justifications put forward by States to explain their behaviour as well as to the reactions these had generated.

Despite of the fact that they had the same definition of customary law and employed the same material to determine the existence and content of customary rules, the 'positivist' literature was very sceptical regarding the way in which 'naturalists' and 'eclectics' had dealt with and interpreted this material. Lawrence and Oppenheim (whose textbooks are particularly thorough in the discussion of methodological issues) were among the most critical. In ten pages he dedicated to the analysis of the respective merits of the 'a priori' and of the 'historical' method, Lawrence strongly denounced the approaches that mixed positivism (induction) and naturalism (deduction). He accused the authors that employed them, of 'produc[ing] in their readers a mode of thought as confused and confusing as their own'[50] and of 'blend[ing] the ideal with the real, [of] confus[ing] what ought to be with what is, and [of] turn[ing] moral rightness into legal right'.[51] Lawrence somewhat reflexively concluded by asserting that the right method for international 'must of necessity be historical' because that was what issued from State practice: States appealed to the rules acknowledged in practice and not to natural law to settle their disputes'.[52] In 1908, in an article entitled '*The Science of International Law: Its Tasks and Method*', Oppenheim similarly directly asked the question of 'which method is the right one?'[53] He affirmed that the science should be based on facts and empirical observation. Like his colleague he deplored the political, humanitarian and other bias that regularly led writers of international law to see rules where there were none, and to fill the lacunae of the law with *de lege feranda* considerations.[54]

Yet, in spite of these discourses, it may be questioned to what extent the 'positivist' approach to custom was truly purged from all deductive and 'wishful' considerations. The answer is complex. On the one hand, while acknowledging the importance of ethics, 'positivist' writings advocated for a clear separation of law and morals but, on the other hand, also had a very idealistic vision of the role of international law and international lawyers.

[50] Lawrence, *The Principles of International Law*, p. 23, see also p. 19.
[51] Ibid., p. 23.
[52] Ibid., p. 23, see also p. 20.
[53] Oppenheim, 'The Science of International Law', 327.
[54] Ibid., pp. 333 and 353.

The idea according to which law could not be completely disconnected from morals because justice was the ideal law had to strive for, was still core in a lot 'positivist' works. As in the 'eclectic' writings, they often regarded ethics as the model to follow and believed that, with the progress of humanity, the laws of society would eventually come to identify with the laws of morality. Social and moral standards of conduct, in sum, could gradually work their way to legal normativity.[55] The line of demarcation between mere usage and proper custom was, hence, delicate to draw. As 'positivists' earnestly recognised, this distinction was highly subjective and rested on the 'sharp eye' of the jurist and on its capacity to understand 'the pulse of his age'.[56] Despite advocating for objectivity, these scholars were therefore aware that even the description of the law as it is, was a process of interpretation in which their personal bias, just as that of the 'naturalists' and the 'eclectics', played a role in the conclusions they reached. The remedy to this inevitable pitfall was to always clearly distinguish 'between the writer's opinion *de lege feranda* and really recognised rules of law'.[57] To summarize, as Lawrence explained:

> we do not imagine that the moral quality of these rules is a matter of indifference, or believe that writers on public law need not trouble themselves about it. All we contend for is that the question what are the rules of International Law on a given subject, and the question whether they are good or bad should be kept distinct.[58]

Still, beyond the simple description of the applicable rules of law, authors regularly thought of themselves as idealists and activists. 'Law', Oppenheim pressingly affirmed, 'is merely a means to certain ends outside itself'.[59] The task of the lawyer, he went on to explain, was to 'criticise the existing law for the purpose, not of pulling it to pieces, but of preparing its *improvement*'.[60] As a consequence, international lawyers were not necessarily impartial observers of the legal order, but active participants to its evolution and, by the same token, to the progress and humanisation of the international society. International law carried a social

[55] Rivier, Principes du droit des gens, vol. 1, p. 25. See also Oppenheim, 'The Science of International Law', p. 334.
[56] Oppenheim, Ibid.
[57] Ibid., p. 335. Emphasis in the original.
[58] Lawrence, *The Principles of International Law*, p. 23. See also Westlake, *International Law*, vol. 2, p. 10.
[59] Oppenheim, 'The Science of International Law', p. 314.
[60] Ibid., p. 356. Emphasis added.

project of orderly and peaceful co-existence of States; law was a tool for social progress and the task of the jurist was to help it achieve its ends.[61] Oppenheim was categorical: '[h]e who has no faith in the possibility of accomplishing it is not wanted among us'.[62] This warning was not meant for legal advisers but for academics. Scholarly writings were perceived as particularly important and influential. Rivier, in reference to French jurist and sociologist Gabriel Tarde, underlined how doctrinal ideas could progressively slide into the legal conscience and into the practice of nations.[63] In *Les transformations du droit* (1893), Tarde explained:

> Most of the laws of war recognized by civilized states have never been deliberated, or have not been unanimously accepted, in international conventions. This right seems to be the glaring realization of this 'morality without obligation or sanction' [...] So where does its effective power really come from? It is quite simple and well known: from the success of the works of Grotius and Vattel in their time, that is to say, from the enthusiastic support given to their formulas by a host of eminent minds, then statesmen, and finally any enlightened person, who successively suffered the salutary contagion of this enthusiasm.[64]

Scholarly writings were considered as capable of playing an important role in the evolution of international law and eventual sprouting of new customary rules. This is also why, it seems, 'positivist' writers deemed it preferable to stick to an inductive approach that followed the methodological canons of 'science'. This balance between legal utopianism and political pragmatism could, in fact, be a manner to galvanise the attention around the need to plug specific legal loopholes. But, at a time when, as Koskenniemi highlights, international lawyers became increasingly self-conscious as to the scientific character of their discipline,[65] it could also be a means to ensure the credibility of the discipline, acceptance of the international legal discourse and, as a result, respect for the existing rules of international law as well as the potential for international lawyers to be incremental in ameliorating these rules.[66] Because they answered the

[61] Kingsbury, 'Legal Positivism as Normative Politics', p. 402.

[62] Oppenheim, 'The Science of International Law', p. 356.

[63] Rivier, *Principes du droit des gens*, vol. 1, pp. 31–32.

[64] Gabriel Tarde, *Les transformations du droit: étude sociologique* (Felix Alcan, 1893), p. 158. Translation by the author.

[65] Koskenniemi, *From Apology to Utopia*, p. 123.

[66] In this sense, see Guillaume Sacriste et Antoine Vauchez, 'La « guerre hors-la-loi », 1919–1910. Note de recherche 'Les origines de la définition d'un order politique international' (2004) 150 *Acte de la recherche sociale* 195; and by the same authors, 'The Force of

criticism that had been addressed to international law from outside the discipline and partly allowed to fill its lack of 'scientific' legitimacy, inductive methodologies were, in a way, viewed as a better strategy to work towards the improvement of international law. This means that the 'positivist' international legal discourse was, among other elements, built bearing in mind how the intended audience would receive it, whether it was other legal scholars or government officials. This might explain why, as we shall now see, writings of positivist inclinations were not always consistent in the methodologies they used to tackle the issue of the use of force.

4.3 A 'Discursive' Approach to Intervention and a 'Factual' Approach to War

The tension between 'traditional' and 'new' methodologies just described was very palpable in the way intervention and the use of force were addressed. The most striking feature was the fact that some authors separated resort to war from the general regime of intervention and, using different methodologies, reached different conclusions regarding their prohibition. These methodologies did not give the same weight to fundamental principles of international law and did not approach State practice in the same way. While the general rule of non-intervention was usually deduced from the principles of independence and equality and then confirmed by an approach to State practice that placed the emphasis on *opinio juris* through the analysis of States' justification discourses ('discursive' methodology), resort to war was analysed from the strict point of view of practice ('factual' methodology).[67]

International Law: Lawyers' Diplomacy on the International Scene in the 1920s' (2007) 32 *Law & Social Inquiry* 103.

67 Focusing on nineteenth-century scholarship, Pieter Kooijmans and Eric Wyler also distinguish two positivist methodologies. Kooijmans speaks of a 'realist' vs. a 'voluntarist' approach and Wyler of a 'factualist' vs. a 'legalist' method. See Pieter H. Kooijmans, *The Doctrine of the Legal Equality of States: An Inquiry into the Foundations of International Law* (A. W. Stijhoff, 1964), p. 108; Eric Wyler, 'L'influence du positivisme sur la doctrine volontariste et objectiviste en droit international: plus qu'un facteur de rapprochement?', in Pierre-Marie Dupuy et Vincent Chetail (eds.), *The Roots of International Law/Les fondements du droit international – Liber Amicorum Peter Haggenmacher* (Martinus Nijhoff, 2013), pp. 352–354. Analysing contemporary literature, Olivier Corten speaks of a 'extensive' and of a 'restrictive' approach, see 'Controversies over the Customary Prohibition on the Use of Force: A Methodological Debate' (2005) 16 *European Journal of International Law* 803–822.

'Positivists' all agreed that intervention was prohibited by the law of nations. In establishing this rule, however, they used a methodology that seemed to be at odds with their rejection of deductive thinking and followed the path carved out by the 'naturalist' and 'eclectic' literature. Despite criticising deductive thinking, the establishment of the rule of non-intervention was the result of a mix of deduction from the fundamental principles of law, and of induction from State practice. State practice, in fact, was considered to be too contradictory and ambiguous to authenticate a rule of non-intervention beyond reasonable doubt. In this respect, Lawrence was particularly clear:

> We can generally deduce the rules of International Law from the practice of States; but in this case it is impossible to do anything of the kind. [...] On this subject history speaks with a medley of discordant voices, and the facts of international intercourse give no clue to the to the rules of international law. We might, indeed, deem that the search for rules of any kind was hopeless, were it not that it is possible to deduce certain clear and unmistakable precepts from principles admitted on all sides. No one doubts the existence of the right of independence, or the duty of self-preservation, and from these we are able by a process of deduction to obtain what we are in search of.[68]

From the principle of independence, the rule of non-intervention necessarily issued. Funck-Brentano and Sorel, for instance, firmly asserted in their 1900 textbook that: 'by intervening, a State fails to respect the sovereignty and independence of the State in whose affairs it intervenes. Intervention is therefore not a right, because there is no right against the law and the sovereignty of State is an essential principle of the law of nations'.[69] Similarly, under the heading of 'the right of independence', Oppenheim and Calvo respectively wrote: that 'intervention is a rule forbidden by the law of nations which protects the International Personality of the State, there is no doubt';[70] and that 'absolute sovereignty necessarily implicates complete independence; from there a right, that of States to freely follow their path towards their own destiny; and an obligation, that of recognising and respecting the rights and independence of other States'.[71]

[68] Lawrence, *The Principles of International Law*, p. 117.

[69] Funck-Brentano et Sorel, *Précis*, p. 216. Translation by the author.

[70] Oppenheim, *International Law*, vol. 1, p. 182.

[71] Calvo, Manuel, vol. 1, p. 100. Translation by the author. See also de Martens, Traité de droit international, vol. 1, pp. 394–395; Hall, *A Treatise*, p. 282; Rivier, Principes du droit

In spite of its controversial nature, 'positivists' still sought to find a confirmation of the rule of non-intervention in State practice. Rivier thus noted how this rule (albeit dispensably) had often been reasserted in treaties such as the Treaty of Lübeck (1629), the Treaty of the Pyreneans (1659) and the Treaty of Nystad (1721).[72] More thoroughly, in his six-volume manual, Calvo delved into a seventy-page long analysis of State practice.[73] At the end this analysis, he concluded that both intervention and non-intervention were part of international law; the main question was to determine which one was the rule and which one was the exception. In his opinion, since behind political interest legal reasons were often given to justify interventions, practice showed that non-intervention was the rule that prevailed in international relations.[74] Oppenheim adopted an analogous position. He wrote:

> Careful analysis of the rules of the Law of Nations regarding intervention and the hitherto exercised practice of intervention make it apparent that intervention is *de facto* a matter of policy just like war. [...] No State will ever intervene in the affairs of another, if it has not some important interest in doing so, and it has always been easy for such State to find or pretend to some legal justification for an intervention, be it self-preservation, balance of power, or humanity.[75]

A few sentences later, Oppenheim once again reaffirmed that 'unjustified intervention violates the very principles of the Law of Nations'.[76] In sum, although law had no influence on the decision to intervene in another State, it nonetheless acted as a framework of reference to make the intervention appear acceptable to the other members of the international society. The fact that States referred to this framework showed their deference and acceptance of the rules it contained. *Opinio juris* here was the determinative element and emphasis was placed on the analysis of discourse rather than bare facts. Intervention was a de facto, but not a de jure, matter of politics.

Oppenheim interestingly reached a diametrically opposite conclusion regarding resorts to armed force that amounted to war. Most writers,

des gens, vol. 1, p. 390; Lawrence, *The Principles of International Law*, p. 117; Mérignhac, *Traité de droit international public*, vol. 1, p. 284.

[72] Rivier, Principes du droit des gens, vol. 1, p. 390.

[73] Calvo, *Le droit international*, vol. 1, pp. 279–351.

[74] Ibid., p. 351. See also Calvo, Manuel, vol. 1, p. 115.

[75] Oppenheim, *International Law*, vol. 1, p. 187.

[76] Ibid., p. 188.

however, did not make this distinction between armed intervention and war: as we saw, war was just one of the forms that armed intervention could take when all other 'peaceful' means had failed.[77] They usually jumped to the analysis of the conditions in which recourse to war was permitted without feeling the need to re-demonstrate or even re-state the principle of respect for independence of foreign nations.[78] Calvo, for instance, strictly held the same discourse regarding intervention and war. He insisted that a difference needed to be made between the 'justifying causes' of war (which referred to the *rules* of the law of nations) and the 'motives' for war (which referred to the *facts*), complaining that writers of international law too often mistook rules and facts, principles of law and mere usage.[79] By contrast, Oppenheim considered that:

> All such rules laid down by writers on International Law as recognising certain causes as just and others as unjust are rules of writers, but not rules of International Law based on international custom or international treaties.
>
> [...]
>
> A State which makes war against another will never confess that there is no just cause of war, and it will therefore, when it has made up its mind to make war for political reasons, always look out for a so-called just cause. Thus frequently the apparent reason of war is only a pretext behind which real causes are concealed.[80]

Oppenheim's position and sudden shift of method is somewhat puzzling: intervention was de facto but not de jure a matter of politics; war was de facto and, hence, de jure a matter of politics. Thomas Lawrence, John Westlake – together with a few German authors – and Anzilotti shared this view.[81] Lawrence considered that: 'modern international law knows nothing of those moral questions. It does not pronounce upon them: it simply ignores them'.[82] Paul Heilborn likewise insisted that: 'modern

[77] See above (Section 1.3). In the 'positivist' literature see Funck-Brentano et Sorel, Précis, p. 232; Hall, *A Treatise*, p. 374; Rivier, Principes du droit des gens, vol. 2, p. 201; Mérignhac, Traité de droit international public, vol. 3, p. 10.

[78] Funck-Brentano and Sorel nonetheless insisted that: 'La guerre n'est pas un droit pour les Etats [. . .] dire qu'elle est un droit pour les Etats équivaut à dire qu'il n'y a entre les Etats d'autre droit que la force', in Précis, p. 232.

[79] Calvo, *Le droit international*, vol. 2, p. 22.

[80] Oppenheim, *International Law*, vol. 2, pp. 69 and 71.

[81] Westlake, *International Law*, vol. 1, p. 7; Dionisio Anzilotti, *Corso di diritto internazionale*, 3 vols. (Anthenaeum, 1915), vol. 3, p. 185

[82] Lawrence, *The Principles of International Law*, p. 292.

international law knows [...] no rule concerning when war may be waged. [...] The use of force is absolutely permitted in inter-state relations'.[83]

What might explain this sudden methodological shift? Why when the fact that States intervened in each other's affairs was not enough to deny the 'reality' of the principle of non-intervention, was the fact that States made war to each other sufficient to discard the principle according to which States should respect their mutual independence? According to Wilhelm Grewe, given their very voluntarist conception of international law, this attitude towards *ius ad bellum* was not all that surprising coming from German scholarship.[84] In fact, if one adopted a neo-Hegelian vision in which international law was viewed as 'external public law' created by the sole will of the State to which it would apply, then the rules of international law were as easily made as unmade depending on the immediate interest of that State. Caricaturally speaking, it was sufficient for a State to declare that it did not recognise any legal limitations to its right to wage war (anymore), for war to become permissible on its part. Grewe felt this attitude to be more surprising coming from the 'empiricist' mainstream Anglo-Saxon literature, which he viewed as more rooted in traditional conceptions of international law.[85] Grewe, however, simply saw it as a sign that Oppenheim, Lawrence and Westlake were more 'positivistic' than their compeers. Then again, is a method based on discourse and *opinio juris* necessarily less empirical and 'positivistic' than a method based on bare factual analysis?

The particularism of the Anglo-Saxon literature, supposedly deeply influenced by John Austin, has also often been underlined.[86] Based on his 'command theory', and because of the absence of a superior international authority capable of enforcing effective sanctions upon recalcitrant States, Austin denied the existence of international law as law.[87] In

[83] Paul Heilborn, *Handbuch des Völkerrechts*, (*W. Kohlhammer*, 1912), vol. 1, p. 23 (English translation in Grewe, The Epochs of International Law, p. 531, (footnote no 28)). See also Westlake, *International Law*, vol. 2, p. 4.

[84] Grewe, *The Epochs of International Law*, p. 533.

[85] Ibid., p. 533.

[86] See Michael Lobban, 'English Approaches to International Law in the Nineteenth Century', in Matthew Craven, Malgosia Fitzmaurice & Maria Vogiatzi (eds.), *Time, History and International Law* (Martinus Nijhoff, 2007), pp. 78–88.

[87] It is worth noting that some international lawyers agreed with Austin. John Norton Pomeroy, for instance, considered that: 'In truth, a large portion of what is generally termed international law has none of the very essential elements of positive human jurisprudence. So far as the administration of human affairs, of political societies, is concerned, it cannot with propriety be termed *law*, but should be called *morality* –

response, British international lawyers almost systematically dedicated a section of their manuals' introduction to criticising Austin's narrow conception of law and to proving that, even though the international legal system indeed lacked autonomous and institutionalised sanction mechanisms, it nevertheless was law proper because of the social sanction it received.[88] Did this social sanction then disappear when a State resorted to full-blown war? Another element of Anglo-Saxon particularism that is often put forward is the pragmatism associated with common-law legal culture. In 1910, Westlake already argued that while continental lawyers tended to refer to international law as an abstract 'standard of right independently from its reception', 'the Englishman appeals primarily to international law as a body of rules considered with regard to their reception'.[89] Said simply, Westlake believed the English-speaking literature to be more in touch with reality; their outlook was more inductive and positivistic whereas continental jurists relied more on grand ideals of justice. Still, this does not explain why Oppenheim, Lawrence and Westlake would switch from one methodology to another. The entanglement of international legal scholars with their respective governments and diplomatic services has also sometimes been underlined and may be another factor to take into consideration. Some have argued that nineteenth century *ius ad bellum* may have been weakened as a result of the colonial wars that took place around the turn of the century.[90] It may also be that these authors were anxious to accommodate 'prevailing ideas', as Calvo suggested, at a time in which the results of The Hague Peace Conferences of 1899 and 1907 had been disappointing in terms of mechanisms for preventing war. Be that as it may, it should be remembered that, for most writers, the legal regime of resort to war did not differ from that of general intervention and, as a consequence, nor did the circumstances in which recourse to them could be had.

international morality', in *Lectures on International Law in Time of Peace* (Houghton, Mifflin and Company, 1886), p. 17. Emphasis in the original.

88 Hall, *A Treatise on International Law*, pp. 14–17; Lawrence, *The Principles of International Law*, pp. 2 and 10–16; Oppenheim, *International Law*, vol. 1, pp. 4–9; Westlake, *International Law*, vol. 1, pp. 8–9. On the overall reaction of English-speaking scholarship to Austin, see Michael Lobban, 'English Approaches to International Law', pp. 80–88.

89 Westlake, *International Law*, vol. 1, p. 10.

90 See Jochen von Bernstorff, 'The Use of Force in International Law before World War I: On Imperial Ordering and the Ontology of the Nation-State' (2018) 29 *European Journal of International Law* 233–260.

4.4 The Exceptions Resulting from State Practice or from the Fundamental Principles of International Law

The fundamental principles of international law played a similarly ambiguous and changing role regarding the exceptions to the rule of non-intervention. Unlike 'naturalists' and 'eclectics', they did not necessarily believe that all the exceptions revolved around the principle of self-preservation. Self-preservation included all the circumstances in which the intervening State responded to or anticipated a threat to its security, interests or rights, but issues such as humanitarian and solicited intervention were not necessarily tested against, or linked back to, this principle. In *A Treatise on International Law* (1890) Hall, for instance, wrote:

> 'The grounds upon which intervention had taken place, or upon which it is said with more or less authority that it is permitted, may be referred to the right of self-preservation, to a right of opposing wrong-doing, to the duty of fulfilling engagements, and to friendship for one of two parties in a state'.[91]

In the same spirit, Lawrence warned his readers that 'we have seen how the duty of self-preservation may override the duty of respect for a neighbour's freedom of action. It must now be pointed out that this is not the only exception to the general principle of non-intervention'.[92] In other words, all the exceptions did not gravitate around the principle of self-preservation, which was only one of the considerations that had been claimed to justify a right of intervention.

As these extracts tend to suggest, 'positivist' writings usually started by identifying the exceptions that had been asserted to exist either in practice or in the scholarship and then proceeded to verify their value. Considering the inductive methodology that this strand of the literature advocated, one would expect this verification to be carried out based on the analysis of State practice in order to determine whether States had truly accepted these circumstances as legal exceptions to the rule of non-intervention. In the 1878 re-edition of *Kent's Commentaries on International Law*, after having exposed the main instances of intervention, Abdy explained that:

> 'Such is the narrative of the most remarkable events in the history of interference or intervention since the year 1818, laid before the reader for

[91] Hall, *A Treatise*, p. 283.

[92] Lawrence, *The Principles of International Law*, p. 118.

> the purpose of enabling him to contrast with the declarations of the statesmen and the opinions of the legists the facts of history, and to obtain, if possible, some definite and rational rule'.[93]

State practice, however, and as we saw nineteenth-century authors themselves underlined, was quite opaque and often contradictory. 'On this subject', Lawrence wrote, 'history speaks with a medley of discordant voices'.[94] Determining the legal exceptions to non-intervention was, therefore, a complex process of detangling and making sense out of State practice. From there, two scenarios could present themselves: either there was enough State practice and a certain coherence could be found within it, in which case the scholarship barely referred to the fundamental principles of international law; or State practice was scarce and inconsistent, in which case the fundamental principles played a decisive role. In other terms, only a widely established and accepted practice could put the principle of independence aside; in the absence of such coherent practice, the legal exceptions to the rule of non-intervention could still be determined by reference to the fundamental principles of international law.

A widely accepted practice could, for example, be encountered at the beginning of the nineteenth century in relations to foreign intervention to repress internal revolutionary movements. The Congresses of Aix-la-Chapelle (1818), Troppau (1820), Laybach (1821) and Verona (1822) had indeed given rise to vivacious and extensive debates on which jurists could rely to determine the content of the law. The lessons writings of positivist inclination drew from these events, however, greatly differed from those of the 'naturalist' and 'eclectic' writings. While the works examined in the first two chapters adopted the British view, the 'positivist' scholarship believed that the 1815 Peace Treaties and subsequent Congresses consecrated a system of systematic intervention to repress international revolts to maintain the old monarchical European order. Writing at the end of the nineteenth century, like Funck-Brentano and Sorel, many authors retrospectively insisted that:

> 'The treaty of the Holy Alliance of 26 September 1815 and above all the Protocol of Aix-la-Chapelle of 15 November 1818, laid down the basis of a system of intervention in the relations of States with their subjects: the purpose of this system of intervention was to maintain the treaties of

[93] Abdy, *Kent's Commentaries*, p. 78. Emphasis added.
[94] Lawrence, *The Principles of International Law*, p. 117.

> 1815 and defend established authorities against the efforts of the revolutionary spirit'.[95]

However morally and politically blameworthy these interventions might have been, according to 'positivist' writings they were at the time perfectly admissible from a legal point of view. The positions and attitudes of States between 1815 and 1822 regarding foreign intervention to repress internal revolts were, in sum, considered as sufficiently clear and univocal to bend the fundamental principle of independence.

For all that, 'positivist' writings still adopted the restrictive view, according to which the sole existence of a revolt in another State did not constitute a sufficiently direct and imminent threat to justify intervention.[96] They simply did not believe that this interpretation had imposed itself from the start: it was the result of a historical evolution. Great Britain had been the first to openly defend this position, which eventually worked its way into the other European courts.[97] During the Congress of Aix-la-Chapelle, the British representatives had, in fact, been the only ones to express their disapproval of the Tsar's note.[98] Again, on the occasion of the Congresses of Troppau, Laybach and Verona, they were the only ones to voice their opposition to the interventions to crush the Carbonari in Naples and against the liberal government of Spain. But even though it did not prevent the Austrian and French expeditions, the British position still had an impact on the 'legal conscience' of its fellow members within the European Concert. Abdy thus noted how in 1823, despite deciding to interfere in the affairs of Spain, the French Minister for Foreign Affairs, René-François de Chateaubriand, declared: 'No government has a right to interfere in the internal affairs of another government *except in the case where the security and immediate interests of the*

[95] Funck-Brentano et Sorel, Précis, p. 213. Translation by the author. See also de Martens, Traité de droit international, vol. 1, p. 396; Calvo, Le droit international, vol. 1, p. 286; by the same author, Manuel, vol. 1, pp. 107–108; Rivier, Principes du droit des gens, vol. 1, p. 399; Westlake, *International Law*, vol. 1, p. 319.

[96] Funck-Brentano et Sorel, Précis, p. 216; Hall, *A Treatise*, p. 283; Calvo, Manuel, vol. 1, p. 116; Rivier, Principes du droit des gens, vol. 1, p. 397; Lawrence, *The Principles of International Law*, p. 118; Mérignhac, Traité de droit international public, vol. 1, p. 292; Oppenheim, International Law, vol. 1, p. 178.

[97] 'L'Angleterre', Calvo explained, 'fut la première à résister aux prétentions de l'Autriche, de la Prusse et de la Russie', in Manuel vol. 1, p. 108. See also Abdy, *Kent's Commentaries*, pp. 43–46.

[98] See above (Section 2.4).

first government are compromised'.[99] To this, Rivier added another statement, made by François Guizot, the head of the Quai d'Orsay from 1840 to 1848, who, in retrospect, looked upon the French intervention as iniquitous because unnecessary.[100] The declaration of the US President Monroe in 1823 and the destitution of the Bourbon monarchy in 1830, were presented as other important markers in the evolution of States' positions towards the dismissal of the right of intervention to repress internal revolts.[101] These led Rivier to conclude, in 1896, that 'it is not something our time anymore'.[102]

State practice also seemed to be regarded as sufficiently clear not to have to resort to the fundamental principles of international law to determine the admissibility of humanitarian intervention. In spite of this, the opinions of writers as to the direction in which this 'clear' practice pointed, obviously, differed. Martens, for instance, despite claiming that international lawyers should work towards the elimination of all exceptions to the rule of non-intervention, was very much in favour of interventions on grounds of humanity.[103] But, in his opinion, the scope of application of this exception was limited to 'civilised nations' *vis-à-vis* nations of a 'lesser rank'.[104] In light of Russia's policies towards Turkey, Martens's acquaintances with the Russian Foreign ministry probably

[99] Chateaubriand's speech regarding the war in Spain as quoted in Abdy, *Kent's Commentaries*, p. 78, footnote no 1. Emphasis added. Also referring to Chateaubriand, see Rivier, Principes du droit des gens, vol. 1, p. 399.

[100] 'En droit, elle était inique, car elle n'était pas nécessaire. La révolution d'Espagne, malgré ses excès, ne faisait courir à la France ni à la Restauration aucun danger sérieux. Les différends qu'elle suscitait entre les deux gouvernements auraient pu aisément être surmontés sans rompre la paix. Les grands et légitimes motifs manquaient donc à cette guerre', quoted in Rivier, Principes du droit des gens, vol. 1, p. 398.

[101] Calvo, for instance, wrote that: 'Cette attitude du gouvernement des Etats-Unis exerça une puissante influence sur les hésitations du gouvernement anglais et sur les projets des Etats absolutistes de l'Europe, qui n'osèrent pas entrer en lutte ouverte contre une force morale et matérielle comme celle qui résultait du concert de l'Angleterre et des Etats-Unis pour la défense des gouvernement constitutionnels', in Manuel, vol. 1, p. 111. For a more detailed account see Calvo, *Le droit* international, vol. 1, pp. 289–292. See also Lawrence, *The Principles of International Law*, p. 181.

[102] Rivier, Principes du droit des gens, vol. 1, p. 391. Translation by the author.

[103] He claimed that: 'Il appartient à la science contemporaine de faire disparaître les exceptions au principe de non-intervention encore admises par des publicistes faisant autorité, exceptions qui diminuent la force même du principe', in de Martens, Traité de droit international, vol. 1, p. 396.

[104] Ibid., p. 398.

were not estranged to his positions in this respect.[105] He was however not isolated. After reviewing the European interventions into the affairs of the Ottoman Empire, Calvo reached a similar conclusion:

> It issues from the facts that we have just reviewed that the interventions of the Great Powers of Europe in the affairs of Turkey are part, so to speak, of the customary law of Europe; this right is grounded in historical precedents as well as in the treaties that regulated the admission of Turkey in the European family [...]. It is in the name of European equilibrium, as in the interest of peace and humanity that we can see Powers interfere in the internal affairs of Turkey...[106]

In this perspective, humanitarian intervention was a legal exception to the rule of non-intervention but only in the relations between Europe and the Ottoman Empire, as well as, to some extent, China and Japan.[107] All the authors in favour of this type of intervention did not share this position. Alexandre Mérignhac, for instance, stressed that the principle of humanitarian intervention should not be pushed too far, as too many authors had transformed it into an unlimited right of interference for the Great Powers into the affairs of 'uncivilised' nations.[108] Giving the note that President Roosevelt sent to Tsar Nicholas II after the first Kishinev pogroms in 1903 as an example, the French jurist believed that humanitarian intervention was a proof of the greater integration and cohesion of the international society.[109] It found its roots in 'international solidarity'[110] and, in a way, it could be argued that it was even more justified among the 'like-minded civilised nations' as a collective sanction of the violation of the law of this 'community'.

[105] In addition to teaching international law at the University of Saint Petersburg, Martens, also served as a diplomat for the Russian Empire.

[106] Calvo, Le droit international, vol. 1, pp. 314–315. Translation by the author.

[107] Lawrence, *The Principles of International Law*, p. 121.

[108] Mérignhac, Traité de droit international public, vol. 1, p. 300. See also Rivier, Principes du droit des gens, vol. 1, p. 397.

[109] Mérignhac, Traité de droit international public, vol. 1, p. 298. About Roosevelt's note to the Tsar Nicholas II in 1903 see the President's message to Congress, 1904 in *The Works of Theodore Roosevelt. Presidential Addresses and State Papers* (P. F. Collier & Son, 1910), vol. 3, pp. 178–179.

[110] Mérignhac wrote: 'Et ce principe, basé sur la solidarité internationale, a depuis été accepté par la plupart des publicistes. En effet, les droits sacrés de l'humanité priment toute considération, en sorte que l'intervention devient ici légitime de plein droit, sans que les intérêts spéciaux de l'intervenant soient menacés', in Traité de droit international public, vol. 1, p. 298.

Contrarily to what Antoine Rougier suggested in his famous 1910 article, '*La théorie l'intervention d'humanité*', the authors that subscribed to the idea of the existence of an 'international society' or of a 'family of nations' did not always endorse intervention on grounds of humanity.[111] Practice, in their opinion, did not confirm it. Lawrence considered humanitarian intervention was 'destitute of technical legality'.[112] Oppenheim noted:

> That the powers have *in the past* exercised intervention on these grounds there is no doubt. Thus Great Britain, France and Russia intervened in 1827 in the revolutionary struggle between Greece and Turkey, because public opinion was horrified at the cruelties committed during this struggle. And many a time interventions have taken place to stop the persecution of Christians in Turkey. *But whether there is really a rule of the law of Nations which admits such intervention may well be doubted.*[113]

In the same vein, Hall considered that 'religious oppression, short of a cruelty which would rank as tyranny, *has ceased to be* recognised as an independent ground of intervention, but it is still used between Europe and the East as an *accessory motive*, . . .'.[114] To support this view, Hall quoted a circular issued by Russia in reaction to the decision of Great-Britain and France in 1856 to suspend their diplomatic relations with Naples as a result of the inhumanity with which the kingdom was ruled. In this circular, the Russian diplomatic services explained that while such considerations may have justified offering advice, 'we believe that to be the furthest limit allowable. [. . .] To endeavour to obtain from the King of Naples concessions as concerns the internal government of his state by threats, or by a menacing demonstration, is a violent usurpation of his authority'.[115] In other words, even though considerations of humanity may, in the past, have been among the circumstances that could justify foreign intervention, practice appeared to have revoked this exception. Rivier, likewise, observed that tyranny and atrocities had barely (if ever) been invoked alone to justify intervention. While the will to put an end to the bloody Greek war of independence, for instance, was certainly among

[111] Antoine Rougier, 'La théorie de l'intervention d'humanité' (1910) 17 *Revue générale de droit international public* 472.

[112] Lawrence, *The Principles of International Law*, p. 121. See also Abdy, *Kent's Commentaries*, p. 81.

[113] Oppenheim, International Law, vol. 1, 1905, p. 186. Emphasis added.

[114] Hall, *A Treatise*, p. 287. Emphasis added.

[115] Quoted in Hall, *A Treatise*, p. 289 (footnote no 2).

the elements that had motivated the European intervention, considerations of self-preservation had essentially been put forward to justify the military actions of 1827.[116] The 1860 French expedition to Lebanon and Syria, for its part, was considered a 'mix of cooperation and intervention'[117] as it had been carried out with the Sultan's consent.[118]

The place reserved to the analysis of practice to determine the admissibility of solicited intervention in a civil war as a legal exception to the rule of non-intervention was, on the other hand, more limited. Strangely enough, authors such as Oppenheim, Rivier and Calvo did not even really mention the hypothesis, even though, as we already saw, it was quite contentious.[119] Hall noted how, in the scholarship, intervention had sometimes been claimed to be lawful if exercised in favour of the government, in favour of either the government or the rebels, or in favour of neither.[120] To settle the debate, he did not refer to any practice but, instead, simply asserted that:

> If intervention on the ground of mere friendship were allowed, it would be idle to speak seriously of the rights of independence. Supposing the intervention to be directed against the existing government, independence is violated by an attempt to prevent the regular organ of the state from managing the state affairs in its own way. Supposing it on the other hand to be directed against rebels, the fact that is has been necessary to call in foreign help in enough to show that the issue of the conflict would without it be uncertain, and consequently that there is doubt as to which side would ultimately establish itself as the legal representative of the state.[121]

Most 'positivist' writings followed this line of thought that relied on the principle of independence to decide on the admissibility of solicited

[116] Rivier wrote: 'Dans l'intervention concernant la Grèce, en 1827, les trois puissances ont voulu, sans doute, mettre un terme à l'oppression des chrétiens. Mais un motif de conservation a pu à juste titre être invoqué: les intérêts des ressortissants étrangers, mis en péril par la guerre civile. La Grande-Bretagne, spécialement, a constaté le caractère exceptionnel de cette intervention, « a departure from the general rule, which forbids other powers to interfere in the contests betwixt sovereign and subjects »; en même temps que l'existence d'un « great evil pressing seriously upon the interests of Her Majesty own subjects »', in Principes du droit des gens, vol. 1, p. 396. See also Abdy, *Kent's Commentaries*, p. 50.

[117] Rivier, Principes du droit des gens, vol. 1, p. 396. Translation by the author.

[118] Ibid., p. 396; Calvo, Le droit international, vol. 1, p. 308.

[119] See above (Section 2.4) and (Section 3.4).

[120] Hall, *A Treatise*, p. 290.

[121] Ibid., p. 291.

intervention as a legal exception to non-intervention.[122] During the 1900 session of the *Institut de droit international* in Neuchâtel, on the occasion of which a resolution on the topic was adopted favouring the doctrine of 'negative equality', no mention was made of practice either.[123]

Even though, as Lawrence claimed, 'intervention at the request of one of the parties to a civil war [was] not uncommon',[124] it seems that this practice was hard to grasp. An example of such intervention could have been the European intermission in the Greek war of independence in 1827, which notably followed a request for good offices and mediation received from the Greek insurgents.[125] But the role that this solicitation had in justifying the intervention was ambiguous. In the same vein, when Russia provided help to Austria against the rebels during the Hungarian war of independence in 1849, the Tsar insisted that he was acting upon considering the security of his own empire.[126] The United States secession war (1861–1865) and the *Alabama Claims* arbitration may also be mentioned to illustrate the practice of States regarding intervention in civil wars. However, when hostilities broke out between the Union and the Confederacy, third States adopted contrasting positions: some issued a declaration of neutrality, others did not.[127] It is also unclear whether the States that did adopt a neutral position did it out of a sense of legal

[122] See Funck-Brentano et Sorel, Précis, pp. 219–221; Lawrence, *The Principles of International Law*, pp. 125–126; Mérignhac, Traité de droit international public, vol. 1, p. 305.

[123] IDI, *Droits et devoirs des Puissances étrangères, au cas de mouvement insurrectionnel, envers les gouvernements établis et reconnus qui sont au prises avec l'insurrection* (Session de Neuchâtel, 1900). For an analysis of the resolution and of the debates see Olivier Corten, 'La rébellion et le droit international: le principe de neutralité en tension' (2014) 374 *Recueil des cours de l'académie de droit international* 90–96.

[124] Lawrence, *The Principles of International Law*, p. 125.

[125] See below (Section 6.1).

[126] 'The Emperor is sorry to quit the passive and expectant position hitherto maintained, but still he remains faithful to the spirit of his former declaration, for in granting to every state the right to arrange its own mind, and refraining from interfering with any alternations of their form of government which such states might think proper to make, his Majesty reserves to himself full liberty of action in case the re-action of revolutions near him should tend to endanger his own safety or the political equilibrium on the frontiers of his empire. Our safety is endangered by what is now doing and preparing in Hungary', 'Note of the Count of Nesselrode, Saint Petersburg, 27th of April 1849', available in *Annual Register* (F. & J. Revington, 1850), vol. xli, pp. 333–334.

[127] See Quincy Wright, 'The American Civil War, 1861–1865', in Richard A. Falk (ed.), *The International Law of Civil War* (John Hopkins University Press, 1971), p. 82. About the American civil war from a legal point of view see also Stephen C. Neff, *Justice in Blue and Grey. A Legal History of Civil War* (Harvard University Press, 2010).

obligation or mere discretionary politics.[128] The *Alabama Claims* do not really shed light on the issue. The legality of the delivery of warships to the Confederacy by Great Britain was, in fact, assessed with respect to the *British Neutrality Act*, not general international law. These are just a few examples showing how nineteenth century authors might have found it difficult to restore coherence into the practice of States regarding solicited intervention in a civil war, which is probably why they resorted to fundamental principles to decide on the legal admissibility of such interventions.

To summarize, the fundamental principles assumed an ambiguous role in the determination of the exceptions to non-intervention. They were both central and peripheral: peripheral because priority was given to State practice and that all the exceptions did not necessarily have to fall within the scope of self-preservation; but central because only a widely accepted practice could infringe upon independence and that, in the absence of such practice, the fundamental principles held the final word.

* * *

This fourth chapter constituted the last step towards the 'deconstruction' of the first of the two backbones that underlies the indifference narrative, i.e. the claim that positivists consecrated the right for Sates to resort to armed force as they pleased, while the writers who considered law limited this right were the naturalist exception. Analysing the writings of the authors whose work can be considered to fall within the 'positivist' category, it aimed to verify whether they truly believed the use of force to be an unrestrained State prerogative, and if so on what basis. It showed that they, for the most part, did not, and that the 'neo-Hegelian' vision of nineteenth century positivism that modern-day doctrine often has is not really justified either.

As today, there were several 'types' of legal positivism in the nineteenth century. The most distinct feature of 'mainstream' positivism (or 'empiricist' positivism to use Neff's expression) was probably its uneasy attitude towards its 'rationalist' heritage. 'Positivists', in fact, adopted a discourse that was heavily critical of the 'naturalist' and 'eclectic' literature, which they deemed 'unscientific'. At the same time, their outlook on the international legal system was built on the same premises of sociability, reason and analogy with the contractualist theories of the State. Their system of law was also structured around three fundamental rights inherent to statehood: independence, equality and self-preservation.

[128] Corten, 'La rébellion et le droit international', p. 98.

They, moreover, shared an idealistic vision of (and project for) international law as a tool for the pacification of international relations and global welfare. In many respects, it thus seems that the 'positivists' violent criticism of naturalism can be interpreted as angst to legitimize the discipline. This is not to say that the differences with the two other strands of the international legal scholarship were purely cosmetic. Mainstream positivist were mostly idealists, but they felt that keeping to a strict description of the law as it truly applied was the best way to serve the project of international law. 'Positivist' literature, therefore, advocated for a strictly inductive methodology grounded in the analysis of State practice. Fundamentally, however, such as method was hard to follow with orthodoxy. The rule of non-intervention, for example, was first deduced from the principle of independence and then confirmed by the examination of State practice. Similarly, all the exceptions were not necessarily induced from practice; some 'positivist' authors occasionally deduced them from other existing rules of international law.

What is nevertheless more important to remember at this stage and for the purpose of this book's argument, is that even the 'positivists', with only a few exceptions, recognised that law established limits to resort to armed force by States, measures short of war and war alike.

Conclusion of Part I

Some Thoughts on the Differences between Past and Present Scholarship on the Use of Force

The aim of this first part of the book was to question the first backbone of the indifference-narrative by testing the assumption according to which the nineteenth and early twentieth century authors who asserted the existence of rules regulating the use of force were foremost naturalists. Modern day literature, indeed, often argues that pre-Versailles international lawyers generally recognised that the use of force was beyond legal regulation and that the authors who did not were the 'naturalist' exception.[1] Trying to have as broad a perspective and encompass as many nineteenth and early twentieth century textbooks as possible, it has not only shown that the idea that rules regulated resort to armed force was widespread among the scholarship, but also that this belief was not the prerogative of the 'naturalists'. With few exceptions, in fact, authors of all theoretical inclinations asserted that the use of force, whether it took the form of 'measures short of war' or of war, was not an absolute right of States. The use of force was legitimate, but only in certain circumstances – that is to say as an exception, not as a rule.

Withal, it is true that the influence of the work of the so-called 'founding fathers' and of the naturalist theories of international law on nineteenth and early twentieth century doctrine cannot be denied. As several authors highlight, classic international law literature was at the crossroad of naturalism and positivism. It built systems of law that oscillated from one pole to another. We saw how 'naturalist', 'eclectic' and even 'positivist' writings

[1] See Maurice Bourquin, 'Le problème de la sécurité internationale' (1934) 49 *Recueil des cours de l'académie de droit international* 477; Bernhard Roscher, 'The "Renunciation of War as an Instrument of National Policy"' (2002) 4 *Journal of History of International Law* 294; Mary Ellen O'Connell, 'Peace and War', in Bardo Fassbender and Anne Peters, *The Oxford Handbook on the History of International Law* (Oxford University Press, 2012), p. 283.

were based upon the same rationalist premises and all integrated descending and ascending elements in their theory of, and methodology for, international law. The literature leaning towards the naturalist pole, for instance, had a more hierarchical and pyramidal conception of the international legal order and ultimately adopted a deductive approach to custom, while also stressing the importance of taking State practice into consideration. On the other side, the doctrine that was more inclined towards positivism adopted a discourse that advocated for a strictly inductive approach and claimed State consent to be the primary source of law, while having a providential vision of law. In various respects, it may be argued that differences between the three models of law presented in this book was more a difference of discourse then actual practice. The rule of non-intervention was always deduced from the fundamental principles of law, and then, more or less confirmed by an analysis of State practice. In a case as in the others, nineteenth century authors seemed to find themselves facing the dilemma of building a system of international law that was sufficiently complete and in touch with reality all the while not relinquishing ideals of justice.

Does this ambivalence, however, mean that the conclusions of nineteenth century authors regarding the use of force should all be viewed as mere naturalist fantasies? Does this duality signify that classic scholarship should altogether be discarded? If a positive answer were to be given to this question, then probably today's literature should be looked upon with caution as well. As Koskenniemi has demonstrated in *From Apology to Utopia* (1989), this relentless movement from induction to deduction is still at the core of international legal argumentation.[2] Broad principles of international law inherited from the natural law tradition continue to play a role, equity being the typical example. Contemporary international law is not gapless and, to fill its lacunae and imprecisions, modern-day lawyers still has recourse to deductive reasoning from broad overbearing principles of law.[3]

The contemporary literature on the use of force offers a good illustration. As we know, the current legal regime on the use of force in international is rooted in articles 2(4), 42 and 51 of the UN Charter. The rules laid down in these three provisions are general, vague and

[2] Martti Koskenniemi, *From Apology to Utopia. The Structure of International Legal Argument* (re-issue with new epilogue) (Cambridge University Press, 2005).

[3] On lacunae, see Jean Salmon, 'Quelques observations sur les lacunes du droit international public' (1967) 3 *Revue belge de droit international* 440–458.

certainly do not encompass all the situations in which resort to force may or not be had. To give them substance, jurists will have to use induction (from the study of precedents) and deduction (usually from general principles of international law or, even, extra-legal considerations). But, again, depending on their theoretical (as well as political, philosophical or religious) preferences and biases, all authors will not rely on induction and deduction equally and, therefore, will not fill the gaps and resolve the indeterminacies of contemporary *ius ad bellum* in the same ways.

Let us take a couple of examples to rapidly demonstrate this point. Today, as in the nineteenth century, the issues of humanitarian intervention and intervention by invitation in a civil war are still particularly controversial. Like a 150 years ago, the advocates of humanitarian intervention usually rely on a nexus of ascending and descending arguments. They will generally refer to a combination of either or of all of these four elements: (i) State practice (Nigeria 1968–1970, Bangladesh 1970, Cambodia 1978–1979, Central Africa 1979 and, more recently, Kosovo 1999, Libya 2011 or even Syria since 2014); (ii) the UN Charter (article 1 read in conjunction with article 2(4)); (iii) the new 'social necessities' of international life; or yet, (iv) to a broad principle of 'humanity' of which the multiplication of human rights protection instruments since 1945 would be an expression.[4] The two first arguments can be said to be of inductive nature and the two latter of deductive

[4] See for e.g. Richard B. Lillich, 'Forcible Self-Help by States to Protect Human rights' (1967–1968) 53 *Iowa Law Review* 325–351; by the same author, 'Intervention to Protect Human Rights' (1969) 15 *McGill Law Journal* 205–219; Jean-Pierre L. Fonteyne, 'The Customary International Law Doctrine of Humanitarian Intervention: Its Current Validity Under the U.N. Charter' (1973–1974) 4 *California Western International Law Journal* 203–270; Robert Meade Chilstrom, 'Humanitarian Intervention under Contemporary International Law: a Policy-Oriented Approach' (1974) 1 *Yale Journal of International Law* 93–147; Thomas E. Behuniak (Capt.), 'The Law of Unilateral Humanitarian Intervention by Armed Force: A Legal Survey' (1978) 79 *Military Law Review* 157–191; Wil D. Verwey, 'Humanitarian Intervention under International Law' (1985) 32 *Netherlands International Law Review* 357–418; Fernando Tesón, *Humanitarian Intervention: An Inquiry into Law and Morality* (Transational Publishers, 1988); Michael Reisman, 'Sovereignty and Human Rights in Contemporary International Law' (1990) 84 *American Journal of International Law* 866–876; Barry M. Benjamin, 'Unilateral Humanitarian Intervention: Legalizing the Use of Force to Prevent Human Rights Atrocities' (1992) 16 *Fordham International Law Journal* 120–158; Adam Robert, 'The So-Called "Right" of Humanitarian Intervention' (2000) 3 *Yearbook of International Humanitarian Law* 3–51; John J. Merriam, 'Kosovo and the Law of Humanitarian Intervention' (2001) 33 *Case Western Reserve Journal of International Law* 111–154; Terry Nardin, 'The Moral Basis of Humanitarian Intervention' (2002) 16 *Ethics and International Affairs* 57–70.

nature.[5] The presence of these 'moral' considerations, however, does not lead the opponents of humanitarian intervention to simply toss their colleagues' contentions to the side. They engage with the pro-humanitarian claims seriously and propose alternative interpretations of the precedents, of the Charter and of their relations to general principles law and human rights.[6] Their outlook on the issue will, generally speaking, be more inclined towards 'voluntarism' (or 'subjectivism') and their methods may appear more inductive. Still, as a final touch, authors will sometimes seek to legitimise their conclusions by grounding them in (collective rather than individual) moral and political (and therefore descending) considerations, especially the fact that humanitarian intervention is too susceptible of being used as a false pretext for intervention and become the tool of the powerful against the weak. Its potential as a destabilising factor of the international order and of the paramount principle of non-intervention is, in other words, too strong.

The same ambiguities are observable concerning the issue of the legality of solicited intervention in a situation of civil war. Three positions currently co-exist in the scholarship: 'positive equality', 'asymmetry' and 'negative equality'. Each relies on its own blend of ascending and descending arguments. According to the most permissive view ('positive equality'), intervention by invitation in a civil war is permissible both on behalf of the government and of the insurgents. This minority opinion is very inductive and 'factual' in its way of approaching the matter. It relies on the observations that there is no specific rules prohibiting solicited intervention in a civil war as such, and that, in practice, States often intervene in such situations, regardless of

[5] See J. L. Holzgrefe, 'The Humanitarian Intervention Debate', in J. L. Holzgrefe and Robert O. Keohane (eds.), *Humanitarian Intervention. Ethical, Legal and Political Dilemmas* (Cambridge University Press, 2003), pp. 15–52.

[6] See for e.g. Thomas M. Franck and Nigel S. Rodley, 'After Bangladesh: The Law of Humanitarian Intervention by Military Force' (1973) 67 *American Journal of International Law* 275–305; Natalino Ronzitti, *Rescuing Nationals Abroad through Military Coercion and Intervention on Grounds of Humanity* (Martinus Nijhoff, 1985), pp. 89–110; Jack Donnelly, 'Human Rights, Humanitarian Crisis, and Humanitarian Intervention' (1993) 48 *International Journal* 607–640; Yoram Dinstein, *War, Aggression and Self-Defence* (5th ed., Cambridge University Press, 2011), pp. 73–75; Olivier Corten, *Le droit contre la guerre* (2e ed., Pedone, 2014), pp. 801–874 (english version: *The Law against War. The Prohibtion of the Use of Force in Contemporary International Law* (Hart, 2010), pp. 495–549); Christine Gray, 'The Use of Force for Humanitarian Purposes', in Nigel D. White and Christian Henderson (eds.), *Research Handbook on International Conflict and Security Law* (Edward Elgar, 2013), pp. 229–255; Nigel Rodley, 'Humanitarian Intervention', in Marc Weller (ed.), *The Oxford Handbook on the Use of Force* (Oxford University Press, 2015), pp. 775–796.

whether the invitation has been issued by the government or the rebels.[7] In this perspective, law is the bare reflection of factual reality, and the rest of scholarship has criticized 'positive equality' for precisely that reason.[8]

The other two positions temper this theory by proposing a different interpretation of practice and by re-introducing elements of deductive reasoning, mainly from the principles of non-intervention and self-determination. For the proponents of the doctrine of 'asymmetry', sight must not be lost of the principle of non-intervention and one of its exceptions: consented intervention. On this basis, they argue that interference in a civil war abroad is permissible only if carried out at the request of the government. The legality of such operations hinges on whether the government was indeed competent to deliver such an invitation. This interpretation, which already relied on a mix of deduction and induction, is believed to be further reinforced and confirmed by State practice which is claimed to be 'replete with instances of detachment of armed forces from one State to another, at the latter's request, in order to help safeguarding law and order in the face of domestic turmoil'.[9] The advocates of 'negative equality', for their part, retort that when intervening third States have never claimed a right of interference in a civil conflict as such. Instead, they generally contend that they are carrying simple 'police operations', 'peace-keeping missions' or acting in the context of a counter-intervention.[10] Moreover, because of the principle of self-determination, consented intervention cannot be mutatis mutandis applied to situations of civil war. The legality of such actions does not

[7] Roger Pinto, 'Les règles de droit international concernant la guerre civile' (1965) 114 *Recueil des cours de l'académie de droit international* 482–499; Richard A. Falk, *The International Law of Civil War* (The Johns Hopkins Press, 1971), p. 15.

[8] Albrecht Randelzhofer, 'Article 2 (4)', in Bruno Simma and al. (ed.), *The Charter of the United Nations: A Commentary*, 2 vols. (2nd ed., Oxford University Press, 2002), vol. 1, p. 122. See also ICJ, *Military and Paramilitary Activities in and aginst Nicaragua* (Nicaragua vs. United-States of America), Merits, Judgment of 27 June 1986, *I.C.J. Reports 1986*, par. 246, p. 126.

[9] Dinstein, War, Aggression and Self-Defence, p. 119. See also Antonio Tanca, *Foreign Armed Intervention in Internal Conflict* (Martinus Nijhoff, 1993), p. 47; Georg Nolte, 'Secession and External Intervention', in Marcelo Kohen (ed.), *Secession. International Law Perspective* (Cambridge University Press, 2006), pp. 76–93; Christopher J. Le Mon, 'Unilateral Intervention by Invitation in Civil Wars: The Effective Control Test Tested' (2002–2003) 35 *NYU Journal of International Law and Politics* 741–793; Christian Walter, Antje von Ungern-Sternberg and Kavus Abushov, *Self-Determination and Secession in International Law* (Oxford University Press, 2014), p. 89.

[10] Corten, Le doit contre la guerre, p. 476; Robert Kolb, *Ius contra bellum. Le droit international relatif au maintien de la paix* (Bruylant, 2009), pp. 328–329; Christine Gray, *International law and the Use of Force* (3rd ed., Oxford University Press, 2008), p. 84.

only depend on whether the government was competent to ask its neighbours for assistance, but also on the purpose of the requested intervention. If the aim is to help repress a revolt that is not fomented from the outside, then the interference contradicts the principle of self-determination and should be deemed unlawful.[11] In other words, States have a duty of neutrality as a (essentially descending) consequence of the general principle of self-determination.

As we can see, contemporary scholarship on the use of force is still caught in the same argumentative tension between 'apology' and 'utopia', to use Koskenniemi's words. The different opinions on the acceptability of humanitarian intervention and of third-party intervention do not appear to solely be the result of different methodologies but also of a deeper divide between interventionist and non-interventionist sensibilities that guide interpretation. Of course, some may be tempted to argue that there remains a major difference between classic and modern-day doctrine, which is that the legal character of the principles of non-intervention and self-determination makes no doubt. Even though authors sometimes use deductive methodologies, their reasoning remains fundamentally grounded in positive law rather than in natural law. While this may be true, this assertion nevertheless needs to be nuanced because nineteenth century scholars equally considered the rights of independence, equality and self-preservation to be part of positive international law. Technically speaking, their approaches and conclusions were just as grounded in positive law as those of contemporary scholars. The only difference between the present and the past is the fact that, today, the main principles governing the relations of States have been codified and set in legal texts, whereas in the nineteenth century they were customary and, consequently, harder to grasp with a similar degree of certainty. In the second part of this book we will see that the similarities between the contemporary and classic ways of thinking about the use of force in international law extend to State practice.

[11] See Art. 2 (1) IDI, Resolution on Principle of non-intervention in civil wars (Wiesbaden Session, 1975); Art. 3 (1), IDI, Resolution on Present problems of the Use of Force in International Law (Rhodes Session, 2011); Independent Fact-Finding Mission on the Conflict in Georgia (IIFFMCG), *Report*, vol. 2, September 2009, pp. 276 ff.. See also Rosalyn Higgins, 'The Legal Limits to the Use of Force by Sovereign States. United Nations Practice' (1961) 37 *British Yearbook of International Law* 309; Louise Doswald-Beck, 'The Legal Validity of Military Intervention by Invitation of the Government' (1986) 56 *British Yearbook of International Law* 242–244; Théodore Christakis et Karine Bannelier, 'Volenti non fit injuria? Les effets du consentement à l'intervention militaire' (2004) 50 *Annuaire français de droit international* 120.

PART II

The Use of Force in Nineteenth-Century Practice

Law beyond Morals and Politics

Introduction: Aim, Methodology and Outline

After having demonstrated that the majority of nineteenth- and early twentieth-century authors, from all theoretical backgrounds, believed that the use of force was restricted by international law, this second part of the book turns to the second backbone of indifference-narrative. It questions the assertion according to which the justifications brought forward by States when they resorted to armed force were merely moral and political and had no effect in positive international law. Contemporary doctrine, in fact, often argues that 'States continued to use the rhetoric of justice when they went to war, but the justification produced no legal reverberations',[1] or yet that:

> 'In the public law of Europe war was admitted without restrictions. The question of legitimate motive probably played a politcal and moral role, but had no legal value. It was not a matter of international law, but a matter of propaganda in defense of national interests'.[2]

[1] Yoram Dinstein, *War, Aggression and Self-Defence* (5th ed., Cambridge University Press, 2011), p. 69.

[2] Hans Wehberg, 'L'interdiction du recours à la force. Le principe et les problèmes qui se posent' (1951) 78 *Recueil des cours de l'académie de droit international* 21. Translation by the author. See also Charles de Visscher, *Théories et réalités en droit international public* (Pedone, 1955), p. 359; Paul Reuter, *Droit international public* (2nd ed., Presses Universitaires de France, 1963), p. 285; Georg Schwarzenberger, *A Manual of International Law* (5th ed., Stevens & Sons Limited, 1967), pp. 181–182; Ian Brownlie, *International Law and the Use of Force by States* (Clarendon Press, 1968), p. 41; Antoine Favre, *Principes du droit des gens* (LGDJ, 1974), p. 709; Wilhelm Grewe, *The Epochs of International Law* (Walter De Gruyter, 2000), p. 531; John H. Currie, *Public International Law* (2nd ed., Irwin Law, 2008), p. 454; (Nguyên Quôc Dinh), Patrick Daillier, Mathias Forteau et Alain Pellet, *Droit international public* (9th ed., LGDJ, 2009), p. 1032; Robert Kolb, *Ius contra bellum. Le droit international relatif au maintien de la paix* (Bruylant, 2009), p. 33; John Duggard, *International Law. A South African Perspective* (4th ed., Juta, 2011), p. 495.

This argument is hard to confront because it is circular. It is based on the premise that, since there was no prohibition of force in international law, the discourses of the States could *a fortiori* not refer to any framework of positive law, while at the same time claiming that if such rules had existed, then they would have been the result of State practice. A second claim has more recently been added to this interpretation of the practice of using force before World War I. Jochen von Bernstorff argues that even if rules ring-fencing the use of force existed before the twentieth century, their normative and binding power was weakened as a result of colonial expansion.[3] He contends that, from the 1870s onwards, European powers gradually developed broader interpretations of the right to self-preservation in order to justify their warring enterprises in the semi-peripheries. The result of this practice was that by 1914 'legal restrictions on the right to wage war [. . .] had lost most of their regulating impact'.[4] Von Bernstorff notes that in the last three decades of the nineteenth century it is estimated that more than 100 interventions backed by force took place in 'non-European' spaces,[5] and grounds his conclusions on the analysis of some of these precedents.

Still, we are forced to observe that modern interpretations of the practice of using force in the nineteenth century is rarely supplemented by a systematic and in-depth analysis of this practice. Seeking to engage in such an analysis, the pages that follow address the two above mentioned claims. They argue that even though law was a consideration amongst others, the discourses of States held distinctively legal features that seemed to suggest that State believed themselves to be bound by rules of international law when resorting to armed force; and that while different patterns of using and justifying force in 'European' and 'non-European' spaces existed, it is unclear whether it can be asserted that the legal framework had become altogether inoperative by the turn of the century.

Considering the number of armed interventions that took place throughout the nineteenth century, it would be unrealistic to conduct an exhaustive review of State practice. A selection of case studies must necessarily be operated. In selecting these case studies several elements

[3] Jochen von Bernstorff, 'The Use of Force in International Law before World War I: On Imperial Order and the Ontology of the Nations States' (2018) 29 *European Journal of International Law* 233–260.

[4] Ibid., p. 257.

[5] von Bernstorff, 'The Use of Force in International Law before World War I', 248.

must be kept in mind. The first element is of temporal nature. In order to have a representative view of nineteenth-century practice of using force and identify potential changing trends, it is indeed paramount to analyse precedents from both the 'beginning' and 'end' of that century. The second element is geographical: to be able to draw general conclusions and verify whether justification for force varied depending on the area in which it was being used, it is vital to examine precedents that took place in the 'centre' but also in the 'semi-peripheries' and 'peripheries'. The third and final element is 'material'. We in fact saw that armed intervention in the nineteenth century could either take the form of armed reprisals (or measures short of war) or of war proper. It is consequently important to diversify the case studies in order to take this difference into account and assess if they were justified on different grounds.

The above stresses two other important methodological questions: (i) how and where can the discourses developed by States be found and (ii) according to what criteria will these discourses be analysed to gauge their nature and potential legal impact? As regards the first issue, the positions expressed by States during the various precedents that will be examined are extracted from internal and external diplomatic correspondence, war declarations and ultimatums, from policy papers and addresses in front of national parliaments or other audiences. The documents cited were either gathered from published records (diplomatic books, official and personal compendiums of correspondence, memoirs, etc.) or through personal research in the diplomatic archives of several States (in particular, *The National Archives* on London, the *Archives diplomatiques* in Paris, and the *Archivo histórico nacional* in Madrid).

When analysing this material, the main criteria used to determine the essence and legal value of the arguments invoked will be 'discursive'. In reference to the different approaches to custom expounded in the first part of this book, one could say that the perspective adopted draws from nineteenth century 'positivist' writings. As a reminder, the authors of the time insisted on the distinction that needed to be made between 'motives' (referring to the political motivations of a particular action) and the 'justifying causes' (understood as the notions and concepts of law mobilised to legitimise that same action).[6] Said differently, the emphasis will here be on determining the existence of an *opinio juris*. It lies on the premise that if States invoked legal arguments to justify and react to a use

[6] See, e.g., Carlos Calvo, *Le droit international théorique et pratique*, 6 vols. (Guillaumin & Cie, 1887), vol. 2, p. 22.

of force, it indicates that they believed force to be ring-fenced by particular rules of international law. In fact, there is no need to justify a behaviour that is, in all circumstances, permitted. Although we may doubt that law plays a role in the decision-making, it is generally agreed that it provides States with a linguistic framework to justify and legitimise their (political) decisions.[7] It follows that international law is considered as a language with a vocabulary of its own; a vocabulary which, in order to convince the recipients of the discourse, must immediately hint towards the nature of the arguments put forth. Focus will thus be placed in spotting the presence of 'key words' that fall within the lexical field of law ('lawful', 'unlawful', 'legal', 'illegal', 'right', 'rule', 'principle', 'duty', etc.).[8] When analysing nineteenth-century justifying discourses, however, it should be kept in mind that some words, which today we tend to interpret as revealing ethical or moral considerations, had a different value. Classic examples are references to what is 'legitimate' or 'just'. At the time, in fact, these terms largely seemed to blend within the vernacular of law.[9] Greater attention will thus have to be given to the broader context of the discourse when they are used.

All this being clear, employing the tools presented above, this second part of the book starts by analysing nineteenth-century practice of justifying force in the 'centre' (Chapter 5), then in the 'semi-peripheries' (Chapter 6), and finally in the 'peripheries' (Chapter 7). The introductions of each chapter offer brief clarifications about what 'areas' of the globe these different appellations encompassed and on what their right and obligations were believed to be.

[7] See, e.g., Olivier Corten, *Le discours du droit international. Pour un positivisme critique*, (Pedone, « Coll. Doctrine(s) », 2009); by the same author, 'Formalization and Deformalization as Narratives of the Law of War', in José María Beneyto and David Kennedy (eds.), *New Approaches to International Law. The European and American Experiences* (T.M.C. Asser Press, 2012), pp. 253–257; Martti Koskenniemi, 'The Place of Law in Collective Security' (1995–1996) 17 *Michigan Journal of International Law* 455–490.

[8] On the second issue, see in particular Olivier Corten et Barbara Delcourt, 'Droit, légitimation et politique extérieure: précisions théoriques et méthodologiques', in Olivier Corten et Barbara Delcourt (dirs.), *Droit, légitimation et politique extérieure: l'Europe et la guerre du Kosovo* (Bruylant, 2001), pp. 26–29.

[9] In this sense, see Olivier Corten, 'Droit, force et légitimité dans une société internationale en mutation', in *Le discours du droit. Pour un positivisme critique* (Pedone, Coll. « Doctrine(s) », 2009), p. 80.

5

Justifying the Use of Force in the 'Centre'

While today all States are said to be equal, such was not always the case. Present-day doctrine cultivates the image of a highly hierarchised nineteenth century legal order. It is said that international society was broken down into different categories of States and entities ('civilised', 'semi-civilised' and 'uncivilised'), whose rights and obligations were not identical. We assume that European States were the main beneficiaries of a law of nations which barely, if at all, applied in their relations with the rest of the world. Stephen Neff, for instance, explains that international law was only applicable between 'civilised' nations, meaning European Christian States and their former colonial dominions in North, Central and South America.[1] The limited scope of application of the international law, Neff argues, was the result of the transition from naturalism (cosmopolitan and universalist by essence) towards positivism (contractualist and relativist). In a positivist mind frame, in fact, States were the main creators of international law and only the rules they had specifically accepted could be considered as binding upon them. Because the law of nations was a product of 'European civilisation', it followed that it was only applied to those entities that had contributed to its making.[2]

Authors have discussed the importance of the religious criteria to define the 'centre'. Wilhelm Grewe, for instance, also considered that classic international law solely applied in the relations between 'civilised' nations, but felt that religion was not a central consideration.[3] This was also the position developed by Antonio Truyol y Serra in his course at the

[1] Stephen C. Neff, Justice *among Nations. A History of International Law* (Harvard University Press, 2014), p. 311.

[2] Ibid., p. 310.

[3] Wilhelm Grewe, *The Epochs of International Law* (Walter de Gruyter, 2000), p. 454.

Hague Academy in 1965.[4] He explained that the change of paradigm from 'Christian civilisation' to 'civilisation' was triggered by the independence of the American colonies and the intensification of trade relations with the Far East. Together with Grewe, they observed how from 1815 onwards references to 'civilised nations' slowly replaced traditional references to 'Christian nations' in international treaties.[5] Even though, in the end, 'civilisation' was still judged by European standards this technically permitted the inclusion of 'non-Christian', 'non-European' and 'non-white' nations into the international legal community.[6] They gave the example of Haiti, Liberia and Turkey, respectively admitted into the realm of international law in 1828,1848 and 1856.[7]

Even though modern-day representations of the nineteenth century as strictly and highly hierarchised may seem to go hand and in hand with the generally over-realist interpretation of this era, it is not without historical grounds. Franz von Holtzendorff, for instance, was positive that the differences of culture and mores prevented the establishment of relations with 'barbarous tribes' and 'semi-civilised' nations on the same ground as with 'civilised nations'.[8] But the most famous 'classification' of States is probably the one operated by James Lorimer. Lorimer argued that humanity was divided into three concentric zones: 'civilised humanity', 'barbarous humanity' and 'savage humanity'.[9] Each zone enjoyed a different level of political recognition and, therefore, of rights and duties. Only the first fully beneficiated from all the guarantees and advantages of international law, public and private. Lorimer considered that the States falling within this category were the European States and the Great Powers, as well as the States of North and South America.[10]

[4] Antonio Truyol y Serra, 'L'expansion de la société internationale aux XIXe et XXe siècles' (1965) 116 *Recueil des cours de l'académie de droit international* 127 ff.

[5] Wilhelm Grewe, *The Epochs of International Law*, p. 445.

[6] On the expansion of the international legal community in the nineteenth century see also Arnulf Becker Lorca, *Mestizio International Law. A Global Intellectual History, 1842–1933* (Cambridge University Press, 2014), pp. 76–77 and 98–136.

[7] Ibid., p. 462.

[8] Franz von Holtzendorff, *Introduction au droit des gens* (Verlagsanstalt und Druckerei A.-G., 1889), pp. 10–18. See also William E. Hall, *A Treatise of International Law* (3rd ed., Clarendon Press, 1890) pp. 42–43; Frédéric de Martens, *Traité de droit international*, 3 vols. (Librairie Marescq Ainé, 1883), vol. 1, pp. 239–240.

[9] James Lorimer, *The Institutes of the Law of Nations. A Treatise of Jural Relations of Separate Political Communities* (W. Blackwood and sons, 1883), p. 101.

[10] Ibid., pp. 101–102.

In the case of South American States, it has nonetheless been argued that the Monroe doctrine of 1823 de facto placed them into the category of the 'semi-peripheries'.[11] The same holds true for Turkey, whose unequal treaties with the European Powers were only abrogated with the Treaty of Lausanne in 1923 despite being officially admitted into the 'family of European nations' with the Treaty of Paris in 1856.[12] This chapter consequently excludes, for the time being, the analysis of interventions that took place in these two regions of the world, and concentrates on uses of force involving States whose membership to the 'centre' was not debated. Some cases, such as the 1841 British embargo on the Kingdom of the Two-Sicilies have already been briefly examined in the first part of the book.[13] To complement these brief analyses, the precedents that will be examined in more details in the pages that follow are: the Austrian intervention to crush the Carbonari Revolt in the Kingdom of the Two-Sicilies in 1821 (Section 5.1); the Crimean War in 1856 (Section 5.2); the Franco-Prussian War of 1870 (Section 5.3); the Spanish-American War of 1898 (Section 5.4); and finally the Austrian war declaration to Serbia in July 1914 (Section 5.5).

5.1 The Austrian Intervention in the Kingdom of the Two-Sicilies (1821)

To understand Austria's intervention in the Kingdom of the Two-Sicilies to crush the Carbonari Revolt in 1821, we first need to resituate this intervention within its broader international political context. We already mentioned in the first part of the book, that the peace settlements of 1814–1815 sought to reorganise international relations after 26 years of instability in Europe triggered by the French Revolution and later coming into power of Napoléon. During the Châtillon-sur-Seine Congress (1814), the Powers had thus solemnly proclaimed that '[i]t is time, at last, that princes may, without foreign interference, ensure the well-being of their people; *that nations respect their mutual*

[11] Jochen von Bernstorff, 'The Use of Force in International Law before World War I: On Imperial Order and the Ontology of the Nations States' (2018) 29 *European Journal of International Law* 250.

[12] Art. 28 of the Treaty of Peace with Turkey, Lausanne on 24 July 1923; Art. 7 General Treaty of Peace between Great Britain, Austria, France, Prussia, Russia, Sardinia and Turkey, Paris, 30 March 1856.

[13] See above (1.3.).

independence'.[14] This new system was formalised at the Congress of Vienna, which is traditionally considered as having borne the constitution the Concert of Europe around the four victorious Allied Powers against Napoléon: Austria, Prussia, Russia and Great Britain, later joined by France in 1818. Presenting the project of the union to the British Parliament in May 1815, the British Foreign Affairs secretary thus explained that the alliance 'should re-establish a comprehensive system of Public Law in Europe' and provide the necessary tools to avoid the re-occurrence of events such as those endured by the continent since 1789.[15] The relations of European nations would now be organised around the principle of non-intervention and the holding of regular meetings to discuss international affairs. But this did not mean that the members of the European Concert had identical views about intervention and non-intervention. We already referred to the debates that opposed the more conservative Powers, chiefly Russia, to Great Britain during the Congress of Aix-la-Chapelle in 1818 in that respect. Wishing to integrated the anti-liberal policies of the Holy Alliance within the framework of the European Concert, Tsar Alexander I issued a '*Mémoire confidentiel*' in which he pleaded for systematic intervention by the Powers to repress liberal revolts and preserve the old monarchical order of Europe.[16] In this memorandum, the Tsar proposed an extensive interpretation of the principle of self-preservation. He was deeply convinced that internal and international politics could not be dissociated and that the rise of any revolutionary movement in Europe represented, in itself, a threat to the peace of the continent and, consequently, to the security of all European States.[17] Great Britain strongly disagreed. In response to the Tsar's memorandum, Lord Castlereagh explained that the Allies 'could only justify interference in the affairs of a Foreign State, upon the ground of

[14] 'Déclaration des Puissances alliées sur la rupture du Congrès de Châtillon-sur-Seine, 16 mars 1814', full text available in Charles de Martens, *Guide diplomatique*, 2 vols. (P. Aillaud, 1837), vol. 2, p. 12. Emphasis added. Translation by the author.

[15] See Cynthia Weber, *Simulating Sovereignty, Intervention, the State and the Symbolic Exchange* (Cambridge University Press, 1995), p. 42.

[16] 'Mémoire confidentiel du Cabinet Russe, Aix-la-Chapelle, le 26 septembre (8 oct.) 1818', full text available in Arthur R. Wellesley (2nd Duke of Wellington) (ed.), *Supplementary despatches, correspondence and memoranda of Field Marshal Arthur Duke of Wellington, K.G.*, 15 vols. (John Murray, 1865), vol. 12, pp. 743–749.

[17] Ibid., p. 746.

considering their own safety compromised and that, independently of such a Consideration, they cannot claim any right of interference'.[18]

It was against this backdrop that Austria, a member of the Holy Alliance, intervened in the Kingdom of the Two-Sicilies to quell the Carbonari revolts in 1821. The origins of the Carbonari movement are not clear. They are sometimes said to have been an off-shoot of the freemasons imported to Southern Italy at the time of the Napoleonic occupation.[19] It is said that members were recruited foremost within the nobility, public servants and small landowners and that after the downfall of Napoleon the movement became popular with the middle classes. They were socialised with the liberal ideas of the French revolution and the restoration of the old monarchy after the defeat of Napoléon contradicted their hopes for the instauration of a constitutional monarchy in the Kingdom of the Two-Sicilies. The Carbonari movement took a decisive anti-Bourbon twist. In early July 1820, following the example of the revolts in Spain, the rebellion forced Ferdinand I to promise political reforms and the adoption of a constitution.[20]

On the 25th, the Austrian Chancellor, Metternich wrote to the different courts of Germany to indicate that the interests of the Emperor were endangered by the situation in Naples.[21] As Cynthia Weber notes, this danger was perceived to stem from two different, albeit related, elements.[22] On the one hand, Austria believed that the Carbonari revolts was proof of revolutionary contagion in Europe. It therefore needed to be promptly supressed, failing which the continent risked revolving back into the chaos the 1814–1815 settlements had sought to put an end to. From this perspective, Vienna was adopting the Russian view according to which intervention was permissible to preserve the general political order of the continent. On the other hand, and maybe to convince Great Britain of the legitimacy of intervention, the Austrian government also

[18] Memorandum on the Treaties of 1814-1815', Aix-la-Chapelle, October 1818, full text available in C. K. Webster (ed.), *The Congress of Vienna 1814-1815* (Oxford University Press, 1918), p. 169.

[19] Editors of the Encyclopaedia Britannica, 'Carbonari', *Encyclopædia Britannica Online* (available at: www.britannica.com/topic/Carbonari, last update: 15 November 2015).

[20] See 'Proclamation by the King of Sicily relative to the nomination of the Prince Regent as his Vicar-General and Alter-Ego, and the adoption of the Spanish constitution, Naples, 7 July 1820', doc. no 1 in FO, *British and Foreign State Papers, 1820–1821* (Printed by Harrison and son, 1830), p. 1129.

[21] 'Circular of the Austrian Government to the different courts of Germany, Vienna, 25 July 1820', doc. no 2 in ibid., p. 1130. Translation by the author.

[22] Cynthia Weber, Simulating Sovereignty, pp. 47–48.

argued that the revolt against Ferdinand I caused a special threat to its security and to its rights. In his letter, Metternich indeed referred to the emperor's close ties with ruling families in Italy, to the treaties that bound him to these families, and to Austria's own territorial possessions in the north of the peninsula. All of this meant that Austria was the 'natural guardian and protector of public tranquillity in Italy'.[23] The emperor thus had 'an important *duty*, to keep all movements tending towards the disturbance of order away from its borders and those of its neighbours, to suffer no encroachment on its rights and relations assured to the Princes of Italy by the Treaties'.[24] Intervention was hence not only a matter of general security warranted as a result of a general threat, but also a matter of 'personal' security warranted as a result of Austria's rights.

The opportunity of intervening in Southern Italy, and elsewhere to quell the liberal uprisings, would be the subject of the Congress of Troppau convened in late October 1820. Only Austria, Prussia and Russia (i.e., the three powers of the Holy Alliance) were present. The Congress resulted in the adoption of a joint declaration (known as the 'Troppau Protocol') in which the three Powers clearly endorsed the Russian interpretation of the 1814–1815 settlements. It provided that:

> The States of the Alliance which have undergone changes of government as result of revolution, the result of which threatens of other States, will cease to be considered as member of the Alliance and will remain excluded until their situation presents guaranties of order and stability. If owing to such alterations, immediate danger threatens other States as a result of their proximity, the Powers bind themselves to bring them back into the bosom of the Alliance, first by using amicable means, and second, coercive force shall the employment of such force become necessary.[25]

On 20 November 1820, the three allied courts sent a Circular reporting on the result of their discussions to London and Paris giving more details about their stand on the Neapolitan question. They explained that the revolution in Naples was 'an evident breach of the Covenant that guarantees all the governments of Europe with the inviolability of their territory and the enjoyment of peaceful relations that excludes any

[23] 'Circular of the Austrian Government to the different courts of Germany, Vienna, 25 July 1820', doc. no 2 in FO, BFSP 1820–1821, p. 1130.

[24] Ibid.

[25] Quoted in Antonin Debibour, *Histoire diplomatique de l'Europe*, 2 vols. (Felix Alcan, 1891), vol. 1, p. 152. Translation by the author.

encroachment on their mutual rights'.[26] As a result, intervention would merely be the result of the Powers' incumbent obligations to protect the 1814–1815 settlements. No concrete action was yet to be taken; Russia wished for the intervention to be carried out under the auspices of the Concert and consequently preferred to wait until it could be discussed with the other Powers.

This was the purpose of the Congress of Laybach, convened on 26 January 1821, to which the King of Naples was also invited, officially to act as a mediator between his subjects and the Allied Courts.[27] Great Britain, however, did not wait until the opening of this new congress to make its disapproval of the Troppau Protocol known. In line with the position that it had already expressed in 1818, London's issue was not so much with intervention in Naples as with the general doctrine of intervention to supress liberal movements the Protocol proclaimed. It reasserted that this interpretation was unsubstantiated by the 1814–1815 treaties but also pointed to the danger of 'incorporat[ing] [it] into the ordinary diplomacy of States, or into the Institutes of the Law of Nations'.[28] To really guarantee general peace and tranquillity, intervention had to remain the exception and acceptable only when a State's 'own immediate security, or essential interests, are seriously endangered'.[29] In the present case, Great Britain did not deny that Austria and the Italian Powers might find themselves in such circumstances:

> The British government did not hesitate to express their strong disapprobation of the mode and circumstances, under which that revolution was understood to have been effected; but they, at the same time, expressly declared to several Allied Courts, that they should not consider themselves called upon, or justified, to advise interference on the part of this country; they fully admitted, however, that other European States, and especially Austria and the Italian Powers, might feel themselves differently circumstanced.[30]

In other words, shall they decide to militarily intervene in Naples, Austria, Prussia and Russia could not pretend to do so on the basis of

[26] 'Court aperçu des premiers résultats des Conférences de Troppau', inclosure to doc. no 8 in FO, BFSP 1820–1821, p. 1150.

[27] 'The Emperor of Austria and Russia, and the King of Prussia, to the King of Sicily, Troppau, 20 November 1820' doc. no 6 in ibid., p. 1147.

[28] 'Viscount Castlereagh to the British Ministers to Foreign Courts, London, 19 January 1821', doc. no 18 in ibid., p. 1162.

[29] Ibid.

[30] Ibid., p. 1161.

the 1814–1815 settlement nor on behalf of the European Concert. Austria's intervention could nevertheless be understood as an application on its own right to self-preservation considering the dangers that the events in the Two-Sicilies potentially posed to its own integrity.

This is why Great Britain did not oppose Austrian intervention at Laybach, even though it refused to give its 'permission' so as to avoid giving the impression this action endorsed the Troppau Protocol. France, despite the restauration was a constitutional monarchy, adopted a similar attitude.[31] It was thus with the approval of its two partners within the Holy Alliance, of the King of the Two-Sicilies (but not of the parliament), and of other Italian Courts (amongst which Piedmont and Sardinia) that Austria launched its intervention on 13 February 1821. On this occasion, the Austrian government declared this action 'was destined to accomplish the resolutions decided at Laybach'.[32] By 7 March, the Austrian troops reached the borders of the Two-Sicilies and the constitutional government was quickly disposed of.[33] When the Laybach Congress was dispersed in May, the Allied Courts issued one final declaration explaining that the intervention in Naples had been the result of their determination to preserve the European continent from disorder and assert the principles on which the 1814–1815 had been created. Their policies, they stated, 'would always be guided by preservation of the independence of the rights of every State, as recognised by existing Treaties'.[34]

Despite the fact that the time of the Holy Alliance is sometimes presented as the epitome of indiscriminate intervention, this first precedent already shows that international was not an absent or irrelevant. The prospect of intervention in Naples reignited the 1818 debates about the meaning of the 1814–1815 treaties and the permissibility of intervention. The Powers all seemed to agree that the rule was non-intervention but disagreed on the nature of the threat that could warrant action on the basis of self-preservation. For the Powers of the Holy Alliance, a general menace to established order was sufficient. Intervention in Naples was

[31] Debibour, Histoire diplomatique de l'Europe, vol. 1, p. 153.

[32] 'Declaration of the Austrian Government, Vienna, 13 February 1820', doc. no 27 in FO, BFSP 1820–1821, p. 1180.

[33] Debibour, Histoire diplomatique de l'Europe, vol. 1, p. 154.

[34] 'Declaration of the Allied Sovereigns of Austria, Prussia and Russia, on the breaking up of the Conferenced at Laybach, Laybach, 12 May 1821', doc. no 38 in FO, BFSP 1820–1821, p. 1200.

thus not only justified, but a mere application of the treaties. Great Britain, on the other hand, opposed the concept of collective intervention in the name of the Concert, insisting that only an immediate and personal threat could push the general principle of non-intervention to the side. The Austrian intervention in Naples, in sum, did not only spur a debate about the opportunity of intervention, but genuine discussions about the legal framework surrounding such action.

5.2 The Crimean War (1853–1856)

The circumstances that led to the outburst of the Crimean War are complex. They find their roots in the famous 'Eastern Question', i.e., the political and strategic competition between the European Powers which emerged as a result of the instability and progressive downfall of the Ottoman Empire.[35] The preservation of the Sublime Porte was seen by most Powers as a *sine qua non* condition of international order. Europeans nations were particularly wary of Russian expansionism. They feared that, taking advantage of the weakness of the Ottoman Empire, Russia would expand to the south leading it not only to control part of the eastern Mediterranean, but also to become too powerful and upset the balance of power in Europe. This fear was not unjustified: Russia indeed hoped to gain greater access to the Mediterranean but also to unite Orthodox Christianity, which made up a third of Ottoman population, under its rule. The downfall of the Sublime Porte is usually identified to have started around the end of the seventeenth century. In the space of around 160 years before the beginning of the Crimean War in 1853, nine wars had already opposed the two empires. Each peace settlement had progressively allowed Russia to reinforce its presence around the Black sea and to be granted ever greater rights of supervision over the Sultan's treatment of his Christian subjects. The violation of these rights would then often be alleged to justify further wars and concessions on the part of Constantinople.

The 1853–1856 war was the result of one of these attempts. In February 1853, Tsar Nicholas I sent a special envoy, Alexander Menchikovto to demand the full and immediate fulfilment of Turkey's obligations towards Russia's protective rights over Christians and seek the negotiation of a new agreement that would reinforce these rights by

[35] See David M. Goldfrank, *The Origins of the Crimean War* (Routledge, 1994).

granting Russia general control of the Ottoman Orthodox Church.[36] While Constantinople was prepared to give further assurances that it would fulfil its treaty obligations towards Russia in good faith, the proposed terms of the new convention were not acceptable. With the support of the British and French ambassadors, the Ottoman government rejected the Russian offer.[37] Diplomatic ties were severed, Russia launched an occupation of the Danubian provinces of Vallachia and Moldova to force Turkey's hand but war was not yet declared.[38] Talks were conducted through the summer in Vienna where the Powers sought to calm the situation down and convince the Russian to evacuate the occupied territories. Fearing revolts in the empire, Sultan Abdülmecid I finally resolved to declare war on Russia on 4 October 1853.

The Powers continued to seek a diplomatic resolution of the conflict by offering their good offices. In a protocol dated 5 December 1853, they warned that 'hostilities could not continue without affecting the interests of their own States' and that 'the existence of Turkey within the limits assigned to it by existing treaties ha[d] become one of the necessary conditions of European equilibrium [and of] the tranquillity of all Powers'.[39] Negotiations under the auspices of Austria, Prussia, France and Great Britain, would continue through the winter. The Powers, however, were forced to observe that the positions of the belligerents were hardly reconcilable. Faced with the repeated defeats of the Ottoman Empire, France and Great Britain sent their fleets to the Black Sea for the purpose of acting as an interposition force by protecting the Ottomans from further attacks and, in so doing, impress the need for peace on Russia.[40] Saint Petersburg was not pleased. It underlined that the

[36] See Alain Goutmann, *La guerre de Crimée, 1853-1856* (SPM, 1995), p. 113 ff; David M. Goldfrank, 'Policy Traditions and the Menshikov Mission', in Hugh Ragsdale (ed.), *Imperial Russian Foreign Policy* (Cambridge University Press, 1993), pp. 119–158; Trevor Royle, *Crimea: The Great Crimean War, 1854–1856* (Palgrave Macmillan, 2000), pp. 34–49.

[37] See Bernadotte E. Schmitt, 'The Diplomatic Preliminaries of the Crimea War' (1919) 25 *The American Historical Review* 36–67.

[38] 'Proclamation du Prince Gortchakoff annonçant l'Occupation de la Principauté de Moldavie par les Troupes Russes, 20 June / 2 July 1853', in FO, *British and Foreign State Papers 1853–1854* (William Ridgway, 1865), vol. 44, p. 1127.

[39] See 'Protocol of Conference between the Plenipotentiaries of Austria, France, Great Britain and Prussia, relative to the Differences between Russia and Turkey', Vienna, 5 December 1853', in ibid., p. 1049. Translation by the author.

[40] See the explanations given by the Earl of Clarendon to the Russian ambassador in 'The Earl to Clanrendon to Baron Brunnow, London, 31 January 1854', doc. no 3 in ibid., pp. 101–102.

presence of the Allied fleet in the Black Sea had the 'blatant character of hostility',[41] was an 'infringement on their belligerent rights',[42] and, insisting that 'this distinction being contrary to the rule of public law',[43] demanded that both belligerents be treated equality by the British and the French. For Russia, in sum, the British and French joint action was contrary to the laws of neutrality.

Great Britain defended itself against these accusations. The Foreign Affairs Secretary, Earl Clarendon, replied:

> '[I]n defending Turkey from the imminent danger that threatens her, Her Majesty's Government uphold the fundamental principle of European policy involved in the maintenance of the Ottoman Empire that has been repeatedly proclaimed by the five Great Powers of Europe'.[44]

In relation to the Russian occupation of Vallachia and Moldova, he further added that 'no injury to the Christian subjects of the Porte affor [ed] even a pretext for such acts' and that, in so doing, 'the Russian government violat[ed] the *status quo* of Europe, contradicting the intentions proclaimed by the Great Powers in 1840 and 1841, and stamping Russia as the disturber of general peace'.[45] Despite appearances, the Earl of Clarendon's response was arguably not solely based on consideration of politics. First, in fact, he was stating that the Russian occupation of the Danubian provinces was groundless because it had not suffered an injury warranting reprisals. The Russian action was thus at odds with the rules regulating the use of coercive measures. This disregard, moreover, not only affected the Ottoman Empire, but the general peace of Europe and, therefore, the Powers' interests. Equally interesting was Clarendon's mention of the 'intentions proclaimed [...] in 1840 and 1841'. He was referring to the Treaty for the Pacification of the Levant (1840) and the London Straights Convention (1841) which had both been signed by Great Britain, Prussia, Austria, Russia, and the Ottoman Empire, for the purpose of ending the Second Egyptian-Ottoman War (1839–1841) and

41 'Count Nesselrode to Baron Brunnow, Saint Petersburg, 4/16 January 1854', doc. no 1 in ibid., p. 99. Translation by the author.

42 Ibid., p. 100. Translation by the author.

43 'Baron Brunnow to the Earl of Clarendon, London, 23 January/4 February 1854', doc. no 5 in ibid, p. 104. Translation by the author.

44 'The Earl to Clanrendon to Baron Brunnow, London, 31 January 1854', doc. no 3 in ibid., p. 102.

45 Ibid., p. 103. Emphasis in the original.

restore the Porte's sovereignty over Syria.[46] The preamble of the 1840 treaty stated that the Powers were 'animated by the desire to maintain the integrity and independence of the Ottoman Empire, in the interest of the preservation of peace in Europe'.[47] To some extent, Clarendon seemed to consider that the Powers had committed themselves to preserving the existence of the Sublime Porte within its current borders for the overall good of the Continent. Russia' actions violated this commitment; Great Britain's and France's were meant to uphold them.

In reaction, the Russian government suspended diplomatic relations with London and Paris in early February 1854. On 27 February 1854, Great Britain and France sent a joint note to the Tsar Nicholas I requiring Russia's withdrawal from Valachia and Moldova before 30 April. The Tsar was to give his response within six days, failing which the Powers would have no other choice but to consider themselves at war with Russia. The Tsar refused to answer; London and Paris declared war 27 March 1854. Napoléon III's message was transmitted to the Senate on that same day. It was brief and mostly indicated that the emperor 'had been forced to take the arms to support an ally'.[48] On 12 March 1854, that is after the expiration of the Franco-British ultimatum to Russia, Great Britain and France had indeed concluded a treaty of alliance and military aid with Turkey. The preamble of this treaty stated that the purpose of the alliance was to 'reject the aggression directed by His Majesty the Emperor of All Russia against the territories of the Ottoman Sublime Porte, an aggression by which the integrity of the Ottoman Empire and the independence of the throne of his imperial majesty the Sultan are threatened'; and that the two Powers had resolved to help the Ottoman Porte 'fully convinced that the existence of the Ottoman Empire within its present limits is essential to maintain the balance of power between the States of Europe'.[49] Other than that, the French declaration made no allusion to

[46] The London Straight Convention is available in FO, *British and Foreign State Papers 1840–1841* (James Ridgway and Sons, 1857), vol. 29, p. 703.

[47] 'Convention between Great Britain, Austria, Prussia, and Russia, and Turkey, for the Pacification of the Levant, signed at London, 15 July 1840', in FO, *British and Foreign State Papers 1839–1840* (Harrison and Sons, 1857), vol. 28, p. 432. Translation by the author.

[48] *Journal des débats politiques et littéraire*, 29 Mars 1854, p. 1. Translation by the author.

[49] 'Treaty between Great Britain, France and Turkey, relative to Military Aid to be given to Turkey, Constantinople, 12 March 1854', in FO, BFSP 1853–1854, p. 7. Translation by the author.

preservation of the European balance of power or to considerations of law. Moreover, the lack of publicity of parliamentary debates during the Second Empire does not allow to assess whether these were subject to discussion within the French Senate.[50]

In Great Britain, Queen Victoria's message announcing war with Russia was read before the Houses on 27 March 1854 and followed by a more thorough presentation by the government on the 31st. The Queen's message was just as succinct as that the French Emperor: 'Her Majesty feels bound to afford active assistance to her ally the Sultan against unprovoked aggression'.[51] Charged with presenting the position of the government to the House of Commons, Lord John Russell gave a detailed account of the events that had led Great Britain to war.[52] He explained that the attitude of Russia had shown that its aim was not to protect the Christian subjects of the Porte, but to seek territorial aggrandisement and the disintegration of the Ottoman Empire. In this context, the object of the war was to help 'an ally, one of the Powers whose integrity and independence are sanctioned by the *public law of Europe*' to repel the Tsar's aggression.[53] Lord Russel added that this was in 'consisten[t] with [Great Britain's] duties to Europe – [and] consisten[t] with the general interest of this country'.[54]

Following the French and British war declaration, the Vienna Conference (which had so far sought to act as a mediator between Russia and Turkey) issued a protocol on 9 April 1854 in which it noted that: 'the change of attitude operated by the two Powers represented in the Vienna Conference as a consequence of the approaches attempted by France and England, [is] supported by Austria and Prussia as being *founded in law*'.[55] The Protocol did not give further indications as to why that was exactly. The fact that France and Great Britain were members of the Vienna Conference, however, allows us understand that

[50] On publicity of parliamentary debates during the French Second Empire, see Bernard Gaudillère, 'La publicité des débats parlementaires (1852–1870)' (2008) 4 *Parlement[s], Revue d'histoire politique* 27–49.

[51] 'Message from Her Britannic Majesty to both Houses of Parliament on the outbreak of War with Russia, 27 March 1854', in FO, BFSP 1853–1854, p. 110.

[52] Hansard, HC vol. 132, cols. 198–217, 31 March 1854.

[53] Ibid., col. 216. Emphasis added.

[54] Ibid., col. 213.

[55] 'Protocol of Conference between Austria, France, Great Britain and Prussia, relative to the non-evacuation of the Danubian principalities by Russia, and the consequent participation of England and France in the war between Russia and Turkey, Vienna, 9 April 1854', in FO, BFSP 1853–1854, p. 83.

the intervention on the side of Turkey was believed to be 'founded in law' for the same reasons these two Powers had previously and consistently put forward since the beginning of the crisis.

It has to be admitted that international law did not appear to be the central consideration. The war was indeed foremost presented as a matter of European politics, order and equilibrium. Yet, it also must be recognised that law was not altogether absent from the debates and diplomatic interactions between the Powers. Even though the vernacular of law was not as explicitly used as during the Austrian intervention in Naples in 1821, it was present between the lines. Great Britain and France indeed considered that Russia, by invading the Danube provinces and refusing to evacuate them, had acted unjustly (not to say illegally), by attacking the Ottoman Empire without a serious cause. In so doing, it had disturbed the principles upon which the Powers had agreed to conduct their affairs with the Sublime Porte. After lengthy attempts to resolve the dispute diplomatically, they had resolve to resort to war to redress this wrongdoing. In that sense, the Crimean War was carried out as a sanction of international law.

5.3 The Franco-Prussian War (1870–1871)

After the Crimean War, the Franco-Prussian War of 1870 was the second major European war that shook the continent during the nineteenth century. This war, which lasted from 19 July 1870 to 28 January 1871, is often said to have been wanted by Otto von Bismarck and decisive for the unification of Germany. As other national movements, 'pan-germanism' originated in the early nineteenth century, the publication of Johann Gottlieb Fichte's *Addresses to the German Nation* in 1807 sometimes being identified as a founding moment.[56] Written during Napoleon's occupation of the German States, this book was a plea for the awakening of national sentiment and for the unification of Germanic nations. After Napoleon's defeat, the Confederation of Germanic States was created at Vienna in 1815. It was a loose political association composed of 39 German-speaking states with a parliament but without executive power, essentially formed for the purpose of

[56] See, e.g., Eric Dorn Brose, *German History 1789–1871. From the Holy Roman Empire to the Bismarckian Reich* (Berghahn Book, 1997), pp. 70–71.

mutual defence.[57] Affected by the rivalry between Prussia and Austria, it is said that the Confederation was rather ineffective. In 1834, a custom union (*Zollverein*) was formed under the patronage of Prussia. The economy of the German States grew more interdependent, nourishing the spread of pan-Germanism among the liberal bourgeoisie. A first attempt at unification was conducted following the 1848 revolutions, but the Prussian King, Friedrich-Wilhelm IV, refused the crown offered to him by the Frankfurt parliament: he did not want to accept an offer from a popularly elected parliament without the consent of German princes and feared it would lead to Austrian or Russian intervention.[58] In 1861, the King died and his brother, Wilhelm I, came into power choosing Bismarck as his Minister-President. Although favourable to German unification, Bismarck was not a liberal. He saw unification as a means to get rid of Austria's domination over the Germanic Confederation as well as to increase Prussian influence, power, and status within the European political system.[59] The Austro-Prussian War of 1866 over the Schleswig-Holstein question, won by Prussia, would see the dissolution of the Germanic Confederation and the creation of the North-German Confederation. Napoléon III grew wary of Bismarck's politics. The Prussian Minister-President was convinced that, due to the then quite recent history of French occupation and strong anti-French feeling, war with France would allow to bring the project of unification to completion. He did not, however, want to declare war on France as that would have branded Prussia as the aggressor. Instead, he endeavoured to create a situation which he knew would lead Paris to initiate hostilities.

This opportunity he found when the throne of Spain was left vacant as a result of the 1868 *Gloriosa* Revolution, which had forced Isabella II out of the country. In concertation with Juan Prim, the strongman of the *Gloriosa*, Bismarck pushed for the candidacy of a cousin of Wilhelm I, Leopold Hohenzollern-Sigmaringen, to fill the position. The French government feared the nomination of a Prussian prince in Spain would lead to its encirclement. For Spain, however, the prince of Hohenzollern

[57] The Editors of Encyclopaedia Britannica, 'German Confederation', *Encyclopaedia Britannica Online* (available at: www.britannica.com/topic/German-Confederation, last update: 16 January 2016).

[58] David E. Barclay, *Frederick Wilhelm IV and the Prussian Monarchy, 1840–1861* (Clarendon Press, 1995), pp. 194–195.

[59] See Louis Leo Snyder and Ida Mae Brown, *Bismarck and the Unification of Germany* (F. Watts, 1966); Otto Pflanze, *Bismarck and the Development of* Germany, 3 vols. (Princeton University Press, 1963), vol. 1.

presented several advantages. As the French ambassador reported Juan Prim to have explained to him: 'he is catholic, of royal race, he is thirty-five years old, has two sons, and is married to a Portuguese princess'.[60] When France received confirmation that Hohenzollern had accepted the throne of Spain on 3 July 1870, it engaged in intense diplomatic efforts to have his candidacy removed. The French ambassador to Madrid, M. Mercier de Lostende, immediately indicated that such a course of events would be seen as a provocation because 'in case of a European war, [France] would have no security for its Pyrenean border if a Prussian prince occupie[d] the throne of Spain'.[61] Prim was sympathetic to the French argument but insisted that Spain was in urgent need of replacement and that there was no viable alternative.[62] In Berlin, the French *Chargé d'affaires*, M. Le Sourd, quickly required an audience with the Prussian Foreign Affairs Minister, Herman von Thile, to discuss Prussia's involvement in this situation. Thile denied the Prussian government had had any hand in the matter, but Le Sourd was not convinced, and neither was the French Minster for Foreign Affairs, the Duc de Gramont.[63] In a letter to his *Chargé* at Berlin, he indeed replied:

> 'No one will ever be led to believe that a Prussian prince can accept the Spanish crown without permission from the King, head of his family. And if the King has authorized it, what becomes of the alleged official ignorance of the Berlin cabinet?'[64]

On 7 July 1870, Gramont resolved to send the French Ambassador, Count Benedetti, to meet the King at Ems in order the shed full light on this affair.[65] Benedetti was asked to make it very clear that the only way war could be avoided was if the King agreed to disapprove and forbid his cousin's accession to the Spanish throne. He was also invited to make it known that it had not been uncommon for monarchs to veto the nomination of princes to vacant thrones and that, in this respect, the demands of France were in conformity with 'well established precedents

[60] 'M. Mercier de Lostende au Duc de Gramont, Madrid, 3 July 1870', doc. no 7 in MAE, *Archives diplomatiques 1871–1872*, 4 vols. (Librairie Diplomatique Ayrot, 1872), vol. 1, p. 13. Translation by the author.

[61] Ibid., p. 14.

[62] Ibid., pp. 14–15.

[63] 'M. Le Sourd au Duc de Gramont, Berlin, 4 July 1870', doc. no 8 in ibid., pp. 16–17.

[64] 'Le Duc de Gramont à M. Le Sourd, Paris, 7 July 1870', doc. no 18 in ibid., p. 28. Translation by the author.

[65] 'Le Duc de Gramont au Conte Benedetti, Paris, 7 July 1870', doc. no 20 in ibid., p. 29.

of the public law of Europe'.[66] The point was that Paris had the right, as matter of protection of its interests and security, to request that the candidacy of Hohenzollern be withdrawn.

Benedetti arrived at Ems on the night of the 8th and met with the King on the following day. Reporting to the Minister for Foreign Affairs, he indicated that Wilhelm I had confirmed that he had given his approval to Leopold Hohenzollern's decision to accept the throne of Spain but had insisted he had done so as head of the family rather than on behalf of the Prussian government. The King, moreover, indicated that he was not willing to forbid his cousin from effectively going to Spain and that the decision would have to be the Prince's own.[67] French public opinion was agitated, and Gramont pressured Benedetti to get a clear response from the King who was waiting to hear from his cousin. On the 12th, France was informed that Prince Hohenzollern had agreed to withdraw his plea, but from Spain instead of Prussia.[68] Wilhelm I confirmed the information and gave his approval on the 13th.[69] The French were only partially relieved by this news. Following his instructions, Benedetti informed the King that this was 'a guaranty for the present, but [that it was] essential to secure the future'.[70] The French government asked the King of Prussia to give his assurance that, shall Hohenzollern come back on his decision, he would not support or authorise it. The King, in Benedetti's words, 'absolutely refused' and the discussion was closed despite the French diplomat other attempts to meet with him.[71] The ambassador left Ems and war preparations started in their earnest.

The Ems dispatch, through which the Prussian government gave its own account of the negotiations, is often said to have played a key role in the outburst of the war. Bismarck, the story goes, modified the dispatch to make it look as though the King had treated the French ambassador with disrespect. The dispatch was leaked to the press, further agitating public opinion in France but rallying national feeling in the German States.[72] For the French government, in any case, war had already become inevitable as a result of Wilhelm's refusal to guarantee that he would oppose the candidacy of a Prussian prince to the throne of Spain

66 'Le Duc de Gramont au Conte Benedetti, Paris, 9 July 1870', doc. no 43 in ibid., pp. 53–54.
67 'Le Conte Benedetti au Duc de Gramont, Ems, 9 July 1870', doc. no 47 in ibid., p. 58.
68 'La Duc de Gramont au Conte Benedetti, Paris, 12 July 1870', doc. no 88 in ibid., p. 92.
69 'Le Conte Benedetti au Duc de Gramont, Ems, 13 July 1870', doc. no 98 in ibid., p. 107.
70 Ibid.
71 Ibid.
72 See H. W. Koch, *A History of Prussia* (Routledge, 2014), p. 267.

in the future. Great Britain tried to offer its good offices to the two powers in the hope of averting war, but the offer was refused.[73]

The French war declaration to Prussia was drafted on 17 July 1870 and communicated to Bismarck on the 19th by M. Le Sourd. The declaration read:

> The Government of His Majesty the Emperor of the French, not being able to look upon the project of putting a Prussian prince on the Spanish throne but as an enterprise directed against the territorial security of France, found itself obliged to ask His Majesty the King of Prussia for an assurance that such a combination could not be carried out without his assent.
>
> His Majesty the King of Prussia having refused to give such assurance [. . .], the Imperial Government has no other choice but to see the King declaration's a proof of an ulterior motive threatening France and balance of Power in Europe. [. . .]
>
> Consequently, His Imperial Majesty's Government has judged that it has an obligation to immediately defend its honour and its compromised interests, and, has resolved to take all the measures required by the situation to this end, it considers itself, as of now, to be in a state of war with Prussia.[74]

The war, in sum, was presented as a situation of self-preservation and self-defence even though the language used in the declaration clearly does not directly refer to law. We may indeed recall that France claimed it was its right to require that a Prussian prince not sit on the throne of Spain. As it is, this element was emphasised in the circular the Duc de Gramont sent to French legations a few days after the war declaration. In this circular, the French Foreign Affairs Minister explained:

> It was this government [the Prussian government], in fact, which not believing itself bound by *common law* and scorning the *rules* to which the greatest powers had the wisdom to submit, tried to impose a dangerous extension of its influence on an abused Europe. [. . .]
>
> Every nation, we like to repeat, is master of its own destiny. This principle, highly affirmed by France, has become one of the *fundamental laws* of modern politics. But the right of each people, as of each individual, is limited by the right of others, and it is forbidden for a nation, under the pretext of exercising its sovereignty, to threaten the existence or security of a neighbouring people. [. . .] when it comes to the choice of a sovereign,

[73] 'Lord Lyon to the Duc of Gramont, Paris, 15 July 1870', annexe 1 to doc. no 151 in MAE, Archives diplomatiques 1871–1872, p. 164.

[74] 'M. Le Sourd au Conte Bismarck, Berlin, 19 July 1870', doc. no 177 in ibid., pp. 189–190. Translation by the author.

> a government never has the right to pretend and always has the right to exclude. This *doctrine* has been accepted by all cabinets in circumstances similar to those in which the candidature of Prince Hohenzollern has placed us, notably in 1831, in the Belgian question, in 1830 and 1862, in the Hellenic question.[75]

5.4 The Spanish-American War (1898)

The story of the rivalry between Spain and the United States over Cuba is a long one.[76] Washington had already contemplated intervening on the island during the Ten Years' War (1868–1878). But at the time of this first attempt of Cuban elites to gain independence from Madrid, the United States was not yet influential enough to confidently defy a European, albeit decaying, Power such as Spain.[77] In the 1890s, the situation was different; the United States had become politically, militarily, and commercially far more powerful (and, hence, also more valuable to the other European Powers). When a new insurrection broke out on 24 February 1895, the United States kept a close eye on the situation. They indeed possessed numerous interests on the island. In 1895, President Grover Cleveland estimated that US investments in plantations, mining, railroad and other enterprises represented around 30 to 50 million dollars, while commercial exchanges with Cuba amount to more than 100 million dollars annually.[78] By 1896 these numbers had been divided by two, and in 1897 by three.[79] The ferocious warfare was met with annoyance, but the Cleveland administration was not willing to

[75] 'Le Duc de Gramont aux agents diplomatiques de la France à l'étranger, Paris, 21 July 1870', doc. no 210 in ibid., p. 230. Emphasis added. Translation by the author.

[76] See Louis A. Perez Jr., *Cuba Between Empires, 1878-1902* (University of Pittsburg Press, 1983); Louis A. Perez Jr., 'Cuba. Sugar and Independence', in Thomas M. Leonard (ed.), *United States-Latin American Relations, 1850–1903* (University of Alabama Press, 1999), pp. 35–57; Esteban Morales Dominguez and Gary Prevost, *United States-Cuban Relations. A Critical History* (Lexington Books, 2008), pp. 21 ff.

[77] About the diplomatic relations between the United States and Spain during the Ten Years' War see French Ensor Chadwick, *The Relations of the United States and Spain. Diplomacy* (Charles Scribner's sons, 1909), pp. 287–410; Jean-David Avenel, *La guerre hispano-américaine de 1898. La naissance de l'impérialisme américain* (Economica, 2007), p. 32.

[78] President Grover Cleveland quoted *in* Howard Zinn, *A People's History of the United States* (Longman, 1980), p. 295.

[79] Chadwick, The Relations of the United States and Spain, p. 37; Elbert J. Benton, *International Law and Diplomacy of the Spanish-American War* (The Johns Hopkins Press, 1908), p. 37.

intervene despite continuous pressure from Congress and public opinion.[80] It said is that Cleveland had no desire for exterior expeditions and was more interested in the development of US internal economy.[81]

Although President William McKinley was not keen on war either, his inauguration marked a changed of paradigm. McKinley was more permeable to public opinion and felt that he needed to take a firmer stand as the conflict was lingering on with no signs of betterment.[82] In June 1897, General Steward Woodward (a lawyer trained at Yale and Columbia) was appointed as the new ambassador to Madrid. His first task was to hand over a note expounding the United States position on the situation in Cuba.[83] The bottom line was that Washington expected peace to be promptly restored, failing which it might feel it had the right to actively address the issue. The note pointed to Spain's inability to put an end to the conflict, to the great prejudices this caused to the United States, and specified that behind this situation 'li[ed] the larger and ulterior problem of intervention'.[84] Has State Secretary Sherman also had the occasion to explain to the Spanish ambassador, the injuries inflicted upon the United States by this war 'give the president the *right* to specific remonstrance'.[85] The grounds on which the United States believed to be justified in intervening were best presented in a letter from State Secretary Sherman to Woodford on 16 July 1897:

> No exception can be taken to the general proposition that a neighbouring nation, however deeply disturbed and injured by the existence of a devastating internal conflict at its doors, may be constrained, *on grounds of international comity*, to disregard its endangered interests [...]. *The onlooking nation needs only wait 'reasonable time' before alleging and*

[80] About the 'yellow press' and the civil war in Cuba see Joseph E. Wisan, *The Cuban Crisis as Reflected in the New York Press (1895–1898)* (Columbia University Press, 1934).

[81] Joseph Smith, *The Spanish-American War. Conflict in the Caribbean and the Pacific, 1895–1902* (Routledge, 1994), p. 30; Jean-David Avenel, La guerre hispano-américaine de 1898, p. 33.

[82] Certain members of McKinley's cabinet, such as State Secretary John Sherman, were themselves pro-war. See Philip S. Foner, *The Spanish-Cuban-American War and the Birth of American Imperialism*, 2 vols. (NYU Press, 1972), vol. 1, p. 208 ff; John L. Offner, *An Unwanted War: The Diplomacy of the United States and Spain over Cuba, 1895–1898* (The University of North Carolina Press, 1992), p. 54.

[83] John L. Offner, An Unwanted War, p. 54.

[84] Ibid., p. 560.

[85] 'Mr. Sherman to Mr. Dupuy de Lôme, Department of State, Washington, 26 June 1897', doc. no 269 in Ministerio de Estado, *Spanish Diplomatic Correspondence and Documents, 1896–1900. Presented to the Cortes by the Minister of State* (translation by the United States Department of State) (Government Printing Office, 1905), p. 26. Emphasis added.

> *acting upon the right which it, too, possesses. This proposition is not only a legal subtlety, but a broad principle of international comity and law.*[86]

Sherman thus stated a principle (non-intervention) and the exception the United States intended to invoke shall Spain fail to pacify the island. More interesting for the purpose of our demonstration, however, is the distinctly legal features of the position expressed by the United States. The fact that a State may intervene in a civil war abroad, in fact, was not only presented as deriving from reason ('comity', 'moral obligation', 'reasonableness') but as a rule of law ('this proposition is not only a legal subtlety, but a broad principle of international [. . .] law'). The United States reiterated with this position on several occasions. In a letter dated 2 December 1897 to the new Spanish Minister of State, Pio Gullón, Woodford, for instance, indicated that the 'actions of [his] government rested [. . .] upon moral and *legal rights*'.[87]

The Spanish government's reaction to the United States pretentions was as straightforward. Madrid openly rejected the doctrine of intervention developed by the McKinley administration. It acknowledged the damages the war in Cuba was causing to the United States, but insisted that while Washington was justified in expressing its desire for peace such situations could 'never [give rise to] interference or intrusion'.[88] This position was repeated in a letter to Woodford dated 1 February 1898, which Gullón concluded by indicating that: 'the United States, [. . .], will not fix a period for the termination of the present Cuban insurrection'; that 'a *limitation of the legitimate and immutable national sovereignty could not be permitted at any time*'; and that 'there remains no reason or pretext for now discussing the duration of that struggle, which is of an exclusively domestic nature'.[89]

Interestingly, the Spanish government also took this occasion to remind the United States about its duties of neutrality. Many Cuban exiles had fled to the United States and Gullón explained that the best

[86] 'Mr. Sherman to Mr. Woodford, Department of State, Washington DC., 16 July 1897', doc. no 4, US Department of State, *Papers Relating to the Foreign Relations of the United States, 1898* (Government Printing Office, 1901), p. 560. Emphasis added.

[87] 'Mr. Woodford to Mr. Gullón, Madrid, 20 December 1897', doc. no 34, in Ministerio de Estado, Spanish Diplomatic Correspondence, pp. 53–54. Emphasis added.

[88] 'Reply of Pio Gullón to Mr. Woodford's note of 23 September 1897, Ministry of State, Madrid, 23 October 1897', inclosure to doc. no 50, in US Department of State, Papers 1898, p. 583.

[89] 'Reply of Pio Gullón to Mr. Woodford's note of 23 September 1897, Ministry of State, Madrid, 23 October 1897', inclosure to doc. no 50 in ibid., p. 660.

way Washington could contribute to achieving peace in Cuba was by abiding to its duty of due diligence as 'demanded by general international friendship'.[90] He noted that:

> *Despite the express provisions of those laws and the doctrine maintained by the American Government in the famous Alabama arbitration with regard to the diligence which should be used to avoid whatsoever aggressive act against a friendly nation*, it is certain that filibustering expeditions have set forth and unfortunately continue to set forth from the United states, [. . .].[91]

In a letter of 1 February 1898, Gullón would further add that:

> the friendship which is founded upon international law obliges all States, to use the words of the famous South American publicist, Calvo, not only to prevent their own subjects from causing injury to a friendly country, but to exert themselves to prevent any plots, machinations, or combinations of any kind tending to disturb the security of those States with which they maintain relations of peace, friendship, and good harmony, from being planned in their territory.[92]

The mention of the *Alabama Claims* arbitration and the direct reference to Calvo, among other elements, are particularly striking and once again revealing of the distinctively legalistic nature of the Spanish-American correspondence during this crisis.

Despite appearances, by the autumn of 1897, the United States felt that its relations with the Spanish Crown were heading in the right direction and that war might, after all, be avoided. The Spanish government, in fact, had started to implement reforms in Cuba and Washington was confident that they would yield the expected results.[93] In February 1898, however, two successive mishaps precipitated the two nations on the path of war. On the 8th, a letter of the Spanish ambassador calling the US President 'weak', 'a bidder for the admiration of the crowd' and a

[90] Ibid., p. 585.

[91] Ibid. Emphasis added.

[92] 'Mr. Gullón to Mr. Woodford, Ministry of State, Madrid, 1 February 1898', inclosure to doc. no 346 in ibid., pp. 661–662.

[93] Talking about the administrative reforms in Cuba in a letter dated 20 November 1897, Sherman wrote that these were a 'hopeful indication of change' and that 'in taking this advanced position, the Government of Spain has entered upon a pathway from which no backward step is possible', 'Mr. Sherman to Mr. Woodford, Department of State, Washington, 20 November 1897', doc. no 72, in ibid., pp. 603 and 606.

'would-be politician' was leaked to the press.[94] A week later, on the 15th, the *USS Maine* (a US battleship sent to the Cuban coasts with the consent of Spain) mysteriously exploded in the Havana harbour, killing 266 of the 354 crew members.[95] Spain was promptly accused of having deliberately destroyed the ship. Although Madrid strongly denied any implication in this unfortunate event and proposed the establishment of a commission of inquiry, of an arbitral tribunal and even mediation, American public opinion had already decided on war, leaving little to no discretion to the President.[96]

The weeks that elapsed between the incident and the beginning of hostilities were dedicated to debating the form of the intervention, drafting the President's message to the Congress, making final military arrangements and preparing the aftermath of the conflict. McKinley addressed the Congress on 11 April 1898. The intervention in Cuba was presented as a 'neutral intervention', meaning an intervention to put an end to the Cuban civil war but not directed against Spain as such. In his address, McKinley emphasised the cruel nature of this conflict, the damages it had already inflicted on American interests and nationals, and Spain's inability to pacify the island. He explained that the United States were acting 'on behalf of endangered American interests which *give us the right and the duty* to speak and to act'.[97] 'The forcible intervention of the United States as a neutral to stop the war', he added,

> . . . is justifiable on rational grounds. [. . .]
>
> Third. The right to intervene may be justified by the very serious injury to the commerce, trade, and business of our people, and by the wanton destruction of property and devastation of the island.
>
> Fourth, and which is of the utmost importance. The present condition of affairs in Cuba is a constant menace to our peace and entails upon this Government an enormous expense.[98]

As can be seen, the United States claimed to have a special interest in the Cuban question because of their proximity and because the injuries its

[94] 'Mr. Dupuy de Lôme to Mr. José Canalejas, Legation of Spain, Washington, December 1897', in ibid., p. 1007.

[95] Donald H. Dyal (ed.), *Historical Dictionary of the Spanish American War* (Greenwood Press, 1996), pp. 200–202.

[96] Elbert J. Benton, International Law and Diplomacy, p. 76; Sebastian Balfour, *The End of the Spanish Empire*, pp. 25–26.

[97] 'President McKinley's message to the Congress, 11 April 1898', in US Department of State, Papers 1898, p. 759. Emphasis added.

[98] Ibid., p. 757.

interests and citizens had endured. But the intervention was also presented as matter of national security. It was about redressing a wrong and preventing its aggravation.

Spain interpreted the United States 'neutral intervention' as a full-blown war declaration and broke all diplomatic relations with the United States on 21 April 1898.[99] Madrid's reaction to President McKinley's address is embodied in two separate memorandums. Both texts are roamed with legal considerations, which consisted in presenting Spain's behaviour as righteous and the United States' as driven by greed, force and arbitrariness. Gullón concluded his first memorandum thus: 'His Majesty's government only desires to make it known to the civilised world that *reason and right* on their side and provocation and injustice on that of the United States'.[100] He opened the second stating that 'few cases can be named in the course of centuries in which the *right is clearer on the one side* and the insult more open on the other'.[101] The story, as told from the Spanish perspective, was one a continuous provocation and interference on the part of the United States. They were accused of having fomented and supported the Cuban revolution and now taking the situation of disorder as an excuse to intervene. This intervention, the memorandums asserted, was an offence 'to the *legitimate sovereignty* of Spain in Cuba',[102] was 'without the support of any argument but force',[103] and that annexation of Cuba by the United States that would result from it was an 'open and criminal robbery [that] will be opposed by the Spanish people with *right* on their side'.[104]

Another element that made the United States action problematic according to Spain, was the absence of necessity. The United States, in fact, had rejected all the propositions of Spain for an amicable resolution of the dispute. Necessity and the exhaustion of all other remedies was

[99] In a letter dated 21 April 1898 Gullón informed the Spanish ambassador in Washington that: 'the president having approved a resolution of both Chambers of the United Sates which, in denying the legitimate sovereignty of Spain and in threatening armed intervention in Cuba, is equivalent to an evident declaration of war, . . .', 'Mr. Gullón to Mr. Polo de Bernabé, Madrid, 21 April 1898', doc. no 146 in Ministerio de Estado, Spanish Diplomatic Correspondence, p. 135.

[100] 'Memorandum', inclosure to doc. no 140, in ibid., p. 132.

[101] 'Memorandum', inclosure to doc. no 149, in ibid., p. 137. Emphasis added.

[102] 'Memorandum', inclosure to doc. no 140, in ibid., p. 131. Emphasis added.

[103] Ibid.

[104] Ibid., p. 132. Emphasis added.

thus deemed a condition for resort to intervention and to war. This necessity, however, was now evident on the part of Spain:

> The Spanish people and Government, arbitrarily and unjustly provoked, *find themselves under the hard necessity of appealing to force in order to repel the scandalous attack of which they are made the object*, and to defend the historical integrity of their country's territory at the same time as their integrity and honour. [. . .] provocation, offense and the declaration of war came from the side of the United States. Spain, *strong in her right*, has confined herself to replying to the attacks and accepting at last the challenge thrown to her [. . .].[105]

The Spanish-American war, as we can observe, was a particularly rich precedent. It gave rise to intricate and thorough debates about the right of intervention and the duties of neutrality. Spain and the United States genuinely engaged in discussion about the nature and the scope of their respective rights and obligations under international law. In the end, both States justified their decision to resort to force on the basis of the right to self-preservation. For the United States, the intervention was warranted by the damages the Cuban civil war was causing to its interests and to those of its nationals as well as by the threat to its security which this ongoing contest represented. For Spain, war had been declared by the United States and its was its duty to react as a matter of self-defence.

5.5. The Austrian Ultimatum to Serbia and the Outbreak of World War I (1914)

A discussion of nineteenth and early twentieth century practice of justifying the use force would not be complete without having a look at the way Austria justified war against Serbia in July 1914, precipitating the World War I. The events at the inception of this devastating conflict are well known. They find their roots in the Balkans. On the eve of Great War, the Austro-Hungarians controlled the current territories of Slovenia, Croatia, Bosnia-and-Herzegovina as well as northern Serbia and western Romania. These areas of the Empire, however, were subject of unrest. As elsewhere in Europe, nationalist movements had emerged in the Balkans calling for the union of the Slav peoples. Some of these movements had crystallised into secret paramilitary societies such as

[105] 'Memorandum', inclosure to no 149, in ibid., pp. 137–138. Emphasis added.

the Black Hand, formed by officers of the Serbian Army in 1911, or yet *Narodna Oblana* ('National Defence') and *Mlada Bosna* ('Young Bosnia') respectively created in 1908 and 1911 following the annexation of Bosnia-and-Herzegovina by the Austro-Hungarian Empire. These societies maintained more or less close ties, but pursued the same ideal of liberating the southern Slavs from Austrian domination in order to create a unitary State. They recruited and trained partisans and spies, conducted anti-Austrian sabotage, assassinations and propaganda. They were connected with Serbian governmental authorities, although historians note that the magnitude this association has so far never been fully uncovered.[106] What is nevertheless known is that these organisations were behind the assassination of Archduke Franz-Ferdinand, heir to the Austro-Hungarian throne, on 28 June 1914 in Sarajevo.

The Archduke and his wife were killed by Gavrilo Princip, a Serb Bosnian student who was a member of Young Bosnia, with weapons provided by the Black Hand. The investigations carried out by the Austro-Hungarian authorities had revealed that Serbian officials might have been involved in the attack. They suspected the terrorists had beneficiated from the help of the Serbian border patrols for exfiltration. As soon as 29 June 1914, the Serbian Minister at Vienna telegraphed his Prime Minister to warn that 'the Vienna press asserts that the magisterial enquiry has already shown that the Sarajevo outrage was prepared at Belgrade; further, that the whole conspiracy in its wider issues was organised at Belgrade among the youths inspired with the Great Serbian idea'.[107] The diplomatic correspondence shows that Serbia immediately endeavoured to assure the Austro-Hungarians of its good faith, promising that it would 'not tolerate within [its] territory the fostering of any agitation or illegal proceedings calculated to disturb [their] already delicate relations with Austria-Hungary', that it would

[106] Alan Cassels, *Ideology and International Relations in the Modern World* (Routledge, 1996), p. 122. See also Barbara Jelavich, 'What the Habsburg Government Knew about the Black Hand' (1991) 22 *Austrian History Yearbook* 131–150; Dušan T. Batakovic, 'Storm Over Serbia. The Rivalry between Civilian and Military Authorities (1911–1914)' (2003) 44 *Balcanica* 307–356.

[107] 'M. Yov. M. Yovanovitch, Minister at Vienna, to M. N. Pashitch, Prime Minister and Minister for Foreign Affairs, Vienna, 16/29 June 1914', doc. no 1 in FO, *Collected Diplomatic Documents Relating to the Outbreak of the European War* (Harisson and sons, 1915), p. 369.

bring those responsible to trial in the 'event of its being proved that there are any in Serbia',[108] and that Serbia had not 'directly or indirectly inspired acts of this kind'.[109]

And, in fact, Austria-Hungary did not seem to hold the Serbian authorities directly responsible for the attack. But as the investigation lingered on without concrete results, it started to feel that Serbia was not duly fulfilling its obligations towards the Empire. This element was clearly stated in the Austrian war ultimatum of 23 July 1914:

> The History of recent years, and in particular the painful events of the 28th June last, have shown the existence of a subversive movement with the object of detaching a part of the territories of Austria-Hungary from the Monarchy. The movement, which had its birth under the eye of the Serbian Government, has gone so far as to make itself manifest on both sides of the Serbian frontier in the shape of acts of terrorism and a serious of outrages and murders.
>
> Far from carrying out the *formal undertakings contained in the declaration of 31st March, 1909*, the Royal Serbian Government has done nothing to repress these movements. It has permitted the criminal machinations of various societies and associations directed against the Monarchy and has tolerated unrestrained language on the part of the press, the glorification of the perpetrators of outrages, and the participation of officers and functionaries in subversive agitation. [...]
>
> This *culpable tolerance* of the Royal Serbian Government has not ceased at the moment when the events of the 28th June last proved its fatal consequence to the whole world. [...]
>
> The above-mentioned results of the magisterial investigation do not permit the Austro-Hungarian Government to pursue any longer the attitude of expectant forbearance which they have maintained for years in face of the machinations hatched in Belgrade, and thence propagated in the territories of the Monarchy. The results, on the contrary, impose on the them the *duty* of putting an end to the intrigues which form a perpetual menace to the tranquillity of the Monarchy.[110]

As can be seen, Austria-Hungary was threatening war based on the Serbian authorities strongly suspected unwillingness to control and supress anti-Austrian movements. The ultimatum presents this as a

108 'M. Yov. M. Yovanovitch, Minister at Vienna, to M. N. Pashitch, Prime Minister and Minister for Foreign Affairs, Vienna, 17/30 June 1914', doc. no 5 in ibid., p. 371.

109 'M. N. Pashitch, Prime Minister and Minister for Foreign Affairs, to all Serbian Royal Legations abroad, Belgrade, 18 June/1 July 1914', doc. no 8 in ibid., p. 373.

110 'Austrian War Ultimatum to Serbia, Vienna, 23 July 1914', doc. no 4 in ibid., pp. 4–5. Emphasis added.

wrongdoing, not just as a general matter but as a result of the 1909 declaration. Forced on Serbia following the annexation of Bosnia-and-Herzegovina, the declaration indeed provided that:

> Serbia, conforming to the advice of the powers agrees to renounce the attitude of protest and opposition which she has taken since the month of October of last year. She agrees to modify the line of her political conduct in regard to Austria-Hungary and to live in the future on good terms with it. In conformity with this declaration [...] [s]he will disband the volunteer bodies and will prevent the formation of irregular bands upon her territory.[111]

In order for Serbia to avert war and to show good will in the fulfilment of its obligations, Austria-Hungary made 11 requests : (i) that the Serbian government publish on the front page of its 'Official Journal' a formal condemnation of anti-Austrian propaganda and official involvement therein; (ii) that it supress any publication which incited hatred of the Austro-Hungarian Monarchy; (iii) that it dissolve *Narodna Obrana* and other societies immediately; (iv) that it eliminate anti-Austrian propaganda from public education; (v) that it remove any officer or public official guilty of conducting anti-Austria propaganda from office; (vi) that it accept the collaboration of Austro-Hungarian representatives for the suppression of subversive movements; (vii) that it take judicial action against the accessories of the June 28 plot and accept the participation of Austro-Hungarian delegates in the process; (viii) that it arrest Major Voija Tankositch and Milan Ciganovitch whose involvement in the plot had been established by the imperial investigation; (ix) that it prevent the cooperation of Serbian official to illicit traffic of arms and explosives; (x) that it furnish explanations regarding the high officials that had expressed hostility towards the Empire after the June 28 events; and finally, (xi) that it notify the Austro-Hungarian government of the execution of these measures without delays.[112] Serbia was given until the 25 July 6 p.m. to respond.

After consulting with Russia, its ally, Serbia answered on the 25th at 5.45 p.m.[113] It accepted all the terms with the exception of the

[111] 'Declaration of the Serbian Government recognizing the fait accompli regarding Bosnia addressed to the Austro-Hungarian Government, Vienna, 31 March 1909', doc. no 43 in Snezana Trifunovska (ed.), *Yugoslavia Through Documents From its Creation to its Dissolution* (Martinus Nijhoff, 1994), p. 113.

[112] 'Austrian War Ultimatum to Serbia, Vienna, 23 July 1914', doc. no 4 in FO, Collected Diplomatic Documents, pp. 6–8.

[113] 'M. N. Pashitch, Prime Minister and Minister for Foreign Affairs, to all Serbian Royal Legations abroad, Belgrade, 12/25 July 1914', doc. no 41 in ibid., p. 390.

participation of Austro-Hungarian delegates to the inquiry as this, the Serbian authorities claimed, would be a 'violation of the Constitution and of the law of criminal procedure'.[114] With the weight of the Russian Empire behind it, Belgrade trusted that, if Vienna sincerely wished to avoid war, it would regard the Serbian reply as sufficiently conciliatory. The Serbs even suggested the dispute be submitted to the 'International Tribunal at The Hague' shall Austria-Hungary not deem their answer satisfactory.[115] Vienna did not react to this suggestion and immediately broke diplomatic relations. On the 28th, it sent a further telegram to notify that:

> The Imperial and Royal government are themselves compelled to see to the *safeguarding of their rights and interests*, and with this object, to have recourse to the force of arms. Austria-Hungary consequently considers herself henceforward in a state of war with Serbia.[116]

This declaration would set in motion the complex game of alliances established since the end of the nineteenth century leading to the general conflagration that we know.

On 30 July 1914, Russia mobilised its troops to support its ally, and refused to comply to the Austro-Hungarian and German demand of withdrawal. On 1 August, Germany declared war on Russia:

> In consequence of this threatening step, [. . .], the German government was faced by a grave and imminent danger. If the German government had failed to guard against this peril they would have compromised the safety and the very existence of Germany. [. . .] His Majesty the Emperor, my august sovereign, accepts the challenge, and considers himself at war with Russia.[117]

Knowing that France was an ally of Russia, Germany also started mobilising troops to its western borders. On 2 August, in reaction, the French government did the same insisting, however, that 'mobilisation is not war'.[118] On the same day, the Germans asked Belgium, a neutral nation,

[114] 'Reply of the Serbian Government to Austro-Hungarian Note', doc. no 39 in ibid., p. 35.

[115] Ibid., p. 37.

[116] 'Count Leopold Berchtold, Austro-Hungarian Minister for Foreign Affairs, to M. N. Pashitch, Serbian Prime Minister and Minister for Foreign Affairs, Vienna, 15/28 July 1914', doc. no 45 in ibid., p. 392.

[117] 'Note presented by the German Ambassador at Saint Petersburg, 19 July/1 August 1914', doc. no 76 in ibid., p. 294.

[118] *'Le Président de la République, Raymond Poincaré et al., "A La Nation Française"', (2 August 1914) 209 Journal Officiel de la République Française 7054.*

for free passage. The German Minister at Brussels claimed that his government had received intelligence that France intended to march on Germany through Belgium. He expressed doubts that Belgium would be able to resist such an attack and argued that 'it [was] essential for the self-defence of Germany' that German troops be allowed to cross the border in order to anticipate the attack.[119] Belgium refused. It not only stated that this would 'violate Belgian territory' but would also be, owing to the Kingdom's neutrality, 'a violation of international law' that no strategic interest would be able to justify.[120] On the 3rd, Germany declared war on France invoking 'flagrantly hostile acts' committed by the French Army and the necessity for the Emperor to reply to these 'acts of aggression'.[121] On the 4th, it declared war on Belgium. On that same day, Brussels appealed to the guardian power of its neutrality, Great Britain, invoking the 1839 Treaty of London.[122] In response, London sought explanations with Berlin and asked that it not carry out this plan: 'His Majesty's Government are bound to protest against this violation of a treaty to which Germany is a party in common with themselves'.[123] Germany recognised without difficulty that was indeed a violation of international law, but argued that her right of self-defence overrode her obligations towards Belgium: 'we are in a state of legitimate self-defence, and necessity knows no law'.[124] In any case, the troops had already crossed the border. In reaction, Great Britain severed diplomatic relations with Germany and entered the war.[125]

Twenty-five more war declarations will rhythm the course of the Great War before the armistice was signed on 11 November 1918. Those

[119] 'Note presented by Herr von Below Saleske, German Minister at Brussels, to M. Davignon, Belgian Minister for Foreign Affairs, Brussels, 2 August 1914', doc. no 20 in FO, Collected Diplomatic Documents, p. 309.

[120] 'Note communicated by M. Davignon, Belgian Minister for Foreign Affairs, to Herr von Below Saleske, German Minister, Brussels, 3 August 1914', doc. no 22 in ibid., pp. 311–312.

[121] 'Letter handed by the German Ambassador to M. René Viviani, President of the Council, Minister for Foreign Affairs, during his farewell audience, Paris, 3 August 1914', doc. no 147 in ibid., p. 240.

[122] 'His Majesty the King of the Belgians to His Majesty King George, Brussels, 3 August 1914', doc. no 25 in ibid., p. 313.

[123] 'Sir Edward Grey to Sir E. Goschen, British Ambassador at Berlin, London, 4 August 1914', doc. no 153 in ibid., p. 107.

[124] 'Baron Beyens, Belgian Minister at Berlin, to M. Davignon, Belgian Minister for Foreign Affairs, Berlin, 4 August 1914', doc. no 35 in ibid., p. 317.

[125] 'Sir E. Goschen, British Ambassador in Berlin, to Sir Edward Grey, London, 8 August 1914', doc. no 160 in ibid., pp. 110–114.

mentioned in the course of this brief analysis nevertheless already give an overview of the tone and language used. All the parties involved justified their behaviours and international law was never very far: Austria-Hungary declared war on Serbia to protect its rights, which Serbia had violated by not abiding by its obligations under the 1909 declaration; Germany declared war on Russia, France and Belgium, invoking self-defence; and Great Britain sided with its allies of the Triple Entente as a result of Germany's violation of international law. Once again, this war was presented as a sanction of law. The German Empire's assertion that 'where there is necessity, there is no law' might appear to contradict this, but it does not fully. Of course, the case of Belgium was particular due its status as neutral guaranteed by a treaty to which Germany was also a party, meaning that Berlin's admission that it had violated international law may not be interpreted as a recognition that such acts of force were 'forbidden' under general customary law. Yet, two other elements likewise need to be emphasised: one, by referring to necessity, Germany was appealing to a concept on which the fundamental right to self-preservation was founded; and, two, even so, Germany seemed to be rather isolated in making such a bold statement.

* * *

Eric Hobsbawm has argued that the 'long nineteenth century' was characterised as a period of relative peace in Europe and exportation of violence in the 'semi-peripheries' and 'peripheries', especially around the turn of the century.[126] Still, some important conflicts between 'central' powers did take place over the period of time spanning from 1815 to 1914. The purpose of this chapter was to analyse some of these precedents in order to understand the nature of the arguments put forward by States when they resorted to armed force. More specifically, the aim was to see whether, as modern-day doctrine usually claims, legal justifications were not brought forward, or only as matter of diplomatic decency rather than legal obligation. With that objective in mind, five cases were studied: the Austrian intervention in Naples (1821–1822), the Crimean War (1853–1856), the Franco-Prussian War (1870–1871), the Spanish-American War of 1898, and finally, the Austrian war ultimatum to Serbia in July 1914. This brief incursion into the practice of justifying force, already allows to bring some nuance of to the traditional narrative

[126] Eric Hobsbawm, *The Age of Empire (1875–1914)* (Vintage Books 1987).

of indifference. In fact, although international law was not necessarily the prime consideration, direct or indirect references to *ius ad bellum* can be found in all five precedents.

In 1821 and 1898, for instance, the Austrian interference to in the Carbonari Revolt and the United States' actions in Cuba both provoked debates about the scope and limits of the right to resort to armed intervention. Austria claimed to have a right to intervene because the situation in the Kingdom of the Two-Sicilies threatened its interests and its security as a result of its presence in the north of Italy. The more liberal powers within the European Concert recognised this right but, in parallel, re-insisted that intervention was permissible when a threat was 'personal', immediate and direct. In other words, only an injured State could use force for the purpose for redressing and preventing a violation of international law, whether this violation resulted from an infringement of treaty obligations or of the said States' right to independence. Similarly, we saw that during the Spanish-American War, both belligerents developed thorough arguments in order to establish or deny the United States right to interfere in Cuba. The use of precedents, references to past arbitrations, and to international legal doctrine, was particularly striking. Clearly, such debates would not have taken place if these States did not somehow believe to be bound by some rules ring-fencing the use of force.

In the three other cases, the use of legal vernacular was maybe less evident. Still, law was far from absent. During the Crimean War, for example, France and Great Britain foremost referred to consideration of European equilibrium and balance of power to explain their decision to enter the war on Turkey's side. But these principles, it seems, were believed to have become part of the law of nations applicable between European powers, as they had been embedded in several treaties to which Russia was also a party. By annexing Vallachia and Moldova, Russia had violated these principles and committed an act of aggression. The Crimean War was a sanction of that violation and a course of action which, as a reminder, the Powers of the Concert deemed 'founded in law'.[127] Likewise, when France declared war on Prussia in 1870, it did so considering that its rights under international law had been violated. Not

[127] 'Protocol of Conference between Austria, France, Great Britain and Prussia, relative to the non-evacuation of the Danubian principalities by Russia, and the consequent participation of England and France in the war between Russia and Turkey, Vienna, 9 April 1854', in FO, BFSP 1853–1854, p. 83.

only was the choice of a Prussian prince for Spain throne a threat to its security, but a violation of the principle according to which Powers could veto the choice of a new sovereign when a European throne was vacant. Even the outburst of the World War I, an event that is often presented as the culmination of the States' unrestricted war prerogatives, was justified by reference to international law. As a matter of fact, Austria-Hungary declared war on Serbia as a result of the latter's alleged inability or unwillingness to fulfil its treaty obligations to repress 'terrorist' pan-Slavic movements that represented a threat to the security of the Empire.

In other words, in all these precedents, force was used as a sanction of law, i.e. to respond to a violation, or threat of violation, of the intervening State's rights. It is also interesting to note how, in all five cases, resort to arms was ultimately presented as a matter of security, of protecting a State's existence within its current borders, even though the treat had not technically reached those borders yet. Self-preservation could be used preventively, but also 'extraterritorially'. The two next chapters extend the analysis of practice to uses of force outside 'European' spaces to see whether Powers also legally justified their actions these areas and, if so, whether the nature of the arguments they developed differed from those used in the 'centre'.

6

Justifying the Use of Force in the 'Semi-peripheries'

The second concentric zone, known as the 'semi-peripheries', was composed by what Lorimer called 'barbarous humanity' and extended to those States 'inferior in quality' but not 'in quantity'.[1] 'Quality', in Lorimer's framework, referred to wealth, culture and morality (to some extent meaning religion); while 'quantity' referred to the size of the population and territory.[2] Western international lawyers deemed European culture and mores intrinsically superior because of their 'attainment in the arts, and science, and commerce, as well as in policy and government'.[3] Yet, because of their size and power, States such as Turkey, Persia, Siam, China and Japan could not be completely excluded from the international system. They were sovereign nations in the sense that they had a definable territory which they were able to defend and on which they could exercise durable authority. But the 'inferiority' of their culture, meant that they could not be treated on a equal footing with the 'West'. For nineteenth-century writers, the full application of international law indeed required the existence 'common legal conscience' – i.e., similar legal cultures, traditions and institutions.[4] Such similarities did not exist with the countries of the near and far east. They therefore enjoyed some rights, but not all of them.

Lorimer argued that they enjoyed 'partial political recognition': they were recognised as sovereign States with an international legal personality (i.e. capacity to have right and obligations under international law),

[1] James Lorimer, *The Institutes of the Law of Nations. A Treatise of the Jural Relations of Separate Political Communities*, 2 vols. (W. Blackwood and Sons, 1883), vol.1, p. 101.
[2] Ibid., vol.1, p. 182 ff.
[3] John T. Abdy, *Kent's Commentaries on International Law* (Deighton and Sons, 1878), p. 8.
[4] Franz von Holtzendorff, *Introduction au droit des gens. Recherches philosophiques, historiques et bibliographiques* (Verlagsanstalt und Druckerei A.-G., 1889) 10. See also Louis Renault, *Introduction à l'étude du droit international* (L. Larose, 1879) 20; Henry Bonfils, *Manuel de droit international public* (Arthur Rousseau, 1894), p. 22.

but this recognition did not extend to their internal legal systems.[5] Concretely, this meant that their domestic legal acts were not considered as having any authority in the domestic legal systems of the 'civilised' world. They could not, for instance, seek the extra-territorial application of their legislation or execution of their judicial decisions, and neither could they hope to prosecute nationals of western State before their own courts and tribunals. This was the object of the 'capitulation' or 'unequal' treaties through which 'civilised' States sought to secure special treatment and privileges as well as the creation of specialised jurisdictions for their citizens present in those countries.[6] For the rest, 'semi-peripheral' States could enter into treaty relations with 'civilised humanity' and were believed to beneficiate from the three fundamental rights inherent to statehood: independence, equality and self-preservation.[7] It follows that the principle of non-intervention was applicable in their relations with the 'Europeans', even though unequal treaties gave the Powers many opportunities to interfere in the affairs of those States supposedly to protect the rights and interests of their nationals. This point was so clear that, in 1879, the IDI decided to change the topic of the 4th Commission from the '*Application aux nations orientales du droit des gens coutumier de l'Europe*' [Application of the customary law of nations to Oriental nations] to the examination of the reforms Oriental States should carry out in order to be granted 'plenary political recognition'.[8] Another way for a State of the semi-periphery to 'jump' category was to be formally accepted into the 'family of civilised nations'. This is what happened with Turkey following the Crimean War in 1856. Article 7 of the Treaty of Paris indeed provided that the European Monarchs 'declare the Sublime Porte admitted to participate in the advantages of Public Law and system

[5] James Lorimer, The Institutes of the Law of Nations, vol. 1, p. 217.

[6] On 'unequal treaties', see, e.g., Matthew Craven, 'What Happened to Unequal Treaties? The Continuities of Informal Empire' (2005) 74 *Nordic Journal of International Law* 335–382.

[7] Renault, Introduction, p. 21; Bonfils, *Manuel*, p. 20; Alessandro Paternostro, 'La révision des traités avec le Japon au point de vue du droit international' (1891) 23 *Revue de droit international et de législation comparée* 5–29 and 176–203; Fyodor Martens, *Traité de droit international*, 3 vols. (Librairie Marescq, 1883), vol. 1, p. 239.

[8] The full name of the 4th Commission became '*Application aux nations orientales du droit des gens coutumier de l'Europe - Examiner quelles réformes sont désirables dans les institutions judiciaires actuellement en vigueur dans les pays de l'Orient, par rapport aux procès dans lesquels un Européen ou un Américain est engagé*', see IDI, 'Notices et notes diverses, Session 1879' (1880) 12 *Revue de droit international et de législation comparée* 98–99.

of Europe'. The practical impact of this recognition was, however, rather limited: the European powers continued to interfere in the Christian affairs of the Porte and the capitulation system only abolished by the Treaty of Lausanne in 1923.[9]

Von Bernstorff argues that the justifications used by the Powers to legitimise their warring enterprises in these areas were different from the ones they employed against each other, especially towards the end of the nineteenth century. He seems to contend that, in the context of colonial expansion, the 'semi-peripheries' served as a sort of testing ground for justifications based on a broader understanding of self-preservation. Interventions were carried out not only in case of threat to the actual existence of a State, but also to its more general interests, those of its citizens and the general equilibrium of the international system.[10] A couple of precedents involving the use of armed force in the 'semi-peripheries' (the Christie Question, the Batsch Affair and the United States occupation of Veracruz) have already been briefly examined in the first part of this book.[11] The pages that follow add four new cases to this analysis: the European intervention in the Greek War of Independence in 1827 (Section 6.1), the French expedition to Lebanon and Syria of 1860 (Section 6.2), the multilateral intervention in China to repress the Boxer Revolt in 1901 (Section 6.3), and the application of the Monroe doctrine (1823) and Roosevelt Corollary (1904) by the United States in Nicaragua in 1909-1912 (Section 6.4). Although not, strictly speaking a precedent, the Monroe Doctrine and the Roosevelt corollary offer some interesting insights into the practice of using force in the Latin American 'semi-periphery'. We will see that Powers, once again, generally sought to legally window-dress their actions, and the discourses developed do not seem to point towards the existence of substantial differences in the nature of the arguments developed in comparison to the 'centre', nor between the beginning and end of the nineteenth century.

[9] Art. 28, Treaty of Peace with Turkey, Lausanne on 24 July 1923, in force 6 August 1924.

[10] The distinction introduced by von Bernstorff is more precisely between 'ontology-related justification' (when the existence of the State as such is directly threatened) and 'order-relations justifications'. See 'The Use of Force in International Law before World War I: On Imperial Order and the Ontology of the Nations States' (2018) 29 *European Journal of International Law* 233–260.

[11] See above (Section 1.2).

6.1 The European Intervention in the Greek War of Independence (1827)

The European intervention during the Greek War of Independence was often mentioned by nineteenth-century literature when discussing the permissibility of solicited intervention in civil wars and intervention on humanitarian grounds. This intervention, in fact, is sometimes presented as the first instance of humanitarian intervention in modern history.[12] As such it has often been used by 1960s and 1970s literature as proof of the existence of a unilateral right of humanitarian intervention.[13] Strongly opposing this view, Ian Brownlie insists that qualifying this intervention as 'humanitarian' is 'ex post factoism' because the 'governments of the time did not use a legal justification'.[14] Although the status under which humanitarian motives were invoked by the intervening powers can indeed appear doubtful, we shall nonetheless see that Great Britain, France and Russia did bring legal justifications forward to explain their action.

According to Greek national history, the revolution against Ottoman rule started on 25 March 1821, when the bishop of Patras, with the help of 1500 peasants, repelled the attack of 60 Turkish riders that had come to arrest him.[15] The late eighteenth and early nineteenth centuries had seen the birth of different nationalist movements across the Greek provinces of the Ottoman Empire. The Greek independentists were part of these movements which the conservative Powers of the Holy Alliance

[12] See, e.g. Davide Rodogno, *Against Massacre. Humanitarian Intervention in The Ottoman Empire, 1815–1914* (Princeton University Press, 2012), p. 63; Simon Chesterman, *Just War or Just Peace? Humanitarian Intervention and International Law* (Oxford University Press, 2002), p. 28.

[13] See Thomas M. Franck and Nigel S. Rodley, 'After Bangladesh: The Law of Humanitarian Intervention by Military Force' (1973) 67 *American Journal of International Law* 275–305; Richard B. Lillich, 'Humaniatrian Intervention: A Reply to Ian Brownlie and a Plea for a Constructive Alternative', *in* John Norton Moore (ed.), *Law and Civil War in the Modern World* (The Johns Hopkins University Press, 1974), pp. 229–251; Jean-Pierre L. Fonteyne, 'The Customary International Law Doctrine of Humanitarian Intervention: Its Current Validity under the U.N. Charter' (1973–1974) 4 *California Western International Law Journal* 203–270; Thomas E. Behuniak (Capt.), 'The Law of Unilateral Humanitarian Intervention by Armed Force: A Legal Survey' (1978) 79 *Military Law Review* 157–191.

[14] Ian Brownlie, 'Humanitarian Intervention', in John Norton Moore (ed.), *Law and Civil War in the Modern World* (Johns Hopkins University Press, 1974), p. 220.

[15] This romanticised account is notably the result of the work of François Pouqueville in *Histoire de la régénération de la Grèce*, 4 vols. (Firmin Didot et frères, fils et cie., 1843), vol. 3, pp. 67–68.

had vowed to combat at the Congress of Troppau and Laybach.[16] It is thus without surprise that, despite the Greeks best effort to obtain their support, the Europeans initially reacted with suspicion. Even their co-religionist and protector of Orthodox Christianity, Tsar Alexander I, did not hesitate to consider the Greek revolt as a rebellion against the rightful and legitimate authority of the Sultan.[17]

Reports of ferocious warfare and gruesome massacres, greatly affecting western public opinion, led some Powers to slowly revise their position. The execution of the Patriarch of Constantinople in the summer of 1821, the massacre of Chios in April 1822, the siege of Missolonghi in 1824, and the calling by the Ottomans of their Egyptian vassal, Ibrahim Pasha, to crush the rebellion in Morea, in particular, provoked strong commotion and philhellenic sympathies in Europe.[18] Rumours spread of a 'barbarisation plan' consisting in systematically displacing or enslaving the population of Morea to replace it with Muslim settlers.[19] For Russia, whose relations with the Ottoman Empire was already strained by several other disputes, inaction was becoming an issue.[20] Dreading a unilateral action by Saint Petersburg, Great Britain drew closer to the new Tsar, Nicholas I, and in 1826 the two nations signed a protocol foreseeing an intervention in Greece.[21] A year later, France joined the Alliance and a new treaty was signed in London on 6 July 1827.[22] Through this treaty, the Powers agreed to offer their mediation to the Greeks and the Sublime

[16] See above (Section 5.1).

[17] Rodogno, Against Massacre, pp. 64–65.

[18] In addition to 'Scène du massacres de Chios' (1824) by Eugène Delacroix, the French poet Victor Hugo wrote a famous poem entitled 'Les têtes du Sérail' as a tribute to the events in Missolonghi in *Les Orientales* (1829). For other examples, see Rodogno, Against Massacre, pp. 72–78.

[19] According to historian John A. Marriott, Ibrahim Pasha was nicknamed the 'exterminator of infidels', in *The Eastern Question. A Historical Study in European Diplomacy* (Clarendon Press, 1917), p. 185.

[20] Among these disputes were questions of demarcation of several branches of the Danube, the refusal of the Porte to recognize the voluntary entry of Abkhazia and Georgia into the Russian Empire, and of the help that the Sultan continued to provide to Muslim rebels fighting Russian domination in the Northern Caucasus. See Francis R. Bridge and Roger Bullen, *The Great Powers and the European State System, 1814–1914* (2nd ed., Pearson Longman, 2005), p. 51.

[21] Protocol relative to the Affairs of Greece, signed in Saint Petersburg, 23 March 1826.

[22] Treaty for the Pacification of Greece, signed between his Majesty, the Most Cristian King, and the Emperor of all Russias, London, 6 July 1827, available in Lady Bourchier (ed.), *Memoir of the Life of Admiral Sir Edward Codrington*, 2 vols. (Longmans Greens & Co., 1873) vol. 1, p. 502.

Porte. An additional and secret article, however, specified that shall the Sultan refuse, Great Britain, Russia and France would establish a pacific blockade around the coasts of Morea in order to intercept military supplies sent from Egypt. The Sultan, Mahmud II, refused the Powers' offer for mediation and the latter promptly sent their ships to the Ionian Sea. In October 1827, the European blockade would inadvertently result in the famous Battle of Navarino, during which the entirety of the Ottoman fleet was destroyed and to occupation by French 'peacekeeping' troops until 1831.

The preamble of the Treaty of London and the diplomatic correspondence that preceded the adoption of this treaty give us some insight into the justifications put forward by the Powers to justify their intervention. Justifications were essentially threefold: first, humanitarian considerations; second, self-preservation; and third, the request for mediation received by the Greek insurgents. The legal status of these arguments, however, differed.

Doctrine favourable to humanitarian intervention has sometimes claimed that the presence of humanitarian considerations in the preamble of the Treaty of London proved that such interventions were legally admissible. Gustave Rolin-Jaquemyns, for instance, argued that through this treaty 'the Powers were not recognising a fact, but dictating a rule'.[23] Along the same lines, Henry Wheaton insisted that this agreement was the 'illustration of the principles of international law authorising interference [...] where the general interests of humanity are infringed'.[24] The preamble stated that the Powers were 'penetrated with the necessity of putting an end to this sanguinary struggle' and 'animated with the desire of putting a stop to the effusion of blood'.[25] At the same time, however, the Powers did not speak of a right of intervention on grounds of humanity.

The negotiations that preceded the adoption of the Protocol of Saint Petersburg and the Treaty of London, do not help clarify the status of the humanitarian argument. The correspondence between London, Saint Petersburg and Paris in 1826 and 1827 shows that the powers were more preoccupied with the form the intervention should take rather than by its

[23] Gustave Rolin-Jaequemyns, 'Le droit international et la phase actuelle de la question d'Orient' (1876) 8 *Revue de droit international et de législation comparée* 507.

[24] Henry Wheaton, *Elements of International Law*, 2 vols. (Carey, Lea & Blanchard, 1836), vol. 1, p. 95.

[25] Pars. 1–2, Preamble, Treaty for the Pacification of Greece.

justification.[26] At most, in a letter to the Russian ambassador, Foreign Secretary George Canning explained that he did not believe the Ottomans turning down mediation would 'giv[e] a *right of war* against the Porte'.[27] But he did feel that:

> the continuance of a contest so ferocious in its details, and so hopeless of termination, and leading to excesses of piracy and plunder so intolerable to civilized Europe, to be an evil of so extraordinary a character, as to *justify extraordinary interposition*; and to *render lawful any expedient short of positive hostility* for impressing upon the recusant party the necessity of reasonable accommodation.[28]

The legal nature of Canning's remarks are here quite evident: he speaks of a 'right' to war and of the 'lawfulness' of resort to measures short of war. Moreover, the extracts above show that, according to Great Britain, it was the injuries the Powers were enduring as a result of the civil war that gave them the right of interference.[29] The preamble to the Treaty of London indeed further stated that this situation 'daily *causes fresh impediments to the commerce of the States of Europe, and gives opportunity for acts of piracy which not only expose the subjects of the high contracting parties to grievous losses, but also renders necessary measures which are burthensome for their observation and suppression*'.[30] The intervention was, therefore, also and foremost presented as a matter of self-preservation of the rights of the three European Courts.

Mention should also briefly be made of the request for mediation the Powers had received from the Greek insurgents. The preamble referred to

[26] Charles W. Crawley, *The Question of Greek Independence. A Study of British Policy in the Near East, 1821–1833* (Howard Fertig, 1973), pp. 74–75.

[27] 'Letter from George Canning to Prince Lieven, 4 September 1826', in Augustus Granville Stapleton, *The Political Life of Right Honourable Georges Canning*, 3 vols. (Longman, Rees, Orme, Brown and Green, 1831), vol. 3, p. 263. Emphasis added.

[28] ibidem. Emphasis added.

[29] In this sense, see Chesterman, *Just War or Just Peace?*, p. 29. See also Martha Finnemore, 'Constructing Norms of Humanitarian Intervention', in Peter Katzenstein (ed.), *The Culture of National Security: Norms and Identities in World Politics* (Columbia University Press, 1996), p. 163; Francis Kofi Abiew, *The Evolution of the Doctrine and Practice of Humanitarian Intervention* (Kluwer Law International, 1999), p. 49; Eliana Augusti, 'L'intervento europeo in Oriente nel XIX secolo: storia contesa di un istituto controverso', in Luigi Nuzzo and Milos Vec (eds.), *Constructing International Law: the Birth of a Discipline* (Klosterman, 2012), p. 289; Katia Boustany, 'Intervention humanitaire et intervention d'humanité: évolution ou mutation en Droit international?' (1979) 8 *Revue québécoise de droit international* 103–111.

[30] Par. 1, Preamble, Treaty for the Pacification of Greece. Emphasis added.

this invitation: 'having moreover received from the Greeks an earnest invitation to interpose their mediation with Ottoman Porte'.[31] Sticking to a textual interpretation, however, this solicitation justified the offer for mediation but not coercive intervention as such.

It is equally interesting to have a look at the reactions the Treaty of London and the establishment of the blockade in August 1827 provoked on the part of the Ottoman Empire and third States. Prussia and Austria-Hungary had been invited to join the initiative. Both Courts refused not only because they did not believe this intervention to be timely, but also because they had doubts regarding its legality. Writing to his ambassador to Paris, Austrian Chancellor, Metternich, insisted that he 'shall *never* recognise' the principle according to which States could intervene in a civil war on the demand of insurgents.[32] This was a question, he added, 'neither more nor less of the foundations of the law of Nations recognized up to this hour. [...] oppressed authority *cannot* be rescued without *manifest violation of the independence of States*'.[33] In a letter to Russia and Great Britain bearing the official Austrian response to their invitation, the Chancellor firmly stressed that:

> His Majesty, accustomed as he is to reply to such confidential overtures with absolute sincerity, cannot abstain from drawing attention to some points which do not agree with his feelings, and on which he will proceed to explain himself with the good faith and candour inseparable from his policy.
>
> These points concern the employment of coercive measures intended to force the *Grand-Seigneur* –
>
> To renounce his sovereignty over the Greek subjects of his Empire and to substitute a state of suzerainty; [...]
>
> The Emperor, in fact, *does not know how he can claim the right in either of these cases to employ such measures, or even to threaten the Porte.*[34]

In a later communication, he would further add that 'we will never violate what we feel to be principles',[35] and that Austria's 'isolation in

[31] Par. 2, Preamble.

[32] Quoted in Harold Temperley, *The Foreign Policy of Canning 1822–1827. England, the Neo-Holy Alliance, and the New World Order* (G. Bell and Sons, 1925), p. 361. Emphasis in the original.

[33] Quoted in ibid., pp. 360–361. Emphasis added.

[34] 'Metternich to Tatistscheff and Wellesley, Vienna, 22 December 1826', in Richard Metternich (ed.), *Memoirs of Prince Metternich*, 5 vols. (Richard Bentley and son, 1881), vol. 4, pp. 339–340. Emphasis in added.

[35] 'Metternich to Esterhazy, Vienna, 14 February 1827', in ibid., p. 360. Emphasis added.

the affair arises solely from the invincible repugnance of our august master to violate what he regards as a *incontestable principle of law*'.[36]

The Ottoman Empire's reaction was analogous. In a manifesto dated 9 June 1827, that is to say, while the Treaty was being negotiated, the Sultan warned the Powers of the negative effect of the foreseen intervention:

> The Greek affair is an internal affair of the Sublime Porte, [. . .] it is for the Sublime Porte alone to take care of it; [. . .] henceforth *no Power should interfere in this affair, and if anyone should do so, he should be asked for a reason, in the interest of the preservation of the rights of Governments, and the Laws of Nations.*[37]

The Ottoman Empire thus unequivocally reminded the Powers of their duties under the law of nations. Once again, the language used by the Turks was the language of law: 'must not', 'he should be asked for a reason', the 'rights of Governments', or yet the explicit reference to the 'laws of nations'.

As mentioned above, the establishment of the pacific blockade would result in the famous battle of Navarino, during which the totally the Ottoman fleet present in the harbour was destroyed. This event confused the European Courts and the Porte as to whether a state of war now existed between them. The Turkish government indeed felt that 'the three Power having thus openly violate the treaties and declared war, the Sublime Porte had the *right* to retaliate'.[38] The situation diffused, but war would eventually break out between the Ottoman Empire and Russia. In reaction to Navarino, Sultan Mahmud II denounced the Convention of Akkerman signed with Russia on 7 October 1826, which granted Saint Petersburg a right of inspection over the treatment by the Porte of its Christian subjects.[39] The Porte explained that it had agreed to sign the Convention only with the intention of breaking it and,

[36] 'Metternich to Ottenfels in Constantinople, Vienna, 3 October 1827', in ibid., p. 403. Translation by the author.

[37] 'Manifesto of the Sublime Porte declining the Pacification with the Greeks proposed by the Mediating Powers, 9 June 1827', in FO, *British and Foreign State Papers 1826–1827* (Harrison and sons, 1828), vol. 14, pp. 1045–1046. Emphasis added. Translation by the author.

[38] 'Hatti Shérif ou proclamation adressée le 18 décembre 1827 aux ayants d'Europe et d'Asie', available in Charles L. Lesur, *Annuaire historique universel pour l'année 1827* (Fantin, 1828), Appendice, p. 119.

[39] Convention explicative et complémentaire du traité de Bucarest de 1812, signed in Akkerman, 25 September/7 October 1826, available in Gabriel Noradounghian, *Recueil*

additionally, called all Muslims to take arms against their sworn enemy: Russia. Four months later, Tsar Nicholas I declared war on Turkey. The Russian war declaration exposed all the grounds for remonstrance the empire had against its southern neighbour, and underlined that it had done everything in its power to avoid direct confrontation:

> It was only after carefully weighting the full extent of their duties, which are based on imperative necessity, and only after having acquired the deepest conviction of the justice of our cause, that we have ordered our armies to march with the help of God against an enemy who violated the *law of nations* and the most sacred commitments. [...]
>
> The Monarch avoided until the most legitimate occasion to redress his own grievances [...]. Such *rights*, such *duties*, become even more positive when they follow an obvious moderation and the striking evidence of the most peaceful intentions.[40]

The war, in sum, found its justifications on the same grounds as the intervention: self-preservation. In 1827, it was about preserving the right to commerce (which nineteenth century authors believed to be a corollary of sovereignty). In 1828, it was about redressing the violations of Turkey's international obligations to Russia and defence against the hostile intentions of the Porte.

6.2 The French Expedition to Lebanon and Syria (1860)

Another European intervention would take place in the dominions of the Ottoman Empire some 30 years later. The configuration of the relations between Europe and Turkey at the time had changed: the Ottoman Empire had now been officially admitted into the 'family of European nations' through the 1856 Treaty of Paris. This status, as previously mentioned, was a fiction rather than a reality. The treaties of capitulation with Turkey granting the Europeans special privileges, in fact, were only abrogated in 1923. In practice, the Ottoman Empire was not yet fully considered on an equal footing. As the tripartite intervention of the European Powers in Greece, the French expedition to Lebanon and Syria is often considered as another example of nineteenth century

des actes internationaux de l'Empire ottoman, 3 vols. (Cotillon et F. Pichon, 1897–1900), vol. 2 pp. 116–121.

40 Manifeste de S.M. l'Empereur de Russie, Déclaration de guerre à la Turquie, Saint-Pétersburg, 14 April 1828, in L. Lesur, Annuaire historique 1828, Appendice, pp. 76 and 78. Emphasis added. Translation by the author.

humanitarian intervention.[41] Once again this interpretation has been challenged, this time not because States supposedly did not bring any legal justifications for their actions but because the intervention was carried out with the consent of Sultan Abdülmecid I.[42] The Porte, in fact, was a party to the Protocol of Paris of 3 August 1860 enacting the decision to allow France to send 12.000 men to restore peace and order in the Levant.[43] That being said, it had not been easy for Paris to obtain the assent of the other Powers and of the Porte to this mission.

This intervention found its roots in the massacres and plunder of the Maronites by the Druzes throughout the spring and summer of 1860. France had a special relation with the Christian Maronites and, in fact, was even considered as their protector. Having fought alongside Godefroy de Bouillon during the first Crusade, King Louis IX had apparently declared them 'to be part of the French nation, because their friendship for the French people resembles the friendship that Frenchmen have for each other'.[44] The Maronites were also France's main partners in the silk trade, an industry that was particularly important to the French economy.[45] Paris was 'bound' to react. But it was not willing to act alone. Napoléon III recent military involvement in the Italian *Risorgimento* against Austria as well as the annexation of Nice and Savoy, indeed, meant he now had the proceed with caution *vis-à-vis*

41 See Ellery C. Stowell, *Intervention in International Law* (John Byrne & Co., 1921), p. 63; Stephen Kloepfer, 'The Syrian Crisis, 1860–1861: A Case Study in Classic Humanitarian Intervention' (1985) 23 *Canadian Yearbook of International Law* 247; Itsvan Pogany, 'Humanitarian Intervention in International Law: The French Intervention in Syria Re-examined' (1986) 35 *International and Comparative Law Quarterly* 183; Abiew, The Evolution, p. 50.

42 See Pogany, 'Humanitarian Intervention in International Law', 189. See also Stowell, Intervention in International Law, pp. 64 and 66; Natalino Ronzitti, *Rescuing Nationals Abroad through Military Coercion and Intervention on Grounds of Humanity* (Martinus Nijhoff, 1985), p. 90. Some authors even discuss whether the expedition in Lebanon and Syria may, as a result, be considered as an 'intervention' altogether, see Kloepfer, 'The Syrian Crisis, 1860–1861', 255.

43 Art. 1 of the Protocols of Conference between Great Britain, Austria, France, Prussia, Russia and Turkey, respecting measures to be taken for the Pacification of Syria, Paris, 3 August 1860, available in FO, *British and Foreign State Papers, 1860–1861* (William Ridgway, 1868), vol. 51, p. 278.

44 Quoted *in* Hermance Dufaux, *Les Maronites et la France* (E. Dentu, 1860), p. 5. Translation by the author.

45 Leila Tarazi Fawaz, *An Occasion for War. Civil Conflict in Lebanon and Damascus in 1860* (University of California Press, 1994), p. 22; John P. Spagnolo, *France and Ottoman Lebanon, 1861–1914* (Ithaca Press, 1977), p. 20; Yves Ternon, *Empire Ottoman: la chute, le déclin, l'effacement* (Editions du Félin, 2002), p. 180; Rodogno, Against Massacre, p. 93.

the other Powers.[46] When the news of the massacres reached the European capitals, the French authorities initiated an intensive diplomatic ballet to convince the others of the necessity of an intervention. The French efforts can be broken down in two phases. In the first phase, Paris essentially pleaded for the establishment of a commission of inquiry to shed some light on the events. Following the massacres of Damascus in August 1860, during which two to three thousand Christians (including European consular personnel) lost their lives, Paris started advocating for a more aggressive approach.[47] We will focus on this second phase.

Echoes of the slaughter and plunder in Damascus reached Paris a round 17 July 1860.[48] Napoléon III and his Foreign Affairs Minister, Edouard Thouvenel, decided France would intervene by sending an expeditionary corps to restore order in Mount Lebanon.[49] Thouvenel believed that if he could get Great Britain's approval the other Powers would follow, and immediately contacted London to present the French position. The French insisted that 'in the presence of these massacres reproducing themselves from city to city and everywhere where Christian reside, it [was] impossible not to recognise that humanity command[ed] the Powers to act',[50] and that the Ottoman authorities had proved unable, if not unwilling, to address the situation accordingly. Yet, the French proposition was not to act against the Porte, but rather to 'come to its help'.[51] And, in fact, as Thouvenel acknowledge, such an operation '[could] only be performed in collaboration with the Porte'.[52]

The French initiative was met with contrasting reactions. Prussia, it seems, was quite uninvolved and subscribed with Thouvenel's suggestions without any particular difficulty.[53] It simply indicated at some point

[46] Spagnolo, France and Ottoman Lebanon, pp. 33–34.
[47] Rodogno, Against Massacre, p. 101; Gary J. Bass, *Freedom's Battle. The Origins of Humanitarian Interventions* (Vintage Books, 2008), p. 174.
[48] Dépêche télégraphique adressée par l'ambassadeur Constantinople au Ministère des Affaires étrangères, Pera, 19 juillet 1860, MAE, *CP de la Turquie*, vol. 345 (133CP/345).
[49] Fawaz, An Occasion for War, p. 110.
[50] 'Le Ministre des Affaires étrangères à M. le Comte de Persigny, Paris, 16 juillet 1860', in MAE, *Documents diplomatiques 1860* (Imprimerie Impériale, 1861), p. 198. Translation by the author.
[51] 'Le Ministre des Affaires étrangères à M. le Comte de Persigny, Paris, 17 juillet 1860', in ibid., p. 199.
[52] ibidem.
[53] Leila Fawaz moreover underlines that 'Prussia's national aspirations made it advantageous to support a supporter of nationalism, as Napoleon III', in An Occasion for War, p. 113.

in the negotiations of the Protocol that it felt 'the Porte did not seem to have been sufficiently consulted'.[54] Russia was very enthusiastic and probably least concerned with obtaining the consent of the Sultan. It perceived the case of Syria as a unique opportunity to set a precedent for an enhanced right of intervention for the Europeans in the affairs of the Sublime Porte.[55]

Russian enthusiasm was a cause of worry to Great Britain. For London, the consent of the Sultan was the *sine qua non* condition for intervention.[56] Of course, its motivation was political: not only did the British Empire have privileged trade relations with the Druzes, but they most of all feared the effect a 'unilateral' intervention would have on future Russian policies towards the Porte.[57] It was paramount that the principle and limits of the expedition be precisely defined in an international agreement. Beyond political considerations, however, Great Britain also presented this as a legal requirement: 'it is *necessary*', they wrote, '*to authorize* an expedition of European troops to Syria'.[58] France would thus need the approval of the four other Great Powers, but also that of Abdülmecid I. Even though the British government eventually agreed to the intervention, it explicitly admitted that it had done so 'with great reluctance'.[59] Its hesitations were not only about obtaining the consent of the Sultan but also in respect to the necessity of the intervention, which it believed was another condition of its legality. When the Foreign Office heard that a peace agreement had been signed between the Druzes and the Maronites, it jumped on this opportunity to temporalize and hopefully neutralise the French initiative. Writing to the ambassador to Paris, Lord Russell thus indicated that: 'it is on these accounts desirable that the *intervention should only be undertaken when the necessity is*

[54] 'Lord Bloomfield to Lord J. Russell, Berlin, 26 July 1860', in FO, *Correspondence relating to the affairs of Syria* (FO 406/10).

[55] 'Le cabinet de Pétersbourg adhère à nos propositions. Le Prince Gortschakov envoie à Constantinople des ordres en conséquence et à Kisselev l'autorisation de négocier la convention; il n'a aucune objection à ce que les troupes à envoyer en Syrie soient en majeure partie françaises', 'Dépêche télégraphique, Saint-Pétersbourg, 20 juillet 1860', MAE, *CP de la Russie* (112CP/221).

[56] 'Lord J. Russell to Earl Cowley, Foreign Office, 28 July 1860', no 46 (FO, 406/10).

[57] 'Persigny à Thouvenel, Londres, 18 Juillet 1860', MAE, *CP de l'Angleterre*, vol. 717 (8CP717).

[58] 'Lord Loftus to Lord Russell, Vienna, 26 July 1860', no 49, (FO, 406/10). Emphasis added.

[59] 'Lord Russell to Earl Cowley, Foreign Office, 23 July 1860', no 23, in ibid.

clearly proved, and that it *should cease as soon as that necessity shall no longer exist*'.[60]

London was not the only Court to insist on the pre-requisites of consent and necessity. Austria-Hungary's stand on the matter was also firm. The ambassador to Paris was asked to inform the French that Vienna would agree to intervention 'provided that the Porte give its full consent, and that the need for the participation of European troops to restore order be fully demonstrated'.[61] Failing this, a later correspondence indicated, 'the European intervention would [not] be completely justified'.[62] As can thus be seen, beyond political propriety, consent and necessity really appeared to be considered as conditions of legality.

This becomes even clearer when we examine the Ottoman reaction to the French design for intervention. Even though the Sultan somewhat squeamishly agreed to the intervention, he insisted until the very end that he did not need the help of the Europeans to restore order in Mount Lebanon. To show his good will, he had immediately dispatched the Minister for Foreign Affairs himself, Mehmed Fuad Pacha, to Mount Lebanon to restore order and punish the culprits.[63] But the Porte was put in front of a *fait accompli*: the Protocol had been negotiated with minimal consultation of the Sultan and he was now summoned, rather than invited, to the sign it. All the same, the Sublime Porte started by rejecting the intervention, and it took the French ambassador to Constantinople a lot of effort to subdue the Abdülmecid I.[64] The reports of the conference held for the signing of the Protocol held in Paris tell of how the Turkish envoy, once again, insisted that the intervention was not necessary. He also emphasised that this absence of necessity technically deprived the Powers of any right of intervention: 'His Excellency further observed, that he did not understand on what *ground* it was proposed to send foreign troops to Syria', there being already sufficient force from the Sultan's army to restore and maintain tranquillity in the country.[65] He also reminded the Powers that: 'the Sublime Porte does not see any necessity to resort to a measure susceptible of leading to great perils, and

[60] ibidem. Emphasis added.

[61] 'Count Rechberg to Prince Metternich, Vienna, 22 July 1860', inclosure 4 in no 37, in ibid. Emphasis added.

[62] ibidem.

[63] Spagnolo, France and Ottoman Lebanon, p. 35; Fawaz, An Occasion for War, p. 139.

[64] 'Lavalette à Thouvenel, Thérapia, 24 juillet 1860', Annexe no 1, MAE, *CP de la Turquie*, vol. 345 (133CP/345).

[65] 'Earl Cowley to Lord Russell, Paris, 26 July 1860', no 39 (FO 406/10). Emphasis added.

which, in any case, would constitute a sort of *infringement to the sovereignty* of his Imperial Majesty of Sultan'.[66] A few days later, however, the negotiations resumed and the Ottoman envoy was instructed to sign the Protocol provided that: (i) the number of soldiers to be deployed be precisely determined; (ii) the use and movement of these troops be coordinated with Mehmed Fuad Pacha; and (iii) that a time frame for the departure of the troops be fixed.[67] These requests respectively became Articles I, III and V of the Protocol signed in Paris on 3 August 1860.

The discourse developed and vernacular used by States on the occasion of the French expedition to Lebanon and Syria may appear less 'legal' than in the case of the intervention in the Greek war of independence. Despite the fact that the Ottoman Empire did refer to the principle of sovereignty, references to 'non-intervention' or to the 'law of nations' cannot, strictly speaking, be found. This may be because the intervention in Mount Lebanon was, all in all, less controversial. That being said, Great Britain's, Austria's and the Porte's insistence on necessity and consent, as well as Russia's hope that the intervention would set a precedent, are interesting. They, in fact, tend to show that these events and the discourses that accompanied them were believed to have influence the evolution of the positive law of nations.

6.3 The Intervention of the Powers in China as a result of the Boxer Uprising (1901)

The Boxer uprising was instigated by the Fists of Harmony and Justice, a secret society created in the mid-1880s opposed to the westernisation of China, to Westerners and to the feudal power of the Qing Dynasty.[68] The expansion of trade with the Far East had led to the establishment of numerous unequal treaties with China, often obtained through 'gunboat' diplomacy. According to Dong Wang there is no consensus about the number of unequal treaties that bound China to foreign powers; estimates run from 500 to 1000.[69] Unequal treaties provided unreciprocated

[66] 'M. Musurus to Lord Russell, London, 30 July 1860', no 55 (FO 406/10). Emphasis added.

[67] 'Dépêche télégraphique, Constantinople, 29 juillet 1860', (MAE133CP/345).

[68] On the Boxer Uprising, see Joseph W. Esherick, *The Origins of the Boxer Uprising* (University of California Press, 1987); Lanxin Xiang, *The Origins of the Boxer War: A Multinational Study* (Routledge, 2003).

[69] Dong Wang, *China's Unequal Treaties. Narrating National History* (Lexington Books, 2008), p. 2.

privileges to foreigners in China (such as tax exemptions, trade privileges, extraterritorial rights, establishment of Christian missionaries, etc.), but also the opening of ports to international commerce and the cession or lease of territories to western powers. China's first 'unequal' treaty is generally considered to have been the Nanjing Treaty, which put an end to the First Opium War in 1842 and ceded the territory of Hong-Kong to Great Britain.[70] Other treaties of cession and lease would follow suit, and historian Immanuel Hsu argues that in course of the nineteenth century China was de facto reduced to a 'semi-colonial' status.[71] Westerners developed their own subcultures within the ceded or leased territories, while Chinese were usually treated as second class citizens and submitted to foreign administration. This inevitably created resentment against westerners as well as against the Qing Dynasty, which was perceived as having been unable to resist external pressures.[72] It was this resentment that fuelled the creation of secret societies and militias, such as the Fists of Harmony and Justice.

The first action of some relevance against foreigners was the assassination of two German missionaries in the province of Shandong, just south of Peking, on All Saints' Day 1897. In its often said that the Germans were looking for a pretext to get their share of Chinese territory and that this episode, known of the Juye incident, gave them the excuse they needed.[73] The Kaiser was informed of the attack on November 6 and promptly requested the dispatch of warships to take possession of the Bay of Jiaozuo. This, he explicitly stated, was meant as a first measure of reprisal ('*Represaillen*') of which others would follow shall the Chinese authorities refuse to pay 'a high monetary compensation, as well as prosecute and punish the criminals'.[74] In a later communication, the

[70] Art. 3 of the Treaty of Peace, Friendship and Commerce between His Majesty the Queen of Great Britain and Ireland and the Emperor of China, Nanjing, 29 August 1842, available in William Frederick Mayer (ed.), *Treaties between the Empire of China and Foreign Powers* (4th ed., North China Herald Office, 1902), p. 1.

[71] Immanuel C. Y. Hsu, *The Rise of Modern China* (3rd. ed., Oxford University Press, 1990), p. 13.

[72] See ibid., p. 533. See also Maria Adele Carrai, *Sovereignty in China. A Genealogy of the Concept since 1840* (Cambridge University Press, 2019).

[73] Esherick, *The Origins of the Boxer Uprising*, p. 124.

[74] 'Kaiser Wilhelm an das Auswärtige Amt, Telegram, Neues Palais, den 6 November 1897', doc. no 3686 in Johannes Lepsius, Albrecht Mendelssohn-Bartholdy and Friedrich Thimme (eds.), *Die Grosse Politik der Europäischen Kabinette, 1871–1914*, 46 vols. (Deutsche Veragsgesellschaft für Politik und Geschichte, 1924), vol. 14, Part 1, p. 67.

German Foreign Affairs Minister, Berhnard von Bülow, would likewise explain that the purpose of the intervention was 'to attain full expiation for the murder of German and Catholic missionaries'.[75] Arguably, Berlin's intervention was rather precipitated: it was launched before a formal request for explanation and reparation had even been issued to the Chinese authorities. But although it felt that that Germany had 'acted arbitrarily', China was not in position to militarily engage the German troops or oppose the Kaiser's requests.[76] Its defeat during the Sino-Japanese War (1894–1895) had strained the country's economy and army, and the Emperor was already struggling to control domestic unrest. As reparation for the assassination of the two missionaries, the Qing government therefore agreed to rather humiliating terms: several high raking state officials from Shandong Province were dismissed, three catholic churches and new residences for the missionaries were built at the expense of the Chinese authorities, financial compensation was given to the attacked Catholic missions, and Germany was granted a 99-year lease over the deep-water port of Jiaozuo.[77] Joseph W. Esherick argues that, while the impact of the German intervention may seem less dramatic than one could have expected, the indirect effects were considerable.[78] The vexatory terms of the agreement, in fact, further weakened the Qing dynasty and nourished anti-western feelings.

It is in this context that support for those who came to be known as the 'Boxers' grew and that hostile actions against foreigners and Christians became ever more frequent. By 1900, the dowager Empress Cixi had moreover managed to turn the animosity of the rebels solely against foreigners, meaning that part of the Chinese authorities were now perceived as accomplices of these attacks. As a result of the unrest, many European nations already had squadrons posted along the coast to conduct punctual rescue missions and 'shows of force'. Guards were also sent to protect the legations in Peking. The records of diplomatic correspondence in the period spanning from January to June 1900 shows constant reports of violence, of murders and of the measures taken by

[75] Quoted in John S. Lowry, *Big Swords, Jesuits, and the Bondelswarts: Wilhelmine Imperialism, Overseas Resistance and German Political Catholicism* (Brill, 2015), p. 116.

[76] Esherick, The Origins of the Boxer Uprising, p. 129.

[77] The Kiachow Convention is available in Mayer (ed.), Treaties between the Empire of China and Foreign Powers, p. 280.

[78] Esherick, The Origins of the Boxer Uprising, p. 130.

the Powers to seek to protect their interests in China. On 4 January, for instance, news of the murder of a British missionary reached London.[79] Chinese authorities promptly offered their condolences and promised to find and punish the culprits.[80] The imperial government would issue several decree reminding the governors of the affected provinces of China's treaty obligations to offer protection to foreigners and not to interfere with the propagation of the Christian faith.[81] The British Prime Minister, the Marquess of Salisbury, nonetheless informed that, shall China fail to give satisfaction and continue its efforts to supress secret societies, 'it will be desirable to resort to naval action when other means of pressure are exhausted'.[82] New reports of murders and attacks continued to reach Europe and the Chinese authorities were perceived as less and less concerned with properly addressing the situation. Writing to the Prime Minister in June 1900, the British ambassador to Peking informed that the Chinese government admitted that it 'was reluctant to deal harshly with the movement which, owing to its anti-foreign character, was popular'.[83] He further indicated that he had informed the Chinese authorities that they 'would be held responsible by Her Majesty's Government for criminal apathy'[84] and that 'this failure to supress the Boxers was, [. . .], leading straight to foreign intervention'.[85] Intervention, in other words, would be the result of China's failure to meet its international obligations.

China, however, was in a delicate situation: caught between a threat of foreign intervention if it did not severely repress the Boxers, on the one side, and at risk of further aggravating the Qing Dynasty's already

[79] 'Sir C. MacDonald to Marquess of Salisbury, Peking, 4 January 1900', doc. no 1 in FO, *Correspondence Respecting the Disturbances in China (China no 1)* (Printed for HMSO by Harrison, 1901), p. 1.

[80] 'Sir C. MacDonald to Marquess of Salisbury, Peking, 5 January, 1900', doc. no 2 in ibidem.

[81] See 'Imperial Decree dated 5 January 1990', inclosure 2 to doc. no 5 in ibid., p. 5; 'Proclamation by the Governor-General of Chih'i, 21 February 1900', inclosure 3 to doc. no 32 in ibid., p. 19.

[82] 'The Marquess of Salisburry to Sir C. MacDonald, Foreign Office, 11 March 1900', doc. no 12 in ibid, p. 6.

[83] 'Sir C. MacDonald to Marquess of Salisbury, Peking, 5 June 1900', doc. no 75 in ibid., p. 36.

[84] 'Sir C. MacDonald to Marquess of Salisbury, Peking, 5 June 1900', doc. no 70 in ibid., p. 35.

[85] 'Sir C. MacDonald to Marquess of Salisbury, Peking, 5 June 1900', doc. no 75 in ibid., p. 36.

precarious position if it did, on the other. The Emperor, moreover, had lost control of part of its army to the Boxer cause. In this context, a particular incident at the Taku Fort, fortifications at the month of the Feiho river leading to Peking, spurred doubts as to whether a state of war now existed between China and the Powers. In the process of sending more guards to protect the legations in Peking, Chinese troops fired on the allied fleet. The emperor quickly contacted the Powers to inform them that the soldiers had acted against their instructions and seek reassurances that this incident would not be interpreted as an act of war.[86] The Allies agreed to assumed that 'the Chinese troops were [not] acting under the instructions of the Chinese government, but by compulsion of the Boxers, [and that] the Powers were [therefore] not in a state of war with China'.[87]

But the crisis truly reached its paroxysm when the Boxers entered Peking mid-June 1900. On 13 June, the Japanese chancellor and the German ambassador were murdered.[88] On the night of that same day, hundreds of converts and servants of foreigners were reported to have been killed and foreign property destroyed.[89] Reports of the first attacks on foreign legations reached the Powers on the 17th, and their siege by the Boxers and dissenting factions of the Chinese army began on the 20th.[90] Following these events, eight nations agreed to coordinate their efforts to rescue the legations. Throughout the month of July, Austria-Hungary, Germany, France, Italy, Russia, Japan, Great Britain and the United States collaborated to put a force of 20,000 men in place to march on Peking. The operation started on 4–5 August and the legations were liberated on the 15th.

The diplomatic correspondence between the Powers suggests that they did not hold Chinese authorities directly accountable for the attacks. They did, however and once again, feel that Peking had failed to fulfil its treaty and customary obligations to protect foreign citizens and that

[86] See 'Marquess of Salisbury to Count Scott, Foreign Office, 22 June 1900', doc. no 173 in ibid., p. 69.

[87] See 'Count Scott to the Marques of Salisbury, Saint Petersburg, 24 June 1900', doc. no 185 in ibid., p. 74.

[88] 'Consul Tratman to the Marquess of Salisburry, Cheffo, 1 July 1900', doc. no 228 in ibid., p. 87.

[89] 'Consul-General Warren to the Marquess of Salisbury, Shangae, 16 June 1900', doc. no 142 in ibid., p. 59.

[90] 'Rear-Adminral Bruce, at Taku, to Admiralty, despatched from Port Arhutr, 17 June 1900', doc. no 186 in ibid., p. 74.

this justified them into taking matters in their own hands. The Russians had thus already indicated that:

> 'the friendly counsels of the Russian Representative as well as those of the other Powers at Peking have failed. [. . .] The life and property of foreign subjects are in danger. [. . .] Consequently, it becomes imperative to take more effective measures to assure the safety of the Imperial Legation and of the Russian subjects residing in the country'.[91]

The Russians, as we can see, emphasised that the Powers had, first of all, sought to resolve the situation through friendly means and that it was the inability of the Chinese authorities to control the unrest that was now forcing them to take more assertive measures. This is not without recalling the warning of the British ambassador to the Emperor that the failure to supress the Boxers would lead to foreign intervention. For sure, there are no explicit references to international law in these extracts of diplomatic correspondence, but they do match the course of action recommended by the law of nations: the presence of an offence warranting the use of friendly measures and, in case those are not sufficient, of measure short of war. Arguably, the actions taken by the Allied Powers were consequently not only a matter of fact and politics, but a matter of law.

The German and the US positions reinforce this point. In response to a *note verbale* of the Chinese legation in Berlin regretting the degradation of the relations between the two countries, Count von Bülow answered that: 'the Chinese imperial Government have not made atonement for the outrageous murder of the Imperial Minister, and given the adequate guarantees that their conduct in the future will be in accordance with the *law of nations*'.[92] Likewise, in a letter to the Emperor dated 23 July 1900, President McKinley explained that:

> The purpose for which we landed troops in China was the rescue of our legation from grave danger and the protection of the lives and property of Americans who were sojourning in China in the enjoyment of *rights guaranteed them by treaty and by international law*. The same purposes are publicly declared by all the powers which have landed military forces in Your Majesty's Empire.[93]

[91] 'Count Moravieff to M. De Staal, Saint Petersburg, 3 (16) June 1900', doc. no 149 in ibid., p. 62.

[92] 'Response of Count von Bülow to the Chinese Note Verbale of 19 1900', inclosure to doc. no 78 in FO, *Correspondence Respecting the Disturbances in China (China no 3)* (printed for HMSO by Harrison, 1901), pp. 31–32. Emphasis added.

[93] 'The President to the Emperor of China, Washington, 23 July 1900', doc. no 6 in US Department of State, *Foreign Relations of the United States 1901. Appendix: Affairs in China* (Government Printing Office, 1902), p. 14. Emphasis added.

6.4 The Monroe Doctrine, the Roosevelt Corollary and the United States' Interventions in Nicaragua (1909–1912)

Latin American countries were not, technically speaking, part of the 'semi-peripheries'. As we indeed saw they were included by nineteenth century scholars into the category of 'civilised humanity', which, as a reminder, Lorimer stated to include the States of North and South America.[94] It has nevertheless been argued that with proclamation of the Monroe doctrine in 1823, followed by the Roosevelt corollary eighty years later, the United States had de facto 'established its own semi-periphery regime for Latin America'.[95] Nineteenth-century scholarship was also divided as to the nature and practical implications of the President James Monroe's annual message to the Congress in December 1823. This message was delivered in the context of the Latin American States wars of independence and the president, pointing to the fundamental differences between the political systems of Europe and that of America, insisted that:

> We owe it, therefore, to candor and to the amicable relations existing between the United States and those powers to declare that we should consider any attempt on their part to extend their system to any portion of this hemisphere as dangerous to our peace and safety. With the existing colonies or dependencies of any European power we have not interfered and shall not interfere, but with the Governments who have declared their independence and maintained it, and whose independence we have, on great consideration and on just principles, acknowledged, we could not view any interposition for the purpose of oppressing them, or controlling in any other manner their destiny, by any European power in any other light than as the manifestation of an unfriendly disposition toward the United States.[96]

Monroe was thus warning the European Powers against any attempt to reconquer lost territories in Central and South America. This declaration was looked upon with suspicion by European international lawyers who felt that, by the same token, the United States had just proclaimed their right to intervene in those same areas.[97] The scope of the Monroe

[94] Lorimer, The Institutes of the Law of Nations, pp. 101–102.

[95] von Bernstorff, 'The Use of Force in International Law before World War I', 250.

[96] 'Message of the President, Washington, 2 December 1823' (available at: https://millercenter.org/the-presidency/presidential-speeches/december-2-1823-seventh-annual-message-monroe-doctrine).

[97] See for e.g. Johann-Caspar Bluntschli, *Le droit international codifié* (Guillaumin et Cie., 1870), p. 254, footnote no 3; Theodor Woolsey, *Introduction to the Study of International*

Doctrine would later be extended by Theodore Roosevelt's address to Congress in December 1904. Roosevelt explained that the United States had no desires for territorial aggrandizement, but that is was in its interest that neighbouring nations should be 'stable, orderly and prosperous'. 'If nations', he continued,

> shows that it knows how to act with reasonable efficiency and decency in social and political matters, if it keeps order and pays its obligations, it need fear no interference from the United States. Chronic wrongdoing, or an impotence which results in a general loosening of the ties of civilized society, may in America, as elsewhere, ultimately require intervention by some civilized nation, and in the Western Hemisphere the adherence of the United States to the Monroe Doctrine may force the United States, however reluctantly, in flagrant cases of such wrongdoing or impotence, to the exercise of an international police power.[98]

At the time, the United States had already conducted several armed interventions in the rest of the Americas on similar basis (the intervention in Cuba in 1898 previously discussed being an example),[99] but as von Bernstorff underlines this policy was now presented as an official doctrine: a threat to the interests of the United States or of its citizens, was a threat to the security of the United States.[100]

The Monroe Doctrine and the Roosevelt corollary are interesting for the purpose of our argument in two respects. First, it shows that the United States' doctrine was not disconnected from legal considerations. It was a political doctrine, for sure, but a legal one as well. As von Bernstorff notes it was connected to one of the fundamental rights of State: self-preservation, which as reminder was the only one capable of pushing the two others (independence and equality) to the side.[101] This point was made clear by Elihu Root who, in addition to being a distinguished international lawyer and president of the *American Society for International Law*, was also Roosevelt's Secretary of War (1899–1904)

Law (2nd ed., Charles Scribner & Co., 1871), p. 68; Paul Pradier-Fodéré, *Traité de droit international public européen et américain suivant les progrès de la science et de la pratique contemporaine*, 9 vols. (Pedone-Lauriel, 1883–1894), vol. 1, p. 557; Henry Bonfils, *Manuel de droit international* (Arthur Rousseau, 1894), p. 157.

98 'Message of the President, Washington, 6 December 1904' in US Department of State, *Papers Relating to the Foreign Relations of the United States 1904* (Government Printing Office, 1905), p. XLI.

99 On American interventionism in Latin America see, e.g., Alan McPherson, *A Short History of US Interventions in Latin America and the Caribbean* (Wiley Blackwell, 2016).

100 von Bernstorff, 'The Use of Force in International Law before World War I', 251.

101 See above (Section 2.4), (Section 3.4) and (Section 4.4).

and then State secretary (1904–1909). In 1914, he indeed clearly indicated that: 'the [Monroe] Doctrine is not international law, but it rests upon the right to self-protection, and that right is recognised by international law'.[102] He further underlined that it was well admitted that this right could apply extraterritorially, that is 'beyond the territorial limits of the State exercising it'.[103] He gave several examples of such exercises, including by European Powers, such as the French opposition to the succession of a German prince to the throne of Spain, which led to the Franco-Prussian War of 1870 previously discussed;[104] the actions taken by the Europeans to prevent the expansion of Russia to the Mediterranean, which we saw was a key consideration in the outburst of the Crimean War of 1856;[105] or yet, the numerous interposition of the Courts into the 'Eastern question', of which the intervention during the Greek War of Independence also examined above is an example.[106] All these actions, he forcefully asserted, were applications of a principle of law: that a State has the right to resort to force to react to the wrongdoings of other States as a matter of preservation.

But Root's argument is also interesting in another respect. In insisting that the Monroe doctrine was merely the application of the principle of self-preservation, he was also denying that the United States had, in any way, created a sort of special regime for its interventions in Latin America. This is notably what he highlighted when writing that:

> If the Monroe Doctrine had never been declared or thought of, the sovereign rights of each American republic would have been limited by the equal sovereign rights of every other American republic, including the United States. The United States would have had a right to demand from every other American state observance of treaty obligations and of the rules of international law. It would have had the right to insist upon due protection for the lives and property of its citizens within the territory of every other American state, and upon the treatment of its citizens in that territory according to the rules of international law. The United States would have had the right as against every other American state to object to acts which the United States might deem injurious to its peace and

[102] Elihu Root, 'The Real Monroe Doctrine' (1914) 8 *American Journal of International Law* 423.

[103] ibidem.

[104] See above (Section 5.4).

[105] See above (Section 5.3).

[106] See above (Section 6.1).

> safety, just as it had the right to object to such acts as against any European Power, and just as all European and American Powers have the right to object to such acts as against one another. All these rights which the United States would have had as against other American states it has now. They are not in the slightest degree affected by the Monroe Doctrine. They exist now just as they would have existed if there had been no Monroe Doctrine. They are neither greater nor less because of that Doctrine. They are not rights of superiority; they are rights of equality. They are the rights which all equal independent states have as against one another.[107]

In sum, the manner in which the United States justified their uses of armed force in the Latin American 'semi-periphery' was consistent with general international law and, furthermore, not at deviance with the way it would justify it against Europeans or for that matter, with the way Europeans had justified it against each other. And, in fact, it was not uncommon for nineteenth-century doctrine to assert that the right to self-preservation extended to the protection of the 'social and economic conditions' of the State.[108] Moreover, the Sulphur Crisis of 1841 gave an example of the use of armed reprisals against a fellow State from the 'centre' (the Kingdom of the Two-Sicilies) for considerations purely connected to trade and economy.[109] It is true, however, that the 'gravity' of the British embargo can be said to be of a lesser extent than some of the measures carried out by Washington in Central and South America. Moreover, in Latin America, the United States had a pattern of justifying intervention on the ground of protecting their nationals that was scarcely encountered in the 'centre'. We, however, saw that a similar justification had been brought forth in the case of the Spanish-American War – i.e., a war opposing two powers from the 'centre'.[110]

As for the United States interventions in Latin America, the case of the occupation of Veracruz in the context of the Tampico affair was briefly examined in the first part of this book.[111] But let us have a quick look at on last precedent, with far-reaching economical stakes: the interventions during the Nicaraguan Civil War in 1909 and 1912.

[107] Root, 'The Real Monroe Doctrine', 436.

[108] See, e.g., William E. Hall, *A Treatise of International Law* (Clarendon Press, 1890), p. 283.

[109] See above (Section 1.2).

[110] See above (Section 5.5).

[111] See above (Section 1.2).

As Karl Bermann notes, after Mexico and Cuba, Nicaragua is the country in which the United States intervened most persistently.[112] The policy of the United States in this Central American State needs to be understood against the backdrop of the Powers' competition for drilling a commercial canal connecting the Atlantic and Pacific Oceans.[113] In the late nineteenth century, several projects for such a canal existed and not only in Panama, but also in Nicaragua. When Washington was granted a 99-year lease over the Panama Canal because of its support for Panama's secession from Colombia, it lost interest in building a new route through Nicaragua. José Santos Zelaya had until then welcomed foreign investments and tolerated some abuses of contracts by US companies, but he changed attitude and progressively turned to European Powers when the project of a Nicaragua Canal was shut down.[114] From then onwards, most of the policies of the United States in Central America would be directed towards protecting this investment and seeking to hinder the other Powers influence in the area.

Another issue for the United States was that Zelaya, now unsympathetic to US interests, was seeking to dominate Central American politics. They viewed him as a destabilising force in the area and this, again, was not just a problem of fact but a problem of law. As State Secretary Philander C. Knox explained to the Nicaraguan *Chargé* in Washington: 'it is notorious that President Zelaya has almost continuously kept Central America in tension or turmoil; that he has repeatedly and flagrantly violated the provisions of the conventions, and, [. . .] has sought to discredit those sacred international obligations'.[115] The State Secretary was referring to the 1907 Washington Conventions, a series of treaties negotiated for the purpose of promoting peace and stability in the Isthmus region.[116] To this first wrongdoing (which arguably affected neighbouring countries more directly than Washington), another issue was added: two American citizens had been arrested and executed on

[112] Karl Bermann, *Under the Big Stick. Nicaragua and the United States since 1848* (South End Press, 1986).

[113] McPherson, *A Short History of US Interventions*, pp. 55–56.

[114] Ibid., p. 62.

[115] 'The State Secretary to Nicaraguan Chargé, Washington, 1 December 1909', doc. no 422 in US Department of State, *Papers Relating to the Foreign Relations of the United States, with the Annual Message of the President Transmitted to Congress December 7, 1909* (Government Printing Office, 1914), pp. 455–456.

[116] See James Brown Scott, 'The Central American Peace Conference of 1907' (1908) 2 *American Journal of International Law* 121–143.

counts of having joined the rebellion and mined the San Juan River, and threats had been made on the US consulate in Managua. In light of these elements, Knox indicated that 'from every point of view it has evidently become difficult for the United States to further delay more active response to the appeals so long made, to its duty to its citizens, to its dignity, to Central America, and to civilization'.[117] Through this letter, the United States also severed diplomatic ties with Nicaragua and explained that the issue of reparations would be postponed until the establishment of a new government to which it would be capable of 'look [ing] for reparations for the Killing of Messrs. Canon and Grove, or, indeed for the protection which must be assured American citizens and interests in Nicaragua'.[118] In the meantime, several ships were dispatched to blockade the Port of San Juan del Norte, and Zelaya resigned from office to avoid invasion.[119] Interestingly, in his address to the parliament, the resigning President pointed to 'the hostile attitude of a powerful nation which, *against all right*, has intervened in our political affairs and publicly furnished the rebels with the aid which they had asked for'.[120]

Estrada seized power in Managua and the United States agreed to recognise the new government provided those responsible for the death of the two American citizens be duly prosecuted. Estrada's presidency, however, was contested and his position precarious. To safeguard American interests, Knox sent Thomas Dawson to secure an agreement (the Dawson Agreement) establishing a form of tutelage over the finances of the country. This was part of the United States' 'dollar diplomacy': offering loans to Central American countries based on the belief that financial stability would bring political stability and prevent the United States from having to engage into new military adventures on the territory of its southern neighbours.[121] President Howard Taft's policy did not yield the expected results. The liberals ousted from power were

[117] 'The State Secretary to Nicaraguan Chargé, Washington, 1 December 1909', doc. no 422 in US Department of State, Papers 1909, p. 456.

[118] ibidem.

[119] McPherson, A Short History of US Interventions, p. 63.

[120] 'Manisfesto of President Zelaya to the National Assembly, Ressigns Power to Deposit it in Whoever May be Named Thereby, 17 December 1909', inclosure 1 to doc. 426 in US Department of State, *Papers 1909*, p. 459. Emphasis added.

[121] Lester D. Langley, The Banana Wars: United States Intervention in the Caribbean, 1898–1934 (SR Books, 2002), pp. 60–61. See also Dana G. Munro, Intervention and Dollar Diplomacy in the Caribbean, 1900–1921 (Princeton University Press, 1964).

seeking to regain it, and dissentions within the conservative party moreover started to emerge. In May 1911, Estrada was forced out of the Presidency by Adolfo Diaz and, in July 1912, Diaz's Minister of War, Luis Mena, began his own revolt to seize power. In this context, to a request for assurances that he 'was willing and able to afford adequate protection to all private property of American citizens in Nicaragua',[122] Diaz replied that 'it was employing every available means to give such protection but that it regretted that, because of the necessity of using forces to put down armed disorders, it was unable for the present to comply with the Legation's requests' and required that the US government send forces.[123] Washington obliged and troops were sent to guard the legation and US interests in Nicaragua. Although this second intervention in the course of a little more than two years was conducted with the approval of Nicaragua's government, it still found its roots in the Monroe doctrine and Roosevelt corollary which, as we saw, the US government considered to be the simple application of the principle of self-preservation and, therefore, of the recognised exception to the principle of non-intervention.

* * *

It is sometimes believed that nineteenth-century international law did not apply to non-western entities, and that, in the context of colonial expansion and competition, European Powers flouted the law in their relations with 'non-white' and 'non-Christian' States. This chapter sought to analyse the Powers' practice of using and justifying force against 'semi-peripheral' States, in order to assess to what extent law was used to justify those actions and how these justifications might have differed from the ones used in the 'centre'. Four precedents were examined to that end: the European intervention in the Greek War of Independence in 1827, the French expedition to Lebanon and Syria in 1860, the Powers multilateral intervention during the Boxer Revolt in 1900, and, finally, the Monroe doctrine and Roosevelt corollary with a special focus on their application in Nicaragua (1909–1912).

122 'The Secretary of State to the President, Washington, 5 August 1912', doc. no 1438 in US Department of State, Papers Relating to the Foreign Relations of the United States, With the Annual Message of the President Transmitted to Congress December 3, 1912 (Government Printing Office, 1919), p. 1032.

123 ibidem.

The analysis shows that Powers usually endeavoured to develop legal arguments to justify their uses of armed force in the 'semi-peripheries'. In all four cases, as in the three precedents mentioned in the first part of book (i.e., the Christie Question, the Batsh Affair and the occupation of Veracruz), intervening Powers sought to demonstrate how the situation affected *their* rights. As in the 'centre', in sum, force was essentially resorted to by injured States to vindicate an alleged previous violation of law, i.e. as a matter of self-preservation. This suggests that resort to armed force in the 'semi-peripheries' relied on the same rationale as between members of the 'European family'.

Yet, although the Sulphur Crisis in 1841 might offer a counterexample, it has to be admitted that resort to armed force was rarely justified on the mere grounds of protecting commerce or nationals when it was used in the 'centre'. As we saw in the previous chapter, considerations of national security ('ontological justifications') were generally brought forth at a point of another, including for World War I. In the 'semi-peripheries', on the other hand, this was not the case. Nevertheless, it is unclear whether this allows to conclude that self-preservation was interpreted more broadly in the 'semi-peripheries'. As in the 'centre', interventions usually found their source in violation of treaties or custom, but because the Powers' rights in these areas were broader as a result of unequal treaties, so were the opportunities to resort to force. Intervention for the protection of commerce or nationals can thus be seen as a reflection of 'partial' political recognition.

This leads us to wonder to what extent *ius ad bellum*, if it at all applied, might have been even more 'deformalized' when force was being employed against 'peripheral entities'. But before proceeding to this last chapter of practice analysis, it is also worth underlining that the examined precedents do not point towards the existence of differences in how the use of force was justified at the beginning or at the end of the nineteenth century. The European Powers' discourse in Greece was not more or less 'legalised', or the principle of self-preservation understood more restrictively, than during the United States interventions in Nicaragua in the early twentieth century.

7

Justifying the Use of Force in the 'Peripheries'

The peripheries were all the remaining spaces. Lorimer referred to them as 'residue of humanity'; areas of land that were neither part of the colonial empires of the western nations, nor under the domination of the semi-peripheral States.[1] This mainly included the peoples and 'tribes' of Africa, Oceania and Asia that were not considered as politically organised and territorially stable enough to be recognized as proper States.[2] Lawrence spoke of the 'wandering tribe[s] with no fixed territory to [their] own'.[3] Using Lorimer's criteria, one could say that they were viewed to lack both 'quality' and 'quantity': not only were their cultures, traditions and mores not considered as lifting up to European standards, but their size and power were deemed too unimportant to allow them to genuinely participate to the international system. Of course, factually, this was not necessarily the case. Citing Taslim O. Elias and Richard Akinjid, Antony Anghie underlines how kingdoms such as Benin, Ethiopia and Mali were politically highly organised entities the Europeans had treated as sovereign and entered into treaty relations with.[4] For nineteenth century lawyers, however, this was not sufficient to claim that they belonged to the category of the 'semi-civilised' States, let alone to that of 'civilised humanity'. Hall and Martens, for instance, noted how Great Powers had had a tendency to treat non-European entities by European standards, but insisted that this had been done out of interest, honour and because the Europeans had to set the example for

[1] James Lorimer, *The Institutes of the Law of Nations. A Treatise of the Jural Relations of Separate Political Communities*, 2 vols. (W. Blackwood and Sons, 1883), vol.1, p. 102.

[2] Henry Bonfils, *Manuel de droit international public* (Arthur Rousseau, 1894), p. 23. See also Antony Anghie, 'Finding the Peripheries: Sovereingty and Colonialism in Nineteenth Century International Law' (1999) 40 *Harvard International Law Journal* 23–30.

[3] Thomas Lawrence, *The Principles of International Law* (D.C. Heath & Co. Publishers, 1900), p. 58.

[4] Antony Anghie, 'Finding the Peripheries', 25.

the rest of humanity.[5] Since they could not be considered as 'States' properly so-called, in theory, 'uncivilised peoples' were not believed to enjoy the guarantees offered by the principles of independence, equality and self-preservation.

Still, this did not mean that they had no rights whatsoever. They had 'human recognition' – i.e., European powers had to respect the 'humanitarian principles of rational law' in their interactions with them.[6] It was not clear what these humanitarian principles might exactly have been, and the authors of the time did not elaborate on this point. Nor did they seem to comment much on the view expressed by John A. Kasson, the US plenipotentiary to the 1884–1885 Berlin Conference, according to which 'modern international law follows closely a line which leads to the recognition of the right of native tribes to dispose freely of themselves and of their hereditary territory' and 'in conformity with this principle my government would gladly adhere to a more extended rule, to be based on a principle which should aim at the voluntary consent of the natives whose country is taken possession of'.[7] It has been suggested that, by insisting on the consent of African chiefs to cessions of territory, Kasson's proposal meant to include the 'native tribes' into the system of international law, granting them some of the attributes of sovereignty.[8] Although some say that there was a tacit agreement of participants on this point, the motion was not included in the Conference's Acts.[9] Likewise, in 1888, while observing that there was a 'practice of conventions with the indigenous chiefs' and that most of the appropriation of territories had actually taken place in that manner, the IDI concluded that this was 'recommendable' but not a requirement.[10] However, as

[5] William E. Hall, *A Treatise of International Law* (Clanrendon Press, 1890), p. 43; Frédéric de Martens, *Traité de droit international*, 3 vols. (Librairie Marescq, 1883), vol. 1, pp. 239–240.

[6] Ibid.

[7] Protocol of 31 January 1885, Parliamentary Papers, c. 4361, p. 209.

[8] See Cathal M. Doyle, *Indigenous Peoples, Title to Territory, Rights and Resources. The transformative role of free, prior and informed consent* (Routledge, 2015), p. 53.

[9] Charles H. Alexandrovitch, *The European-African Confrontation. A study in treaty-making* (Martinus Nijhoff, 1973), p. 47.

[10] IDI, *Projet de déclaration internationale relative aux occupations de territoire* (Session de Lausanne, 1888). See also 'Sixième Commission – Examen de la théorie de la Conférence de Berlin' (1888) 10 *Annuaire de l'Institut de droit international* 177 and 181–182. On the relations between treaties and sovereignty see Anghie, 'Finding the Peripheries', pp. 1–71; Isabelle Surun, 'Une souveraineté à l'encre sympathique? Souveraineté autochtones et appropriations territoriale dans les traités franco-africains au XIXe siècle' (2014) 69 *Annales. Histoire, Sciences Sociales* 313–348; Mamadou Hébié, *Souveraineté territoriale*

James Crawford underlined, a resolution proposed by Ferdinand von Martitz stating that these territories fell altogether outside the realm of international law was also defeated.[11]

The peripheries, in sum, seemed to be in a situation of 'limbo': neither inside nor completely outside the system. They could conclude treaties with the 'civilised' States but were not themselves considered as proper States. How did this translate, if at all, in the way the Powers justified their warring enterprises against 'peripheral' entities? As Inge Van Hulle underlines, the use of force in the imperial context has, so far, been somewhat overlooked by international legal scholarship.[12] In her book on British colonial practices in Western Africa, she notes how the use of force in the 'peripheries' accelerated from the 1880s onwards as a result of inter-European colonial competition. This is the period that von Bernstorff also identifies has having marked a progressive shift in practices of justifying force.[13] Van Hulle nevertheless suggests that the colonisers generally sough to legally 'window-dress' their actions. The first part of this chapter starts by presenting Van Hulle's findings regarding the logics of use of force for the purpose of British colonial in West Africa, with particular reference to the cession of Lagos in 1861 (Section 7.1). It then endeavours to complete this analysis with new precedents, which as we shall see, largely confirm her argument. The additional precedents studied in this chapter are as follows: the Anglo-Zulu War (Section 7.2), the French constitution of its Indochina colony (Section 7.3), and the US annexation of Hawaii (Section 7.4).

7.1 British Colonial Expansion in West Africa and the Cession of Lagos (1861)

British colonial expansion in Western Africa started in the late eighteenth century and accelerated during the second half of the nineteenth

par traité. Une étude des accords entre puissances coloniales et entité politiques locales (Presses Universitaire de France, 2015).

11 James Crawford, *The Creation of States in International Law* (Oxford Univertisy Press, 2005), p. 264, footnote no 48. See IDI, 'Sixième Commission – Examen de la théorie de la Conférence de Berlin' (1888) 10 *Annuaire de l'Institut de droit international* 177.

12 Inge Van Hulle, *Britain and International Law in West Africa. Empire and Legal Experimentation* (Oxford University Press, *forthcoming*), 165.

13 Jochen von Bernstorff, 'The Use of Force in International Law before World War I: On Imperial Order and the Ontology of the Nations States' (2018) 29 *European Journal of International Law* 233–260.

century.[14] When Great Britain proceeded to bring Lagos within the bosom of the Empire, it was already well established on several points of the Gulf of Guinea's coasts, mainly in modern-day Gambia and Sierra Leone. Competition for resources with France, among other elements, would lead London to seek the aggrandizement of its dominions in Western Africa. Inge Van Hulle argues that, in this context, three typologies of arguments would generally be used to justify the use of force and obtain new cessions of territories: racialized necessity, humanitarianism and reprisals.[15] 'Racialized necessity' referred to the fact that African populations were often depicted as savage, cruel and warmongers, suggesting that they understood no other language but force. Closely connected to this first type of argument, humanitarianism was connected to the idea of the European 'civilising mission', but also to the British efforts to supress the slave trade on which the economy of many African nations rested. Since the adoption of the Slave Trade Act in 1807, Great Britain was indeed posing as a champion of abolitionism. Adopted by the Parliament, this act forbade slave trade in the British Empire. In application of this act, the West Africa Squadron would be created for the purpose of patrolling Western African coasts and seize any ship (including foreign) transporting slaves.[16] In parallel, it is estimated that around 50 anti-slavery treaties were pushed on African chiefs,[17] the violation of which was then sometimes used as a third justification for the use of force: reprisals.[18] The conquest of Africa by Great Britain (and other European nations) thus often seemed to follow a cycle of concluding treaties of cession and commerce, use of force to vindicate the alleged

[14] Fabrice Bensimon, *L'Empire Brittanique* (PUF, coll. « Que sais-je ? », 2013), pp. 49–68.

[15] Van Hulle, *Britain and International Law in West Africa*, 167.

[16] See Kenneth Morgan, *Slavery and the British Empire: From Africa to America* (Oxford University Press, 2007), p. 202; Christopher Lloyd, *The Navy and the Slave Trade: The Suppression of the African Slave Trade in the Nineteenth Century* (Routledge, 2012).

[17] In this respect, some authors have insisted that African agency in the signing of treaties with Europeans should not be underestimated. See above footnote no 10 and Van Hulle, *Britain and International Law in West Africa*, 24.

[18] See Edward Keene, 'A Case Study of the Construction of International Hierarchy: British Treaty-Making against the Slave Trade in the Early Nineteenth Century' (2007) 61 *International Organization* 311–339; Howard Hazen Wilson, 'Some Principal Aspects of British Efforts to Crush the African Slave Trade, 1807–1912' (1950) 44 *American Journal of International Law*, 505–526. On anti-slavery and international more generally, see Michel Erpelding, *Le droit international anti-esclavagiste des 'nations civilisée' (1815–1845)* (Institut Universitaire de Varenne, 2017).

disregard of those treaties, and acquisition of new cessions and privileges through issuing peace settlements, and so on.

In this sense, it has been argued that anti-slavery was decisive in solidifying Great Britain's grip on Western Africa. Historian Richard Huzzey shows how anti-slavery played a key role in the transition of the British colonial politics from indirect rule towards direct rule.[19] Until the mid-nineteenth century, in fact, British presence in Africa mostly took the form of indirect rule, meaning that London essentially relied on alliances with local chiefs and administration to conduct daily affairs. Anti-slavery, of course, was not the sole motivation; economic and political interests were also at stake. In her book, Van Hulle underlines how British colonial expansion in Western Africa needs to be understood against the complex background of Franco-British rivalry and competition for the control of the increasing commodity trade in the area.[20] Be that as it may, Huzzey considers that it would be too simple to reduce anti-slavery as a mere cynical pretext or *excuse* for intervention. The 'ideology' of anti-slavery, as he calls it, was deeply entrenched in Victorian mentality. Putting an end to the slave trade was thus truly construed as a *motive* for intervention, which, incidentally, appealed to public opinion and allowed to get its support.[21] The British government progressively acquired the conviction that the only way to effectively curb slave-trade was to permanently establish themselves in the region.[22] Huzzey argues that annexation of Lagos was a prime example and that this event 'marked a shift from commerce and slave-trade diplomacy to British occupation'.[23]

The British seizure of Lagos in 1861 is also the main case study used by Van Hulle to evidence the logics of justifying force in Western Africa.[24] She explains that the anti-slave trade agreement that would later be invoked by Great Britain to justify armed action against Lagos was concluded following of the dethronement of the then Oba (King) of Lagos, Kosoko, by his cousin, Akitoye. In 1851, Great Britain helped Akitoye seize power in exchange of a treaty through which the new Oba committed himself to control and put an end to slave trade in Lagos and

[19] See, e.g., Richard Huzzey, *Freedom Burning. Anti-Slavery and Empire in Victorian Britain* (Cornell University Press, 2012), p. 132 ff.
[20] Van Hulle, *Britain and International Law in West Africa*, 187.
[21] Huzzey, *Freedom Burning*, p. 133.
[22] Ibid., p. 146.
[23] Ibid., p. 147.
[24] Van Hulle, *Britain and International Law in West Africa*, 177–182.

surrounding areas.[25] Van Hulle shows that, already in 1851, although 'humanitarianism' was the prime argument put forward for the 'Reduction of Lagos', legal arguments were also present. In a pro-government pamphlet distributed after the events two arguments were more specifically developed. The arguments were somewhat contradictory: one, it was questioned whether African entities could be considered as sovereign States, and other, pointed towards the past destruction of British subjects' properties. This last element is not without recalling the arguments developed by the Powers to intervene in 'semi-peripheral' States, which they considered as sovereign.[26] From this perspective, the 1851 attack on Lagos can be argued to have been a use of reprisals.

But with the anti-slavery treaty they had concluded with the new Oba, Akitoye, Great Britain now had a more solid ground to justify future interventions. The provisions of the treaty were diverse. Not only did the Oba commit himself to abolish the slave trade on his territories and to grant trading privileges to British merchants,[27] but the treaty also stated that: 'if at any time it shall appear that the slave-trade has been carried on through or from the territory of the King and Chiefs of Lagos, the slave-trade may be put down by Great Britain by force upon that territory'.[28] In the years that followed the death of Akitoye in 1853 and his replacement by his son, Docemo, Great Britain sought to conclude a new treaty that would cede the territory of Lagos to British colonial rule. Docemo refused the terms of the treaty. Pressured by France's expansion in the area, London resolved to take a more aggressive attitude.[29] The 1852 Treaty of Lagos gave them the opening they needed. After some 'hard bargaining', to use the expression of Antony G. Hopkins, Docemo signed the Treaty of Cession in Lagos on 6 August 1861.[30]

[25] See Preye Adekoya, 'The Succession Dispute to the Throne of Lagos and the British Conquest and Occupation of Lagos' (2016) 10 *African Research Review* 217–218; Robin Law, 'International Law and the British Suppression of the Atlantic Slave Trade', in Derek Peterson, *Abolitionism and Imperialism in Great Britain* (Cambridge University Press, 2010), pp. 150–174.

[26] See above Chapter 6.

[27] Arts. 1 and 4, Treaty between Great Britain and Lagos, Lagos, 1 January 1852, available in Robert Sydney Smith, *The Lagos Consulate, 1851–1861* (University of California Press, 1979), Appendix A, pp. 135–137.

[28] Art. 3.

[29] Smith, *The Lagos Consulate, 1851–1861*, p. 121.

[30] Antony G. Hopkins, 'Property Rights and Empire Building: Britain's Annexation of Lagos, 1861' (1980) 40 *The Journal of Economic History 780*.

As Van Hulle highlights, the cession of Lagos provoked debates at the House of Commons and the government was asked to provide some explanations. It must be noted, as previously mentioned, that direct rule was not part of the normality British colonial policy in Africa. Many still felt that it offered few advantages in comparison to indirect rule, which allowed Great Britain to take advantage of the resources without the burden of daily administration. The discussion in the House started with the expenses the Crown would have to endure to maintain the Lagos colony. But it quickly shifted to issues of international law when Sir Francis Baring, a Whig MP, rose to the stand. He narrated the events that had led Docemo to agree to the treaty of cession under duress.[31] He also noted that two days after the treaty was signed, Docemo had sent a formal letter of protest indicating that he had never intended to cede his territories to Great Britain and did so only 'because if I do not, he [Captain Bedingfield] is ready to fire on the Island of Lagos, and to destroy it in the twinkling of an eye'.[32] In addition, seeing that the annexation of Lagos had essentially been justified by the breach of the 1852 treaty, Baring wondered whether any complaint had been addressed to Docemo in this respect, as he believed that 'by international law, where a treaty existed, due complaint must be made of any breach of that treaty before hostilities were resorted to'.[33] Although he did not fully agree with his colleague's reading of the situation, Mr Freeland, also remarked that:

> 'surely the smaller and the weaker the State concerned, the more important it was that a Government like that of England should respect, as far as possible, its independence, and endeavour conscientiously to apply the same principles to it as they would apply in their intercourse with a more powerful community'.[34]

Other MPs more frontally disagreed with Baring and defended the attitude adopted by the government. Mr Gregory, for instance, pointed to the fact that Docemo 'if willing, had been unable' to restrain the slave trade in his kingdom'.[35] Mr Layard, the Under-Secretary of State for Foreign Affairs, was also present to clarify the situation. He agreed that 'in their dealings with the natives of Africa, as, indeed, with all the world, they should be guided by strict maxims of equity and justice', and insisted

[31] Hansard, HC vol. 127, col. 505, 12 June 1862.

[32] Baring quoted Docemo' letter of 8 August 1861, Ibid.

[33] Ibid., col. 503.

[34] Ibid., col. 511.

[35] Ibid., col. 507.

that he felt 'confident it would appear that they had dealt both justly and most kindly with Docemo'.[36] He rejected the accusations of Sir Baring against the Government:

> [Our] right hon. Friend accused the Government of violating international law; but he really made a great deal of a very small matter. He spoke as if the King of Lagos were the head of a great independent State, instead of a petty chief exercising doubtful authority over a few people. [...] At length Lagos became a resort of the partisans of the King of Dahomey, and a depot for the arms and powder furnished to him to enable him to carry on the slave trade and his horrible human sacrifices. It became, at length, absolutely necessary either that Lagos should be abandoned or that we should take possession of it altogether.[37]

As Van Hulle points out, this debate shows that the use of force against 'peripheral' entities was not without raising legal issues for the Powers. By the same token, the British attitude in the context of its legal expansion in Western Africa also offers a good illustration of the 'limbo' situation of these nations within the international legal system: not inside, but not outside either. On the one hand, in fact, it was questioned whether the rules that applied to 'civilised nations' could be considered to apply in their relation with African kingdoms. But, on the other hand, and has Van Hulle underlines, it seems that the Powers generally sought to legally 'window-dress' their actions by arguing that these were warranted as a result of treaty violation (i.e., reprisals). This suggests that they somehow felt as though they were bound by rules of *ius ad bellum* even in their dealings with the 'periphery'. The following case studies will tend confirm this feeling.

7.2 The Anglo-Zulu War (1879)

The use of reprisals as an argument for colonial expansion was not limited to Western Africa. When Great Britain invaded Zululand in 1879, the High Commissioner for South Africa and governor for the Cape Colony, Sir Henry Bartle Frere, also sought to construct a *casus bello*. Bartle Frere, it said, was a convinced colonialist with a substantial experience of colonial administration. He had started as a writer with the Bombay Civil Service, eventually rising to the position of governor of Bombay in 1862–1867. When he was chosen as the new governor of the

36 Ibid., col. 508.
37 Ibid., cols. 508–509.

Cape Colony in 1877, he thus already had an accomplished career and had just been granted the title of Baronet by the Queen in recognition of his service. It was because of his reputation that the State Secretary for the Colonies, Earl Carnarvon, had chosen him for the task of accomplishing the establishment of a grand South African Confederation.[38] The idea of uniting the States of South Africa was not new. Sir George Grey, the governor of the Cape colony from 1854 to 1862, had already nourished such projects. He believed that the political division between the different 'white-controlled' territories weaken them against the natives and that the constitution of a federation would also strengthen Great Britain's hold in the region.[39] At the time, however, the Colonial Office rejected the project. The idea was taken over by Earl Carnarvon in the 1870s who proposed the establishment of a confederation under the same model as the one just established in Canada.[40] Historians do not agree on what Carnarvon's motivations might have been. Some stress that it was to have a 'uniform native policy'; others emphasise the need to secure the route to India; others still, point to the discovery of diamonds in the Orange and Vaal rivers and the perceived need to develop a capitalist economic system.[41] Because of the discovery of diamonds, however, competition for resources and tensions between the different 'European' communities of South Africa had risen. Great Britain's plan was not greeted with enthusiasm by the Boers of the Orange Free State and Transvaal, also because British policy in the area had grown more aggressive. In 1871, Griqualand West (an area bordering the Cape Colony, the Orange Free State and Transvaal in the North) had been taken possession of, and in 1877 Transvaal was annexed.[42]

It was in this context that Carnarvon chose to send Bartle Frere to the Cape, believing that his experience would allow him to bring the project of the confederation to completion. Carnarvon hoped this could be

[38] Ian Knight, *A Companion to the Anglo-Zulu War* (Pen & Sword Military, 2008), p. 4.

[39] See Bruce A. Knox, 'The Rise of Colonial Federation as an Object of British Policy, 1850–1870' (1971) 11 *Journal of British Studies* 92–112.

[40] The South African Act of 1877 can be found in Arthur Percival Newton (ed.), *Selected Documents Relating to the Unification of South Africa* (Routledge, 1968), pp. 51–69.

[41] R. L. Cope, 'Local Imperatives and Imperial Policy: The Sources of Lord Carnarvon's South African Confederation Policy' (1987) 20 *The International Journal of African Historical Studies* 601–602.

[42] The annexation was resisted by part of the Boer population, who took up the arms to reclaim independence. In 1884, Transvaal freed itself from British domination and the South African Republic was created.

completed before the end of his term, and Bartle Frere was determined to fulfil his mission within two years of his appointment.[43] When the new governor arrived in the Cape Colony, Britain possessed most of modern-day South Africa. Squeezed between Transvaal to the north-east and Natal in the South was the Zulu Kingdom. The border between the Kingdom and Natal had been defined in the Anglo-Zulu Treaty of 1843: the Thukela river to the south, and its confluent the uMziyathi river (also known as the 'Buffalo river') to the west.[44] The Zulu Kingdom, in sum, stood in the way of Bartle Frere for the completion of the South African Union.

It is said that the Zulu King, Cetewayo, at the head of an army of 40.000 men, was determined to resist European designs for expansion, especially the Boers'.[45] There was delimitation agreement with Transvaal and for decades Boers farmers had started to establish themselves on Zulu lands, between the uMziyathi and Blood rivers. This gave rise to a territorial dispute for which Cetewayo regularly sought British mediation while, at the same time, reinforcing his army for the eventuality of confrontation and conducting punctual raids to scare the Boers away. But when Transvaal was annexed in April 1877, Great Britain cessed to be a 'neutral' party: the lands claimed by the Boers would have *ipso facto* fallen under British rule.[46] It is in this context that Bartle Frere arrived at the Cape. He interpreted Cetewayo's determination to reclaim the disputed territories as hostile and quickly acquired the conviction that war with the Zulus would be the best way to 'pacify' the region in addition to bringing about the Union he had been sent to put in place. Worried by the bellicose designs of the new High Commissioner, the Governor of Natal, Sir Henry Bulwer, suggested the establishment of a commission of inquiry to settle the dispute instead.[47] Sure of his title, Cetewayo promptly agreed; Bartle Frere was not averted by the idea: after all, as long as the legal status of the territory was unclear, he could not claim that Cetewayo's incursions

[43] Andrew Porter, *The Oxford History of the British Empire*, 3 vols. (Oxford University Press, 1999), vol. 3, p. 606.

[44] John Laband, *Historical Dictionnary of the Zulu Wars* (The Scarcecrow Press Inc., 2009), p. 183.

[45] The Editors of Encyclopaedia Britannica, 'Cetshewayo', *Encyclopaedia Britannica Online* (available at: www.britannica.com/biography/Cetshwayo, last updated on 4 February 2020).

[46] See John Martineau, *The Life and Correspondence of the Right Hon. Sir Bartle Frere*, 2 vols. (John Murray, 1895), vol. 2, p. 230.

[47] Ibid., pp. 235–236.

offended the Crown; but if the Commission ruled in favour of the Boers and Zulu attacks continued, he could. Moreover, he was convinced that if the findings were not favourable to the Zulus, the King would not abide by the Commission's decision, giving him a motive for war. The verdict was delivered in July 1878 and, against Bartle Frere's expectations, the Commission ruled in favour of the Zulus. It is said the High Commissioner willingly withheld the award, seeking to have it modified all the while looking for another reason to justify the invasion of the Zulu Kingdom.[48]

Two incidents, taking place over the summer of 1878, gave him the excuse he was looking for. First, on 25 July, Zulu warriors crossed the Tugela river to capture two wives of local chief, Sirayo, who had fled to Natal with their lovers. They had been followed by Sirayo's sons, who took them back to their village were, it is said, they were executed. Second, two British engineers were captured while on the Zulu side of the border where they were very briefly detained before being sent back.[49] Bartle Frere and the Government of Natal requested reparations for these outrages. Cetewayo apologised and offered financial compensation but refused to surrender the culprits for trial in Natal. This offer was rejected. In parallel, Bartle Frere sought to obtain reinforcements from London.[50] This request was also rejected; and the new Secretary of State for the Colonies invited the High Commissioner to adopt a resilient attitude in order 'to avert the very serious evil of war with Cetewayo'.[51] London, in other words, was making it clear that it did not want war with the Zulus. This was in October, but Bartle Frere seemed profoundly convinced that the Zulu 'problem' needed to be addressed and, therefore, continued to push his agenda forward.

Faced with Cetewayo's refusal to give the reparations the Administrators of the South African colonies sought, the High Commissioner issued an ultimatum on 11 December 1878. In addition to the surrender of those responsible for the kidnapping of Sihayo's wives and arrest of the two British engineers, Bartle Frere also asked for Cetewayo to introduce governmental reforms, to disband the Zulu Army and to swear allegiance to Queen Victoria.[52] Cetewayo was given 30 days to answer to the first set of

[48] See Hansard, HC vol. 244, cols. 1869–1870, 27 March 1879.

[49] Ibid., cols. 1877–1878.

[50] John Martineau, Life and Correspondence, vol. 2, p. 258.

[51] Cited in ibid., p. 261.

[52] Frances Colenso and Edward Dunnford, *History of the Zulu War and Its Origins* (Cambridge University Press, original ed.: 1880, 2011), pp. 237–238.

requests and 30 additional days for the remaining two. The Zulu King did not respond, and war broke out on 11 January 1879. Considering the Zulus' silence, Bartle Frere had notified the government of the imminence of the war a week before. He explained that he had no hope Cetewayo would 'afford the redress Her Majesty's government has the right to demand' and that is was clear that 'the Zulu King's intentions are not friendly to the British government'.[53] He carried on stating that war was necessary 'to protect the British territory from further aggression, and compel the Zulu King to comply with all the demands made on him, whether for satisfaction due to the British government, or for the security of British territory'.[54]

The Anglo-Zulu War was controversial: Bartle Frere had acted against the wishes of the government and did not obtain the quick victory he had anticipated. The war lasted almost seven months and the British were defeated on several occasions, such as in the battle of Isandlawa ten days only after the beginning of the hostilities. Following this debacle, a motion was adopted to the effect of declaring that although it supported the government's war effort in South Africa, the House of Lords

> 'regret[ted] that the ultimatum which was calculated to produce immediate war should have been presented to the Zulu King without authority from the responsible advisers of the Crown, and that an offensive war should have been commenced without imperative and pressing necessity or adequate preparation'.[55]

The motion was discussed at length at the House of Commons.[56] Some members of parliament felt as though the High Commissioner had deliberately provoked the war, looking for any excuse to build a *casus bello*, and issuing an ultimatum whose terms he knew the Zulus could not meet. The discussions thus indicate that some believed war to have been waged on fallacious motives, but unlike the debates that followed the cession of Lagos, issues of international law were not explicitly discussed. Ernest Noel, a member of the Liberal party, however, interestingly pointed to the sovereign status of Cetewayo. He asked whether the 'Government thought it was right, just, and fair of an English officer to

53 John Martineau, *Life and Correspondence*, vol. 2, p. 261.
54 Ibid.
55 Hansard, HL vol. 244, cols. 1404–1405, 21 March 1879.
56 See Hansard, HC vol. 244, cols. 1606–1697, 25 March 1879; cols. 1865–1950, 27 March 1879; cols. 1991–2090, 28 March 1879.

send to an independent Sovereign this message [the ultimatum]'.[57] Yet, it is hard to say whether Noel's question was in any manner informed by international law or motivated by purely internal consideration of colonial and administrative law. In fact, although pointing to Bartle Frere's manipulations, the members of the parliament were foremost interested in knowing whether the government supported the High Commissioner's course of action or whether he had acted against his instructions. Sir Hicks Beach, Secretary of State for the Colonies, gave no straightforward answer. Although he admitted that war had not been the government's desire, he also pointed to the fact that there 'was sufficient proof of the danger to the neighbouring communities from the existence of an Army such as that maintained by the Zulu King'.[58]

In this sense, Bartle Frere's determination to find a cause for war with the Zulus can be seen as a discourse meant for internal consumption, aimed at showing that he was acting within his powers as Governor and High Commissioner. In fact, according to rule 35 of the Regulation for the Colonial Service of 1867: 'He [a governor] is not to declare or make war against any Foreign State, or against the Subjects of any Foreign State. Aggression he must always repel to the best of his ability'.[59] Precedents had also made it clear that the war prerogatives of Governors were strictly limited to defence. During the Second Ashanti War (1863–1864), for instance, the Secretary of State for the Colonies had reminded the governor of the Gold Coast that he was only allowed to act as a matter of defence, and that:

> it is upon this principle alone that the Governors are authorized to make war, and no invasion of neighbouring territories can be sanctioned, unless it can be shown that it is really a defensive measure, safer, less costly in blood and money, and more likely to be decisive in its results than waiting for an attack which is being prepared.[60]

Still, we may also wonder to what extent these rules and regulations were the translation into colonial policy of the general rules of international law according to which force could only be used for the purpose of defending a State interest and security.

[57] Hansard, HC vol. 244, col. 2082, 28 March 1879.

[58] Hansard, HC vol. 244, col. 1926, 27 March 1879.

[59] Rule 35, Colonial Office, Rules and Regulations for Her Majesty's Colonial Service (Harrison and Sons, 1867), p. 10.

[60] See Hansard, HC vol. 175, col. 549, 20 May 1864.

7.3 French Expansion in Southeast Asia and the Tonkin Expeditions (1870s–1880s)

The French first arrived in Southeast Asia in the seventeenth century. The conquest of the current territories of Vietnam, Cambodia and Laos, however, would only start in the 1850s through a process that Pierre-Jean Simon describes as rhythmed 'by a series of *coup de main*, skirmishes, battles and treaties with local authorities'.[61] The development of commerce and establishment of Christian communities, which accompanied it, would serve as a pretext for the gradual expansion of the French colonial empire. In 1858, in fact, Napoleon III would take the persecution of Christians as a pretext to launch a first punitive expedition. At the time, the Emperor was looking to establish a French base in the Far East similar to those possessed by the British in Hong Kong, the Portuguese in Macao and the Spanish in Cavite.[62] The special envoy he had sent to negotiate with various local nations had been particularly badly received by the Emperor of Annam, Tu Duc, and had failed to obtain the commercial and political privileges sought by Napoleon III. Over the course of 25 years, it is said that 7 bishops and 15 priests (13 of which were French) had been executed in Annam. Moreover, due to its participation to the operations carried out by Great Britain against China during the Second Opium War (1856–1860), France had troops in the vicinity. The French Emperor took this opportunity to complete his project by force. The operations did not go as smoothly has he had anticipated: it would take three years to submit Tu Duc.[63] On 5 July 1862, the Treaty of Saigon was signed. The Emperor of Annam recognised freedom of religion, authorised the opening of three ports (Tourane, Balat and Quang An) to French trade, granted French ships the right to sail and commerce along the Mekong river, and ceded the southern province the Bien Hoa, Gia Dinh, Vinh Tuong as well as the island of Poulo Condore to France.[64] This treaty marked the beginning of the Cochinchina colony and of France's colonial expansion in Southeast

[61] Pierre-Jean Simon, 'L'indochine française: bref apperçu de son histoire et représentations coloniales' (2001) 1234 *Homme & Migrations* 15.

[62] Auguste Thomazi, *La conquête de l'Indochine* (Payot, 1934), pp. 26–27.

[63] See Blandine Boltz, 'La conquête de Tourane, 1858–1860. L'expérience d'une défaite coloniale au Vietnam' (2019) 49 *Bulletin de l'Institut Pierre Renouvin* 17–27.

[64] Traité de paix et d'amitié, conclu à Saïgon entre la France et l'Espagne, d'une part et le Royaume d'Annam, d'autre part, 5 June 1862 available in L. De Reinach (ed.), *Recueil des traités conclus par la France en Extrême-Orient (1684–1902)* (Ernest Leroux, 1902), p. 94.

Asia. The region was unstable and troubled by piracy. The Cochinchina administration quickly acquired the conviction that the only way to secure the colony would be to take possession of the tormented areas.[65] In 1863, a treaty by which Cambodia was placed under the protection of France was signed with King Norodom I and, three years later, the region of the Mekong Delta and the three southernmost provinces of Vinh Long, Chau Doc and Hu Tien were annexed. But the completion of what was to become French Indochina was truly brought about by the Tonkin expeditions of 1872–1873 and 1883–1885.

The Tonkin consists in the Northern part of Vietnam centred around the city of Hanoi and the Hong River (also known as the 'Red River'), an important commercial water way taking its source in the Chinese province of Yunnan. Control of this river was thus strategic to increase the French participation in the China trade, object of most of the inter-European competition in Southeast Asia. At the time, however, the river was closed to international trade in addition to being dominated by armed bands such as the Black Flags and Yellow Flags, which had fled China after the Taiping Rebellion (1850–1864) and now defied the authority of the Emperor of Annam in Tonkin. This situation troubled France in various respects: political instability in Annam sometimes spilled over into its possessions, but most importantly it feared other European Powers, in particular Germany, would take advantage of the situation to obtain territorial cessions and commercial advantages from Tu Duc. This fear was reinforced by the fact that the Emperor was still refusing to sign a new treaty recognising the sovereignty of France over the provinces annexed in the mid-1860s and promising not to let other European power settle in Annam. As colonial competition grew in the area, the Governor of Cochinchina, Admiral Dupré, grew more and more convinced that France needed to take action in the Tonkin in order to secure its position and reputation.

On 22 December 1872, Governor Dupré wrote to the Minister of Navy (also responsible for colonial affairs). He informed him that the situation was degrading, that the German had been to Hue to meet Tu Duc, and that it was paramount to clarify relations with Annam through a new treaty and to address the situation in Tonkin with more energy. He suggested that an expeditionary force be sent to occupy Hanoi and the

[65] Stefan Eklöf Amirell, *Pirates of Empire. Colonisation and Maritime Violence in Southeast Asia* (Cambridge University Press, 2019), pp. 173–174.

estuary of the Hong River.[66] The Minister was not opposed to the idea, but felt he needed to consult with his colleague, the Minister for Foreign Affairs, as Dupré's proposition 'raise[d] issues that need[ed] to be thoroughly examined by both our departments'.[67] The main issue was whether 'this threat [was] imminent' enough to prompt such an action.[68] While he also agreed that the situation in Annam needed to be addressed, he did not believe Tu Duc's refusal to sign a new treaty 'would *authorize* the use of coercion' and indicated that 'he had hesitations as to whether, in the current circumstances, we [France] should carry out an enterprise of this type, as long as its expediency has not been fully demonstrated by the *necessity of safeguarding our existing interests*'.[69] In other words, the Minister for Foreign Affairs was unsure the current threat to French interests was sufficient to justify armed intervention. It is in those terms that the Minister of Navy would also inform Governor Dupré to continue negotiations: 'my colleague does not think that the present circumstances *allow us to have recourse to violent means of coercion* against Emperor Tu Duc'.[70] Although international law is not explicitly mentioned, we can sense how these considerations might have resulted from an application of the regime of reprisals and of the principle of self-preservation. And, in fact, in 1924, colonial historian Maurice Dutreb opined that this position resulted from the Minister for Foreign Affairs' 'western conception of diplomacy' in which pacific means were the '*deus ex machina* of all problems'.[71]

The Cochinchina governor would, however, find another opportunity to intervene in Tonkin. In 1872, a French trader, Jean Dupuis, mounted a private expedition aimed at forcingly opening the Hong river to commerce.[72] At first, the Governor was willing to support Dupuis to avoid the benefices of the expedition from falling into the hands of competing Powers. But a better opportunity presented itself when, on the last day of August 1873, the government of Annam officially solicited the Governor's help to expel Dupuis from Tonkin. Dupré obliged and sent

[66] Cited in Maurice Dutreb (Marthe Du Bert), *L'amiral Dupré et la conquête du Tonkin* (Société de l'histoire des colonies françaises, 1924), pp. 14–18.

[67] Cited in ibid, p. 19. Translation by the author.

[68] Ibid. Translation by the author.

[69] Cited in ibid., pp. 20–21. Emphasis added. Translation by the author.

[70] Cited in ibid., p. 22. Emphasis added. Translation by the author.

[71] Ibid., p. 20. Translation by the author.

[72] See Claire Villemagne, 'Commerçant et colons français au Tonkin, les pioniers oubliés de la colonisation' (2003) 340–341 *Outre-Mers. Revue d'histoire* 297–317.

Captain Francis Garnier with about 60 men and three small boat to the north.[73] Garnier was instructed to remove Dupuis, but also to stay at Hanoi and take the measures he would deem necessary to impress the need to open the Hong River to Franco-Chinese trade on the Annamites.[74] Face with the refusal of the local authorities to engage talks about the Hong River, Garnier gave them an ultimatum on 19 November 1873: either they agreed to open the river to commerce, to disarm the Hanoi citadel, and to grant safe passage for Dupuis to Yunnan, or the French troops would resort to the arms. The Annamite did not answer. On the 20th, Garnier and his men took possession of the Hanoi citadel and of several strongholds on the river. On 1 December, the Annamite government agreed to start the negotiations for a new treaty and, even though Garnier was killed by Black Flags on government payroll on the 21st, negotiations continued.

The new treaty was signed at Saigon on 15 March 1874.[75] France recognised the independence of Annam and promised financial, military and economic aid to quell disorders in the north. Tu Duc, for his part, recognised French sovereignty over the six southern provinces of Cochinchina and agreed to open the Hong River to French commerce and navigation in exchange for custom duties. The new treaty did little to better the situation in Tonkin and it was the alleged violation by Tu Duc of his new conventional obligations that would provoke a second intervention in 1883.[76]

The increased transit of goods and commodities, in fact, only augmented pirate activities on the river. Paris accused Annam of plotting with China and of hiring Black Flags to disturb European trade. The Cochinchina administration felt that Tu Duc was not only unable, but also unwilling, to control banditry in Tonkin forcing France to maintain troops in the region. This was costly and ineffective. In a letter to the French *Chargé d'affaires* at the Hue Court, the governor of Cochinchina, Charles Le Myre de Vilers, indeed explained that: 'The Royal Government, either by impotence, or by considerations of which I do not need to look for the origin, has been unable to drive out of its

[73] Dutreb, L'amiral Dupré, pp. 46–47; Amirell, Pirates of Empire, pp. 177–178.

[74] See Dupré's letter of instructions to Garnier in Dutreb, L'amiral Dupré, pp. 48–49.

[75] Traité de paix et d'alliance conclu à Saigon entre la France et le Royaume d'Annam, 15 March 1874 available in MAE, *Documents diplomatiques. Affaire du Tonkin, 1ere partie (1874–1882)* (Imprimerie Nationale, 1883), p. 1.

[76] See Charles Fourniau, 'La genèse et l'évolution de l'affaire du Tonkin' (1971) 246 *Revue Historique* 377–402; Paul Deschanel, *La question du Tonkin* (Berger-Lerault, 1883).

territory the bands of Black Flags, which *in violation of the treaties*, collect taxes on the navigation of the Hong River'.[77] While contemplating intervention and pressuring the government of Annam, France insisted that it had no belligerent intentions, and that the purpose of its actions was solely to ensure 'the scrupulous execution of the 1874 treaties'[78] or yet the 'loyal and sincere execution of the 1874 treaties'.[79] At first, the government in Paris was not keen on another campaign in the Tonkin. For the anti-imperialists, the death of Garnier was seen as proof of the perils and futility of colonial adventures.[80] In this respect, nineteenth century French colonial policy has sometimes been described as inconsistent and the result of isolated and individual enterprises (such as Dupré's in 1873) rather than following a precise plan.[81]

Be that as it may, historian Stefan Eklöf Amirell argues that by the 1880s the rhetoric of piracy became so entrenched in colonial discourse that politicians and public opinion grew convinced that France simply needed to take possession of Annam and Tonkin.[82] After many months of hesitation, dissent, and debates, the Government eventually made up its mind that the best way to ensure the faithful application of 1874 agreement was, indeed, for France to permanently establish itself in Tonkin.[83] The Minister for Foreign Affairs, Paul-Armand Challemel-Lacour, presented the government's new position to the Senate on 13 March 1883. In his speech, he explained that the dispositions of the 1874 treaties,

> have too often been forgotten, distorted, or violated by the King of Annam. [...] For the past nine years, facts have demonstrated and continue to demonstrate that the government and the King of Annam is *incapable of fulfilling the obligations imposed upon them by this treaty*, in particular that of maintaining and restoring order in their territories by

[77] 'Le Gouverneur de Cochinchine à M. Rheinart, Saïgon le 17 janvier 1882', annexe to doc. no 102 in MAE, Affaire du Tonkin, p. 201. Emphasis added. Translation by the author.

[78] 'M. de Freycinet, Ministre des Affaires étrangères, à l'Amiral Jauréguiberry, Ministre de la Marine et des Colonies, Paris le 16 mars 1882', doc. no 105 in ibid., p. 208. Translation by the author.

[79] 'Le Gouverneur de Cochinchine à M. Rheinart, Saïgon le 17 janvier 1882', annexe to doc. no 102 in ibid., p. 202. Translation by the author.

[80] Amirell, Pirates of Empire, p. 224.

[81] C. M. Andrew and A. S. Kanya-Forstner, 'Centre and Periphery in the Making of the Second French Empire, 1815-1920', in Andrew Porter and Robert Holland (eds.), *Theory and Practice in the History of European Expansion Overseas. Essays in Honour of R.E. Robinson* (Frank Cass, 1988), p. 9.

[82] Amirell, Pirates of Empire, pp. 224–225.

[83] Fourniau, 'La genèse et l'évolution de l'affaire du Tonkin', pp. 395–396.

> protecting their borders from Chinese incursions as well as ensuring the security of transit on the Hong River. This task [now] belongs to us, and we intend to fulfil it. [. . .] It will suffice that instead of being in Tonkin as foreigners, [. . .], we get established there on a permanent basis as protectors of public order, security and tranquillity'.[84]

Once again, although no direct reference to international law can be found in this discourse, it is clear that the intervention was presented and justified as a sanction (or reprisal) for an offence: the incapacity and suspected unwillingness of Tu Duc to respect the 1874 Treaty. Nine thousand men were sent to take possession of key points on the Hong River's delta and, in August 1883, a new treaty was signed at Hue establishing French Protectorates over Annam and Tonkin. The Indochinese Union would officially be created five years later, on 17 October 1887.

7.4 The Overthrow of the Kalakua Dynasty and the United States' Annexation of Hawaii (1893–1898)

The annexation of Hawaii by the United States took place in 1898, five years after the overthrow of the Kalakua Dynasty in 1893, and four years after the establishment of the Hawaiian Republic in 1894. The revolt against Queen Liliuokalani was the doing of European and American settlers who had come in numbers to the island since the early 1800s because of the sugar cane and whaling industries, as well as the islands strategic position as a refuelling port in the middle of the Pacific Ocean. A particularity of Hawaii in comparison to other 'peripheral' entities, was that labour was imported rather than recruited among the local population. It is estimated that, by the 1850s, 2,130 of the 84,165 inhabitants of the islands were foreigners.[85] By the early 1890s, this number had grown to 41,873 for a total population of 89,990, among which 13,205 European and US citizens, and 5,734 Hawaiian-born white foreigners.[86] As trade developed and 'white' populations took control of the islands' economy, so did consular relations with the powers and their entanglement in

[84] 'Sénat, Débats parlementaire, compte-rendu in extenso, Séance du mardi 13 mars 1883' (1883) 71 *Journal official de la République Française* 292–293. Translation by the author.

[85] Andrew W. Lind, *Hawaii's People* (4th ed., University Press of Hawaii, 1980), p. 6.

[86] See official census of 1890 in 'Mr Blount to Mr Gresham, Honlulu, 17 July 1893', doc. no 17 in US Department of State, *Foreign Relations of the United States, Affairs in Hawaii, 1894* (Government Printing Office, 1895), Appendix II, p. 598.

Hawaiian politics under the pretext of protecting nationals. In 1843, for instance, Great Britain occupied the archipelago for five months as a result of a land dispute involving the British consul, Richard Charlton.[87] France had undertaken a similar action in 1848, to protest the alleged persecutions of Catholics and imposition of new tariffs on French trade by Hawaiian authorities.[88]

The United States grew more and more weary of European imperialism and progressively reinforced its economic and military presence in the area. In 1842 already, Secretary of State Daniel Webster had sent a letter to the agents of the Sandwich Islands (as they were then called) in which he recognised the independence of the local government and declared that 'no power ought either to take possession of the islands as a conquest, or for the purpose of colonization, and that no power ought to seek for any undue control over the existing Government'.[89] This letter, and the later message of President Tyler to Congress in which he emphasised the United States' special interests on the islands, extended the Monroe Doctrine to the North Pacific.[90] In the wake of these declarations new treaties were concluded with Hawaii: in 1849, a treaty of friendship, commerce and navigation providing for a 'most-favoured nation' clause was signed;[91] in 1875, a treaty of commercial reciprocity providing for the suppression of duty rights on a series of goods was adopted;[92] it was renewed in 1884, moreover, granting the

[87] The correspondence relative to this dispute is available in FO, *British and Foreign State Papers, 1842–1843* (Ridgway and sons, 1858), vol. 31, pp. 1023–1029. About the 'Paulet Affair', see also Ralph S. Kuykendall, *The Hawaiian Kingdom*, 3 vols. (Hawaii University Press, 1938), vol. 1, pp. 208–230.

[88] About French presence in Hawaii, see Christian Huetz de Lemps, 'La France et les français aux îles Hawaii au XIXe siècle' (1989) 284–285 *Outre-Mers. Revue d'histoire* 131–141; George Verne Blue, 'The Project for a French Settlement in the Hawaiian Islands, 1824–1842' (1933) 2 *Pacific Historical Review* 85–99; Mary Ellen Birkett, 'Forging French Colonial Policy in the Pacific' (2007) 8 *French Colonial History* 155–169.

[89] 'The Secretary of State to the agents of the Sandwich Islands, Washington, 12 December 1842', in US Department of State, Affairs in Hawaii, Appendix II, p. 44.

[90] See Tyler's special message in ibid., pp. 39–41.

[91] Treaty of Friendship, Commerce and Navigation, Washington, 20 December 1849, in force 9 November 1850 available in Charles I. Bevans (ed.), *Treaties and other International Agreements of the United States of America, 1776–1949*, 13 vols. (Department of State Publications, 1971), pp. 864–871.

[92] Treaty of Commercial Reciprocity, Washington, 30 January 1875, in force 9 September 1876 available in ibid., pp. 874–877.

United States exclusive rights for the establishment of a coaling and repair station in the harbour of the Pearl River.[93]

But the important presence of foreign nationals also came with increased demands for political participation and representation in local politics. It is in these demands, sometimes backed by foreign entanglements, that the deposition of the Hawaiian monarchy in 1893 finds its source. Queen Liliuokalani came into power following the death of her brother in 1891. She sought to introduce political reforms to undo some of the elements of the 'Bayonet Constitution' of 1887, so-called due to the fact that it was adopted under the threat of armed revolt on the part of 'white' business-owners.[94] The 1887 constitution had largely stripped the monarchy of its power, in addition to replacing universal male suffrage with selective suffrage based on ownership, income and literacy and opening the right to vote and be elected to non-naturalised foreigners.[95] In practice this excluded most of the native population from local politics. When the Queen attempted to promulgate a new constitution restoring the powers of the monarchy and amending the voting system in January 1893, white elites once more rebelled and openly called for the United States to annex the islands.

The US minister to the Kingdom of Hawaii, John L. Stevens supported the plan. In March 1892, he had already written to Secretary of State Blaine to inquire whether in case of a revolt 'the present minister and naval commander here may deviate from established *international rules* and precedents that normally restricted the use of force to the protection of nationals in case of disorder'.[96] Stevens was hence well aware that direct intervention in the affairs of Hawaii was, in theory, not lawful. The answer given to him is not available in diplomatic records, but when the time came, Stevens did not hesitate to have the USS *Boston* dispatched to Honolulu, officially for protection American lives and property. Two companies of sailors landed, but instead of being positioned around US citizens' quarters, the soldiers were deployed around the royal palace and

[93] Treaty of Commercial Reciprocity, Washington, 6 December 1884, in force 9 November 1887 available in ibid, pp. 878–879.

[94] See Jon Kamakawiwo'ole Osorio, *Dismembering Lahui. A History of the Hawaiian Nation to 1887* (University of Hawaii Press, 2002), pp. 193–248.

[95] Art. 59, Constitution of the Hawaiian Kingdom, granted by Kalakua, 6 July 1887 available in Robert C. Lydecker (ed.), *Roster Legislature of Hawaii, 1841–1918* (Hawaiian Gazette Co., Ltd., 1918), pp. 166.

[96] 'Mr Stevens to Mr Blaine, Honolulu, 9 March 1892', doc. no 48 in US Department of State, Affairs in Hawaii, *Appendix II*, p. 354. Emphasis added.

government buildings. Immediately after the Queen was overthrown, Stevens recognised the new provisional government established by Sanford B. Dole. Two weeks later, on 1 February 1893, Stevens raised the American flag on government buildings thus proclaiming Hawaii to be a protectorate of the United States and a demand for 'full and complete political union' was filed with Washington by the provisional government.[97] This policy was to some extent supported by President Benjamin Harrison's Administration. Secretary of State Forster, and Blaine before him, were in fact both in favour of annexation.[98] In a letter dated 11 February 1893, Forster nevertheless indicated that, while US troops could remain on the islands as long as they were necessary to for the protection of US citizens and interests, he reproved Stevens' actions tending towards the establishment of a protectorate over Hawaii: 'no step should be taken by you, or will be sanctioned by this Government', he wrote, 'which might tend to derogate in any way from the independence of the Government of the Hawaiian Islands, which the United States have recognized as sovereign and with which they treat on terms of sovereign equality'.[99] If Hawaii was to become part of the United States it had to be properly done. In the meantime, a treaty of annexation was submitted by the Harrison administration to the Senate for consideration, and Forster hoped it would be swiftly approved before the elected president, Grover Cleveland, took office.[100] His wish was not granted.

When Cleveland came into office, in March 1893, he withdrew the annexation treaty from examination by the Senate and, preoccupied by the alleged involvement of Stevens and of the State Department in the coup, called for an investigation. Former Congressman James H. Blount was entrusted with this task and submitted his report on 17 July 1893. He noted that Hawaiians generally supported the Queen, that this was the 'first time American troops were ever landed on these islands at the instance of a committee of safety without notice to the existing government', and concluded that American Minister had colluded with white

[97] 'The Hawaiian special commissioners to Mr. Foster, Washington, 3 February 1893', doc. no 11 in ibid. pp. 224–226.

[98] Adam Burns, *American Imperialism: The Territorial Expansion of the United States, 1783–2013* (Edinburgh University Press, 2017), p. 74; Michael J. Devine, *Forster and the Struggle for the Annexation of Hawaii* (University of California Press, 1977), pp. 29–50.

[99] 'Mr Forster to Mr Stevens, Washington, 11 February 1893', doc. no 18 in US Department of State, Affairs in Hawaii, *Appendix II*, p. 240.

[100] Adam Burns, *American Imperialism*, p. 75.

settlers to overthrow the local government.[101] Stevens was recalled and Cleveland announced that the United States would not annex Hawaii. In his message to the Senate and the Congress on 18 December 1893, Cleveland stated that Stevens's recognition of the provisional government was 'wrongful';[102] that the US occupation of Hawaii was 'wholly without justification',[103] had been conducted 'upon false pretexts',[104] and was 'lawless';[105] and that:

> By an *act of war*, committed with the participation of a diplomatic representative of the United States and without authority of Congress, the Government of a feeble but friendly and confiding people has been overthrown. A substantial wrong has thus been done which a due regard for our national character as well as the rights of the injured people requires we should endeavor to repair.
>
> The *law of nations* is founded upon reason and justice, [...]. The considerations that *international law* is without a court for its enforcement, and that obedience to its commands practically depends upon good faith, instead of upon the mandate of a superior tribunal, only give additional sanction to the law itself and brand any deliberate *infraction* of it not merely as a wrong but as a disgrace. A man of true honor protects the unwritten word which binds his conscience more scrupulously, if possible, than he does the bond a breach of which subjects him to legal liabilities; and the United States in aiming to maintain itself as one of the most enlightened of nations would do its citizens gross injustice if it applied to its international relations any other than a high standard of honor and morality. On that ground the United States cannot properly be put in the position of countenancing a wrong after its commission any more than in that of consenting to it in advance. On that ground it cannot allow itself to refuse to redress an injury inflicted through an abuse of power by officers clothed with its authority and wearing its uniform; and on the same ground, if a feeble but friendly state is in danger of being robbed of its independence and its sovereignty by a misuse of the name and power of the United States, the United States cannot fail to vindicate its honor and its sense of justice by an earnest effort to make all possible reparation.[106]

[101] 'Mr Blount to Mr Gresham, Honolulu, 17 July 1893', doc. no 17 in US Department of State, Affairs in Hawaii, Appendix II, pp. 588 and 594.
[102] 'President Message relating to the Hawaiian Islands, Washington, 18 December 1893', in ibid., p. 453.
[103] Ibid., p. 452.
[104] Ibid., p. 455.
[105] Ibid.
[106] Ibid., pp. 456–457. Emphasis added.

In fewer words, Cleveland asserted that the United State had violated international law, and that he now meant to repair this injury by working towards the reinstatement of Liliuokalani. Geopolitically, the annexation of Hawaii was in the United States' interest, but we can see how legal considerations, in this case, overrode considerations of political opportunity.

Pro-annexation movements, however, lobbied the largely pro-annexation Senate into ordering another investigation under the auspices of Senator John T. Morgan, chair of the Senate Foreign Relations Committee. Presented to the Houses on 26 February 1894, the Morgan Report contradicted Blount's. Interestingly, one of the points of divergence concerned the rules applicable in the relations between the United States and the Kingdom of Hawaii. The report, indeed, insisted that:

> In no sense, and at no time, has the Government of the United States observed toward the domestic affairs of Hawaii the *strict impartiality and the indifference enjoined by the general law of non-interference, in the absence of exceptional conditions. We have always exerted the privilege of interference in the domestic policy of Hawaii to a degree that would not be justified, under our view of the international law, in reference to the affairs of Canada, Cuba, or Mexico.* The cause of this departure from our general course of diplomatic conduct is the recognized fact that Hawaii has been all the time under a virtual suzerainty of the United States, which is, by an apt and familiar definition, a paramount authority, not in any actual sense an actual sovereignty, but a de facto supremacy over the country. This sense of paramount authority, of supremacy, with the *right to intervene in the affairs of Hawaii*, has never been lost sight of by the United States to this day.[107]

This meant that: 'the diplomatic officers of the United States in Hawaii have the right to much larger liberty of action in respect to the internal affairs of that country than would be the case with any other country with which we have no peculiar or special relations'.[108] Stevens, in other words, had not acted beyond his powers and the actions of the United States were perfectly legal (not just opportune) owing to the special status of Hawaii. In sum, the international rules that applied to this 'peripheral' entity were not the same, but this did not mean that a right of intervention did not somehow have to be established.

[107] 'Senate Report No. 227, 53rd Congress, 2nd session, 26 February 1894' in US Senate, *Reports of the Committee on Foreign Relations, 1789–1901*, 8 vols. (Government Printing Office, 1901), vol. 6, p. 383. Emphasis added.

[108] Ibid., p. 382.

The Republic of Hawaii was officially proclaimed on 4 July 1893 and Sanford B. Dole became its first president. While he continued to refuse annexation, Cleveland agreed to recognise this new government. Annexation would not be effected until a new President, William McKinley, came into office and after the United States' victory in the Spanish-American War of 1898. Historians are still divided on the reasons that pushed the new administration to take this decision.[109] Some emphasise trade, others Hawaii's strategic value as a stopover on the way to newly acquired territories in the Philippines. Be that as it may, Hawaii officially became an American 'territory' with the adoption of the Newlands resolution by Congress on 4 July 1898.

* * *

The status of 'peripheral' entities in the system of international law was paradoxical. On the one hand, they were not considered as sovereign, meaning that they were not believed to enjoy the corollaries of sovereignty: the right of independence, equality and self-preservation. Considering that the principle of non-intervention resulted from the combination of these rights, we could have expected it not to be applied in the relations between western Powers and the 'periphery'. Yet, on the other hand, as many nineteenth century authors noted, Powers often treated 'peripheral' entities as sovereign. Most territorial cessions had indeed taken place through treaties and were embedded in treaties. Ironically, these same treaties, or rather their alleged violation, would later serve to justify the use of force and further territorial cessions. In relation to Western Africa, some authors have thus underlined how colonial expansion followed a pattern in which international law, more particularly the institution of reprisals, was instrumental.

The cession of Lagos in 1861, used by Van Hulle and presented in this chapter, illustrates this pattern well. The cession, in fact, was obtained through threat of force and based on Docemo's allege inability to control the slave trade as provided by the 1851 treaty. This event, moreover, provoked debates at the House of Commons as to whether Great Britain in so doing had respected international law. In this chapter, we saw that it was not limited to Western Africa but seemed to be the standard procedure of European colonial expansion. The Anglo-Zulu War, in fact, was also justified by the alleged violation of a treaty: the 1843 Anglo-Zulu

109 See Adam Burns, *American Imperialism*, p. 75.

treaty signed after the annexation of Natal. It was also interesting to see how the High Commissioner sought a *casus belli* at all costs. France's colonial adventures in Indochina likewise found their sources in previous violations of law and in the Annamite authorities' alleged inability to deliver the privileges they had granted to the French. In the case of Hawaii as well issues of international law were debated. The United States had formally recognized the sovereignty of the archipelago, which prompted Cleveland to assert that Stevens' decision to land troops was illegal as American lives and interests were not threatened. The pro-annexation Senate overturned this conclusion by arguing that Hawaii had a special status that gave the United States a broader right of interference into its internal affairs as a result of the many treaties existing between the two entities.

This limited survey of practice tends to show that, as in the 'centre' and in the 'semi-peripheries', States justified their actions when they used force in the 'peripheries' using international law. Moreover, despite the debates that sometimes emerged concerning the extent to which the law of nations truly applied in the Powers' relations with 'peripheral' entities, it must be noted that, no State claimed a general unrestricted right to resort to force. Such effort would not have been necessary if they did not believe that some positive rules constraining armed reprisals and war did not exist. The language of international law, in sum, was also spoken with the nations of Africa, Asia and Oceania.

Conclusion of Part II

Some Thoughts on the Differences between Past and Present Practice of Justifying Force

What lessons can be drawn from the analysis of the arguments put forward by States when using force in the nineteenth century? First, it may confidently be asserted that law, beyond morals and politics, held an important role. In fact, whether in the 'centre', the 'semi-peripheries' or the 'peripheries', it seems that States systematically appealed to international law to justify or explain their actions. Sometimes references to international law were very clear and direct, sometimes less so. The Austrian intervention in Naples in 1821, the Spanish-American War of 1898, as well as, to a certain extent, the European intervention in Greece in 1827 and the annexation of Hawaii gave rise to rather 'theoretical' debates about the scope and limits of the right to resort to force. In other cases, international law might seem to have played a lesser role, but was always in the background; for instance, when a State claimed to be acting in reaction to a previous violation of law. In all the examined precedents, the intervening Power(s) followed the same procedure consisting in alleging that they were protecting or vindicating their rights, whether they issued from treaties or from customary international law. Fundamentally, all these actions were presented as sanctions of law – i.e. as the exercise of the right to self-preservation.

Picking up on this last observation, some may be tempted to argue, as Ian Brownlie and von Bernstorff, that the arguments put forward by States were 'stereotyped pleas' mobilising a concept of self-preservation that admitted so many *casus belli* that it was actually devoid of any legal significance.[1] In other words, even if self-preservation might at some

[1] Ian Brownlie, *International Law and the Use of Force by States* (Clarendon Press, 1968), p. 41; Jochen von Bernstorff, 'The Use of Force in International Law before World War I: On Imperial Order and the Ontology of the Nations States' (2018) 29 *European Journal of*

point have had a legal existence, the uses and abuses that it underwent emptied it from any palpable juridical content, relegating it to a mere 'catch-all' political notion. While it is certainly true that the nineteenth and early twentieth century notion of self-preservation was much broader than its closest contemporary equivalent – self-defence – Brownlie and cie.'s contention does not fundamentally call into question the fact that States used the vocabulary of international law to justify their behaviour on the basis of self-preservation. Said differently, it does not challenge the fact that States presented it as a question of law, not just of morals or politics. It follows that, albeit the States' discourses were indeed stereotyped pleas, they nonetheless showed deference to a certain idea that the unbridled use of armed force was not socially or legally acceptable.

In this respect, one may more fundamentally wonder to what extent the nineteenth and early twentieth-century practice of justifying the use of force is truly different from nowadays.[2] Of course, the Charter of the United Nations now lays out an a priori much more clearly defined and determinate set of rules than nineteenth-century customary law. When justifying resort to armed measures, States will usually refer to one or the other of the Charter's provisions, instantaneously giving their discourses undisputable legal content and significance. At the same time, however, the adoption of the UN Charter is far from having solved problems of indeterminacy. Articles 2(4) and 51 are regularly submitted to different and divergent interpretations. Is there, for instance, a threshold for the prohibition of the use of force? May the Security Council retroactively legalise a use of armed force? Who may consent to a foreign intervention? Can self-defence be used preventively and/or against non-state actors?. Scholars do not agree on the answers that should be given to these questions and States continue to play with these indeterminacies to coat their decision to go to war with the appearances of legality. The exceptions to the rule of the prohibition of the use of force, as well as the rule itself, still get used and abused to the point where one might (and some indeed do) believe them to be devoid of legal content.[3] All this to

International Law 244. See also James L. Brierly, *The Law of Nations: An Introduction to the International Law of Peace* (Clarendon Press, 1949), p. 293; Robert Kolb, *Ius contra bellum. Le droit international relatif au maintien de la* paix (Bruylant, 2009), p. 33.

2 *Contra* see Tom Ruys, 'From *passé simple* to *futur imparfait*? A response to Verdebout' (2015) 2 *Journal on the Use of Force and International Law* 14.

3 See for example Michael J. Glennon, *Limits of Law, Prerogative of Power. Intervention after Kosovo* (Palgrave Macmillan, 2001); and by the same author 'The Limitations of the

say that the States' pleas probably are just as stereotyped today as they were then, and if the nineteenth century practice and the principle of self-preservation must be considered to have been legally irrelevant, then the current practice of justifying force and the current principle of self-defence should maybe not be given too much credit either.

The positions adopted and discourses recently deployed by States in relation to the current situation in Syria should help clarify this point. The ongoing civil war in Syria and the international reactions to it have caused a lot of ink to flow in the scholarship. The crisis started in March 2011, when the Arab Spring reached the cities of Daara, Aleppo and Damascus, sparking protests to demand democratic reforms and the destitution of President Bashar Al-Assad. The demonstrations were met by violent repression from the government precipitating the deterioration of the situation into armed insurrection and, eventually, into full-scale civil war by the end of summer. Since the very beginning of the insurrection, the international community has voiced its concerns regarding the ill treatment of civilians, political opponents and rebels by governmental authorities. The chemical attacks against the rebel strongholds of Ghouta in August 2013 and of Khan Sheikhun in April 2017, in particular, resulted in worldwide outrage, stirring the debate around the opportunity of intervening militarily in Syria to protect the civilian population.[4] The situation even further degraded and complexified when, taking advantage of the general state of chaos, jihadi groups got involved in the conflict and started using the Syrian territory as a rear base for international terrorism. The presence of these groups, and

Traditional Rules and Institutions Relating to the Use of Force', in Marc Weller (ed.), *The Oxford Handbook on the Use of Force in International Law* (Oxford University Press, 2015), pp. 79–95. In response to Glennon, see James Crawford and Rowan Nicholson, 'The Continued Relevance of the Established Rules and Institutions Relating to the Use of Force', in Marc Weller (ed.), *The Oxford Handbook on the Use of Force in International Law* (Oxford University Press, 2015), pp. 96–113.

4 About the international response to the use of chemical weapons in Syria, see Jillian Blake and Aqsa Mahmud, 'A Legal "red line"?: Syria and the Use of Chemical Weapons in Civil Conflict' (2013) 61*UCLA Law Review Discourse* 244-260; Carsten Stahn, 'Between Law-Breaking and Law-Making: Syria, Humanitarian Intervention and 'What the Law Ought to Be"' (2013) 19 *Journal of Conflict and Security Law* 25–48; Anders Henriksen and Marc Schack, 'The Crisis in Syria and Humanitarian Intervention' (2014) 1 *Journal on the Use of Force in International Law* 122–147; Mika Hayashi, 'Reacting to the Use of Chemical Weapons: Options for Third States' (2014) 1 *Journal on the Use of Force and International Law* 80–121; Anne Lagerwall, 'Threats of and Actual Military Strikes against Syria – 2013 and 2017', in Tom Ruys and Olivier Corten (eds.), *International Law and the Use of Force. A Case-Based approach*, Oxford: Oxford University Press, pp. 828–854.

especially of the Islamic State in Iraq and the Levant ('ISIL' or 'ISIS'), caught international attention when, in June 2014, Iraq alerted the UN Security Council of the group's exactions on its territory and called for international help to defeat ISIS.[5] Bagdad's request prompted the US-led coalition to bombard the Islamic State's positions, first in Iraq, and then in Syria as of late September 2014.[6]

There are thus two components to the current situation and international response to the Syrian crisis. On the one side, there has been a debate on the propriety of intervening militarily against the Al-Assad regime to protect the civilian population. On the other, air strikes have effectively been carried out against ISIS on Syrian soil in the name of the fight against international terrorism. Although the target (government vs. rebels), the objective (protect civilians vs. defeat ISIS) and the justification (humanitarian consideration vs. terrorism) for interference vary, both components gave rise to a practice of justifying force that combined moral, political and legal arguments.

Following the attack in the Ghouta neighbourhood of Damascus in 2013, the United States, Great Britain and France seriously contemplated the possibility of intervening against the Syrian authorities accused of being responsible for the raid. Although the three States agreed that the use of chemical weapons should be met with a forceful response, the justifications they brought forth were neither uniform nor clear.[7] The United Kingdom claimed a right 'under international law to take exceptional measures in order to alleviate the scale of the overwhelming humanitarian

[5] UN Security Council, Letter dated 25 June 2014 from the Permanent Representative of Iraq to the United Nations addressed to the Secretary-General, 25 June 2014, UN. Doc. S/2014/440.

[6] About the military intervention against ISIS, see Christian Henderson, 'Editorial Comment. The Use of Force and the Islamic State' (2014) 1 *Journal on the Use of Force and International Law* 209–222; Olivia Flasch, 'The legality of the air strikes against ISIL in Syria: new insights on the extraterritorial use of force against non-state actors' (2016) 3 *Journal on the Use of Force and International Law* 37–69; Laurie O'Connor, 'Legality of the use of force in Syria against Islamic State and the Khorasan Group' (2016) 3 *Journal on the Use of Force and International Law* 70–96; Franck Latty, 'Le brouillage des repères du ius contra bellum. A propos de l'usage de la force de la France contre Daech' (2016) 120 *Revue générale de droit international public* 11–39; Olivier Corten, 'L'argumentation des Etats européens pour justifier une intervention militaire contre l' « Etat Islamique » en Syrie: vers une reconfiguration de la notion de légitime défense?' (2016) 49 *Revue belge de droit international* 31–68.

[7] In this sense, see Olivier Corten and Agatha Verdebout, 'Les interventions militaires récentes en territoire étranger: vers une remise en cause du *jus contra bellum*?' (2014) 60 *Annuaire français de droit international* 157.

catastrophe in Syria'[8] and that 'a legal basis is available under the doctrine of humanitarian intervention'[9] when the Security Council is blocked. But Washington and Paris were reluctant to go this far. François Hollande's declaration that 'international law must evolve'[10] and Barack Obama's assertion that the United States would feel 'comfortable going forward without the approval of the United Nations Security Council',[11] can, in fact, be interpreted as an admission that, in its current state, the law did not recognise interference on grounds of humanity.

What is more intriguing, however, are the arguments France and the United States resorted to in the absence of a recognized doctrine of humanitarian intervention to explain their military designs against Damascus. Three elements were mainly put forward: (i) considerations of humanity; (ii) the Syrian government's lack of respect for the international treaties banning the use of chemical weapons; and (iii) the threat which the continuing civil war in Syria posed to international security as well as to their own national security. Both presidents, indeed, started their allocutions by underlining the Syrian regime's 'appalling decision to gas innocent people',[12] or yet the fact that 'the world watched in horror as men, women and children were massacre in Syria in the worst chemical weapons attack of the 21st century'.[13] Both presidents then also moved on to explain that in so acting, Bashar Al-Assad had 'ma[de] a mockery of the global prohibition on the use of chemical weapons'[14] and inaction would cause the risk for 'eroding the ban on chemical

[8] Prime Minister's Office, 'Chemical Weapon use by the Syrian Regime: UK Government's Legal Position', 29 August 2013, par. 4 (available at: www.gov.uk/government/publications/chemical-weapon-use-by-syrian-regime-uk-government-legal-position/chemical-weapon-use-by-syrian-regime-uk-government-legal-position-html-version).

[9] Ibid. For a comment of the United Kingdom's position, see Christian Henderson, 'The UK Government's Legal Opinion on Forcible Measures in Response to the Use of Chemical Weapons by the Syrian Government' (2015) 64 *International and Comparative Law Quarterly* 179–196.

[10] 'Présidence de la République, Discours de M. Président de la République, à l'occasion de la XXIe Conférence des Ambassadeurs', Palais de l'Elysée, 27 August 2013 (available at: https://es.ambafrance.org/XXIe-Conference-des-ambassadeurs).

[11] White House, Office of the Press Secretary, 'Statement by the President on Syria', 31 August 2013 (available at: www.whitehouse.gov/the-press-office/2013/08/31/statement-president-syria).

[12] 'Présidence de la République, Discours de M. Président de la République, à l'occasion de la XXIe Conférence des Ambassadeurs', Palais de l'Elysée, 27 August 2013.

[13] White House, Office of the Press Secretary, 'Statement by the President on Syria', 31 August 2013.

[14] Ibid.

weapons'.[15] The erosion of the ban on chemical weapons, in turn, would pose a threat not only to international peace and security but equally 'to our own national security',[16] Obama finally argued, as 'over time, our troops would again face the prospect of chemical warfare on the battlefield [a]nd it could be easier for terrorist organizations to obtain these weapons'.[17] The positions expressed by France and the United States in 2013 actually take over all the major elements of nineteenth century State practice of justifying humanitarian intervention: a pathos articulated around considerations of humanity, a claim that treaties were violated, and a loose conception of what constitutes a threat to international or national security. In the end, the plan for intervention was abandoned when Prime Minister Cameron's motion to use force was rejected by the House of Commons on 29 August 2013, and it became clear that Obama would not get the Congress' approval either.

A year later, western and other Powers would eventually come to get involved in the conflict, although to fight the ISIS presence in Syria rather than for humanitarian reasons. The first air strikes of the US-led coalition on Syrian soil were launched on 22 September 2014. At first glance, these operations could not be grounded in any of the classically recognized exceptions to the prohibition of the use of force. Indeed, the Syrian government had not called or even consented to the intervention, the UN Security Council had not authorized the use of force, and neither the United States nor its allies had been subject to an act of aggression in the sense of definition of Resolution 3314, opening the right for self-defence under Article 51 of the Charter. Adopting a strict reading, in fact, self-defence is only relevant *between States* and provided that an act of aggression has *actually* been committed.

To take action in Syria, justifications had to be looked for elsewhere, or, at least, in alternate interpretations of the Charter. The coalition chose to rely on the combination of three controversial arguments: (i) legitimate self-defence against a non-State actor; (ii) preventive legitimate

[15] White House, Office of the Press Secretary, 'Remarks by the President in Address to the Nation on Syria', 10 September 2013 (available at: www.whitehouse.gov/the-press-office/2013/09/10/remarks-president-address-nation-syria).

[16] White House, Office of the Press Secretary, 'Statement by the President on Syria', 31 August 2013. See also 'Présidence de la République, Discours de M. Président de la République, à l'occasion de la XXIe Conférence des Ambassadeurs', Palais de l'Elysée, 27 August 2013.

[17] White House, Office of the Press Secretary, 'Remarks by the President in Address to the Nation on Syria', 10 September 2013.

self-defence; and (iii) the 'unwilling or unable' doctrine. In the letter dated 23 September 2014 to the UN Secretary General, the United States thus explained that:

> ISIL and other terrorist groups in Syria are a threat not only to Iraq, but also to many other countries, including the United States and our partners in the region and beyond. States must be able to defend themselves, in accordance with the inherent right of individual and collective self-defence, as reflected in Article 51 of the Charter of the United Nations, when, as is the case here, the government of the State where the threat is located is unwilling or unable to prevent the use of its territory for such attacks.[18]

Some of Washington's traditional allies were initially reluctant to follow suit on this position and decided to limit their operating grounds to Iraq. Slowly, however, more and more States joined the coalition efforts in Syria, taking up one aspect or another of the arguments developed by the US. The United Kingdom, for example, insisted that Iraq's collective right of self-defence under Article 51 enabled it took attack ISIS's position in Syria as well.[19] France, in addition to Iraq's request for assistance, invoked a 'direct and extraordinary threat to [its own] security', and this even before the 13 November 2015 terrorist attacks in Paris.[20] Turkey, Canada and Australia endorsed the 'unwilling or unable' doctrine, claiming that 'States must be able to act in self-defence when the Government of the State where the threat is located is unwilling or unable to prevent [the] attacks'.[21] Other States, still, did not refer to

[18] UN Security Council, Letter dated 23 September 2014 from the Permanent Representative of the United States of America to the United Nations addressed to the Secretary-General, 23 September 2014, UN Doc. S/2014/695.

[19] UN Security Council, Identical letters dated 25 November 2014 from the Permanent Representative of the United Kingdom of Great Britain and Northern Ireland to the United Nations addressed to the Secretary-General and the President of the Security Council, 25 November 2014, UN Doc. S/2014/851.

[20] UN Security Council, Identical letters dated 8 September 2015 from the Permanent Representative of France to the United Nations addressed to the Secretary-General and the President of the Security Council, 9 September 2015, UN Doc. S/2015/745.

[21] UN Security Council, Letter dated 9 September 2015 from the Permanent Representative of Australia to the United Nations addressed to the President of the Security Council, 9 September 2015, UN Doc S/2015/693. See also UN Security Council, Letter dated 24 July 2015 from the *Chargé d'affaires a.i.* of the Permanent Mission of Turkey to the United Nations addressed to the President of the Security Council, 24 July 2015, UN Doc. S/2015/563; UN Security Council, Letter dated 31 March 2015 from the *Chargé d'affaires a.i.* of the Permanent Mission of Canada to the United Nations addressed to the President of the Security Council, 31 March 2015, UN Doc S/2015/221.

any specific Charter provision or doctrine, simply noting that 'terrorist organizations and such regimes [the Syrian regime] are two sides of the same coin; both work against the interests of people and against peace, security and stability in the world'[22] or that 'Syria has been unable to protect the borders from its side'.[23] This shows at least two things: first, that, even now, States do not always feel the urge to refer to the Charter's legal framework to justify resort to armed force; and, second, that self-defence remains an inherently vague, indeterminate and therefore 'catch-all' notion. The difference between past and present practices of justifying the use of force must, therefore, not be overemphasised. If we admit that present discourses produce legal reverberations then we should probably soften our interpretation of nineteenth century practice and recognise that such might have equally been the case before 1919.

[22] This was the opinion expressed by Qatar: UN Security Council, Verbatim Record, 7271st Meeting, 19 September 2014, UN Doc. S/PV.7271, p. 31.

[23] Jordan's position is quoted in Olivier Corten and Agatha Verdebout, 'Les interventions militaires récentes', 150.

PART III

The Narrative of Indifference in the Twentieth Century

Disciplinary Identity and Legitimacy

Introduction: Aim, Methodology and Outline

The First World War and the adoption of the Covenant of the League of Nations marked a turning point in international legal historiography. The nineteenth century became the past and the establishment of a new institutionalised collective security system was felt as having inaugurated a new 'era' for international law. It was then, during the interwar years, that the narrative of indifference first surfaced in scholarship. Why did the adoption of the Covenant's collective security system need to be presented as a revolution rather than as an evolution of international law? Why did the interwar legal scholars sometimes need to go as far as to deny the existence of any legal provisions restricting the use of force before 1919? In other words, where does our oversimplified narrative of indifference come from? For what purpose did it emerge? How did it become the commonly accepted version of the history of the use of force in international law upheld up to this day? The first part of the book has ruled out the assumption according to which the apparition of the indifference narrative in the twentieth century may simply be summed up to a shift of paradigm from naturalism to positivism. As a matter of fact, nineteenth-century authors generally integrated the analysis of State practice into their methodology; a State practice that, as we saw in the second part of the book, beyond moral and political considerations appeared to have genuine legal reverberations. The idea that international law suddenly became a positivist discipline and finally saw the nineteenth century for what it truly was is, as a result, unconvincing. Instead, it is argued that the indifference narrative finds its roots outside the purely legal sphere, in the very beliefs that underlie the identity of international law as an academic discipline and profession.

This final part of the book draws from mnemohistory framework presented in the general introduction of the book.[1] Based on the post-modern premises, mnemohistorians contend that historical accounts are social constructions whose content is contingent upon the social and political conditions of their production. Jan Assmann, for instance, considers that the deeply founded beliefs about self and other that determine the identity of a particular society or group, act as 'mythomoteurs' (or 'story-generators'). They shape the way in which a given group understands and rationalises its surroundings.[2] They organise the world in a manner that is cognitively consistent with our underpinning prejudices and representational biases;[3] i.e., they provide a logical explanation to overcome a contradiction. Following this line of thought, this book contends that the emergence the narrative of indifference in international legal doctrine can be seen as the product of the discipline's pre-existing intellectual traditions and beliefs about international law confronted with the traumatic events of the World War I. In order to understand 'indifference', we therefore need to start by fathoming the core values and latent cognitive frames that bind international law as a field and as a professional group in order to then assess their impact on the narrative of indifference and examine how this narrative may have helped the discipline make sense of its history.

This raises two important methodological questions: How can the core values and latent cognitive frames of the discipline and profession be identified? Second, how can their impact on the narrative of indifference be assessed?

Determining the content of a group's subconscious dispositions – gaining 'knowledge about background knowledge',[4] as Herbert and Irene Rubin put it – is not an easy task. In international law, a few studies have more or less directly touched upon this delicate issue. In 1999, Kennedy, for instance, explained how a certain disciplinary identity can be said to have consolidated around international lawyers' constant

[1] See *supra* General Introduction (point III).

[2] Jan Assmann, *Moses and the Egyptian.* The Memory of Egypt in Western Monotheism (Harvard University Press, 1997), p. 15. See also Wulf Kansteiner, 'Finding Meaning in Memory: A Methodological Critique of Collective Memory Studies' (2002) 41 *History and Theory* 180.

[3] See also Duncan Bell, 'Writing the World: Disciplinary History and Beyond' (2009) 85 *International Affairs* 3–22.

[4] Herbert J. Rubin and Irene Rubin, *Qualitative Interviewing: The Art of Hearing Data* (Sage, 1995), p. 20.

strife to improve the international legal system and strengthen the rule of law.[5] In *The Gentle Civilizer* (2001) and in *The Liberal-Welfarist Law of Nations* (2012), Koskenniemi and Tourme-Jouannet similarly underline how the profession federated around a common project; 'civilising' on the one side, 'liberal-welfarist' on the other.[6] Generally speaking, however, the question of 'identity' was not necessarily the core concern of these studies. The methodology one might want to follow to make the beliefs of the discipline surface is, as a consequence, not presented. The constructivist literature in international relations, where the impact of identity and representational biases on practices has more often been investigated offers some useful indications as to how one may want to proceed.[7] Most authors recommend ethnographical observations. The researcher should immerse themselves in the milieu he or she wishes to understand. If ethnographical observations are not possible, then one should look for the 'nearest vantage point'.[8] Usually this will mean conducting qualitative interviews, but if this is not an option either, relying on archival documents, interviews, memoirs and other carriers of discourse may also provide a good alternative.[9] When selecting these documents, it is furthermore recommended to prefer texts that have enjoyed wide readership or were aimed at a wide audience, because they are more likely to have a role in defining the dominant discourse or in bearing the dominant discourse.[10] In our case, when the aim is to define

[5] David Kennedy, 'When Renewal Repeats: Thinking against the Box' (1999–2000) 32 *New York Journal of International Law and Politics* 340–348.

[6] Martti Koskenniemi, *The Gentle Civilizer of Nations. The Rise and Fall of International Law, 1870–1960* (Cambridge University Press, 2001) pp. 11–97; Emmanuelle Jouannet, *The Liberal-Welfarist Law of Nations. A History of International Law* (Cambridge University Press, 2012). See also Martti Koskenniemi, *From Apology to Utopia: The Structure of International Legal Argument* (re-issue with new epilogue) (Cambridge University Press, 2005), pp. 17–23.

[7] For an 'inventory' of the different methods, see Vincent Pouliot, 'Methodology. Putting Practice Theory Into Practice', in Rebecca Adler-Nissen (ed.), *Bourdieu in International Relations. Rethinking Key Concept in IR* (Routledge, 2013), pp. 50–52; Vincent Pouliot, '"Sobjectivism": Toward a Constructivist Methodology' (2007) 51 *International Studies Quarterly* 368–370.

[8] Edward Schatz, 'What Kind(s) of Ethnography Does Political Science Need?', in Edward Schatz (ed.), *Political Ethnography: What Immersion Contributes to the Study of Power* (Chicago University Press, 2009), p. 307.

[9] Diane Vaughan calls this type of enquiry 'historical ethnography', in 'Bourdieu and Organizations: The Empirical Challenge' (2008) 37 *Theory and Society* 71.

[10] Lene Hansen, *Security as Practice. Discourse Analysis and the Bosnian War* (Routledge, 2006), p. 76; Pouliot, 'Sobjectivism', 371–372; Iver B. Neumann, 'Discourse analysis', in

the underlying mindset of an academic field, textbooks, once more, seem to offer a particularly suited material for analysis. Not only are they targeted towards a large audience, but they are also aimed at educating the new generations of international lawyers: i.e., ensure that they adopt the discipline's *ethos* and internalise its *doxa*. But what should we be looking for when examining manuals? International relations literature advises to interrogate what makes 'common sense' – that is what 'speaks of itself', is recurrent and taken for granted.

Once the latent cognitive frames that underlie the identity of the discipline have been identified, the next issue is that of how to assess and measure the impact that these frames have had (and still have) on the narrative of indifference. Assmann argues that not only does the identity of a group influence the content of the historical accounts it produces, but also that these accounts, in turn, aim to reinforce that identity. This is also why they will usually be built using the 'codes' of that identity.[11] This idea is reminiscent of Pierre Bourdieu and his claim that practices, including discursive practices, 'always tend to reproduce the objective structures of which they are the product'.[12] It follows that if a particular account is indeed the result of a group's pre-existing representational biases, it will tend to reproduce these biases. Neither Assmann nor Bourdieu, however, give any indication as to how one may want to proceed to make the underlying structures of the discourse emerge to assess to what extent they mimic the beliefs at their inception. In this respect, the research will proceed by drawing inspiration from Claude Lévi-Strauss's work on myths. The similarities of the anthropologist's work with that of the mnemohistorians' must, in passing, be underlined. Lévi-Strauss understood 'myths' very broadly as any sort of story aimed to explain an otherwise inexplicable event or situation. In his own words, they provided 'a logical model capable of overcoming a contradiction'.[13] History, he felt, fitted that description. It is, in fact, often used and organised in such a way as for a society or a group to make sense of its past, of its position and choices in the present

Audie Klotz and Deepa Prakash (eds.), *Qualitative Methods of International Relations* (Palgrave, 2008), p. 67.

[11] Jan Assmann, 'Collective Memory and Cultural Identity' (1995) 65 *New German Critique* 130.

[12] Pierre Bourdieu, *Outline of a Theory of Practice* (original ed.: 1972) (Cambridge University Press, 1977), p. 72. See also Vaughan, 'Bourdieu and Organizations', p. 70.

[13] Claude Lévi-Strauss, *Structural Anthropology* (original ed.: 1958) (Basic Books, 1963), p. 229.

world.[14] Lévi-Strauss's interest for mythological accounts more specifically laid in their narrative (syntagmatic) and rhetorical (paradigmatic) structures. He felt that highlighting the structures of myths was the best way to understand the meaning and function of these stories. As myths are expressed and communicated through language (words, sentences and interconnection of sentences), Lévi-Strauss naturally chose to base his method on linguistic analysis. Insisting that the 'function of repetition is to render the structure of the myth apparent',[15] he more specifically suggested superposing the different versions of a same account and conducting a paradigmatic discourse analysis in order to make the 'structural law' of the myth surface. For didactic reasons, the details of Lévi-Strauss's method will be explained when it is mobilised. Still, to summarize in just a few words, particular attention will be given to the vocabulary and lexicon employed by the proponents of the indifference-narrative to see to what extent its structures mimic the profession's deep-founded beliefs about international law.[16]

Keeping these considerations in mind, Chapter 8 endeavours to outline the core values and to evidence the latent cognitive frames that underlie the identity of international law as a discipline and measure their impact on the rhetorical structures of our traditional historical account on the use of force. It shows how the narrative of indifference mirrors international law's more general representation of itself and, in particular, evidence how they are built on the same idea that law is a remedy against disorder and a vector of social progress. Chapter 9 addresses the question of the function of the narrative of indifference in the scholarship – what contradiction was it trying to resolve? It argues that 'indifference' mainly served as a coping mechanism aimed at preserving the identity of the discipline by restoring its credibility as an effective tool for the maintenance of international peace and security, following the traumatic events of the World War I.

[14] In an interview with Bernard Pivot on French television in 1984, Lévi-Strauss indeed wondered whether 'au fond, est ce que nous n'utilisons pas l'histoire un peu à la façon d'un mythe, en l'organisant de telle façon qu'elle nous aide – ou nous croyons qu'elle nous aide – a mieux comprendre notre passé, notre position actuelle dans le monde et les choix politiques que nous faisons', Archives INA, *Apostrophe: Claude Lévi-Strauss répond à Bernard Pivot*, 4 May 1983.

[15] Lévi-Strauss, *Structural Anthropology*, p. 229.

[16] See below (8.2.1.) and (8.2.2.).

8

Disciplinary Beliefs about International Law and the Narrative of Indifference

A Mirror Effect

The aim of this chapter is to highlight the core beliefs that underlie the identity of international law as a discipline and examine their impact on the narrative of indifference. Focusing on the analysis of international law textbooks from the interwar period to the present day, it will start by showing that the field of international law appears to have been (and to still be) deeply rooted in the idea that rules of law are a vector of social order and progress (Section 8.1.). The second part will then turn to the analysis of the literature dating from 1919 to the present day dealing with the history of the use of force. Analysing the content and the rhetoric of the narrative of indifference, it illustrates how the traditional historical account on the use of force, built on the opposition of law and order to politics and anarchy, unmistakably reproduces the discipline's more general structural representational biases about itself (Section 8.2.).

8.1 Disciplinary Beliefs about International Law: Law as a Vector of Social Order and Progress

Some may be skeptical or plainly dislike the idea of making broad claims about the beliefs and values that underlie international law as a disciplinary and professional field. After all, the discipline is traversed by many different theoretical approaches, outlooks and sub-specialties that seem to have little in common. There might also be national differences in the way international law is taught and, consequently, thought about and understood.[1] Some may further question what an international lawyer today might have in common with a nineteenth-century or interwar lawyer. Still, as Oscar Schachter and others in his wake have argued, it seems that the profession appears to share a set of common references

[1] See, e.g., Anthea Roberts, *Is International Law International?* (Oxford University Press, 2017).

that enable us to communicate and debate with each other.[2] Kennedy even adds that 'an international lawyer from 1875 could converse easily with one from 1995' and 'might well agree both where the field has failed and what steps were necessary to get things back on the right track'.[3] Chapters 2–4 have already insidiously shown how, beyond theoretical divides, nineteenth century scholars generally seemed to have the same idealistic vision of international law. Whether their outlook was closer to the 'naturalist' or 'positivist' end of the spectrum, they shared the conviction that the aim of international law was to ensure the peaceful co-existence of States and viewed themselves as the craftsmen of that project.

Skimming through international law textbooks from the interwar to the present day, we will see that this providential vision of international law and, by extension, of the international legal profession has survived far beyond the nineteenth and early twentieth century. The idea that law is the carrier of order is, in fact, still pivotal in modern day literature. Three grand themes, common to most textbooks from the first half of the twentieth century to the present day, can be considered as especially revealing of how international lawyers view their own discipline in this respect. The first of these themes lies in the way international law is consistently defined as an indispensable system whose function is to ensure the peaceful and orderly co-existence of States (Section 8.1.1.). A second pro-eminent feature of most textbooks throughout the twentieth century is the 'effectivity complex' from which international law seems to suffer *vis-à-vis* municipal law. As a matter of fact, it appears that scholars feel quasi-systematically compelled to justify the truly legal nature of their discipline (Section 8.1.2.). These two first recurrent features of international law textbooks, furthermore, find an expression in the way the general history of the discipline is presented, i.e., as a story *of* a constant progress of law and *through* law (Section 8.1.3.).[4]

[2] Oscar Schachter, 'The Invisible College of International Lawyers' (1977–1978) 72 *Northwestern University Law Review* 217–226. See also David Kennedy, 'When Renewal Repeats: Thinking against the Box' (1999–2000) *NYU Journal of International Law and Politics* 340–348; Mario Prost, *The Concept of Unity in International Law* (Hart Publishing, 2012), p. 141.

[3] Kennedy, 'When Renewal Repeats', 340.

[4] See Thomas Skouteris, *The Notion of Progress in International Law Discourse* (TMC Asser Press, 2010); Tilmann Altwicker and Oliver Diggelmann, 'How Progress Is Constructed in International Legal Scholarship' (2014) 25 *European Journal of International Law* 425–444.

8.1.1 *The Function(s) of International Law: Injecting Order in an Otherwise Chaotic International Society*

The question of the function of international law cannot be detached from the broader question of the function of law in general. In the dictionary, 'disorder' and 'disorganisation' are sometimes offered as antonyms of 'law'.[5] A society without law is hence a 'disorderly' society. But, in turn, 'order' and 'organisation' are presented as synonyms of 'society'. It follows that: (i) speaking of 'disorderly society' is somewhat oxymoronic and (ii) that the existence of a 'proper' society requires law. This common idea that law and society are co-depend, Eric Wyler tells us, goes back to Greek mythology; to the episode of the Titanomachy, to be more precise.[6] The story goes that after defeating his father Cronos and putting an end to the reign of the Titans, Zeus gave *philia* (brotherly love) to humans thus indicating that the time of *cosmos* (order) has finally come to replace the time of *chaos* (void). Wyler concludes that: 'of sacred origin, law immediately appears connected to peace and to order'.[7] It is in this spirit that first year law students will often be taught that law is the body of rules that governs the relations between the members of a same group and that it is also the necessary condition of life in society.[8]

International law is not conceived differently. The *Max Planck Encyclopaedia* defines international law as the 'legal order which is meant to *structure* the interaction between entities participating in and shaping international relations'[9] and claims that 'without a minimum of compliance with international law rules, international relations, [. . .], are unworkable. *Anarchy*, complete *instability*, and *chaos* would be the consequence'.[10] The belief that international law is a condition for the existence of an international society and the keeper of international order

[5] In that spirit, Jackson H. Ralston wrote in 1941 that law 'suggests peace, order, regularity' in *A Quest for International Order* (John Byrnes and Company, 1941), p. 77.

[6] Eric Wyler, 'La Paix par le droit. Entre réalité, mythe et utopie', in Laurence Boisson de Chazournes et Marcelo Kohen (eds.), *International Law and the Quest for its Implementation / Le droit international et la quête de sa mise en œuvre. Liber Amicorum Vera Gowlland-Debbas* (Brill, 2010), p. 472.

[7] Ibid. Translation by the author.

[8] See, e.g., N. A. Maryan Green, *International Law* (3rd ed., Pitman Publishing, 1987), pp. 2–3.

[9] Rüdinger Wolfrum, 'International Law', *Max Planck Encyclopaedia of Public International Law Online* (last update: November 2006), par. 1. Emphasis added.

[10] Ibid., par. 16. Emphasis added.

will, of course, remind us of the 'theories of the State' and social contract that many nineteenth century lawyers used to explain (and justify) the existence of interstate rules.[11] Although, modern textbooks will less often, or less explicitly, refer to these theories, the idea that international law is a necessary protection against chaotic international relations is widespread and has remained relatively stable throughout our period of interest. In 1932, Georges Scelle, for instance, considered that: 'all composite societies, all these inter-social communities *generate*, by the very fact that they exist, their own legal norms, in order to ensure the maintenance and development of the solidarity on which they are based'.[12] In 1974, Julius Stone, offered a similar account:

> 'With the increasing complexities of international life, and the growing sense of interdependence of nations, all of us must yearn for a reliable world *order*, under settled criteria of right and wrong, and of obligation and responsibility – in short some universally understood and effective law of all mankind'.[13]

Ten years later, Joseph G. Starke spoke of international law as 'that indispensable body of rules [. . .] without which it would be virtually impossible for them [States] to have steady and frequent intercourse'.[14] Today, in the same spirit, Malcolm Shaw's widely read *International Law* tells us that 'in the long march of mankind from the cave to the computer a central role has always been played by the idea of law – the idea that *order* is necessary and *chaos* inimical to a just and stable existence'[15] and

[11] For a critique of this idea see Philip Allott, 'International Law and the Idea of History' (1999) 1 *Journal of the History of International Law* 10–11.

[12] Georges Scelle, *Précis de droit des gens* (Librairie du Recueil Sirey, 1932), p. 30. Emphasis in the original. Translation by the author. See also Ellery C. Stowell, *International Law. A Restatement of Principles in Conformity with Actual Practice* (Henry Holt and Company, 1931), p. 1; Erich Kaufmann, *Règles générales du droit de la paix* (Librairie du Recueil Sirey, 1936), p. 151 ff;

Marcellus Donald A. R. von Redlich, *The Law of Nations* (2nd ed., World League for Permanent Peace, 1937), p. 1; James L. Brierly, 'Règles générales du droit de la paix' (1936) 58 *Recueil des cours de l'académie de La Haye* 234.

[13] Julius Stone, *Of Law and Nations. Between Power Politics and Human Hopes* (William S. Hein & Co., 1974), p. 41. Emphasis added.

[14] Joseph G. Starke, *Introduction to International Law* (9th ed., Butterworths, 1984), pp. 14–15.

[15] Malcolm N. Shaw, *International Law* (6th ed., Cambridge University Press, 2008), p. 1. Emphasis added. For a more detailed analysis of this passage of Shaw's textbook, see Skouteris, The Notion of Progress, pp. 18–19.

that 'international law aims for *harmony*'.[16] Even Jan Klabbers's manual of 2013, with its critical overtones, reads that:

> the bottom line should be clear: the existence of international relations, of whatever kind, entails the existence of international law. As the ancient Romans knew, wherever there is a society, there will be law (*ubi societas, ibi jus*), and the rules regulating contacts within the society of states are generally called international law.[17]

Unlike others, however, Klabbers's manual takes some distance regarding this assertion, informing the reader that this idea that law is an irremediable consequence of but also condition for the existence of a 'peaceful' society is certainly one of the dominant assumptions international lawyers have about their discipline.[18] Klabbers echoes a fair share of the aforementioned studies that have, from near or far, touched upon the issue of identity. As a reminder, Kennedy indeed argues that international lawyers, in spite of their differences of approach and opinion, can be said to share the common goal of strengthening international rule of law.[19] Likewise, when Koskenniemi talks of the 'civilising' mission, he refers to international lawyers' strife and belief in the possibility to discipline international relations through law. Still in the same vein, Thomas Skouteris notes that the Kantian mantra of social progress through legal internationalism seems to lay the groundwork for many of the profession's premises and is, indeed, 'central to the identity of the international jurist and the reason why many of us joined the field'.[20] Mario Prost, finally, is also of the opinion that the question of 'how to order the world under the rule of law' forms the fundamental enigma of

[16] Shaw, International Law, p. 12. Emphasis added.

[17] Jan Klabbers, *International Law* (Cambridge University Press, 2013), p. 3. See also Marcel Sibert, *Traité de droit international public*, 2 vols. (Dalloz, 1951), vol. 1, p.3; Green, International Law, pp. 2–3; Rosalyn Higgins, *Problems and Process. International Law and How We Use It* (Clarendon Press, 1994), p. 1; J.-Maurice Arbour, *Droit international public* (3rd ed., Yvon Blais, 1997), p. 25; Marcel Sikondo, *Introduction au droit international public* (Ellipse, 1999), p; 74; John O'Brien, *International Law* (Cavendish Publishing, 2001), p. 34; Martin Dixon, *International Law* (6th ed., Oxford University Press, 2007), pp. 1, 3 and 18; Anthony Aust, *Handbook of International Law* (2nd ed., Cambridge University Press, 2010), pp. 205–206; Lung-chu Chen, *An Introduction to Contemporary International Law. A Policy-Oriented Perspective* (3rd ed., Oxford University Press 2015), p. 4.

[18] Klabbers, International Law, pp. 3–4.

[19] Kennedy, 'When Renewal Repeats', 340 westphalian terms 348.

[20] Skouteris, *The Notion of Progress*, p. 1.

international law, an enigma that guides much of the profession's practices.[21]

Yet, 'order' is an indeterminate notion. The meaning international lawyers have vested in it has not necessarily been stable and the notion has often been used as a receptacle for the legitimation of a wide-ranging, not always consistent, array of projects.[22] At this stage it would be beyond the point of this research to trace the evolution of how the international legal community has understood 'order'. It is nonetheless interesting to note that the concept seems to have broadened with time as international law's areas of concern multiplied. It is, for instance, intriguing how a lot of textbooks still define international law in classical Westphalian terms as the rules regulating the intercourse of States to quickly underline the out-dated nature of that definition.[23] States, they say, despite remaining the main protagonists of international relations and law, now co-exist with other actors. The role of and the place given to international organisations, non-governmental organisations but also private groups and individuals, in particular, need to be acknowledged. The underlying postulate is that we have been, and still are, moving from an inter-State dynamic to transnational dynamics.

This movement obviously has had, and still has, repercussions on the way 'order' has been and is conceptualised. More importantly for us, it may have impacted the place that the classically understood notion of peace (negatively defined as absence of armed conflict) held and holds within international law's framework. Some authors have thus noted how a 'positive' understanding of peace – based on the cooperation rather than co-existence of States and on the creation of transnational synergies among peoples – has slowly come the supersede its negative counterpart. Using Hersch Lauterpacht's claim according to which international law should have as a premise the establishment of inter-state peace and the protection of human rights as a joint purpose, they note how: 'while the protection of human rights steadily gained support as a primary purpose of international law, international legal literature largely abandoned promoting the establishment of peace as an independent, overarching

[21] Prost, *The Concept of Unity*, p. 145.

[22] See Anne Orford, 'Constituting order', in James Crawford and Martti Koskenniemi (eds.), *The Cambridge Companion to International Law* (Cambridge University Press, 2012), pp. 271 westphalian terms 289.

[23] See, e.g., Joe Verhoeven, *Droit international public* (Larcier, 2000), p. 17.

aim of international law'.[24] The replacement of the 'liberal' model of international order by a 'welfarist' model of transnational order, operates at the detriment of the traditional understandings of the *ius ad bellum*. The concept of 'humanity' will sometimes be opposed to that of 'sovereignty' – the State becomes the enemy of the people – to plead in favour of the 'enhancement of the lawful use of force to meet [so-called] modern challenges'.[25]

We will have the occasion to come back in further details on the question of the interconnections between the notion of order and of peace later in the course of this dissertation.[26] We shall, in particular, see how, in the years that preceded and those that followed the Great War, the idea of order was intrinsically linked to inter-state peace. For the time being, however, what is most important to remember, is how the international legal profession's rhetoric associated the idea of law with that of order, whatever the meaning one puts behind that concept. The function of international law is to inject *order* in an otherwise *chaotic* international society. Whether it is truly able to achieve that end (and, hence, 'law' in the proper sense of the term) is another issue.

8.1.2 The 'Effectivity Complex' of International Law: John Austin's Enduring Spectre and the Refuge of Formalism

All international lawyers have, at some point, been confronted with the assertion that international law is not real law. The argument is familiar. In the fashion of John Austin, our interlocutor will, most probably, contend that in the absence of a superior authority capable of laying down determinate obligations and forcefully enforce them through an effective mechanisms of sanction, international law is incapable of controlling the behaviour of States. The application of, and respect for, international rules, they will continue, purely depends on the good will of States. Consequently, international law cannot be said to be 'binding' in the legal sense of the term. At best, it creates a vague feeling of moral and ethical obligation. Moreover, the frequency with which States violate

[24] Cecilia M. Bailliet and Kjetil Mujezinović Larsen, 'Introduction: Promoting Peace Through International Law', in Cecilia M. Bailliet and Kjetil Mujezinović Larsen (eds.), *Promoting Peace through International Law* (Oxford University Press, 2015), p. 1.

[25] 'Enhancing the lawful use of force to meet modern challenges', is the title of section IV (A) of Antonio Cassese's edited volume entitled *Realizing UtopiaL The Future of International Law* (Oxford University Press, 2012), p. 343.

[26] See below (9.1.1.).

their engagements just comes as a final illustration of how ineffective international law is in fulfilling its tasks, of how unable it is to act as vector of order in international relations, and of the little importance that States themselves give to it. Confronted with these claims, even the sceptics among us, might find themselves defending the legal nature of international law. An attack on the effectivity of international law as law is an attack on the legitimacy of the discipline and, by extension, on the utility of the profession.[27] It is personal and has been for a while.[28]

Since John Austin made his claim in 1832, that international is 'law improperly so-called',[29] this issue, as Frédéric Mégret remarks, has 'provoked a long series of responses and counter-responses, evidence that, if anything, international lawyers were piqued by the suggestion'.[30] Nineteenth century scholarship was fast to react to Austin's attack on, and depreciation of, their discipline. As soon as 1836, Wheaton thus noted that a disciple of Jeremy Bentham had observed how the rules adopted for the conduct of independent States could not be called 'laws' in the strict sense of the term.[31] At that point, however, Wheaton did not endeavour to answer to Austin's arguments. A few years later, in 1839, Manning was more thorough in his rejection of his fellow Englishman's assertions. 'My objection', he wrote, 'is that the word law, which has, in our language, so long been employed in a much wider sense, should, by a single writer, be declared to be only "properly" used with [his] restricted meaning'.[32]

Thenceforth, textbooks quasi-systematically have a part of their introductory section dedicated to the question of 'is international law, 'law'? and to the demonstration that it, of course, is.[33] The tone of some

27 In this sense, see Frédéric Mégret, 'International Law as Law', in James Crawford and Martti Koskenniemi (eds.), *The Cambridge Companion to International Law* (Cambridge University Press, 2012), p. 72. On the question of legitimacy see John Tasioulas, 'The Legitimacy of International Law', in Samantha Benson and John Tasioulas (eds.), *The Philosophy of International Law* (Oxford University Press, 2010), pp. 97–116.

28 For an illustration of this see Anthony D'Amato, *International Law: Process and Prospect* (Transnational Publishers Inc., 1995), pp. 358–370.

29 John Austin, *The Province of Jurisprudence Determined* (John Murray, 1832), p. 147.

30 Frédéric Mégret, 'International Law as Law', p. 72. See also Emmanuelle Jouannet, 'Regards sur un siècle de doctrine française du droit international' (2000) 46 *Annuaire français de droit international* 8 ff.

31 Henry Wheaton, *Elements of International Law*, 2 vols. (Lea & Blanchard, 1836) vol. 1, pp. 46–47.

32 William Oke Manning, *Commentaries on the Law of Nations* (S. Sweet, 1839), p. 5.

33 See, e.g., Ernest Nys, *Les origines du droit international* (Alfred Castaigne, 1894), p. I ff; Amos S. Hershey, *The Essentials of International Public Law* (MacMillan, 1919), p. 5;

manuals is even, at times, defensive. Authors will, for example, regret that 'unfortunately, this question is still being asked, and not only by law students',[34] or warn that:

> Those who approach international law after having studied a national legal system (municipal law) may feel the need either to revise their conception of 'law' or to take the view, as many do, that 'international law is not law'. Those who take the latter view may be surprised to learn that every state in the world, that is to say their statesmen and governments, acts on the assumption that inter-state relations are governed by law. The reader may thus be advised to do likewise.[35]

The profession's response is as familiar as the initial argument. It usually goes as follows: Austin's definition of 'law' is unnecessarily restrictive and relies too heavily on the idea of vertical punitive sanction; although it is true that international society lacks centralised authorities, other types of sanctions, in particular social sanctions, can be just as effective in ensuring compliance with obligations; States recognise the existence of international law; municipal law is not always respected either; and, in any case, States actually proportionally respect more than they violate their

Charles G. Fenwick, *International Law* (The Century Co., 1924), pp. 40–41; Franz von Litszt, *Le droit international. Exposé systématique* (Pedone, 1928), pp. 8–11; Karl Strupp, *Eléments du droit international universel, européen et américain*, 2 vols. (Les éditions internationales, 1930), vol. 1, p. 3; Sibert, *Traité de droit international public*, vol. 1, pp. 4–8; Hans Kelsen, *Principles of International Law* (Rinehart & Company Inc., 1952), pp. 18 ff; Louis Cavaré, *Le droit international public positif*, 2 vols. (2nd ed., Pedone, 1961), vol. 1, p. 9; Paul Guggenheim, *Traité de droit international public*, 2 vols. (Librairie de l'Université de Genève, 1967), vol. 1, pp. 21–24; Charles Rousseau, *Droit international public*, 5 vols. (Editions Siray, 1970–1983), vol. 1, p. 25; Gerhard von Glahn, *Law Among Nations. An Introduction to Public International Law* (3rd ed., MacMillan Publishing Co., 1976), p. 6; Starke, Introduction to International Law, pp. 15–17; Arbour, Droit international public, pp. 29–32; Peter Malanczuk, *Akehurst's Modern Introduction to International Law* (7th ed., Routledge, 1997), pp. 3–6; Sikondo, Introduction au droit international public, p. 54; Verhoeven, Droit international public, pp. 21–24; O'Brien, *International Law*, pp. 28–33; James H. Wolfe, *Modern International Law. An Introduction to the Law of Nations* (Prentice Hall, 2002), p. 1; Richard K. Gardiner, *International Law* (Pearson Longman, 2003), p. 3; Dixon, *International Law*, pp. 4–6; Shaw, International Law, pp. 2–8; (Nguyên Quôc Dinh), Patrick Daillier, Mathias Forteau et Alain Pellet, *Droit international public* (8th ed. LGDJ, 2009), pp. 100–102; Aust, Handbook of International Law, pp. 3–5; Dejo Olowu, *International Law. A Textbook for the South Pacific* (CD Publishing, 2010), pp. 18–20; John Duggard, *International Law. A South African Perspective* (Juta, 2011), pp. 7–9; Klabbers, *International Law*, pp. 9–11. Exception, see Ian Brownlie, *Principles of Public International Law* (4th ed., Clarendon Press, 1990).

[34] Aust, *Handbook of International Law*, p. 3.

[35] Green, *International Law*, p. 1.

international obligations. In this respect, modern textbooks will equally underline the role played by the media, which, by only covering spectacular (but exceptional) cases of violations of international law rather than the ordinary course of business, offer a twisted image of the field.[36]

More interesting than the arguments that international lawyers have put forth for the past two hundred years to defend and prove the 'truly' legal nature of their discipline, is the fact that they still feel compelled to do so. Unlike municipal law, the effectivity, and consequently, legitimacy of international law is still not taken for granted and this, somehow, upsets international lawyers. Of course, this does not mean that international lawyers necessarily believe international law always has great or imperative influence on the behaviour of States, especially when questions of high politics are involved. Still, as Koskenniemi observes, most cannot help but feel slightly irritated when governments disregard their obligations.[37] To illustrate this point, Koskenniemi refers to the debate about the US intervention in the Dominican Republic that took place in the mid-1960s between A. J. Thomas and Adolf A. Berle, on the one side, and Wolfgang Friedmann, on the other. To briefly summarize, Thomas and Berle argued that the intervention was justified as a matter of self-defence, the revolution in the Dominican Republic being so clearly in contradiction with US interests, but also that, in any case, legal technicalities were beside the point when matters of such high political stake were involved. Faced with these arguments, Koskenniemi notes how, even a lawyer labelled a 'realist' such as Friedman, could not refrain from adopting a formalistic stand. More than the substance of Thomas and Berle's contentions, 'perharps what Friedman f[ound] objectionable', Koskenniemi argues, 'is the nonchalance with which [they] treat[ed] his profession, the (to him) self-evident hypocrisy that accompanied their reasoning and that seemed to fatally undermine the profession's faith and integrity'.[38] Formalism acts as an argumentative reflex and

[36] This preoccupation was already expressed by James L. Brierly in 1936. In his course at The Hague Academy, the British professor indeed wrote that: 'Les violations du droit international, lorsqu'elles se produisent aujourd'hui, ont souvent un caractère sensationnel et risquent donc de faire perdre de vue, dans une certaine mesure, aux observateurs superficiels que l'obéissance à la loi est la coutume normale des Etats', in 'Règles générales du droit de la paix', 11. See also Malanczuk, Akehurst's, p. 6; Aust, Handbook of International Law, p. 3.

[37] Martti Koskenniemi, *The Gentle Civilizer of Nations. The Rise and Fall of International Law, 1870–1960* (Cambridge University Press, 2001), p. 498 ff.

[38] Ibid., p. 499.

refuge for the international lawyer faced with the practical lack of effectivity and indetermination of his or her discipline. This reflex is clearly reminiscent of the Kantian idealism about the power of law evoked in the previous section, as it is a form of expression of the belief that law can be a shield against arbitrariness.

Beyond formalism, however, international lawyers are prompt to recognise that their field does not always set effective standards of conduct for States and that its sanction mechanisms certainly leave room for improvement. Accordingly, international law is said to be 'true but imperfect law'[39] and 'weaker than municipal law';[40] in sum a 'primitive' legal system still in the early stages of its development.[41] Once more, municipal law serves as a point of comparison: it is stronger, it is more 'perfect', more sophisticated, because it is more ancient. The underlying claim is that international law follows the same trajectory as national legal systems but simply finds itself a few steps behind. The greater effectivity of international law, in other terms, is merely a question of time.[42] Although the evolution of international institutions is slow, Paul Guggenheim for instance tells us, it is 'certain'.[43]

8.1.3 *Historiographies of International Law: A Story of Constant Progress of the Law and* Through *Law*

The two previous sections showed how international law is envisioned as an indispensable tool to ensure order on the international place, but also how its capacity to effectively do so remains contested and precarious. The way the history of international law is generally presented in textbooks acts as a synthesis of that ideal and of that reality. It also appears as yet another manifestation of the cosmopolitan idealist mantra that roams

[39] von Glahn, Law among Nations, p. 6.

[40] Malanczuk, Akehurst's, p. 6.

[41] Oscar Svarlien, *An Introduction to the Law of Nations* (McGraw-Hill Book Company, 1955), p. 3; Stone, Of Law and Nations, p. 43. On the primitivism of international law see Michel Virally, 'Sur la prétendue « primitivité » du droit international', in *Le droit international en devenir* (Graduate Institute Publications, 1990), pp. 91–101.

[42] In this sense see Richard Collins, *The Institutional Problem in Modern International Law* (Hart, 2016), p. 38.

[43] 'Les institutions encore primitives du droit international public sont cependant soumises à une évolution lente mais certaine', Guggenheim, Traité de droit international public, vol. 1, p. 23. In the same vein, James L. Brierly stated in 1936 that: 'A longue échéance nous pouvons donc nous attendre, avec quelques raisons, à un renforcement international du règne du droit', in 'Règles générales du droit de la paix', 11.

the field. As Oliver Diggelmann puts it, traditional historiographies of international law seem to be guided, on the one hand, by the 'idea that there is simply no alternative to the success of international law', and, on the other, by the will to 'immunize the discipline against the challenges of its relevance'.[44] The story told is thus one of the correlative progress *of* international law and of the international society *through* international law. What is meant by this is that, over time, international law is shown to have gradually evolved and consolidated into a genuine normative system, an evolution and consolidation that has enabled the overall amelioration of international and transnational dynamics. The slow but steady development of law – through the establishment and emergence of new rules, the creation of international fora of discussion or institutions, and the codification of existing rules – has, in sum, served as a catalyst of order against chaos. In this respect, let us simply recall the opening sentence to Shaw's manual. 'In the long march of mankind from the cave to the computer', it tells us, 'a central role has always been played by the idea of law'.[45] This excerpt not only suggests that, from the cave to the computer, law has always existed, but also that it has been a leading factor in the evolution of mankind from pre-history to modernity.[46] In other words, even though international law is not yet perfectly effective in bringing order to the world, its history shows that it has been able to continuously grow as a legal system and that this growth has been objectively beneficial. More international law, in a way, equates to a better international society.[47]

Following this general narrative weave, the history of international law is divided into a series of historical periods, each representing an improvement from the previous. In this frame, modern international law is usually said to have originated about 400 years ago, around the time of the Treaty of Westphalia (1648) and the writings of the so-called

[44] Oliver Diggelmann, 'The Periodization of the History of International Law', in Bardo Fassbender and Anne Peters (eds.), *The Oxford Handbook on the History of International Law* (Oxford University Press, 2012), pp. 1008–1009.

[45] Shaw, *International Law*, p. 1.

[46] See Skouteris, *The Notion of Progress*, p. 19.

[47] In this respect Koskenniemi highlights the 'Messianic structure to international law, the announcement of something that remains eternally postponed' and that 'this 'to-come' that enables the criticism of the law's own violence, its biases and exclusions', 'What Is International Law For?', in Malcolm D. Evans (ed.), *International Law* (1st ed., Oxford University Press, 2003), p. 111.

'founding fathers'.[48] Of course, rules regulating the relations independent political entities probably existed in the past. The Greeks, the Romans, the Egyptians likely knew of an 'international law' of some sort,[49] but the legacy of the antiquity for the current system is generally considered to have been rather limited.[50] From the seventeenth century onwards, the history of international law is divided into a series of time lapses symbolising specific moments in the advancement of the discipline. Despite some variations,[51] there seems to be a general agreement in the literature as to the periodisation of international law as well as to the elements that mark the limits of those periods.[52] Four 'ages', whose beginnings and ends are determined by the cycles of large-scale violent conflict and issuing wide-ranging peace settlements, are traditionally distinguished: 1648 to 1815, 1815 to 1914, 1919 to 1939 and 1945 to more or less the

[48] Henry Wheaton, *History of the Law of Nations in Europe and America* (Gould, Banks & Co., 1845), p. 69; Lassa Oppenheim, *International Law*, 2 vols. (Longman Green, 1905), vol. 1, p. 44; Hershey, *The Essentials*, p. 26 and § 54, p. 56; von Redlich, *The Law of Nations*, p. 2; Starke, *Introduction to International Law*, p. 7; Malanczuk, Akehurst's, p. 9; Cesár Sepúlveda, *Derecho internacional* (Editorial Porrúa, 2004), p. 7; Shaw, International Law, p. 14; Duggard, International Law, p. 9; Jan Klabbers, International Law, p. 4.

[49] On international law in antiquity see David J. Bederman, *International Law in Antiquity* (Cambridge University Press, 2001). See also Wolfgang Preisner, 'History of International Law, Ancient Times to 1648', *Max Planck Encyclopaedia for Public International Law Online*, (last update: August 2008).

[50] See Louis Le Fur, 'Règles générales du droit de la paix' (1935) 58 *Recueil des cours de l'académie de droit international* 9; Arthur Nussbaum, *A Concise History of the Law of Nations* (MacMillan, 1947), pp. 7 ff.

[51] For an 'inventory' of the different periodisations that can be encountered in the scholarship since the eighteenth century see William E. Butler, 'Periodization and International Law', in Alexander Orakhelashvili (ed.), *Research Handbook on the Theory and History of International Law* (Edward Elgar, 2011), pp. 379–393. For 'soviet' periodisation, see Kazimierz Grzybowski, *Soviet Public International Law* (A. W. Stijhoff, 1970), pp. 3–4; William E. Butler, 'Some Reflections on the Periodization of Soviet Approaches to International Law', in Donald D. Barry, William E. Butler and George Ginsburg (eds.), *Contemporary Soviet Law: Essays in Honor of John N. Hazard* (Martinus Nijhoff, 1974), pp. 213–225.

[52] Wilhelm G. Grewe underlines that 'there is agreement as to the periodization of the history of international law, and above all as to the question of where one locates the limits of those periods', in *The Epochs of International Law* (Walter de Gruyter, 2000), p. 6. For a critique of periodisation in international law see Ingo J. Hueck, 'The Discipline of the History of International Law – New Trends and Methods for the History of International Law' (2001) 3 *Journal of the History of International Law* 194–217. Also discussing Grewe's periods see Randall Lesaffer, 'The Grotian Tradition Revisited: Change and Continuity in the History of International Law' (2002) 73 *British Yearbook of International Law* 103–139.

present day.[53] Most of the time, the adoption of this particular division of time will not be a conscious choice of the author. It has, as Diggelmann notes, acquired a 'quasi-objective' status; a status that is also reinforced by the fact that international law's conventional periods correspond to the conventional periods of western international history.[54] Two things issue from this. The first, is that the (hi)story of international law follows the same story line as general history. The second, is that the assumptions that motivate this particular division of time are, as the period themselves, objectivised and internalised. But the division of time in periods, although a useful pedagogical and organisational tool, carries specific interpretations of the past.

The conventional periodisation of the history of international law, for instance, places a lot of emphasis on formal settlements and on the creation of institutions – as we know, 1648 marks the Treaty of Westphalia and the establishment of a system based on the existence of sovereign States; 1815 is the Congress of Vienna and the inauguration of the European Concert; 1919 corresponds to the Covenant of the League of Nations and 1945 to the Charter of the United Nations. This priority given to the 'treaty criteria', as William Butler calls it, has several effects.[55] First, it probably overemphasizes the role of formal statements and institutions for the existence of international law. It suggests that the field needs some sort of wide-ranging agreement to lay down the ground rules of international relations. This can seem odd considering how international law is also said to be, above all, customary. But it is not completely surprising. the Thirty Years' War, the Napoleonic invasions, the two world wars and the peace agreements that issued from them, surely contributed to reshuffling the cards of international relations. But the fact that law is a discipline that traditionally heavily relies on authorities is another factor to take into account. Custom is unstable and elusive, while treaties offer tangible texts and determinate dates, in addition to giving an impression of organisation and effectivity. They give clear and reassuring elements for the jurist to build the history of his or her field.[56]

[53] See, e.g., Nussbaum, A concise history of the law of nations; Grewe, The Epochs; Malanczuk, Akehurst's, p. 9 ff.

[54] Diggelmann, 'The Periodization of the History of International Law', pp. 999 and 1001.

[55] Butler, 'Periodization and International Law', p. 385.

[56] On the role of codification in history see Olivier Corten, 'Les aspects idéologiques de la codification du droit international', in *Le discours du droit international* (Pedone, 2009), pp. 153–172.

Institutions work in the same way. It is, for example, interesting to note how the first two periods of 'modern' international law are characterized by the doctrine that supposedly dominated the era. We often speak of the seventeenth and eighteenth centuries as the age of 'naturalism' and of a law of nations still closely intertwined with philosophy. Manuals will generally focus on exposing the work of the major authors, starting with Grotius and ending with Wolf and Vattel. The nineteenth century, as we already saw, is presented as the 'positivist century'. International law is then associated with power politics and, even though they often underline that the field underwent a significant expansion at the time,[57] textbooks will place the emphasis on the political history of European imperialism and balance of power. The Holy Alliance and European Concert will, of course be mentioned, but to underline the ephemeral existence of the first, and the aleatory and loose functioning of the second. The interwar and post-1945 periods, on the other hand, are respectively presented as the 'League era' and the 'Charter era'. The description will talk less of philosophy or politics, but instead engage in a positivistic appraisal of the rules that existed and of the functioning of the institutions. This contrast in the way the 'content' of the periods of international law is presented conveys the idea that international law needs formal institutions to properly exist and that it only became a self-standing legal discipline in the twentieth century.

Another interpretation of history that the classic periodisation of international law insidiously carries, is the sense that international law trips but never falls; it gets back on its feet in an ever more vigorous form. Instead of destroying international law, major wars contributed to its progress and to the development of better international structures. Abiding by this narrative, but underlining its odd character in the meantime, Louis Cavaré thus noted how:

> Despite the apparent paradox of this assertion, external events, such as wars, especially general wars, have determined significant progress in international law. As we have seen, it was after the long period of the

[57] Georges Scelle, for instance, emphasised: 'au cours du XIXe siècle tant décrié, l'évolution de l'ordre juridique international se poursuit, [. . .]. *L'intégration de la communauté internationale* est, en effet, le résultat du prodigieux effort de production et de commerce qui résulte du développement du *machinisme* et du *régime capitaliste*', in *Manuel élémentaire de droit international public* (Editions Domat-Montchrestien, 1943), p. 41. Emphasis in the original. See also Carlton J. H. Hayes, 'The Historical Background', in Stephen Pierce Duggan (ed.), *The League of Nations. The Principles and the Practice* (The Atlantic Press, 1919), pp. 35–39.

> wars of the Revolution and the Empire that the era of law-treaties began: it was especially after the World War of 1914-1918 that the greatest progress was made, followed by another regression, but this was followed by an attempt at an even more sophisticated world organization.[58]

This brings us back to the narrative of progress that roams the history of the discipline and which, actually, is a common side effect of most periodisations. Dividing history into periods, indeed, suggests that these different time frames have an internal coherence, which can result in overemphasizing discontinuity. That said, discontinuity does not necessarily induce progress narratives; it could equally give rise to stories of decline or of cyclical patterns. The reasons why evolutionary histories still prevail in international law are linked, as already mentioned, to the profession's core residual idealism, as well as to the field's continuing search for recognition and legitimacy. But another element also needs to be highlighted. In addition to borrowing the traditional periods of European history, international law also follows the same overall 'eudemonistic' and 'teleological' historical philosophy, inherited from eighteenth-century enlightenment, which still dominates most of contemporary western historiographies.[59] The extract from Cavaré's textbook, for instance, could be said to be reminiscent of Georg Wilhelm Friedrich Hegel's philosophy of history. In *Phenomenology of the Spirit* (1807), Hegel argued that history advances by means of dialectic clashes, i.e., the encounter of a thesis and of an antithesis whose contradiction is eventually sublated by a synthesis dictated by reason.[60] Here, the thesis would be that international law is a vector of order, the antithesis would be that wars still happen and the synthesis is the emergence of a new system of international relations after each major conflict, which, learning from the shortcomings of the previous period, enables the system to carry on under another, better, form.[61]

[58] Louis Cavaré, *Le droit international public positif*, 2 vols. (Pedone, 1961), vol. 1, p. 246.

[59] Diggelmann, 'The Periodization of the History of International Law', pp. 999 and 1009.

[60] Georg Wilhelm Friedrich Hegel, *The Philosophy of History*, original ed.: 1837 (Dover Publications, 1956), p. 56.

[61] In 1937, Charles Dupuis introduced his course at The Hague Academy by observing how international history is one of constant oscillation between 'l'organisation internationale' and 'l'anarchie des souveraineté'. 'Chacune des grandes crises belliqueuses qui ravagèrent l'Europe', he added, 'a provoqué l'éclosion de projets destinés à porter remède à l'anarchie des souverainetés', in 'Les antécédents de la Société des Nations' (1937) 60 *Recueil des cours de l'académie de droit international* 5. In the beginning of the twentieth century legal historian, Robert Redslob, for his part, used a wave metaphor to speak of the general movement of international law: 'on dirait les vagues d'une marée montante qui tantôt se

As the excerpt from Cavaré's textbook also suggests, that is exactly the narrative that the literature has adopted regarding the use of force and the disturbing events of the World War I. This is, however, not where the resemblance between the disciplinary beliefs about international law and the traditional discourse about the history of the use of force stops. Indeed, we shall now see how the rhetoric of the narrative of indifference mimics, in almost every aspect, the structures upon which the whole professional discourse about international law just expounded is built.

8.2 The Narrative of 'Indifference': Law and Order vs. Politics and Anarchy

The narrative of indifference did not emerge in a univocal manner. Authors did not (and still do not) fully agree on how to tell the story of recourse to armed force before the World War I. Immediate after-war textbooks continued to be written under the same model as nineteenth century textbooks and carried the same discourse as the pre-war scholarship. Jan de Louter's *Le droit international public positif* (1920) and Paul Fauchille's eighth edition of *Traité de droit international public* (written from 1921 to 1926), for instance, were still organized around the 'fundamental rights and duties' of States,[62] and still addressed the use of force (from retorsions and reprisals to war as the measure of absolute last resort) as unamicable means of settling international disputes, while making no mention of the Covenant of the League of Nations.[63] The Covenant was adopted on 28 June 1919 and came into force 10 January 1920. It took a few years for the literature to incorporate the outcome of the Versailles settlements, for the new generation of international lawyers

jettent à l'assaut du ravage, tantôt retombent dans le néant, mais qui suivent tout de même, à la longue, une marche ascendante', in *Histoire des grands principes du droit des gens depuis l'antiquité jusqu'à la veille de la Grande Guerre* (Rousseau & Cie. Éditeurs, 1923), p. 547. On a more critical note, Kennedy, likewise notices that disciplinary history of international law is characterised by cycles of 'anxiety and disputation' and 'consensus and renewal', see 'When Renewal Repeats', 342.

62 Jan de Louter, *Le droit international public positif*, 2 vols. (Imprimerie de l'Université, 1920), vol. 1, pp. 232–250; Paul Fauchille, *Traité de droit international public*, 2 vols. (8th éd., Arthur Rousseau, 1922), vol. 1, pp. 394 ff.

63 de Louter, Le droit international public positif, vol. 2, pp. 212–234; Fauchille, Traité de droit international public, vol. 1, pp. 685 ff.

to occupy the forefront of the scene and for the feelings of war vendetta to decisively give way to the desire for peace. Even then, however, the narrative of indifference did not appear in a cohesive, organised and uncontested fashion. It came, and still comes, in different versions.

This section will start by highlighting the characteristics of the different versions of the narrative of 'indifference'; present their content and ambiguities (Section 8.2.1.). It will then show that, despite seemingly telling a different (hi)story, they all share the same rhetorical structure and, as a result, tell the same story. This resemblance, we shall moreover see, is not limited to the indifference-narrative different iterations. Structurally, in fact, they all mimic the discipline's more general discourse about international law, its functions and its history. Using a method based on Claude Lévi-Strauss's structural and linguistic analysis of myths, we shall see how all the different version of the history of the use of force are built on the axiomatic opposition of law and order to politics and anarchy (Section 8.2.2.). This observation confirms the hypothesis according to which mainstream historical accounts on the prohibition of the use of force in international law are products of the discipline's core beliefs about itself. Finally, even though the narrative of indifference (in one or the other of its versions) is widely shared in the scholarship, this section would not be complete without having a look at the works, which from the 1920s onwards, have questioned it (Section 8.2.3.).

8.2.1 *Different (Hi)Stories: Content and Ambiguities of the Narrative(s) of Indifference*

The narrative of indifference is not a homogenous and unitary discourse. Different accounts of classical international law's nonchalant attitude towards the right to resort to military force exist in contemporary doctrine and can be gathered under the general appellation of 'narrative of indifference'. A quick look at the literature dating from 1919 to the present-day shows that three sub-narratives of indifference can be identified: 'total' indifference, 'partial' indifference, and 'practical' indifference. The simple fact that doctrine does not actually exactly agree on what the rules on the use of force in the nineteenth century consisted (or did not consist) is already quite perplexing. But, beyond the discrepancies that exist between the different versions of the narrative of indifference, we shall see that all three accounts are themselves not devoid of ambiguities.

The Sub-Narrative of 'Total' Indifference

The main ambiguity that surrounds the narrative of 'total indifference' is linked to terminology. The writings that adopt this version of the indifference-narrative barely seem to make a distinction between war and measures short of war. They either broadly talk of the 'use of force' in general or of 'war' in an extensive fashion that seemingly embraces any type of resort to armed force. It may thus be read that 'in the Westphalian legal order, it was admitted that States could *resort to force*. *War* was considered as an ordinary and legitimate political instrument';[64] that 'in the international society [before 1919], resort to force was legal. It has often been justified by considering war as an inevitable action of the existence'.[65] Knowing that the use of force in the nineteenth century could take different forms that produced different legal consequences,[66] this interchangeable use of the expression 'use of force' and 'war' is confusing. Do these authors really mean to talk about the use of force in general (war and measures short of war) and use the word 'war' as a commodity of language, or do they actually only intend to talk about war restrictively understood?

[64] Nico Schrijver, 'Article 2, paragraphe 4', in Jean-Pierre Cot et Alain Pellet (eds.), *La Charte des Nations Unies. Commentaires articles par articles* (3e ed., Economica, 2005), p. 440. Emphasis added. Translation by the author.

[65] Mme. Paul Bastid, *Cours de droit international public* (Les cours de droit, 1976–1977), p. 987. Emphasis added. Translation by the author. See also Sibert, Traité de droit international public, vol. 2, p. 625; Louis Delbez, *Les principes généraux du droit international public* (3rd ed., LGDJ, 1963), p. 395; Antoine Favre, *Principes du droit des gens* (LGDJ, 1974), pp. 711–713; Starke, Introduction to International Law, p. 508; Antonio Cassese, *International Law* (Oxford University Press, 2001), pp. 27 and 33; O'Brien, International Law, pp. 676–677; Modesto Seara Vásquez, *Derecho internacional público* (Editorial Porrúa, 2004), pp. 361–362; Dixon, International Law, p. 310; Robert Kolb and Richard Hyde, *An Introduction to the International Law of Armed Conflicts* (Hart Publishing, 2008), pp. 9–10; John H. Currie, *Public International Law* (2nd ed., Irwin Law, 2008), pp. 452–453; Alina Kaczorowska, *Public International Law* (4th ed., Routledge, 2010), p. 689; Duggard, International Law, p. 465; Yoram Dinstein, *War, Aggression and Self-Defence* (5th ed., Cambridge University Press, 2011), pp. 77–78; Gideon Boas, *Public International Law. Contemporary Principles and Perspectives* (Edward Elgar, 2012), pp. 310–311; Pierre-Marie Dupuy et Yann Kerbat, *Droit international public* (Dalloz, 2012), p. 615; Rebecca M. Wallace and Olga Martin-Ortega, *International Law* (7th ed., Sweet & Maxwell, 2013), p. 294; Oliver Dörr, 'Prohibition of the Use of Force', *Max Planck Encyclopeadia of Public International Law Online* (last update: September 2015), par. 4.

[66] See above Chapter 1.

This ambiguity was already present in the interwar literature. After the World War I, most authors focused their attention on war.[67] They were quite adamant that the system of collective security of the League was, in this respect, revolutionary. Nicolas Politis spoke of 'an unlimited right of war' before 1919;[68] Hans Wehberg claimed that '*ius publicum europaeum* admitted war regardless of any *justa causa*';[69] Maurice Bourquin that 'classical international law, has it began to emerge in the nineteenth century, admitted, in sum, the legality of war';[70] Louis Le Fur that 'in this system [that of the nineteenth century], we refuse to distinguish between the war that are just and those that are unjust, there are only wars that succeed or that fail, success is proof of law';[71] Hersch Lauterpacht that 'war was in law a natural function of the State and a prerogative of its uncontrolled sovereignty'.[72] On the other hand, measures short of war were barely spoken of from a historical perspective.[73] It may be that the trauma caused by the Great War made the measures short of war appear as an issue of secondary importance. It may also be that, since the Covenant of the League of Nations only explicitly dealt with war, the incentive was greater to comment on the evolution of the elements that were most visibly new.

The legal status of coercive measures was, in fact, uncertain during the interwar years. The Covenant of the League of Nations, and later the Briand-Kellogg Pact (1928), generated extensive debates concerning the

[67] See, e.g., Quincy Wright, 'Changes in the Conception of War' (1924) 18 *American Journal of International Law* 755–767; Joachim von Elbe, 'The Evolution of the Concept of Just War in International Law' (1939) 33 *American Journal of International Law* 665–688; Arthur Nussbaum, 'Just War – A Legal Concept?' (1943) 42 *Michigan Law Review* 453–459.

[68] Nicolas Politis, 'Le problème des limitations de la souveraineté et la théorie de l'abus des droits dans les rapports internationaux' (1925) 6 *Recueil des cours de l'académie de droit international* 40.

[69] Hans Wehberg, 'L'interdiction du recours à la force. Le principe et les problèmes qui se posent' (1951) 78 *Recueil des cours de l'académie de droit international* 25–26. Translation by the author.

[70] Maurice Bourquin, 'Le problème de la sécurité internationale' (1934) 49 *Recueil des cours de l'académie de droit international* 477. Translation by the author.

[71] Louis Le Fur, *Précis de droit international public* (4th éd., Librairie Dalloz, 1939), p. 302. Translation by the author.

[72] (Lassa Oppenheim) Hersch Lauterpacht (ed.), *International Law – A Treatise*, 2 vols. (5th ed., Longman Greens, 1935), p. 148.

[73] Exceptions are P. H. Winfield, 'The History of Intervention in International Law' (1922–1923) 3 *British Yearbook of International Law* 130–149; Nicolas Politis, 'Les représailles entre les Etats membres de la SdN' (1924) 31 *Revue générale de droit international public* 7–8. But these authors were proponents of 'partial indifference'.

scope of the prohibition of the use of force they contained. With the Covenant, the crux of the problem revolved around Article 10 – according to which member States should respect and preserve each other's '*territorial integrity*' and '*political independence*' against external aggression –[74] and Articles 12 and 15 – which provided for mandatory recourse to pacific mechanisms of dispute resolution (arbitration, judicial settlement or enquiry by the Council) when a disagreement susceptible of leading to a '*rupture*' appeared between member States and imposed a moratorium of three months after the judicial decision before '*resort to war*' could be had.[75] Some writers contended that there were many other ways to damage the sovereignty and political independence of a State besides war and that Article 10 consequently extended the 'prohibition' of the use of force beyond the mere hypothesis of war.[76] The same reasoning was applied to Articles 12 and 15. They argued that the word 'rupture' was, by definition, very broad and should consequently be understood as including all the situations in which the good mutual relations of States were endangered.[77] Others, the minority, considered that these provisions needed to be read in conjunction with the rest of the Covenant, which textually only referred to 'war' and never explicitly mentioned armed coercive measures.[78] The preamble, in fact, spoke of 'the acceptance of obligations not to resort to war', and the second half of

[74] Art. 10, Covenant of the League of Nations, Paris, 28 June 1919, in force: 10 January 1920. For an overview of the controversies surrounding the interpretation of Article 10, see Agatha Verdebout, 'Article 10', in Robert Kolb (ed.), *Commentaire sur le Pacte de la Société des Nations* (Bruylant, 2015), pp. 430–432.

[75] Arts. 12 and 15, Covenant of the League of Nations.

[76] See Ciriaque G. Tenekides, 'L'évolution de l'idée des mesures coercitives et la Société des Nations' (1926) 53 *Revue de droit international et de législation compare* 410–411; J. M. Yepes et Pereira da Silva, *Commentaire théorique et pratique du Pacte de la Société des Nations et des Statuts de l'Union Panaméricaine*, 3 vols. (Edition A. Pedone, 1934), vol. 1, p. 284.

[77] Charles de Visscher insisted: 'ce terme ne désigne pas seulement la guerre ou le danger prochain de la guerre, [. . .]; il s'applique également à toute situation que les parties ne parviennent pas à régler par leur propre effort et qui, en se prolongeant, est de nature à mettre en danger leurs bonnes relations mutuelles', in 'L'interprétation du Pacte au lendemain du différend italo-grec' (1924) 51 *Revue de droit international et de législation comparée* 215. See also Walther Schücking and Hans Wehberg, *Die Satzung des Völkerbundes*, 2 vols. (F. Vahlen, 1924), pp. 507–508; Politis, 'Les représailles entre les Etats membres de la SdN', 14; Zygmunt Gralinski, *Le règlement pacifique obligatoire des différends internationaux suivant le Pacte de la Société des Nations* (Pedone, 1925), p. 194.

[78] See Titus Kormanicki, *La question de l'intégrité territoriale dans le Pacte de la Société des Nations* (Les presses universitaires de France, 1923), p. 176; Karl Strupp, 'L'incident de Janina entre la Grèce et l'Italie' (1924) 31 *Revue générale de droit international public*

Article 12 likewise specified what was meant by 'rupture' by forbidding resort to '*war*' within a period of three months following the judicial decision. To this, the first group retorted with a teleological argument. They claimed that with the adoption of the Covenant, the distinction between the different types of use of force had lost its *raison d'être*.[79] An act of war could hardly be distinguished from an act of armed reprisals; from which it followed that any use of force, regardless of the intention that accompanied it, should be deemed contrary to the desire for peace expressed by the States when they signed the Covenant in 1919. Moreover, the availability of pacific mechanisms for dispute settlement (Articles 12 to 15) meant that measures of self-help were no longer a necessary institution of international law – States had other (new) ways to ensure respect for their rights.

Seized with this thorny issue following the bombardment and occupation of the island of Corfu by Mussolini as retaliation for the assassination of three Italian officers, the League's Commission of jurists avoided settling the debate.[80] It concluded that: 'coercive measures which are not intended to constitute an act of war, may or may not be consistent with the provisions of Articles 12 to 15 of the Covenant, and it is for the Council, when the dispute has been submitted to it, to decide'.[81] Critical, Quincy Wright and Ciriaque Tenekides felt that the Commission's tentatively cautious opinion was, in practice, tantamount to admitting that States could still have recourse to armed coercive measures under the League of Nations' framework.[82] The attempts by the member States to enlarge the scope of the Covenant's prohibition of the use of force, through the Geneva Protocol (1924), the Treaties of Locarno (1925)

283–284; Olof Hoijer, *Le Pacte de la Société des Nations. Commentaire théorique et pratique* (Editions Spes, 1926), pp. 185–186.

[79] See Hans Wehberg, 'Le Protocole de Genève' (1925) 7 *Recueil des cours de l''académie de droit international* 38–39; Politis, 'Les représailles entre les Etats membres de la SdN', 11; de Visscher, 'L'interprétation du Pacte au lendemain du différend italo-grec', 384; Tenekides, 'L'évolution de l'idée des mesures coercitives', 410–411; Nicolas N. Petrascu, *Les mesures de contrainte internationale qui ne sont pas la guerre entre les Etats membres de la Société des Nations* (Jouve & Cie., 1927), p. 193; Brierly, 'Règles générales du droit de la paix', 122–125; Scelle, Manuel élémentaire, pp. 645–646.

[80] On the Corfu incident see Quincy Wright, 'Opinion of the Commission of Jurists on Janina-Corfu Affairs' (1924) 18 *American Journal of International Law* 536–544; de Visscher, 'L'interprétation du Pacte au lendemain du différend italo-grec', 213–230 and pp. 377–397; Strupp, 'L'incident de Janina', 255–284; James Barros, *The Corfu Incident of 1923. Mussolini and the League of Nations* (Princeton University Press, 1965).

[81] Quoted *in* Wright, 'Opinion of the Commission of Jurists', 541.

[82] Ibid.; Tenekides, 'L'évolution de l'idée des mesures coercitives', 403.

and bilateral non-aggression pacts, as well as the resurgence of the debate after the adoption of the Briand-Kellogg Pact in 1928, also tended to confirm the literal restrictive interpretation.[83]

But what do these debates tell us about what interwar authors thought of the use of force below the threshold of war before the Great War and the Covenant? For the authors that claimed that armed reprisals were an anachronistic institution of self-help, it is safe to assume that they believed their use to have been permitted before 1919. The answer is more delicate in what concerns the tenants of the literal interpretation. The fact that they considered armed coercive measures to be beyond the reach of the Covenant does not, in fact, imply that they thought they were permitted, then or before. To have an answer, we would need to know what these authors thought customary law provided regarding these more limited uses of military force. If they claimed them permitted in the 1920s and 1930s, it may, in fact, be assumed that they believed such was equally the case before the war. Karl Strupp was one of the few scholars to uphold the literal view, and he deemed armed reprisals were authorised under general customary law. Permitted, however, did not mean unregulated nor that international law was indifferent to them. In relation to the Corfu incident, for instance, Strupp was of the opinion that *if* Greece had truly violated its obligations, then Italy was perfectly entitled to occupy the island.[84] The use of force short of actual war was thus lawful, but only because it intervened as a reaction to a previous violation of law. In this perspective, coercive measures were only procedurally regulated – meaning that they could be resorted to if a certain number of material and formal conditions were met – but regulated nonetheless. This classical understanding of armed reprisals as a measure of self-help was generally shared by the interwar doctrine, defenders of the teleological interpretation of the Covenant included.[85]

83 On the debate regarding the scope of the prohibtion of the use of force contained in the Briand-Kellogg Pact, see, e.g., David H. Miller, *The Peace Pact of Paris. A Study of the Briand-Kellogg Pact* (G. P. Putnam's Sons, 1928), pp. 121–129; Charles G. Fenwick, 'War as an instrument of national policy' (1928) 22 *American Journal of International Law* 826–829; Miroslas Gonsiorowski, 'The Legal Meaning of the Pact for the Renunciation of War' (1936) 30 *American Political Science Review* 653–680; Victor H. Rutgers, 'La mise en harmonie du Pacte de la Société des Nations avec le Pacte de Paris' (1931) 38 *Collected Recueil des cours de l'académie de droit international* 61–79.

84 Strupp, 'L'incident de Janina', 283.

85 See for e.g. Politis, 'Les représailles entre les Etats membres de la SdN', 7–8; Georges Scelle, 'Règles générales du droit de la paix' (1933) 46 *Recueil des cours de l'académie de droit international*, 670; Petrascu, Les mesures de contrainte, p. 116.

From this point of view, it seems that the discourse of 'total indifference' essentially consolidated in the doctrine after the World War II, and one may wonder to what extent this discourse and its terminological ambiguities are the result of the simplification of an otherwise hardly readable interwar discourse. The generalization of 'indifference' from war to the use of force in general can equally be explained by the fact that, with the adoption of Article 2(4) of the UN Charter, the distinction between war and measures short of war resolutely lost its reason to be. For works whose main concern is not history, 'total indifference' offers a concise historical introduction to the principle of the prohibition of the use of force that avoids getting into the complexities of the past regime and of the past debates. This prompts the question of whether this first version of the traditional historical narrative can truly be considered as different and independent from the second version – partial indifference –, which, as we shall soon see, postulates the indifference of international law to war but not to measures short of war. The answer is yes, because even among the carriers of the narrative of 'total indifference' some authors made a clear distinction between war and coercive measures to claim that neither one nor the other was regulated before the twentieth century. Such was the case in Jan Verzijl's *International law in Historical Perspective* (1968), James Brierly's *The Law of Nations* (1949) and Charles de Visscher's *Théorie et réalités en droit international* (1955).[86] Verzijl made clear what he meant by use of force. He wrote:

> Never until the 20th century has the use of force been banned by positive international law, nor would it have been possible to ban it in a society without any central authority to enforce the ban. It was practised in various forms: forcible annexation of foreign territory, extortion of political concessions, reprisals, so-called pacific blockades, military invasion, individual or collective intervention and formal war.[87]

For Brierly, the absence of regulation of measures short of war was a logical consequence of the absence of such regulations for war:

> the extremest form of intervention is war, and until recently modern international law, as we have seen, has not attempted to distinguish

[86] See also Nigel D. White, *Advanced Introduction to International Conflict and Security Law* (Edward Elgar, 2014), pp. 26–27.

[87] Jan Verzijl, *International Law in Historical Perspective*, 5 vols. (A. W. Stijhoff, 1968), vol. 1, p. 215 and p. 224.

> between legal and illegal occasions of making war. As long as this was the attitude of law to war, it is not surprising that there should have been little agreement on the principles which regulated the less extreme measures of coercion by which one state might assume to dictate a certain course of action to another.[88]

De Visscher, for his part, discussed the issue of reprisals and of war in separate sections. He considered, on the one hand, that in the nineteenth century coercive measures were merely an 'afterall moderate [exercise] of a sovereign right, that to use armed force'.[89] On the other, he asserted that 'indifferent to its causes [the causes of war], law will only become interested with its consequences',[90] and that 'immobilised in this 'defeatist' attitude, international law bandwagoned behind governments down a dead-end path'.[91] The use of the words 'defeatist' and 'dead-end' already gives a glimpse into the nature of the lexicon used by this strand of the scholarship to describe and characterize the classical system of international law.[92]

Sub-Narrative of 'Partial' Indifference

The sub-narrative of 'partial' indifference claims that international law did not regulate resort to war but did limit the use of armed coercive measures. It follows the path traced at the end of the nineteenth century by Oppenheim, Westlake, Lawrence and a few others.[93] It is hence not surprising that this account should generally be the one found in the later version of these authors' textbooks, especially in Oppenheim's landmark treatise. For the third and fourth editions, Ronald Roxburgh, in 1921, and Arnold McNair, in 1928, did not really comment on the history of the use of force, but their position is not too hard to determine. As nineteenth-century doctrine, they spoke of reprisals and other minor recourses to military force as falling within the scope of the coercive means of settling an international dispute. For their use to be lawful, they explained that, substantially, a damage needed to exist, and, procedurally, every amicable means of resolving the dispute had to have been unsuccessfully

[88] James L. Brierly, *The Law of Nations. An Introduction to the International Law of Peace* (Clarendon Press, 1949), pp. 284–285.

[89] Charles de Visscher, *Théorie et réalités en droit international* (Pedone, 1955), p. 360. Translation by the author.

[90] Ibid., p. 362. Translation by the author.

[91] Ibid., p. 363. Translation by the author.

[92] See below (Section 8.2.2.).

[93] See above (4.3.).

exhausted.[94] To illustrate their sayings, Roxburgh and McNair furthermore referred to nineteenth century State practice, which prompts the conclusion that they considered measures short of war to have been already governed by classical international law. As concerns war, even if they somewhat seemed to present the introduction of procedural thresholds by articles 12 to 15 of the League of Nations Covenant as a novelty, the stand of the two British scholars is blurrier.[95] Owing to this, as well as to the adoption of the Briand-Kellogg Pact in 1928 – which, for the first time, went beyond mere procedural regulations of resort to war – Hersch Lauterpacht's 1935 edition of the famous textbooks clarified that point. Fleshing out the historical part by a few paragraphs, Lauterpacht notably concluded that:

> International law regulated in time of peace the relations of states on the basis of the scrupulous respect for the independence and dignity of each of them. It made the limited invasion of the sphere of interests of states through the institution of reprisals dependent upon a number of more or less clearly defined conditions. But, by the exercise of a purely discretionary right of declaring war, a state could with one stroke release itself, as against the attacked member of the society of states, from all the obligations of international law save those appertaining to the conduct of war.[96]

'Partial indifference', as already hinted, dominated most of the interwar scholarship. In addition to the authors just mentioned, it was for instance also present in the writings of Georges Scelle, Karl Strupp, Quincy Wright, Charles Fenwick and Edwin Borchard.[97] After the

[94] (Lassa Oppenheim) Ronald H. Roxburgh (ed.), *International Law – A Treatise*, 2 vols. (3rd ed. Longman Greens, 1920), vol. 2, pp. 44–60; (Lassa Oppenheim) Arnold McNair (ed.), *International Law – A Treatise*, 2 vols. (4th ed. Longman Greens, 1928), vol. 2, pp. 84–100.

[95] Without exploring the history of war in international law, the third and fourth edition simply read that: 'It [international law] does not object to states which are in conflict waging war upon each other, provided they have – in compliance with the Covenant of the League of Nations – previously submitted the dispute to an inquiry by the Council of the League', in Roxburgh (ed.), *International Law*, vol. 2, p. 66 and McNair (ed.), International Law, vol. 2, p. 114.

[96] Lauterpacht (ed.), *International Law*, vol. 2, p. 149.

[97] Fenwick, *International Law*, pp. 383 and 428; Wright, 'The Changes in the Conception of War', 756; Quincy Wright, 'The Outlawry of War' (1925) 19 *American Journal of International Law* 89; Edwin M. Borchard, 'The Multilateral Treaty for the Renunciation of War' (1929) 23 *American Journal of International Law* 118; Strupp, *Eléments de droit international public*, vol. 2, p. 506; Scelle, 'Règles générales' du droit de la paix', 670; Scelle, *Manuel élémentaire*, pp. 645–646. See also, von Elbe, 'The Evolution of the Concept of Just War', 685; Tenekides, 'L'evolution de l'idée des mesures coercitives', 401.

World War II, 'partial indifference', it seems, gave away to 'total indifference', but it could still be found in the works of renowned authors. The names of Ian Brownlie, Philip Jessup, Nguyen Quoc Din, and Alain Pellet can be mentioned.[98] Brownlie, who allocated numerous pages to the history of the use of force in his reference *ius ad bellum* textbook, thus considered that the nineteenth century 'was dominated by the right to go to war as an attribute of the sovereign state',[99] but that States 'had to pay for the luxury of avoiding the consequences of a state of war by submitting to some measure of legal regulation of the lesser means of coercion'.[100] In the same way, a well-known French textbook on international law, authored by Nguyen Quoc Dinh and edited by Patrick Daillier, Mathias Forteau and Alain Pellet, teaches that:

> 'In order to be able to use force without having to provide any justification, states only had to decide to use the extreme means of war. If, on the other hand, they stuck to the more moderate form of 'armed reprisals', then they had to have a valid legal basis for their action'.[101]

This account, it should also be noted, is defended by legal historians, some of which have written specialised studies on the history of the use of force in international law, and whose voice have, thereupon, become particularly authoritative. In French-speaking academia, one may in particular think of Robert Kolb, who asserts that 'the law of peace limited measures short of war',[102] but that 'the opportunity and liceity of war became a political matter of fact, not a question of law'.[103] In the English-speaking world, one may more easily think of Stephen Neff's *War and*

[98] Ian Brownlie, *International Law and the Use of Force by States* (Clarendon Press,1968), pp. 19–50; Philip C. Jessup, *A Modern Law of Nations. An Introduction* (The MacMillan Company, 1950), p. 157; (Quôc Dinh), Daillier, Forteau et Pellet, *Droit international public*, p. 1032. See also Anthony Clark Arend and Robert J. Beck, *International Law and the Use of Force: Beyond the UN Charter* (Routledge, 1993), pp. 16–17; Kinga Tibori Szabó, *Anticipatory Action in Self-Defence. Essence and Limits under International Law* (TMC Asser Press, Springer, 2011), pp. 68–72; Chen, *An Introduction*, p. 378.

[99] Brownlie, *International Law and the Use of Force*, p. 49. By the same author see also *Principles of Public International*, p. 729.

[100] Brownlie, *International Law and the Use of Force*, p. 28.

[101] (Quôc Dinh), Daillier, Forteau et Pellet, Droit international public, p. 1032.

[102] Robert Kolb, *Ius contra bellum: Le droit international relative au maintien de la paix* (Bruylant, 2009), p. 32. By the same author see also 'La légitime défense et les Etats au XIXe siècle et pendant l'époque de la Société des Nations', in Robert Kolb (dir.), *Commentaire du Pacte de la Société des Nations* (Bruylant, 2014), pp. 1301–1302. Translation by the author.

[103] Kolb, *Ius contra bellum*, p. 29. Translation by the author.

the Law of Nations (2005), which, to date, probably is the most comprehensive monograph specifically dealing with the history of resort to armed force in international law. In this book, Neff explains that 'the decision to resort to war was a prerogative of policy, not of law',[104] and that 'what distinguished measures short of war from a true state of war was – very broadly speaking – their overall nature as measures of law enforcement as opposed to measures of national policy'.[105] In fewer words, measures short of war were instituted and regulated by international law, whereas war was beyond its reach.

Even though strictly speaking more convincing considering historical evidence than the sub-narrative of 'total indifference', 'partial indifference' is, once again, not devoid of ambiguities. There is, in fact, something rather counter-intuitive in claiming that international law restricted smaller, and not major, violations of another State's sovereignty and independence. Most of the advocates of this version of the history of the use of force, especially in the post–World War II literature, do not fail to notice this apparent inconsistency. Daillier, Forteau and Pellet call this situation 'paradoxical'.[106] Jessup refers to it as 'strange'.[107] Paul Reuter as 'absurd',[108] and Kolb as 'incongruous' and 'contradictory'.[109] Jessup was the only one to go past this observation and to suggest a logical explanation for it. Adopting a very positivistic and formalistic outlook, the American professor argued that this peculiar situation was simply 'illustrative of the manner in which international law ha[d] developed over the centuries in a world of sovereign states'.[110] He explained that, while, over time, States had come to accept the necessity of restraining the use of armed force, they never managed to reach such an agreement as to give up their ultimate right to wage war. In any case, for all the symbolisms and consequences surrounding it, war was never entered upon lightly. As a result, the incentive to give up such an

[104] Stephen C. Neff, *War and the Law of Nations. A History* (Cambridge University Press, 2005), p. 164.

[105] Ibid., p. 216.

[106] (Quôc Dinh), Daillier, Forteau et Pellet, *Droit international public*, p. 1032. See also Chen, *An Introduction*, p. 378.

[107] Jessup, *A Modern Law of Nations*, p. 157.

[108] Paul Reuter, *Droit international public* (Presses Universitaires de France,1963), p. 286.

[109] Kolb, Ius contra bellum, p. 31.

[110] Jessup, *A Modern Law of Nations*, p. 157. Adopting Jessup's argument, Chen, equally claims that 'this apparent paradox illustrates the manner in which international law has developed over the centuries in a world of sovereign states', *An Introduction*, p. 378.

important last resort political tool was never heavy enough. To further ground his assertions, he added that 'justification for war itself ha[d] been more frequently placed on moral grounds or high political aspirations and ideals [as a consequence of which] customary law ha[d] at best characterised war as un-legal – neither legal nor illegal'.[111] By contrast, 'justifications for the lesser uses of force ha[d] been generally couched in legal terms – [. . .] – and the customary law developed tests of propriety of such conduct'.[112] Jessup's reasoning, however, could also be said to apply a double standard to the analysis of State practice. The second part of this thesis has in fact shown that that the nature of the justification brought forth to justify the use of measures short of war or of war did not fundamentally differ. Yet, for some reason, the firsts are considered has having produced legal effects and the seconds are not.[113]

The difficulty of resolving the inner contradictions of 'partial indifference' might explain why it is far from being the most popular version of the history of the use of force in international law. It is a challenging position to defend, not only because it would (ideally) require the author to elucidate its incongruities, but also because it requires bringing a number of technical legal precisions about classical international law. 'Partial indifference' suggests clarifying the difference between the 'state of war' and the 'state of peace', explaining how to determine the difference between measures short of war and war, commenting on the role of war declarations as well as on a series of other complicated issues upon which nineteenth century scholarship, itself, rarely reached a common position.[114] All this, in sum, does not always fit the purpose of the short and straightforward historical introduction that most textbooks understandably seek. Besides, even though classical international law is believed to have been more restrictive with regards to the use of force, it does not mean that it is perceived as having been better suited to handle the realities of nineteenth century international relations. The existence of procedural rules, did not in fact and in the absence of a

[111] Jessup, *A Modern Law of Nations*, p. 158.

[112] Ibid.

[113] In this respect also, Jessup's argument follows the path of Oppenheim who, as a reminder, used a methodology based on practice and *opinio juris* to analyse the issue of intervention in general and measures short of war, but switched to a method that seemed exclusively based on the material practice of States when it came to war. See above (4.3.).

[114] See above Chapter 1.

central authority, prevent reprisals from being abused and the tool of the powerful against the weak.[115] Consequently, in spite of not being *formally* totally indifferent to the use of force, classical international law could be said to have been so *in practice*, because the appreciation of whether an injury had been suffered or not ultimately rested with the States. This argument also underlies the sub-narrative of 'practical' indifference.

The Sub-Narrative of 'Practical' Indifference

While 'partial' indifference can be said to follow the tide of the writings of Oppenheim, Westlake and Lawrence, the sub-narrative of 'practical' indifference, for its part, can be said to draw from the rest of the nineteenth century scholarship. Like them, in fact, the proponents of this last version of the indifference-narrative claim that before the twentieth century the use of force was essentially construed as a dispute settlement mechanism.[116] Unlike the two previous iterations of the narrative of indifference, it therefore does not claim that classical international law was *de jure* indifferent to the use of force. Rules existed and these rules were procedural: there needed to be previous violation of international law and amicable means had to be exhausted before resort to measures short of war then war could be had. The use of force, in sum, was a measure of self-help not technically speaking an unregulated prerogative of States. This third version of the narrative of indifference might appear fundamentally different from the two others and some may doubt it should be studied in connection with 'total' and 'partial' indifference. But, in the end, the proponents of this third sub-narrative of indifference also believe classical international law was powerless. They adopted the same attitude as the advocates of 'partial' indifference concerning measures short of war. The issue was not that there were not any rules, but rather that a central authority, superior to the States, was lacking to ensure they were correctly applied. States were free to decide for themselves whether they had suffered an injury and whether that injury justified resorting to measures short of war and, as last remedy, to war. As Enzo Cannizaro underlines, in the long run, there is little difference between the position according to which the use of force was an absolutely discretionary prerogative, and that according to which it was a discretionary prerogative to protect one's rights.[117] In both cases,

[115] Chen, *An Introduction*, p. 378.
[116] See above (1.1.), (2.3.), (2.4.), (Section 3.3.), (3.4.), (4.3.) and (4.4.).
[117] Enzo Cannizaro, *Corso di diritto internazionale* (Giuffrè Editore, 2011), p. 1.

law's constrain is deemed to have been inexistent: if not in theory, at least in practice.

This account, it seems, was not widespread in the interwar years. Some might think this odd considering that nineteenth-century writings were closer in time (and consequently better known) then and they are now. At the same time, admitting that there were rules before the Great War was tantamount to admitting that these had failed – which, as we shall later see, was exactly what the discipline wished to avoid.[118] Moreover, blaming the inefficacy the classical *ius ad bellum* on the absence of a supranational authority was giving credit to the Austinian critique of international law according to which it is not law proper precisely because it lacked enforcement mechanisms. In the interwar years, the discipline was moreover still relatively new, as was the organisation of the international society into an international institution (the League of Nations).[119] It should also be underlined, that the present discourse on the absence of a 'proper' international organisation before 1919 was not necessarily prevalent during the interwar. Of course, the League of Nations was believed to be a great progress but its origins were often traced back to the Holy Alliance and to the European Concert, if not further back. In his course at the Hague Academy entitled '*Les antécédents de la Société des Nations*' (1937), Charles Dupuis, thus stressed how the system of diplomatic conferences established with the peace settlements of 1814–1815 took the form of a 'stable institution' even though it was not permanent.[120] More recently, historian Matthias Schulz went a step further arguing that the European Concert functioned like a nineteenth-century 'Security Council'.[121] Although this last claim might seem exaggerated, this is to say that it is not because the workings of international society were not institutionalised into a permanent organisation that no mechanisms of peer control existed whatsoever.

The closest account to the sub-narrative of 'practical' indifference that can be found in the interwar literature is the work of Robert Redslob (1882–1962). But, again, his writings are not without ambiguities. On the

118 See below Chapter 9.

119 See above (Section 8.1.2.).

120 Charles Dupuis, 'Les antécédents de la Société des Nations' (1937) 60 *Recueil des cours de l'académie de droit international* 77. See also Pittman B. Potter, 'Développement de l'organisation internationale (1815–1914)' (1938) 64 *Recueil des cours de l'académie de droit international* 71–121.

121 Matthias Schulz, Normen und Praxis. Das Europäische Konzert der Großmächte als Sicherheitsrat, 1815–1860 (Oldenbourg Wissenschaftsverlag, 2009).

one hand, in *Histoire des grands principes du droit des gens* (1923), Redslob wrote that 'war too is a means to settle disputes between peoples' and that:

> there is a certain contact between war and the law of nations. Just as the sun sometimes illuminates the earth with its rays and sometimes abandons it to darkness, so the law of nations approves one type of use of force and condemns another. A struggle may be in contradiction with the law of nations, it may be a violation of its principles. War is then illegitimate. Or yet recourse to force, without being prompted by international law, may be accepted as an extreme measure, because there is no other way to obtain satisfaction from an illegal act. In such cases war is just.[122]

This idea, he further indicated, was already included in the Peace of Westphalia – article 12 § 5 and 7 of the Treaty of Osnabrück and § 116 and 117 of the Treaty of Munster, to be more precise –[123] and '[was] so well and so profoundly encored in reason, that it has always been recognised by diplomacy'.[124] He thus appeared to claim that 'war as a sanction' and as an *ultima ratio* measure of reprisal had transcended the domain of ethics and philosophy to become part of the positive law of nations as recognised by nations. On the other hand, however, he considered that the theories of just war were 'too idealistic to govern human realities' and had remained 'confined to the domain of science'.[125] He also insisted that war was a 'cataclysm of nature', 'lived in another world' and 'outside the periphery of law'.[126] Redslob maintains this double discourse throughout his work,[127] and does not really give any indication as to how to reconciliate these contradictory claims. A hint of an answer might be that he felt classical international law lacked an 'international league' that would put an end to every illegitimate use of force.[128] Even if rules existed, the absence of central enforcement mechanisms was enough to outdo them and make war, in last analysis, extra-legal.

122 Redslob, Histoire des grands principes, p. 469.
123 Robert Redslob, *Les principes du droit des gens moderne* (Librairie Arthur Rousseau, 1937), pp. 229–230.
124 Ibid., p. 230. Translation by the author.
125 Ibid., p. 234. Translation by the author.
126 Redslob, *Histoire des grands principes*, p. 469.
127 See also Robert Redslob, *Traité de droit des gens* (Librairie du Recueil Sirrey, 1950), pp. 265–266.
128 Redslob, *Histoire des grands principes*, p. 471.

In post-1945 and modern-day scholarship, the ambiguities that characterised Redslob's work did not disappear. Krzysztof Skubiszewski, for example, explained that:

> the study of the last millennium [. . .] [does not] warrant the conclusion that until 1919 or 1928 international law licensed war as an always perfectly lawful means of settling a dispute or changing existing rights. [. . .] In the early law of nations states had a right of war (ius ad bellum), but that right was not identical with a licence to wage war.[129]

But he also further added that in that system:

> The state remained for centuries the sole judge of what constituted a valid and sufficient cause. As long as the state was, in fact, free to determine the object of its obligation, *the element of legal obligation did not exist*. Hence the frequent practice of States to resort to war whenever the national interests so demanded, and the general acceptance among the positivist writers of the view that, prior to 1919, states had an unlimited right of war.[130]

Skubiszewski, in sum, affirms that international law did not authorise war in all circumstances, not even to settle a dispute. But he quickly nuances this assertion by arguing that since there was no superior authority to control the behaviour of States and sanction the recalcitrant, 'the element of legal obligation did not exist'. War, after all, remained beyond the reach of law. Slim Laghmani (who strongly relies on Redslob's work), Peter Malanczuk and Georg Schwarzenberger have held similar views.[131]

More recently, Oona Hathaway and Scott Shapiro have equally adopted this third version of the 'indifference'-narrative in their book *The Internationalists* (2017).[132] The purpose of this book is to restore the Briand-Kellogg Pact of 1928 – officially known as the 'General Treaty for

[129] Krzysztof Skubiszewski, 'Use of Force by States and Collective Security. Law of War and Neutrality', in Max Sørensen (ed.), *Manual of Public International Law* (MacMillan, 1968), pp. 741–742.

[130] Ibid., p. 742. Emphasis added.

[131] Slim Laghmani, *Histoire du droit des gens du jus gentium impérial au jus publicum europeanum* (Pedone, 2003), pp. 180–182; Malanczuk, Akehurst's, p. 10; Georg Schwarzenberger, *International Law as Applied by International Courts and Tribunals*, 2 vols. (Stevens and Sons, 1968), vol. 2, pp. 38–39. See also Stamir Alexandrov, *Self-Defence against the Use of Force in International Law* (Kluwer Law International, 1996), pp. 11–13.

[132] Oona Hathaway and Scott Shapiro, *The Internationalists. How a Radical Plan to Outlaw War Remade the World* (Simon & Schuster, 2017).

Renunciation of War as an Instrument of National Policy' – to its rightful place in history. Even though the Pact obviously did not eradicate war, Hathaway and Shapiro claim that it marked the transition from a *ius ad bellum* to a *ius contra bellum* logic – that is, from war as a dispute settlement mechanism towards the prohibition of war.[133] The system of the 'old world order' (as they call it) was based on Grotius's theories of just war, according to which war could only be waged to vindicate or prevent a violation of law.[134] 'War', they emphasised, 'could not be entered for any reason whatsoever'.[135] They also note how this was reflected in practice. States were careful to bring a justification forth when they resorted to force, and their war manifestoes, they argue, acted as sorts of 'law suit complaints'.[136] In the end, however, they still insist that the 'old world order' was 'a world where states [were] sovereign and war [was] legal, [and where] it is impossible to adjudicate between just and unjust wars'.[137] According to Hathaway and Shapiro, this state of things truly changed in the 1930s with the gradual establishment of enforcement mechanisms for the Peace Pact, especially the doctrine of non-recognition that was first invoked following Japan's invasion of Manchuria.[138] The effectivity – and, by extension, the legal nature – of the rules of *ius ad* (or *contra*) *bellum* is thus once more made to rest on the presence of enforcement mechanisms. Without them, law is still presented as characterised by a 'privilege to use force', a 'right to conquest', 'gunboat diplomacy' and a 'licence to kill'.[139]

The narrative of 'practical' indifference is the closest to historical sources. In claiming that resort to measures short of war and war were accepted when all other means of obtaining satisfaction for a legal claim had failed, it is consistent with nineteenth century doctrine and State practice. It is also clear that, as the proponents of this narrative suggest, the rules of classical *ius ad bellum* lacked effectivity and that the systems of enforcement established during the interwar years (whether through article 16 of the LN Covenant or the doctrine of non-recognition) probably made law more 'constraining'. They, at least, made the cost of disrespecting rules more predictable and visible. But, by eventually

[133] Ibid., pp. xi–xiii.
[134] Ibid., pp. 3–30.
[135] Ibid., p. 44.
[136] Ibid., pp. 31–55.
[137] Ibid., p. 55.
[138] Ibid., pp. 163–168.
[139] Ibid., p. 97.

denying the legal nature of the rules because of their supposed lack of sanction, the third version of the 'indifference' narrative could be said to amalgamate two separate issues: the existence of the rule, and its effectivity. It could also be said to adopt Austin's restrictive definition of law; a definition they otherwise reject when it comes to the analysis of contemporary international law and the inefficacy of its current enforcement mechanisms.[140] In any case, the underlying message of 'practical' indifference remains the inexistence of rules on the use of force in the nineteenth century. This becomes even clearer when we analyse the narrative and rhetorical structures of the discourse of indifference. All three version, as we shall see, share the same construction articulated around the opposition of a nineteenth century portrayed as that of anarchy and chaos, to a twentieth century presented as the time of law and order. This structure is where the core of the traditional account of indifference lies; in spite of telling different histories, the sub-narratives of indifference each ultimately tell the same story. This story is not only a story about the advent of the prohibition of force, but also a story about how law, more generally, overcame chaos and brought order to the international plane.

8.2.2 Same Story: How Law Overcame Chaos and Brought International Order

The contradictions between the different versions of the 'indifference' narrative and their inner ambiguities contrast with the clarity of their discursive structures. The extracts cited in the previous section, the vocabulary the literature uses to describe the pre-war and post-war periods, and the bleak image of the nineteenth century that they contribute to create already gives an indication as to what these structures might be. We might thus remember how de Visscher described the attitude of the classical international law to the use of force as 'defeatist'.[141] He also spoke of an era characterised by 'persistent individualism' and 'extra-legality'.[142] He presented the nineteenth century *ius ad bellum* as an ill-adapted and unsustainable system whose only possible outcome was the World War I – a war of a magnitude no one had foreseen and that made governments realise that, for their own sake as well as for the prosperity

[140] See above (Section 8.1.2.).
[141] de Visscher, *Théorie et réalités*, p. 363.
[142] Ibid., p. 358.

all, there was no other option but enhanced international cooperation.[143] The Great War, in other words, forced States to replace co-existence with genuine cooperation. Along the same lines, Verzijl considered that in the nineteenth century:

> 'the time was not ripe for resolute steps in this direction [that of a prohibition of the use of force] until the First World War plunged humanity into a catastrophe despite The Hague Peace Conferences, and the liquidation of that war in 1919 called world-wide co-operation against future aggression'.[144]

In the 1930s, Redslob and Bourquin also agreed that:

> 'This state of mind [war as a legal prerogative] lasted until the Great War, and we can even say that it found its fatal outcome in it. After the giant battle that engendered an upheaval in human values, there was a rebirth of conceptions of the international order';[145]

and that:

> 'It was not until the cataclysm of 1914 that the movement was given the decisive impetus and that the now well-established principle that the use of force, far from being an intangible prerogative, constitutes, at least under certain conditions, a crime against which the international community must rise, was introduced into the world's legal consciousness'.[146]

In more recent literature, Hathaway and Shapiro, as well as Neff, wrote that 'the war that began in 1914 was the terrible culmination of the Old World Order',[147] and that:

> 'In reaction to the manifold horrors of the Great War of 1914–1918, the Statemen and people of the world showed a commendable determination to place legal restrictions on future resort to war, to replace the anarchic Hobbesian world with more regulated order'.[148]

This storyline is not without recalling the more general narrative sequence of international legal history. It indeed takes a major conflict as a pivotal point of transition from one period to another and follows a

[143] Ibid., pp. 363–364.
[144] Verzijl, International Law in Historical Perspective, vol. 1, p. 217.
[145] Redslob, Les principes du droit des gens moderne, p. 236.
[146] Maurice Bourquin, 'Règles générales du droit de la paix' (1931) 35 *Recueil des cours de l'académie de droit international* 178.
[147] Hathaway and Shapiro, The Internationalists, p. 97.
[148] Neff, War and the Law of Nations, p. 285. See also Kolb, *Ius contra bellum*, p. 31.

'trial and error' pattern.[149] This pattern forms the syntagmatic (i.e., diachronic or chronological) chain of the discourse of indifference. From the paradigmatic (i.e., synchronic) point of view, each of the three elements of the chain – the nineteenth century, the Great War and the twentieth century – can, moreover, be seen to be associated with a particular lexicon that echoes the discipline's more fundamental belief about the power of international law as a vector of order and social progress.

This syntagmatic-paradigmatic correlation and similarity between the discourse of indifference and the discipline's broader narrative becomes even more evident if we apply the method proposed by Claude Lévi-Strauss to examine the structure and meaning of mythological accounts to the narrative of indifference. The anthropologist analysed myths like language. Insisting that meaning was in structures and that structures were in repetitions, he suggested gathering the different versions of a same myth and conducting paradigmatic discourse analysis. He argued that by superimposing the different versions of a same story and conducting this type of analysis, the structure of the account would surface through the layers.[150] To this end, Lévi-Strauss more specifically proposed using a classical tool of linguistic analysis: a two-axes word association table. In linguistics, these tables are used to highlight the relation between the syntagmatic and paradigmatic structures of a given account. On the syntagmatic (horizontal) axis, the different units that constitute the narrative frame of the account are placed in chronological order, while the paradigmatic (vertical) axis indexes the words and expressions that are used to characterise each of the units of the studied discourse.[151] If we want 'to tell the myth', Lévi-Strauss explained, 'we would disregard the columns and read the rows from left to right'.[152] But 'if we want to *understand* the myth', the anthropologist carries on, 'then we will have to [. . .] read from left to right, column after column'.[153]

Applied to each of the sub-narratives of indifference and brought together, Lévi-Strauss's proposed method gives us the table below (Table 1).

[149] See above (Section 8.1.2.).

[150] Claude Lévi-Strauss, *Structural Anthropology*, p. 218. See also Walter Burkert, *Structure and History in Greek Mythology and Ritual* (University of California Press, 1979), p. 11; Wendy D. O'Flaherty, Asceticism and Eroticism in the Mythology of Śiva, Oxford: Oxford University Press, 1973, p. 17.

[151] Claude Lévi-Strauss calls the different units of the syntagmatic chain 'mythèmes'.

[152] Claude Lévi-Strauss, *Structural Anthropology* (original ed.: 1958) (Basic Books, 1963), p. 214.

[153] Ibid.

Table 1. *Syntagmatic-paradigmatic word association table*

Syntagmatic (diachronic) axis

Paradigmatic (synchonic) axis	*Nineteenth Century* (old world order)	*World War I*	*Twentieth Century* (new world order)	
	persistan individualism		cooperation	'Total' indifference
	rivalry		solidarity	
	uncontrolled sovereign liberty			
	anarchy of sovereingties	carnage	obligations	
	regime of improvision			
	constant war		stable organisation	
	violence and hegemony		peace and security	
	cult of violence			
	barbarity	catastrophe		
	political' international law			
	negation of law		new chapter of international law	
	war as state policy			'Partial' indifference
	collision of naked ineterests		quest for justice	
	interstate rivalry	devastation	new world	
	contest for power			
	anarchic hobbessian society	horrors	just war reborn	
	generalised *ius ad bellum*			
	absolute sovereignty	catastrophe	solidarity	
	lack of well-developped international organisation		global international organisation	
	might is right		might no longer makes right	'Practical' indifference
	ulimited / unrestricted right to war			
	freedom of war	giant struggle	rebirth	
	conquest			
	territorial competition			
	consacrated violence		justice	
	international anarchy			
	realm of violence			
	disorder absence of (efficient) rules	*breaking point*	***order*** new (efficient) rules	

The horizontal axis represents the narrative pattern of the discourse of indifference; that is its syntagmatic (or diachronic) structure. As we saw from the excerpts cited above, it is divided into three units or '*mythèmes*': before the war (the nineteenth century), the war, and after the war (twentieth century). The World War I is the breaking point between the first and third units. As the table shows, the first unit (the nineteenth century) and third unit (the twentieth century) are presented as clear and definite opposites. The paradigmatic axis indexes the words and expressions used by the proponents of each of the sub-narratives of indifference – 'total', 'partial' and 'practical' - to characterise the different constitutive units of the story. The table shows that, whether in the sub-narrative of 'total', 'partial' or 'practical' indifference, the nineteenth century is systematically associated with words such as 'rivalry',[154] 'anarchy',[155] 'war',[156] 'violence'[157] and 'politics'.[158] It was a time when might is said to have made right, and in which insecurity and disorder prevailed.[159] In his 1924 courses to the freshly created *Hague Academy of International Law*, Otfried Nippold even qualified the policies that prevailed beforehand as the 'antogonist[s] of law', as a 'negation of international law'.[160] Schwarzenberger, for his part, spoke of the 'impotence of international law'.[161] This image of the pre-1919 era clearly echoes the idea that without law there is only chaos, and that without law humanity is bound to fall into the 'carnage',[162] 'horrors'[163] and 'catastrophe'[164] of war. The twentieth century, on the other hand, is associated with words such as 'cooperation',[165] 'solidarity',[166] 'justice',[167] 'peace and security'[168] and 'law'.[169] This was 'the moment of history', in Redslob's emphatic style, 'when the will for justice, [...] rose with all its superb majesty to break the realm of violence'.[170] All this conveys a sense of organisation, of stability and of

[154] See, e.g., Otfried Nippold, 'Le développement historique du droit international depuis le Congrès de Vienne' (1924) 2 *Receuil des cours de l'académie de droit international* 27; Hoijer, Le Pacte de la Société des Nations, p. 1; Sibert, Traité de droit international public, vol. 2, p. 616; Neff, War and the Law of Nations, p. 167.

[155] See, e.g., Hoijer, Le Pacte de la Société des Nations, p. 4.

[156] See, e.g., Sibert, Traité de droit international public, vol. 2, pp. 625–626; Skubiszewski, 'Use of Force by States and Collective Security', p. 741; Kolb, Ius contra bellum, p. 28.

[157] See, e.g., Redslob, *Histoire des grands principes*, p. 561; Sibert, Traité de droit international public, vol. 2, p. 627; de Visscher, *Théorie et réalités*, p. 362; Laghmani, Histoire du droit des gens, p. 181.

[158] See, e.g., Kormanicki, La question de l'intégrité territorial, p. 30; Nippold, 'Le développement historique du droit international', 53 and 100; Hoijer, Le Pacte de la Société des Nations, p. 4; de Visscher, Théorie et réalités, p. 362.

[159] Hathaway and Shapiro, The Internationalists, pp. 15, 23–26 and 28.

[160] Nippold, 'Le développement historique du droit international', 16.

[161] Schwarzenberger, *International Law*, vol. 2, p. 38.

[162] Schrijver, 'Article 2, paragraphe 4', p. 441.

[163] Neff, *War and the Law of Nations*, p. 285.

[164] Verzijl, *International Law in Historical Perspective*, vol. 1, p. 217.

[165] Ibid.; Schrijver, 'Article 2, paragraphe 4', p. 441.

[166] Sibert, *Traité de droit international public*, vol. 2, p. 621.

[167] Neff, *War and the Law of Nations*, p. 167; Redslob, Histoire des grands principes, p. 561.

[168] Hoijer, *Le Pacte de la Société des Nations*, p. 1; Schrijver, 'Article 2, paragraphe 4', p. 441.

[169] Hoijer, *Le Pacte de la Société des Nations*, p. 5.

[170] Redslob, *Histoire des grands principes*, p. 561.

order. This appeasement is presented as the consequence of the introduction of (new) rules of international law thanks, among other elements, to the adoption of the Covenant of the League of Nations. Of course, even interwar scholars were not naïve and did not believe the League's system to be perfect. It had many limitations. Nevertheless, it was the beginning of international law's movement towards the prohibition of the use of force. It was the first step on the road to further progress, and it remains that under the schema of indifference, the pre-war era becomes synonymous to the rule of force, while the post-war era is synonymous to the rule of law.

We stand at the heart of the binary rhetorical structures that Lévi-Strauss identified as the rhetorical structure of most mythological accounts.[171] The reason for recurrence of binary constructions, he argued, is that they offer simple, straightforward, didactic and lasting models of explanations for complex events. It is also for these reasons of simplicity and durability that myths, or in this case a historical account, will tend to be built on pre-existing endemic cognitive schemes.[172] The presence of the international legal profession's representational biases is, here, particularly evident. Paradigmatically, the narrative of indifference is, in fact, built on the belief that law is the remedy against disorder. Syntagmatically it relies on the idea that with the sophistication and humanisation of the international society, law will eventually prevail over disorder and anarchy. More than an account on the history of the use of force, the narrative of indifference consequently appears as the story of the triumph of law over selfish politics and as proof, as we shall later emphasise, of international law's capacity to evolve into a 'proper' legal order.

What does all this tell us? First of all, by showing that the narrative of indifference reproduces the structure of the discipline's general discourse about its function and its history, it enables to conclude that it is a product of the traditional beliefs and fears that underlie the identity of the field. By the same token, it also indicates that an explanation for the emergence of the narrative of indifference can most probably be found in these beliefs.

[171] As some authors, nonetheless, underline, binary structures are not in any way particular to, or distinctive of, myths. See Alan Dundes, 'Binary Opposition in Myth: The Propp/Lévi-Strauss Debate in Retrospect' (1997) 56 *Western Folklore* 46–47.

[172] See Pierre Swiggers, 'Le mythe: vers une typologisation structurelle « profonde »', in Christophe Vielle, Pierre Swiggers et Guy Jucquois (eds.), *Comparativisme, Mythologies, Langages* (Peeters, 1994), pp. 23–31.

8.2.3 *Questioning the Content and Rhetorics of Indifference: A Brief Overview of Critiques*

The narrative of indifference did not only emerge in an equivocal manner because it came in different versions, but also because it was always contested, in one or the other of its aspects, by a handful of authors. Three types of challenges to the traditional account can be found in the literature since the interwar: a theoretical challenge that was the work of Hans Kelsen and of the normativists; an ideological challenge that can be found in the writings of Carl Schmitt and in Soviet scholarship; and, finally, a historical challenge that started with Leo Strisower and recently resurfaced.

A Theoretical Challenge: Hans Kelsen and the Normativists

The main challenge to the narrative of indifference came from the normativist literature. Leading figure of the movement, Hans Kelsen never actually frontally addressed the question of the history of the use of force in international law in his writings. His critique, however, is evident from his work on resort to armed force under general (customary) international law. In spite of the adoption of the Covenant, and more intriguingly of the United Nations Charter, Kelsen, continued to comment on the state of the use of force under general international law; a law that he did not necessarily seem to believe to have been affected by the two aforementioned instruments. He explained that, as far as war was concerned, the scholarship advocated for two diametrically opposed theories.[173] According to the first, war was an attribute of sovereignty and States were consequently free to resort to it for whichever reason they pleased. According to the second, as the more limited uses of armed force, war was a sanction and could therefore only be used to respond to a previous violation of international law. Kelsen resolutely pledged his allegiance to the second view. His position, obviously, was not based on naturalist considerations (with which the 'just war' theories are usually associated) nor on an empirical analysis of state practice, but was the result of logical deduction from the manner in which he understood law as a normative system.

The notions of coercion and sanction were pivotal in Kelsen's theory of law. Without mechanisms to sanction deviant behaviour and compel

[173] Kelsen, Principles of international law, pp. 33–34; from the same author see also *Collective Security Under International Law* (Government Printing Office, 1957), pp. 35–39; and 'Théorie du droit international public' (1953) 84 *Recueil des cours de l'académie de droit international* 41–42.

respect for rules, a system of norms could not, in fact, qualify as 'law' properly so called.[174] The same was true of international law, and the absence of a centralised authority to impose and enforce sanctions, meant that the use of force (of war, in particular) as a measure of self-help, was even more crucial to determine whether international law could, or not, be viewed as a proper legal order.[175] In this context, Kelsen argued that if, as the dominant doctrine suggests, one is to claim that general international law was 'indifferent' to resort to war – that is, if war is neither a delict nor a sanction – then 'general international law is not law in the specific sense of the term'.[176] This is because admitting this theory has two consequences in Kelsen's normativist framework. The first is that being a decentralised system, the international community cannot ensure respect for international law and, by the same token, its own survival if law is not construed as a sanction mechanism. Kelsen believed that when a State waged war on another State as a reaction to a previous violation of international law, the actions of that first State extended beyond its individual interests. By resorting to war in order to protect its legal rights, a State was, in fact, also acting more generally in defence of international law and, by extension, of the international community.[177] The second consequence of 'indifference' in Kelsen's framework, is that, if war is not considered a delict, the principle of *pacta sunt servanda* – which Kelsen, for a time, considered to be the '*grund-norm*' of international law – loses all relevance and meaning. If a State can legally wage war at any time, for any reason, and impose its will to others, then respect for one's obligations becomes but a vain maxim. In Kelsen's opinion it even becomes 'doubtful whether it can be assumed that under general international law states have any rights – that is, legally protected interests'.[178] The dominant doctrinal view was, more specifically, in direct contradiction with the principles of respect for the independence and territorial integrity of other States, which Kelsen held to be part of general customary international law.[179]

[174] See Hans Kelsen, *The Pure Theory of Law* (University of California Press, 1970), p. 33.
[175] Kelsen, *Principles of International Law*, pp. 3–6.
[176] Kelsen, *Collective Security*, p. 36.
[177] Ibid. See also Kelsen, *Principles of International Law*, p. 36.
[178] Kelsen, *Collective Security*, p. 36.
[179] Ibid. See also Alfred Von Verdross, 'Règles générales du droit international de la paix' (1929) 30 *Recueil des cours de l'académie de droit international* 496; Ellery C. Stowell, *The Diplomacy of the War of 1914* (Houghton Mifflin Company, 1916), pp. 301–302; and by the same author, *International Law*, p. 489.

Kelsen's arguments could, however, be criticised on the ground that his understanding of sanctions was quite (probably too) restrictive.[180] Advocates of 'partial indifference', in particular, may retort that his insistence that war could only and absolutely needed to be considered as a measure of sanction in order for international law to be a genuine legal order, is a little extreme considering the existence of armed reprisals. But, for Kelsen and the normativists, claiming that international law governed the limited use of armed force (reprisals) and not the unlimited use of armed force (war), was an incongruity that could not be overcome, and that invalidated the discourse of 'partial indifference'.[181] In 1929, Alfred Von Verdross was particularly thorough in exposing his objections. He insisted that this doctrine reversed the burden of proof by requiring the demonstration of the existence of special rules limiting the right to wage war, instead of asking if and to what extent the generally accepted principle of respect for the territorial integrity of other States suffered from exceptions. 'But', he continued,

> no one has yet proved that under positive international law, the principle of respect for foreign territory fades in the face of war. Nor could such an interpretation be accepted, for want of an express provision, since it would lead to the absurd consequence that minor violations of foreign territory would be strictly prohibited, while any hostile aggression would have to be tolerated. The principle of respect for foreign territory would thus cease to apply in the case of the most serious violation of the property protected by this fundamental rule.[182]

Paul Guggenheim, whose *Traité de droit international public* (1953-1954) used normativist premises, also took this view. Like Von Verdross, he considered that 'it would be contradictory to admit coercive measures as an act of reprisal only if it is motivated by a previous violation of law and to consider, on the other hand, that war is authorised in all circumstances';[183] and, like Kelsen, he insisted that admitting such a position would be 'irreconcilable with the idea of international law as a legal order'.[184] In the normativist mind-set, claiming that there was no

[180] See François Rigaux, 'Kelsen et le droit international' (1996) 32 *Revue belge de droit international* 396–401; for the English version, see 'Kelsen on International Law' (1998) 9 *European Journal of International Law* 325–343.

[181] Kelsen, *Principles of International Law*, p. 36; and by the same author: Collective Security, p. 35.

[182] Von Verdross, 'Règles générales', 497.

[183] Guggenheim, *Traité de droit international public*, vol. 2, p. 94. Translation by the author.

[184] Ibid. Translation by the author.

'prohibition' of the use of force before the twentieth century was, in a way, equivalent to claiming that there was no international law before 1919. Although not through the same method, the normativists, in sum, came to the same conclusion as most of nineteenth- and early twentieth-century scholarship, which is that the use of force, war included, was a sanction mechanism that could only be employed as an *ultima ratio* to seek repair for a previous violation of the law.

A Political Challenge: Carl Schmitt and Soviet Scholarship

Carl Schmitt's and Soviet international legal scholarship's critique of the narrative of indifference deployed on very different level from that of the normativists. Schmitt and Soviet authors did not criticise the content of the narrative as much as they did its underlying 'liberal-democratic' rhetorics. Their critique, however, concerned different aspects of these rhetorics: Schmitt's was focused on the paradigmatic structure of the account, while the Soviet lawyers concentrated on its syntagmatic structure.

In his seminal book, *The Nomos of the Earth* (1950), Schmitt's aim was not to offer a technical history of the rules of international law, but to present an account of the *jus publicum europaeum* as a system for the spatial organisation of the earth. He was of the opinion that 'as feuds, reprisals and applications of force of various kinds', war needed to be recognised, and was indeed recognised, as an acceptable means of effecting territorial changes.[185] But even though war was a sovereign prerogative of every State, Schmitt stressed that it was 'incorrect to characterize the order of interstate international law from the 17th to the 20th century as anarchy because it permitted war'.[186] For Schmitt it was the opposite. From 1815 to 1914, war was regulated because bracketed by the Great Powers and a legalised procedure. The aim of international law was not to abolish war but to circumvent it; an aim that the *jus publicum europaeum* had, in his view, achieved by replacing the feudal and religious order of the Middle Ages by secular sovereign States that recognized each other as equals, and by relying on a political system of balance of power. Civil and religious wars (which were characterized by the annihilation of the enemy) had been replaced by interstate wars (whose aim was not destruction, but merely to make one's will prevail),

[185] Carl Schmitt, *The Nomos of the Earth in the International Law of Jus Publicum Europaeum* (Telos Press, 2003), p. 186.

[186] Ibid.

thus humanising war from the inside as well as limiting its disruptive effects on the outside while, at the same time, enabling the adaptation of the spatial order to necessities.[187]

This is why, according to Schmitt, it was a profound mistake to indiscriminately designate any use of force as anarchy and, by extension, to characterise the nineteenth century as anarchical. The wars of that time, he insisted, 'represent[ed] the highest form of order within the scope of human power',[188] and, he continued, 'the great problems of international law cannot be disposed of as easily as the pacifism of the League of Nations and its anarchy slogan would have it'.[189] On the contrary, the parallel movements towards the outlawry of war and the creation of international organisations would mark the return to total warfare. Schmitt feared that the 'liberal-democratic' rhetorics, by masking the real economic and political stakes, would contribute to distorting the image of the enemy as well as the perception and practice of war. When war is waged on considerations of world order and humanity, the enemy becomes the enemy of humanity as a whole and, the objective of war, instead of being the procurement of a determinate advantage, becomes the annihilation of the enemy.[190] The League of Nations and the efforts for the legal limitation of war, in this perspective, represented not a progress but a leap backwards. The paradigmatic structure of the indifference-narrative is completely reversed: politics and balance of power are associated with order; law and international integration are associated with chaos.

Soviet scholarship's critique of the mainstream account might seem less essentialist. It did not necessarily reverse the order of the paradigmatic opposition of order and chaos but was likewise suspicious of the 'liberal-democratic' rhetoric of the account. It did not think of war as a positive tool of international order, and like 'mainstream' western

[187] Ibid., pp. 141–144.

[188] Ibid., p. 187.

[189] Ibid.

[190] See Anthony Carty, 'Carl Schmitt's Critique of Liberal International Legal Order between 1933 and 1945' (2001) 14 *Leiden Journal of International Law* 25–76; Jean-Claude Monod, 'La destabilisation humanitaire du droit international et le retour de la « guerre juste »: une lecture critique du *Nomos de la terre*' (2004) 68 *Les études philosophiques* 40–47; Emmanuel Pasquier, 'Carl Schmitt et la circonscription de la guerre: Le problème de la mesure dans la doctrine des « grands espaces »' (2009) 40 *Etudes internationales* 55–72; Stephen Legg, 'Interwar Spatial Chaos? Imperialism, Internationalism and the League of Nations', in Stephen Legg (ed.), *Spatiality, Sovereignty and Carl Schmitt: Geographies of the Nomos* (Routledge, 2011), pp. 106–122.

literature felt that it was important to ban resort to the arms as much as possible. The Soviet authors' representation of the history of the use of force, however, differed in two essential ways: in its breaking point – the event at the origin of the change of orientation of international law – and in its representation of the twentieth century.

The 1917 October Revolution, instead of World War I, was considered the turning point from 'old' to 'new' international law. In his textbook of 1962, Grigory Tunkin thus taught that 'before the Great October Socialist Revolution international law had recognized the right of States to go to war (*jus ad bellum*), pursuant to which one State could resort to war against another whenever it considered this advisable'.[191] In Tunkin's work, as in the 'bourgeois' narrative, the 'old' international legal order was characterised as that of the rule of force, while the 'new' legal order presented as anti-colonialist and directed against war.[192] This shift, however, was not the result of a sort of immanent universal social necessity revealed by the excesses of the Great War. The post-war international society was not viewed as one of cooperation either, but one of co-existence between the capitalist States, on the one hand, and the socialist States, on the other. It was not harmonious and homogenous but plural and conflictual, and, in this context, the progressive prohibition of the use of force in the interwar years was not the result of a 'natural' or objective drive but that of power relationships and struggles.

In these struggles, the USSR was presented as the progressive force carrying the project of the ban of the use of force.[193] Throughout the interwar, Soviet Russia, which had proclaimed the search for just and durable peace as the guiding principle of its foreign policy as soon as November 1917, indeed, tried to push more ambitious agreements for the prohibition of the use of force in general and not only of war as

[191] Grigory I. Tunkin, *Theory of International Law*, original ed.: 1962 (Harvard University Press, 1974), p. 50. See also Grzybowski, *Soviet Public International Law*, p. 453.

[192] See Lauri Mälksoo, 'The History of International Legal Theory in Russia: A Civilizational Dialogue with Europe' (2008) 19 *European Journal of International Law* 229. For intellectual histories of Soviet international law, see Ivo Lapenna, *Conceptions soviétiques de droit international public* (Pedone, 1954); Lauri Mälksoo, *Russian Approaches to International Law* (Oxford University Press, 2015).

[193] Sergei B. Krylov, 'Les notions principales du droit des gens (La doctrine soviétique du droit international)' (1947) 70 *Recueil des cours de l'académie de droit international* 424–427; Tunkin, Theory of International Law, pp. 50–52. See also Bernard Dutoit, *Co-existence et droit international à la lumière de la doctrine soviétique* (Pedone, 1966), pp. 42–43; Jean-Yves Calvez, *Droit international et souveraineté en URSS* (Armand Collin, 1953), p. 217.

such.[194] Of course, Russia had its own political interests in trying to lock as much as feasible the legal possibilities for States to resort to the arms. From the 1920s until the World War II, Moscow was militarily weak and recovering a five-year civil war (1917–1922) in which the European nations had recurrently intervened in support of the counter-revolutionary forces. Still, Soviet Russia was presented as the voice of the weak against the strong and the prohibition of force as a major achievement of the socialist states. We can see how this account diverged quite substantially from the western 'universalist' narrative that somehow erased the conflictual dimension of law. Although on different premises, Soviet scholars (and the adepts of Marxist approaches to international law) shared this characteristic of accepting the political dimension of law and warn against the 'western' depoliticisation of legal history with Schmitt.

A Historical Challenge: Leo Strisower and Contemporary Scholarship

The third type of challenge posed to the narrative of indifference is of historical nature. It started with Leo Strisower's *Der Krieg und die Völkerrechtsordnung* in 1919.[195] In this book, the Austrian jurist expounded his theory that war, under customary international law, could only be fought in response to a previous violation of international law. Professor of legal theory to Hans Kelsen in Vienna, his book had an important influence on the positions later developed by the normativists.[196] Strisower's demonstration, however, was not based on logical deductions from a theoretical model of international law, but from historical sources. Mónica García-Salmones Rovira notes how 'he employed an extensive range of literature of diplomatic relations and official government texts'.[197] And, indeed, Strisower referred to numerous authors, such as Kaltenborhn, Heffter, Geffcken, Bluntschli, Neumann, Bonfils, Fauchille, Pradier-Fodéré, Fiore, Twiss, Hall,

194 On Soviet efforts for peace, see Timothy A. Taracouzio, *The Soviet Union and International Law* (The MacMillan Company, 1935), pp. 301–308.

195 Leo Strisower, *Der Krieg und die Völkerrechtsordnung* (Manz, 1919), pp. 20–27.

196 On the influence of Strisower, see Josef L. Kunz, 'Bellum justum and Bellum Legale' (1951) 45 *American Journal of International Law* 529; Monica García-Salmones Rovira, *The Project of Positivism in International Law* (Oxford University Press, 2013), pp. 186–187.

197 García-Salmones Rovira, *The Project of Positivism*, p. 187.

Halleck and Woolsey, to name just a few.[198] In terms of practice, the Austrian lawyer gave the Third Italian War of Independence against Austria in 1866, the Franco-Prussian War of 1870, the Russo-Turkish War of 1877, the Spanish-American War of 1898, the Russo-Japanese War of 1905 and the Balkan Wars of 1912–1913 as main examples.[199] Von Verdross thought Strisower's study particularly thorough and as 'providing proof that the customary law of nations also corresponded to the classic doctrine on the legitimacy of war'.[200] But, except for the normativists, it seems that Strisower's demonstration somehow failed to convince his contemporaries. Josef L. Kunz, for example, and despite also having been educated in Vienna, felt that 'his argumentation [was] moral rather than legal'.[201]

It appears that it was not until 1992 that yet another Austrian lawyer from the University of Vienna, Stephan Verosta, attempted to question the narrative of indifference based on historical evidence.[202] He noted how the scholarship welcomed the prohibition of aggressive war in the Covenant of the League of Nations, but overlooked the fact that these rules had actually been in force since the peace settlements of 1814–1815.[203] To prove his point, Verosta chose to concentrate on the analysis of State practice, but only analysed one precedent: the Greco-Turkish War of 1897 during which, taking advantage of a Christian revolt in Crete, Greece tried to seize the island. Verosta gathered documents deposited in the archives of the Austro-Hungarian Foreign Ministry in Vienna in order to determine and analyse the positions expressed by the Powers of the Concert in response to Greece's aggression of the Porte. Emphasising the discontent expressed by the Powers at the actions of Athens, Verosta concluded that: 'this short study has proved that even before the League of Nations any war in Europe had

[198] Strisower, *Der Krieg*, p. 21.

[199] Ibid., pp. 22–23, footnote no 5.

[200] von Verdross, 'Règles générales', 497. Transaltion by the author.

[201] Kunz, 'Bellum justum and Bellum Legale', 529. For a critique of Kunz's critique, see García-Salmones Rovira, *The Project of Positivism*, p. 188, footnote no 172.

[202] Stephan Verosta, 'The Unlawfulness of Wars of Aggression Before 1914', in Emmanuel G. Bello and Prince Bola A. Ajibola, *Essays in honour of Judge Taslim Olawale Elias*, 2 vols. (Martinus Nijhoff, 1992), vol. 1, pp. 117–124.

[203] 'The outlawry of the war of aggression under the Covenant was hailed by many as a decisive progress in international law and in international relations. [. . .] At the same time, it was overlooked that basic rules now laid down in the Covenant had been in force since 1815, especially respect of the territorial integrity and the political independence of states', Ibid., p. 117.

to have a justifying cause or reason'.[204] But, once more, Verosta's article did not convince the rest of the scholarship. Dinstein, for instance, considers the evidence provided by his Austrian colleague 'not persuasive'.[205]

As pointed out in the general introduction, more recently, Mary Ellen O'Connell, Emmanuelle Tourme-Jouannet, Olivier Corten and Randall Lesaffer have again taken upon themselves to question the indifference narrative on historical premises. O'Connell is the most succinct. In 2013, noting that the nineteenth-century scholarship generally seemed to think resort to war to be within the domain of international law, she considered that 'this fact should raise doubts about the core proposition that with the rise of positivism in the 18th and 19th centuries, restraints on war faded'.[206] In this piece, however, O'Connell does not venture pass the interrogation stage to actually challenge the traditional account of indifference. Tourme-Jouannet goes a step further. Her observations are founded on the extensive study of the nineteenth century scholarship she carries out in *The Liberal-Welfarist Law of Nations* (2011). Expounding how the system of classical international law was generally structured around the theory of the fundamental rights of States, she notes how, even though 'just war' had been abandoned, the right to wage war was nonetheless 'closely ring-fenced and confined'.[207] It could only be used in the hypothesis of a previous violation of a fundamental right and if the dispute could not be diplomatically resolved. Tourme-Jouannet, moreover, traces the apparition of the contemporary standard narrative to the period of the interwar and reproves the authors of the time for misinterpreting the writings of their predecessors. 'In truth', she wrote,

> criticism [is] once again excessive and too prompt to disqualify classical international law. In an over-hasty amalgam, commentators infer that States legally had the right to trigger any war at any time. Nothing could be more mistaken. In classical international law – as in the modern law of nations – the right to resort to war was no more the right to do anything than sovereignty was itself absolute.[208]

[204] Ibid., p. 124.

[205] Dinstein, *War, Aggression and Self-Defense*, p. 78, footnote no 431.

[206] Mary Ellen O'Connell, 'The Prohibition of the Use of Force', in Nigel D. White and Christian Henderson (eds.), *The Research Handbook on International Conflict and Security Law* (Edward Elgar, 2013), p. 95.

[207] Emmanuelle Jouannet, *The Liberal Welfarist Law of Nations. A History of International Law* (Cambridge University Press, 2012), p. 129.

[208] Ibid., p. 130.

To these critiques foremost based on the analysis of pre-Versailles doctrine, Corten and Lesaffer add an appraisal based on State practice. Corten thus underlines how a look at practice shows that the positions of States were consistent with those expressed in the scholarship.[209] When they resorted to armed force, he insists, governments never claimed to have an indiscriminate right to do so, but instead brought legal justifications forth and always denied wishing to infringe upon the sovereignty of another State. Lesaffer likewise notes how 'wars were by and large justified as reactions to prior unwarranted action',[210] and criticises how, in contemporary literature,

> 'everything that corroborates the 'Hobbesian' or 'Westphalian' interpretation of the law of nations since 1648 is placed in the spotlight and called fundamental to the system; everything that detracts from it is pushed into the shadows and rejected as exceptional'.[211]

This book is in the continuation of this tendency – which nonetheless remains a minority within the scholarship – that challenges the narrative of indifference on historical grounds. The first two part of the books insisted on the discrepancy that exists between the commonly accepted narrative of indifference and historical sources. Analysing nineteenth century doctrine and State practice, they demonstrated that the overwhelming majority of authors asserted that the right to use force was not an absolute sovereign prerogative and that, States too, admitted that rules existed that limited the use of war and measures short of war.

* * *

Starting from constructivist-structuralist premise that historical accounts reflect the identity and culture of the society in which they emerge, this chapter sought to verify if, and to what extent, the narrative of

[209] Olivier Corten, 'Droit, force et légitimité dans une société internationale en mutation' (1996) 37 *Revue interdisciplinaire d'études juridiques* 77. See also by the same author, 'Formalization and Deformalization as Narratives of the Law of War', in José Maria Beneyto and David Kennedy (eds.), *New Approaches to International Law. The European and American Experiences* (TMC Asser Press, 2012), pp. 260–264.

[210] Randall Lesaffer, 'Too Much History: From War as Sanction to the Sanctioning of War', in Marc Weller (ed.), *The Oxford Handbook on the Use of Force in International Law* (Oxford University Press, 2015), p. 46.

[211] Randall Lesaffer, 'International Law and Its History: The Story of an Unrequited Love', in Matthew Craven, Malgosia Fitzmaurice and Maria Vogiatzi (eds.), *Time, History and International Law* (Martinus Nijhoff, 2007), p. 36.

indifference can be considered as product of the beliefs that underlie the identity of international law as a discipline. To this end, a two-step approach was adopted. The first step consisted in trying to identify the logics that structure the profession's representation of itself by examining how it defines and portrays international law in general. Focusing on the analysis of textbooks – because they carry and determine of the dominant discourse – three main features have surfaced: (i) the conviction that law is indispensable to bring order to an otherwise conflictual international society; (ii) the 'effectivity complex' from which international law still seems to suffer regarding its capacity to fulfil that mission; and (iii) a historiography which, by relying on the idea of progress, synthesises the two previous elements. These three elements are part of international law's foundational beliefs, and, as such, influence the way international lawyers, as a group, interpret events and make sense of the world that surrounds them. To re-use the term employed by Jan Assmann, they are the master narratives that act as the '*mythomoteurs*' of the discipline.[212] Bearing this in mind, the aim of the second part of the inquiry was to verify the hypothesis according to which the content of the historical accounts about the use of force is a product of the field's more general beliefs about international law by examining the rhetorical structures upon which the narrative of indifference is built. We saw that the paradigmatic and syntagmatic structures of all versions of the narrative of indifference clearly mimic the first and third elements of the discipline's more general discourse about international law – that is, the idea that law is a remedy against chaos and that time ineluctably brings progress. The following chapter interrogates the function of this narrative in the discipline and argues that it finds its roots mostly in the second element highlighted above, that is to say, the effectivity or credibility complex of international law.

[212] Jan Assman, *Moses and the Egyptian. The Memory of Egypt in Western Monotheism* (Harvard University Press, 1997), p. 15.

9

The Emergence of the Narrative of Indifference in the Interwar

Preserving Identity by Restoring Credibility

Mnemo-historians, cultural historians, and constructivists all agree that, in addition to being mirrors of the identity of the society that produces them, historical narratives also fulfil a social function within that society. Assmann and Lévi-Strauss, for instance, respectively argue that they aim to preserve the beliefs that unite a community and to offer a logical model of explanation to resolve a contradiction.[1] To synthetize these two not so different claims, one could say that historical accounts aim to bring a logical explanation for an event that is otherwise incompatible with the latent cognitive frames through which a group traditionally perceives reality. Events are rationalised in a way fitting with the group's deep founded beliefs about self and others. As indicated in the conclusion of the previous chapter, this book argues that the 'effectivity complex' of international law is fundamental to understand the *raison d'être* of the narrative of indifference. This narrative essentially holds the same function as international law's general history – that is, to show that with time international law has consolidated, and continues to consolidate, into a more and more sophisticated system of rules, which concomitantly suggests that it is more and more capable of bringing order on the international plane. In the aftermath of the World War I, it was paramount to restore the credibility of international law, which had not been able to prevent the 1914–1918 outburst of violence, as a tool for interstate peace.

To fully understand why, in the pursuit of that aim, part of the interwar doctrine felt the need to go as far as to deny the existence of any sort of rules on the use of force before 1919, the next sections will put the spotlight on two elements. First, it is important to grasp the meaning that was, at the time, vested in the notion of 'order'. Order, we shall see,

[1] Claude Lévi-Strauss, *Structural Anthropology* (original ed.: 1958) (Basic Books, 1963), p. 229.

was essentially conceived as a synonym for peace amongst the nations, which meant that the prime function of international law was to preserve that peace. In this context, the World War I represented a total failure of international law; a failure for which only a narrative as extreme as that of 'indifference' could provide remedy (Section 9.1). The second element lies in the fact that the war prevention system of the Covenant of the League of Nations was largely the consecration of the pre-war logics that had been advocated for by international lawyers for years. Many authors indeed believed that the establishment of formalized judicial mechanisms for dispute resolution was how international law would be able to fulfil its task of preserving peace. One cannot, therefore, help but see the indifference-narrative also as a product of the emotional reaction caused by the culmination of the profession's work in favour of the idea of 'peace through law' (Section 9.2).

9.1 International Order as Inter-State Peace, the Great War and the Failure of International Law: 'Indifference' as a Narrative Remedy

Point 8.1.1. of the previous chapter showed how the notion order was, and still is, central to the way the function of international law is defined. Installing and maintaining 'factual' order is, in fact, seen as the primary aim of law, and so installing and maintaining 'factual' international order is conceived as the primary objective of international law. But the content vested in the notion of order is highly indeterminate.[2] The meaning given to it has evolved through time and is not the same today as it was at the beginning of the twentieth century. This means that the way in which we perceive the function of international law has equally evolved and is not the same today as it was a hundred years ago. In the decades that preceded the World War I, interstate peace was almost held to be a synonym for international order; installing and maintaining peace among the nations was, therefore, perceived as being the primary function of international law (Section 9.1.1). In this context, the outburst of the Great War in the month of August 1914 represented a total failure of international law to fulfil its main task and was lived as yet another

[2] Anne Orford opposes 'factual order', understood as the alternative to anarchy, to 'order' as an authoritative regime that exists beyond the States. See 'Constituting Order', in James Crawford and Martti Koskenniemi (eds.), *The Cambridge Companion to International Law* (Cambridge University Press, 2012), p. 272.

demonstration of its outright lack of effectivity. Within the profession, these events clashed with the belief that law could be a shield against brutal force and disorder. The indifference-narrative provided the international legal community with a cognitively consonant explanation that reduced that contradiction (Section 9.1.2). The war was not the failure of international law, which did not restrict the use of force, but of international politics. This narrative, moreover, also appeared to pursue aims outside the profession. Many scholars were worried that the war had rattled the public's trust in international law and further degraded the already precarious image of the discipline. 'Indifference', it therefore seems, equally served as a narrative remedy to compensate that feared loss of credibility (Section 9.1.3).

9.1.1 *The Meaning of 'Order': Ensuring Inter-State Peace as the Prime Function of International Law*

Late nineteenth- and early twentieth-century scholarship placed a heavy emphasis on the existence of a general state of peace between the sovereign States of the world as the fundamental condition for 'factual' international order. Writers insisted that the objective of international law was to achieve 'world peace order',[3] 'to consolidate peace on earth, having eliminated war from the domain of inter-state relations',[4] or, in Oppenheim's words to ensure 'peace among the nations'.[5] Even professional societies such as the *Institut de droit international* and the *American Society for International Law* inscribed the idea of working towards the promotion of that aim in their statutes. Article 1 of the IDI Statute, for instance, provides that it would 'promote the progress of international law [...] by contributing, within the limits of its competence, either to the *maintenance of peace*, or observance of the laws of war'.[6] The ASIL, for its part, declared its purpose to be the 'promot[ion] [of] the establishment of relations on the basis of law and justice',[7] which,

[3] Karl Gareis, *Encyclopädie und Methodologie des Rechtswissenschaft* (Roth, 1887), p. 160.

[4] Vladimir E. Hravar (1893) quoted in William E. Butler, 'On the History of International Law in England and Russia', in William E. Butler (ed.), *The Non-Use of Force in International Law* (Martinus Nijhoff, 1989), p. 13.

[5] Lassa Oppenheim, Lassa Oppenheim, 'The Science of International Law: Its Tasks and Methods' (1908) 2 *American Journal of International Law*, p. 314.

[6] Art. 1 (2) d) IDI Statute. Emphasis added.

[7] Art. 2, Constitution of the American Society of International Law, available in (1907) 1 *American Journal of International Law*, 131–135.

as George Flinch noted, roughly speaking meant 'substituting reason for force in the settlement of international controversies'.[8]

For all that, pre-war scholars did not think that war could always be avoided, but the task of international law was to limit as much as possible the opportunities for States to have legal recourse to armed force. We may recall from Chapter 4 that Russian lawyer Fyodor Martens explained that the progressive assertion of the principle of non-intervention during the nineteenth century had been one of the great conquests of international law, and that the profession now needed to work towards making the remaining exceptions to the principle disappear as they hampered the power of the rule.[9] 'The exceptions to the principle of non-intervention are a danger',[10] Martens warned. Interferences often degenerated into open hostilities, and the more exceptions to the rule, the more opportunities for States to manipulate the law to further their own interests. Still, the imminent Russian scholar did not believe that all the excuses for the use of armed force should be suppressed. In a world without central authority, the right of self-defence and in protection of the intervening State's positive rights had to be preserved, as well as the right of humanitarian intervention to protect the Christian populations living in 'non-civilized' nations.[11] As we however also saw, numerous nineteenth century jurists expressed doubts as regard the desirability of interference on grounds of humanity as an exception to the rule of non-intervention, precisely because they feared it would open the door wide for abuse.[12] So, even though these writers were not always as direct as Martens or Oppenheim in asserting that the task of international law was to limit the legal occurrences of war, this belief seemed subjacent in the concerns they expressed regarding humanitarian intervention.

Four interconnected elements shed some light on why 'negative' peace was so central to the definition of the function of international law, while

[8] George A. Finch, 'The American Society of International Law, 1906–1956' (1956) 50 *American Journal of International Law*, 293.

[9] Fréderic de Martens, *Traité de droit international*, 3 vols. (Librairie Marescq Ainé, 1883), vol. 1, p. 396.

About Martens, see Vladimir V. Pustogarov, *Our Martens. F. F. Martens International Lawyer and Architect of Peace*, edited and translated from Russian by W. E. Butler (Kluwer Law International, 2000).

[10] de Martens, *Traité de droit international*, vol. 1, p. 397. Translation by the author.

[11] Ibid., pp. 397–398.

[12] See above (Section 2.4), (Section 3.4), (Section 4.4).

also continuing to illustrate the centrality of war prevention for international law.

First is the fact that international law at the time was still generally presented as a purely inter-state law.[13] States were the only subjects and actors of the international scene. As a result, the order that international law was supposed to inject on that scene was foremost conceived as an order between States. In this one-dimensional vision of the international society 'factual' order, hence, instinctively referred to the idea of peace amongst the nations. As a matter of fact, linguistically, 'disagreement', 'fighting', and by extension, 'combat', 'conflict' and 'war' are presented as the antonyms to 'order'. 'Peace', on the other hand, is mentioned as one of its synonyms. As Georg Schwarzenberger noted in *International law and Order* (1971), this means that 'at its lowest [that is to say, in an international *society* of *States*], [order suggests] a negative form of peace'.[14] In a multidimensional society, the merger of the notion of 'order' with that of 'peace' has different consequences. If, as today, international law is said to apply to a variety of different actors (individuals, international organisations, non-governmental organisations and so forth) the meaning of international order, indeed, changes: harmony not only needs to be as far as possible achieved between States, but also between the other actors. Inter-state peace becomes less preponderant in defining the function of international law and downgrades as an objective amongst others.[15] Human rights, democracy and other 'providential' aspects of international legal project, for example, become more

[13] See for e.g. Théophile Funck-Brentano et Albert Sorel, *Précis de droit des gens* (E. Plon et Cie, 1877), p. 1; Travers Twiss, *The Law of Nations Considered as Independent Political Communities*, 2 vols. (2nd ed., Clarendon Press, 1884), vol. 1, p. 2; Charles Calvo, *Le droit international théorique et pratique*, 6 vols. (4th ed., Guillaumin et Cie., 1887), vol. 1, p. 139; William E. Hall, *A Treatise on International Law* (3rd ed., Clarendon Press, 1890), p. 1; Alphonse Rivier, *Principes du droit des gens*, 2 vols. (Arthur Rousseau, 1896), vol.1, pp. 3–4; Thomas Lawrence, *The Principles of International Law* (D.C. Heath and Co., 1900), p. 1; Alexandre Mérignhac, *Traité de droit international public*, 3 vols. (LGDJ, 1905), vol. 1, p. 6; Lassa Oppenheim, *International Law. A Treatise*, 2 vols. (Longman Green, 1905), vol. 1, p. 3; John Westlake, *International Law*, 2 vols. (Cambridge University Press, 1910), vol. 1, p.1.

[14] Georg Schwarzenberger, *International Law and Order* (Stevens and Sons, 1971), p. 10.

[15] In this sense, see Allen Buchanan, 'The Legitimacy of International Law', in Samantha Bensson and John Tasioulas (eds.), *The Philosophy of International Law* (Oxford University Press, 2010), p. 89.

important. But, as long as international law was defined in inter-state terms, international order could be said to equate to inter-state peace.

The second element to be taken into consideration is the use of the analogy with national law and with the 'contractualist' theories of State to explain the birth and the necessity of international law. As we saw, the model of the social contract was regularly used in the nineteenth-century scholarship to illustrate the idea of the existence of an international society and of international rules of conduct.[16] As it turns out, security and force have a protagonist role in the 'contractualist' theories of the State.[17] Individuals are, in fact, said to have given up part of their freedom and submit to law in order to escape a state of nature, characterised by the war of all against all, in exchange for the protection of the State. Above all, they delegated their right to use force (private war, vengeance, etc.) in favour of a central authority whose task, as the new detainer of the 'monopoly of legitimate violence', is to ensure the security of the entities that created it and compose it. The limitation of the use of individual force is thus the pivotal clause of the social contract, and the elimination of violence at the national level the prime function of domestic law.[18] The analogy of the international with the national legal phenomenon through the use of these theories of social contract suggests that the function of international law was likewise viewed as that of restraining as much as possible the use of force, in order to ensure the security of the members of the international society. In this framework, security was the reason for which States had accepted to give up part of their sovereignty and inter-state security was, therefore, the domain in which international law chiefly needed to perform.

In link with the second point, the third point to be made regarding the centrality of inter-state peace as the main function of international law according to the profession before the Great War, lies with the external perceptions of the discipline. As point 8.1.2. of the previous chapter has shown (and the paragraph just above also indicates), international law is a field that compares itself a lot to national law. People outside the field also operate this comparison. More often than not, jurists are primarily trained in domestic law, and the public, overall, has more contact with national rules. Domestic legal orders end-up serving as the yardsticks

[16] See above (Section 2.1), (Section 3.1) and (Section 4.1).

[17] See Cécile Tournaye, *Kelsen et la sécurité collective* (LGDJ, 1995), pp. 11–12.

[18] See Hans Kelsen, 'Théorie du droit international' (1953) 84 *Recueil des cours de l'académie de droit international* 27.

against which the truly legal character of international law is measured by public opinion. Even though writers liked to emphasise the different nature of international law, an irresistible desire to show that, as a still primitive legal order, international law was maybe not as deficient as it is generally thought to be, stems from the literature.[19] The profession was (and still is) preoccupied by the 'others' perceptions of the discipline and, therefore, also took these perceptions into account when defining the field. The classical reproach formulated against international law was its lack of a central authority and sanction mechanism. Said differently, the issue with international law was essentially that it remained a system based on self-help in which, to use Abdy's words, 'there [was] but one real remedy, the sword'.[20] In some way, the use of force was hence determinant in the external belief that international law was not 'law proper'. Peace was what the discipline thought the population expected international law to bring.[21] Consequently, even though maybe not deliberately, international lawyers felt that the more international law would be able to control the use of force by States, the more the discipline would finally be recognised by its 'others' with the legal prestige it deserved.

Fourthly, and finally, the consequences that war had on trade and on the legal relations of States need to be highlighted. For the profession, preventing war was not the only function of international law, but it was the one upon which the capacity of international law to fulfil its other tasks depended. We saw how international law has generally perceived itself as a vehicle of and tool for the social and human progress of society.[22] Free trade, it seems, was very often considered by the late nineteenth century scholarship as an objectively and intrinsically positive value for humanity. Writers of international law claimed that by encouraging the interaction and cooperation of States, free trade was an agent of

[19] See above (Section 8.1.2) and (Section 8.1.3).

[20] John T. Abdy, *Kent's Commentaries on International Law* (2nd ed., Deighton and sons, 1878), p. 4.

[21] Miloš Vec underlines that: 'Some contemporary writers rejected the aims of peace movements vigorously, yet even for them it was clear that a certain part of the population expected international law and international lawyers to devote their activities to "peace"', in 'From Invisible Peace to the Legitimation of War. Paradoxes of a Concept in Nineteenth Century International Law Doctrine', in Thomas Hippler and Miloš Vec (eds.), *Paradoxes of Peace in the Nineteenth Century Europe* (Oxford University Press, 2015), p. 34.

[22] See above (Section 8.1.3.).

greater cultural understanding, of general prosperity and of international integration.[23] Capitalism promoted the 'global common good'; it was a vector of international socialisation.[24] The relation between international law and international trade was a mutually beneficial one. By bringing nations into more frequent and closer contact, sixteenth century mercantilism was, in fact, viewed as having given the impulsion for the development of international law.[25] In the interest of humanity, but also of international law itself, the smooth and efficient conduct of trade thus needed to be facilitated and protected. In manuals, whether it was in the sections dealing with international waterways, freedom of the seas, rules of diplomacy, but also war and neutrality, commerce was an omnipresent preoccupation. Rivier even considered that the interests of global trade were of 'a higher nature' than those of international politics.[26] International law, however, could only deploy its full potential as a facilitator of trade, and, by the same token, as a promoter of the 'global common good', in time of peace. In fact, not only did war put an end to the normal treaty, diplomatic and commercial relations of the belligerents, it also heavily affected the trade of other nations.[27] As a result, to remain a driving force of social progress by protecting commerce, international law, once again, essentially needed to make sure that States were not too easily allowed to resort to armed force against each other.

In this context, the problem with the Great War was not that it was a war, but that it was a generalised war. It had replaced the ideal of 'world peace order' by a state of 'world war anarchy'. The hostilities were not limited to two belligerents like in the Franco-Prussian War (1870) or the Russo-Japanese War (1905), nor was the fighting territorially circumvented or taking place in faraway lands. The profession and the discipline

[23] Lawrence, for instance, wrote: 'Commerce, intermarriage, scientific discovery, community of religion, [...] – all these, and countless other causes, tend to knit states together in a social bound somewhat analogous to the bound between the individual man and its fellows', in *The Principles of International Law*, p. 3. For more examples see also Rivier, *Principes du droit des gens*, vol. 1, p. 259.

[24] See B.S. Chimni, 'Capitalism, Imperialism, and International Law in the Twenty-First Century' (2012) 14 *Oregon Review of International Law* 17–45.

[25] See Martti Koskenniemi, 'International Law and the Development of Mercantile Capitalism', in Pierre-Marie Dupuy et Vincent Chetail (dirs.), *The Roots of International Law/Les fondements du droit international – Liber Amicorum Peter Haggenmacher* (Martinus Nijhoff, 2013), pp. 3–37.

[26] Rivier, *Principes du droit des gens*, vol. 1, p. 109.

[27] See, e.g. Oppenheim, *International Law*, vol. 2, p. 106.

could deal with these smaller contradictions, but not with a general conflagration at the heart of the international system.

9.1.2 *The Great War and the Failure of International Law (i): 'Indifference' as a Narrative Remedy for a Cognitive Dissonance Within the Profession*

Without naming it, when Assmann and Lévi-Strauss argue that historical narratives aim to rationalise events that would otherwise be in conflict with the core beliefs of the group that creates these narratives, they actually refer to a classical concept of social psychology: cognitive dissonance. Introduced by Leon Festinger in the 1950s, cognitive dissonance is defined as the state of psychological discomfort caused by two conflicting cognitions – i.e., beliefs, opinions, values, knowledge or behaviours.[28] Festinger's theory starts from the premises that individuals, as a general rule, seek consistency within themselves.[29] Faced with a contradiction, they will therefore strive to restore coherence by putting mechanisms of rationalisation in place in order to reduce the tension of the dissonance.

The tension of the dissonance may be reduced in several ways that usually involve adapting one or the other of the conflicting cognitions. In *A Theory of Cognitive Dissonance* (1957), Festinger identified three essential modes of reducing a cognitive dissonance: (i) changing one of the two cognitions, (ii) forget or diminish the importance of one of the cognitions or (iii) acquire a new cognition to neutralise the contradiction between the two preceding cognitions.[30] The 'choice' of the mode of reduction will depend on the strength and resistance to change of the cognitions involved. The more a cognition is subjectively important to a person, the less likely it is to change; similarly, the more a cognition is objectively resistant (e.g., the fact that the grass is green or that it is raining) the less likely it is to change too.[31] To use the example of smoking put forth by Festinger, if this behaviour is deeply anchored in the habits of the smoker (subjectively resistant cognition) and considering that the knowledge that smoking is bad is also hard to ignore or reverse (objectively resistant cognition), a heavy smoker is more likely to

[28] Leon Festinger, *A Theory of Cognitive Dissonance* (Stanford University Press, 1957), p. 9.
[29] Ibid., p. 1.
[30] Ibid., pp. 18–24.
[31] Ibid., pp. 24–28.

use the second or third model of reducing the dissonance. Another important element that needs to be taken into consideration is the overall context in which the dissonance occurs, such as the social environment. Studies have indeed shown that if the dissonance touches group beliefs and is experienced collectively, the responses to the contradiction will not be the same because the rationalisation is not individual but collective. In short, groups are less likely to adapt their beliefs to new cognitions, especially if these beliefs are directly linked to the social identity of the said group. The pre-existing cognition will most often be reinforced in response to contradiction.[32]

A pioneering work in this respect has been that of Leon Festinger, Henry Ricken and Stanley Schacter in *When Prophecy Fails* (1956).[33] In 1954, the three psychologists decided to infiltrate a religious sect in order to study what would happen when their leader's doomsday prophecy failed. Marion Keech, the founder and leader of the Seekers, claimed that she had received information from the people of the planet Clarion that life on earth would come to an end on 21 December 1954. The world would be flooded and only her followers saved. In preparation for disaster, she encouraged her disciples to sell their belongings, quit their jobs and abandon the non-believing members of their families to gather in Lake City. On 21 December 1954, however, nothing happened. A dissonance appeared between the Seekers' doomsday belief, on the one side, and the fact that nothing actually happened, on the other. Instead of leading to the disintegration of the group as one might have expected, Festinger and his colleagues observed that the non-realisation of the prophecy reinforced the Seekers' social cohesion and pre-existing convictions. At first, the members of the cult were distressed at the disconfirmation of their belief, but they rapidly accepted the rationalisations provided to them by Mrs Keech.[34] She said that it was the strength of their faith that had saved humanity from annihilation. Through this new information, the meaning of the non-realisation of the prophecy was reversed: rather than contradicting the Seekers' core belief, it comforted and reinforced them.

[32] See in particular Joel Cooper and Diane Mackie, 'Cognitive Dissonance in an Intergroup Context' (1983) 44 *Journal of Personality and Social Psychology* 536–544.

[33] Leon Festinger, Henry W. Ricken and Stanley Schacter, *When Prophecy Fails* (University of Minnesota Press, 1956).

[34] ibid., pp. 193–215.

This study was the first time (and one of rare occasions) where scientists were able to analyse this type of group phenomenon in near-experimental conditions. But it should be emphasised that maintenance of 'invalid' beliefs in spite of hard contradicting evidence has also been observed in situations involving a priori more rational beings than the followers of a 'UFO cult'.[35] Festinger, Ricken and Schacter, concluded that in order for that type of reaction to take place five elements needed to be present: (i) there must be a conviction, (ii) there must be commitment to that conviction, (iii) the conviction needs to be amenable to univocal disconfirmation, (iv) the conviction must, in fact, be disconfirmed and (v) there needs to be a sufficient number of persons experiencing this disconfirmation to provide easy social support.[36]

The situation of international lawyers in 1914–1918, and shortly after, fits with this overall description: there was a strong conviction, commitment to that conviction, disconfirmation through the World War I of that conviction and a social support network to face the disconfirmation of that conviction.

The nature and content of the discipline's conviction have already been sufficiently addressed and it therefore does not appear necessary to elaborate much further on that matter.[37] The question of the profession's commitment to the belief that international law is a vector of social order and more specifically of international peace, on the other hand, has, so far, only been examined to a lesser extent. The second section of this chapter will deal with the investment of jurists for the promotion of international law as a tool for peace in further details, but it is already important to note that this investment was substantial. As we saw, professional societies were created with the aim of promoting international law and peace through the pacific settlement of disputes. Some scholars became active members or supporters of pacifist movements, whose role in the convening of the Hague Peace Conferences has often been highlighted. During the Hague Conferences as well, international lawyers were present in force to push the cause of arbitration (within the limits of their governments' instructions).[38] This is to say that the project of international law as an instrument for peace was an ideal in which many scholars had deep personal faith and to which they devoted

[35] See Festinger, *A Theory of Cognitive Dissonance*, pp. 243–246.
[36] Festinger, Ricken and Schacter, *When Prophecy Fails*, p. 216.
[37] See above (Section 8.1.1) and (Section 9.1.1).
[38] See below (Section 9.2.2.).

personal time. Of course, unlike the Seekers, international lawyers did not give up their homes and families, but their dedication was great, nonetheless. It was their professional life and sometimes even more.

The disconfirmation of that belief brought about by the World War I was, as a result, quite severe. There was a dissonance between the cognition of the events of World War I and the belief that international law would be effective in bringing 'world peace order'. If international law regulated the use of force, how could the war and all its excesses, in fact, take place? And if international law truly had an ordering and pacifying power how could these horrors not be prevented? International law had failed its main and most important mission. The contradiction was even greater considering the recent progresses of international arbitration and other pacific mechanisms of dispute resolution notably achieved in the Hague, and the scope and intensity of the conflict. More than forty States were involved in World War I. Fighting took place in Europe, Africa, Asia and Oceania, resulting in an estimated total of 17 million dead and 20 million wounded.

International lawyers acknowledged the disconfirmation of international law's pacifying motto by the war. They feared the effects it might have, both inside and outside the profession. Reacting to Sir Edward Carson's – an Anglo-Irish barrister, judge and politician – claim that the law of nations had been destroyed, Root noted, as soon as 1915, that 'the incidents of the great war now raging affect[ed] seriously the very foundations of international law'.[39] A year later, Pillet seemed equally troubled when writing that: 'nothing subsists of what seemed most clearly established and we, the servants of international law, have come to wonder if, after this great destruction, something can be rebuilt'.[40] His disenchantment led him to abandon public international law in favour of private international law.[41] After the war, Alvarez, Ralston, Fenwick and Politis expressed similar anxieties. Alvarez worried that international law had been 'discredited'.[42] Ralston feared that people might, from now on, think international law to be nothing more but a

[39] Elihu Root, 'The Outlook for International Law' (1915) 9 *Proceedings of the American Society for International Law* 2.

[40] Antoine Pillet, 'La guerre actuelle et le droit international' (1916) 23 *Revue générale de droit international public* 6. Translation by the author.

[41] Albert de Lapradelle, *Maîtres et doctrines du droit des gens* (2nd ed., Editions internationales, 1950), p. 320.

[42] Alejandro Alvarez, Preface to Karl Strupp, *Eléments de droit international public universel, européen et américain*, 2 vols. (Les Editions Internationales, 1930), vol. 1, p. xvii.

'paper creation'.[43] Fenwick was concerned that the term 'international law' might not seem to bear 'any relations to the realities' anymore.[44] Politis, for his part, wrote that:

> The world war deeply troubled people's minds about the value, effectiveness and even existence of international law. Seeing so many treaties violated, so many rules disregarded, so much arbitrariness reigning in the relations of peoples, we have allowed ourselves to be overcome by doubt and pessimism. There has been talk of the ruin and bankruptcy of international law, of the impossibility of subjecting the activities of States to binding rules of law.[45]

The war was decisively felt as being the antithesis of the belief on which the existence of international law lied, just as the fact that the world did not come to an end on 21 December 1954 was the plain opposite of the belief upon which the existence the Seekers rested.

Because faith in the ordering power of international law was so directly linked to the existence of international law as a discipline and of international lawyers as a professional group, however, this cognition was not going to be the one to change. Changing this cognition would have been tantamount to signing international law's and the international legal profession's death warrants. And, in fact, the core conviction in the power of law was not recanted, quite the opposite. As with the Seekers, it was the meaning of the events that was adapted to fit with the pre-existing cognition. The Great War was transformed from a failure of international law to a triumph of international law. Thanks to the narrative of indifference according to which classical *ius ad bellum* did not truly regulate the use of force, the World War I was not the fault of international law, but the result of the absence of (sufficient) rules and of selfish power politics. To go even further, without the war, the governments of the world might have never come to realise the urgent need for more order through more international rules. In this perspective, although tragic, the World War I had actually been quite beneficial from the strict point of view of the battle for international rule of law. It had enabled the transition from a state of generalised anarchy towards a

43 Jackson H. Ralston, *Democracy's International Law* (John Byrne & Co., 1922), foreword.
44 Charles G. Fenwick, *International Law* (The Century Co., 1924), p. 30.
45 Nicolas Politis, *Les nouvelles tendances du droit international* (Librairie Hachette, 1927), pp. 9–10. Translation by the author. See also Olof Hoijer, *Le Pacte de la Société des Nations. Commentaire théorique et pratique* (Editions Spes, 1926), p. 172.

world order which, guided by law, would lead to a more just and peaceful international society.[46] In this sense, 'indifference' clearly acted as a narrative remedy to the cognitive dissonance experienced by international lawyers as a consequence of World War I.

As mentioned, the propensity to maintain pre-existing conviction despite contradicting evidence is even more likely when the dissonance is shared as a group. The members of the group do not necessarily need to be under the same roof (like the Seekers) for social support to contribute to the reduction of the contradiction. Only two elements have to be present: (i) several persons experiencing the same dissonance and (ii) contact between these persons.[47] It has already been shown that at least six members of the profession, and not the least among them, shared a feeling of unease at the events of the Great War. Most of them were in contact with each other, as well as with others. Root, Ralston and Fenwick were all active within the ASIL, which met regularly during and after the war. Alvarez, Pillet and Politis were members of the IDI, which resumed its sessions in 1919. Other members of these societies around these years included Moore, Scott, Borchard, Bustamente, Schuecking, Dupuis, Kaufmann, Lapradelle, Le Fur, de Visscher, Wehberg, Max Huber, Baty, Higgins or yet de Louter, Albéric Rolin and Edouard Rolin-Jaecquemyns to name just a few. Many international lawyers were equally present as members of their States' delegations to the peace negotiations of 1919 in Paris. It is undeniable that all these people were in contact. It is probable that they discussed and shared their experience of the war, and, given the widespread character of the belief in the social necessity of law, it is presumable that the majority of these men felt unease as to the impact that these four years of extreme violence might have on the still young discipline of international law.

Of course, as we saw, this does not mean that the indifference-narrative imposed itself immediately or uniformly. Some scholars, Kelsen and Strisower for instance, opposed it from the very start.[48] Even amongst its tenants, 'indifference' came in slightly different versions. It was a process of formulation, reception and mediation. How, then, did this process work and how did 'indifference' (in one or the other of its versions) come to be shared by most of the profession? Just

[46] See above (Section 8.2.1.) and (Section 8.2.2.).

[47] Festinger, *A Theory of Cognitive Dissonance*, pp. 198–200.

[48] See above (Section 8.2.3.).

like individuals, groups seek internal coherence. If members of a group disagree, a pressure to bridge the disagreement will arise, especially if the difference of opinion touches upon a core definitional issue. One may adapt his or her opinions to those of the rest of group, try to persuade others to change their opinions, or if this fails, make the other person not comparable to one's self (by attributing different characteristics, or plainly rejecting, that other person).[49] Thus, for instance, if someone claims that international law regulated the use of force before the Great War, one of three things may happen. Supposing that this person belongs to the minority, the easiest option to reduce the dissonance will be for that person to change his/her opinion or adapt his/her discourse to make it acceptable to the rest of the community. He/she may also try to convince others to adopt his/her views. But, his/her capacity to do so will be greater if he/she is not isolated (in which event the pressure to reduce the dissonance will, in any case, be lower), and/or holds substantial power and influence – in our case, as a leading scholar and respected authority for example. If neither of these mechanisms work, there remains to find an explanation as to why people disagree. In international law, differences of opinion will most often be attributed to a divergence of conception as to how the law works. When Kelsen, for instance, placed himself against the tide of the dominant interwar scholarly discourse about the use of force, the dissonance between him and 'mainstream' international lawyers could be reduced by tracing his position to his peculiar and highly hierarchized vision of the international legal order. By the same logics, Schmitt's heavy criticism of the rhetoric surrounding the narrative of indifference and his exaltation of war as a potential stimulator of international order could be imputed to his antiformalist and decisionist theories.[50] The Soviet dissent could be explained away by ideology and its Marxist reading of international law. Strisower‘s claims, as we saw, were pushed away as being 'moral rather than legal'. By doing so, the general harmony of the group could be preserved even though different opinions continue(d) to (co-)exist.

[49] Festinger, *A Theory of Cognitive Dissonance*, p. 182.

[50] On decisionism, see Carl Schmitt, *On the Three Types of Juristic Thought* (Praeger Publishers, 2004). About Carl Schmitt and international more generally, see Martti Koskenniemi, 'Carl Schmitt and International Law', in Jens Meierhenrich and Oliver Simons (eds.), *The Oxford Handbook of Carl Schmitt* (Oxford University Press, 2017), pp. 592–611.

For the rest, it would be hard to give an account of the interpersonal dynamics of communication and persuasion that actually took place in Paris and elsewhere in the 1920s and 1930s. In addition to the fact that interwar lawyers, at least in their writings, rarely directly spoke of the history of the use of force in the nineteenth century, there are no records of corridor and private talks. Either way, the process is often subtler. Beyond words, it involves attitudes, behaviours and feelings that are complicated to observe in non-experimental conditions. It is, nevertheless, worth noting that President Wilson opened the 1919 session of the IDI using the following terms:

> this great and unprecedented war was fought to consolidate international law, to prove that it is a reality [. . .] If we can now give international law the kind of vitality that it can only have if it is a real expression of our moral judgments, we will have completed, in a sense, the work that this war was intended to solemnly enshrine.[51]

The US president was very well respected within the international legal circles and his words certainly found echo. His discourse was consonant with the cognitions of the people he was addressing and with the rationalizations that they had themselves probably already elaborated. Moreover, the fact that men of influence, such as Wilson (a man of State), shared their view of the Great War was obviously comforting. The role of social support in reducing a dissonance, in fact, lies on the idea that the more people believe in something, the most certainly it must be true.[52] As a result, the group might sometimes seek to further reduce the dissonance it has experienced by seeking additional support for its views outside the group ('proselyting' activities). This also happens if the group is worried it might get ridiculed or its image get degraded because of the disconfirmation of its system of belief by the facts. Such phenomenon could be observed with the narrative of indifference in the interwar years. It was not only about reconciling the belief in the power of law with the actual events of 1914–1918 within the profession, but also about (re) building trust in international law by 'exporting' this narrative and belief outside the strict limits of the profession.

[51] IDI (1919) 27 *Annuaire* x (Session extraordinaire de Paris, Mai 1919). Translation by the author.

[52] Festinger, *A Theory of Cognitive Dissonance*, p. 200.

9.1.3 The Great War and the Failure of International Law (ii): 'Indifference' as Narrative Remedy for a Loss of Credibility Outside the Profession

In the way it perceives itself and defines its function, international law appears as a self-conscious discipline. It is insecure because of its reputed lack of effectivity in comparison to national legal systems, and defines its function according, among other things, to what it believes people await from it.[53] We indeed saw that the profession had this idea that public opinion, by analogy to the domestic level, expected international law to organise the peaceful relations of sovereign States. The outside legitimacy and credibility of the discipline therefore rested on the capacity of international rules to effectively fulfil that mission, or, at least, to seem to fulfil it.

In addition to scattering the discipline's system of belief, the World War I also had it worried about the impact that these events might have on the public's perception of the discipline. This apprehension was, for instance, apparent in the extract from Politis's previously quoted. He considered that war had profoundly agitated '*les esprits*' regarding the value and efficacy of international law as a result of the repeated violations of international treaties and rules.[54] Fenwick worried that war, and more particularly the violation of Belgium's neutrality, had made a 'mockery' of law and that 'in the *popular mind* the term "international law" [. . .] was a term that no longer bore any relation to the realities or the needs of international life'.[55] Alvarez was still more explicit. He had the impression that: 'public opinion, overwhelmed by this cataclysm and above all by the repeated violation of international law, believed that this law had gone bankrupt: at least it fell into disrepute in its eyes'.[56] Surely, the war traumatised western society as a whole, but one may doubt whether people were truly aware of the violations of international law as such. Rational or not, these fears testify of the imperious need felt by the profession to bolster its image and, in so doing, preserve its integrity. It was about remedying the perceived loss of credibility of the discipline and convincing the public that international law and the League of Nations would guarantee lasting peace.

[53] See above (Section 8.1.2.) and (Section 9.1.1.).

[54] Nicolas Politis, *Les nouvelles tendances du droit international* (Librairie Hachette, 1927), pp. 9–10.

[55] Fenwick, *International Law*, p. 30. Emphasis added.

[56] Alvarez, 'Preface to Karl Strupp', p. xvii. Translation by the author.

It was easy for international lawyers to find social support outside the field's strict limits. Their needs and interests meet with those of other, sometimes powerful, spheres. Demands for lasting peace emanated from all the strands of society, and, after a slaughter of four years, the legitimacy of many (European) governments rested on their capacity to deliver on that promise. Like international lawyers, but for different reasons, they needed to reassure the public that the League and the legal framework that they had put in place would prevent another war.[57] But most of the activities for the promotion of the League were carried out not by the governments but by the civil society. The idea of 'peace through law' had, indeed, been the credo of many pacifist movements before the war.[58] In addition to some legal scholars, these organisations usually included, wealthy and influential persons, such as industrials and politicians. Andrew Carnegie, Leon Bourgeois, Lord Robert Cecil and many deputies involved with the *Inter-parliamentary Union* – created in 1889 by Frédéric Passy and William Randal Cremer with the aim of promoting arbitration as a substitute for war – come to mind.[59] In 1910, steel tycoon Andrew Carnegie created the *Carnegie Endowment for International Peace* nominating Elihu Root at its head, for the purpose of 'promoting a global acceptance of the peaceable methods in the settlement of international disputes'.[60] Trained lawyers, Bourgeois (an honorary member of the IDI as of 1908) and Cecil were also firm believers in the principles of 'legal pacifism'.[61] In light of their commitment to the pacifist cause, it is

57 The French government did not publicly endorse any action in favour of a League of Nations before peace was concluded, as they feared that the pacifist propaganda might demotivate the troops on the front and sometimes suspected the pacifist movements of being infiltrated by the enemy. See Jean-Michel Guieu, '«Pour la paix par la Société des Nations ». La laborieuse organisation d'un mouvement français de soutien à la Société des Nations (1915–1920)' (2006) 22 *Guerres mondiales et conflits contemporains* 89–102; Christian Birebent, *Militants de la paix et de la SDN. Les mouvements pacifistes de soutien à la Société des Nations en France et au Royaume-Uni 1918–1925* (L'Harmattan, 2007), pp. 45 and 55–56.

58 See below (Section 9.2.).

59 About the Inter-parliamentary Union, see inter alia Christian L. Lange, 'The Interparliamentary Union' (1924) 86 *Advocates for Peace through Justice* 474–478.

60 Carnegie Endowment for International Peace, *Report of the Director of the Division of International Law* (26 October 1911), p. 1.

61 See Alexandre Niess, 'Leon Bourgeois (1851–1925), juriste et ange de la paix' (2009) 11 *Parlement[s], Revue d'histoire politique* 135–148; Stanilas Jeannesson, 'Léon Bourgeois aux Conférences de La Haye de 1899 et 1907: solidarisme et démocratisation des relations internationales' (2014) 33 *Histoire, économie & société* 107–120; Gaynor Johnson, *Lord Robert Cecil: Politician and Internationalist* (Routledge, 2013). On the doctrine of

imaginable that such individuals as well experienced a certain disconfirmation of their conviction as a result of World War I, and that this shock further convinced them of the urgency to develop international rule of law. They had the power and resources to carry out wide-ranging actions to sway public support for the League of Nations and its framework.

Both closely involved with the establishment of the League by their governments, Cecil and Bourgeois respectively founded the *League of Nations Union* (LNU) in October 1918 and the *Association française pour la Société des Nations* (AFSdN) in November 1918.[62] Other such organisations included the *Groupement universitaire pour la Société des Nations* (GUSdN) and the *Association de la paix par le droit* (APD) in France, as well as the American *League to Enforce Peace* (LEP) created in 1915 and headed by former US President William Howard Taft.[63] Pro-League movements were present in the four corners of the world. Established in late 1919, the *International Union of League of Nations Associations* (IULNA) brought together societies from over forty countries. The aim of these organisations – some of which had already been involved in the reflection process on the establishment of the League – was to promote and raise public awareness on the work of the League of Nations. Robert Cecil and Gilbert Murray, the leading instances of the LNU, were convinced that the people would undoubtedly support the League if it was honestly and clearly explained to them.[64] In its first tract, the AFSdN likewise declared that in order to be efficient, the League of Nations needed 'popular support, a vast movement of faith' and that its role in this context was one 'of study and of propaganda'.[65] Still in the same vein, the IULNA stated that 'making plans for educational and propaganda work was the very *raison d'être* for the federation'.[66]

'solidarism' initiated by Bourgeois and international law, see Martti Koskenniemi, *The Gentle Civilizer of Nations. The Rise and Fall of International Law, 1870–1960* (Cambridge University Press, 2001), pp. 284–291.

[62] The LNU was the successor of the League of Nations Society (LNS) formed in 1915.

[63] On the GUSdN, see Christophe Birebent, 'Le Groupement universitaire pour la Société des Nations face aux crises des années trente' (2004) 74 *Matériaux pour l'histoire de notre temps* 14–19.

[64] Helen McCarthy, *The British People and the League of Nations. Democracy, citizenship and internationalism, c. 1918–1948* (Manchester University Press, 2011), p. 20.

[65] AFSdN, Notre programme, Tracte no 1, p. 2. Translation by the author.

[66] Quoted in Birebent, *Militants de la paix et de la SDN*, p. 94.

International lawyers were involved within the pro-League societies and made themselves available for their 'propaganda' activities. Scelle, for instance, was responsible for the AFSdN's local section of Dijon, and Jules Basdevant presided the GUSdN for a time. Politis, Scelle, René Cassin, Ferdinand Larnaude and Albert de Lapradelle all gave conferences on behalf of the ADFSdN.[67] Besides public conferences, the actions carried out were diverse. In addition to the traditional tracts, papers, posters and pamphlets, radio talk shows and public screenings were also organised. The LNU even had a subcommittee in charge of cinema that contributed to the production of two movies, the *Star of Hope* in 1925 and the *World War and After* in 1926.[68] These two movies were essentially aimed towards the youth, which constituted one of the main targets of the pro-League movements. According to the LNU education committee, an estimated one million children saw these movies between 1925 and 1930.[69] The strategy laid on building lasting peace by educating the new generations to the principles of internationalism and to the workings of the League. And so, inter-war pacifist movements developed ambitious programs specially aimed at schools and universities. Drawing and essay contests were organised, the creation chairs and pro-League clubs in the universities was encouraged and supervised.

But the major project put in place by pro-League societies was the revision of school textbooks in order to integrate the pacifist 'liberal-democratic' account of the World War I and of its outcomes.[70] The LNU, for instance, drew up a list of adequate textbooks and materials, which it

[67] See ibid., pp. 83 and 88; Jean-Michel Guieu, 'Les juristes français, la Société des Nations et l'Europe', Communication présentée le 14 octobre 2005 à l'occasion du Colloque 'Aristide Briand, la SdN et l'Europe, 1919–1932', p. 5.

[68] McCarthy, *The British People and the League of Nations*, p. 114. On the use of radio and cinema, see Jean-Jacques Renoliet, *L'UNESCO oubliée. La Société des Nations et la coopération intellectuelle (1919–1946)* (Publication de la Sorbonne, 1999), pp. 305–307.

[69] B. J. Elliott, 'The LNU and History Teaching in England: A Study in Benevolent Bias' (1977) 6 *History of Education* 131–141.

[70] On the revision of textbooks in the interwar, see *inter alia* Maria-Cristina Guintella, 'Enseignement de l'histoire et révision des manuels scolaires dans l'entre-deux-guerres', in Marie-Christine Basques, Annie Bruter et Nicole Tutiaux-Guillon (eds.), *Pistes didactiques et chemins d'historiens. Textes offerts à Henri Moniot* (L'Harmattant, 2003), pp. 161–189; Marcelo Verga, 'Manuels d'histoire pour la paix en Europe', in Marta Petricioli and Donnatella Cherubini (eds.), *For Peace in Europe. Institutions and Civil Society Between the World Wars* (PIE Peter Lang, 2007), pp. 503–524; Christophe Bechet, 'La révision pacifiste des manuels scolaires. Les enjeux de la mémoire de la guerre 14–18 dans l'enseignement belge de l'Entre-deux-guerres' (2008) 20 *Cahiers d'histoire du temps présent* 49–101.

circulated amongst the education circles. In the early 1920s, the *Carnegie endowment* – whose president, Elihu Root, was deeply convinced of the necessity of familiarising the masses with the working of international relations in general and of international law in particular – commissioned an extensive inquiry into European history schoolbooks.[71] The aim of the study was to pinpoint the good and bad practices and alert the public authorities of the need to modify the passages that might sustain hatred and distrust between the former belligerents.[72] The civil society initiatives were monitored and sometimes directly encouraged by the League of Nations itself.[73] In 1923 and in 1924, the League's Assembly adopted resolutions that respectively 'urge[d] the Governments of the States Members to arrange that the children and youth in their respective countries where such teaching is not given be made aware of the existence and aims of the League of Nations and of the terms of its Covenant',[74] and stressed the need to 'train the younger generation to regard international co-operation as the normal method of conducting world affairs'.[75] In 1925, the League's Committee on Intellectual Cooperation would pass yet another (similar) resolution and create a sub-committee of experts charged with the task of assessing the implementation of the resolutions by the member States. In 1927, the sub-committee – in which Alfred Zimmern, amongst others, sat – issued a report that, in addition to providing children with knowledge of the League as soon as primary school, suggested making the study of public international law mandatory for all law students.[76]

Historians agree that member States were, by and large, well disposed towards the League's recommendations, especially after the Treaties of Locarno were signed in 1925 and Germany joined the League of Nations

[71] Elihu Root, 'The Need for Popular Understanding of International Law' (1907) 1 *American Journal of International Law* 1–3.

[72] Dotation Carnegie pour l'Europe, *Enquête sur les manuels scolaires d'après-guerre* (Centre européen de la dotation Carnegie, 1923), pp. 2 and 27. About the Carnegie inquiry, see Tomás Irish, 'Peace through History? The Carnegie Endowment for International Peace's Inquiry into European schoolbooks, 1921–1924' (2016) 45 *Journal of the History of Education Society* 38–56.

[73] On the action of the League of Nations, see UNESCO, *A Handbook for the Improvement of Textbooks and Teaching Materials as Aids to International Understanding* (UNESCO, 1949), pp. 16–23; John E. Harley, *International Understanding. Agencies Educating for a New World* (Stanford University Press, 1931), pp. 137–151.

[74] Quoted in ibid., pp. 140–141.

[75] Ibid.

[76] Ibid., p. 142.

in 1926. In Belgium, for example, the Minister for Education, Camille Huysmans, adopted a ministerial circular in which he stated that history courses will be considered incomplete 'if the pacifying mission of the League of Nations is not highlighted'.[77] A small syllabus containing a lesson on the League of Nations for primary school was annexed to the circular. The lesson, in addition to describing the organisation of the League, notably taught that its aim was to preserve the hard-earned peace of 1918:

> 'The victorious nations wanted to show that they had pursued the ideal of establishing a lasting peace based on justice and the recognition of the law. The League of Nations is, in fact, an institution designed to guarantee the Rule of Law in international politics and thus stabilize the Peace that the soldiers of 1914 so dearly acquired'.[78]

The content of British school textbooks was similar. One of the manuals recommended by the LNU thus explained that the League was 'born out of the realisation of the need to end all wars, control [the States'] passions and desire for conquest'.[79] It emphasised the cardinal role of judicial mechanisms of dispute settlement. Talking about arbitration, it read:

> We have seen that a great many disputes before 1914 had already been settled that way, and that there were great many promises between nations to submit certain kinds of disputes to arbitration. The Court at The Hague, also, could have been called to settle the quarrel. [. . .] The armies were ready, and the means of peaceful settlement were not.
>
> So war came.[80]

It then carried on to expound the security system put in place by the Covenant of the League of Nations:

> Most important of the promise is Article 12. By it the nations agree that if any dispute arises amongst them likely to lead to war they will submit the matter either to arbitration or judicial settlement or to inquiry by the Council, and they agree in no case to resort to war until three months after the award had been given. [. . .] [This period] would most likely mean that at the end of it all they would make up their quarrel some other way.

77 'Circulaire ministérielle du 10 avril 1926' (1926) 20 *Bulletin du Ministère des Sciences et des Arts* 44–45. Emphasis added. Translation by the author.

78 Ibid., p. 51. Translation by the author.

79 Kathleen Innes, *The Story of the League of Nations Told for Young People* (The Hogarth Press, 1925), p. 37.

80 Ibid.

> Very important, too, is the article which asks the Council to set up a Court, known as the Permanent Court of International Justice, because it is always ready to judge any case that is brought to it. [. . .] Perhaps, if a permanent Court had been sitting there [the Peace Palace] in 1914, [. . .] the Great War would have been avoided'.[81]

We can see how these textbooks clearly reproduced the rhetorics of indifference and conveyed the idea that law would provide the necessary framework to preserve the world from another generalised war.

Of course, international lawyers were not directly responsible for the content of school manuals and for their revision. At the same time, as we saw, they were closely connected to the pro-League movements as well as to the League itself. The whole idea behind these educational campaigns seemed to be the belief that by training new generations to peace, war would, in the long run, disappear from habit. But the insistence on the law and on its pacifying power also indicates that the pro-League of Nations lobby pursued a more immediate aim: rebuilding public trust in the capacity of international law to ensure international peace.

9.2 The Covenant of the League of Nations as the Consecration of Pre-War War-Prevention Logics: 'Indifference' as an Expression of Emotions

With the theories of cognitive dissonance, the focus was put on the traumatic event – i.e. the event that disconfirmed the belief heretofore held as certitude –, in the present case, the World War I. Besides the war, however, it cannot be denied that the establishment of the League of Nations, and the adoption of the Covenant, marked an important material and symbolic evolution for international law. The impact of this other significant event on the emergence of the narrative of indifference cannot, as a consequence, be ignored. In continuation with Assmann and others' claim that (hi)stories find their roots in the identity and core beliefs of the societies that create them, this section wishes to put the emphasis on the role of emotions on the apparition of 'indifference'. Not that theories of cognitive dissonance do not involve emotions; as we saw, the feeling of discomfort is key as it triggers mechanisms for rationalisation of the contradiction.[82] Here the perspective is slightly different and

[81] Ibid., pp. 39–40.

[82] While differences exist between the notions of 'emotion' and 'feeling', it is not necessary for the present research to get into the details of these differences.

consists in approaching the narrative of indifference as an expression of emotion rather than as a reaction to an emotion.

More concretely, it is argued that 'indifference' is a form of expression of the positive emotions provoked by the adoption of the Covenant and the establishment of the first integrated international organisation. In many ways, the legal framework of the League was the consecration of the 'peace through law' motto and of the pre-war war-prevention logics for which the international law community had advocated for many years. As from the 1870s and the success of the *Alabama Claims* arbitration, international lawyers became increasingly involved with the pacifist projects and lobby for the promotion of judicial means for dispute resolution, in particular arbitration (Section 9.2.1). The pacifist movements' two main demands were the establishment of a Permanent Court and of mandatory arbitration. In this context, the holding of the Hague Conferences of 1899 and of 1907 yielded grand expectations. To the disappointment of many, however, few were actually met (Section 9.2.2). With the adoption of the Covenant of the League of Nations, on the other hand, all the pacifist demands on arbitration were finally consecrated, which is why the narrative of indifference and its rhetorics can also be interpreted as an expression of relief and pride at the culmination of fifty years of activism (Section 9.2.3).

9.2.1 From (the) Alabama *to The Hague: Arbitration Becomes the Project of International Lawyers*

In the first part of this book, we saw how in classical international law the use of armed force was generally considered by the nineteenth-century scholarship as a mechanism of dispute resolution. In order to be lawful, any resort to military measures depended on the material existence of a dispute and on the reunion of a set of procedural thresholds. The sequence was as follows: first, the injured State had to have recourse to the amicable and non-coercive means to resolve the dispute (such as diplomatic negotiations, mediation or arbitration); then, if non-coercive means had failed, resort to amicable but coercive means (retorsions, reprisals, pacific blockade or embargo) could be had; finally, only if satisfaction had still not been attained and if there existed no other way to obtain redress, war could become a legal option. International legal scholars, indeed, often insisted that war was a measure of absolute last resort.[83] In practice, however and despite the procedural limitations, States ultimately remained the sole judges of the opportunity of resorting to force and to war.

In this context, the peace movements of the nineteenth century, as well as academia, strove to advocate for a greater role of judicial mechanisms of dispute resolution, in particular arbitration, as an alternative to the use of violence.[84] The practice of arbitration was ancient, but enjoyed a sort of second youth as of the mid-1800s.[85] The *Alabama Claims* arbitration of 1871–1872 between the United States and Great Britain, in particular, was viewed as a great success and an example to be followed.[86] Mérignhac took this case as proof that 'arbitration has pacified many quarrels that, without it, would have, for sure, been emptied by resorting to the arms'.[87] The *Alabama Claims* arbitration reinforced the belief that arbitration could efficiently avoid disputes from degenerating into armed conflicts and, it seems, also gave a new impulsion to pacifist movements.[88] Some authors have indeed underlined how, after a slowdown of their activities as a result of the wars of the 1860s, peace societies enjoyed resurgence, and their advocacy entered a 'more distinctively legal phase' centred around the promotion of arbitration.[89] Reflecting this new

[83] See above (1.3.), (2.3.), (3.3.), and (4.3.).

[84] About peace movements and arbitration, see Sandi E. Cooper, *Patriotic Pacifism. Waging War on War in Europe, 1815–1914* (Oxford University Press, 1991), pp. 91–115; Jackson H. Ralston, *Arbitration from Athens to Locarno* (Stanford University Press, 1929), pp. 137–140; David D. Caron, 'War and International Adjudication: Reflections on the 1899 Peace Conference' (2000) 94 *American Journal of International Law* 8–13; Cecilie Reid, 'Peace and Law – Peace Activism and International Arbitration, 1895–1907' (2004) 29 *Peace & Change* 527–548.

[85] On the history of international arbitration see Henry S. Fraser, 'Sketch of the History of International Arbitration' (1926) 11 *Cornell Law Review* 179–208; Ralston, *Arbitration from Athens to Locarno*.

[86] See, for example, the enthousiastic accounts of the *Alabama Claims* arbitration made by J. T. Abdy, *Kent's Commentaries*, vol. 1, pp. 316–321; Mérignhac, *Traité*, vol. 1, pp. 454–464; Joseph B. Moore, 'International Arbitration' (1909) 7 *Michigan Law Review* 549.

[87] Mérignhac, *Traité*, vol. 1, p. 320.

[88] In this sense, see Caron, 'War and International Adjudication', 9.

[89] James L. Tyron, 'The Rise of Peace Movements' (1911) 20 *The Yale Law Review* 363. See also Randall Lesaffer, 'Peace through Law. The Hague Conferences and the Rise of *ius contra bellum*', in Maartje Abbenhuis, Christopher Ernest Barber and Annalise R. Higgins (eds.), *War, Peace and International Order? The Legacies of The Hague Conferences of 1899 and 1907* (Routledge, 2017), p. 33; Cecelia Flynch, 'Peace Movements, Civil Society and the Development of International Law', in Bardo Fassbender and Anne Peters (eds.), *The Oxford Handbook of the History of International Law* (Oxford University Press, 2012), p. 209.

orientation, groups such as the *Société française pour l'arbitrage international* in 1867, the *International Arbitration and Peace Association* in 1881, the association *La Paix par le Droit* in 1887 or yet the *Inter-parliamentary Union* and the *International Peace Bureau* (IPB), in 1887 and 1888, were created.

With time, and with the professionalisation of the discipline of international law, although they might have initially been wary, international lawyers became more and more involved with these movements.[90] In Europe, the names of Otfried Nippold, Walther Schücking and Louis Renault – who received the 1907 Nobel Prize in recognition for his work in favour of arbitration – are often mentioned.[91] In the United States, scholars such as Edwin Borchard, John Bassett Moore, Jackson Ralston, George Grifton Wilson, James Brown Scott or yet Elihu Root were also connected to the pre-war pacifist movements. As already specified, in fact, Root was chosen as the first president of the *Carnegie Endowment for International Peace*, whose aim was to 'promote a global acceptance of the peaceable methods in the settlement of international disputes',[92] after its creation in 1910. From 1901 to 1905, most of the authors mentioned above also attended the Lake Mohonk Conferences on International Arbitration, a series of meetings held every summer from 1895 to 1916 by a group of wealthy and influent men to discuss and direct public sentiment in favour of judicial mechanisms for dispute settlement.[93] It was during one of these Lake Mohonk sessions that, dissatisfied with the poor level of discussion on international law, the

[90] See Vec, 'From Invisible Peace to the Legitimation of War', pp. 33–36; Lesaffer, 'Peace through Law', p. 33; Randall Lesaffer, 'Too Much History: From War as a Sanction to the Sanctioning of War', in Marc Weller (ed.), *The Oxford Handbook on the Use of Force in International Law* (Oxford University Press, 2015), p. 48; C. Roland Marchand, *The American Peace Movements and Social Reforms, 1889–1918* (Princeton University Press, 1972), p. 40; Ingo Venzke, *How Interpretation Makes International Law. On Semantic Changes and Normative Twists* (Oxford University Press, 2012), pp. 140–144.

[91] See Vec, 'From Invisible Peace to the Legitimation of War', p. 35; Tyron, 'The Rise of Peace Movements', 363. See also Jean-Michel Gieu, 'Les juristes internationalistes français, l'Europe et la paix à la Belle époque' (2012) 149 *Relations internationales* 27–41; Marilena Papadaki, 'L'action des juristes internationalistes au service de la paix internationale à la fin du XIXe siècle: le cas de Nicolas Politis (1872–1942)' (2015) 91 *Cahiers de la Méditérrannée* 21–31. About Walther Schücking, see Mónica García Salmones, 'Walther Schücking and the Pacifist Tradition of International Law' (2011) 22 *European Journal of International Law* 755–782.

[92] Carnegie Endowment for International Peace, Report of the Director (26 October 1911), p. 1.

[93] Marchand, *The American Peace Movements*, pp. 39–40.

idea of creating a professional society to discuss the same issues and pursue the same aims is said to have burgeoned.[94] In 1906, the *American Society for International Law* was founded. Four years later, yet another organisation, the *American Society of the Judicial Settlement of Disputes*, aimed at the establishment of a Permanent Court was created under the impulsion of James Brown Scott.[95] Even the *Institut* made the issue of arbitration one of its first preoccupations and fields of action. As Bo Stråth and Cecelia Lynch note, peace societies were influential in defining the contours of the 'project' of international law.[96] If the aim of international law was to bring 'world peace order', arbitration was certainly felt to be one of the crucial ways to achieve that aim. The idea of 'peace through law' – or 'peace through arbitration' – in other words, became the project of international law and of the international legal profession.

But the influence was not just that of peace movement on the profession of international law; it was mutual. The emergence of the discipline as a profession distinct from diplomacy, in fact, probably was not estranged from the juridification of the pacifist discourse. Committed to the cause of the peaceful settlement of international disputes, international lawyers were happy to offer their legal expertise. By the turn of the century, about a dozen serious projects systematising the organisation of arbitration existed according to historian Sandi E. Cooper.[97] International lawyers had an important role in shaping these projects. In addition to some personal undertakings by jurists of renown – for example, Leonid Kamarowsky's *Le Tribunal international* (1887) or Alexandre Mérignhac's *Traité théorique et pratique de l'arbitrage international* (1895) –[98] one of the first important texts on arbitration was the IDI's '*Projet de règlement pour la procédure arbitrale internationale*' (1875). Adopted barely two years after the creation of the *Institut*, the '*projet*' was aimed at facilitating the process of resorting to arbitration by

[94] See Editorial Comment, 'Introduction' (1907) 1 *American Journal of International Law* 129–130. See also Marchand, *The American Peace Movements*, p. 41.

[95] Editorial Comment, 'American Society of the Judicial Settlement of Disputes' (1910) 4 *American Journal of International Law* 930–932. See also *Ralston, Arbitration from Athens to Locarno*, p. 137.

[96] Bo Stråth, 'Perpetual Peace as Irony, as Utopia and as Politics', in Thomas Hippler and Miloš Vec (eds.), *Paradoxes of Peace in Nineteenth Century Europe* (Oxford University Press, 2015), p. 282; Flynch, 'Peace Movements, Civil Society, and the Development of International Law', p. 198.

[97] Cooper, *Patriotic Pacifism*, p. 91.

[98] Leonid Kamarowsky, *Le Tribunal international* (Pedone, 1887); Alexandre Mérignhac, *Traité théorique et pratique de l'arbitrage international* (L. Larose, 1895).

providing the States with ready-made rules of procedure.[99] This work will have direct influence on the 'Code of International Arbitration' proposed by Henri La Fontaine – a Belgian lawyer, scholar, politician and president of the IPB from 1907 to 1943 –at the Sixth Universal Peace Congress held in Antwerp in 1894.[100] The most famous of all arbitration project, however, was the *Inter-parliamentary Union*'s 'Draft for the organisation of a Permanent Court of Arbitration' (1894). Written by the Baron Edouard Descamps – yet another Belgian lawyer, politician and pacifist – the draft provided for the establishment of a permanent court to which States would be able to voluntarily submit their quarrels. The judgements issued by the court were to be given an executory form.[101] As is known, the 'Draft' would later serve as a working document during the Hague Peace Conference of 1899.

The motivation behind the wish to create a permanent court rather than continue to rely on ad hoc tribunals was twofold. Despite its many successes, arbitration had also enjoyed its fair share failures. It was felt that the establishment of a permanent judicial institution would permit to avoid all the instances in which States had been unable to agree on arbitration in a timely fashion, as well as those in which, dissatisfied with the outcome of the procedure, one of the parties would question the validity of the award and unilaterally declare it to be null.[102] As Henry S. Maine in his *Whewell lectures* of 1887, many indeed thought that, although it would not solve all the problems of arbitration, a permanent court might, at least, vest the arbitrator's decisions with greater prestige and, hence, authority.[103]

[99] The preamble of the project read: 'Désirant que le recours à l'arbitrage pour la solution des conflits internationaux soit de plus en plus pratiqué par les peuples civilisés, espère concourir utilement à la réalisation de ce progrès en proposant, pour les tribunaux arbitraux, le règlement éventuel suivant. Il recommande à l'adoption entière ou partielle des Etats qui concluraient des compromis', IDI, 'Projet de règlement pour la procédure arbitrale internationale', Session de La Haye, 1875.

[100] 'Code de l'arbitrage international', available in *Bulletin officiel, VIe Congrès Universel de la Paix*, Anvers, 1894, Annexe 1 (Imprimerie de la Veuve Backer, 1895), pp. 109–116. About Henri La Fontaine, see Nadine Bernard, 'Henri La Fontaine (1854–1943) ou la paix par le droit' (1995) 31 *Revue belge de droit international* 343–356.

[101] Ralston, *International Arbitration from Anthens to Locarno*, p. 140.

[102] See Caron, 'War and International Adjudication', 10.

[103] 'Such a court would be free from the infirmity which afflicts all such additions to international system. It would have no force at its back. But I think it would be better constituted. I think it would be more free from prejudice, and would soon be recognised as freer, than the present occasional adjudicators', Henry S. Maine, *International Law. The Whewell Lectures* (John Murray, 1888), p. 219.

9.2.2 *The Hague Peace Conferences: Disappointment and Persistent Optimism in the Face of Semi-Successes*

The pacifist movements and international legal community's wishes were only partially granted with the adoption of Articles 20 to 57 of Convention (I) for the pacific settlement of international dispute in the Hague on 29 July 1899.[104] Article 20 provided for the organisation of a Permanent Court of Arbitration, and the following provisions laid down the rules of operation and procedure. The Court, however, was only 'permanent' and a 'court' in name. As a result of some delegations' staunch opposition to the creation of an actual stable institution, States were only able to agree on the establishment of a general list of arbitrators, from which the parties willing to judicially settle their disputes could choose from.[105] In sum, even though Convention (I) provided for a certain framework, a 'new' tribunal had to be put in place for each new arbitration. The hopes of the pacifists were also frustrated in that, despite the Russian delegation's best efforts, the idea of obligatory arbitration had equally been pushed to the side.[106]

All in all, the results of the first Peace Conference were deemed a little disappointing, including to the many international lawyers present in The Hague as members of their countries delegations.[107] Reflecting on the outcome of the Conference, Dutch scholar, Tobias Asser complained that 'the Convention of 1899 gave only a phantom of a court, an

[104] Convention (I) for the pacific settlement of international disputes, The Hague, 29 July 1899, in force: 4 September 1900.

[105] Arts. 23 and 24 Convention (I) for the pacific settlement of international disputes. For an account of the 3rd commission's discussions about the establishment of the Permanent Court of Arbitration, see Frederick W. Holls, *The Peace Conferences at The Hague, and its bearing on International Law and Policy* (The Mac Millan Company, 1900), pp. 233–276; William I. Hull, *The Two Hague Conferences, and Their Contribution to International Law* (Ginn & Company, 1908), pp. 370–387; Albert de Lapradelle, 'La Conférence de la Paix (La Haye, 18 mai–29 juillet 1899)' (1900) *Revue générale de droit international public* 148–157.

[106] See de Lapradelle, 'La Conférence de la paix', 130–148; Hull, The Two Hague Conferences, pp. 297–311; William I. Hull, 'Obligatory Arbitration and The Hague Conferences' (1908) 2 *American Journal of International Law* 731–734; Caron, 'War and International Adjudication', 17–18.

[107] Among the international lawyers present at The Hague in 1899 were Nagao Ariga (Japan), Tobias M. C. Asser (Netherlands), Frederick W. Holls (United States), Heinrich Lammasch (Austria-Hungary), Set Low (United States), Fyodor Martens (Russia), Ichiro Motono (Japan), Ch. Corragioni d'Orelli (Siam), Louis Renault (France), Edouard Rolin-Jaeqmyns (Siam), Baron Von Stegel (Germany), Voïslave Veljkovitch (Serbia) and Philip Zorn (Germany).

impalpable spectre or, to speak more clearly, a secretariat and a list'.[108] Fyodor Martens was saddened by the delegations' incapacity to agree on obligatory arbitration, not even for claims relating to pecuniary damages that were, in practice, already often voluntarily referred to arbitration.[109] At the same time, Martens, as well as others, remained optimistic about the outcome of the Conference and the process which it had set in motion. Recognizing that sacrifices had to be made and that the agreement on arbitration was a 'practical result',[110] Martens insisted that the Conference had been a defining moment for international law as it would now form the basis for any future discussion on matters of peace and war.[111] Other international legal scholars present at the Hague, such as Louis Renault and Seth Low, also defended their delegations' record arguing that Convention (I) represented a step in the right direction.[112]

In the rest of the scholarship as well, feelings were mixed. Felix Stoerk – professor at the University of Greifswald in Germany and member of the IDI – considered that the Conference was a semi-success and that no grand prospects should be nourished as to its practical efficacy.[113] He was moreover convinced that the delegations failure to live up to the expectations would cause the public to lose faith in the idea of 'peace through law', severely dampening the movement towards the greater integration of international law and of the 'civilised people' of the world.[114] Most authors, while admitting that the Conference may, in fact, have been perceived as a failure outside the profession, did not share Stoerk's pessimism. Franz Despagnet, for instance, although conceding that at first glance Convention (I) may be perceived as nothing more than the expression of 'platonic wishes', was convinced that 'positive results,

108 Quoted in Hull, The Two Hague Conferences, p. 410.

109 Ibid., pp. 349–350.

110 Fyodor Martens, 'International Arbitration and the Peace Conference at The Hague' (1899) 169 *The North American Review* 606.

111 Ibid., p. 623.

112 Louis Renault, *'L'oeuvre de La Haye 1899 et 1907', Conférence faite à l'Ecole libre des sciences politiques, le 5 juin 1908* (Paris: Félix Alcan, 1908), pp. 6–14; Seth Low, 'The International Conference of Peace' (1899) 169 *The North American Review* 625–639.

113 Felix Stoerk, 'La Conférence de La Haye et ses résultats. Opinion' (1900) *Revue générale de droit international public* 204. See also Louis Le Fur, 'La paix perpétuelle et l'arbitrage international' (1900) *Revue générale de droit international* 443.

114 'L'insuccès paralyse l'activité: l'espérance lorsqu'elle est déçue, se trouve pour de longues années dépouillée de sa force. Nous sommes aujourd'hui dans un cercle de dépression de cette nature; nous sommes dégoutés pour longtemps du vol téméraire vers l'idéal', Stoerk, 'La Conférence de La Haye et ses résultats', 205.

prodromal to a more encompassing reform, had been obtained'.[115] Ramon de Olivart, Alexandre Mérignhac and Emiliano Brusa, for their part, stressed the symbolic and practical importance of the creation of the PCA. 'The most important achievement of the Peace Conference and that which made it worthy of that name', de Olivart wrote, 'is the organization of international arbitration under the form of a visible institution'.[116] Still along the same lines, authors such as Thomas Lawrence regretted that a truly permanent court with mandatory jurisdiction could not be established, but nevertheless claimed that Convention (I) offered the truly desirous States all the necessary tools to abate war.[117] Oppenheim and Hershey shared this opinion.[118] Despite the shortcomings of the 1899 Hague Conference and contrary to Stoerk's gloomy predictions, the idea of peace through law and arbitration, it thus seems, was still going strong.

It was therefore 'natural', as Heinrich Lammasch said, that the issue of arbitration was once more on the top of the agenda during the second Hague Peace Conference in 1907.[119] The aim, this time, was to ameliorate the system agreed upon eight years earlier. Since 1899, many States had taken on their own initiative to conclude bilateral treaties providing for obligatory arbitration (e.g., the Porter Conventions).[120] This led many to think that time was finally ripe for a comprehensive agreement on

[115] Franz Despagnet, 'La Conférence de La Haye et ses résultats. Opinon' (1900) *Revue générale de droit international public* 230.

[116] Ramon de Olivart, 'La Conférence de La Haye et ses résultats. Opinion' (1900) *Revue générale de droit international public* 208. See also Mérignhac, 'La Conférence de La Haye et ses résultats. Opinion' (1900) *Revue générale de droit international public* 236; Emiliano Brusa, 'La Conférence de La Haye et ses résultats. Opinion' (1900) *Revue générale de droit international public* 245.

[117] Lawrence, *Principles of International Law*, pp. 676–677. See also Hannis Taylor, *A Treatise on International Public Law* (Callaghan & Company, 1901), pp. 48–49; Frederick E. Birkenhead, *International Law* (G. N. Morang, 1901), pp. 177–178.

[118] Oppenheim, *International Law*, vol. 2, p. 6; Amos S. Hershey, 'Convention for the Peaceful Adjustment of International Differences' (1908) 2 *American Journal of International Law* 30.

[119] Heinrich Lammasch, 'Compulsory Arbitration at the Second Hague Conference' (1908) 2 *American Journal of International Law* 83, and by the same author 'L'arbitrage obligatoire entre les deux conférences de la paix' (1909) 16 *Revue générale du droit international public* 690.

[120] Around 140 bilateral treaties providing for mandatory arbitration were concluded between 1899 and 1907 according to James L. Tyron's calculations, see 'The Hague Conferences', 477. See also Albert de Lapradelle et Nicolas Politis, 'La deuxième conférence de la paix. Origine, convocation, organisation' (1909) 16 *Revue générale de droit international public* 385–437.

international arbitration. Accordingly, the creation of a genuinely permanent court – i.e., with nominated members holding regular meetings – and the question of obligatory arbitration were back on the negotiations table. Despite elaborate debates and several proposals put to the vote, the 44 delegations present at the Hague in 1907 could not reach a definitive agreement on either of these two issues.[121] The main obstacles lied in the method for the appointment of the judges and with the continued reluctance of several States to accept obligatory arbitration.[122] The contribution of the 1907 Conference to arbitration was, as a result, rather modest. It took the form of two declarations: one inviting the willing States to recognize that some disputes are susceptible of being submitted to obligatory arbitration; and another, recommending that States adopt the Convention for the creation of a Judicial Arbitration Court drafted by the Conference, and bring it into force 'as soon as an agreement has been reached respecting the selection of judges and the constitution of the Court'.[123]

Once more, expectations were vexed. But, once more also, the international law community tried to put the 'failure' of the Second Hague Peace Conference into perspective.[124] Lammasch, who acted as a 'scientific delegate' for Austria-Hungary during the Conference, for example, acknowledged that the declarations had no 'practical value' but was of the opinion that 'the discussions that preceded their adoption have not been worthless for the future, we could not appreciate them enough'.[125] He argued that Germany's, among other nations, opposition to arbitration might even turn out to be salutary in that, by highlighting the issues posed by the other delegations' proposals, they would help elaborate better solutions to be discussed at the Third Peace Conference.[126]

[121] For accounts of the discussions, see Hull, *The Two Hague Conferences*, pp. 387–390 and 311–348; Lammasch, 'Compulsory Arbitration', 83–94; Caron, 'War and International Adjudication', 20–22.

[122] The nations opposing obligatory arbitration essentially were Germany, Austria-Hungary, Romania, Greece, Turkey, Belgium, Bulgaria and Switzerland.

[123] Wish no 1, Final Act of the Second Peace Conference held at The Hague in 1907.

[124] The international lawyers present at the Hague in 1907 included: Philip Zorn (Germany), James Brown Scott (United States), Heinrich Lammasch (Austria-Hungary), Antonio Sanchez des Bustamente (Cuba), Louis Renault (France), Georges Streit (Greece), Pierre Hudicourt (Haïti), Francis Hagerup (Norway), Tobias M. C. Asser (Netherlands), Fyodor Martens (Russia), Ch. Corragioni d'Orelli (Siam) and Max Huber (Switzerland).

[125] Lammasch, 'L'arbitrage obligatoire', 698. Translation by the author.

[126] It is worth noting that, like Germany, Austria voted against the proposals for obligatory arbitration put forth by the British, French and Russian delegations, see Hull, 'Obligatory Arbitration', 740.

In the same spirit, but with no praise for the Germans, Renault, who was part of the French delegation, emphasised that even though an agreement could not be reached, 'the discussion has not been useless, because it had slowly narrowed the elements of incertitude down, enabling to see exactly what remains to be discussed'.[127] He moreover enthusiastically insisted that it was on the modalities and not on the principles of a permanent court and of obligatory arbitration that negotiations had come to a deadlock. In this perspective, the outcome of the 1907 Conference was altogether positive because it had showed that States concurred on the principles of arbitration and it had permitted to identify the few remaining points of discord. Renault was optimistic that the Conference had laid down all the groundwork for the project of international arbitration to be soon realised.[128] James Brown Scott, also at the Hague with the US delegation, shared his French colleague's views. He believed the absence of tangible agreement to be an issue of secondary importance. The declarations, particularly the one on the court, was, according to him, already a 'great result' because, through them, States had all accepted the principle of the permanent judicial body composed of permanent judges and of obligatory arbitration.[129]

These results, in sum, were thought to bode well for the future and slow progress was not an issue. One way or another, in fact, the aims would be achieved. The World War I, however, put a harsh stop to the process, preventing the Third Peace Conference from ever taking place.

9.2.3 *In Paris: Relief and Pride at the Culmination of Fifty Years of Pro-Arbitration Efforts*

All of the above explains why, in many ways, the adoption of the Covenant of the League of Nations in 1919 represented the crowning of the peace movements' and the profession's relentless efforts in favour of judicial mechanisms of dispute resolution. Article 14 finally provided for the establishment of a truly permanent court, the Permanent Court of International Justice (PCIJ) and Articles 12 to 15 established an instance

[127] Renault, 'L'œuvre de La Haye 1899 et 1907', 20. Translation by the author.

[128] Ibid., pp. 24–27.

[129] James Brown Scott, 'The Proposed Court of Arbitral Justice' (1908) 2 *American Journal of International Law* 806. See also Hull, 'Obligatory Arbitration and The Hague Conferences', 742; Hershey, 'Convention for the Peaceful Adjustment of International Differences', 49.

of mandatory judicial settlement.[130] Through these last three provisions, in fact, the members of the League committed to: (i) submit their disputes to arbitration (if suitable) or to the Council of the League and (ii) wait for a period of three months until after the award of the arbitrators, judicial decision or report of the Council before resorting to war. Article 17, furthermore, opened the possibility of submitting disputes to the Council for non-member States as well, in which case the procedures described in Articles 12 to 15 applied *mutatis mutandis*. In the hypothesis one of the members did not abide by its obligations, Article 16 finally provided for the imposition of commercial, financial or, if need be, military sanctions. The sanction system was a new element compared to the philosophy that had presided during the Hague Conferences that did not supply for any collective mechanisms to ensure respect for law. But, by reinforcing the procedural thresholds that needed to be met before resort to arms could be had, the Covenant merely further differed the legal occurrence of war. The absence of a more encompassing prohibition of war was not necessarily viewed as problematic. In truth, it was in line with the temporisation logics that had dominated international legal thought for the past few decades. Since the establishment of 'cooling-off' periods would suffice to prevent the outburst of any conflict, a rule of prohibition was felt to be superfluous. With the Covenant, the two main demands of the pacifist movements (and even more) had, in sum, finally come to fruition. This simple fact helps shed some additional light on the narrative of indifference in at least two interconnected ways: as an expression of relief, and as an expression of pride.

The Narrative of Indifference as an Expression of Relief

Relief is commonly defined as the positive feeling that occurs once a distressing or unpleasant situation has come to an end.[131] As such, it is dependent upon a pre-existing negative state, such as stress and anxiety.[132] Lexically, relief is associated with words such as 'finally' or 'fortunately', with the idea of better, of satisfaction or of accomplishment, as well as with semantics and syntaxes that convey an overall sense of

[130] About Articles 12 to 15 of the Covenant see above (Section 8.2.1.).

[131] The *Oxford English Dictionary* defines 'relief' as the 'feeling of reassurance and relaxation following release from anxiety of distress' (http://en.oxforddictionaries.com/definition/relief).

[132] See Richard S. Lazarus, *Emotion and Adaptation* (Oxford University Press, 1991), p. 280; Kate Sweeny and Kathleen D. Vohs, 'On Near Misses and Completed Tasks: The Nature of Relief' (2012) 23 *Psychological Science* 464.

appeasement and of resolved expectancies. We already saw how the narrative of indifference, by opposing an anarchical nineteenth century to a peaceful twentieth century, carried a general impression of alleviation of international tensions with the World War I and the Covenant as tipping points.[133] Similarly, statements such as those claiming that it took the World War for the idea of the prohibition of force to fully penetrate the legal conscience of States or emphasising the inadequacy of classical international law with the necessities of international life, also contributed to creating this sense of accomplishment. But to really understand the narrative of indifference as an expression of relief, two elements have to be highlighted because they influence the type and magnitude of the response: (i) the nature of the event that puts an end to the negative emotional state and (ii) the intensity of that negative emotional state.

As concerns the event that puts an end to the negative emotional state, psychologists Kate Sweeny and Kathleen D. Vohs have identified two broad types of reliefs: the *near-miss relief* and the *task-completion relief*.[134] The first type of relief response is triggered by the avoidance of an unpleasant situation, while the second is the result of the completion of an unpleasant task or end of an unpleasant situation. Sweeny and Vohs argue that depending on the type of relief one experiences, the memory of the events and the future behaviour in reaction to these events will vary. Near-miss relief, for example, will tend to produce more counter-factual thinking – i.e., engaging in 'what-if' scenarios – and dwelling on the negative experience. When the negative aspects of the experience leave the stronger mark, relief will usually prompt people to strategise about how to avoid similar situations in the future.[135] Task-completion relief has the opposite effect. It tends to provoke less downward counter-factual thinking and allows to focus on the positive rather than the negative aspects of the experience. As a consequence, it also increases the chances that people will be willing to repeat the unpleasant experience because the they consider the outcome to be worthwhile – the positive, in other words, surpasses the negative.[136] It follows that, in terms of narrative – of how the experience is recalled and told – near-miss relief will usually create speculative and negative accounts about

[133] See above (Section 8.2.1.) and (Section 8.2.2.).

[134] Sweeny and Vohs, 'On Near Misses and Completed Tasks', 464.

[135] Ibid., p. 467.

[136] Ibid.

what could have been, while task-completion relief will produce narratives that focus more on the positive character of the outcome.

From this, it is quite evident that the narrative of indifference can appear as an expression of task-completion relief. As the two previous sections illustrated, the Covenant was, in fact, the consecration of several decades of efforts in favour of arbitration. This is also the way in which the scholarship itself seemed to have lived the event. Von Redlich, for instance, claimed that 'the Covenant of the League of Nations [and] the Statute of the Permanent Court of International Justice) [. . .] were the greatest *triumph* of International Law over warfare'.[137] Redslob, likewise, considered that 'the silencing of Germany in the council of nations had been a happy effect of the world war, [because], defeated, it could not hinder on the *great task* facing the world anymore [and] the League of Nations could be created'.[138] The establishment of the League was a necessity and a task; a task that was finally completed when the Covenant was adopted in June 1919. Moreover, the narrative of indifference clearly focused on the outcome rather than on the negative emotional experience that preceded the completion of the task. The very bleak image of the nineteenth century drawn by the inter-war scholarship, in fact, does not so much serve to illustrate the hardship or anxiety as it is meant to emphasise the revolutionary character and, consequently, worthwhile nature of the achievement. The technique is common and, as we saw, recurrent in the history of international law.[139] The past is easy to manipulate and, by depreciating the past in addition to praising the present, the contrast between the old and the new is amplified. The achievement becomes more extraordinary, more miraculous; a liberation in sum.

One may however wonder whether the relief felt by the profession following the adoption of the Covenant was truly great enough to trigger such an extreme reaction as the narrative of indifference. This is where the issue of the intensity of emotions comes into play. The sensation of relief, as mentioned, exists because of a pre-existing state of anxiety. But it also exists in proportion to it. Said differently, the intensity of the

[137] Marcellus Donald A. R. von Redlich, *The Law of Nations* (2nd ed., World League for Permanent Peace, 1937), p. 492. Emphasis added.

[138] Robert Redslob, *Histoire des grands principes du droit des gens depuis l'antiquité jusqu'à la veille de la Grande Guerre* (Rousseau & Cie. Éditeurs, 1923), p. 558. Emphasis added. Translation by the author.

[139] See above (Section 8.1.3).

positive affect is equivalent to the intensity of the negative affect. This co-relation of intensity is particularly well reflected in French philosopher Pierre Livet's concept of '*soulagement exultant*' – or 'exultant relief'.[140] To better understand the interaction between anxiety and relief, Livet emphasises the role of two additional elements: stakes and time. The argument is simple and, indeed, intuitive: the higher the stakes, the greater the anxiety, and the longer the anxiety-provoking situation lasts, the more anxiety provoking it gets, and so, by contrast, the more exultant is the relief once the situation finally comes to term.[141] In these sorts of situations, the expression of the positive feelings can act as a stress-coping mechanism that buffers the negative emotional experience.[142] It follows that, to fully and efficiently exorcise the stressful experience, the expression of the positive emotion will commensurate the intensity the anxiety felt. Livet's use of the term 'exultance' suggests exuberance, excess and exaggeration. The expression of 'exultant relief' may thus imply storytelling patterns that emphasise and distort certain elements of reality to reflect the strength of the feelings experienced.

In this perspective, 'indifference' and its amplified narrative can be understood as an expression of 'exultant' relief. Stakes were high, time was long and anxiety was deep. The challenge, in fact, went far beyond the mere question of arbitration. The establishment of judicial mechanisms of dispute resolution, as we saw, was pictured as essential for international law to be able to fulfil its pacifying function.[143] This is to say that with the project of a Permanent Court and of mandatory arbitration, it was the discipline and its credibility that were on the line. Of course, in the fifty years of advocacy in favour of judicial mechanisms of dispute settlement, progress had been made. But the achievements of the two Hague Conferences were not felt to be fully satisfactory. Although the scholarship was resilient and had faith that a third peace conference would finally yield the expected results, the outburst of the World War I shook the profession's beliefs to their very core.[144] In this context, the adoption of the Covenant showed that, despite events, international law was still considered relevant and that it was finally

[140] Pierre Livet, 'Emotions, rationalité, densité temporelle et manifestation de valeurs' (2009) 144 *Revue européenne des sciences sociales* 7–23.

[141] Ibid., 18–21, especially 21.

[142] See Michelle Skinner, 'Emotional Expression', in Marc D. Gellman and J. Rick Turner (eds.), *Encyclopaedia of Behavioural Medicine* (Springer, 2013), pp. 673–674.

[143] See above (Section 9.2.1.).

[144] See above (Section 9.1.1.) and (Section 9.1.2.).

given the necessary tools to fulfil its mission. The contrast between the nineteenth and the twentieth century of the 'indifference'-narrative can, in sum, be read as a reflection of the profession's emotional rollercoaster.

Narrative of 'Indifference' as an Expression of Pride

But the narrative of 'indifference' can, additionally, also be interpreted as an expression of pride. Pride, as relief, is a positive emotion that pertains to the category of happiness. It has the particularity that its causal event confirms and increases one's sense of worth.[145] As a result, it will usually be linked to an object or an achievement that is the product of one's own work or of that of a group he or she identifies with. Said differently, the event that triggers a reaction of pride will usually be more personal. From there, we can thus see how pride can be linked to task-completion relief and how the expression of this type of relief can also be interpreted as a reflection of pride. Task-completion relief, Sweeny and Vohs indeed tell us, is 'satisfaction in the completion of a job well done (or a job done, in any case)'.[146] It follows that, when a narrative focuses on the positive character of an achievement and that this achievement is the result of the storyteller's own work, it is hard not to see this account as somewhat self-congratulatory. By accentuating the 'miraculous' character of the accomplishment, the agent's own role is, by the force of things, simultaneously emphasised and re-valued. From this point of view, the narrative of indifference can, in parallel, also be analysed as an expression of personal or professional pride on the part of international lawyers from seeing their project of judicial settlement of international disputes consecrated by the Covenant.

In addition to their implication alongside the peace movements, some international lawyers were directly involved with the drafting of the League's Covenant and, later, with the PCIJ Statute. The Statute, in fact, was in large part drafted by the Advisory Committee of Jurists nominated by the Council of the League of Nations on 12–13 February 1920. Composed of eleven specialists of international law – Mineichiro Adatci (Japan), Rafael Altamira (Spain), Clovis Beviláqua (Brazil), Edouard Descamps (Belgium), Francis Hagerup (Norway), Albert de Lapradelle (France), Bernard Loder (Netherlands), Walter Phillimore (Great Britain), Arturo Ricci-Busatti (Italy) and Elihu Root assisted by James Brown Scott (United States) – the Committee was charged with

145 Lazarus, *Emotion and Adaptation*, p. 271.

146 Sweeny and Vohs, 'On Near Misses and Completed Tasks', 467.

the task of providing the League and its member States with a project for the organisation of the new court.[147] The Council furthermore authorised the creation of a secretariat of experts to assist the Committee in its endeavour. The secretariat was placed under the supervision of Anzilotti and composed of Otfried Nippold, Bohdan Winiarski of the University of Poznań and Åke Hammarskjöld, who became the first Registrar of the Court and was later appointed as a judge. Working through the summer of 1920 based on a text prepared beforehand by Root and Phillimore, the Committee was fast to deliver. On 24 July 1920, the eleven jurists transmitted the result of their work to the Council. After just a few modifications, the Statute was adopted by the Assembly on 13 December 1920, and ready to be signed by the States three days later.[148]

But let us concentrate on the drafting of the League of Nations Covenant, which bore the creation of the Court as well as of the other mechanisms of war prevention. As is well known, the Covenant was the synthesis of several different 'national' projects, many of which had been elaborated in consultation with at least a few international lawyers. Often considered as one of the most influential League projects, the *Interim Report* of the Phillimore Committee, for instance, was the result of collaboration between historians (Albert Pollard, John Holland Rose and Julian Corbett), diplomats (Eyre Crowe and William Tyrell) and lawyers.[149] The two lawyers present in the Committee were Walter

[147] PCIJ, Advisory Committee of Jurists, *Procès-verbaux of the Proceedings of the Committee*, June 16th–July 24th 1920, The Hague: Van Langenhuyssen Brothers, 1920, p. III.

[148] On the drafting process of the CPIJ Statute, see John Bassett Moore, *The Project of a Permanent Court of International Justice and Resolutions of the Advisory Committee of Jurists: Report and Commentary* (The Carnegie Endowment, 1920); and by the same author, 'The Organization of the Permanent Court of International Justice' (1922) 22 *Columbia Law Review* 497–526; Mandley O. Hudson, 'The Permanent Court of International Justice' (1922) 35 *Harvard Law Review* 245–275; and by the same author, *The Permanent Court of International Justice. A Treatise* (The MacMillan Company, 1934), pp. 85–121; Antonio Sánchez de Bustamente y Sirvén, La Cour permanente de Justice internationale (Recueil Sirey, 1925), pp. 96–113; Gleider I. Hernandez, *The International Court of Justice and the Judicial Function* (Oxford University Press, 2014), pp. 20–34; Mark Weston Janis, *America and the Law of Nations 1776–1939* (Oxford University Press, 2010), pp. 203–204.

[149] See David H. Miller, *The Drafting of the Covenant*, 2vols. (G. Putnam's Sons, 1928), vol. 1 p. 9; Felix Morley, *The Society of Nations* (The Brookings Institution, 1932), p. 10; Florian Couveinhes-Matsumoto, 'Les travaux préparatoires', in Robert Kolb (ed.), *Commentaire sur le Pacte de la Société des Nations* (Bruylant, 2015), p. 42.

Phillimore – son of Robert Phillimore – who chaired the Committee, and Cecil Hurst – a legal adviser at the Foreign Office who later became a judge at the PCIJ and presided the said Court from 1934 to 1936. The Committee, it should also be mentioned, had been created under the initiative of Lord Robert Cecil, a law graduate from Oxford and under-secretary of State for Foreign Affairs from 1915 to 1919, whose role in the interwar pro-league movements and propaganda has already been emphasised.[150] The system proposed by the Phillimore Committee's *Interim Report* consisted in a combination of prohibiting certain wars, institutionalising cooperation and organising mechanisms for the pacific settlement of international disputes.[151]

Chronologically, the next outline for the creation of a League was the report submitted on 8 June 1917 by the *Commission interministérielle d'étude pour la Société des Nations* (CIESDN) established by the French government about a year earlier.[152] The Commission was Leon Bourgeois's idea and, given his curriculum – as a peace activist, as a former Minister for Foreign Affairs, as head of the French delegation at the two Hague Conferences and as an honorary member of the IDI – the radical senator was quite naturally chosen as its president.[153] The rest of the members were nominated by the government following Bourgeois's recommendations and requests. From the start, the objective had been to gather a team of military men, economists, diplomats and jurists. Amongst the 22 members of the commission, four were specialists of international law: Louis Renault, who has already been mentioned several times in the course of this research; André Weiss, who became a judge and vice president of the PCIJ from 1922 to 1928; Jules Basdevant, a famous professor from the University of Paris; and, Charles Lyon-Caen, another professor at the University of Paris and member of the IDI as well as of the Hague Academy's curatorium. In addition to the prohibition of certain wars, the institutionalisation of cooperation and the organisation of judicial mechanisms of dispute settlement, the French

[150] See above (Section 9.1.3.).

[151] The text of *Interim Report* of the Phillimore Committee is available in Miller, *The Drafting of the Covenant*, vol. 2, pp. 3–6.

[152] On the French project and the CIESDN, see ibid., vol. 1, pp. 10–12; Scott G. Blair, 'Les origines en France de la SDN. La Commission interministérielle d'étude pour la Société des Nations 1917–1919' (1993) 75 *Relations internationales* 277–292; Sami Saré, *The League of Nations and the Debate on Disarmement* (Edizioni Nuova Cultura, 2013), pp. 41–48; Couveinhes-Matsumoto, 'Les travaux préparatoires', pp. 44–45.

[153] On Bourgeois and the CIESDN, see Alexandre Niess, 'Leon Bourgeois', 135–148.

plan preconized the creation of a system of sanctions (diplomatic, legal, economic and military), implemented, if need be, by a unified international force.[154]

On the other side of the Atlantic too, international lawyers were closely associated with the projects for a League of Nations. The American prospects for the future organisation resembled the United Kingdom's. They relied on arbitration more than on a genuine system of collective security.[155] Edward Mandel House, whom Wilson had charged with the task of drafting the US project, used the Phillimore Committee's report as a starting point. To adapt the British project to Washington's view, House called on the assistance of David Hunter Miller (an international lawyer specialised in treaties) and William Wiseman (an English naval officer and head of British intelligence in the United States who acted as a liaison officer between House and Lord Cecil in London).[156] The secretary of state, Robert Lansing (a lawyer who had experience with international arbitration and was an active member of the ASIL)[157] and Elihu Root (former secretary of state and president of the ASIL), are also said to have had an influence on the content of the plan House handed to the president on 16 July 1918.[158] The House Plan was not the United States' final, but it had an important impact on subsequent projects. It served as a basis for Wilson's first draft, which the President then modified on several occasions following Lansing's, Miller's and James Brown Scott's observations, as well as the reception of General Jan Smuts's famous *Practical Suggestion* in December 1918.[159]

[154] The Text of the French 'Projet de Pacte' is available in Miller, The Drafting of the Covenant, vol. 2, pp. 397–403.

[155] See Peter Raffo, 'The Anglo-American Preliminary Negotiations for a League of Nations' (1974) 9 *Journal of Contemporary History* 153–176.

[156] On the 'House project' see Miller, The Drafting of the Covenant, vol. 1, pp. 12–15; Wilton B. Fowler, *British-American Relations 1917–1918: The Role of Sir William Wiseman* (Princeton University Press, 1969), pp. 207–208; Lloyd E. Ambrosius, *Woodrow Wilson and the American Diplomatic Tradition: The Treaty Fight in Perspective* (Cambridge University Press, 1987), p. 43.

[157] Robert Lansing was the Counsel of the United States during the *Bering Sea Arbitrations* that opposed the United States to the United Kingdom in 1892–1893. On the role of Robert Lansing during the peace negotiations, see Robert Lansing, *The Peace Negotiations. A Personal Narrative* (Houghton Mifflin Company, 1921).

[158] Couveinhes-Matsumoto, 'Les travaux préparatoires', p. 45.

[159] See ibid., pp. 46–47. On Jan Smuts's *Practical Suggestion*, see Miller, *The Drafting of the Covenant*, vol. 1, pp. 34–39; Georges Curry, 'Woodrow Wilson, Jan Smuts, and the Versailles Settlement' (1961) 66 *The American Historical Review* 968–986.

But the text discussed at the Hotel Crillon during the first round of negotiations (3–13 February 1919) was not a 'pure' American product. It was the result of the fusion of the British and US projects. A week or so before the Conference opened, the British and the Americans engaged in an intensive diplomatic ballet with the aim of presenting a common project and front during the negotiations in order to increase their chances of imposing their views on the other delegations.[160] Although Wilson is said to have been reluctant to have international lawyers play too big a part, they were, once more, among the lead dancers.[161] The merger of the US and British plans was, in fact, essentially the work of David Hunter Miller and Cecil Hurst. The Miller-Hurst draft served as the main working document during the first rounds of discussions.[162] The discussions of the Commission charged with the League of Nations took place in Colonel House's rooms at the Hotel Crillon. According to the records, present to discuss the Miller-Hurst draft were, amongst others: Wilson and House for the United States; Cecil and Smuts for Great-Britain; Bourgeois and Ferdinand Larnaude (international lawyer and dean of the Faculty of Law of the University of Paris) for France; the Italian prime minister Vittorio Emmanuelle Orlando; the Belgian Minister for Foreign Affairs Paul Hymans; and Wellington Koo, who held a PhD in international law from University of Columbia, representing China.[163] There to observe, report and prepare the debates on the Covenant were also David Hunter Miller, Cecil Hurst and Henri Rolin, who acted as a personal secretary to Paul Hymans during the Conference. More generally, also present in Paris as plenipotentiaries or legal adviser to their country's delegation were, to name a few, Anzilotti (Italy), Politis

[160] Miller recalled: 'House told me he wanted me to meet with Cecil and go as far possible in having an agreement with the British on the basis of the Covenant [. . .]. He said that if we could get an agreement with the British we could get the Japanese and Italians to assent to it and then the French', in *The Drafting of the Covenant*, vol. 1, p. 54. See also Couveinhes-Matsumoto, 'Les travaux préparatoires', p. 49.

[161] See Benjamin Allen Coates, *Legalist Empire: International Law and American Foreign Relations in the Early Twentieth Century* (Oxford University Press, 2016), p. 153.

[162] See Miller, *The Drafting of the Covenant*, vol. 1, pp. 65–71.

[163] Other members of the Commission on the League of Nations were Vittorio Scialoja (Italian Minister for Foreign Affairs), Baron Makino Nobuaki (former Japanese Minster for Foreign Affairs), Viscount Chinda Sutemi (Japanse ambassador in London), Epitacio Lindolfo de Silva Pessoa (former Brazilian Minister of Justice), Jayma Batalha Reis (Portugese ambassador to Russia) and Milenko R. Vesnić (Sebian ambassador in Paris). See Minutes (French) of the Commission on the League of Nations, in Miller, *The Drafting of the Covenant*, vol. 2, pp. 395–396.

and Stelios Séfériadès (Greece), Bodhan Winiarski (Poland), Schücking (Germany), Rudolf Laun (Austria), Bourquin and de Visscher (Belgium), La Pradelle and Henri Fromageot (France), Mandley O. Hudson (United States) and Alexander Pierce Higgins (United Kingdom). As we can thus see, international lawyers were not estranged from the elaboration process of the League of Nations. The war-prevention system of the Covenant was, in substance, the result of their work as sanctioned by the States.

This is not to say that all international lawyers were 'proud' or even content with the shape that the League of Nations' security system finally took. The Anglo-American vision, based on the judicial settlement of disputes, dominated the Covenant to the disappointment of some, including the younger generation of US lawyers, who would have preferred a more collective and centralised war-prevention framework – i.e., closer to the French proposals.[164] But, even amongst the disappointed, everything was not negative. Von Redlich, for instance, felt that 'the Covenant of the League of Nations was a compromise and therefore not entirely satisfactory',[165] but that 'on the whole, however, it constituted another great advance of international law'.[166] In other terms, they adopted the same attitude of resilient optimism and 'developmentalist rhetorics', to use Guillaume Sacriste's and Antoine Vauchez's expression, as they had following the mitigated results of the Hague Conferences of 1899 and 1907.[167] The Covenant was not perfect, but it was better than whatever prevailed before and needed to be praised for at least that.

* * *

This chapter sought to examine the reasons for the emergence of the narrative of indifference during the interwar period. Two concomitant explanations were brought forth: one linked to the negative experience of the outburst of the World War I, and another to the positive experience of the adoption of the Covenant of the League of Nations. On the one

[164] See Hatsue Shinohara, *US International Lawyers in the Interwar Years. A Forgotten Crusade* (Cambridge University Press, 2012), pp. 26 ff. See however Antoine Pillet, *Le traité de paix de Versailles: conférences faites au Collège Libre des Sciences-sociales* (Marcel Rivière et Cie., 1920).

[165] von Redlich, *The Law of Nations*, p. 502.

[166] Ibid.

[167] Guillaume Sacriste and Antoine Vauchez, 'The Force of International Law: Lawyers' Diplomacy on the International Scene in the 1920s' (2007) 32 *Law & Social Inquiry* 103.

hand, 'indifference' can be understood as a narrative remedy to resolve a contradiction experienced by international lawyers as a result of World War I. The events of 1914–1918, in fact, scattered the discipline's foundational belief about the pacifying power of international law and were perceived as posing an existential threat on the discipline. The narrative of indifference, and its diffusion outside the boundaries of the profession, erased the contradiction between events and beliefs, and, in so doing: (i) restored coherence in the representation that international law had of itself and (ii) remedied the loss of credibility, which it felt it suffered from outside the profession. But, the narrative of indifference can also be understood as an expression of relief and pride triggered by the adoption of the League of Nations' Covenant, which, by and large, consecrated the internationalists' own work in favour of judicial mechanisms of dispute settlement. This was a long process, and one that saw the hopes of activists deceived on several occasions. Adding the surplus of stress caused by the World War I to this, the 'exaggerations' carried by the narrative of indifference appear as a reflection of the intensity of the differential emotional gap between the period that preceded the adoption of the Covenant, when the future of international law was uncertain, and the period that followed the adoption of the Covenant, when international law was finally given the means to fulfil its pacifying mission.

Interestingly, some interwar authors readily recognised the excesses of their own accounts on the laws on the use of force before the Great War. Bourquin in 1931, for example, criticised the authors who, 'by attachment to tradition' minimised the change undergone by international law as a result of the 1919 settlements, but admitted that 'for sure, everything more or less lines up in the development of societies, and revolutions, in spite of appearances, weld themselves with the state of things they aim to destroy'.[168] More explicitly, Kaufman in 1935 noted that: 'it seems to be the consequence of any codification that, at least for a certain time, the scientific work has the tendency to exaggerate the new elements and the absorptive character of the new regulation'.[169] Today, however, while continuing to uphold the narrative of indifference, the literature seems to have lost awareness of its hyperbolic character.

168 Bourquin, 'Règles générales', 5. Translation by the author.

169 Erich Kaufmann, 'Règles générales du droit de la paix' (1935) 54 *Recueil des cours de l'académie de droit international* 589. Translation by the author.

Conclusion of Part III

Some Thoughts on the Persistence of the Narrative of Indifference in Modern-Day Doctrine

After having evidenced the discrepancy between the past and modern discourse about the use of force, the third and final part of this book aimed at pin-pointing the nature, the apparition, and the raison d'être of the narrative of indifference in twentieth century international legal scholarship. It upheld the hypothesis according to which today's commonly accepted history of the use of force finds its roots in the beliefs that underlie the identity of international law as a discipline confronted with the events of the World War I and immediate post-war. Guided by the work of Jan Assmann and Claude Lévi-Strauss, the demonstration was carried out in two main steps. The first, Chapter 8, wished to verify if and to what extent the narrative of indifference could, indeed, be considered to be an emanation of the discipline's assumptions about itself and others. In this context, we saw that the common account of the history of the use of force in international law mimics, in several aspects, the discipline's more general discourse about itself and about the power of international law to order international relations and bring progress to humanity. The purpose of Chapter 9 was, then, to interrogate the social function of the narrative of indifference and of the exaggerated contrast between pre- and post-war era that it upholds. It has been argued that this traditional account is linked to the events of the World War I, and that in at least two interconnected ways: (i) as a result of the negative experience caused by the outburst of the war and the concomitant need to salvage the little credibility international law had left by finding another culprit and (ii) as a result of the positive experience caused by the adoption of the Covenant of the League of Nations and the conviction that international law had finally been given the means of its ambitions.

But a crucial question remains: if the narrative of indifference is so closely related to the post-World War I context, how an we explain that it has subsisted to today and even become the commonly accepted version of the history of the use of force in international law? The elements of response are to be found in the considerations set out in the two last chapters. Three lines of explanation can, more particularly, be brought forth: (i) a structural explanation, (ii) a functional explanation and (iii) a methodological explanation.

The *structural explanation* emphasises the long-term impact of the narrative's rhetorical structures on the perception schemes of the discipline and of its members. If we go back to Lévi-Strauss and Assmann, we might remember how these authors claimed that while myths and historical accounts are stories on the past created to meet present needs, they simultaneously relate to the future.[1] In order to fulfil their task and efficiently preserve the group's identity, the narratives, in fact, need to be able to durably shape the way in which the said group understands its past and, therefore, itself. This is why, as already mentioned, the discursive structure of these accounts will most often be built up from pre-existing beliefs and assumptions, as well as on Manichean binary schemes that offer simple and didactic explanations for complex events. This is to say that the foundations of the account are, by definition, meant to have a lasting impact, and subsist beyond the content of the actual story because that is where the core of the message resides. We thus saw how the 'indifference' narrative came in different versions and how these could, themselves, be considered as versions of a deeper and more encompassing myth about law and its harmonising power. And so, the narrative of indifference is not so much a story about the use of force in particular, as it is a story about the indispensability of international law in general.

This being said, the structure does not endure by itself. It needs to be nurtured and transmitted to retain its influence. The crucial role of education in this respect has frequently been highlighted and we pointedly saw how the rhetoric of law and order *vs.* politics and anarchy penetrated all strands of society after the Great War.[2] It, most notably, ran through school history textbooks to illustrate the changes that international relations underwent in the first half of the twentieth century. The beliefs that underlie the narrative of indifference thus go far beyond

[1] Claude Lévi-Strauss, *Structural Anthropology*, (original ed.: 1958) (Basic Books, 1963), p. 209; Jan Assmann, 'Collective Memory and Cultural Identity' (1995) 65 *New German Critique* 130.

[2] See above (Section 9.1.3.).

the discipline of international law. Their roots are deeper but also wider and carried by many materials besides international law textbooks. Public and disciplinary creeds about law confirm and reinforce each other, making them even more persuasive and lasting because hard to question. This, Leon Festinger argues, is precisely the result proselyting activities aim to achieve, for 'if more and more people can be persuaded that the system of belief is correct, then clearly it must, after all, be correct'.[3]

Interestingly, more than to endure, it seems that the structures of 'indifference' also had an influence on the evolution of the historical narrative on the use of force in international law. The account has, indeed, simplified over time. While 'partial indifference' dominated the interwar years, 'total indifference', which now seems to have outdone it, only appeared later, in post–WWII literature.[4] On close observation, in buffering the legal difference between war and measures short of war, the second version of the traditional account offers a (hi)story that is actually more in tune with the binary rhetoric of the overall account. In presenting international law as indifferent to all forms of use of armed force, it reinforces the contrast between the pre-1914 and the post-Versailles periods. It presents classical international law as even less sophisticated and, by the same token, the legal framework of the peace settlements as even more revolutionary and grandiose. The account, in sum, crystallised and tightened around its discursive structure, thus not only preserving the core message of the narrative but also, in a way, making it stronger.

The simplification of the account, however, cannot simply be traced back to the cognitive power of the structure. Accounts evolve to respond to a change in circumstances, especially a change in historical circumstances.[5] With the end of the World War II and the adoption of the UN Charter, the criticism of the immediate past (the interwar) became more relevant than the critique of the more distant past (the nineteenth century) to legitimise the new system. In other terms, the deficiencies of classical international law were less important than those of the League of Nations and, therefore, deserved less attention. And, in fact, if we look at most contemporary textbooks the space allotted to the discussion of the use of force in the League era will be far greater than that dedicated to

[3] Leon Festinger, Henry W. Riecken and Stanley Schacter, *When Prophecy Fails* (University of Minnesota Press, 1956), p. 28.

[4] See above (Section 8.2.1.) and (Section 8.2.2.).

[5] Walter Burkert, *Structure and History in Greek Mythology and Ritual* (University of California Press, 1979), pp. 26–29.

the discussion of nineteenth century *ius ad bellum*. Of course, some may argue that this is simply because, objectively speaking, more conventions and pacts dealing with the use of force were concluded from 1919 to 1939 than from 1815 to 1914. But again, this argument lays too much emphasis on formal agreements at the expense of other sources of international law. Many events of importance punctuated the evolution of *ius ad bellum* in the nineteenth century, from the 1814–1815 peace settlements to the Monroe doctrine, the Drago doctrine, the *Caroline* incident, the Bryan treaties, the *Alabama claims* or yet the Hague Conventions. 'Total indifference' usefully synthetized the interwar discourse of 'partial indifference' in a way that met the needs of the discipline and of the scholarship after WWII, while keeping the same underlying message about the strength, the necessity and, consequently, the legitimacy of international law.

This question of the 'needs' brings us to the second explanation for the persistence of 'indifference' past the interwar years: the *functional explanation*. As reminded earlier, this third part of the book has been guided by the idea that historical accounts appear at a given time to fulfil a specific social function. In the present case, it has been argued that the narrative of indifference can be understood as a way of preserving the representation that the discipline international law had of itself in the face of the disconfirming and traumatic events of the Great War. In the same line of thought, it may be assumed that 'the reason for th[e] "living on" [of the narrative] lies in the continuous relevance of these events'.[6] Said differently, as long as a given account endures, it may be presumed that it continues to hold a specific function in the society that sustains it. What might the function of 'indifference' for international law be nowadays? It actually seems that the function of 'indifference' has not changed much in over a hundred years; it continues to contribute to the preservation of the identity and legitimacy of international law as a legal discipline.

In this perspective, the narrative of indifference is inseparable from international law's more general historiography. The traditional account on the use of force, indeed, mimics the storytelling patterns of the discipline's 'autobiography'.[7] It is only a piece of this larger ensemble, and the function of the (hi)story of the use of force is the same as that of the overall (hi)story of international law. In telling a tale of gradual

[6] Jan Assmann, *Moses and the Egyptian. The Memory of Egypt in Western Monotheism* (Harvard University Press, 1997), p. 10.

[7] See above (Section 8.2.1.) and (Section 8.2.2.).

formalisation and progress, we saw how the discipline's historiography appears as a grand justification for the necessity of international law and its existence as law proper.[8] It reconciles theory and practice; the way international law defines its social purpose and the fact that it does not always manage to achieve this purpose or, at least, visibly seem to achieve it. The media have sometimes been blamed for this: 'it is only when serious breach of international law is alleged to have occurred that the media take notice. This can give a distorted impression of the nature of international law',[9] Anthony Aust, for instance, deplores. The discipline's general historiography remedies this misconception by conveying the idea that things would be even worse without international law, notwithstanding its imperfections and the fact that it is not yet as sophisticated as domestic law.

Due to its 'sensational' character, the use of force (and, more generally, warfare) concentrates much of this unwanted media attention. It bears a heavy responsibility in the public's 'distorted impression' of international law. Aside from the media, a quick look at how the rules of *ius ad bellum* are usually depicted in popular culture suffices to demonstrate their lack of credibility in the public's eyes. Analysing more than a hundred movies, Olivier Corten thus notes how international law is either absent from any consideration or represented as ill adapted, irrelevant and useless if not foolish.[10] This depiction, Corten further remarks, 'is miles away from the perspective that runs through most legal writings and emphasises the importance of the Charter of United Nations for international peace and security'.[11] The public's perception of the rules of the use of force, in sum, contrasts with, and challenges, that of internationalists'. In this context, the narrative of indifference remains as relevant as ever to preserve the inside coherence and outside credibility of international law. The discipline still needs to justify its existence and, because of the attention war receives, an important part of doing this is by proving its ability to

[8] See above (Section 8.1.3.).

[9] Anthony Aust, *Handbook of International Law* (2nd ed., Cambridge University Press, 2010), p. 3. See also James L. Brierly, 'Règles générales du droit de la paix' (1936) 58 *Recueil des cours de l'académie de droit international* 11; Peter Malanczuk, *Akehurst's Modern Introduction to International Law* (7th ed., Routledge, 1997), p. 6.

[10] Olivier Corten, 'Mais où est donc passée la Charte des Nations Unies ? Représentation et sous-représentation des règles sur l'usage de la force dans les films d'action', in Olivier Corten and François Dubuisson (dirs.), *Du droit international au cinema* (Pedone, 2015), pp. 89–127.

[11] Ibid., pp. 90–91. Translation by the author.

somehow control this phenomenon. Just as international law's general history, the narrative of indifference conveys the idea that although the current collective security system has its flaws, without it, wars might be even more frequent and destructive.

Finally, there is also a *methodological explanation* for the persistence of the narrative of indifference in modern day doctrine. Traditional international historiography and the narrative of indifference have become objective facts, part of what makes common sense within the discipline. This means that, generally speaking, they are not questioned; as just mentioned, they shape the way in which internationalists a priori approach historical matters. And this is where more trivial (or practical) considerations of methodology come into play. It is, for example, significant that when asserting that international law did not regulate the use of force before the twentieth century, authors do not always feel the need to reference their claim. Those who do, seldom refer to original sources of the time, doctrine or State practice. Instead, they tend to rely on what a great authority or another has written. James Brierly and Ian Brownlie are most often cited. When pre-1914 sources are used, Oppenheim, who clearly continues to hold a particular aura in international legal scholarship, is top of the charts. It may be that this is characteristic of a discipline such as law, and especially international law, which gives a particularly high value to the 'teachings of the most highly qualified publicists'.[12] There is an overreliance on secondary sources, which is perfectly understandable when the main concern of the research is not the history of international law.[13] As legal historians, indeed, wholeheartedly admit, historical and archival work is tedious and time-consuming.[14] But still, its absence, favours the reproduction and, by the same token, the naturalisation and depoliticisation of historical narratives.

[12] Art. 38 (1) d), ICJ Statute.

[13] As Jan Verzijl noted, the literature 'leans too much on the writings or elaborations of sources by others and too seldom shows signs of an independent and systematic research in the available immediate sources', in *International law in Historical Perspective*, 5 vols. (A. W. Stijhoff, 1968), vol. 1, p. 407.

[14] Ibid. See also Randall Lesaffer, 'International Law and Its History: The Story of an Unrequited Love', in Matthew Craven, Malgosia Fitzmaurice and Maria Vogiatzi (eds.), *Time, History and International Law* (Martinus Nijhoff, 2007), pp. 27–41.

Conclusion

It has been argued that every major crisis of international law has seen a return of the discipline to its history.[1] There indeed appears to be an urge to go back to the foundations and to the fundamentals in periods of transition and uncertainty; a need to take stock of the past in order to know how to situate one's self in the present and plan for the future. Returns to the past, are, in sum and in most instances, guided by present social, political or even psychological needs. In the course of this research, we have seen how the narrative of the indifference of international law to the use of force before the twentieth century emerged in the interwar scholarship as a means to rationalize the events of the World War I and enable the discipline to move past the failure which they represented.

Commentators usually agree that international law's latest turn to history was, for its part, triggered by the end of the Cold War.[2] The reconfiguration of political dynamics following the termination of the East-West confrontation was felt as opening new possibilities for international law and, especially, as an opportunity to redeploy its liberal and cosmopolitan project.[3] Neff thus notes how 'a fresh spirit was in the air',[4] 'rais[ing] the tantalizing possibility of ending the long deadlock of the UN Security Council, enabling that body to perform its role as a global

[1] Randall Lesaffer, 'International Law and Its History: The Story of an Unrequited Love', in Matthew Craven, Malgosia Fitzmaurice and Maria Vogiatzi (eds.), *Time, History and International Law* (Martinus Nijhoff, 2007), pp. 27–41.
p. 29.

[2] ibidem; Martti Koskenniemi, 'Why History of International Law Today?' (2004) 4 *Rechtsgeschichte*. 63; Emmanuelle Tourme Jouannet and Anne Peters, 'The *Journal of the History of International Law*: A Forum for New research' (2014) 16 *Journal of the History of International Law* 2.

[3] In this sense, see Martti Koskenniemi, 'Why History of International Law Today?', 63.

[4] Stephen C. Neff, *Justice Among the Nations. A History of International Law* (Harvard University Press, 2014), p. 443.

watchmen against aggression and other threats to peace'.[5] In the early 1990s, some authors believed that 'some of the traditional norms and practices of international law that were suppressed during the Cold War can now be revived'[6] and predicted a renewed support for, as well as an acceleration in the development of, international institutions.[7] Many also felt that it was an occasion to finally (and this time truly) move past the Westphalian model towards a system that privileged cooperation and promoted human rights and welfare.[8] Concepts such as 'human security', 'responsibility to protect', 'positive peace', 'right to development' or yet to 'democracy', made their way into the vocabulary of international law and relations.

But if the fall of the iron curtain provoked a surge of enthusiasm within the discipline, it also came with a certain dose of anxiety. It was important to give this 'new world order' the 'right' impulsion and make sure that everybody understood the stakes of the on-going changes. As Reisman amongst others emphasized in 1990, the end of the Cold War 'd [id] not mean the beginning of peace, nor d[id] it signal a new international stability'.[9] On the contrary, the dislocation of the USSR was susceptible of resulting – and, in fact, did result – in territorial instability and reorganisation. As Lea Brilmayer argues, it also meant that the West had now lost its traditional (and reliable) enemy by opposition to which it had defined its foreign policy and identity for the past forty years.[10]

[5] Ibid., p. 444

[6] Michael Reisman, 'International Law and the Cold War' (1990) *Faculty Scholarship Series*, Paper no 873, 861. See also Nicholas Rostow, 'The International Use of Force After the Cold War' (1991) 32 *Harvard International Law Journal* 411-421.

[7] See, e.g., Mark W. Janis, 'International Law?' (1991) 32 *Harvard International Law Journal* 370–372.

[8] On the place of human rights in the 'new world order' see, for e.g. Jack Donnelly, 'Human Rights in the New World Order' (1992) 9 *World Policy Journal* 249–277; Nicolas Guilhot, *The Democracy Makers: Human Rights and International Order* (Columbia University Press, 2005), pp. 69–100; Joseph Raz, 'Human Rights in the Emerging World Order' (2012) 1 *Transnational Legal Theory* 31–47; Mortimer Sellers, *New World Order; Sovereignty, Human Rights and Self-Determination of Peoples* (Berg Publishers, 1996); Jean Salmon, 'Vers l'adoption d'un principe de légitimité démocratique?', in Olivier Corten et al. (eds.), *A la recherche du nouvel ordre mondial. Le droit international à l'épreuve* (Editions Complexe, 1993), pp. 59–89.

[9] Reisman, 'International Law and the Cold War', 863. See also Gennady M. Danilenko, 'The Changing Structure of International Law: Constitutional Implications' (1992) 32 *Harvard International Law Journal* 353–362.

[10] Lea Brilmayer, 'The Odd Advantage of Reliable Enemies' (1991) 32 *Harvard International Law Journal* 331–338.

There were new uncertainties concerning who the new enemies and the new allies were. Direction and purpose were needed and this is where (hi) story, once more, came into play. The previous period (the Cold War era) was, again, deprecated and the possibilities brought forth by the new international order met with idealist expressions of hope for the future. Expressions such as 'gridlock'[11] and 'balance of terror',[12] were used to present the late 1940s to the early 1990s period, while the new era was spoken of in terms of 'new found freedom of action',[13] of 'a trend towards democracy'[14] and of 'renewed possibility for cooperation'.[15]

This discourse, once again, was not a prerogative of the international legal profession. In the manner of Wilson in 1918, Georges H. W. Bush, for instance, declared to the Congress on 11 September 1990 that:

> A hundred generations have searched for this elusive path to peace, while a thousand wars raged across the span of human endeavor. Today, that new world is struggling to be born, a world quite different from the one we have known, *a world where the rule of law supplants the rule of the jungle*, a world in which nations recognize the shared responsibility for freedom and justice, a world where the strong respect the rights of the weak.[16]

Whatever the hidden or cynical motives behind this rhetoric,[17] it is striking to see how the post-Cold War discourse mimics that which followed the end of the World War I. This just comes as a further illustration of the cyclic pattern of international law's tale about its history, and of how much the discipline's interest in its history, indeed, finds its roots in present necessities rather than 'disinterested' historical curiosity.[18] Every crisis, every challenge, is turned into an opportunity for

11 Rostow, 'The International Use of Force After the Cold War', 411.

12 Reisman, 'International Law and the Cold War', 859.

13 Mohammed Bedjaoui, *The New World Order and the Security Council. Testing the Legality of its Acts* (Martinus Nijhoff, 1994), p. 37.

14 Judith H. Bello and Alan F. Holmer, 'After the Cold War: Whither International Economic Law' (1991) 32 *Harvard International Law Journal* 323.

15 Brenda Cossman, 'Reform, Revolution, or Retrenchment – International Human Rights in the Post-Cold War Era' (1991) 32 *Harvard International Law Journal* 339.

16 'President Bush, "Toward a New World Order", Address before a joint session of Congress' (17 September 1991) 1 *US Department of State Dispatch*.

17 See Patrick Herman, 'Le monde selon Bush: genèse d'un nouvel order mondial', in Olivier Corten et al. (dirs.), *A la recherche d'un nouvel order mondial. Le droit internartional à l'épreuve* (Editions Complexe, 1993), pp. 7–20.

18 In this sense, see David Kennedy, 'Turning to Market Democracy: A Tale of Two Architectures' (1991) 32 *Harvard International Law Journal* 374.

the discipline to prove its worth and social utility. In the 1990s, of course, it was not about creating new rules or establishing a new collective security system. Formally speaking, international law was believed to have all the required tools to fulfil its cosmopolitan and pacifying mission. It rather was about finally giving the framework of 1945 the opportunity to function as its founders had intended and enable the UN to pursue its benevolent action.

International law's latest turn to history, however, has taken a particular twist. From the second half of the 1990s onwards, international legal history indeed seems to have become the field of predilection of critical scholars. As it is, the premises and aims of critical legal histories oppose those of conventional legal history. While conventional history is, in fact, often built on the assumptions that there is a historical truth that can be objectively be accounted for and follow 'whiggish' patterns of storytelling, critical histories rely on the idea that legal history is a socially and politically determined discourse and that humanity does not necessarily follow a linear path towards progress.[19] From there, critical legal historians have generally sought to 'liberate the field from the grip and structural bias hegemonic historical narratives'[20] produced by classical mainstream history. This enterprise has taken several forms, from 'contextualised' intellectual histories to third-world histories of rules and institutions, to post-modern analyses of historical accounts as such. Each of these approaches seek, in their own way, to highlight the power relationships and struggles at play behind international law and its narratives. Said differently, instead of building certainties about international law, critical scholars' impulse to historicise aims to deconstruct these certainties in an attempt to demystify the discipline and highlight its indeterminate and political nature.

But if inquiring into the past is never fortuitous and always 'a political act',[21] one may wonder what purpose(s) – or 'hidden agenda' to use Assmann's words – critical legal histories pursue behind their 'deconstructionist' endeavours. As Emmanuelle Tourme Jouannet and Anne Peters point out, the epistemological factor cannot be ignored as an

[19] Thomas Skouteris, 'Engaging History in International Law', in José Maria Beneyto and David Kennedy (eds.), New Approaches to International Law. The European and American Experiences (TMC Asser Press, 2012), pp. 106–116.

[20] Ibid., p. 111.

[21] George Rodrigo Bandeira Galindo, 'Martti Koskenniemi and the Historiographical Turn in International Law' (2005) 16 *European Journal of International Law* 543.

explanation for the rise of critical histories. The decline of the pragmatist outlook on international law that accompanied the Cold War period, they say, finally enabled for the development of more theoretically inclined and post-modern perspectives.[22] The field was just following a trend, a more general movement, which had started in social sciences a few decades before and had already gained traction in domestic legal histories, especially in the United States.[23] It is as if technicality and dogmatism became less essential to the survival of the discipline, allowing space for cynicism and doubt.

At the same time, critical legal scholars' scepticism does not seem to be the expression of enmity towards the discipline. Instead, it can be interpreted as the symptom of profound, albeit frustrated, idealism. Aside from the fact that one seeks to construct and the other to deconstruct, the aims of classical historiography and of 'newstream' histories are indeed quite similar: understand the past to plan for a better future. The introductions to several critical international legal histories thus start by noting that 'it seems at times as if we have lost sight of what international law is';[24] by stating that they 'hope to make our present situation clearer to us and sharpen our own ability to act in the professional contexts that are open to us as we engage in our practices and projects';[25] or that they aim

> to facilitate and further the reconstructive project which a number of scholars, working within the tradition of Critical race Theory, Feminism, Lat-Crit theory or Third World approaches to International Law, have in common, the project of an international law that is responsive to the needs of variously disadvantaged peoples[26]

[22] Tourme Jouannet and Peters, 'The *Journal of the History of International Law*', 2. See also Skouteris, 'Engaging History in International Law', pp. 102–103.

[23] See, e.g., Robert W. Gordon, 'Critical Legal Histories' (1984) 36 *Stanford Law Review* 57–125.

[24] Emmanuelle Jouannet, *The Liberal-Welfarist Law of Nations. A History of International Law* (Cambridge University Press, 2012), p. 1. See also by the same author, 'The Critique of Classical Thought During the Interwar Period. Vattel and Van Vollenhoven', in Anne Orford and Florian Hoffmann (eds.), *The Oxford Handbook on the Theory of International Law* (Oxford University Press, 2016), p. 102.

[25] Martti Koskenniemi, *The Gentle Civilizer of Nations. The Rise and Fall of International Law* (Cambridge University Press, 2001), p. 10.

[26] Antony Anghie, *Imperialism, Sovereignty and the Making of International Law* (Cambridge University Press, 2007), p. 8.

From this point of view, the purpose of the 'new' histories of international law is far from being that of 'raz[ing] everything in [their] path, even the good stuff'.[27] They deconstruct to lay the foundations for reconstruction. They wish to evidence the structural flaws of international law to eventually remedy them and create a system that is more inclusive and respectful of cultural and political diversity, even though critical scholars, themselves, might not have a clear idea how to achieve this. On the other hand, it is also possible to see these proclamations of intentions as somewhat cynical. Appealing to the present appears as quite a conventional and consensual manner of justifying historical research. It sometimes seems that interest in the past for its own sake is barely understood. History is only useful if it can bring lessons for the present and the future. Claiming to wish to illuminate present experiences and issues with historical light might, thus, also be a way to anticipate criticism and the daunting 'so what?' question.

Beyond cynicism, however, knowledge of the past is essential for the discipline to carry out constructive self-examination. International law needs to be aware of its representational biases and of the limits of its discourse. In this respect, this study of the narrative indifference has more specifically demonstrated that, in its efforts to prove itself 'law proper', the discipline may have sometimes shown overconfidence in its capacity to ensure the peaceful co-existence of States, as well as a tendency to be disdainful of politics. International law has, indeed, constantly defined itself by opposition to politics; one is presented as the guarantee of order and cooperation, whereas the other is depicted as synonymous to anarchy and egoism.[28] Traditional historiography, thus conveys the idea that politics is the 'enemy' of law and, in so doing, conceals the very political nature of law by suggesting the latter to be a neutral, universal and, consequently, necessarily positive force for social progress.

These representations and 'latent cognitive frames' do not only impact (hi)story. They also have an influence on the way we think and talk about international law on a daily basis. This is particularly visible in the current literature and debates about *ius contra bellum* in at least two connected ways.

First, they somehow suggest that law is more often part of the solution than part of the problem. If the twentieth century has shown one thing,

[27] Skouteris, 'Engaging History in International Law', p. 118.
[28] See *supra* Chapter 8 (8.2.1.) and (8.2.2.).

however, it probably is that the formalisation and codification of the rules on the use of force have not prevented conflict from taking place. The twentieth century is in fact frequently considered as one of the deadliest in recorded history, and the first two decades of the twenty-first century have so far not indicated a change of trend. Of course, international lawyers are not naïve and know that rules alone cannot bring peace to the international plane, but this is nevertheless the story carried by traditional historiography. The occurrence of wars in the nineteenth century (and in particular of the Great War) is blamed on the absence of rules. The weakness of the League of Nations system is presented as responsible for the instability of the interwar years. The political immobilisation of the United Nations as a result of the Cold War is held liable for the organisation's incapacity to live up to expectations. Today, it is the inadequacy and rigidity of the current structures and rules on the use of force, as well as a few States' unwillingness to reform them, that are being finger-pointed for the present state of insecurity.[29] Once again, it is as if politics impeded the 'good' development of international law, which in parallel suggests that any human activity is susceptible of being efficiently ring-fenced by law if it is given the opportunity. And so, the development of rules through legal technique sometimes seems to have become an end (or achievement) in itself. As Kennedy and Corten indeed argue, there appears to be a certain 'cult of rules' in contemporary scholarship.[30]

The second way the narrative of indifference appears to impact the contemporary discourse on the use of force is in implying that there is an end (a precise, although yet unknown, point of arrival) to the evolution of law. In presenting the metamorphosis of *ius ad bellum* into *ius contra bellum* as a story of constant progress towards a better, more accurate and more adequate legal system, it indeed gives the impression that we (international lawyers) will eventually manage to find the 'perfect' set of

[29] This is especially true in what concerns the reform of the UN Security Council veto system, see, e.g., Jan Wouters and Tom Ruys, 'Security Council Reform: A New Veto for a New Century?', *KU Leuven Institute for International Law Working Paper*, no 78, June 2005, p. 2; Paul Kennedy and Bruce Russett, 'Reforming the United Nations' (1995) 74 *Foreign Affairs* 56–71.

[30] David Kennedy, *Of War and Law* (Princeton University Press, 2006), pp. 141 ff; Olivier Corten, 'Formalization and Deformalization as Narratives of the Law of War', Randall Lesaffer, 'International Law and Its History: The Story of an Unrequited Love', in Matthew Craven, Malgosia Fitzmaurice and Maria Vogiatzi (eds.), *Time, History and International Law* (Martinus Nijhoff, 2007), p. 252.

rules, that is, the perfect balance in the classic 'state *vs.* community *vs.* individual' trichotomy. Although probably not fully conscious, this belief helps coat any and every proposal for reform or discourse on the necessity to adapt international law to current necessities and 'new challenges' with almost natural and dogmatic authority.[31]

Yet, the first two parts of this book have shown that these 'new challenges' so often spoken of by scholarship (mass human rights violations, transnational terrorism, etc.) are, by no means, new. The same hopes and fears (hopes for a fairer and more humane international society and fears that rules will be abused) have animated doctrinal debates about the legality of humanitarian intervention, of preventive self-defence, of self-defence against non-State actors and so forth, for at least the past two hundred years.[32] Only the answer some authors choose to provide have changed. In fact, while nineteenth century international lawyers forcefully pleaded for a restrictive approach and for the formalisation of the rules on the use of force, we are today witnessing the opposite movement towards an extensive outlook and the deformalisation of *ius contra bellum*. This shifting balance probably comes as a further illustration of the profoundly precarious nature of any attempt to create a comprehensive or 'perfect' system of collective security.

[31] On the rhetorics of 'new' challenges and interventionism, see, e.g. Anne Orford, 'Muscular Humaniatrianism: Reading the Narratives of New interventionism' (1999) 10 *European Journal of International Law* 679–711; Olivier Corten, 'Formalization and Deformalization', pp. 264–265.

[32] See above Conclusion to Part 1.

BIBLIOGRAPHY

Treaties, Conventions and Other International Agreements

Traité de paix, d'amitié et de commerce entre François Ier et Suleyman Ier, dit « le Magnifique », Constantinople, February 1535.

Treaty of Kütchük Kaynarca, Kütchük Kaynarca, 10/21 July 1774.

Protocol relative to the Affairs of Greece, signed in Saint Petersburg, 23 March 1826.

Convention explicative et complémentaire du traité de Bucarest de 1812, signed in Akkerman, 25 September/7 October 1826.

Treaty for the Pacification of Greece, signed between His Majesty, the Most Cristian King, and the Emperor of all Russias, London, 6 July 1827.

Treaty of Peace, Friendship and Commerce between His Majesty the Queen of Great Britain and Ireland and the Emperor of China, Nanjing, 29 August 1842.

Treaty of Friendship, Commerce and Navigation, Washington, 20 December 1849.

General Treaty of Peace between Great Britain, Austria, France, Prussia, Russia, Sardinia and Turkey, Paris, 30 March 1856.

Protocols of Conference between Great Britain, Austria, France, Prussia, Russia and Turkey, respecting measures to be taken for the Pacification of Syria, Paris, 3 August 1860.

Treaty between Great Britain and Lagos, Lagos, 1 January 1852.

Treaty between Great Britain, France and Turkey, relative to Military Aid to be given to Turkey, Constantinople, 12 March 1854.

General Treaty of Peace between Great Britain, Austria, France, Prussia, Russia, Sardinia and Turkey, Paris, 30 March 1856.

Protocols of Conference between Great Britain, Austria, France, Prussia, Russia and Turkey, respecting measures to be taken for the Pacification of Syria, Paris, 3 August 1860.

Traité de paix et d'amitié, conclu à Saïgon entre la France et l'Espagne, d'une part et le Royaume d'Annam, d'autre part, 5 June 1862.

Traité de paix et d'alliance conclu à Saigon entre la France et le Royaume d'Annam, 15 March 1874.

Treaty of Commercial Reciprocity, Washington, 30 January 1875.

Treaty of Commercial Reciprocity, Washington, 6 December 1884.
Convention (I) for the pacific settlement of international disputes, adopted in The Hague, on 29 July 1899.
Convention (III) relative to the opening of hostilities, signed in The Hague, 18 October 1907.
Covenant of the League of Nations, Paris, 28 June 1919, in force 10 January 1920.
Treaty of Peace with Turkey, Lausanne on 24 July 1923, in force 6 August 1924.
Charter of the United Nations, adopted in San Francisco, on the 26 June 1945.

Case Law

Alabama Claims of the United States of America against Great Britain, Award rendered on 14 September 1872 by the Tribunal of arbitration established by Article 1 of the Treaty of Washington of May 1871, UN *Reports of Arbitral Awards* (RIAA), vol. XXIX, pp. 125–134.
ICJ, North Sea Continental Shelf (Federal Republic of Germany vs. Denmark; Federal Republic of Germany vs. Netherlands), Judgment of 20 February 1969, ICJ Reports 1969, p. 3.
Military and paramilitary activities in and against Nicaragua (Nicaragua vs. United-States of America), Merits, Judgment of 27 June 1986, ICJ Reports 1986, p. 14.

Archives, State Papers and Official Compendiums of Diplomatic Correspondence

Colonial Office (UK), Rules and Regulations for Her Majesty's Colonial Service (J. Harrison and Son, 1867).
Foreign Office (FO), British and Foreign State Papers 1826–1827 (J. Harrison and Son, 1828), vol. 14.
Papers relative to the Affairs of Greece, 1826–1830 (J. Harrison and Son, 1831).
Papers relative to the affairs of Greece, 1826–1832 (J. Harrison and Son, 1835).
Affairs of Syria. Disturbances (FO 78/1557).
Correspondence relating to the affairs of Syria (FO 406/10).
British and Foreign State Papers 1839–1840 (J. Harrison and Son, 1857), vol. 28.
British and Foreign State Papers 1842–1843 (Ridgway and Sons, 1858), vol. 31.
British and Foreign State Papers 1853–1854 (William Ridgway, 1865), vol. 44.
British and Foreign State Papers, 1859–1860 (William Ridgway, 1867), vol. 50.
British and Foreign State Papers, 1860–1861 (William Ridgway, 1868), vol. 51.
Collected Diplomatic Documents Relating to the Outbreak of the European War (J. Harrison and Son, 1915).
Correspondence respecting the disturbances in China (China n°1) (Printed for HMSO by Harrison, 1901).

Correspondence respecting the disturbances in China (China n°3) (printed for HMSO by Harrison, 1901).

Hansard, Parliamentary Debates (UK), House of Commons vol. 132, 31 March 1854.

House of Commons vol. 127, 12 June 1862.

House of Commons, vol. 244, 27 March 1879.

House of Commons, vol. 244, 25 March 1879.

House of Commons, vol. 244, 28 March 1879.

House of Commons, vol. 175, 20 May 1864.

House of Lords, vol. 244, 21 March 1879.

Ministère des affaires étrangères (MAE), Correspondence politique de l'Angleterre, vol. 717.

Correspondence politique de l'Autriche, vol. 477.

Correspondence politique de la Prusse, vol. 336.

Correspondence politique de la Russie, vol. 221.

Correspondence politique de la Turquie, juin-juillet 1860 (345).

Documents diplomatiques 1860 (Imprimerie Impériale, 1861).

Archives diplomatiques 1871–1872 (Librairie Diplomatique Ayrot, 1872).

Documents diplomatiques. Affaire du Tonkin, 1ere partie (1874–1882) (Imprimerie Nationale, 1883).

Ministerio de Estado, *Spanish Diplomatic Correspondence and Documents, 1896–1900. Presented to the Cortes by the Minister of State*, [United States Department of State, translation] (Government Printing Office, 1905).

Parliamentary debates (France).

Journal des débats politiques et littéraire, 29 March 1854.

Journal official de la République Française, vol. 71, 13 March 1883.

Journal Officiel de la République Française, vol. 209, 2 August 1914.

United State Department of State, *Foreign Relations of the United States, Affairs in Hawaii, 1894* (Government Printing Office, 1895), Appendix II.

Papers Relating to the Foreign Relations of the United States (1898), Washington (Government Pinting Office, 1901).

Papers Relating to the Foreign Relations of the United States, with the annual message of the President transmitted to the Congress, 5 December 1898, (Government Printing Office, 1901).

Papers Relating to the Foreign Relations of the United States, With the Annual Message of the President Transmitted to Congress, 7 December 1909 (Government Printing Office, 1914).

Papers Relating to Foreign Affairs 1914 (Government Printing Office, 1922).

US Department of State, *Foreign Relations of the United States 1901. Appendix: Affairs in China* (Government Printing Office, 1902).

United States Senate, *Reports of the Committee on Foreign Relations, 1789–1901*, 8 vols. (Government Printing Office, 1901).

Private Collections of Documents

Bassett Moore, John, *A Digest of International Law*, 8 vols. (Government Printing Office, 1906).

Bevans, Charles I. (ed.), *Treaties and Other International Agreements of the United States of America, 1776–1949*, 13 vols. (Department of State Publications, 1971).

Bourchier (Lady) (ed.), *Memoir of the Life of Admiral Sir Edward Codrington*, 2 vols. (Longmans Greens & Co., 1873).

Ghillany, Friedrich W. et Schnitzer, Jean-Henri, *Manuel diplomatique. Recueil des traités de paix européens les plus importants, des actes des Congrès et autres documents relatifs à la politique internationale, depuis le traité de Westphalie jusqu'à ces derniers temps*, 2 vols. (Treuteel & Würtz, 1856).

Lepsius, Johannes, Mendelssohn-Bartholdy, Albrecht and Thimme, Friedrich (eds.), *Die Grosse Politik der Europäischen Kabinette, 1871–1914*, 46 vols. (Deutsche Veragsgesellschaft für Politik und Geschichte, 1924).

Lesur, Charles L., *Annuaire historique universel pour 1821* (Libraire Fantin, 1822).

Londonberry, Charles W. V. (Marquess of) (ed.), *Correspondence, Despatches and other papers of the Viscount Castlereagh* (John Murray, 1853).

Lydecker, Robert C. (ed.), *Roster Legislature of Hawaii, 1841–1918* (Hawaiian Gazette Co., Ltd., 1918).

Martens, Charles de (ed.), *Guide diplomatique*, 2 vols. (J. P. Aillaud, 1837).

Martineau, John (ed.), *The Life and Correspondence of the Right Hon. Sir Bartle Frere*, 2 vols. (John Murray, 1895).

Mayer (ed.), William Frederick, *Treaties between the Empire of China and Foreign Powers* (4th ed., North China Herald Office, 1902).

Metternich, Richard (ed.), *Memoirs of Prince Metternich*, 5 vols. (Richard Bentley and Son, 1881).

Milovaniwitch, Milan, *Les Traités de garanties au XIXe siècle. Etudes de droit international et d'histoire diplomatique* (Arthur Rousseau, 1888).

Newton, Arthur Percival (ed.), *Selected Documents Relating to the Unification of South Africa* (Routledge, 1968).

Noradounghian, Gabriel (ed.), *Recueil des actes internationaux de l'Empire ottoman*, 3 vols. (Librarie Cotillon et F. Pichon, 1897).

Reinach, L. de (ed.), *Recueil des traités conclus par la France en Extrême-Orient (1684–1902)* (Ernest Leroux, 1902).

Testa (de), Ignace (Baron) (ed.), *Recueil des traités de la Porte Ottomane avec les Puissances étrangères*, 9 vols. (Amyot, 1864).

Trifunovska, Snezana (ed.), *Yugoslavia through Documents From Its Creation to Its Dissolution* (Martinus Nijhoff, 1994).

Webster, C. K. (ed.), *The Congress of Vienna 1814–1815* (Oxford University Press, 1918).

Wellesley, Arthur R. (2nd Duke of Wellington) (ed.), *Supplementary Despatches, Correspondence and Memoranda of Field Marshal Arthur Duke of Wellington, K.G.*, 15 vols. (John Murray, 1865).

League of Nations and United Nations Documents

International Law Commission, Wood, Michael (Special Rapporteur), *First Report on Identification of Customary International Law*, International Law Commission, Sixty-fifth session, Geneva 6 May–7 June and 8 July–9 August 2013 (17 May 2013), A/CN.4/663.

Identical letters dated 25 November 2014 from the Permanent Representative of the United Kingdom of Great Britain and Northern Ireland to the United Nations addressed to the Secretary-General and the President of the Security Council, 25 November 2014, UN Doc. S/2014/851.

Identical letters dated 8 September 2015 from the Permanent Representative of France to the United Nations addressed to the Secretary-General and the President of the Security Council, 9 September 2015, UN Doc. S/2015/745.

Letter dated 9 September 2015 from the Permanent Representative of Australia to the United Nations addressed to the President of the Security Council (9 September 2015) UN Doc. S/2015/693.

Letter dated 31 March 2015 from the *Chargé d'affaires a.i.* of the Permanent Mission of Canada to the United Nations addressed to the President of the Security Council (31 March 2015) UN Doc. S/2015/221.

Letter dated 23 September 2014 from the Permanent Representative of the United States of America to the United Nations addressed to the Secretary-General, 23 September 2014, UN Doc. S/2014/695.

Letter dated 24 July 2015 from the *Chargé d'affaires a.i.* of the Permanent Mission of Turkey to the United Nations addressed to the President of the Security Council, 24 July 2015, UN Doc. S/2015/563.

Permanent Court of International Justice, Advisory Committee of Jurists, *Procès-verbaux of the Proceedings of the Committee*, 16 June–24 July 1920 (Van Langenhuyssen Brothers, 1920).

Second Report on identification of customary international law, International Law Commission, Sixty-sixth session, Geneva 5 May–6 June and 7 July–8 August 2014 (22 May 2014), A/CN.4/672.

United Nations Educational and Scientific Cooperation Organization, *A Handbook for the Improvement of Textbooks and Teaching Materials as Aids to International Understanding* (UNESCO, 1949).

United Nations Security Council, Letter dated 25 June 2014 from the Permanent Representative of Iraq to the United Nations addressed to the Secretary-General, 25 June 2014, UN Doc. S/2014/440.

Verbatim Record, 7271st Meeting, 19 September 2014, UN Doc. S/PV.7271.

International Law Manuals, Treatises and Textbooks

Abdy, John T. (ed.), *Kent's Commentaries on International Law* (2nd ed., Deighton and sons, 1878).

Abou-Al-Wafa, Ahmed, *Public International Law* (Dar-Al-Nahda Al Arabia, 2002).

Akehurst, Michael, *A Modern Introduction to International Law* (Geroges Allen and Unwin Ltd., 1970).

Alcorta, Amancio, *Cours de droit international public*, 2 vols. (L. Larose et Forcel, 1887).

Amos, Sheldon, *Lectures on International Law* (Stevens and Sons, 1876).

Anzilotti, Dionisio, *Corso di diritto internazionale*, 3 vols. (Anthenaeum, 1915).

Cours de droit international (translation and reproduction of the 3rd edition from 1929) (LGDJ, 1999).

Arbour, J. Maurice, *Droit International Public* (3rd ed., Yvon Blais, 1997).

Aspiazu, Agustin, *Dogmas del derecho internacional* (Imprenta de Hallet & Breen, 1872).

Aust, Anthony, *Handbook of International Law* (2nd ed., Cambridge University Press, 2010).

Bastid, Mme. Paul, *Cours de droit international public* (Les Cours de droit, 1976–1977).

Bello, Andrés, *Principios de derecho de gentes* (Librería de la señora Viuda de Calleja y hijos, 1844).

Benadava, Santiago, *Derecho internacional publico* (3rd ed., Editorial Jurídico de Chile, 1989).

Birkenhead, Frederik E., *International Law* (G. N. Morang, 1901).

Bluntschli, Johann-Caspar, *Le droit international codifié* (Guillaumin et Cie., 1870).

Boas, Gideon, *Public International Law: Contemporary Principles and Perspectives* (Edward Elgar, 2012).

Bonfils, Henry, *Manuel de droit international public* (Arthur Rousseau, 1894).

Bonfils, Henry et Fauchille, Paul, *Manuel de droit international public* (7th ed., Arthur Rousseau, 1914).

Brierly, James L., *The Law of Nations: An Introduction to the International Law of Peace* (Clarendon Press, 1949).

Brownlie, Ian, *Principles of Public International Law* (4th ed., Clarendon Press, 1990).

Principles of Public International Law (7th ed., Oxford University Press, 2008).

Calvo, Charles, *Le droit international théorique et pratique*, 6 vols. (4th ed., Guillaumin & Cie., 1887).

Manuel de droit international public et privé, 2 vols. (Arthur Rousseau, 1892).

Carnazza-Amari, Giuseppe, *Trattato sul diritto internazionale di pace* (V. Maisner e compagnia, 1875).

Cannizzaro, Enzo, *Corso di diritto internazionale* (Giuffrè Editore, 2011).

Casanova, Ludovico, *Del diritto internazionale* (Stabilimento tipografico Ludovico Lavagnino, 1858).

Cassese, Antonio, *International Law* (Oxford University Press, 2001).

Cavaré, Louis, *Le droit international public positif*, 2 vols. (2nd ed., Pedone, 1961).

Chen, Lung-chu, *An Introduction to Contemporary International Law. A Policy-Oriented Perspective* (3rd ed., Oxford University Press, 2015).

Combacau, Jean et Sur, Serge, *Droit International Public* (Montchrestien, 1997).

Conforti, Benedetto, *Diritto internazionale* (7th ed., Editoriale Scientifica, 2006).

Conforti, Benedetto, and Labella, Angelo, *An Introduction to International Law* (Martinus Nijhoff, 2012).

Corbett, P. E., *Law and Society in the Relations of States* (Harcourt, Brace and Company, 1951).

Corten, Olivier, Dubuisson, François, Koutroulis, Vaios et Lagerwall, Anne, Une, *Introduction critique au droit international* (Editions de l'Université de Bruxelles, 2017).

Creasy, Edward, *First Platform of International Law* (John Van Voorst, 1876).

Currie, John H., *Public International Law* (2nd ed., Irwin Law, 2008).

Daillier, Patrick, Forteau, Mathias et Pellet, Alain, *Droit International Public* (8th ed., LGDJ, 2009).

D'Amato, Anthony, *International Law: Process and Prospect* (Transnational Publishers Inc., 1995).

Davis, Cushman K., *A Treatise on International Law, including American Diplomacy*, (annotated and revised by Peter J. Healy) (Keefe-Davidson Law Book Co., 1901).

Davis, Georges B., *Elements of International Law, with an Account of Its Origins and Historical Development* (Harper & Brothers Publishers, 1900).

Delbez, Louis, *Les principes generaux du droit international public* (3rd ed., LGDJ, 1963).

Dixon, Martin, *International Law* (6th ed., Oxford University Press, 2007).

Duggard, John, *International Law. A South African Perspective* (4th ed., Juta, 2011).

Fauchille, Paul, *Traité de droit international public*, 2 vols. (8th ed., Arthur Rousseau, 1921–1926).

Favre, Antoine, *Principes du droit des gens* (LGDJ, 1974).

Fenwick, Charles G., *International Law* (The Century Co., 1924).

Field, David Dudley, *Projet d'un code de droit international proposés aux diplomates, aux hommes d'Etat, et aux jurisconsultes* (Pedone-Lauriel, 1881).

Fiore, Pasquale, *Nouveau droit international public*, 3 vols. (2nd ed., Auguste Durand, Pedone-Lauriel, 1885).

Il diritto internazionale codificato e la sua sanzione giuridica (Union Tipograpfico-Editrice, 1890).

Focarelli, Carlo, *Digesto del diritto internazionale* (Editoriale Scientifica, 2004).

Funck-Brentano, Théophile et Sorel, Albert, *Précis de droit des gens* (E. Plon et Cie., 1877).

Gallaudet, Edward Miner, *A Manual of International Law* (Barnes, 1879).

Garden (Comte de), Guillaume, *Traité complet de la diplomatie ou théorie générale des relations extérieures des puissances de l'Europe*, 2 vols. (Librairie Treutel et Würtz, 1833).

Gardiner, Richard K., *International Law* (Pearson Longman, 2003).

Gentili, Alberico, *De Iure Belli Libri Tres* (translation from the 1612 edition by John C. Rolfe), 3 vols. (Clarendon Press, 1933).

Glenn, Edwin F., *Handbook of International Law* (West Publishing Co., 1895).

González Campos, Julio D., Sánchez Rodríguez, Luis I. y Sáenz de Santa María, Paz Andrés, *Curso de Derecho Internacional Público* (4th ed., Thomson Civitas, 2008).

Grotius, Hugo, *The Rights of War and Peace* (translated from Latin by Jean de Barbeyrac, original ed.: 1625) (W. Innys & al., 1738).

Grybowski, Kazimierz, *Soviet Public International Law* (A. W. Stijhoff, 1970).

Guggenheim, Paul, *Traité de droit international public*, 2 vols. (Librairie de l'Université de Genève, 1953–1954).

Hall, William E., *A Treatise on International Law* (3rd ed., Clarendon Press, 1890).

Halleck, Henry, *International Law: or Rules Regulating the Intercourse of States in Peace and War* (D. Van Nostrand, 1861).

Elements of International Law and the Laws of War (J. B. Lippincott & Co., 1866).

Heffter, August-W., *Le droit international de l'Europe* (E.-H. Schroeder, 1873).

Heilborn, Paul, *Handbuch des Völkerrechts* (W. Kohlhammer, 1912).

Hershey, Amos S., *The Essentials of International Public Law* (The MacMillan Company, 1912).

Holland, Thomas E., *Studies in International Law* (Clarendon Press, 1898).

Holtzendorff (von), Franz, *Introduction au droit des gens: Recherches philosophiques, historiques et bibliographiques* (Verlagsanstalt und Druckerei A.-G., 1889).

Janis, Mark Weston, *International Law* (6th ed., Walters Kluwer, 2012).

Jessup, Philip C., *A Modern Law of Nations. An Introduction* (The MacMillan Company, 1950).

Kaczorowska, Alina, *Public International Law* (4th ed., Routledge, 2010).

Kaufmann, Erich, *Règles générales du droit de la paix* (Librairie du Recueil Sirey, 1936).

Kelsen, Hans, *Principles of International Law* (Rinehart & Company, 1952).

Kent, James, *Commentaries on American Law*, 4 vols. (9th ed., Little, Brown and Company, 1858).

Klabbers, Jan, *International Law* (Cambridge University Press, 2013).

Klüber, Johann Ludwig, *Droit des gens moderne de l'Europe*, 2 vols. (Librairie J. G. Cotta, 1819).

Lauterpacht, Hersch (edited by Elihu Lauterpacht), *International Law. Collected Papers*, 4 vols. (Cambridge University Press, 1975).
Lawrence, Thomas, *The Principles of International Law* (D. C. Heath & Co. Publishers, 1900).
Le Fur, Louis, *Précis de droit international public* (4th ed., Librairie Dalloz, 1939).
Levi, Leone, *International Law: With Materials for a Code of International Law* (D. Appleton and Company, 1888).
Litz, Franz (von), *Le droit international* (translation of the 9th German edition of 1913) (A. Pedone, 1927).
Lopez Sanchez, Pedro, *Elementos de derecho internacional público* (Imprenta de Revista de Legislación, 1866).
Lorimer, James, *The Institutes of Law. A Treatise of the Principles of Jurisprudence, as Determined by Nature* (T. & T. Clark Publishers, 1872).
The Institutes of the Law of Nations – A Treatise of the Jural Relations of Separate Political Communities, 2 vols. (W. Blackwood and sons, 1883).
(de) Louter, Jan, *Le droit international public positif*, 2 vols. (Imprimerie de l'Université, 1920).
Lowe, Vaughan, *International Law* (Oxford University Press, 2007).
Maine, Henry S., *International Law (the Whewell lectures)* (John Murray, 1890).
Malanczuk, Peter, *Akehurst's Modern Introduction to International Law* (7th ed., Routledge, 1997).
Manin, Philippe, *Droit international public* (Masson, 1979).
Manning, William Oke, *Commentaries on the Law of Nations* (S. Sweet, 1839).
Martens (de), Frédéric, *Traité de droit international*, 3 vols. (Librairie Marescq Ainé, 1883).
Martens (von), Georg-Friedrich, *A Compendium of the Law of Nations* (2nd ed., Corbett and Morgan, 1802).
Précis de droit des gens moderne de l'Europe fondé sur les traités et l'usage (3rd ed., Librairie de Dietrich, 1821).
Maryan Green, N. A., *International Law* (3rd ed., Pitman Publishing, 1987).
Maxey, Edwin, *International Law with Illustrative Cases* (The F. H. Thomas Law Book Co., 1906).
Merignhac, Alexandre, *Traité de droit international public*, 3 vols. (LGDJ, 1905).
Moser, Johann Jakob, *Versuch des Neuesten Europäischen Völk-Rechts in Friedens- und Kriegs-Zeiten* (Varrentrapp und Wenner, 1779).
Neumann (von), Léopold, *Eléments de droit des gens moderne européen* (Arthur Rousseau, 1886).
Nys, Ernest, *Les origines du droit international* (Alfred Castaigne, 1894).
Le droit international. Les principes, les théories, les faits, 3 vols. (Alfred Castaigne, 1906).
O'Brien, John, *International Law* (Cavendish Publishing Limited, 2001).
Olowu, Dejo, *International Law. A Textbook for the South Pacific* (CD Publishing, 2010).

Oppenheim, Lassa, *International Law. A treatise*, 2 vols. (Longmans, Green & Co., 1905–1906).

(edited by Ronald H. Roxburgh), *International Law. A treatise*, 2 vols. (3rd ed., Longman Greens, 1920).

(edited by Arnold D. McNair), *International Law. A treatise*, 2 vols. (4th ed., Longman Greens, 1928).

(edited by Hersch Lauterpacht), *International Law. A treatise*, 2 vols. (5th ed., Longman Greens, 1935).

Ortolan, Théodore, *Règles de droit international et de diplomatie de la mer*, 2 vols. (J. Dumaine, cosse et N. Delamotte, 1845).

Pando, José María, *Elementos de derecho internacional* (Imprenta de Alegría y Charlain, 1843).

Phillimore, Robert, *Commentaries upon International Law*, 3 vols. (T. & J. W. Johnson, 1854).

Pistoye (de), Alphonse, et Duverdy, Charles Denis, *Traité des prises maritimes*, 2 vols. (Librairie Auguste Durand, 1855).

Pradier-Fodéré, Paul, *Traité de droit international public européen et américain suivant les progrès de la science et de la pratique contemporaine*, 6 vols. (Pedone-Lauriel, 1883–1894).

Polson, Archer, *Principles of the Law of Nations* (John Joseph Griffin & Co., 1848).

Pomeroy, John Norton (edited by Theodore Salisbury Woolsey), *Lectures on International Law in Time of Peace* (Houghton, Milfin and Company, 1886).

Pufendorf (von), Samuel, *Of the Law of Nature and Nations* (translated from Latin by Mr. Carew) (original edition: 1672) (Printed for J. Walthoe, R. Wilkin, J. and J. Bonwicke, S. Birt, T. Ward, and T. Osborne, 1729).

Reddie, James, *Inquiries in International Law, public and private* (2nd ed., Blackwood, 1851).

Redlich (von), Marcellus Donald A. R., *The Law of Nations* (2nd ed., World League for Permanent Peace, 1937).

Redslob, Robert, *Les principes du droit des gens moderne* (Librairie Arthur Rousseau, 1937).

Traité de droit des gens (Librairie du Recueil Sirrey, 1950).

Remiro Brotons, Antonio, *Derecho internacional público*, 2 vols. (Tecnos, 1982).

Renault, Louis, *Introduction à l'étude du droit international* (L. Larose, 1879).

Reuter, Paul, *Droit International Public* (2nd ed., Presses Universitaires de France, 1963).

Droit International Public (5th ed., Presses Universitaires de France, 1976).

Riquelme, Antonio, *Elementos de derecho público internacional*, 2 vols. (Imprenta de D. Santiago Saunaque, 1849).

Rivier, Alphonse, *Principes du droit des gens*, 2 vols. (Arthur Rousseau, 1896).

Romanos, Angel, *Elementos de derecho internacional público* (Tipografía de Mariano Salas, 1904).

Rousseau, Charles, *Droit International Public*, 5 vols. (Sirey, 1980).
Saénz, Antonio, *Instituciones elementales sobre el derecho natural y de gentes* (curso dictado en la Universidad de Buenos Aires en los años 1822–23) (A. Boica y cia., 1939).
Scelle, Georges, *Précis de droit des gens* (Librairie du Recueil Sirey, 1932).
Manuel élémentaire de droit international public (Editions Domat-Montchrestien, 1943).
Schwarzenberger, Georg, *A Manual of International Law* (5th ed., London: Stevens & Sons Limited, 1967).
International Law as Applied by International Courts and Tribunals, 4 vols. (Stevens & Sons Limited, 1968).
Schwarzenberger, Georg, and Brown, E. D., *A Manual of International Law* (6th ed., Professional Books Limited, 1976).
Seara Vásquez, Modesto, *Derecho internacional público* (Editorial Porrúa, 2004).
Sepúlveda, Cesár, *Derecho internacional* (Editorial Porrúa, 2004).
Shaw, Malcolm, *International Law* (6th ed., Cambridge University Press, 2008).
Sibert, Marcel, *Traité de droit international public*, 2 vols. (Librairie Dalloz, 1951).
Sikondo, Marcel, *Introduction au droit international public* (Ellipses, 1999).
Slomanson, William R., *Fundamental Perspectives on International Law* (5th ed., Thomson Wadsworth, 2007).
Starke, Joseph G., *Introduction to International Law* (9th ed., Butterworths, 1984).
Stockton, Charles H., *Outlines of International Law* (Scribner's sons, 1914).
Stone, Julius, *Of Law and Nations. Between Power Politics and Human Hopes* (William S. Hein &Co., 1974).
Stowell, Ellery C., *International Law. A Restatement of Principles in Conformity with Actual Practice* (Henry Holt and Company, 1931).
Strupp, Karl, *Eléments du droit international universel, européen et américain*, 2 vols. (Les éditions internationales, 1930).
Svarlien, Oscar, *An Introduction to the Law of Nations* (McGraw-Hill Book Company, 1955).
Taylor, Hannis, *A Treatise on International Public Law* (Callaghan & Company, 1901).
Torres Campos, Manuel, *Elementos de derecho internacional publico* (Librería Fernando Fé, 1890).
Triepel, Heinrich, *Droit international et droit interne* (Pedone, 1920).
Tunkin, Grigory I., *Theory of International Law* (Harvard University Press, 1974).
Twiss, Travers, *The Law of Nations Considered as Independent Political Communities*, 2 vols. (2nd ed., Clarendon Press, 1884).
Vattel (de), Emer, *The Law of Nations; or, Principles of the Law of Nature Applied to the conduct and Affairs of Nations and Sovereigns* (translated by Charles J. Fenwick) (The Carnegie Institution of Washington, 1916).
Verhoeven, Joe, *Droit International Public* (Larcier, 2000).

von Glahn, Gerhard, *Law Among Nations. An Introduction to Public International Law* (3rd ed., MacMillan Publishing Co., 1976).

Walker, Thomas A., *The Science of International Law* (C. J. Clay and Sons/ Cambridge University Press, 1893).

A Manual of Public International Law (Cambridge University Press, 1895).

Wallace, Rebecca M. and Martin-Ortega, Olga, *International Law* (7th ed., Sweet & Maxwell, 2013).

Westlake, John, *International Law*, 2 vols. (Cambridge University Press, 1910–1913).

Wharton, Francis, *A Digest of International Law of the United States*, 3 vols. (Government Printing Office, 1886).

Wheaton, Henry, *Elements of International Law*, 2 vols. (Carey, Lea & Blanchard, 1836).

Wildman, Richard, *Institutes of International Law*, 2 vols. (William Benning & Co., 1849).

Wilson, George G., *Handbook of International Law* (West Publishing Company, 1910).

Wilson, George G., and Tucker, George F., *International Law* (Silver, Burdett and Company, 1910).

International Law (9th ed., Silver Burbett and Company, 1935).

Woolsey, Theodor D., *Introduction to the Study of International Law* (2nd ed., Charles Scribner & Co., 1871).

Monographs

Abiew, Francis Kofi, *The Evolution of the Doctrine and Practice of Humanitarian Intervention* (Kluwer Law International, 1999).

Abkariyus, Iskander, *The Lebanon in Turmoil. Syria and the Powers 1860* (translated by J. F. Scheltema) (Yale University Press, 1920).

Alexandrov, Stamir A., *Self-Defence against the Use of Force in International Law* (Kluwer Law International, 1996).

Alexandrovitch, Charles H., *The European-African Confrontation. A Study in Treaty-Making* (Martinus Nijhoff, 1973).

Alvarez, Alejandro, *Le droit international de l'avenir* (Institut américain de droit international, 1916).

Ambrosius, Lloyd E., *Woodrow Wilson and the American Diplomatic Tradition: The Treaty Fight in Perspective* (Cambridge University Press, 1987).

Amirell, Stefan Eklöf, *Pirates of Empire. Colonisation and Maritime Violence in Southeast Asia* (Cambridge University Press, 2019).

Anaya, S. James, *Indigenous People in International Law* (Oxford University Press, 2004).

Anghie, Antony, *Imperialism, Sovereignty and the Making of International Law* (Cambridge University Press, 2007).

Anzilotti, Dionisio, *Teoria generale della responsabilità dello Stato nel diritto internazionale* (F. Lumachi, 1902).

Arend, Anthony Clark and Beck, Robert J., *International Law and the Use of Force: Beyond the UN Charter Paradigm* (Routledge, 1993).

Armitage, David, *The Foundations of Modern International Thought* (Cambridge University Press, 2013).

Assmann, Jan, *Moses and the Egyptian: The Memory of Egypt in Western Monotheism* (Harvard University Press, 1997).

Cultural Memory and Early Civilization. Writing, Remembrance and Political Imagination (Cambridge University Press, 2011).

Austin, John, *The Province of Jurisprudence Determined* (John Murray, 1832).

Avenel, Jean-David, *La guerre hispano-américaine de 1898. La naissance de l'impérialisme américain* (Economica, 2007).

Bachand, Rémi, *Les théories critiques de droit international aux Etats-Unis et dans le monde anglophone* (Pedone, 2015).

Balfour, Sebastian, *The End of the Spanish Empire, 1898–1923* (Clarendon Press, 1997).

Barclay, David E., *Frederick Wilhelm IV and the Prussian Monarchy, 1840–1861* (Clarendon Press, 1995).

Barros, James, *The Corfu Incident of 1923: Mussolini and the League of Nations* (Princeton University Press, 1965).

Bass, Gary J., *Freedom's Battle: The Origins of Humanitarian Intervention* (Vintage Books, 2008).

Bassett Moore, John, *The Principles of American Diplomacy* (Harper & Brother Publishers, 1918).

Becker Lorca, Arnulf, *Mestizo International Law: A Global Intellectual history, 1842–1933* (Cambridge University Press, 2014).

Bederman, David J., *International Law in Antiquity* (Cambridge University Press, 2001).

Bedjaoui, Mohammed, *The New World Order and the Security Council. Testing the Legality of Its Acts* (Martinus Nijhoff, 1994).

Beede, Benjamin B., *The Small Wars of the United States, 1899–2009* (2nd ed., Routledge, 2010).

Bensimon, Fabrice, *L'Empire Brittanique* (PUF, col. « Que sais-je ? », 2013).

Benton, Elbert J., *International Law and Diplomacy of the Spanish-American War* (The Johns Hopkins Press, 1908).

Bermann, Karl, *Under the Big Stick. Nicaragua and the United States since 1848* (South End Press, 1986).

Bernard, Montague, *On the Orinciple of Non-intervention. A Lecture* (J. H. and Jas. Parker, 1860).

A Historical Account of the Neutrality of Britain during the American Civil War (Longmans, Green, Reader, and Dyer, 1870).

Birebent, Christian, *Militants de la paix er de la SDN. Les mouvements pacifistes de soutien à la Société des Nations en France et au Royaume-Uni 1918–1925* (L'Harmattan, 2007).

Bobbio, Norberto, *Essais de théorie du droit (recueil de textes)* (LGDJ, 1998).

Bourdieu, Pierre, *Outline of a Theory of Practice* (original ed.: 1972) (Cambridge University Press, 1977).

et Passeron, Jean-Claude, *Reproduction in Education, Society and Culture* (original ed.: 1970) (2nd ed., Sage Publications, 1990).

Pascalian Meditations (original ed.: 1997) (Stanford University Press, 2000).

Bowett, Derek W., *Self-Defence and International Law* (Manchester University Press, 1958).

Bowring, Bill, *The Degradation of the International Legal Order. The Rehabilitation of Law and the Possibility of Politics* (Routledge, 2008).

Brewer, David, *The Greek War of Independence. The Struggle for Freedom from the Ottoman Oppression* (Overlook Press, 2001).

Bridge, Francis R. and Bullen, Roger, *The Great Powers and the European State System, 1814–1914* (2nd ed., Pearson Longman, 2005).

Brierly, James L., *The Outlook for International Law* (Clarendon Press edition of 1945).

Brose, Eric Dorn, *German History 1789–1871. From the Holy Roman Empire to the Bismarckian Reich* (Berghahn Book, 1997).

Brownlie, Ian, *International Law and the Use of Force by States* (Clarendon Press, 1968).

Brunet de Presle, Charles-M.-W. et Blanchet, Alexandre, *Grèce depuis la conquête romaine jusqu'à nos jours* (Firmin Didot et frères, fils et cie., 1860).

Burkert, Walter, *Structure and History in Greek Mythology and Ritual* (University of California Press, 1979).

Burns, Adam, *American Imperialism: The Territorial Expansion of the United States, 1783–2013* (Edinburgh University Press, 2017).

Caplan, Richard, *A New Trusteeship? The International Administration of War-Torn Territories* (Routledge, 2002).

Carrai, Maria Adele, *Sovereignty in China. A Genealogy of the Concept since 1840* (Cambridge University Press, 2019).

Cassels, Alan, *Ideology and International Relations in the Modern World* (Routledge, 1996).

Chadwick, French Ensor, *The Relations of the United States and Spain. Diplomacy* (Charles Scribner's sons, 1909).

(de) Charnisay, Philippe, *L'insurrection hellénique et la diplomatie européenne* (A. Fayolles, 1904).

Chartier, Roger, *Au bord de la falaise. L'histoire entre inquiétude et certitude* (Albin Michel, 1998).

Chesterman, Simon, *Just War or Just Peace? Humanitarian Intervention and International Law* (Oxford University Press, 2002).

Christie, William Douglas, *Notes on the Brazilian Question* (McMillan 1865).

Churchill, Charles, *The Druzes and the Maronites under the Turkish Rule from 1840 to 1860* (Bernard Quadrich, 1862).

Clavin, Patricia, *Securing World Economy. The Reinvention of the League of Nations, 1920–1946* (Oxford University Press, 2013).

Coates, Benjamin Allen, *Legalist Empire. International Law and the American Foreign Relations in the Early Twentieth Century* (Oxford University Press, 2016).

Collins, Richard, *The Institutional Problem in Modern International Law* (Hart, 2016).

Corten, Olivier, *The Law against War: The Prohibition of the Use of Force in Contemporary International Law* (Hart, 2010).

Le droit contre la guerre (2nd ed., Pedone, 2014).

Cooper, Sandi E., *Patriotic Pacifism. Waging War on War in Europe, 1815–1914* (Oxford University Press, 1991).

Crawford, James, *The Creation of States in International Law* (Oxford Univertisy Press 2005).

Crawley, Charles W., *The Question of Greek Independence. A study of British policy in the Near East, 1821–1833* (Howard Fertig, 1973).

Culler, Jonathan, *On Deconstruction. Theory and Criticism after Structuralism* (Cornell University Press, 1982).

Dakin, Douglas, *The Greek Struggle for Independence, 1821–1833* (University of California Press, 1973).

Debibour, Antonin, *Histoire diplomatique de l'Europe*, 2 vols. (Felix Alcan, 1891).

De Lima, F. X., *Intervention in International Law, with reference to the organisation of American States* (Uitgeverij Pax Nederland, 1971).

Denieuil, Pierre-Noël, *Culture et société: intinéraire d'un sociologue* (L'Harmattan, 2008).

Derrida, Jacques, *Positions* (University of Chicago Press, 1981).

Margins of Philosophy (University of Chicago Press, 1982).

Deschanel, Paul, *La question du Tonkin* (Berger-Lerault, 1883).

Detter, Ingrid, *The Law of War* (2nd ed., Cambridge University Press, 2000).

Devine, Michael J., *Forster and the Struggle for the Annexation of Hawaii* (University of California Press, 1977).

Dickinson, Edwin de Witt, *The Equality of States in International Law* (Harvard University Press, 1920).

Dinstein, Yoram, *War, Aggression and Self-Defense* (6th ed., Cambridge University Press, 2011).

Doyle, Cathal M., *Indigenous Peoples, Title to Territory, Rights and Resources. The Transformative Role of Free, Prior and Informed Consent* (Routledge 2015).

Dufaux, Hermance, *Les Maronites et la France* (E. Dentu, 1860).

Dutoit, Bernard, *Co-existence et droit international à la lumière de la doctrine soviétique* (Pedone, 1966).

Dutreb, Maurice (Marthe Du Bert), *L'amiral Dupré et la conquête du Tonkin* (Société de l'histoire des colonies françaises, 1924).

Erpelding, Michel, *Le droit international anti-esclavagiste des 'nations civilisée" (1815–1845)* (Institut Universitaire de Varenne, 2017).

Esherick, Joseph W., *The Origins of the Boxer Uprising* (University of California Press, 1987).

Eyffinger, Arthur, *The 1899 Peace Conference. 'The Parliament of Man, the Federation of the World'* (Kluwer Law International, 1999).

Falk, Richard A., *The International Law of Civil War* (The Johns Hopkins Press, 1971).

Falcke, Horst P., *Le blocus pacifique* (Rossberg, 1919).

Farah, Caesar E., *The Politics of Interventionism in Ottoman Lebanon 1830–1861* (I. B. Tauris, 2000).

Fawaz, Leila Tarazi, *An Occasion for War. Civil Conflict in Lebanon and Damascus in 1860* (University of California Press, 1994).

Fenwick, Charles G., *The Neutrality Laws of the United States* (The Carnegie Endowment for International Peace, 1913).

Ferrer, Ada, *Insurgent Cuba. Race, Nations and Revolution, 1868–1898* (The University of North Carolina Press, 1999).

Festinger, Leon, *A Theory of Cognitive Dissonance* (Stanford University Press, 1957).

(with) Ricken, Henry W. and Schacter, Stanley, *When Prophecy Fails* (University of Minnesota Press, 1956).

Focarelli, Carlo, *International Law as a Social Construct* (Oxford University Press, 2012).

Foner, Philip S., *The Spanish-Cuban-American War and the Birth of American Imperialism*, 2 vols. (NYU Press, 1972).

Fowler, Wilton B., *British-American Relations 1917–1918: The Role of Sir William Wiseman* (Princeton University Press, 1969).

Ganji, Manouchehr, *International Protection of Human Rights* (Librairie E. Droz, 1962).

Garcia Arias, Luis, *Estudios de Historia y Doctrina del Derecho Internacional* (Instituto de Estudios Políticos, 1964).

García-Salmones Rovira, Mónica, *The Project of Positivism in International Law* (Oxford University Press, 2013).

Garner, James Wilford, *International Law and the World War*, 2 vols. (Longmans, Green & Co., 1920).

Glennon, Michael J., *Limits of Law, Prerogative of Power – Interventionism after Kosovo* (Palgrave Macmillan, 2001).

Goebel, Julius, *The Equality of States: A Study in History of Law* (Columbia University Press, 1923).

Goldfrank, David M., *The Origins of the Crimean War* (Routledge, 1994).

Gordley, Matthew E., *Teaching through Song in Antiquity: Didactic Hymnody Among Greeks, Romans, Jews and Christians* (Mohr Siebeck, 2011).

Goutmann, Alain, *La guerre de Crimée, 1853–1856* (SPM, 1995).

Goyard-Fabre, Simone, *Les embarras philosophiques du droit naturel* (J. Vrin, 2002).

Gralinski, Zygmunt, *Le règlement pacifique obligatoire des différends internationaux suivant le Pacte de la Société des Nations* (Pedone, 1925).

Gray, Christine, *International Law and the Use of Force* (3rd ed., Oxford University Press, 2008).

Grewe, Wilhelm G., *The Epochs of International Law* (Walter de Gruyter, 2000).

Grzybowski, Kazimierz, *Soviet Public International Law* (A. W. Stijhoff, 1970).

Guilhot, Nicolas, *The Democracy Makers: Human Rights and International Order* (Columbia University Press, 2005).

Halbwachs, Maurice, *La mémoire collective* (édition critique établie par Gérard Namer) (Albin Michel, 1997).

Hallett, Brien, *Les cadres sociaux de la mémoire* (Librairie Félix Alcan, 1925).

The Lost Art of Declaring War (University of Illinois Press, 1998).

Hansen, Lene, *Security as Practice. Discourse Analysis and the Bosnian War* (Routledge, 2006).

Harley, John E., *International Understanding. Agencies Educating for a New World* (Stanford University Press, 1931).

Hathaway, Oona and Shapiro, Scott *The Internationalists. How a Radical Plan to Outlaw War Remade the World* (Simon & Shuster, 2017).

Hébié, Mamadou, *Souveraineté territorial par traité. Une étude des accords entre puissances coloniales et entités politiques locales* (Presses Universitaire de France, 2015).

Hendel, Ronald, *Remembering Abraham: Culture, Memory and History in the Hebrew Bible* (Oxford University Press, 2005).

Hernandez, Gleider I., *The International Court of Justice and the Judicial Function* (Oxford University Press, 2014).

Hernandez, José M., *Cuba and the United States. Intervention and militarism, 1868–1933* (University of Texas Press, 1993).

Hewitt, Marsha Aileen, *Freud on Religion* (Routledge, 2014).

Higgins, Rosalyn, *Problems and Process. International Law and How We Use It* (Clarendon Press, 1994).

Hobsbawm, Eric, *The Age of Empire (1875–1914)* (Vintage Books, 1987).

Hoijer, Olof, *La solution pacifique des litiges internationaux avant et depuis la Société des Nations* (Edition Spes, 1925).

Le Pacte de la Société des Nations. Commentaire théorique et pratique (Editions Spes, 1926).

Holland, Thomas E., *The European Concert and the Eastern Question. A Collection of Treaties and Other Public Acts Edited with Introduction and Note* (Clarendon Press, 1885).

Holls, Frederick W., *The Peace Conference at The Hague, and Its Bearings on International Law and Policy* (The MacMillan Company, 1900).

Hsiung, James C., *Anarchy & Order. The Interplay of Politics and Law in International Relations* (Lynne Rienner Publishers, 1997).

Hsu, Immanuel C. Y., *The Rise of Modern China* (3rd ed., Oxford University Press, 1990).

Hudson, Mandley O., *The Permanent Court of International Justice. A Treatise* (The MacMillan Company, 1934).

Hull, William I., *The Two Hague Conferences, and Their Contribution to International Law* (Ginn & Company, 1908).

Hutton, Peter H., *The Memory Phenomenon in Contemporary Historical Writing* (Palgrave MacMillan, 2016).

Huzzey, Richard, *Freedom Burning. Anti-Slavery and Empire in Victorian Britain* (Cornell University Press, 2012).

Jacobini, H. B., *A Study of the Philosophy of International Law as Seen in Works of Latin American Writers* (Martinus Nijhoff, 1954).

Janis, Mark W., *America and the Law of Nations 1776–1939* (Oxford University Press, 2010).

Jarrett, Mark, *The Congress of Vienna and Its Legacy. War and Power Diplomacy after Napoleon* (Oxford University Press, 2014).

Johnson, Gaynor, *Lord Robert Cecil: Politician and Internationalist* (Routledge, 2013).

Jordan, Donaldson and Pratt, Edwin Judson, *Europe and the American Civil War* (Oxford University Press, 1931).

Jouannet, Emmanuelle, *The Liberal-Welfarist Law of Nations. A History of International Law* (Cambridge University Press, 2012).

Joyner, Christopher, *International Law in the 21st Century. Rules for Global Governance* (Rowman & Littlefield Publishers, 2005).

Kamakawiwo'ole Osorio, Jon, *Dismembering Lahui. A History of the Hawaiian Nation to 1887* (University of Hawaii Press, 2002).

Kamarowsky, Leonid, *Le Tribunal international* (Pedone, 1887).

Kelsen, Hans, *Collective Security Under International Law* (Government Printing Office, 1957).

Knight, Ian, *A Companion to the Anglo-Zulu War* (Pen & Sword Military, 2008).

Koch, H. W., *A History of Prussia* (Routledge, 2014).

Kolb, Robert, *Ius contra bellum. Le droit international relatif au maintien de la paix* (Bruylant, 2009).

Kolb, Robert, and Hyde, Richard, *An Introduction to the International Law of Armed Conflicts* (Hart Publishing, 2008).

Kooijmans, Pieter H., *The Doctrine of the Legal Equality of States: An Inquiry into the Foundations of International Law* (A. W. Stijhoff, 1964).

Kormanicki, Titus, *La question de l'intégrité territorial dans le Pacte de la Société des Nations* (Les presses universitaires de France, 1923).

Koskenniemi, Martti, *The Gentle Civilizer of Nations. The Rise and Fall of International Law, 1870–1960* (Cambridge: Cambridge University Press, 2001).

From Apology to Utopia. The Structure of International Legal Argument, (re-issue with new epilogue) (Cambridge University Press, 2005).

Kuehl, Warren F. and Dunne, Lynne K., *Keeping the Covenant. American Internationalists and the League of Nations, 1920–1939* (The Kent State University Press, 1997).

Kuykendall, Ralph S., *The Hawaiian Kingdom*, 3 vols. (Hawaii University Press, 1938).

La Fontaine, Henri, *The Great Solution. Magnissima Charta* (World Peace Foundation, 1916).

Laghmani, Slim, *Histoire du droit des gens du jus gentium impérial au jus publicum europeanum* (Pedone, 2003).

Laity, Paul, *The British Peace Movement 1870–1914* (Clarendon Press, 2001).

Lane, Jeremy F., *Pierre Bourdieu: A Critical Introduction* (Pluton Press, 2000).

Langley, Lester D., *The Banana Wars. United States Intervention in the Caribbean, 1898–1934* (SR Books, 2002).

Lansing, Robert, *The Peace Negotiations. A Personal Narrative* (Houghton Mifflin Company, 1921).

Lapenna, Ivo, *Conceptions soviétiques de droit international public* (Pedone, 1954).

(de) Lapradelle, Albert, *Maîtres et doctrines du droit des gens* (2nd ed., Editions internationales, 1950).

Laqua, Daniel, *The Age of Internationalism and Belgium, 1880–1930. Peace, Progress and Prestige* (Manchester University Press, 2015).

Laurent, Pierre, *Pufendorf et la loi naturelle* (Librarie Philosophique J. Vrin, 1982).

Lauterpacht, Hersh, *The Function of International Law in the International Community* (original ed.: 1933) (Oxford University Press, 2011).

Lazarus, Richard S., *Emotion and Adaptation* (Oxford University Press, 1991).

Lenormant, François, *Les derniers événements de Syrie* (Ch. Douniol, E. Dentu, 1860).

Lentacker, Antoine, *La science des institutions impures. Bourdieu critique Lévi-Strauss* (Editions Raison d'agir, *Coll. « Cours et travaux »*, 2010).

Lévi-Strauss, Claude, *Structural Anthropology* (original ed.: 1958) (Basic Books, 1963).

Lieblich, Eliav, *International Law and Civil Wars – Intervention and Consent* (Routledge, 2013).

Lind, Andrew W., *Hawaii's People* (4th ed., University Press of Hawaii, 1980).

(von) Litsz, Franz, *Le droit international. Exposé systématique* (Pedone, 1928).

Lloyd, Christopher, *The Navy and the Slave Trade: The Suppression of the African Slave Trade in the Nineteenth Century* (Routledge, 2012).

Lowry, John S., *Big Swords, Jesuits, and the Bondelswarts: Wilhelmine Imperialism, Overseas Resistance and German Political Catholicism* (Brill, 2015).

Mälksoo, Lauri, *Russian Approaches to International Law* (Oxford University Press, 2015).

Marchand, C. Roland, *The American Peace Movement and Social Reforms, 1898–1918* (Princeton University Press, 1972).

Marc-Lipiansky, Mireille, *Le structuralisme de Lévi-Strauss* (Payot, 1973).

Marriott, John A., *The Eastern Question. An Historical Study in European Diplomacy* (Clarendon Press, 1917).

Marrou, Henri-Irénée, *De la connaissance historique* (Editions du Seuil, 1954).

Maurice, J.F. (Brevet Lieutenant Colonel), *Hostilities Without Declaration of War* (H.M. Stationary Office 1883).

Mattéi, Jean-Mathieu, *Histoire du droit de la guerre (1700–1819)*, 2 vols. (Presses universitaire d'Aix-Marseille, 2006).

McCarthy, Helen, *The British People and the League of Nations. Democracy, Citizenship and Internationalism, c. 1918–1948* (Manchester University Press, 2011).

Mérighnac, Alexandre, *Traité théorique et pratique de l'arbitrage international* (L. Larose, 1895).

L'autonomie cubaine et le conflit hispano-américain (Chevalier-Marescq, 1898).

Merriam, Charles E., *History of the Theory of Sovereignty since Rousseau* (The Lawbook Exchange Ltd., 1999).

Miller, David H., *The Peace Pact of Paris. A Study of the Briand-Kellogg Pact* (G. P. Putnam's sons, 1928).

The Drafting of the Covenant, 2 vols. (G. P. Putnam's Sons, 1928).

Mol, Hans, *Identity and the Sacred. A Sketch for a New Social-Scientific Theory of Religion* (Free Press, 1976).

Moore, John Bassett, *The Principles of American Diplomacy* (Harper & Brother Publishers, 1918).

The Project of a Permanent Court of International Justice and Resolutions of the Advisory Committee of Jurists: Report and Commentary (The Carnegie Endowment, 1920).

Morales Domingez, Esteban and Prevost, Gary, *United States-Cuban Relations. A Critical History* (Lexington Books, 2008).

Morgan, Kenneth, *Slavery and the British Empire. From Africa to America* (Oxford University Press, 2007).

Morley, Felix, *The Society of Nations* (The Brookings Institution, 1932).

Mower, Edmund C., *International Government* (D. C. Heath and Company, 1931).

Munro, Dana G., *Intervention and Dollar Diplomacy in the Caribbean, 1900–1921* (Princeton University Press, 1964).

Murphy, Sean D., *Humanitarian Intervention. The United Nations in an Evolving World* (University of Pennsylvania, 1996).

Neff, Stephen C., *War and the Law of Nations. A General History* (Cambridge University Press, 2005).

Justice in Blue and Grey. A Legal History of Civil War (Harvard University Press, 2010).

Justice among Nations. A History of International Law (Harvard University Press, 2014).

Noel-Baker, Philip, *The Geneva Protocol: For the Pacific Settlement of International Disputes* (P.S. King and Sons, 1925).

Nussbaum, Arthur, *A Concise History of the Law of Nations* (MacMillan, 1947).

N'Zatioula Grovogui, Siba, *Sovereigns, Quasi-sovereigns, and Africans: Race and Self-Determination in International Law* (University of Minnesota Press, 1996).

Offner, John L., *An Unwanted War: The Diplomacy of the United States and Spain over Cuba, 1895–1898* (The University of North Carolina Press, 1992).

O'Flaherty, Wendy D., *Asceticism and Eroticism in the Mythology of Śiva* (Oxford University Press, 1973).

Ory, Pascal, *L'histoire culturelle* (Presses Universitaires de France, Coll. « Que sais-je ? », 2007).

Pélissier du Rausas, Gérard, *Le régime des capitulations dans l'Empire ottoman*, 2 vols. (Arthur Rousseau, 1905).

Perez, Louis A. Jr., *Cuba between Empires, 1878–1902* (University of Pittsburg Press, 1983).

Petrascu, Nicolas N., *Les mesures de contrainte internationale qui ne sont pas la guerre entre les Etats membres de la Société des Nations* (Jouve & Cie, 1927).

Pflanze, Otto, *Bismarck and the Development of Germany. The Period of Unification, 1815–1871*, 3 vols. (Princeton University Press, 1963).

Pillet, Antoine, *Les lois actuelles de la guerre* (Arthur Rousseau, 1898).

Recherches sur les droits fondamentaux des Etats dans l'ordre des rapports internationaux et des conflits qu'ils font naître (A. Pedone, 1899).

Le traité de paix de Versailles: conférences faites au Collège Libre des Sciences-sociales (Marcel Rivière et Cie., 1920).

Porter, Andrew, *The Oxford History of the British Empire*, 3 vols. (Oxford University Press, 1999).

Pouqueville, François, *Histoire de la régénération de la Grèce*, 3 vols. (Firmin Didot et frères, fils et cie., 1843).

Poyo, Gerald E., *"With All, and for the Good of All". The Emergence of Popular Nationalism in the Cuban Communities of the United States, 1848–1898* (Duke University Press, 1989).

Prost, Mario, *The Concept of Unity in International Law* (Hart Publishing, 2012).

Pustogarov, Vladimir V., *Our Martens. F. F. Martens International Lawyer and Architect of Peace* (edited and translated by W. E. Butler) (Kluwer Law International, 2000).

Ralston, Jackson H., *Democracy's International Law* (John Byrnes & Co., 1922).

International Arbitration from Athens to Locarno (Stanford University Press, 1929).

A Quest for International Order (John Byrnes and Company, 1941).

Redslob, Robert, *Histoire des grands principes du droit des gens depuis l'antiquité jusqu'à la veille de la Grande Guerre* (Rousseau & Cie. Éditeurs, 1923).

Reed-Danahay, Deborah, *Locating Bourdieu* (Indiana Universtiy Press, 2005).

Renault, Louis, *L'oeuvre de La Haye 1899 et 1907 (Conférence faite à l'Ecole libre des sciences politiques, le 5 juin 1908)* (Félix Alcan, 1908).

Renoliet, Jean-Jacques, *L'UNESCO oubliée. La Société des Nations et la coopération intellectuelle (1919–1946)* (Publication de la Sorbonne, 1999).

Rigaux, François, *Guerres et interventions dans le sud-est européen* (Editions A. Pedone, 2004).

Roberts, Anthea, *Is International Law International?* (Oxford University Press, 2017).

Robinson, Albert G., *Cuba and the Intervention* (Young People's Missionary Movement of the United States and Canada, 1910).

(de) Rochemonteix, Camille, *Le Liban et l'expédition française en Syrie (1860–1861)* (Librairie Auguste Picard, 1921).

Rodogno, Davide, *Against Massacre. Humanitarian Intervention in the Ottoman Empire, 1815–1914* (Princeton University Press, 2012).

Ronzitti, Natalino, *Rescuing Nationals Abroad through Military Coercion and Intervention on Grounds of Humanity* (Martinus Nijhoff, 1985).

Rubin, Herbert J. and Rubin, Irene, *Qualitative Interviewing: The Art of Hearing Data* (Sage, 1995).

Sainlaude, Stève, *Le gouvernement impérial et la guerre de sécession, 1861–1865: l'action diplomatique* (L'Harmattant, 2011).

Sánchez de Bustamente y Sirvén, Antonio, *La Cour permanente de Justice international* (Recueil Sirey, 1925).

Sauter, Johan, *Die philosophischen Grundlagen des Naturrechts* (J. Springer, 1932).

Schmitt, Carl, *The Nomos of the Earth in the International Law of Jus Publicum Europaeum* (Telos Press, 2003).

On the Three Types of Juristic Thought (Praeger Publishers, 2004).

Schücking, Walther und Wehberg, Hans, *Die Satzung des Völkerbundes*, 2 vols. (F. Vahlen, 1924).

Schulz, Matthias, *Normen und Praxis. Das Europäische Konzert der Großmächte als Sicherheitsrat, 1815–1860* (Oldenbourg Wissenschaftsverlag, 2009).

Schwarzenberger, Georg, *International Law and Order* (Stevens and Sons, 1971).

Šedivý, Miroslav, *The Decline of the Congress System. Metternich Italy and European Diplomacy* (I.B. Tauris, 2018).

Sellers, Mortimer, *New World Order; Sovereignty, Human Rights and Self-Determination of Peoples* (Berg Publishers, 1996).

Shinohara, Hatsue, *US International Lawyers in the Interwar Years. A Forgotten Crusade* (Cambridge University Press, 2012).

Simpson, Gerry, *Great Powers and Outlaw States: Unequal Sovereigns in the International Legal Order* (Cambridge University Press, 2004).

Skouteris, Thomas, *The Notion of Progress in International Law Discourse* (TMC Asser Press, 2010).

Small, Michael, *The Forgotten Peace. Mediation at Niagara Falls, 1914* (University of Ottawa Press, 2009).

Smith, Jospeh, *The Spanish-American War. Conflict in the Caribbean and the Pacific, 1895–1902* (Routledge, 1994).

Smith, Robert Sydney, *The Lagos Consulate, 1851–1861* (University of California Press, 1979).

Snyder, Louis Leo, and Brown, Ida Mae, *Bismarck and the Unification of Germany* (F. Watts, 1966).

Sohn, Louis B., and Buergenthal, Thomas, *International Protection of Human Rights* (The Bobbs-Merrill Company Inc., 1973).

Sontag, Susan, *Regarding the Pains of Others* (Picador, 2003).

Spagnolo, John P., *France and Ottoman Lebanon, 1861–1914* (Ithaca Press, 1977).

Stapleton, Augustus Granville, *Intervention and Non-Intervention or the Foreign Policy of Great Britain from 1790 to 1865* (Murray, 1866).

Stowell, Ellery C., *The Diplomacy of the War of 1914* (Houghton Mifflin Company, 1916).

Intervention in International Law (John Byrne & Co., 1921).

Tanca, Antonio, *Foreign Armed Intervention in Internal Conflict* (Martinus Nijhoff, 1993).

Tanoviceano, Jean, *De l'intervention au point de vue du droit international* (L. Larose et Forcel, 1884).

Taracouzio, Timothy A., *The Soviet Union and International Law* (The MacMillan Company, 1935).

Temperley, Harold, *The Foreign Policy of Canning 1822–1827 – England, the Neo-Holy Alliance, and the New World Order* (G. Bell and Sons, 1925).

England and the Near East. The Crimea (Longman Green & Co., 1936).

Temperley, Harold and Penson, Lilian, *Foundations of British Foreign Policy from Pitt (1792) to Salisbury (1902)* (Cambridge University Press, 1923).

Ternon, Yves, *Empire Ottoman: la chute, le déclin, l'effacement* (Editions du Félin, Michel de Maule, 2002).

Genèse du droit international. Des pères fondateurs aux conférences de la Haye (Editions Karthala, 2016).

Tesón, Fernando, *Humanitarian Intervention: An Inquiry Into Law and Morality* (Transational Publishers, 1988).

Thompson, Edward P., *Customs in Commons* (Penguin Books, 1993).

Tibori Szabó, Kinga, *Anticipatory Action in Self-Defence. Essence and Limits under International Law* (TMC Asser Press, Springer, 2011).

Tournaye, Cécile, *Kelsen et la sécurité collective* (LGDJ, 1995).

Trevor Royle, *Crimea: The Great Crimean War, 1854–1856* (Palgrave McMillan, 2000).

Triepel, Heinrich, *Droit international et droit interne* (French translation of the 1899 German ed.) (Pedone, 1920).

Van Hulle, Inge, *Britain and International Law in West Africa. Empire and Legal Experimentation* (Oxford University Press, 2020).

Venzke, Ingo, *How Interpretation Makes International Law. On Semantic Changes and Normative Twists* (Oxford University Press, 2012).

Verzijl, Jan H. W., *International law in Historical Perspective*, 5 vols. (A. W. Stijhoff, 1968).

Vincent, R. J., *Nonintervention and International Order* (Princeton University Press, 1974).

Visscher (de), Charles, *Théories et réalités en droit international public* (Pedone, 1955).

Vos, Jan Anne, *The Function of Public International Law* (Springer, 2013).

Walter (von), Christian, Ungern-Sternberg, Antje and Abushov, Kavus, *Self-Determination and Secession in International Law* (Oxford University Press, 2014).

Walters, Francis P., *A History of the League of Nations*, 2 vols. (Oxford University Press, 1952).

Wang, Dong, *China's Unequal Treaties. Narrating National History* (Lexington Books, 2008).

Ward, Adolphus W. and Gooch, George P., *The Cambridge History of British Foreign Policy (1783–1919)*, 3 vols. (Cambridge University Press, 1923).

Weber, Cynthia, *Simulating Sovereignty. Intervention, the State and the Symbolic Exchange* (Cambridge University Press, 1995).

Wheaton, Henry, *History of the Law of Nations in Europe and America* (Gould, Banks & Co., 1845).

White, Hayden, *Metahistory: The Historical Imagination in Nineteenth Century Europe* (The Johns Hopkins University Press, 1973).

Wilde, Ralph, *International Territorial Administration. How Trusteeship and the Civilizing Mission Never Went Away* (Oxford University Press, 2010).

Wisan, Joseph E., *The Cuban Crisis as Reflected in the New York Press (1895–1898)* (Columbia University Press, 1934).

Woolsey, Theodore S., *America's Foreign Policy. Essays and addresses* (The Century co., 1898).

Wright, Quincy, *A Study of War*, 2 vols. (University of Chicago Press, 1942).

Xiang, Lanxin, *The Origins of the Boxer War: A Multinational Study* (Routledge, 2003).

Yepes, J. M. et Pereira da Silva *Commentaire théorique et pratique du Pacte de la Société des Nations et des Statuts de l'Union Panaméricaine*, 3 vols. (Edition A. Pedone, 1934).

Zimmern, Alfred, *The League of Nations and the Rule of Law, 1917–1935* (MacMillan, 1939).

Zinn, Howard, *A People's History of the United States* (Longman, 1980)

Book Chapters

Abi-Saab, Georges, 'International Law and International Community: The Long Road to Universality,' in Ronald St. John MacDonald (ed.), *Essays in Honour of Wang Tieya* (Martinus Nijhoff Publishers, 1994), pp. 31–41.

Alvarez, Alejandro, 'Preface to Karl Strupp,' in *Eléments du droit international public universel, européen et américain* (Les Editions Internationales, 1930), vol. 1, pp. xvii–xxxi.

Augusti, Eliana, 'L'intervento europeo in Oriente nel XIX secolo: storia contesa di un instituto controverso,' in Vec (eds.), *Constructing International Law. The Birth of a Discipline* (Vittorio Klostermann, 2012), pp. 277–330.

Bailliet, Cecilia M. and Mujezinović Larsen, Kjetil, 'Introduction: Promoting Peace Through International Law,' in Cecilia M. Baillet and Kjetil Mujezinović Larsen (eds.), *Promoting Peace Through International Law* (Oxford University Press, 2015), pp. 1–18.

Becker Lorca, Arnulf, 'Eurocentrism in the History of International Law,' in Bardo Fassbender and Anne Peters (eds.), *The Oxford Handbook on the History of International Law* (Oxford University Press, 2012), pp. 1034–1057.

(von) Bernstorff, Jochen, 'International Legal History and Its Methodologies: How (not) to Tell the Story of the Many Lives and Deaths of ius ad bellum,' in Andres von Arnauld (ed.), *Völkerreschtgeschichten, Veröffentlichungen des Walter-Schücking-Instituts für Internationales Recht*, vol. 196, 2017, pp. 39–52.

Brownlie, Ian, 'Humanitarian Intervention,' in John Norton Moore (ed.), *Law and Civil War in the Modern Wolrd* (The Johns Hopkins University Press, 1974), pp. 217–228.

Buchanan, Allen, 'The Legitimacy of International Law,' in Samantha Bensson and John Tasioulas (eds.), *The Philosophy of International Law* (Oxford University Press, 2010), pp. 79–96.

Butler, William E., 'Some Reflections on the Periodization of Soviet Approaches to International Law,' in Donald D. Barry, William E. Butler and George Ginsburg (eds.), *Contemporary Soviet Law: Essays in Honor of John N. Hazard* (Martinus Nijhoff, 1974), pp. 213–225.

'On the History of International Law in England and Russia,' *in* William E. Butler (ed.), *The Non-Use of Force in International Law* (Martinus Nijhoff, 1989), pp. 3–16.

'Periodization and International Law,' in Alexander Orakhelashvili (ed.), *Research Handbook on the Theory and History of International Law* (Edward Elgar, 2011), pp. 379–393.

Cahin, Gérard, 'Traité-contrat et traité-loi à partir d'Heinrich Triepel,' in *Grandes pages du droit international* (Editions A. Pedone, 2016), vol. 2, pp. 21–54.

Capps, Patrick, 'Natural Law and the Law of Nations,' in Alexander Orakhelashvili (ed.), *Research Handbook on the Theory and History of International Law* (Edward Elgar, 2011), pp. 61–92.

Collins, Richard, 'Classical Legal Positivism in International Law Revisited,' in Jörg Kammerhofer and Jean d'Aspremont (eds.), *International Legal Positivism in a Post-Modern World* (Cambridge University Press, 2014), pp. 23–49.

Conforti, Benedetto, 'The Principle of Non-Intervention,' in Mohammed Bedjaoui (ed.), *International Law: Achievements and Prospects* (Martinus Nijhoff Publishers, 1991), pp. 467–482.

Conveinhes-Matsumoto, Florian, 'Les travaux préparatoires,' in Robert Kolb (ed.), *Commentaire sur le Pacte de la Société des Nations* (Bruylant, 2015), pp. 7–78.

'Hans Kelsen, « Théorie du droit international coutumier »,' in *Les Grandes pages du droit international* (Pedone, 2016), vol. 2, pp.103–181.

Corten, Olivier, 'Droit, force et légitimité dans une société internationale en mutation,' in *Le discours du droit. Pour un positivisme critique* (A. Pedone, CERDIN Coll. « Doctrine(s) », 2009), pp. 72–104.

'Les aspects idéologiques de la codification du droit international,' *Le discours du droit. Pour un positivisme critique* (A. Pedone, CERDIN Coll. « Doctrine (s) », 2009), pp. 153–172.

'Formalization and Deformalization as Narratives of the Law of War,' in José María Beneyto and David Kennedy (eds.), *New Approaches to International Law. The European and American Experiences* (T.M.C. Asser Press, 2012), pp. 253–257.

'Mais où est donc passée la Charte des Nations Unies ? Représentation et sous-représentation des règles sur l'usage de la force dans les films d'action,' in Olivier Corten and François Dubuisson (eds.), *Du droit international au cinema* (Pedone, 2015), pp. 89–127.

Craven, Matthew, 'Theorizing the Turn to History in International Law,' in Anne Orford and Florian Hoffman (eds.), *The Oxford Handbook of the Theory of International Law* (Oxford University Press, 2016), pp. 21–37.

Crawford, James and Nicholson, Rowan, 'The Continued Relevance of the Established Rules and Institutions Relating to the Use of Force,' in Marc Weller (ed.), *The Oxford Handbook on the Use of Force in International Law* (Oxford University Press, 2015), pp. 96–113.

Deer, Cécile, 'Doxa,' in Michael Greenfell (ed.), *Pierre Bourdieu: Key Concepts* (Acumen, 2008), pp. 114–130.

et Delcourt, Barbara, « Droit, légitimation et politique extérieure: précisions théoriques et méthodologiques », in Olivier Corten et Barbara Delcourt (dirs.), *Droit, légitimation et politique extérieure: l'Europe et la Guerre du Kosovo* (Bruylant, 2001), pp. 19–30.

Diggelmann, Oliver, 'The Periodization of the History of International Law,' in Bardo Fassbender and Anne Peters (eds.), *The Oxford Handbook on the History of International Law* (Oxford University Press, 2012), pp. 997–1011.

Dostian, I., 'L'attitude de la société russe face au mouvement de librération national grec,' in *Les relations gréco-russe pendant la domination turque et la guerre d'indépendance grecque*, Actes du colloque tenu à Thessalonique (23–25 Septembre 1981) (Institute for Balkan Studies, 1983), pp. 63–84.

Druelle-Korn, Clothilde, 'The Great War: Matrix of the International Chamber of Commerce, a Fortunate Business League of Nations,' in Andrew Smith, Simon Mollan and Kevin D. Tennent (eds.), *The Impact of the First World War on International Business* (Routledge, 2016), pp. 103–120.

Dunn, Kevin C., 'Historical Representations,' *in* Audie Klotz and Deepa Prakash (eds.), *Qualitatives Methods of International Relations* (Palgrave, 2008), pp. 78–92.

Flynch, Cecelia, 'Peace Movements, Civil Society, and the Development of International Law,' in Bardo Fassbender and Anne Peters (eds.), *The Oxford Handbook of the History of International Law* (Oxford University Press, 2012), pp. 198–221.

Forchtner, Bernhard, 'Historia Magistra Vitae: The Topos of History as a Teacher in Public Struggles over *Self* and *Other* Representation,' in Christopher Hart and Piotr Cap (eds.), *Contemporary Critical Discourse Studies* (Bloomsbury, 2014), pp. 19–44.

Foucault, Michel, 'The Order of Discourse,' in Robert Young (ed.), *Untying the Text: A Post-Structuralist Reader* (Routledge, 1981), pp. 51–78.

Fox, Gregory H., 'Intervention by Invitation,' in Marc Weller (ed.), *The Oxford Handbook of the Use of Force in International Law* (Oxford University Press, 2015), pp. 816–840.

Glennon, Michael J., 'The Limitations of the Traditional Rules and Institutions Relating to the Use of Force,' in Marc Weller (ed.), *The Oxford Handbook on the Use of Force in International Law* (Oxford University Press, 2015), pp. 79–95.

Goldfrank, David M., 'Policy Traditions and the Menshikov Mission,' in Hugh Ragsdale (ed.), *Imperial Russian Foreign Policy* (Cambridge University Press, 1993), pp. 119–158.

Gray, Christine, 'The Use of Force for Humanitarian Purposes,' in Nigel D. White and Christian Henderson (eds.), *Research Handbook on International Conflict and Security Law* (Edward Elgar, 2013), pp. 229–255.

Grbich, Judith, 'Secrets of Fetish in International Law's messianism,' in Anne Orford (ed.), *International Law and Its Other* (Cambridge University Press, 2006), pp. 197–220.

Guieu, Jean-Michel, « Les juristes français, la SdN et l'Europe », in Jacques Bariety (dir.), *Aristide Briand, la SdN et l'Europe, 1919–1932* (Presses Universitaires de Strasbourg, 2007), pp. 185–199.

Guintella, Maria-Cristina, 'Enseignement de l'histoire et révision des manuels scolaire dans l'entre-deux-guerres,' in Marie-Christine Basques, Annie Bruter et Nicole Tutiaux-Guillon (dirs.), *Pistes didactiques et chemins d'historiens. Textes offerts à Henri Moniot* (L'Harmattant, 2003), pp. 161–189.

Haggenmacher, Peter, 'Grotius and Gentili: a Reassement of Thomas E. Holland Inaugural Lecture 1,' in Hedley Bull, Benedict Kingsbury and Adam Roberts (eds.), *Hugo Grotius and International Relations* (Clarendon Press, 1990), pp. 133–176.

Hamamoto, Shotaro, 'A propos de deux clichés sur l'histoire du droit international en Asie de l'Est,' in Pierre-Marie Dupuy et Vincent Chetail (dirs.), *The Roots of International Law/Les fondements du droit international – Liber Amicorum Peter Haggenmacher* (Martinus Nijhoff, 2013), pp. 743–756.

Hayes, Carlton J. H., 'The Historical Background,' in Stephen Pierce Duggan (ed.), *The League of Nations. The Principles and the Practice* (The Atlantic Press, 1919), pp. 18–49.

Holzgrefe, J. L., 'The Humanitarian Intervention Debate,' in J. L. Holzgrefe and Robert O. Keohane (eds.), *Humanitarian Intervention. Ethical, Legal and Political Dilemmas* (Cambridge University Press, 2003), pp. 15–52.

Jouannet, Emmanuelle, 'Présentation critique,' in Martti Koskenniemi, *La politique du droit international* (Pedone, Coll. « Doctrine(s) », 2007), pp. 7–46.

Kattago, Siobhan, 'Introduction: Memory Studies and Its Companions,' in Siobhan Kattago (ed.), *The Ashagate Companion to Memory Studies* (Routledge, 2015), pp. 1–19.

Kemmerer, Alexandra, 'Turning Aside: On International Law and Its History,' in Russell L. Miller and Rebecca M. Bratspies (eds.), *Progress in International Law* (Martinus Nijhoff, 2008), pp. 71–93.

Kessedjian, Catherine, 'Culture et droit: influence de la culture sur le droit international et ses developments,' in Paul Meerts (ed.), *Culture and International Law* (TMC Asser Press, 2008), pp. 23–42.

Kingsbury, Benedict and Robert, Adam, 'Introduction: Grotian Thought in International Relations,' in Hedley Bull, Benedict Kingsbury and Adam Robert (eds.), *Hugo Grotius and International Relations* (Clarendon Press, 1990), pp. 1–64.

Klein, Pierre, 'Le droit aux élections libres en droit international: mythes et réalités,' in Olivier Corten et al. (dirs.), *A la recherché du nouvel ordre mondial. Le droit international à l'épreuve* (Editions Complexe, 1993), pp. 93–121.

Kolb, Robert, 'La légitime défense et les Etats au XIXe siècle et pendant l'époque de la Société des Nations,' in Robert Kolb (dir.), *Commentaire du Pacte de la Société des Nations* (Bruylant, 2014), pp. 1299–1330.

Koskenniemi, Martti, 'Between Committment and Cynicism: Outline for a Theory of International Law as Practice,' in United Nations, Office of Legal Affairs (ed.), *Collection of Essays by Legal Advisers of States, Legal Advisers of International Organisations and Practitionners in the Field of International Law* (United Nations Publication, 1999), pp. 495–523.

'What Is International Law For?,' in Malcolm D. Evans (ed.), *International Law* (Oxford University Press, 2003), pp. 89–114.

'The Ideology of International Adjudication and the 1907 Hague Conference,' in Yves Daudet (ed.), *Topicality of the 1907 Hague Conference, the Second Peace Conference* (Martinus Nijhoff, 2008), pp. 127–152.

'The Legacy of the Nineteenth Century,' in David Armstrong (ed.), *Routledge Handbook of International Law* (Routledge, 2009), pp. 141–153.

'Hersch Lauterpacht,' in Jack Beatson and Reinhard Zimmermann (eds.), *Jusrists Uprooted: German-Speaking Emigré Lawyers in Twentieth Century Britain* (Oxford University Pess, 2010), pp. 601–661.

'International Law and the Development of Mercantile Capitalism,' in Pierre-Marie Dupuy et Vincent Chetail (dirs.), *The Roots of International Law/Les fondements du droit international – Liber Amicorum Peter Haggenmacher* (Martinus Nijhoff, 2013), pp. 3–37.

'Carl Schmitt and International Law,' in Jens Meierhenrich and Oliver Simons (eds.), *The Oxford Handbook of Carl Schmitt* (Oxford University Press, 2017), pp. 592–611.

Lagerwall, Anne, 'Threats of and Actual Military Strikes against Syria – 2013 and 2017,' in Tom Ruys and Olivier Corten (eds.), *International Law and the Use of Force: A Case-Based Approach* (Oxford University Press, 2018), pp. 828–854.

Law, Robin 'International Law and the British Suppression of the Atlantic Slave Trade,' in Derek Peterson, *Abolitionism and Imperialism in Great Britain* (Cambridge University Press, 2010), pp. 150–174.

Legg, Stephen, 'Interwar Spatial Chaos? Imperialism, Internationalism and the League of Nations,' in Stephen Legg (ed.), *Spatiality, Sovereignty and Carl Schmitt: Geographies of the Nomos* (Routledge, 2011), pp. 106–122.

Lesaffer, Randall, 'International Law and Its History: The Story of an Unrequited Love,' in Matthew Craven, Malgosia Fitzmaurice and Maria Vogiatzi (eds.), *Time, History and International Law* (Martinus Nijhoff, 2007), pp. 27–41.

'Too Much History: From War as Sanction to the Sanctioning of War,' in Marc Weller (ed.), *The Oxford Handbook on the Use of Force in International Law* (Oxford University Press, 2015), pp. 35–55.

'Peace through Law. The Hague Conferences and the Rise of *ius contra bellum*,' in Maartje Abbenhuis, Christopher Ernest Barber and Annalise R. Higgins (eds.), *War, Peace and International Order? The Legacies of the Hague Conferences of 1899 and 1907* (Routledge, 2017), pp. 31–51.

Lillich, Richard B., 'Humaniatrian Intervention: A Reply to Ian Brownlie and a Plea for a Constructive Alternative,' in John Norton Moore (ed.), *Law and*

Civil War in the Modern Wolrd (The Johns Hopkins University Press, 1974), pp. 229–251.

Lobban, Michael, 'English Approaches to International Law in the Nineteenth Century,' in Matthew Craven, Malgosia Fitzmaurice and Maria Vogiatzi (eds.), *Time, History and International Law* (Martinus Nijhoff Publishers, 2007), pp. 65–90.

Mégret, Frédéric, 'International Law as Law,' in James Crawford and Martti Koskenniemi (eds.), *The Cambridge Companion to International Law* (Cambirdge University Press, 2012), pp. 64–92.

Migliori, Margarita, 'Europe, the Classical Polis, and the Greek Nation: Philhellenism and Hellenism in Nineteenth Century Britain,' in Roderick Beaton and David Ricks (eds.), *The Making of Modern Greece* (Ashgate, 2009), pp. 65–77.

Narotchnitzki, A. L. 'La diplomatie russe et la préparation de la conférence de Saint-Pétersbourg sur la Grèce en 1824,' *Les relations gréco-russe pendant la domination turque et la guerre d'indépendance grecque*, Actes du colloque tenu à Thessalonique (23–25 Septembre 1981) (Institute for Balkan Studies, 1983), pp. 87–97.

Neff, Stephen C., « Introduction », in *Hugo Grotius. On the Laws of War and Peace* (edited and annotated by Stephen C. Neff) (Cambridge Unversity Press, 2012), pp. xiii–xxxv.

'Jurisprudential Polyphony: The Three Variations on the Positivist Theme in the 19th Century,' in Pierre-Marie Dupuy et Vincent Chetail (dirs.), *The Roots of International Law/Les fondements du droit international – Liber Amicorum Peter Haggenmacher* (Martinus Nijhoff, 2013), pp. 301–334.

'A Short History of International Law,' *in* Malcolm D. Evans (ed.), *International Law* (4th ed., Oxford University Press, 2014), pp. 3–28.

Neumann, Iver B., 'Discourse Analysis,' in Audie Klotz and Deepa Prakash (eds.), *Qualitatives Methods of International Relations* (Palgrave, 2008), pp. 61–77.

Nolte, Georg, 'Secession and External Intervention,' in Marcelo Kohen (ed.), *Secession. International Law Perspective* (Cambridge University Press, 2006), pp. 65–93.

Noyes, John E., 'Christianity and Theories of International Law in Nineteenth-Century Britain,' in Mark W. Janis and Carolyn Evans (eds.), *Religion and International Law* (Martinus Nijhoff Publishers, 1999), pp. 235–258.

O'Connell, Mary Ellen, 'War and Peace,' in Bardo Fassbender and Anne Peters (eds.), *The Oxford Handbook on the History of International Law* (Oxford University Press, 2012), pp. 272–293.

'The Prohibition of the Use of Force,' in Nigel D. White and Christian Henderson (eds.), *The Research Handbook on International Conflict and Security Law* (Edward Elgar, 2013), pp. 89–119.

Orakhelashvili, Alexander, 'The Origins of Consensual Positivism: Pufendorf, Wolff and Vattel,' in Alexander Orakhelashvili (ed.), *Research Handbook on the Theory and History of International Law* (Edward Elgar, 2011), pp. 93–110.

Orford, Anne, 'Constituting Order,' in James Crawford and Martti Koskenniemi (eds.), *The Cambridge Companion to International Law* (Cambridge University Press, 2012), pp. 271–289.

'International Law and the Limits of History,' in Wouter Werner, Alexis Galán and Marieke de Hoon (eds.), *The Law of International Lawyers: Reading Martti Koskenniemi* (Cambridge University Press, 2017), pp. 297–320.

Özsu, Umut, 'Ottoman Empire,' in Bardo Fassbender and Anne Peters (eds.), *Oxford Handbo ok on the History of International Law* (Oxford University Press, 2012), pp. 429–448.

Perez, Louis A. Jr. 'Cuba. Sugar and Independence,' in Thomas M. Leonard (ed.), *United States-Latin American Relations, 1850–1903* (University of Alabama Press, 1999), pp. 35–57.

Perreau-Saussine, Amanda, 'Three Ways of Writing A Treatise on Public International Law: Textbooks and the Nature of Customary International Law,' in Amanda Perreau-Saussine and James B. Murphy (eds.), *The Nature of Customary Law. Legal, Historical and Philosophical Perspective* (Cambridge University Press, 2007), pp. 228–255.

Pouliot, Vincent, 'Methodology. Putting Practice Theory into Practice,' in Rebecca Adler-Nissen (ed.), *Bourdieu in International Relations. Rethinking Key Concept in IR* (Routledge, 2013), pp. 45–58.

Randelzhofer, Albrecht, 'Article 2 (4),' in Bruno Simma (ed.), *The Charter of the United Nations: A Commentary* (2nd ed., Oxford University Press, 2002), vol. 1, pp. 112–136.

Reisman, Michael, and McDougal, Myres 'Humanitarian Intervention to Protect the Ibos' in Richard B. Lillich, *Humanitarian Intervention and the United Nations* (University of Virginia Press, 1973), pp. 167–196.

Rodley, Nigel, 'Humanitarian Intervention,' in Marc Weller (ed.), *The Oxford Handbook on the Use of Force* (Oxford University Press, 2015), pp. 775–796.

Rodogno, Davide, 'The 'Principles of Humanity' and the European Powers' Intervention in Ottoman Lebanon and Syria in 1860–1861,' in Brendan Simms and D. J. B. Trim (eds.), *Humanitarian Intervention. A History* (Cambirdge University Press, 2011), pp. 159–183.

Salmon, Jean, 'Vers l'adoption d'un principe de légitimité démocratique?,' in Olivier Corten et al. (dirs.), *A la recherché du nouvel ordre mondial. Le droit international à l'épreuve* (Editions Complexe, 1993), pp. 59–89.

Santulli, Carlo, 'Quels sont les pères volontaristes du droit international? Anzilotti et Triepel,' in *Grandes pages du droit international* (Pedone, 2016), vol. 2, pp. 5–19.

Schatz, Edward, 'What Kind(s) of Ethnograpy Does Political Science Need?,' in Edward Schatz (ed.), *Political Ethnography: What Immersion Contributes to the Study of Power* (Chicago University Press, 2009), pp. 303–318.

Schrijver, Nico, 'Article 2, paragraphe 4,' in Jean-Pierre Cot et Alain Pellet (dirs.), *La Charte des Nations Unies. Commentaires articles par articles* (3e ed., Economica, 2005), pp. 437–466.

Skouteris, Thomas, 'Engaging History in International Law,' in José María Beneyto and David Kennedy (eds.), *New Approaches to International Law. The European and American Experiences* (T.M.C. Asser Press, 2012), pp. 99–121.

Skubiszewski, Krzysztof, 'Use of Force by States,' in Max Sørensen (ed.), *Manual of Public International Law* (MacMillan, 1968), pp. 739–854.

Storti, Claudia, 'Empirismo e scienza: il crocevia del diritto internazionale nelle prima metà dell'Ottocento,' in Luigi Nuzzo and Milos Vec (eds.), *Constructing International Law. The Birth of a Discipline* (Vittorio Klostermann, 2012), pp. 51–145.

Stråth, Bo, 'Perpetual Peace as Irony, as Utopia, and as Politics,' in Thomas Hippler and Miloš Vec (eds.), *Paradoxes of Peace in the Nineteenth Century Europe* (Oxford University Press, 2015), pp. 261–284.

Swiggers, Pierre, 'Le mythe: vers une topologisation structurelle « profonde »,' *in* Christophe Vielle, Pierre Swiggers et Guy Jucquois (dirs.), *Comparatisme, Mythologies, Langages. En hommage à Claude Lévi-Strauss* (Petters, 1994), pp. 23–31.

Tamm, Marek, 'Introduction: Afterlife of Events: Perspectives on Mnemohistory" in Marek Tamm (ed.), *Afterlife of events: Perspectives on Mnemohistory* (Palgrave MacMillan, 2015), pp. 3–23.

Tasioulas, John, 'The Legitimacy of International Law,' in Samantha Benson and John Tasioulas (eds.), *The Philosophy of International Law* (Oxford University Press, 2010), pp. 97–116.

Tourme-Jouannet, Emmanuelle, 'Des origines coloniales du droit international: à propos du droit des gens moderne au XVIIIe siècle,' in Pierre-Marie Dupuy et Vincent Chetail (eds.), *The Roots of International Law/Les fondements du droit international – Liber Amicorum Peter Haggenmacher* (Martinus Nijhoff, 2013), pp. 649–671.

'The Critique of Classical Thought during the Interwar Period. Vattel and Van Vollenhoven,' in Anne Orford and Florian Hoffmann (eds.), *The Oxford Handbook on the Theory of International Law* (Oxford Univerity Press, 2016), pp. 101–122.

Vec, Miloš, 'From Invisible Peace to the Legitimation of War. Paradoxes of a Concept in Nineteenth Century International Law Doctrine,' in Thomas Hippler and Miloš Vec (eds.), *Paradoxes of Peace in the Nineteenth Century Europe* (Oxford University Press, 2015), pp. 19–36.

Verdebout, Agatha, 'Article 10,' in Robert Kolb (dir.), *Commentaire sur le Pacte de la Société des Nations* (Bruylant, 2014), pp. 425–446.

Verga, Marcelo, 'Manuels d'histoire pour la paix en Europe,' in Marta Petricioli and Donnatella Cherubini (eds.), *For Peace in Europe. Institutions and Civil Society between the World Wars* (PIE Peter Lang, 2007), pp. 503–524.

Verosta, Stephan, 'The Unlawfulness of Wars of Aggression Before 1914,' in Emmanuel G. Bello and Prince Bola A. Ajibola, *Essays in Honour of Judge Taslim Olawale Elias* (Martinus Nijhoff, 1992), vol. 1, pp. 117–124.

Viraly, Michel, 'Sur la prétendue « primitivité du droit international,' in *Le droit international en devenir* (Graduate Institute Publications, 1990), pp. 91–101.

Vité, Sylvain, 'Article 12,' in Robert Kolb (ed.), *Commentaire sur le Pacte de la Société des Nations* (Bruylant, 2015), pp. 555–570.

Wright, Quincy 'The American Civil War, 1861–1865,' in Richard A. Falk (ed.), *The International Law of Civil War* (John Hopkins University Press, 1971), pp. 30–110.

Wyler, Eric, 'La Paix par le droit. Entre réalité, mythe et utopie,' in Laurence Boisson de Chazournes et Marcelo Kohen (eds.), *International Law and the Quest for Its Implementation / Le droit international et la quête de sa mise en œuvre. Liber Amicorum Vera Gowlland-Debbas* (Brill, 2010), pp. 467–488.

'L'influence du positivisme sur la doctrine volontariste et objectiviste en droit international: plus qu'un facteur de rapprochement?,' in Pierre-Marie Dupuy et Vincent Chetail (eds.), *The Roots of International Law/Les fondements du droit international - Liber Amicorum Peter Haggenmacher* (Martinus Nijhoff, 2013), pp. 335–364

Articles

Adekoya, Preye, 'The Succession Dispute to the Throne of Lagos and the British Conquest and Occupation of Lagos" (2016) 10 *African Research Review* 207–226.

Allott, Philip, 'International Law and the Idea of History' (1999) 1 *Journal of the History of International Law* 1–21.

Altwicker, Tilman and Diggelmann, Oliver, 'How Progress Is Constructed in International Legal Scholarship' (2014) 25 *European Journal of International Law* 425–444.

Anghie, Antony, 'Finding the Peripheries: Sovereignty and Colonialism in Nineteenth Century International Law' (1999) 40 *Harvard Law Review* 1–80.

Angrili, Alessandro, Cherubini, Paolo, Pavese, Antonella and Manfredini, Sara, 'The Influence of Affective Factors on Time Perception' (1997) 59 *Perception & Psychophysics* 972–982.

Arcidiacono, Bruno, 'La paix par le droit international dans la vision de deux juristes du XIXe siècle: le débat Lorimer-Bluntschli' (2012) 149 *Relations internationales* 13–26.

Armstrong, S. W., 'The Doctrine of the Equality of Nations in International Law and the Relation of the Doctrine to the Treaty of Versailles' (1920) 14 *American Journal of International Law* 540–564.

Assmann, Aleida, 'Transformations between History and Memory' (2008) 75 *Social Research* 49–72.

Assmann, Jan, 'Collective Memory and Cultural Identity' (1995) 65 *New German Critique* 125–133.

Atwicker, Tilmann and Diggelmann, Oliver, 'How Is Progress Constructed in International Legal Scholarship?' (2014) 25 *European Journal of International Law* 425–444.

Auxier, George W., 'The Propaganda Activities of the Cuban Junta in Precipitating the Spanish-American War, 1895–1898' (1939) 19 *The Hispanic American Historical Review* 286–305.

Baldwin, Simeon E., 'The Evolution of a World Court' (1921) 1 *Boston University Law Review* 6–12.

Balkin, Jack M., 'Deconstructive Practice and Legal Theory' (1989) 96 *Yale Law Journal* 743–791.

Bandeira Galindo, George Rodrigo, 'Martti Koskenniemi and the Historiographical Turn in International Law' (2005) 16 *European Journal of International Law* 539–559.

Barry, Benjamin M., 'Unilateral Humanitarian Intervention: Legalizing the Use of Force to Prevent Human Atrocities' (1992) 16 *Fordham International Law Journal* 120–158.

Batakovic, Dušan T., 'Storm Over Serbia. The Rivalry between Civilian and Military Authorities (1911–1914)' (2003) 44 *Balcanica* 307–356.

Bechet, Christophe, 'La révision pacifiste des manuels scolaire. Les enjeux de la mémoire de la guerre 14–18 dans l'enseignement belge de l'Entre-deux-guerres' (2008) 20 *Cahier d'histoire du temps présent* 49–101.

Behuniak, Thomas E. (Capt.), 'The Law of Unilateral Humanitarian Intervention by Armed Force: A Legal Survey' (1978) 79 *Military Law Review* 157–191.

Bell, Duncan, Writing the World: Disciplinary History and Beyond' (2009) 85 *International Affairs* 3–22.

Bello, Judith H. and Holmer, Alan F., 'After the Cold War: Whither International Economic Law' (1991) 32 *Harvard International Law Journal* 323–330.

Bernard, Nadine, 'Henri La Fontaine (1854–1943) ou la paix par le droit' (1995) 31 *Revue belge de droit international* 343–356.

Bingham, Tom, 'The Alabama Claims Arbitration' (2005) 54 *International and Comparative Law Quarterly* 1–25.

Birebent, Christophe, 'Le Groupement universitaire pour la Société des Nations face aux crises des années trente' (2004) 74 *Matériaux pour l'histoire de notre temps* 14–19.

Birkett, Mary Ellen, 'Forging French Colonial Policy in the Pacific' (2007) 8 *French Colonial History* 155–169.

Birn, Donald S., 'The League of Nations Union and Collective Security' (1974) 9 *Journal of Contemporary History* 131–159.

Blake, Jillian and Mahmud, Aqsa, 'A Legal 'Red Line'?: Syria and the Use of Chemical Weapons in Civil Conflict' (2013) 61 *UCLA Law Review Discourse* 244–260.

Blair, Scott G., 'Les origines en France de la SDN. La Commission interministérielle d'étude pour la Société des Nations 1917–1919' (1993) 75 *Relations internationales* 277–292.

Blue, George Verne, 'The Project for a French Settlement in the Hawaiian Islands, 1824–1842' (1933) 2 *Pacific Historical Review* 85–99.

Bluntschli, Johan-Caspar, 'Droit de la guerre et coutume de guerre. A propos de des attaques du Colonel Von Rustow contre le droit des gens' (1876) 8 *Revue de droit international et de législation comparée* 663–672.

Boltz, Blandine, 'La conquête de Tourane, 1858–1860. L'expérience d'une défaite coloniale au Vietnam' (2019) 49 *Bulletin de l'Institut Pierre Renouvin* 17–27.

Borchard, Edwin M., 'The Mutlilateral Treaty for the Renunciation of War' (1929) 23 *American Journal of International Law* 116–120.

Bowden, Brett, 'The Colonial Origins of International Law. European Expansion and the Classical Standard of Civilization' (2005) 7 *Journal of the History of International Law* 1–24.

Brilmayer, Lea, 'The Odd Advantage of Reliable Enemies' (1991) 32 *Harvard International Law Journal* 331–338.

Brusa, Emilio, 'La Conférence de La Haye et ses résultats. Opinion' (1900) *Revue générale de droit international public* 237–255.

Carnazza-Amari, Giuseppe, 'Nouvel exposé du principe de non-intervention' (1873) 5 *Revue de droit international et de législation comparée* 352–389.

Caron, David D., 'War and International Adjudication: Reflections on the 1899 Peace Conference' (2000) 94 *American Journal of International Law* 4–30.

Carty, Anthony, 'Critical International Law: Recent Trends in the Theory of International Law' (1991) 2 *European Journal of International Law* 1–27.

'Carl Schmitt's Critique of Liberal International Legal Order between 1933 and 1945' (2001) 14 *Leiden Journal of International Law* 25–76.

Chartier, Roger, 'Le monde comme representation' (1989) 44 *Annales. Economies, Sociétés, Civilisations* 1505–1520.

Chilstrom, Robert Meade 'Humanitarian Intervention Under Contemporary International Law: A Policy-Oriented Approach' (1974) 1 *Yale Journal of International Law* 93–147.

Chimni, B. S., 'Capitalism, Imperialism, and International Law in the Twenty-First Century' (2012) 14 *Oregon Review of International Law* 17–45.

Chopin, Alain, 'L'histoire des manuels scolaires: un approche globale' (1980) 9 *Histoire de l'éducation* 1–25.

Christakis, Théodore et Bannelier, Karine, '*Volenti non fit injuria*? Les effets du consentement à l'intervention militaire' (2004) 50 *Annuaire français de droit international* 102–137.

Craven, Matthew, 'What Happened to Unequal Treaties? The Continuities of Informal Empire' (2005) 74 *Nordic Journal of International Law* 335–382.

Confino, Alon, 'Collective Memory and Cultural History: Problems of Method' (1997) 102 *American Historical Review* 1386–1403.

Cooper, Joel and Mackie, Diane, 'Cognitive Dissonance in an Intergroup Context' (1983) 44 *Journal of Personality and Social Psychology* 536–544.

Cope, R. L., 'Local Imperatives and Imperial Policy: The Sources of Lord Carnarvon's South African Confederation Policy' (1987) 20 *The International Journal of African Historical Studies* 601–626.

Corten, Olivier, 'Droit, force et légitimité dans une société internationale en mutation' (1996) 37 *Revue interdisciplinaire d'études juridiques* 71–112.

'La persistance de l'argument légaliste. Eléments pour une typologie contemporaine des registres de légitimité dans une société libérale' (2002) 50 *Droit et société* 185–203.

'The Controversies Over the Customary Prohibition on the Use of Force: A Methodological Debate' (2005) 16 *European Journal of International Law* 803–822.

et Verdebout, Agatha, 'Les interventions militaires récentes en térritoire étranger: vers une remise en cause du jus contra bellum?' (2014) 60 *Annuaire français de droit international* 135–169.

'The 'Unwilling or Unable' Theory: Has It Been, and Could It Be, Accepted?' (2016) 29 *Leiden Journal of International Law* 777–799.

'L'argumentation des Etats européens pour justifier une intervention militaire contre l' "Etat islamique" en Syrie: vers une reconfiguration de la notion de légitime défense?' (2016) 49 *Revue belge de droit international* 31–67.

Cossman, Brenda, 'Reform, Revolution, or Retrenchment – International Human Rights in the Post-Cold War Era' (1991) 32 *Harvard International Law Journal* 339–354.

Cunningham, Allan, 'The Philhellenes, Canning and Greek Independence' (1978) 14 *Middle Eastern Studies* 151–181.

Curry, Georges, 'Woodrow Wilson, Jan Smuts, and the Versailles Settlement' (1961) 66 *The American Historical Review* 968–986.

Cutler, A. Claire, 'The Grotian Tradition in International Relations' (1991) 17 *Review of International Studies* 41–65.

Danilenko, Gennady M., 'The Changing Structure of International Law: Constitutional Implications' (1991) 32 *Harvard International Law Journal* 353–362.

David, Eric 'Portée et limite du principe de non-intervention' (1990) 26 *Revue belge de droit international* 351–367.

Davison, Roderic H., 'Russian Skill and Turkish Imbecility": The Treaty of Kuchuk Kainardji Reconsidered' (1976) 35 *Slavic Review* 463–483.

Despagnet, Franz, 'La Conférence de La Haye et ses résultats. Opinon' (1900) *Revue générale de droit international public* 215–234.

Dickinson, Edwin D., 'Changing Concepts and the Doctrine of Incorporation' (1932) 26 *American Journal of International Law* 239–260.

Donnelly, Jack, 'Human Rights in the New World Order' (1992) 9 *World Policy Journal* 249–277.

'Human Rights, Humanitarian Crisis, and Humanitarian Intervention' (1993) 48 *International Journal* 607–640.

Doswald-Beck, Louise, 'The Legal Validity of Military Intervention by Invitation of the Government' (1986) 56 *British Yearbook of International Law* 242–244.

Droit-Volet, Sylvie and Meck, Warren, 'How Emotions Colour Our Perception of Time' (2007) 11 *Trends in Cognitive Science* 504–513.

Dubin, Martin, 'The Carnegie Endowment for International Peace and the Advocacy of a League of Nations, 1914–1918' (1979) 123 *Proceeding of the American Philosophical Society* 344–368.

Dudley Field, David, 'De la possibilité d'appliquer le droit international européen aux nations orientales' (1875) 7 *Revue de droit international et de législation comparée* 639–668.

Dundes, Alan, 'Binary Opposition in Myth: The Propp/Lévi-Strauss Debate in Retrospect' (1997) 56 *Western Folklore* 39–50.

Einstein, Lewis, 'British Diplomacy in the Spanish-American War' (1964) 76 *Proceedings of the Massachussetts Historical Society* 30–54.

Falk, Richard A., 'Kosovo, World Order, and the Future of International Law' (1999) 93 *American Journal of International Law* 847–857.

Fenwick, Charles G., 'War as an Instrument of National Policy' (1928) 22 *American Journal of International Law* 826–829.

'The Development of Collective Security, 1914–1954' (1954) 48 *American Society of International Law Proceedings* 2–13.

Féraud-Giraud, Louis-J.-D., 'Des hostilités sans déclaration de guerre' (1885) 18 *Revue de droit international et de législation comparée* 19–49.

Fisher, William W. (III), '"Texts and Context": The Application to American Legal History of the Methodologies of Intellectual Histories' (1997) 49 *Stanford Law Review* 1065–1110.

Flasch, Olivia, 'The Legality of the Air Strikes against ISIL in Syria: New Insights on the Extraterritorial Use of Force against Non-State Actors' (2015) 2 *Journal on the Use of Force and International Law* 37–69.

Fleury Graff, Thibaut, 'Droit d'intervention et révolutions en droit international. Les enseignements de la Sainte Alliance' (2012) 56 *Revue française de théorie, de philosophie et de culture juridique* 111–128.

Franck, Thomas M. and Rodley, Nigel S., 'After Bangladesh: The Law of Humanitarian Intervention by Military Force' (1973) 67 *American Journal of International Law* 275–305.

Fraser, Henry S., 'Sketch of the History of International Arbitration' (1926) 11 *Cornell Law Review* 179–208.

Fonteyne, Jean-Pierre L., 'The Customary International Law Doctrine of Humanitarian Intervention: Its Current Validity Under the U.N. Charter' (1973–1974) 4 *California Western International Law Journal* 203–270.

Fourniau, Charles, 'La genèse et l'évolution de l'affaire du Tonkin' (1971) 246 *Revue Historique* 377–402.

Franck, Thomas M., and Rodley, Nigel S. 'After Bangladesh: The Law of Humanitarian Intervention by Military Force' (1973) 67 *American Journal of International Law* 275–305.

Gaja, Giorgio, 'Positivism and Dualism in Dionisio Anzilotti' (1992) 3 *European Journal of International Law* 123–138.

Gamarra Chopo, Yolanda, 'History of the Historiography of Spanish Textbooks and Treatise on International Law of the 19th Century' (2011–2012) 17 *Spanish Yearbook of International Law* 1–22.

Garner, James W., 'La reconstruction du droit international' (1921) 28 *Revue générale de droit international public* 413–440.

Gathii, James Thuo, 'Imperialism, Colonialism, and International Law' (2007) 54 *Buffalo Law Review* 1013–1066.

Gaudillère, Bernard, 'La publicité des débats parlementaires (1852–1870)' (2008) 4 *Parlement[s], Revue d'histoire politique* 27–49.

Gentner, Dedre, 'Structure-Mapping: A Theoretical Framework for Analogy' (1983) 7 *Cognitive Science* 155–170.

Geslin, Albane, 'Du justum bellum au jus ad bellum: glissements conceptuels ou simples variations sémantiques?' (2009) 64 *Revue de métaphysique et de moral* 459–468.

Glick, Mary L. and Holoyak, Keith H., 'Schema Induction and Analogical Transfer' (1983) 15 *Cognitive Psychology* 1–38.

Goebel, Julius (Jr.), 'The Equality of States,' *Columbia Law Review* (1923) 23 247–277.

Goldsmith, Jack L. and Posner, Eric A., 'Understanding the Resemblance between Modern and Traditional Customary International Law' (1999) 40 *Virginia Journal of International Law* 639–672.

Gonsiorowski, Miroslas, 'The Legal Meaning of the Pact for the Renunciation of War' (1936) 30 *American Political Science Review* 653–680.

Gordon, Robert W., 'Critical Legal Histories' (1984) 36 *Stanford Law Review* 57–125.

Greenwood, Christopher, 'The Concept of War in Modern International Law' (1987) 36 *The International and Comparative Law Quarterly* 283–306.

Guggenheim, Paul, 'La sécurité collective et le problème de la neutralité' (1945) 2 *Annuaire Suisse de droit international* 9–47.

Guieu, Jean-Michel, '« Pour la paix par la Société des Nations ». La laborieuse organisation d'un mouvement français de soutien à la Société des Nations (1915–1920)' (2006) 22 *Guerres mondiales et conflits contemporains* 89–102.

"L'« insécurité collective ». L'Europe et la Société des Nations dans l'entre-deux-guerres' (2009) 30 *Bulletin de l'Institut Pierre Renouvin* 21–43.

'Les juristes internationalistes français, l'Europe et la paix à la Belle Époque' (2012) 149 *Relations internationales* 27–41.

Haferkamp, Hans-Peter, 'Positivism as a Concept of Legal Historians' (2010) 17 *Juridica International* 100–107.

Hall, Stephen, 'The Persistent Spectre: Natural Law, International Order and the Limits of Legal Positivism' (2001) 12 *European Journal of International Law* 269–307.

Hart, Herbert L. A., 'Positivism and the Separation of Law and Morals' (1958) 71 *Harvard Law Review* 593–629.

Hayashi, Mika, 'Reacting to the Use of Chemical Weapons: Options for Third States' (2014) 1 *Journal on the Use of Force and International Law* 80–121.

Henderson, Christian, 'Editorial Comment. The Use of Force and the Islamic State' (2014) 1 *Journal on the use of Force and International Law* 209–222.

'The UK Government's Legal Opinion on Forcible Measures in Response to the Use of Chemical Weapons by the Syrian Government' (2015) 64 *International and Comparative Law Quarterly* 179–196.

Henriksen, Anders and Schack, Marc, 'The Crisis in Syria and Humanitarian Intervention' (2014) 1 *Journal on the Use of Force in International Law* 122–147.

Hershey, Amos S., 'Convention for the Peaceful Adjustment of International Differences' (1908) 2 *American Journal of International Law* 29–49.

Higgins, Rosalyn, 'The Legal Limits to the Use of Force by Sovereign States. United Nations Practice' (1961) 37 *British Yearbook of International Law* 269–319.

Hopkins, Antony G., 'Property Rights and Empire Building: Britain's Annexation of Lagos, 1861' (1980) 40 *The Journal of Economic History* 777–798.

Hornung, Joseph, 'Civilisés et barbares' (1885) 18 *Revue de droit international et de législation comparée* 5–18.

Hudson, Mandley O., 'The Permanent Court of International Justice' (1922) 35 *Harvard Law Review* 245–275.

Hueck, Ingo J., 'The Discipline of the History of International Law – New Trends and Methods for the History of International Law' (2001) 3 *Journal of the History of International Law* 194–217.

Huetz de Lemps, Christian, 'La France et les français aux îles Hawaii au XIXe siècle' (1989) 284–285 *Outre-Mers. Revue d'histoire* 131–141.

Hull, William I., 'Obligatory Arbitration and The Hague Conferences' (1908) 2 *American Journal of International Law* 731–742.

Issitt, John, 'Reflections on the Study of Textbooks' (2004) 33 *History of Education* 683–696.

Irish, Tomás, 'Peace through History? The Carnegie Endowment for International Peace's Inquiry into European schoolbooks, 1921–1924' (2016) 45 *Journal of the history of Education Society* 38–56.

Janis, Mark W., 'International Law?' (1991) 32 *Harvard International Law Journal* 363–372.

Jeannesson, Stanilas, 'Léon Bourgeois aux Conférences de La Haye de 1899 et 1907: solidarisme et démocratisation des relations internationales' (2014) 33 *Histoire, économie & société* 107–120.

Jelavich, Barbara, 'What the Habsburg Government Knew about the Black Hand' (1991) 22 *Austrian History Yearbook* 131–150.

Jouannet, Emmanuelle, 'Regards sur un siècle de doctrine française du droit international' (2000) 46 *Annuaire français de droit international* 1–57.

Kansteiner, Wulf, 'Finding Meaning in Memory: A Methodological Critique of Collective Memory Studies' (2002) 41 *History and Theory* 179–197.

Keene, Edward, 'A Case Study of the Construction of International Hierarchy: British Treaty-Making against the Slave Trade in the Early Nineteenth Century' (2007) 61 *International Organization* 311–339.

Kennedy, David, 'Turning to Market Democracy: A Tale of Two Architectures' (1991) 32 *Harvard International Law Journal* 373–398.

'International Law in the Nineteenth Century: History of an Illusion' (1996) 65 *Nordic Journal of International Law* 385–420.

'When Renewal Repeats: Thinking against the Box' (1999–2000) 32 *NYU Journal of International Law and Politics* 335–500.

Kennedy, Paul and Russett, Bruce, 'Reforming the United Nations' (1995) 74 *Foreign Affairs* 56–71.

Kloepfer, Stephen, 'The Syrian Crisis, 1860–1861: A Case Study in Classic Humanitarian Intervention' (1985) 23 *Canadian Yearbook of International Law* 246–260.

Knox, Bruce A., 'The Rise of Colonial Federation as an Object of British Policy, 1850–1870' (1971) 11 *Journal of British Studies* 92–112.

Koller, David, '. . . and New York and The Hague and Tokyo and Geneva and Nuremberg and. . .: The Geographies of International Law' (2012) 23 *European Journal of International Law* 97–119.

Koselleck, Reinhard, 'Gibt es ein kollektives Gedächtnis?' (2004) 19 *Divanatio* 1–6.

Koskenniemi, Martti, 'The Place of Law in Collective Security' (1995–1996) 17 *Michingan Journal of International Law* 455–490.

'Why History of International Law Today?' (2004) 4 *Rechtsgeschichte* 61–66.

'Into Positivism: Georg Friedrich von Martens (1756–1821) and the Modern International Law' (2008) 15 *Constellations* 189–207.

'Histories of International Law: Dealing with Eurocentrism' (2011) 19 *Rechtgeschichte* 152–177.

Kunz, Josef L., 'The Problem of Revision in International Law' (1939) 33 *American Journal of International Law* 33–55.

'Bellum justum and Bellum Legale' (1951) 45 *American Journal of International Law* 528–534.

Lammasch, Heinrich, 'L'arbitrage obligatoire et les deux conférences de la paix' (1909) 16 *Revue générale de droit international* 689–698.

'Compulsory Arbitration at the Second Hague Conference' (1910) 4 *American Journal of International Law* 83–94.

Lange, Christian L., 'The Interpaliamentary Union' (1924) 86 *Advocates of Peace through Justice* 474–478.

(de) Lapradelle, Albert, 'La Conférence de la Paix (La Haye, 18 mai-29 juillet 1899)' (1900) *Revue générale de droit international public* 5–200.

et Politis, Nicolas 'La deuxième conférence de la paix. Origine, convocation, organisation' (1909) 16 *Revue générale de droit international* 385–437.

Latty, Franck, 'Le brouillage des repères du ius contra bellum. A propos de l'usage de la force de la France contre Daech' (2016) 120 *Revue générale de droit international public* 11–39.

Lauterpacht, Hersch, 'The Grotian Tradition in International Law' (1946) 23 *British Yearbook of International Law* 1–53.

Le Fur, Louis, 'La paix perpétuelle et l'arbitrage international' (1909) 16 *Revue générale de droit international* 437–463.

Le Mon, Christopher J., 'Unilateral Intervention by Invitation in Civil Wars: The Effective Control Test Tested' (2002–2003) 35 *NYU Journal of International Law and Politics* 741–793.

Lesaffer, Randall, 'The Grotian Tradition Revisisted: Change and Continuity in International Law' (2002) 73 *Bristish Yearbook of International Law* 103–139.

Lillich, Richard B., 'Forcible Self-Help by States to Protect Human Rights' (1967–1968) 53 *Iowa Law Review* 325–351.

"Intervention to Protect Human Rights' (1969) 15 *McGill Law Journal* 205–219.

Lingelbach, W. E., 'The Doctrine and Practice of Intervention in Europe' (1900) 16 *The Annals of the American Academy of Political and Social Science* 1–32.

Livet, Pierre, 'Emotions, rationalité, densité temporelle et manifestation de valeurs' (2009) 144 *Revue européenne des sciences sociales* 7–23.

Low, Seth, 'The International Conference of Peace' (1899) 169 *The North American Review* 625–639.

Mälksoo, Lauri, 'The History of International Legal Theory in Russia: A Civilizational Dialogue with Europe' (2008) 19 *European Journal of International Law* 211–232.

Mandelbaum, David G., 'Myths and Myth Maker: Some Anthropological Appraisal of the Mythological Studies of Lévi-Strauss' (1987) 26 *Ethnology* 31–36.

(de) Martens, Fyodor, 'International Arbitration and the Peace Conference at The Hague' (1899) 169 *The North American Review* 604–624.

Martineau, Anne-Charlotte, 'Concerning Violence: A Post-Colonial Reading of the Debate on the Use of Force' (2016) 29 *Leiden Journal of International Law* 95–112.

McKinnon Wood, Hugh, 'The Treaty of Paris and Turkey's Status in International Law' (1943) 37 *American Journal of International Law* 262–274.

McNair, Arnold D., 'Equality in International Law' (1927) 26 *Michigan Law Review* 131–152.

Mérignhac, Alexandre, 'La Conférence de La Haye et ses résultats. Opinion,' (1900) *Revue générale de droit international public* 234–237.

Merriam, John J., 'Kosovo and the Law of Humanitarian Intervention' (2001) 33 *Case Western Reserve Journal of International Law* 111–154.

Milliken, Jennifer, 'The Study of Discourse in International Relations: A Critique of Research and Method' (1999) 5 *European Journal of International Relations* 225–254.

Monod, Jean-Claude, 'La destabilisation humanitaire du droit international etle retour de la « guerre juste »: une lecture critique du *Nomos de la terre*' (2004) 68 *Les études philosophiques* 39–56.

Moore, John Bassett, 'The Organization of the Permanent Court of International Justice' (1922) 22 *Columbia Law Review* 497–526.

Moore, Joseph B., 'International Arbitration' (1909) 7 *Michigan Law Review* 547–556.

Murphy, Cornelius F., 'The Grotian Vision of World Order' (1982) 76 *American Journal of International Law* 477–498.

Nardin, Terry, 'The Moral Basis of Humanitarian Intervention' (2002) 16 *Ethics and International Affairs* 57–70.

Niess, Alexandre, 'Leon Bourgeois (1851–1925), juriste et ange de la paix' (2009) 11 *Parlement[s], Revue d'histoire politique* 135–148.

Nussbaum, Arthur, 'Just War – A Legal Concept?' (1943) 42 *Michigan Law Review* 453–459.

Nys, Ernest, 'Le Concert européen et la notion de droit international' (1899) 31 *Revue de droit international et de législation comparée* 273–313.

O'Connor, Laurie, 'Legality of the Use of Force in Syria against Islamic State and the Khorasan Group' (2016) 3 *Journal on the Use of Force and International Law* 70–96.

Offner, John L., 'McKinley and the Spanish-American War' (2004) 34 *Presidential Studies Quarterly* 50–61.

(de) Olivart, Ramon 'Le différend entre l'Espagne et les Etats-Unis au sujet de la question cubaine' (1898) 5 *Revue général de droit international public* 358–422.

'La Conférence de La Haye et ses résultats. Opinion' (1900) *Revue générale de droit international* 205–214.

Oppenheim, Lassa, 'The Science of International Law: Its Tasks and Methods' (1908) 2 *American Journal of International Law* 313–356.

Orford, Anne, 'Muscular Humaniatrianism: Reading the Narratives of New interventionism' (1999) 10 *European Journal of International Law* 679–711.

'On international Legal Method' (2013) 1 *London Review of International Law* 166–197.

Palabiyik, Mustafa Serdar, 'The Emergence if the Idea of 'International Law' in the Ottoman Empire before the Treaty of Paris (1856)' (2014) 50 *Middle Eastern Studies* 233–251.

Papadaki, Marilena, 'L'action des juristes internationalistes au service de la paix internationale à la fin du XIXe siècle: le cas de Nicolas Politis (1872–1942)' (2015) 91 *Cahiers de la Méditérrannée* 21–31.

Paternostro, Alessandro, 'La révision des traités avec le Japon au point de vue du droit international' (1891) 23 *Revue de droit international et de législation comparée* 5–29 and 176–203.

Pillet, Antoine, 'La guerre actuelle et le droit international' (1916) 23 *Revue général de droit international public* 5–31.

Pogany, Itsvan, 'Humanitarian Intervention in International Law: The French Intervention in Syria Re-Examined' (1986) 35 *International and Comparative Law Quarterly* 182–190.

Pouliot, Vincent, '"Sobjectivism": Toward a Constructivist Methodology' (2007) 51 *International Studies Quarterly* 359–384.

Raffo, Peter, 'The Anglo-American Preliminary Negotiations for a League of Nations' (1974) 9 *Journal of Contemporary History* 153–176.

Ralston, Jackson H., review article of *International Law* by Charles Fenwick (1924) 18 *American Journal of International Law* 853–855.

Rasilla del Moral, (de la) Ignacio, 'El estudio del Derecho internacional en el corto siglo XIX español' (2013) 21 *Rechtsgeschichte* 48–65.

Raz, Joseph, 'Human Rights in the Emerging World Order' (2012) 1 *Transnational Legal Theory* 31–47.

Reid, Cecilie, 'Peace and Law – Peace Activism and International Arbitration, 1895–1907' (2004) 29 *Peace & Change* 527–548.

Reisman, Michael, 'Sovereignty and Human Rights in Contemporary International Law' (1990) 84 *American Journal of International Law* 866–876.

'International La wand the Cold War' (1990) *Faculty Scholarship Series*, Paper n °873, 859–866.

Rigaux, François, 'Kelsen et le droit international' (1996) 32 *Revue belge de droit international* 381–408.

'Kelsen on International Law' (1998) 9 *European Journal of International Law* 325–343.

Robert, Adam, 'The So-called 'Right' of Humanitarian Intervention' (2000) 3 *Yearbook of International Humanitarian Law* 3–51.

Roberts, Anthea, 'Traditional and Modern Approaches to Customary International Law: A Reconciliation' (2001) 95 *American Journal of International Law* 757–791.

Rolin-Jaequemyns, Gustave, 'Le droit international et la phase actuelle de la question d'Orient' (1876) 8 *Revue de droit international et de législation comparée* 293–385.

'Note sur la théorie du droit d'intervention. A propos d'une lettre de M. le Professeur Arntz' (1879) 8 *Revue de droit international et de législation comparée* 675–682.

Root, Elihu, 'The Outlook for International Law' (1915) 9 *Proceedings of the American Society of International Law* 2–11.

Roscher, Bernahrd, 'The "Renunciation of War as an Instrument of National Policy"' (2002) 4 *Journal of History of International Law* 293–309.

Rosenau, James N., 'The Concept of Intervention' (1968) 22 *Journal of International Affairs* 165–176.

Rostow, Nicholas, 'The International Use of Force After the Cold War' (1991) 32 *Harvard International Law Journal* 411–421.

Roxburgh, Ronald H., 'The Sanction of International Law' (1920) 14 *American Journal of International Law* 26–37.

Ruys, Tom, 'The Meaning of 'Force' and the Boundaries of Jus ad Bellum: Are 'Minimal' Uses of Force Excluded from the UN Charter Article 2(4)?' (2014) 108 *American Journal of International Law* 159–210.

'From *passé simple* to *futur imparfait*? A response to Verdebout' (2015) 2 *Journal on the Use of Force and International Law* 3–16.

Sacriste, Guillaume et Vauchez, Antoine, 'The Force of International Law: Lawyers' Diplomacy on the International Scene in the 1920s' (2007) 32 *Law & Social Inquiry* 83–107.

'La « guerre hors-la-loi », 1919–1910. Note de recherche: Les origines de la définition d'un order politique international' (2014) 150 *Acte de la recherche sociale* 91–95.

Sadaa, Julie, 'Pacifisme ou guerre totale ? Une histoire politique du droit des gens: les lectures de Vittoria au XXe siècle' (2009) 6 *Astérion* [on line].

Salmon, Jean, 'Quelques observations sur les lacunes du droit international public' (1967) 3 *Revue belge de droit international* 440–458.

Schachter, Oliver, 'The Invisible College of International Lawyers' (1977) 72 *Northwestern University Law Review* 217–226.

Schmitt, Bernadotte E., 'The Diplomatic Preliminaries of the Crimea War' (1919) 25 *The American Historical Review* 36–67.

Scott, James Brown, 'The Proposed Court of Arbitral Justice' (1908) 2 *American Journal of International Law* 772–810.

'The Central American Peace Conference of 1907' (1908) 2 *American Journal of International Law* 121–143.

Šedivý, Miroslav, 'Metternich and the Anglo-Neapolitan Sulphur Crisis of 1840' (2011) 16 *Journal of Modern Italian Studies* 1–18.

Skinner, Quentin, 'Meaning and Understanding in the History of Ideas' (1969) 8 *History and Theory* 3–53.

Smiley, Will, 'War Without War: The Battle of Navarino, the Ottoman Empire, and the Pacific Blockade' (2016) 18 *Journal of History of International Law* 42–69.

Smith, Munroe, 'The Nature and Future of International Law' (1918) 12 *American Political Science Review* 1–16.

Stahn, Carsten, 'Between Law-Breaking and Law-Making: Syria, Humanitarian Intervention and 'What the Law Ought to Be'' (2013) 19 *Journal of Conflict and Security Law* 25–48.

Stoerk, Felix, 'La Conférence de La Haye et ses résultats. Opinion,' (1900) *Revue générale de droit international public* 201–205.

Strupp, Karl, 'L'incident de Janina entre la Grèce et l'Italie' (1924) 31 *Revue générale de droit international public* 255–284.

Sullivan, Alice, 'Bourdieu and Education: How Useful Is Bourdieu's Theory for Researchers?' (2002) 38 *The Netherlands' Journal for Social Science* 144–166.

Summers, Robert S., 'The New Analytical Jurists' (1966) 41 *New York University Law Review* 861–896.

Surun, Isabelle, 'Une souveraineté à l'encre sympathique? Souveraineté autochtones et appropriations territoriale dans les traités franco-africains au XIXe siècle' (2014) 69 *Annales. Histoire, Sciences Sociales* 313–348.

Sweeny, Kate and Vohs, Kathleen D., 'On Near Misses and Completed Tasks: The Nature of Relief' (2012) 23 *Psychological Science* 464–468.

Tamm, Marek, 'History as Cultural Memory: Mnemohistory and the Construction of the Estonian Nation' (2008) 39 *Journal of Baltic Studies* 499–516.

'Beyond History and Memory: New Perspectives in Memory Studies' (2013) 11/6 *History Compass* 458–473.

Tenekides, Ciriaque G., 'L'evolution de l'idée des mesures coercitives et la Société des Nations' (1926) 53 *Revue de droit international et de legislation comparée* 398–418.

Tourme Jouannet, Emmanuelle and Peters, Anne, 'The *Journal of the History of International Law*: A Forum for New Research' (2014) 16 *Journal of the History of International Law* 1–8.

Toyoda, Tetsuya, 'L'aspect universaliste du droit international européen du 19ème siècle et le statut juridique de la Turquie avant 1856' (2006) 8 *Journal of the History of International Law* 19–37.

Tryon, James L., 'The Rise of Peace Movements' (1911) 20 *The Yale Law Review* 358–371.

'The Hague Conferences' (1911) 20 *The Yale Law Journal* 470–485.

Vaughan, Diane, 'Bourdieu and Organizations: The Empirical Challenge' (2008) 37 *Theory and Society* 65–81.

Vec, Miloš, 'Universalization, Particularization, and Discrimination. European Perspectives on a Cultural History of 19th Century International Law' (2012) 3 *InterDisciplines* 79–102.

Verwey, W. D., 'Humanitarian Intervention Under International Law' (1985) 32 *Netherlands International Law Review* 357–418.

Villemagne, Claire, 'Commerçant et colons français au Tonkin, les pioniers oubliés de la colonisation' (2003) 340–341 *Outre-Mers. Revue d'histoire* 297–317.

(de) Visscher, Charles, 'L'interprétation du Pacte au lendemain du différend italo-grec' (1924) 51 *Revue de droit international et de législation comparée* 213–230 and 377–397.

von Bernstorff, 'The Use of Force in International Law Before World War I: On Imperial Ordering and the Ontology of the Nation-State' (2018) 29 *European Journal of International Law* 233–260.

von Elbe, Joachim, 'The Evolution of the Concept of Just War in International Law' (1939) 33 *American Journal of International Law* 665–688.

Wacquant, Loïc, 'A Concise Genealogy and Anatomy of Habitus' (2016) 64 *The Sociological Review* 64–72.

Wallace-Bruce, Nii Lante, 'Africa and International Law – The Emergence to Statehood' (1985) 23 *The Journal of Modern African Studies* 575–602.

White, Hayden, 'The Question of Narrative in Contemporary Historical Theory' (1984) 23 *History and Theory* 1–33.

Wilson, George G., 'Insurgency and International Maritime Law' (1907) 1 *American Journal of International Law* 46–60.

Wilson, Howard Hazen, 'Some Principal Aspects of British Efforts to Crush the African Slave Trade, 1807–1912' (1950) 44 *American Journal of International Law* 505–526.

Winfield, P. H., 'The History of Intervention in International Law' (1922–1923) 3 *British Yearbook of International Law* 130–149.

Worster, William Thomas, 'The Inductive and Deductive Methods in Customary International Law Analysis: Traditional and Modern Approaches' (2014) 45 *Georgetown Journal of International Law* 445–521.

Wright, Quincy, 'Effects of the League of Nations Covenant' (1919) 13 *American Journal of International Law* 556–576.

'Opinion of the Commission of Jurists on Janina-Corfu Affairs' (1924) 18 *American Journal of International Law* 536–544.

'Changes in the Conception of War' (1924) 18 *American Journal of International Law* 755–767.

'The Outlawry of War' (1925) 19 *American Journal of International Law* 76–103.

Zammito, John H., 'Are We Being Historical Yet? The New Historicism, the New Philosophy of History, and 'Practising Historians'' (1993) 65 *Journal of modern History* 783–814.

Zeller, Gaston, 'Une legende qui a la vie dure: les Capitulations de 1535' (1955) 2 *Revue d'Histoire moderne et contemporaine* 127–132

Hague Academy Collected Courses

Bourquin, Maurice, 'Règles générales du droit de la paix' (1931) 35 *Recueil des cours* 5–232.

'Le problème de la sécurité internationale' (1934) 49 *Recueil des cours* 473–542.

Brierly, James L., 'Règles générales du droit de la paix' (1936) 58 *Recueil des cours* 1–242.

Cavaglieri, Arrigo, 'Règles générales du droit de la paix' (1929) 26 *Recueil des cours* 311–585.

Chaumont, Charles, 'Cours général de droit international' (1970) 129 *Recueil des cours* 335–527.

Corten, Olivier 'La rébellion et le droit international: le principe de neutralité en tension' (2014) 374 *Recueil des cours* 88–100.

Dupuis, Charles, 'Les antécédent de la Société des Nations' (1937) 60 *Recueil des cours* 1–106.

Gaillard, Emmanuel, 'Aspects philosophiques du droit de l'arbitrage international' (2007) 329 *Recueil des cours* 49–216.

Kaufmann, Erich, 'Règles générales du droit de la paix' (1935) 54 *Recueil des cours* 309–639.

Kelsen, Hans, 'Théorie du droit international public' (1953) 84 *Recueil des cours* 1–203.

Krylov, Sergei B., 'Les notions principales du droit des gens (La doctrine soviétique du droit international' (1947) 70 *Recueil des cours* 411–476.

Le Fur, Louis, 'Règles générales du droit de la paix' (1935) 54 *Recueil des cours* 1–307.

Nippold, Otfried, 'Le développement historique du droit international depuis le Congrès de Vienne' (1924) 2 *Recueil des cours* 1–120.

Pinto, Roger, 'Les règles de droit international concernant la guerre civile' (1965) 114 *Recueil des cours* 455–553.

Politis, Nicolas, 'Le problème des limitations de la souveraineté et la théorie de l'abus des droits dans les rapports internationaux' (1925) 6 *Recueil des cours* 5–121.

Potter, Pitman B., 'Développement de l'organisation internationale (1815–1914)' (1938) 64 *Recueil des cours* 71–121.

Rauchberg, H., 'Les obligations juridiques des membres de la Société des Nations pour le maintien de la paix' (1931) 37 *Recueil des cours* 83–204.

Rutgers, V. H., 'La mise en harmonie du Pacte de la Société des Nations avec le Pacte de Paris' (1931) 38 *Recueil des cours* 1–123.

Scelle, Georges, 'Règles générales du droit de la paix' (1933) 46 *Recueil des cours* 327–703.

Von Verdoss, Alfred, 'Règles générales du droit international de la paix' (1929) 30 *Recueil des cours* 271–518.

Wehberg, Hans, 'Le Protocole de Genève' (1925) 7 *Recueil des cours* 1–150.

'L'interdiction du recours à la force. Le principe et les problèmes qui se posent' (1951) 78 *Recueil des cours* 7–121.

Dictionnairies and encyclopedias

Boczek, Boleslaw A. (ed.), *International Law. A dictionary* (Scarecrow Press, 2005).

Dyal, Donald H. (ed.), *Historical Dictionary of the Spanish American War* (Greenwood Press, 1996).

in Encyclopaedia Britannica Online (available at: www.britannica.com/).

- 'Carbonari,' by the Ediotrs (last update: 15 November 2015).
- 'Cetshewayo,' by the Editors (last update: 4 February 2020).
- 'Eclecticism – Philosophy and Theology,' by the Editors (last update: 25 July 2015).
- 'German Confederation,' by the Editors (last update: 16 January 2016).
- 'United States Occupation of Vera Cruz,' by Niheer Dasandi (last update: 14 April 2019).

in Gellman, Marc D. and Turner, J. Rick (eds.), *Encyclopaedia of Behavioural Medicine* (Springer, 2013).

- 'Emotional Expression,' by Michelle Skinner, pp. 673–675.

Gareis, Karl, *Encyclopädie und Methodologie des Rechtswissenschaft* (Roth, 1887).

Laband, John, *Historical Dictionnary of the Zulu Wars* (The Scarcecrow Press Inc., 2009).

Salmon, Jean (dir.), *Dictionnaire de droit international public* (Bruylant, 2001).

in Wolfrum, Rüdiger (ed.), *Max Planck Encyclopaedia of Public International Law* (Oxford University Press, 2012).

- 'Alabama Arbitration,' by Tom Bingham, vol. 1, pp. 272–275.

in Wolfrum, Rüdiger (ed.), *Max Planck Encyclopaedia of Public International Law* (available at: http://opil.ouplaw.com/home/epil).

- 'Bryan Treaties (1913–14),' by Hans-Jürgen Schlochauer (August 2007).

– 'History of International Law, Ancient Times to 1648,' by Wolfgang Preisner (August 2008).
– 'History of International Law, 1648 to 1815,' by Stephan Verrosta (June 2007).
– 'History of International Law, 1815 to World War I,' by Hans-Ulricht Scupin (May 2011).
– 'History of International Law, World War I to World War II,' by Martti Koskenniemi (June 2011).
– 'History of International Law, since World War II,' by Martti Koskenniemi (June 2011).
– 'International Law,' by Rüdinger Wolfrum (November 2006).
– 'Intervention, Prohibition of,' by Philip Kunig (April 2008).
– 'League of Nations,' by Christian J. Tams (September 2006).
– 'Use of Force, Prohibition of,' by Oliver Dörr (September 2015).

Other

American Society for International Law, 'Constitution of the American Society of International Law' (1907) 1 *American Journal of International Law* 131–135.

Carnegie Endowment for International Peace, Report of the Director of the Division of International Law, 26 October 1911.

VIe Congrès Universel de la Paix, *Bulletin officiel*, Anvers 1894 (Imprimerie de la veuve Backer, 1895).

Dotation Carnegie pour l'Europe, *Enquête sur les manuels scolaires d'après guerre* (Centre européen de la dotation Carnegie, 1923).

Editorial Comment, 'American Society for the Judicial Settlement of International Disputes' (1910) 4 *American Journal of International Law* 930–932.

Editorial Comment, 'Introduction' (1907) 1 *American Journal of International Law* 129–130.

Institut de droit international (IDI), 'Application aux nations orientales du droit des gens coutumier de l'Europe,' Notices et Notes diverses, Institut de droit international, Session de 1879 (1880) 12 *Revue de droit international et de législation comparée* 98–99.

'Report of M. Perels, Rapporteur de la sixième commission d'étude – Droit de blocus en temps de paix' (1887) 9 *Annuaire de l'Institut de droit international* 282–283.

'Counter-Report of M. Geffecken' (1887) 9 *Annuaire de l'Institut de droit international* 286–295.

Declaration concernant le blocus en dehors de l'état de guerre, 7 September 1887, Heidelberg Session.

Droit et devoirs des Puissances étrangères, au cas de mouvement insurrectionnel, envers les gouvernement établi et reconnu qui sont aux prises avec l'insurrection, 8 september 1900, Neuchâtel Session.

Resolution on Principle of Non-intervention in Civil Wars, 14 August 1975, Wiesbaden Session.

Resolution on Present problems of the Use of Force in International Law, 8 September 2011, Rhodes Session.

Independent Fact-Finding Mission on the Conflict in Georgia (IIFFMCG), *Report*, 3 vols., September 2009.

Innes, Kathleen, *The Story of the League of Nations Told for Young People* (The Hogarth Press, 1925).

INA Archives, 'Réflexion faites, *Entretiens avec Claude Lévi-Strauss*,' 4 May 1984

INDEX

Cambridge Studies in International and Comparative Law

Books in the Series

160 *Rewriting Histories of the Use of Force: The Narrative of 'Indifference'* Agatha Verdebout
159 *The League of Nations and the Protection of the Environment* Omer Aloni
158 *International Investment Law and Legal Theory: Expropriation and the Fragmentation of Sources* Jörg Kammerhofer
157 *Legal Barbarians: Identity, Modern Comparative Law and the Global South* Daniel Bonilla Maldonado
156 *International Human Rights Law Beyond State Territorial Control* Antal Berkes
155 *The Crime of Aggression under the Rome Statute of the International Criminal Court* Carrie McDougall
154 *Minorities and the Making of Postcolonial States in International Law* Mohammad Shahabuddin
153 *Preclassical Conflict of Laws* Nikitas E. Hatzimihail
152 *International Law and History: Modern Interfaces* Ignacio de la Rasilla
151 *Marketing Global Justice: The Political Economy of International Criminal Law* Christine Schwöbel-Patel
150 *International Status in the Shadow of Empire* Cait Storr
149 *Treaties in Motion: The Evolution of Treaties from Formation to Termination* Edited by Malgosia Fitzmaurice and Panos Merkouris
148 *Humanitarian Disarmament: An Historical Enquiry* Treasa Dunworth
147 *Complementarity, Catalysts, Compliance: The International Criminal Court in Uganda, Kenya, and the Democratic Republic of Congo* Christian M. De Vos
146 *Cyber Operations and International Law* François Delerue
145 *Comparative Reasoning in International Courts and Tribunals* Daniel Peat
144 *Maritime Delimitation as a Judicial Process* Massimo Lando
143 *Prosecuting Sexual and Gender-Based Crimes at the International Criminal Court: Practice, Progress and Potential* Rosemary Grey
142 *Capitalism as Civilisation: A History of International Law* Ntina Tzouvala
141 *Sovereignty in China: A Genealogy of a Concept Since 1840* Adele Carrai
140 *Narratives of Hunger in International Law: Feeding the World in Times of Climate Change* Anne Saab
139 *Victim Reparation under the Ius Post Bellum: An Historical and Normative Perspective* Shavana Musa
138 *The Analogy between States and International Organizations* Fernando Lusa Bordin
137 *The Process of International Legal Reproduction: Inequality, Historiography, Resistance* Rose Parfitt
136 *State Responsibility for Breaches of Investment Contracts* Jean Ho

135 *Coalitions of the Willing and International Law: The Interplay between Formality and Informality* Alejandro Rodiles
134 *Self-Determination in Disputed Colonial Territories* Jamie Trinidad
133 *International Law as a Belief System* Jean d'Aspremont
132 *Legal Consequences of Peremptory Norms in International Law* Daniel Costelloe
131 *Third-Party Countermeasures in International Law* Martin Dawidowicz
130 *Justification and Excuse in International Law: Concept and Theory of General Defences* Federica Paddeu
129 *Exclusion from Public Space: A Comparative Constitutional Analysis* Daniel Moeckli
128 *Provisional Measures before International Courts and Tribunals* Cameron A. Miles
127 *Humanity at Sea: Maritime Migration and the Foundations of International Law* Itamar Mann
126 *Beyond Human Rights: The Legal Status of the Individual in International Law* Anne Peters
125 *The Doctrine of Odious Debt in International Law: A Restatement* Jeff King
124 *Static and Evolutive Treaty Interpretation: A Functional Reconstruction* Christian Djeffal
123 *Civil Liability in Europe for Terrorism-Related Risk* Lucas Bergkamp, Michael Faure, Monika Hinteregger, and Niels Philipsen
122 *Proportionality and Deference in Investor-State Arbitration: Balancing Investment Protection and Regulatory Autonomy* Caroline Henckels
121 *International Law and Governance of Natural Resources in Conflict and Post-Conflict Situations* Daniëlla Dam-de Jong
120 *Proof of Causation in Tort Law* Sandy Steel
119 *The Formation and Identification of Rules of Customary International Law in International Investment Law* Patrick Dumberry
118 *Religious Hatred and International Law: The Prohibition of Incitement to Violence or Discrimination* Jeroen Temperman
117 *Taking Economic, Social and Cultural Rights Seriously in International Criminal Law* Evelyne Schmid
116 *Climate Change Litigation: Regulatory Pathways to Cleaner Energy* Jacqueline Peel and Hari M. Osofsky
115 *Mestizo International Law: A Global Intellectual History 1842–1933* Arnulf Becker Lorca
114 *Sugar and the Making of International Trade Law* Michael Fakhri
113 *Strategically Created Treaty Conflicts and the Politics of International Law* Surabhi Ranganathan
112 *Investment Treaty Arbitration as Public International Law: Procedural Aspects and Implications* Eric De Brabandere
111 *The New Entrants Problem in International Fisheries Law* Andrew Serdy
110 *Substantive Protection under Investment Treaties: A Legal and Economic Analysis* Jonathan Bonnitcha

109 *Popular Governance of Post-Conflict Reconstruction: The Role of International Law* Matthew Saul
108 *Evolution of International Environmental Regimes: The Case of Climate Change* Simone Schiele
107 *Judges, Law and War: The Judicial Development of International Humanitarian Law* Shane Darcy
106 *Religious Offence and Human Rights: The Implications of Defamation of Religions* Lorenz Langer
105 *Forum Shopping in International Adjudication: The Role of Preliminary Objections* Luiz Eduardo Salles
104 *Domestic Politics and International Human Rights Tribunals: The Problem of Compliance* Courtney Hillebrecht
103 *International Law and the Arctic* Michael Byers
102 *Cooperation in the Law of Transboundary Water Resources* Christina Leb
101 *Underwater Cultural Heritage and International Law* Sarah Dromgoole
100 *State Responsibility: The General Part* James Crawford
99 *The Origins of International Investment Law: Empire, Environment and the Safeguarding of Capital* Kate Miles
98 *The Crime of Aggression under the Rome Statute of the International Criminal Court* Carrie McDougall
97 *'Crimes against Peace' and International Law* Kirsten Sellars
96 *Non-Legality in International Law: Unruly Law* Fleur Johns
95 *Armed Conflict and Displacement: The Protection of Refugees and Displaced Persons under International Humanitarian Law* Mélanie Jacques
94 *Foreign Investment and the Environment in International Law* Jorge E. Viñuales
93 *The Human Rights Treaty Obligations of Peacekeepers* Kjetil Mujezinović Larsen
92 *Cyber Warfare and the Laws of War* Heather Harrison Dinniss
91 *The Right to Reparation in International Law for Victims of Armed Conflict* Christine Evans
90 *Global Public Interest in International Investment Law* Andreas Kulick
89 *State Immunity in International Law* Xiaodong Yang
88 *Reparations and Victim Support in the International Criminal Court* Conor McCarthy
87 *Reducing Genocide to Law: Definition, Meaning, and the Ultimate Crime* Payam Akhavan
86 *Decolonising International Law: Development, Economic Growth and the Politics of Universality* Sundhya Pahuja
85 *Complicity and the Law of State Responsibility* Helmut Philipp Aust
84 *State Control over Private Military and Security Companies in Armed Conflict* Hannah Tonkin
83 *"Fair and Equitable Treatment" in International Investment Law* Roland Kläger

82 *The UN and Human Rights: Who Guards the Guardians?* Guglielmo Verdirame
81 *Sovereign Defaults before International Courts and Tribunals* Michael Waibel
80 *Making the Law of the Sea: A Study in the Development of International Law* James Harrison
79 *Science and the Precautionary Principle in International Courts and Tribunals: Expert Evidence, Burden of Proof and Finality* Caroline E. Foster
78 *Transition from Illegal Regimes under International Law* Yaël Ronen
77 *Access to Asylum: International Refugee Law and the Globalisation of Migration Control* Thomas Gammeltoft-Hansen
76 *Trading Fish, Saving Fish: The Interaction between Regimes in International Law* Margaret A. Young
75 *The Individual in the International Legal System: Continuity and Change in International Law* Kate Parlett
74 *"Armed Attack" and Article 51 of the UN Charter: Evolutions in Customary Law and Practice* Tom Ruys
73 *Theatre of the Rule of Law: Transnational Legal Intervention in Theory and Practice* Stephen Humphreys
72 *Science and Risk Regulation in International Law* Jacqueline Peel
71 *The Participation of States in International Organisations: The Role of Human Rights and Democracy* Alison Duxbury
70 *Legal Personality in International Law* Roland Portmann
69 *Vicarious Liability in Tort: A Comparative Perspective* Paula Giliker
68 *The Public International Law Theory of Hans Kelsen: Believing in Universal Law* Jochen von Bernstorff
67 *Legitimacy and Legality in International Law: An Interactional Account* Jutta Brunnée and Stephen J. Toope
66 *The Concept of Non-International Armed Conflict in International Humanitarian Law* Anthony Cullen
65 *The Principle of Legality in International and Comparative Criminal Law* Kenneth S. Gallant
64 *The Challenge of Child Labour in International Law* Franziska Humbert
63 *Shipping Interdiction and the Law of the Sea* Douglas Guilfoyle
62 *International Courts and Environmental Protection* Tim Stephens
61 *Legal Principles in WTO Disputes* Andrew D. Mitchell
60 *War Crimes in Internal Armed Conflicts* Eve La Haye
59 *Humanitarian Occupation* Gregory H. Fox
58 *The International Law of Environmental Impact Assessment: Process, Substance and Integration* Neil Craik
57 *The Law and Practice of International Territorial Administration: Versailles to Iraq and Beyond* Carsten Stahn
56 *United Nations Sanctions and the Rule of Law* Jeremy Matam Farrall
55 *National Law in WTO Law: Effectiveness and Good Governance in the World Trading System* Sharif Bhuiyan

54 *Cultural Products and the World Trade Organization* Tania Voon
53 *The Threat of Force in International Law* Nikolas Stürchler
52 *Indigenous Rights and United Nations Standards: Self-Determination, Culture and Land* Alexandra Xanthaki
51 *International Refugee Law and Socio-Economic Rights: Refuge from Deprivation* Michelle Foster
50 *The Protection of Cultural Property in Armed Conflict* Roger O'Keefe
49 *Interpretation and Revision of International Boundary Decisions* Kaiyan Homi Kaikobad
48 *Multinationals and Corporate Social Responsibility: Limitations and Opportunities in International Law* Jennifer A. Zerk
47 *Judiciaries within Europe: A Comparative Review* John Bell
46 *Law in Times of Crisis: Emergency Powers in Theory and Practice* Oren Gross and Fionnuala Ní Aoláin
45 *Vessel-Source Marine Pollution: The Law and Politics of International Regulation* Alan Khee-Jin Tan
44 *Enforcing Obligations Erga Omnes in International Law* Christian J. Tams
43 *Non-Governmental Organisations in International Law* Anna-Karin Lindblom
42 *Democracy, Minorities and International Law* Steven Wheatley
41 *Prosecuting International Crimes: Selectivity and the International Criminal Law Regime* Robert Cryer
40 *Compensation for Personal Injury in English, German and Italian Law: A Comparative Outline* Basil Markesinis, Michael Coester, Guido Alpa, and Augustus Ullstein
39 *Dispute Settlement in the UN Convention on the Law of the Sea* Natalie Klein
38 *The International Protection of Internally Displaced Persons* Catherine Phuong
37 *Imperialism, Sovereignty and the Making of International Law* Antony Anghie
35 *Necessity, Proportionality and the Use of Force by States* Judith Gardam
34 *International Legal Argument in the Permanent Court of International Justice: The Rise of the International Judiciary* Ole Spiermann
32 *Great Powers and Outlaw States: Unequal Sovereigns in the International Legal Order* Gerry Simpson
31 *Local Remedies in International Law* (second edition) Chittharanjan Felix Amerasinghe
30 *Reading Humanitarian Intervention: Human Rights and the Use of Force in International Law* Anne Orford
29 *Conflict of Norms in Public International Law: How WTO Law Relates to Other Rules of International Law* Joost Pauwelyn
28 –
27 *Transboundary Damage in International Law* Hanqin Xue
26 –
25 *European Criminal Procedures* Edited by Mireille Delmas-Marty and J. R. Spencer

24 *Accountability of Armed Opposition Groups in International Law* Liesbeth Zegveld
23 *Sharing Transboundary Resources: International Law and Optimal Resource Use* Eyal Benvenisti
22 *International Human Rights and Humanitarian Law* René Provost
21 *Remedies against International Organisations* Karel Wellens
20 *Diversity and Self-Determination in International Law* Karen Knop
19 *The Law of Internal Armed Conflict* Lindsay Moir
18 *International Commercial Arbitration and African States: Practice, Participation and Institutional Development* Amazu A. Asouzu
17 *The Enforceability of Promises in European Contract Law* James Gordley
16 *International Law in Antiquity* David J. Bederman
15 *Money Laundering: A New International Law Enforcement Model* Guy Stessens
14 *Good Faith in European Contract Law* Reinhard Zimmermann and Simon Whittaker
13 *On Civil Procedure* J. A. Jolowicz
12 *Trusts: A Comparative Study* Maurizio Lupoi and Simon Dix
11 *The Right to Property in Commonwealth Constitutions* Tom Allen
10 *International Organizations before National Courts* August Reinisch
9 *The Changing International Law of High Seas Fisheries* Francisco Orrego Vicuña
8 *Trade and the Environment: A Comparative Study of EC and US Law* Damien Geradin
7 *Unjust Enrichment: A Study of Private Law and Public Values* Hanoch Dagan
6 *Religious Liberty and International Law in Europe* Malcolm D. Evans
5 *Ethics and Authority in International Law* Alfred P. Rubin
4 *Sovereignty over Natural Resources: Balancing Rights and Duties* Nico Schrijver
3 *The Polar Regions and the Development of International Law* Donald R. Rothwell
2 *Fragmentation and the International Relations of Micro-States: Self Determination and Statehood* Jorri C. Duursma
1 *Principles of the Institutional Law of International Organizations* C. F. Amerasinghe

www.ingramcontent.com/pod-product-compliance
Lightning Source LLC
LaVergne TN
LVHW011701200926
848484LV00004B/1021